INTERNATIONAL POLICY AND POLITICS IN CANADA

Kim Richard Nossal
Queen's University

Stéphane Roussel
Université du Québec à Montréal

Stéphane Paquin
Université de Sherbrooke

Pearson Canada
Toronto

Library and Archives Canada Cataloguing in Publication

Nossal, Kim Richard
    International policy and politics in Canada/Kim Richard Nossal, Stéphane Roussel, Stéphane Paquin.

Includes bibliographical references and index.
ISBN 978-0-13-608972-8

    1. Canada—Foreign relations—Textbooks.   I. Roussel, Stéphane, 1964–
II. Paquin, Stéphane, 1973–   III. Title.

FC242.N68 2011   327.71   C2009-906265-8

ISBN 978-0-13-608972-8

Vice President, Editorial Director: Gary Bennett
Editor-in-Chief: Ky Pruesse
Editor, Humanities and Social Sciences: Joel Gladstone
Executive Marketing Manager: Judith Allen
Assistant Editor: Jordanna Caplan
Managing Editor: Söğüt Y. Güleç
Copy Editor: Rodney Rawlings
Proofreaders: Sally Glover, Tara Tovell
Production Coordinator: Söğüt Y. Güleç
Composition: Integra
Art Director: Julia Hall
Cover Design: Quinn Banting
Cover Image: Janet Foster/Masterfile

1 2 3 4 5   14 13 12 11 10

Printed and bound in USA.

To James G. Eayrs and André Donneur,
pioneers in the study and teaching
of Canadian foreign policy

Contents

Chapter 7   The Prime Minister and Summit Diplomacy   177

Chapter 8   Widening the Circle: Other Ministers   205

Chapter 9   The International Policy Bureaucracy   227

Acronyms and Abbreviations

3D	diplomacy/defence/development
ABM	anti-ballistic missile
ACCT	Agence de coopération culturelle et technique
ALCM	air-launched cruise missile
APEC	Asia-Pacific Economic Cooperation
ASEAN	Association of Southeast Asian Nations
AU	African Union
AUF	Agence universitaire de la Francophonie
BMD	ballistic missile defense
BNA	British North America
BQ	Bloc Québécois
CAF	Canadian Armed Forces
CARICOM	Association of Caribbean Commonwealth countries
CAW	Canadian Auto Workers
CCC	Canadian Chamber of Commerce
CCCE	Canadian Council of Chief Executives
CCF	Cooperative Commonwealth Federation
CCME	Canadian Council of Ministers of Education
CCND	Canadian Committee for Nuclear Disarmament
CENTCOM	Central Command (US)
CEO	chief executive officer
CF	Canadian Forces
CHOGM	Commonwealth Heads of Government Meetings
CIDA	Canadian International Development Agency
CIIPS	Canadian Institute for International Peace and Security
CLC	Canadian Labour Congress
CME	Canadian manufacturers and exporters
C-NAFTA	Federal–Provincial Committee on the North American Free Trade Agreement
CNAFTN	Committee for North American Free Trade Negotiations

CND	Campaign for Nuclear Disarmament (UK)
CSIS	Canadian Security Intelligence Service
CSN	Confédération des syndicats nationaux
C-TPAT	Customs-Trade Partnership against Terrorism
C-Trade	Federal/Provincial/Territorial Committee on Trade
CUPE	Canadian Union of Public Employees
CUSO	Canadian University Service Overseas
DAC	Development Assistance Committee (OECD)
DART	Disaster Assistance Response Team
DEA	Department of External Affairs
DEW	Distant Early Warning line (NORAD)
DFAIT	Department of Foreign Affairs and International Trade
DHS	Department of Homeland Security (US)
DISC	Domestic International Sales Corporation
DM	deputy minister
E&I	Department of Employment and Immigration
EAITC	External Affairs and International Trade Canada
EAO	External Aid Office
FAO	Food and Agriculture Organization
FAST	Free and Secure Trade program
FCCC	Framework Convention on Climate Change
FLQ	Front de libération du Québec
FSF	Financial Stability Forum
G-4	The Quad
G8	Group of Eight
G-20	Group of 20 (finance ministers/central bank governors)
G-20	Group of 20 (leaders)
GATT	General Agreement on Tariffs and Trade
GDU	Garrison Diversion Unit
GNP	gross national product
GO5	Coalition Gestion de l'offre 5
IAE	International Assistance Envelope
IBRD	International Bank for Reconstruction and Development

ICBL	International Campaign to Ban Landmines
ICBM	Inter-continental ballistic missile
ICCS	International Commission for Control and Supervision
ICER	Interdepartmental Committee on External Relations
ICISS	International Commission on Intervention and State Sovereignty
ICJ	International Court of Justice
ICSC	International Commission for Supervision and Control
IETCD	International Economic and Technical Cooperation Division
IFI	international financial institution
IFOR	NATO Implementation Force, Bosnia
IGGI	Inter-governmental Group on Indonesia
ILO	International Labour Organization
INS	Immigration and Naturalization Service (US)
IPS	International Policy Statement
IR	international relations
ISAF	International Security Assistance Force (Afghanistan)
IT&C	Department of Industry, Trade and Commerce
ITW/AA	Integrated Tactical Warning/Attack Assessment
JI	Jemaah Islamiyah
KFOR	Kosovo Force
KGB	Komitet Gosudarstvennoye Bezopastnosti
KMT	Kuomintang (Nationalist Party, China)
KLA	Kosovo Liberation Army
MAD	mutual assured destruction
MAIQ	Ministère des Affaires intergouvernmentales du Québec
MEF	Major Economies Forum on Energy and Climate Change
MEQ	Manufacturiers et exportateurs du Québec
MITT	Ministry of Industry, Trade and Technology (Ontario)
MP	member of parliament
MRI	Ministère des Relations internationales (Québec)
NACC	North Atlantic Cooperation Council (NATO)
NAFTA	North American Free Trade Agreement
NATO	North Atlantic Treaty Organization

NDP	New Democratic Party
NEG/ECP	New England Governors/Eastern Canadian Premiers
NEP	National Energy Program
NERC	North American Electricity Reliability Council
NGO	nongovernmental organization
NORAD	North American Aerospace Defence Agreement
NORTHCOM	Northern Command (US)
NRC	National Research Council
NWS	North Warning System (NORAD)
OAS	Organization of American States
ODA	Official Development Assistance
OECD	Organisation for Economic Cooperation and Development
OEF	Operation Enduring Freedom (Afghanistan)
OIC	Organisation of the Islamic Conference
OIF	Organisation internationale de la Francophonie
OIRP	Office of International Relations and Protocol (Ontario)
OSCE	Organization for Security and Cooperation in Europe
P&P	Priorities and Planning Committee of Cabinet
P-5	permanent five members of the UN Security Council
PC	Progressive Conservative
PCO	Privy Council Office
PFP	Partnership for Peace (NATO)
PJBD	Permanent Joint Board on Defence
PLO	Palestine Liberation Organization
PMO	Prime Minister's Office
PQ	Parti Québécois
PRC	People's Republic of China
PRT	Provincial Reconstruction Team (Afghanistan)
R2P	responsibility to protect
RCMP	Royal Canadian Mounted Police
SDI	Strategic Defense Initiative (US)
SFOR	Stabilization Force
SM5	Supply Management 5

SPP	Security and Prosperity Partnership
SSEA	secretary of state for external affairs
SUCO	Service universitaire canadien outré-mer
TBS	Treasury Board Secretariat
TEIGA	Ministry of Treasury, Economic and Intergovernmental Affairs (Ontario)
TNO	Trade Negotiations Office
TRIPs	trade-related intellectual property rights
UNCED	United Nations Conference on Environment and Development
UNCHR	UN Commission on Human Rights
UNESCO	UN Economic, Social and Cultural Organization
UNFCCC	UN Framework Convention on Climate Change
UNFICYP	UN Peacekeeping Force in Cyprus
UNICEF	UN International Childrens' Emergency Fund
UNOSOM	UN Operation in Somalia
UNPROFOR	UN Protection Force, former Yugoslavia
UNTAC	UN Transitional Authority in Cambodia
UPA	Union des produceurs agricoles
USCG	United States Coast Guard
USSR	Union of Soviet Socialist Republics
VOW	Voice of Women
WHO	World Health Organization
WTO	World Trade Organization

Preface

This book had its origins in the mid-1980s as *The Politics of Canadian Foreign Policy*. That book went through two further editions, in 1989 and 1997. In the early 2000s, the three of us decided to rewrite that book in French, not only updating it, but also expanding references that would be useful and relevant for students studying in French. While the basic structure was retained, *Politique internationale et défense au Canada et au Québec*, which appeared in 2007, was much more than just a translation of *The Politics of Canadian Foreign Policy*, bringing as it did the fresh perspective of two scholars who are not only younger (and younger still) than the original author but also the viewpoint of francophone scholars of international relations. We decided to rewrite it once again in English. Like *Politique internationale*, *International Policy and Politics in Canada* is not just a translation of its predecessor, but an updated and revised version.

In the quarter-century that has passed since the original version of this book first appeared, much has changed. In the fall of 1983, when *The Politics of Canadian Foreign Policy* went to press, the international system was marked by severe crisis and Canadian politics by the prospect of change. Internationally, relations between the United States and its allies in the Cold War on the one hand and the Soviet Union on the other were extremely tense. In March 1983 the administration of Ronald Reagan had outlined plans for a Strategic Defense Initiative designed to make the United States immune from attack by nuclear weapons. In September Soviet jet fighters shot down a Korean Air Lines Boeing 747, killing all 269 on board. In November, the North Atlantic Treaty Organization launched Operation Able Archer, which was intended as an exercise to simulate the start of a nuclear war between East and West. All of NATO's militaries went to DEFCON1, the highest nuclear alert; as part of the exercise, Margaret Thatcher, the British prime minister, and Helmut Kohl, the German chancellor, were spirited away to secure locations and disappeared from public view. Indeed, the exercise was so realistic that the Soviet leadership in Moscow believed the West was about to launch a nuclear attack, and readied its own nuclear weapons for war. The war scare was heightened by the broadcast just days later of a made-for-TV movie, *The Day After*, that portrayed in grim detail a nuclear exchange between East and West.

In Canada, the Constitution, entrenching a new Charter of Rights and Freedoms, had been patriated the year before—but Québec, still governed by a Parti Québécois freshly reelected after the substantial rejection of sovereignty-association in the 1980 referendum, was still outside the Constitution. In the fall of 1983, the long tenure of Pierre Elliott Trudeau was coming to an end and Brian Mulroney had just ousted Joe Clark as leader of the Progressive Conservative party, bringing with him hopes that his leadership would end the long domination of Canadian politics by the Liberal party. The effects of the crushing recession of the early 1980s, marked by high interest rates, the migration of manufacturing, and high levels of American protectionism, were still being felt. Levels of anti-American sentiment in Canada were high, galvanized not only by American protectionism but also by such transborder issues as acid rain. There was also deep opposition to the Reagan administration's Strategic Defense Initiative and to the testing by the United States Air Force of cruise missiles over the snowy stretches of Canada's north.

In the autumn of 2009, as we finish this book, both the world and Canada look radically different. Contemporary global politics is no longer marked by intense rivalry between great powers. The Soviet Union collapsed in the late 1980s, an event marked most vividly by the breaching of that iconic symbol of division between East and West, the Berlin Wall, in November 1989. The Soviet Union's successor state, the Russian Federation, reprogrammed its nuclear weapons and joined the former enemies of the Soviet Union in an expanded Group of Eight, while most members of the rival alliance that the Soviet Union created, the Warsaw Pact, have joined a hugely expanded NATO. The People's Republic of China, which had cooperated with the United States and the West in the 1980s in a de facto anti-Soviet coalition, is now the major trading partner of the United States and of a number of other countries, cooperating in the management of the 2008 global financial crisis. The architecture of global politics is marked by summit diplomacy, with the emergence of new groupings that have grown to crowd the annual agendas of many world leaders. Instead of great-power rivalry, global politics in 2009 continues to be marked by the challenge of radical Islamism, the July 2009 bombings in Jakarta being the latest in a series of attacks since the early 1990s.

In Canada, the most important of these attacks, those launched in the United States on September 11, 2001, continues to cast a long shadow. Over the summer of 2009, 13 more Canadian soldiers were killed in the mission that began in 2001, when the Canadian government joined NATO allies in an attack on Afghanistan for harbouring those who had planned and financed 9/11. Likewise, the effects of 9/11 continue to cause the United States to "thicken" its borders, affecting the transborder flows that accelerated after the embrace of the North American Free Trade Agreement. In Canadian politics, the landscape has also changed. Three minority governments in a row attest to the radical shifts in the party system that have marked the past quarter-century: the collapse of the Progressive Conservative party as a result of challenges from the rise of the Reform party in the west and a party in Québec committed to the *souverainiste* cause rising to be the Official Opposition; the fragmentation of the vote that sustained the Liberal party through three majorities in the 1990s; the "reuniting" of the Conservative Party of Canada under Stephen Harper that ended Liberal dominance but has not to date produced a sufficient shift among voters to produce a majority.

But despite all the profound changes in both global and Canadian politics, it can be argued, as we did in all previous versions of this book, that for those who make (and study) the international policies of a particular country, the essence of their task has not changed much in the intervening years. Only the milieu, the problems of the time, and the personalities have changed (and even then, some of the personalities have proved exceedingly long-lived, such as Fidel Castro Ruz of Cuba). The tasks of those who make international policy in Canada in the post-9/11 era remain not all that different from the tasks that faced their predecessors during the Cold War period—or indeed in the eras before that. Those tasks are to grapple with the anarchical nature of global politics; to cope with the greater power of other political communities, particularly the United States; to protect Canada from the predations of others; to protect and advance the interests of Canadians; and to wrestle with the competing and contending demands Canadians impose on their governors. This is the enduring essence of international policy, regardless of the era.

Our purpose in this book is to provide a heuristic framework for analyzing the foreign policy behaviour of one country in the international system. We argue that a country's international policy is forged in the nexus of politics at three levels—the global, the domestic, and the governmental—and that to understand how and why Canada's international policies look as they do, one has to look at the interplay of all three.

SUPPLEMENTS

CourseSmart for Instructors

CourseSmart goes beyond traditional expectations—providing instant, online access to the textbooks and course materials you need at a lower cost for students. And even as students save money, you can save time and hassle with a digital eTextbook that allows you to search for the most relevant content at the very moment you need it. Whether it's evaluating textbooks or creating lecture notes to help students with difficult concepts, CourseSmart can make life a little easier. See how when you visit **www.coursesmart.com/instructors.**

CourseSmart for Students

CourseSmart goes beyond traditional expectations—providing instant, online access to the textbooks and course materials you need at an average savings of 50%. With instant access from any computer and the ability to search your text, you'll find the content you need quickly, no matter where you are. And with online tools like highlighting and note-taking, you can save time and study efficiently. See all the benefits at **www.coursesmart.com/students.**

PEARSON mysearchlab

MySearchLab offers students extensive help with their writing and research project and provides round-the-clock access to credible and reliable source material.

Research

Content on MySearchLab includes immediate access to thousands of full-text articles from leading Canadian and international academic journals, and daily news feeds from The Associated Press. Articles contain the full downloadable text—including abstract and citation information—and can be cut, pasted, emailed, or saved for later use.

Writing

MySearchLab also includes a step-by-step tutorial on writing a research paper. Included are sections on planning a research assignment, finding a topic, creating effective notes, and finding source material. Our exclusive online handbook provides grammar and usage support. Pearson SourceCheck™ offers an easy way to detect accidental plagiarism issues, and our exclusive tutorials teach how to avoid them in the future. And MySearchLab also contains AutoCite, which helps to correctly cite sources using MLA, APA, CMS, and CBE documentation styles for both endnotes and bibliographies.

To order this book with MySearchLab access at no extra charge, use ISBN 978-0-13-208816-9.

Take a tour at **www.mysearchlab.com**.

ACKNOWLEDGMENTS

We owe a deep debt of gratitude to numerous people who helped bring this project to completion. We would like to thank all members of the team at Pearson Canada—Laura Pratt, Joel Gladstone, Söğüt Güleç, Megan Burns, and Jordanna Caplan—for their consistent support for the project over the past two years, and their hard work on our behalf. Our thanks to the 10 reviewers engaged by Pearson for providing us with incisive criticisms and excellent suggestions:

B. Greg Anderson
University of Alberta

Donald Barry
University of Calgary

C. Brian Bow
Dalhousie University

Duane Bratt
Mount Royal College

D. Hevina Dashwood
Brock University

Dr. Andrew Lui
McMaster University

A. Elizabeth Riddell-Dixon
University of Western Ontario

Heather Smith
University of Northern British Columbia

Denis Stairs
Dalhousie University

Donald Story
University of Saskatchewan

Finally, Rodney Rawlings, our copy editor, and Sally Glover and Tara Tovell, our proof-readers, improved the manuscript in numerous ways, making us appear far more polished than we really are.

KRN/SR/SP
Howe Island/St-Sauveur/Montréal
October 2009

A Note to Students

It is customary in books such as this to include "Suggested Readings" or something similar, intended to direct students to key sources. Students of international policy in Canada are fortunate to be able to draw on a rich array of primary and secondary sources, in English and in French. However, the burgeoning literature in the field makes this an increasingly daunting task. For example, when Stephen J. Randall and John Herd Thompson put together such a list for their work on Canadian–American relations, it turned into a 19-page bibliographical essay that discusses over 300 sources.[1]

We take a somewhat different approach in this book. While we do provide a brief discussion below with some illustrative sources for further research, our "suggested readings" are to be found in each chapter's notes. Notes serve two purposes. First, they are the traditional means of providing readers with the source of quotations, research, interpretation, or ideas. Second, notes act as a form of hypertext, providing additional information about a topic in the text (and because they do this best when they appear as footnotes at the bottom of the page, Pearson Canada deserves thanks for its far-sighted decision to incorporate them here). We use notes for both these purposes, and we are hoping that our readers will not only explore the footnotes for additional information, but will also use the notes in this book as a bibliographical guide. We have tried to ensure that the references are as full as possible, not to be pedantic, but to point the way to those scholars who have treated subjects in greater depth than is possible in a survey such as this one.

We also provide a number of sources in French, a reflection of the vibrant scholarship on international policy and politics in Canada that often remains largely invisible to many students at English-speaking universities. We hope that just as students at French-language universities routinely read the work of English-speaking scholars, readers of this book will read the contributions of francophone scholars.

FURTHER RESEARCH: ADDITIONAL SOURCES

The purpose of this brief bibliographical survey is to provide a guide to some of the general literature. A full bibliography on international policy in Canada is available at http://www.pedc.uqam.ca | Publications | Bibliography.

Histories

The best general histories of Canada and international policy are: C.P. Stacey's two-volume series, *Canada and the Age of Conflict*, vol. 1: *1867–1921* (Toronto: Macmillan, 1977) and vol. 2: *1921–1948: The Mackenzie King Era* (Toronto: University of Toronto Press, 1981); James Eayrs's five-volume series, *In Defence of Canada*, that covers from the end of the

---

[1] John Herd Thompson and Stephen J. Randall, *Canada and the United States: Ambivalent Allies*, 4th ed. (Montréal and Kingston: McGill-Queen's University, 2008), "Bibliographical Essay," 409–28.

First World War until the 1950s; John W. Holmes's two-volume history of the immediate postwar decade, *The Shaping of Peace: Canada and the Search for World Order, 1943–1957;* Paul Painchaud, ed., *De Mackenzie King à Pierre Trudeau: Quarante ans de diplomatie canadienne (1945–1985)* (Québec: Presses de l'Université Laval, 1989); and Robert Bothwell, *Alliance and Illusion: Canada and the World, 1945–1984* (Vancouver: UBC Press, 2007). On the history of Canadian–American relations, see John Herd Thompson and Stephen J. Randall, *Canada and the United States: Ambivalent Allies*, 4th ed. (Montréal and Kingston: McGill-Queen's University Press, 2008).

Annual Reviews

For the period 1939–1984, the Canadian Institute of International Affairs published a series, *Canada in World Affairs.* The final volume in this series covers the Trudeau years: J.L. Granatstein and Robert Bothwell, *Pirouette: Pierre Trudeau and Canadian Foreign Policy* (Toronto: University of Toronto Press, 1990). Students should also consult the international affairs section of the *Canadian Annual Review.* Since 1984, members of the Norman Paterson School of International Affairs at Carleton University have edited an annual series, *Canada Among Nations.* Each volume features essays on both the foreign policy process and key issues in international policy.

Journals and Periodicals

Scholarly articles on international policy in Canada can be found in the following journals: *International Journal*, the quarterly of the Canadian International Council; *Canadian Journal of Political Science*, the journal of the Canadian Political Science Association; *Études internationales*, published by the Institut québécois des hautes Études internationales; *Canadian Foreign Policy*, published by the Norman Paterson School of International Affairs at Carleton University; and the journal of the Association for Canadian Studies in the United States, *American Review of Canadian Studies.* Shorter articles with a policy focus can be found in *Policy Options*, published by the Institute for Research on Public Policy (http://www.irpp.org), and *bout de papier: Canada's Magazine of Diplomacy and Foreign Service*, published by the Professional Association of Foreign Service Officers (http://pafso.com/magazine.cfm). For military issues, consult the *Canadian Military Journal* (http://www.journal.dnd.ca/index-eng.asp).

Diaries, Memoirs, Biographies

There are numerous diaries, memoirs, and biographies of the major political and bureaucratic figures in Canadian international policy. *The Mackenzie King Record* is edited in four volumes by J.W. Pickersgill and D. Forster. Lester B. Pearson's memoirs are in *Mike: The Memoirs of the Rt. Hon. Lester B. Pearson*, in three volumes; John English has published a two-volume biography of Pearson. Basil Robinson's *Diefenbaker's World* is a foreign policy memoir written by Diefenbaker's External Affairs liaison officer; a lengthier and more scholarly treatment may be found in Denis Smith, *Rogue Tory: The Life and Legend of John G. Diefenbaker.* Paul Martin, Sr., Mitchell Sharp, and Pierre Elliott Trudeau have all published memoirs. Trudeau and his foreign affairs adviser, Ivan Head, published a memoir dealing specifically with foreign policy: Ivan Head and Pierre Trudeau, *The Canadian Way: Shaping Canada's Foreign*

Policy, 1968–1984 (Toronto: McClelland & Stewart, 1995). Some parts of Christina McCall and Stephen Clarkson's two-volume *Trudeau and Our Times* deal with foreign policy.

All four prime ministers who served from September 1984 to 2006 have published memoirs: Brian Mulroney, *Memoirs* (Toronto: McClelland & Stewart, 2007); Kim Campbell, *Time and Chance: The Political Memoirs of Canada's First Woman Prime Minister* (Toronto: Seal Books, 1997); Jean Chrétien, *My Years as Prime Minister* (Toronto: Alfred A. Knopf Canada, 2007); Paul Martin, *Hell or High Water: My Life in and out of Politics* (Toronto: McClelland & Stewart, 2008).

Also of note are memoirs of Canadian officials: Allan Gotlieb, *"I'll Be with You in a Minute, Mr. Ambassador": The Education of a Canadian Diplomat in Washington* (Toronto: University of Toronto Press, 1991); Allan Gotlieb, *The Washington Diaries, 1981–1989* (Toronto: McClelland & Stewart, 2006); Charles Ritchie, *Storm Signals: More Undiplomatic Diaries, 1962–1971* (Toronto: Macmillan, 1983); James Bartleman, *Rollercoaster: My Hectic Years as Jean Chrétien's Diplomatic Adviser, 1994–1998* (Toronto: McClelland & Stewart, 2005).

Primary Sources

Edited selections of speeches and documents on Canadian international policy are also available: Walter A. Riddell, ed., *Documents on Canadian Foreign Policy, 1917–1939* (Toronto: University of Toronto Press, 1962); R.A. MacKay, ed., *Canadian Foreign Policy, 1945–1954* (Toronto: McClelland & Stewart, 1971). Arthur E. Blanchette edited three volumes of *Canadian Foreign Policy: Selected Speeches and Documents*—for 1955–65, 1966–76, and 1977–1992.

The Department of Foreign Affairs and International Trade publishes a full historical record in the series *Documents on Canadian External Relations*, a selection of memoranda and dispatches. Volume 1 begins in 1909; at present, volumes are available for the early 1960s. All volumes are fully searchable online at http://www.international.gc.ca/department/history-histoire/dcer/browse-en.asp.

Government Websites

Department of Foreign Affairs and International Trade: http://www.international.gc.ca

Department of National Defence/Canadian Forces: http://www.forces.gc.ca

Canadian International Development Agency: http://www.acdi-cida.gc.ca

Prime Minister's homepage: http://www.pm.gc.ca

Parliament:

> House of Commons:
> http://www2.parl.gc.ca/HouseChamberBusiness/ChamberHome.aspx

> House of Commons Standing Committee on Foreign Affairs and International Development: http://www2.parl.gc.ca/CommitteeBusiness/CommitteeHome.aspx?Cmte=FAAE

> House of Commons Standing Committee on National Defence:
> http://www2.parl.gc.ca/CommitteeBusiness/CommitteeHome.aspx?Cmte=NDDN

Library and Archives Canada maintains archived collections of all the above websites: http://www.collectionscanada.gc.ca

Ministère des Relations internationales du Québec: http://www.mri.gouv.qc.ca

International Policy and Politics in Canada Website

For further resources on international policy in Canada, visit our website: http://ip-pi.ca.

About the Authors

Kim Richard Nossal is Sir Edward Peacock Professor of International Relations, Department of Political Studies, Queen's University, Kingston. He is a former editor of *International Journal*, the quarterly journal of the Canadian International Council, Canada's institute of international affairs. He has served as president of both the Australian and New Zealand Studies Association of North America and the Canadian Political Science Association. Since 2006 he has been the chair of the Academic Selection Committee of the Security and Defence Forum program of the Canadian Department of National Defence.

Nossal has authored or edited twelve books and monographs, and published a number of articles in scholarly journals and chapters in books on Canadian and Australian foreign and defence policy. Besides *International Policy and Politics in Canada*, he is the author of *Politique internationale et défense au Canada et au Québec* (with Stéphane Roussel and Stéphane Paquin, 2007), *The Patterns of World Politics* (1998), *Rain Dancing: Sanctions in Canadian and Australian Foreign Policy* (1994), *Relocating Middle Powers: Australia and Canada in a Changing World Order* (with Andrew Cooper and Richard A. Higgott, 1993), and has co-edited *Architects and Innovators: Building the Department of Foreign Affairs and International Trade, 1909–2009* (with Greg Donaghy, 2009) and *Diplomatic Departures: The Conservative Era in Canadian Foreign Policy, 1984–1993* (with Nelson Michaud, 2001).

At present, he is engaged in a project on the domestic politics of the Afghanistan mission in Australia and Canada. His webpage is at **http://post.queensu.ca/~nossalk/**.

Stéphane Roussel is an associate professor in the Department of Political Science at the Université du Québec à Montréal (UQAM) and Canada Research Chair in Canadian Foreign and Defence Policy. He graduated from Université de Montréal (Ph.D., 1999). Professor Roussel is a member of the Centre d'études des politiques étrangères et de sécurité (CEPES, UQAM), and a Fellow at the Canadian Defence and Foreign Affairs Institute (CDFAI, Calgary). He is also an external associate of the York Centre for International and Security Studies (YCISS), York University; the Research Group in International Security (REGIS), Université de Montréal/McGill University; and the Réseau francophone de recherche sur les opérations de paix, Université de Montréal.

Roussel has published several articles and books on Canadian international policy, including *L'aide canadienne au développement* (with François Audet and Marie-Eve Desrosiers, 2008), *Politique internationale et défense au Canada et au Québec* (with Kim Richard Nossal and Stéphane Paquin, 2007), *Culture stratégique et politique de défense: l'expérience canadienne* (2007), and *The North American Democratic Peace: Absence of War and Security Institution-Building in Canada–US Relations, 1867–1958* (2004).

He currently directs three research programs: "Competing Views of Emerging Threat in the Arctic," "Canada–US Relations during Periods of Crisis," and "Quebec's Public Opinion Attitude toward International Security." His webpage is at **www.pedc.uqam.ca/**.

Stéphane Paquin is professor of applied politics at the Université de Sherbrooke. He holds a Ph.D. in international relations from the Institut d'études politiques de Paris (Sciences-po) and an M.A. from Université de Montréal. In 2006 he served as the interim Secretary General of the International Political Science Association (IPSA). He previously taught at the Institut d'études politiques de Paris, Northwestern University in Chicago, and Université de Montréal.

In addition to *International Policy and Politics in Canada,* Paquin is the author or co-author of seven books, including *La nouvelle économie internationale* (2008), *Pourquoi La Francophonie* (with Louise Beaudoin, 2008), *Politique internationale et défense au Canada et au Québec* (with Kim Richard Nossal and Stéphane Roussel, 2007), *Paradiplomatie et relations internationales* (2004), and *Paradiplomatie identitaire en Catalogne* (2003); and editor or co-editor of eight volumes, including *Introduction aux relations internationales: Théories, pratiques et enjeux* (with Dany Deschênes, 2009), *Les relations internationales du Québec depuis la doctrine Gérin-Lajoie (1965-2005)* (2006), *Histoire des relations internationales du Québec* (with Louise Beaudoin, 2006), and *Mastering Globalization: New Sub-States' Governance and Strategies* (with Guy Lachappelle, 2005). His articles have appeared in the *Canadian Journal of Political Science, Canadian Public Administration, Nationalism and Ethnic Politics, Études internationales, Revue internationale de politique comparée, Guerres mondiales et conflits contemporains,* and *Politique et Sociétés.*

Paquin lectures on international relations, international political economy, comparative politics, and Canadian and Québec international policy. His webpage is at **www.usherbrooke .ca/politique_appliquee/nous_joindre/personnel/enseignant/paquin_.html**.

CHAPTER 1

Introduction: Analyzing International Policy in Canada

Most citizens experience their country's international relations in a kaleidoscopic way—as a series of seemingly disconnected fragments that tumble into particular, apparently unpredictable, patterns, but then are gone. Headlines about the prime minister's latest summit travels; television images of a flag-draped coffin arriving home from overseas; sound-bites of an opposition leader proposing an alternative policy on greenhouse-gas emissions; talking heads commenting on the government's response to the latest financial crisis; getting caught in a street demonstration about an overseas war—these experiences capture our attention, and provoke our interest and perhaps our emotions, but only briefly. Today's issues are quickly eclipsed by new and more pressing concerns. But these, in turn, become yesterday's news, quickly forgotten, and if remembered at all are considered vaguely irrelevant. Little thought tends to be given to the longer-term coherence of the current events of their country's engagement in international affairs, or their connections with the past. Even less thought is devoted to putting these issues into a broader analytical perspective, or to understanding what forces shape the numerous issues that appear on the agenda.

The purpose of this chapter is to suggest a way in which Canada's engagement in the world can be analyzed methodically. While we do not base our discussion on an explicit theory of foreign policy—sharing as we do Christopher Hill's skepticism that "an overarching single theory of foreign policy can ever be achieved without being bland and tautological"[1]—the analysis here owes a clear intellectual debt to the work of those many scholars in the subfield of foreign policy analysis[2] who have sought to render the study of foreign policy more systematic and whose work has influenced our own thinking.[3] It proposes to examine a number of analytical issues and to offer a heuristic framework for analysis: a set of guideposts to how we might think about this country's external policy, how we might organize

---

1 Christopher Hill, *The Changing Politics of Foreign Policy* (London: Palgrave Macmillan, 2003), 10.

2 Foreign policy analysis as a subfield of international relations has a long pedigree that has gone through several "generational" changes: for overviews of the subfield, see Walter Carlsnaes, "Foreign Policy," in Walter Carlsnaes, Thomas Risse-Kappen, and Beth A. Simmons, eds., *Handbook of International Relations* (London: Sage, 2002), 331–49; Kim Richard Nossal, "Opening Up the Black Box: The Decision-Making Approach to International Politics," in David G. Haglund and Michael K. Hawes, eds., *World Politics: Power, Interdependence and Dependence* (Toronto: Harcourt Brace Jovanovich, 1990), 531–552; Steve Smith, "Theories of Foreign Policy: An Historical Overview," *Review of International Studies* 12:1 (January 1986), 13–29; Don Munton, "Comparative Foreign Policy: Fads, Fantasies, Orthodoxies, Perversities," in James N. Rosenau, ed., *In Search of Global Patterns* (New York: Free Press, 1976), 257–71.

3 For example, Richard C. Snyder, H.W. Bruck and Burton Sapin, *Foreign Policy Decision-Making* (1962), republished in 2002 as Richard C. Snyder, H.W. Bruck, Burton Sapin, Valerie M. Hudson, Derek H. Chollet, and James M. Goldgeier, *Foreign Policy Decision-Making (Revisited)* (New York: Palgrave Macmillan, 2002); Joseph Frankel, *The Making of Foreign Policy* (1963); Michael Brecher, Blema Steinberg and Janice Stein, "A Framework for Research on Foreign Policy Behaviour," *Journal of Conflict Resolution* 13:1 (March 1969), 75–101; James N. Rosenau, "Pre-theories and Theories of Foreign Policy," in Rosenau, *The Scientific Study of Foreign Policy* (New York: Free Press, 1971), 95–149; Graham T. Allison, *Essence of Decision: Explaining the Cuban Missile Crisis* (Boston: Little, Brown, 1971); Robert Jervis, *Perception and Misperception in International Politics* (Princeton: Princeton University Press, 1976); Irving J. Janis, *Victims of Groupthink: Psychological Studies of Policy Decisions and Fiascoes* (Boston: Houghton Mifflin 1982); Walter Carlsnaes,

and filter observations about Canada's international behaviour, and how we can better understsand the determinants and sources of policy in Canada. In essence, it seeks to answer two questions: What is international policy, and what determines a country's course in international politics?

WHAT IS INTERNATIONAL POLICY?

It may seem odd to begin with so elementary a question. Indeed, the question raises two issues: Why do we use "international policy" in this book instead of the more usual term "foreign policy," and what is the subject matter of this study? For reasons that will become apparent, it is not possible to answer these questions separately.

Over the past decade, "international policy" has become increasingly used as a synonym for "foreign policy," particularly by some government officials, in large measure because they believed that "foreign policy" no longer accurately conveyed what governments actually do in international politics. This of course brings up a prior question: What exactly *is* foreign policy, and why has that term become so problematic?

The subfield of foreign policy analysis has always been bedevilled by the difficulty of agreeing on what foreign policy is. There are two sources of definitional muddle. First, many students of foreign policy acknowledge that it is a frustratingly undefined concept; as Laura Neack puts it, many foreign policy analysts have been content to take the view that "we know it when we see it."[4] As a result, the term gets used in a variety of ways. Don Munton has complained that "it is seldom clear whether it refers to actions, goals, decisions, objectives, strategies, interests, orientations, initiatives, attitudes, plans, undertakings, or whatever."[5] His complaint is quite accurate; the term *is* used in all those frequently inconsistent ways, by the practitioners of statecraft themselves, by academics who study their behaviour, by the media, and by the general public. But while it may be maddening to students of foreign policy, who need to put a premium on definitional clarity, the problem cannot be satisfactorily resolved. One might try to propose a more precise definition, and insist that all other definitions of the term were wrong, but this would defy common usage, if not common sense. One just has to live with the multifaceted usage of the term in common parlance.

"The Agency-Structure Problem in Foreign Policy Analysis," *International Studies Quarterly* 36 (1992), 245–70; Alexander L. George, *Bridging the Gap: Theory and Practice in Foreign Policy* (Washington: United States Institute of Peace, 1993); Frédéric Charillon, "Introduction," in Charillon, ed., *Politique étrangère: Nouveaux regards* (Paris: Presses de Science po, 2002), 13–29; Dario Battistella, "La politique étrangère," in Battistella, ed., *Théories des Relations internationales* (Paris: Presses de Sciences Po, 2003), 303–33; Hill, *Changing Politics*; Walter Carlsnaes, "Comparative Foreign Policy Analysis in a Historical and Contemporary Context," in Margaret G. Hermann and Bengt Sundelius, eds., *Comparative Foreign Policy Analysis: Theories and Methods* (Englewood Cliffs, NJ: Prentice-Hall, 2004); Valerie M. Hudson, *Foreign Policy Analysis: Classic and Contemporary Theory* (Lanham, MD: Rowman and Littlefield, 2006); Laura Neack, *The New Foreign Policy: Power Seeking in a Globalized Era*, 2nd ed. (Lanham, MD: Rowman and Littlefield, 2008).

4 Neack, *New Foreign Policy*, 25.

5 Munton, "Comparative Foreign Policy," 258.

That said, however, it is necessary to make one minimal distinction between foreign policy and other phenomena. The word "policy" connotes the actions, goals, and decisions of authoritative political actors—or, more commonly, governments. To note that foreign policy lies only in the realm of governments (and only those governments with the authority to make "foreign policy") is to make a critical distinction. For it excludes from consideration the foreign behaviour of nongovernmental or transnational actors, such as civil society organizations or firms. Not that these actors do not play an important role in global politics, that such groups do not have significant impact on the formulation and execution of the international behaviour of governments, or that they do not pursue international policies. They do. But foreign policy, properly speaking, is concerned with the explanation of the behaviour of those who have the capacity to exercise supreme political authority over a given set of issue areas for a given people in a given territory. That is why we exclude the external policies of governments like Toronto or Montréal, the elected councils of which declared their cities as nuclear-free zones in the 1980s. These declarations commanded no authority, and they had no effects other than symbolism, for the simple reason that municipal governments are not empowered to decide such matters, even for those who live within their boundaries. Such decisions can be, and were, overridden by the legitimate authority on such matters, the federal government. But that is why, in the case of Canadian foreign policy, we must include the provincial governments in a consideration of foreign policy—for the provinces do have such competence in certain areas, as we will see in Chapters 11 and 12.

If we follow this distinction with trying to define the foreign nature of governmental behaviour, we run into the second difficulty with the term "foreign policy": the lack of agreement on which policy matters are to be included and which excluded. The difficulty is that other policy areas are defined in purely *functional* terms: fisheries policy, forestry policy, correctional policy, industrial policy, and so on. While there will inevitably be some overlaps among policy areas, a functional delineation makes differentiation between "fisheries" policy and "forestry" policy relatively easy. However, "foreign" policy suggests a delineation on fundamentally *geopolitical* terms: it begins where the territorial jurisdiction of the state ends. For some, therefore, "foreign" policy is likened to any other type of governmental policy—the programs and instruments used by governments to achieve their political objectives. It is not so much "foreign policy" as "policy that is foreign," the argument goes, in the sense that it is assumed to be little more than the external dimension of domestic policy, the projection of the government's interests beyond the boundaries of the state. "Foreign policy is not a thing in itself," Canada's foreign minister declared in 1969, "but an external dimension of domestic policy."[6] In other words, any aspect of governmental policy that extends beyond the geopolitical boundaries of the state is, ipso facto, foreign policy.

There is, however, a dissenting view that "foreign" policy is in fact a functional, not a geographical, category, with its own distinct subject matter, just like other functional policy areas. Hans J. Morgenthau is the most unabashed proponent of this realist view. International *politics*, he argues, is not the same as international *relations*. International politics is about power. Thus, only when a state's behaviour is directed toward the maintenance or expansion

---

6 D.C. Thomson and R.F. Swanson, *Canadian Foreign Policy: Options and Prospects* (Toronto: McGraw-Hill Ryerson, 1971), 9. Such a sentiment, as we shall see in Chapter 2, has enjoyed a venerable history in Canada's foreign relations.

of its power is it acting politically. Not all foreign policy behaviour, he claims, is political. He cites the kind of international activities that are part of a country's foreign relations but not its foreign policy: the negotiation of extradition treaties, trading in goods and services, providing humanitarian assistance, and promoting one's culture abroad.[7]

A less exclusionary perspective would focus not so much on power alone, but on the associated elements of power politics. In this view, the proper realm of foreign policy is the realm of "high politics." This is what Rudyard Kipling termed the "Great Game" of international politics: the juggling, conspiring and, if necessary, fighting that states engage in for dominance and control in an anarchic system. Leaders of states balance and counterbalance power, aligning and combining, to avoid the inexorable consequences of losing power: domination, conquest, enslavement, or death at the hands of their rivals.[8] But international politics is also an arena in which states cooperate with one another in limited ways, erecting in the process the rudimentary elements of what Hedley Bull has termed an "anarchical society."[9] In this view, foreign policy is mainly concerned with three dominant questions of high politics: international order, peace, and war.

The realist perspective, resting as it does on the concept of power, was increasingly derided as outmoded. In an era of globalization, market forces and revolutions in technology and communications diminish the autonomy of states and increase their dependence and interdependence, and create issues of global magnitude beyond the capacity of any one state to address. In this era, issues of "high" politics have given way in importance to the "low" issues of international relations: the distribution of wealth; the exchange of goods, services, capital, and knowledge; the protection of the environment; the maintenance of adequate global food supplies; the management of global threats to health; and such issues as international communications, the transnational trade in drugs and sex workers, money laundering, and the protection of copyright. In short, realists would have us believe that international politics and foreign policy is only about power and "high" politics, with the economic concerns of "low" politics in their own separate domain. But, as Geoffrey Underhill has put it crisply, "the political and economic domains cannot be separated in any real sense."[10] In this view, to exclude from the area of "foreign policy" the profound transformations taking place in the international system no longer makes much sense (if it ever did).[11]

The rejection of such high/low politics and politics/economics dichotomies makes particular sense in Canada's case, mainly because those who make foreign policy for Canada have always been concerned about *both* domains, high and low. They have never been able to avoid the consequences of the rivalries of the great powers, nor the systemic wars into

---

7 Hans J. Morgenthau, *Politics Among Nations: The Struggle for Power and Peace*, 5th ed. (New York: Alfred A. Knopf, 1948, 1973), 27–28.

8 This argument is put most baldly in the work of Kenneth N. Waltz, *Theory of International Politics* (Reading, MA: Addison-Wesley, 1979), chap. 9; Stephen Walt, *The Origins of Alliances* (Ithaca: Cornell University Press, 1987).

9 Hedley Bull, *The Anarchical Society: A Study of Order in World Politics* (New York: Columbia University Press, 1977).

10 Geoffrey R. D. Underhill, "State, Market, and Global Political Economy: Genealogy of an (Inter-?) Discipline," *International Affairs* 76:4 (October 2000), 806.

11 See Steve Smith and Michael Smith, "The Analytical Background: Approaches to the Study of British Foreign Policy," in Michael Smith, Steve Smith, and Brian White, *British Foreign Policy: Tradition, Change and Transformation* (London: Unwin Hyman, 1988), 15; Hill, *Changing Politics*, 4.

which the global community has periodically been plunged since 1867. Canadian governments have always been concerned with peace, war, and the nature of the international order. At the same time, however, they have never been able to escape an abiding concern with the low politics of economics, trade, the environment, and social affairs.

Our examination of the Canadian case will thus focus on issues of both high and low politics and a range of different functional issue areas, from alliance politics to trade relations. But this more expansive approach does not solve the terminological conundrum. The Canadian government pursues policies that have a "foreign" component in a wide variety of policy areas, making distinctions between those various policy areas problematic. Is "defence policy," which consumes $19 billion per year and is implemented by the Canadian Armed Forces (CAF)—or, as they are also called, the Canadian Forces (CF)[12]—and administered by the Department of National Defence, "foreign policy"? The same question can be asked about development assistance policy, which accounts for approximately $4.5 billion and is administered by the Canadian International Development Agency (CIDA)—or about trade policy, fisheries policy, or any other area with an international reach.

The answer in all cases is: yes and no. On the one hand, all these areas of policy are part of the Canadian government's engagement with the international system, and in that sense a corporal on patrol in Kandahar province, an official from Agriculture and Agri-Food Canada posted in Tigray implementing a CIDA project on food security, and an official from the Department of Foreign Affairs and International Trade attending a meeting in Paris on anti-counterfeiting measures are all engaged in Canadian "foreign" policy. On the other hand, there is still a tendency to conceive of defence, development assistance, trade, and other policy areas with a "foreign" element as something different from "foreign policy."[13]

To grapple with the phenomenon of "departmentalism"—the tendency of government agencies to pursue their own mandates and resist centralized coordination—a number of governments in the late 1990s and early 2000s adopted what was called a "whole-of-government" approach to policy, in which different agencies would work to provide integrated policy that crossed department lines.[14] This integrated approach was implemented during the North Atlantic Treaty Organization (NATO) mission in Afghanistan in the 2000s by Britain and Canada. The so-called "3D approach" was designed to combine the efforts of the main agencies of the NATO states who were involved in Afghanistan—the defence forces, the development assistance agencies, and the diplomats from the foreign office.

---

12 Section 14 of the National Defence Act, 1985 reads: "The Canadian Forces are the armed forces of Her Majesty raised by Canada and consist of one Service called the Canadian Armed Forces." The purposely ambiguous wording is deeply political: it permits both the political elites in Canada, and the military itself, to "disappear" the armed essence of this agency of the Canadian state, in keeping with the mythology we explore below that Canada is "peaceable kingdom" and Canadians are an "unmilitary people."

13 Academic explorations tend to mirror these "silos": David B. Dewitt and David Leyton-Brown, eds., *Canada's International Security Policy* (Scarborough: Prentice-Hall Canada, 1995); Cranford Pratt, ed., *Canadian International Development Assistance Policies: An Appraisal*, 2nd ed. (Montréal and Kingston: McGill-Queen's University Press, 1996); and Michael Hart, *A Trading Nation: Canadian Trade Policy from Colonialism to Globalization* (Vancouver: UBC Press, 2003).

14 See Tom Christensen and Per Lægreid, "The Whole-of-Government Approach to Public Sector Reform," *Public Administration Review* 67:6 (2007), 1059–66. The related notion of "joined-up-government" introduced by the government of Tony Blair in 1997 was designed to address intractable social problems that could not be solved by a single government agency alone.

This shift in practice had an impact on language, as governments sought terminology that more accurately reflected the interconnections between the different elements of the state's operations that had international connections. In 2001, for example, Peter Hain, minister of state in the British Foreign and Commonwealth Office, published a pamphlet entitled "The End of Foreign Policy?" that predicted that "as the concept of 'foreign' becomes ever harder to define," foreign ministries would be renamed Departments of Global Affairs, and "international policy" would "no longer be split into arbitrary compartments."[15]

The Canadian government of Paul Martin also embraced this change of language. The result of his government's review of different aspects of Canada's international engagement in 2004 and 2005 was entitled the *International Policy Statement*. It consisted of reviews of each of the three Ds (diplomacy, development assistance, and defence)—plus a T (for international trade), with an overview presented by the prime minister himself.[16] Likewise, the government of Québec embraced this more expansive terminology in its 2006 policy statement.[17] It has also made its appearance in the academic literature: Brian W. Tomlin, Norman Hillmer, and Fen Osler Hampson used it for their examination of a range of different "international policies."[18] In this book, we follow their lead and use "international policy" to describe the external objectives of the Canadian government; its orientation to the international system; its relations with other governments; its positions and attitudes on world politics; and its actions, programs, and decisions.

WHAT DETERMINES INTERNATIONAL POLICY?

To explain a country's foreign policy, the analyst must not only take into account what happens at the international level, but also be familiar with the pattern and context of domestic politics, and with the nature, structure, and process of government. As James N. Rosenau has argued, "those who study foreign policy must, perforce, concern themselves with politics at every level."[19] We argue that because international policy is forged in the nexus of three political environments—the international, domestic, and governmental—it cannot be analyzed unless each level of politics is examined. It is within these three spheres that the sources, or the determinants, of a state's foreign policy are to be found.

---

15 Peter Hain, *The End of Foreign Policy: Britain's Interests, Global Linkages and Natural Limits* (London: Fabian Society, 2001), 61.

16 Canada, *A Role of Pride and Influence in the World: Canada's International Policy Statement*, overview booklet (Ottawa, April 2005).

17 Québec, Ministère des Relations internationales, *Québec's International Policy: Working in Concert* (Québec: Gouvernement du Québec, 2006), available http://www.mri.gouv.qc.ca/en/pdf/Politique.pdf.

18 Brian W. Tomlin, Norman Hillmer, and Fen Osler Hampson, *Canada's International Policies: Agendas, Alternatives, and Politics* (Toronto: Oxford University Press, 2008). See also Victoria Honeyman, "Gordon Brown and International Policy," *Policy Studies* 30:1 (2009), 85–100.

19 James N. Rosenau, "New Directions and Recurrent Questions in the Comparative Study of Foreign Policy," in Charles F. Hermann, Charles W. Kegley, Jr., and James Rosenau, eds., *New Directions in the Study of Foreign Policy* (Boston: Allen and Unwin, 1987), 1.

The International Setting

The first important source of foreign policy for any state is the international setting, or what is sometimes known as the "external environment." There are two distinct but inter-related aspects to the international setting. The first is the environment in which the state must operate; the second is the condition in which the state finds itself in that environment. An assessment of the external environment has to address a number of general questions about the nature of the international system itself. What is the nature of the units that constitute the system—in other words, what political form do the units take: City-states? Empires? Monarchies? Democracies? How many states are there within the system? What is the nature of the international order, hierarchical or anarchic? What is the nature and degree of cooperation and institutionalization within the system? The effects of all these factors on a particular state's foreign policy will be considerable. For example, the polarity of the system is likely to structure the general orientation of inter-national policy, since polarity has an impact on alliance politics. Likewise, the degree and strength of international institutions will have a comparable impact, for strong institu-tionalization is likely to offer greater opportunities for active diplomacy aimed at strengthening international order.

We also need to know the state's geographic location, its status relative to other states, its external economic linkages, its alignments and alliances, its capabilities, and its power. It will be obvious that these are "external" sources only in the sense that these attributes of the state, when they interact in the context of international politics, have an effect on that state's behaviour. It will also be obvious that these factors tend to be the givens, or *relative invariants*, in a state's foreign policy in the sense that every foreign policymaker has to confront them without being able to change them easily or rapidly. To a brief examination of each of these factors we now turn.

Location

Most students of international policy begin with the obvious aspect of setting, the state's "location" in global politics. Location refers not only to its physical or geographic loca-tion, but also to its location in a broader political sense. The importance of geographic location is clear. It determines not only some of the attributes of capability, such as arable land and natural resources, but also neighbourhood and the state's security. Clearly, the foreign policy concerns of a state with no neighbours will be different from those of a state with numerous other states on its borders; a state physically remote from others will have an outlook on security different from that of a state surrounded by aggressive, bel-ligerent, or expansionist neighbours. Likewise, distance or proximity to the centres of great power rivalry will condition a state's external policy, if not its very existence. Living next to a great power complicates a country's foreign policy, as Afghanis, Mexicans, Poles, Vietnamese, and, of course, Canadians, have discovered.

But location also refers to a state's position in the international hierarchy and the impact that has on international policy outcomes. A superpower such as the United States will obviously have a different perspective on international politics than smaller states. That country has interests, preoccupations, and influence that extend across the globe; the pattern of its international relationships will reflect its status at the apex of the international hierarchy. Smaller countries will have narrower interests and a narrower focus.

Economic Structure

A country's location in the global economy will bear heavily on the pattern of its international relations, for economic structure and complexity will affect its capacity for independence in foreign policy and its weaknesses and strengths. It will also determine the dominant patterns of its trading relations, sources of capital for investment, and the health of its national currency in global currency markets. A state with a minimally developed economy or a single-crop economy will have different international priorities than one with a highly mixed and relatively strong economic structure. Such issues as dependence (or lack of it) on international trade, financial flows, technology, or natural resources like food, fuel, or raw materials will also have a bearing on foreign policy orientations, as will diversification (or lack of it) of the state's trade.

Dynamics of Group Membership

By definition, a state's international policy is about its relations with other states in international affairs. Rare is the state that keeps utterly to itself (such as Albania or Burma during the Cold War) or is deemed a "pariah" by the international community (such as North Korea). Group dynamics defines how the government and people of a political community engage the international community; how that community affiliates itself in international society—who are considered "friends" and who "enemies" and who are treated with indifference. Alignments can take different forms, from simple notions of friendship between governments or peoples to formal military alliances between governments. The nature of alignment will vary depending on the broader international context. Thus, for example, during the Cold War period, when the focus of many governments was on military and strategic issues, the world was divided into three camps: the East, led by the Soviet Union; the West, led by the United States; and a fluid and heterogeneous group, the neutral and nonaligned states. By contrast, during the post–Cold War era, when the rivalry between the Soviet Union and the United States had dissipated, economic factors assumed a greater importance in global politics. For some, however, the post–Cold War era was marked by divisions between what Samuel Huntington called "civilizations."[20] In the post-9/11 era, the administration of George W. Bush tended to see alignments according to the attitude of governments toward the "global war on terror."

A state's alignments in international affairs will have a profound influence on its international policy. Alignment, particularly a military alliance, brings with it the advantages of the enhanced physical security that comes with membership in a collective. But it also brings obligations that limit its capacity for independent action. The fear of being abandoned at a critical juncture can prompt a government into a servile loyalty to its allies. Alliances protect, but they also constrain. Moreover, alignments tend to be inertial: once aligned, a state will find it exceedingly difficult to realign. Finally, alignments for smaller states tend to define friends and enemies: the adversaries of their friends become their adversaries, sometimes drawing them into conflicts in which they may not have any interests at stake.

---

20 Samuel P. Huntington, *The Clash of Civilizations and the Remaking of World Order* (New York: Simon and Schuster, 1996).

Capabilities

Analyzing the international policy of a state requires an examination of the resources a state has to act in international politics. Relative to others in the international system, what is its population? Its wealth? Its level of development? Its industrial structure? Its level of urbanization? Its capacity to apply military force or economic coercion? How dependent or vulnerable is it, economically or militarily? These data are often used to establish a state's rank in the international hierarchy; we will return to this question in Chapter 3.

There are other types of resources that are much more difficult to quantify, but nevertheless have a considerable influence on a state's the ability to act internationally. These include a state's reputation in the international community, its ideological or religious beliefs, or its willingness to pursue justice as a goal.

Power

All these factors—geographic location, economic structure, group dynamics, and capability—have a crucial impact on a state's power. International politics is first and foremost an anarchic system: there is no sovereign to arbitrate disputes and only a loose arrangement of rules to which states attach themselves; each state must seek to maximize its goals as best it can, either unilaterally or multilaterally, in cooperation with other states. All states have to rely on power to achieve the one goal of all political communities: the capacity to make decisions for themselves. A careful consideration of power as a critical determinant of both a state's subsidiary foreign policy goals and its capacity to attain them is integral to understanding its international policy.

Domestic Politics

Some theorists of international politics assert that the only external factor that is important for understanding the orientation of states in global politics is the relative power of states. In this view, it is the nature of the international system itself that drives the behaviour of states, and therefore the domestic setting of foreign policy is of little importance. Regardless of the political regime in place, and regardless of the personality or the ideology of the state's political leaders, the state will always adopt policies that will maximize its gains in an anarchic environment.

Kenneth Waltz, who is the primary exponent of this "structural realist" theory, compares the systemic forces of the international system to those of a market. Firms have structural constraints that ensure they act in a manner to further their survival; those that do not go bankrupt. So too in international politics, Waltz argues; units that do not act according to the international system's requirements will perish. The structure of the international environment, therefore, determines the general behaviour of states.[21]

Structural realism seeks to explain (i.e., predict) international politics at a macro level—the interactions of states as a whole. As Waltz acknowledges, "structures never tell us all that we want to know. Instead they tell us a small number of big and important things."[22] In other words, his theory is not meant as a micro theory that will predict the

---

21 Waltz, *Theory of International Politics*, esp. 89–91.

22 Kenneth N. Waltz, "A Response to My Critics," in Robert O. Keohane, *Neorealism and Its Critics* (New York: Columbia University Press, 1986), 329.

exact course of a particular state's international policy. That, he suggests, would be like expecting the law of gravity to predict the exact path of a leaf falling from a tree.

By contrast, in this book we are interested in the path of the leaf: understanding the external behaviour of a particular state at a particular time in history. So we cannot ignore the impact domestic politics has on the international policies of the government in Ottawa.

Our exploration is guided by those who argue a position diametrically opposed to that of the structural realists, particularly historians, who use empirical and inductive models. According to Pierre Milza, historians work on the assumption that the internal politics of states provide "a major key" to explaining international politics, adding that "history and political science have gone [. . .] in different directions on the issue of the Hobbesian doctrine that there should be a difference between politics 'outside' and politics 'inside.'"[23] Liberal approaches to international relations have gone in the same direction. For them, the kind of political regime, relations between different groups within the state, as well as the relationship between the state and its citizens are all important determinants of the international behaviour of a state. In particular, democratic peace theory, which seeks to explain the absence of war between liberal democracies, is in large part based on the assumption of the predominance of internal factors in international policy.[24]

Other approaches take an intermediate position. Classical realist authors, such as Hans Morgenthau or Raymond Aron,[25] claimed to explain the individual behaviour of states but continued to insist on a very clear separation between internal and external factors—and placing greater importance on the latter. However, supporters of a modern form of realism, which Gideon Rose has called "neoclassical realism," argue that, even though relative power relations always constitutes the most important factor in understanding international relations, certain domestic factors are crucial for explaining particular decisions and policies of states.[26] Likewise, constructivists examine ways in which a state's behaviour in global politics is socially constructed rather than simply being determined by structural or external forces. Constructivism seeks to expose how the interactions of political communities are shaped intersubjectively through a process of social interaction, both within the

---

23 Pierre Milza, "Politique intérieure et politique étrangère," in René Rémond, ed., *Pour une histoire politique* (Paris: Seuil, 1996), 316 and 319. To be sure, some political scientists object to the constructions of "insides" and "outsides." See, in particular, R.B.J. Walker for a critique of what he calls the "double move" of international relations to construct "insides" (politics within the state where sovereignty applies) and "outsides" (anarchic politics between sovereign states): *Inside/Outside: International Relations as Political Theory* (Cambridge: Cambridge University Press, 1993), esp. 171–72.

24 For surveys of liberal approaches to international relations, see Tim Dunne, "Liberalism," in John Baylis and Steve Smith, eds., *The Globalization of World Politics: An Introduction to International Relations*, 3rd ed. (Oxford: Oxford University Press, 2005), 185–203; Stéphane Roussel and Dan O'Meara, "Le libéralisme classique: une constellation de theories," in Alex Macleod and Dan O'Meara, eds., *Théories des relations internationales: Contestations et resistances* (Montréal: Athéna Éditions, 2007), 89–110.

25 Morgenthau, Politics Among Nations; Raymond Aron, *Peace and War: A Theory of International Relations* (Garden City, NY: Doubleday, 1966).

26 Gideon Rose, "Neoclassical Realism and Theories of Foreign Policy," *World Politics* 51:1 (October 1998), 144–172. See, for example, Randall L. Schweller, *Unanswered Threats: Political Constraints on the Balance of Power* (Princeton: Princeton University Press, 2006).

state and outside. The focus of constructivism is on the *ideational*—the importance of ideas in the shaping of action, decisions, and policy.[27]

Because we are interested in understanding one state in particular, our analysis focuses on a number of possible explanatory variables related to domestic politics. We have to take into account the nature, composition, and background of Canadian society, and particularly the historical cleavages within the Canadian political system. As we will see, the uneasiness of the relationship between French-speaking and English-speaking Canadians has, not surprisingly, inserted itself into questions of international policy over the course of Canadian history. Likewise, we must take into account the liberal-democratic nature of politics in Canada, and the impact liberal-democratic norms have had on the international behaviour of policymakers in Ottawa. Representative government means that Canada's governors are accountable to the citizenry not only through periodic elections but also through the media and civil society organizations. The role the "electoral connection" and civil society play in the formulation of international policy in Canada will be examined in Chapter 4.

Finally, we examine societal demands for particular directions in international policy behaviour. Such demands emanate in two distinct ways. On the one hand, there is the unorganized and largely uncoordinated expression of public or elite opinion about international affairs and the proper policies that the Canadian government should pursue. On the other hand, organized interests will articulate particular demands. How the demands of both organized and unorganized interests are aggregated and managed by the state affects the course of foreign policy.

To be sure, the conclusions one draws about the impact of domestic politics on Canada's international policies will largely depend on the initial working assumptions one brings to the analysis. There are three broad approaches to the analysis of the relationship between the governors and the governed, and each employs very different assumptions.

The liberal-pluralist approach assumes that the state is essentially an extension of society, and therefore it works in the interests of society as a whole. In this perspective, the state is somewhat like a referee, reacting to numerous demands made by the different individuals and groups that make up society, adjudicating between conflicting demands, and making political decisions based on a "marketplace" calculus of what policies will be supported by the greatest number.[28]

Approaches that focus on class, by contrast, assume that the behaviour of the democratic state is intimately bound to the capitalist mode of production and to the inherent conflict between the dominant or hegemonic class—those who control capital—and other classes in society. Some see the state merely as the governing instrument of the bourgeoisie, always making decisions that serve the interests of the capitalist class. Others, by contrast, have a more nuanced view of the relations between the bourgeoisie and the state

---

27 The constructivist literature is considerable. For overviews, see Chris Reus-Smit, "Constructivism," in Scott Burchill et al., *Theories of International Relations*, 4th ed. (New York: Palgrave Macmillan, 2009); Dan O'Meara, "Constructivisme: Sa place, son rôle, sa contribution et ses debats," in Macleod and O'Meara, *Théories*, 181–206; for an excellent application of theory to a well-known case, see Jutta Weldes, *Constructing National Interests: The United States and the Cuban Missile Crisis* (Minneapolis: University of Minnesota Press, 1999).

28 For the classic formulation of pluralist theory, see Robert A. Dahl, *Who Governs? Democracy and Power in an American City*, 2nd ed., with Douglas W. Rae (New Haven: Yale University Press, 2005), which is a reprinting of the 1961 original with a new preface by Dahl and an assessment by Rae.

in capitalist society. They see the state as being relatively autonomous from those who actually own and control capital. The state's dominant interest, in this view, is the long-term maintenance of the capitalist system itself, not the short-term enrichment of individual capitalists. Thus, the state seeks to be as autonomous as possible in order to mediate inter-class conflict, frequently embracing in the process policies (such as social welfare policies) that are not in the short-term interests of individual capitalists. However, to the extent that such policies forestall disaffection or revolution, and give the system legitimacy in the eyes of other classes, they save greedy capitalists from themselves, and are thus in the long-term interests of the capitalist system.[29]

The unifying theme of these theories of the democratic state is that the state's behaviour is understandable only by reference to interests in society. In contrast with this perspective is the neo-Weberian, or statist, approach, which assumes a rather different relationship between the state and societal interests. It somewhat turns around Winston Churchill's assertion that, in a democratic society, politicians and bureaucrats "are proud to be the servants of the state and would be ashamed to be its masters": state officials are both the servants of the state *and* its masters. Drawing on the perspectives of the German political sociologist Max Weber, statism argues that the group of men and women charged with making authoritative decisions for the polity, and who make up the state, are not mere automata, robotically pursuing the interests dictated to them by others. Rather, they have their own conceptions of the national interest, conceptions that include a calculus about their own personal interests, those of the institution, department, or agency to which they are attached, and the interests of the government as a whole. They certainly will have their own ideas about how best to achieve these. Statist scholars further assume that the policy preferences embraced by the state as a whole may differ considerably from the interests and preferences being articulated by individuals, groups, organizations, and classes in society. Moreover, statist theory asserts, where there is a clash between the state's preferences and those of society, it is the state that has both the willingness and the capacity to ensure that state preferences prevail. On this view, the governors are fully or partially autonomous from the governed.[30]

Clearly, these paradigms offer starkly different predictions about the importance of domestic sources as an influence on the making of international policy in Canada.[31] The

---

29 Linda Freeman, "CIDA, Wheat, and Rural Development in Tanzania," *Canadian Journal of African Studies* 16:3 (1982), 479–504; Rand Dyck, *Canadian Politics: Critical Approaches* (Toronto: Nelson Canada, 1993), 11ff; Cranford Pratt, "Competing Perspectives on Canadian Development Assistance Policies," *International Journal* 51:2 (Spring 1996), 235–58.

30 The statist literature includes Eric A. Nordlinger, *On the Autonomy of the Democratic State* (Cambridge: Harvard University Press, 1981) and Theda Skocpol, "Bringing the State Back In: Strategies of Analysis in Current Research," in Peter B. Evans, Dietrich Rueschemeyer, and Theda Skocpol, *Bringing the State Back In* (Cambridge: Cambridge University Press, 1985), 3–43. John M. Hobson, by contrast, develops a "non-realist theory of international agential state power" that seeks to show that the state has considerable "agential power"—that is, the capacity to shape the international system—but also seeks to locate the state in a co-constitutive way with society and the broader international system in a way that reveals that it is only partially autonomous. See "The Two Waves of Weberian Historical Sociology in International Relations," in John M. Hobson, ed., *Historical Sociology of International Relations* (Cambridge: Cambridge University Press, 2002), 63–81.

31 Kim Richard Nossal, "Analyzing the Domestic Sources of Canadian Foreign Policy," and Cranford Pratt, "Dominant Class Theory and Canadian Foreign Policy: The Case of the Counter-consensus," both in *International Journal* 39:1 (Winter 1983–4), 1–22, 9–135. Pratt revisits this debate in "Competing Perspectives."

liberal-pluralist approach predicts a maximal role for domestic sources: the interests, preferences, and demands of individuals and groups in society will be reflected in Canada's international behaviour. Classist approaches predict that the key explanatory variable in policymaking will be either the interests of the capitalist class or the interests of the capitalist system writ large. Statism predicts little or no impact: international policy will be explained by either external factors or governmental sources, or both. Thus the prism employed is significant, for it will have an inevitable impact on one's conclusions about the importance of the domestic sources of policy.

Governmental Politics

The international and domestic environments set the parameters within which the government makes international policy decisions. Both external and domestic factors will establish the general boundaries of viable policy options. But it is the government—the state—that makes the decisions that shape a country's course in international politics. However, while the government makes decisions in the name of the state, it is not a unitary, monolithic actor, thinking, moving, and speaking with any singularity of purpose. Within the government apparatus, there are competing conceptions of the national interest, contending views on which is the best course to follow. Moreover, these diverging opinions articulated by officials, both elected and bureaucratic, are heavily influenced by their position within the government structure. And decisions made by the government are not necessarily and always based on assumptions of pure means–end rationality: frequently, decision outcomes are the product of bureaucratic politics—saw-offs and compromises by officials from different parts of the government negotiating on a particular foreign policy issue.[32]

Because the process of decision-making will so markedly affect the decisions themselves, we must examine the governmental setting of international policymaking, and the politics within the state apparatus that influences those outcomes. The institutional and organizational structures that exist for the making of authoritative decisions, the lines of authority within those institutions, and the political relationships within and between different organizations of government—these must all be examined. Politics within the executive (between cabinet ministers, between the cabinet and the bureaucracy, and between departments and agencies of government) and between the executive and those members of the legislature not in cabinet, both in the House of Commons and the Senate, will be important in explaining policy.

There is, in Canada's case, one additional aspect to the governmental setting that must be examined: the impact of the federal structure on the conduct of international policy. The constitutions of most federal states allow only a limited role in international affairs for the constituent units in the federation. In Canada, however, the Constitution Acts of 1867–1982 are now silent on the question of whether the federal government has exclusive jurisdiction

---

32 On bureaucratic politics, see Graham T. Allison and Philip Zelikow, *Essence of Decision: Explaining the Cuban Missile Crisis* (New York: Longman, 1999); Nelson Michaud, "Graham Allison et le paradigme bureaucratique: vingt-cinq ans plus tard est-il encore utile?," *Études internationales* 27:4 (December 1996), 769–94; for an application to the Canadian system, see Kim Richard Nossal, "Allison Through the (Ottawa) Looking Glass: Bureaucratic Politics and Foreign Policy in a Parliamentary System," *Canadian Public Administration* 22:4 (Winter 1979), 610–26.

in all matters of foreign policy.[33] Consequently, we must examine the politics between levels of government and the impact this has on the making of international policy.

IDENTITY AND HISTORY

The evolution of Canada's international policy presents a mixture of both change and continuity. Despite the massive changes that have occurred since Confederation both within Canada (in society, technology, the economy, the state, political ideas, and attitudes) and internationally (the distribution of power in the international system, the advent and then the eclipse of nuclear rivalry, the emergence of a globalized economy, the collapse of bipolarity, and the emergence of different power struggles), a number of facets of Canada's external relations have remained remarkably constant over a period of time, in some cases for generations. The constraints imposed by Canada's relations with the great powers have always been a preoccupation for policymakers in Canada concerned to preserve the country's autonomy. There is no less ambivalence about the relationship with the United States in 2010 than there was about the relationship with Britain before the Second World War. Canadians still exhibit a reluctance to spend on national defence during peacetime as did their predecessors in the decades between the world wars or before the Boer War. Canadians were as concerned about international trade in the era of competitive national trade at the end of the nineteenth century as they were in the contemporary era of globalization.

This element of continuity is particularly evident in how Canada has managed its relationship with the United States. The neighbourly quarrels over fish, environmental pollution, boundary security, and trade irritants of numerous sorts have kept prime ministers and presidents occupied for more than a century. Canadians have shown a persistent preoccupation with the country's trading relationship with the United States. Persistent Canadian desires for greater and more guaranteed access to American markets have coexisted with persistent fears of what impacts on Canada such access would have. To paraphrase J.L. Granatstein, trade is one issue that just will not go away,[34] not even after the signing of the free trade agreement with the United States in 1988, the North American Free Trade Agreement (NAFTA) in 1993, and the different agreements concluded after the attacks of September 11, 2001 to secure the Canadian–American frontier.

These observations prompt two comments. First, they underscore how important national identity has been, and continues to be, in the formulation of international policy. Identity is not only a matter of asserting sovereignty, but is also an important part of expressing a distinctive Canadian essence. Indeed, most citizens do not hesitate to claim that one of the main characteristics of being Canadian is not being American, and they expect the policies of their government to reflect this need to stand out. In this sense, it is

---

33 The British North America Act of 1867 did include Article 132, dealing with treaty implementation, which was subsequently repealed: we discuss this in Chapter 11. See also Hans Michelmann, ed., *Foreign Relations in Federal Countries* (Montréal and Kingston: McGill-Queen's University Press, 2009).

34 J.L. Granatstein, "Free Trade Between Canada and the United States: The Issue That Will Not Go Away," in Canada, *Royal Commission on the Economic Union and Development Prospects for Canada, The Collected Research Studies, vol. 29: The Politics of Canada's Economic Relationship with the United States*, Denis Stairs and Gilbert R. Winham, eds. (Toronto: University of Toronto Press, 1985), 11–54.

impossible to study Canada's international policy without looking at the degree to which it reflects Canadian values and culture, and how, in turn, distinctive values contribute to the formation of a national identity. That said, we must also bear in mind that international policy is another arena where we see divisions between English-speaking and French-speaking Canadians play out. Conflict over language and the national question in Québec are factors that cannot be overlooked in understanding Canada's international policy.

Second, evidence of both change and continuity prompts the observation that a nation's history will always play an important part in shaping policy, even if policymakers—not to mention analysts—are not always completely conscious of it. But the heritage of the past continues to influence, even imperceptibly, the broad orientations and the little decisions, for there can be no denying or forgetting what has gone before. Moreover, policymakers often try to apply to their problems to solutions that worked for their predecessors, even if circumstances have changed. History is one of the givens (or relative invariants), like geographical location or geostrategic alignment, impossible to change except over the course of generations. As Christopher Hill put it, "A state's past successes and failures, friendships and enmities, live on in the minds of present-day decision-makers both at home and abroad."[35] Thus the historical continuity in Canadian–American relations, John W. Holmes reminds us, is hardly surprising, for no nation can escape the inexorable consequences of its history: "Coping with the fact of the USA is and always has been an essential ingredient of being Canadian. It has formed us just as being an island formed Britain."[36]

It is because a country's international policy is affected by its past that we do not proceed as though there were an obvious "starting point," such as the achievement of sovereign status with the Statute of Westminster in 1931, or the end of the Second World War in 1945, or the end of the Cold War in 1991, or the transformations wrought by 9/11. Certainly no government in Ottawa ever started with a clean slate in its external policies, not even the government of the new self-governing dominion created by the British North America Act in 1867. Sir John A. Macdonald had to deal with the remnants of the past that imposed themselves on his present, as has every prime minister since. It is with the importance of the past in mind that the analysis here, while not a history of Canada's international policies, nonetheless attempts to take a somewhat broader view of the Canadian experience in international politics in order to tease out of historical examples the determinants and causes that have continuing relevance for understanding Canada's external policies today and in the future.

CONCLUSION

The discussion in this chapter—identifying the three political settings in which policy is made—is intended as a framework to guide analysis of Canada's international policies. The framework itself has no explanatory (that is, predictive) capability. Nor have we tried to provide a normative framework to determine what policies *should* be embraced by the

---

35 Christopher Hill, "The Historical Background: Past and Present in British Foreign Policy," in Smith, Smith, and White, *British Foreign Policy*, 33.

36 John W. Holmes, *Life with Uncle: The Canadian–American Relationship* (Toronto: University of Toronto Press, 1981), 107–108.

Canadian government. Finally, we have purposely not tried to enter, much less settle, the debate over whether the internal or the external is more important as a determinant of policy. Rather, our view is that, in an area as broad as international policy, there is no one factor that occurs so continuously that it becomes the lone determinant of a decision or set of decisions. Any research program on the international policy of a particular state should be multidimensional and flexible, since it rarely happens that isolated decisions or long-term policies are based on a single cause; explaining Canada's international policies, whether contemporary historical, requires a persistent attachment to the possibility that more than one factor is at play.

PART 1

The Policy Setting

The international policy of any state in the international system is by its very nature political. It emerges from the interplay of conflicting interests, divergent objectives, contending perceptions, and different prescriptions about the most appropriate course of action. Such interplay occurs at two distinct but interrelated levels: the conflicts and contentions occur both at a domestic level, between and among members of the political community, and at an international level, between and among the different governments of the states that make up the international community.

Thus, any state's course in world affairs is constrained and impelled by those two environments in which the state's policymakers must operate. Canada is no different: international politics and domestic politics both push and pull those who have to make foreign policy decisions for this country. The first part of the book thus focuses on an examination of the setting of international policy—in other words, the parameters within which Canada's policymakers must operate.

We begin with a discussion Canada's of "location" in global politics. In this book, "location" is used in several senses. First, it is used in its most obvious sense—geographical location. A country's geography—its physical attributes and where it is situated geopolitically—imposes unyielding and invariant parameters on all aspects of policy, including foreign policy. But we also look at Canada's economic "location," for how a state's economy is enmeshed in the larger international political economy will have a profound impact on most aspects of its foreign policy. Finally, we examine what might be thought of as Canada's diplomatic "location"—how the government in Ottawa interacts with other governments, both singly and in groups, in the contemporary international system. As we will see, the dynamics of group membership play a critical role in shaping the limits and the possibilities of Canadian statecraft. We also look at how these various factors determine Canada's capabilities in international politics.

We then turn to the issue of power, and how the exercise and possession of power in the international system constrains and impels policymakers. Historically, both practitioners and students of Canadian foreign policy have been concerned about Canada's role in international affairs: Is Canada a great power, a middle power, or a small power? We survey this debate, and suggest that determining what kind of "power" Canada is in fact does not really tell us much about Canada's power in international politics. Instead, an alternative view is explored. Using a power analysis approach, we examine the different tools of statecraft available to Canadian policymakers, in the process painting a rather different picture of Canadian power.

We then turn to the impact of domestic politics on the making of international politics in Canada. Policymakers are no less constrained and impelled by domestic politics—the interplay of the contending interests of societal actors, or, more plainly, the individuals who make up the Canadian political community. Canadians have interests in foreign policy issues and invariably seek to influence policy on a range of issues. We explore those interests and the influence that societal actors can bring to bear on foreign policy issues, drawing a distinction between the decision-making *process* and the decision-making *environment*.

The decision-making environment is the one, we argue, that most consistently influences policymakers. In particular, policymakers are constrained and impelled by dominant ideas—ideas that Canadians have about international policy and the proper place of their country in global politics. We then explore a century of dominant ideas about foreign policy: imperialism in the years before the First World War, isolationism in the years between the First and Second World Wars, internationalism in the Cold War era, and ending with a discussion of the shifts in dominant ideas that occurred with the end of the Cold War and the era that began after the attacks of September 11, 2001.

CHAPTER 2

Canada's International Location

The idea that there is an intimate link between domestic and international policy has been deeply embedded in the discourse of Canadian policy and politics for almost a century. In January 1922, Canada's prime minister, William Lyon Mackenzie King, attended a lecture by O.D. Skelton, professor of political and economic science at Queen's University; afterwards he noted in his diary that it was "an excellent address, pointing out that foreign policy was the extension of domestic policy."[1] In January 1948, Lester B. Pearson, who was at the time the undersecretary of state for external affairs— the senior civil servant in the Department of External Affairs—had had similar thoughts: "Foreign policy, after all, is merely 'domestic policy with its hat on'. . . . Canada's foreign policy, in so far as it is Canadian policy at all, is, in fact, largely the consequences of domestic factors. . . ."[2] The foreign policy review conducted by Pierre Elliott Trudeau after he assumed the prime ministership asserted that foreign policy was "the extension abroad of national policies."[3] A similar theme was sounded by the government of Brian Mulroney when it embarked on a review of foreign policy in 1985: "Canadian domestic issues are unavoidably bound up with international developments. Accordingly, the policies we develop—foreign and domestic—must address both Canadian and international realities. The two are inseparable elements of a truly national policy."[4] A parliamentary committee established by Jean Chrétien was even more blunt: "There is little distinction any more between foreign and domestic policies," it noted in November 1994. "Foreign policy *is* domestic policy."[5] Paul Martin's *International Policy Statement* of 2005 made the linkage explicit: "Our security, our prosperity and our quality of life all stand to be influenced and affected by these global transformations and by the challenges they bring—from the spectre of international terrorism to the threats of virulent disease, climate change and disappearing fish stocks."[6] It was a theme sounded again by Stephen Harper soon after he assumed the prime ministership in 2006:

> If there is any one thing that has struck me for the short time I have been in this job, it is how critically important foreign affairs has become in everything that we do. . . . And virtually every significant challenge we face—economic, environmental, demographic, security, health, energy, you name it—contains an important, if not critical, international dimension.[7]

---

1 Quoted in James Eayrs, *The Art of the Possible: Government and Foreign Policy in Canada* (Toronto: University of Toronto Press, 1961), 40n.

2 Lester B. Pearson, *Words and Occasions* (Toronto: University of Toronto Press, 1970), 68.

3 Canada, Secretary of State for External Affairs, *Foreign Policy for Canadians*, main booklet (Ottawa: Information Canada, 1970), 9.

4 Canada, Secretary of State for External Affairs, Competitiveness and Security: Directions for Canada's International Relations (Ottawa, 1985), 3.

5 Canada, Parliament, Special Joint Committee Reviewing Canadian Foreign Policy, *Canada's Foreign Policy: Principles and Priorities for the Future* (Ottawa: November 1994), 6.

6 Canada, A Role of Pride and Influence in the World: Canada's International Policy Statement, overview booklet (Ottawa, April 2005), unpaginated.

7 Stephen Harper, "Reviving Canadian Leadership in the World," speech to Woodrow Wilson International Center for Scholars, Ottawa, October 5, 2006, available http://www.pm.gc.ca/eng/media.asp?category=2&id=1343.

These perspectives reflect two sides of a single coin: They imply that Canada's international policies are deeply influenced by domestic policy and politics, and that Canada's domestic policies are as deeply affected by external influences. But if left unqualified, the idea that the international and domestic policy spheres are affected by each other does not help us understand how these dynamics actually work.

Governments cannot simply "go outside" and pursue their policy objectives in the way they can domestically. Within Canada, governments achieve political objectives by exercising authority and by using the coercive power of the state. In international policy, by contrast, Canada's authority stops abruptly at the border: one can no longer simply command obedience to Canadian wishes. One reason for this is the essentially anarchical nature of the international system, in which numerous independent political communities are all seeking to achieve their own political objectives, but without one superordinate sovereign political authority to regulate political relations among them or to make *political* decisions for the global community as a whole. The other reason is the increasingly "denationalized" and globalized economy over which national governments have diminishing control.[8]

By the same token, Canadian policy, domestic or international, is not simply dictated by external factors. While the forces of globalization may limit the autonomy of sovereign states and push governments to harmonize policies with one another, Linda Weiss has argued that states are not entirely powerless in the face of globalization.[9] On the contrary: states actually have considerable room to manoeuvre, as Jean Daudelin and Daniel Schwanen put it, despite the rigidities of the international environment.[10]

In short, this is hardly the raw and brutal state of nature so beloved by structural realist theories of international politics. While the "state of nature" analogy outlined by Thomas Hobbes in *Leviathan* continues to remain popular in theorizing about international relations, Hedley Bull argued over three decades ago that there is considerable order in what he called the "anarchical society" of nation-states.[11] Even if, as Alexander Wendt put it, anarchy is always socially constructed,[12] there is no escaping the anarchical essence of politics at a global level. In the final analysis, every state in the international system is the ultimate arbiter of its own interests: no one is entitled to command, and no one is obliged to obey.

It is one thing to decide one's own interests and formulate one's own objectives, as all sovereign states have the ability to do; it is another to be able to achieve these objectives. All governments will find that the ability to achieve their objectives is severely limited not only by the existence of other states also actively pursuing *their* own interests, but also by

8 Michael Hart, "The End of Trade Policy?," in Fen Osler Hampson and Christopher J. Maule, *Canada Among Nations 1993–94: Global Jeopardy* (Ottawa: Carleton University Press, 1993), 85–105; Stephen McBride, *Paradigm Shift: Globalization and the Canadian State* (Toronto: Fernwood Books, 2001).

9 Linda Weiss, *The Myth of the Powerless State: Governing the Economy in a Global Era* (Cambridge: Polity Press, 1998).

10 Jean Daudelin and Daniel Schwanen, "Room for Manoeuvre and the Paradox of Globalization," in Daudelin and Schwanen, eds., *Canada Among Nations 2007: What Room for Manoeuvre?* (Montréal and Kingston: McGill-Queen's University Press, 2007), 3–28.

11 Hedley Bull, *The Anarchical Society: A Study of Order in World Politics* (New York: Columbia University Press, 1977).

12 Alexander Wendt, "Anarchy Is What States Make of It: The Social Construction of Power Politics," *International Organization* 46:2 (Spring 1992), 391–425.

the often unforgiving nature of a globalized economy. And those who make international policy in Canada cannot simply fashion a world to their liking by wishing away the realities of the contemporary international political economy. Canadian objectives must therefore always be crafted to fit what is attainable. The means adopted to achieve goals must be appropriate to a political environment where success depends not on authority, but on power and influence. The purpose of this chapter is to explore the constraints and imperatives imposed by the international system.

RELATIVE INVARIANTS

Those who make Canada's international policy must always take into account what R.J. Sutherland termed "invariants,"[13] the unchanging conditions usually beyond the capacities of governments in Ottawa to modify. However, such factors might more properly be thought of as *relatively* invariant: while they are generally impervious to change, these conditions might well shift. For example, the bipolar international system that appeared in 1945 constituted a relatively stable "given"—until the unexpected collapse of the Soviet Union in 1991.

In this chapter we look at five invariants that affect Canada's international policies. We begin with geographic location, since geography is one of the primary constraints that policymakers must take into account. Geographic location determines a country's *neighbourhood*, and the communities on the borders with which Canada must deal. But geography also determines *geostrategic location*, and we examine how this location has shifted with shifting patterns of world politics. We then look at Canada's *economic structure* and its impact on policy. The third relative invariant is the influence that *group dynamics*—in particular, Canada's membership in multilateral organizations—exercises on policymakers. Finally we look at *material capabilities*—the resources that the Canadian government can bring to bear in the pursuit of international policy.

NEIGHBOURHOOD

Canada has four neighbours, but demography, culture, language, economic structure, and ideology have combined to make the United States a more important focal point of Canadian policy than the Russian Federation, Greenland, or the French overseas collectivity of Saint-Pierre-et-Miquelon. While Canada's "nordicity" is often celebrated,[14] and governments routinely claim that Canada is an Arctic nation,[15] in fact Canadians have a distinctly southern orientation. Most Canadians live in a thin band along the southern frontier—as far as

---

13 R.J. Sutherland, "Canada's Long Term Strategic Situation," *International Journal* 17:3 (Summer 1962), 199–201; for a reassessment of Sutherland's analysis, see Paul Buteux, "Sutherland Revisited: Canada's Long-Term Strategic Situation," *Canadian Defence Quarterly* 24:1 (Autumn 1994), 5–9.

14 The notion of "nordicity" was developed by the geographer Louis-Edmond Hamelin: see his *Canadian Nordicity: It's Your North Too*, trans. William Barr (Montréal: Harvest House, 1979).

15 In 1985, the Mulroney government's green paper asserted that "we are an Arctic nation. The North holds a distinct place in our nationhood and sense of identity. We view it as special, and ourselves as special because of it." Secretary of State for External Affairs, *Competitiveness and Security: Directions for Canada's International Relations* (Ottawa: Supply and Services Canada, 1985), 1. The 1994 foreign policy review echoed this sentiment, asserting that as a northern country, Canada had

possible from Arctic reaches. Most Canadians live within 300 kilometres of what Roger Swanson once called the "cellophane border,"[16] creating an inexorably southern exposure to American culture, mass media, society, and economics. Americans and three-quarters of Canadians share a common language. Even more importantly, an overwhelming majority of anglophone and francophone Canadians alike share the liberal bourgeois values dominant throughout North America, a sociopolitical homogenization that transcends Canada's fundamental linguistic and national cleavages. Patterns of economic activity—in particular the degree of trade and investment flows between Canada and the United States—are other attributes that direct attention southward.

Such obvious observations about the structure, nature, and location of Canadian society bear repeating if only to explain why the focus of foreign policy in Canada has always been fixed so firmly on the United States. This fixation has been a feature of British North American politics since the 1770s, when those in the northern half of North America chose to forge a separate political community. But it has steadily intensified over the course of the twentieth century with the rise of the United States as the preeminent power in world politics, the global expansion of American culture and economic power, and the increasing integration of the North American economy since the Second World War.

These observations also underscore another attribute of Canada's neighbourhood: its loneliness. The other states contiguous to Canada are neighbours in name only. Efforts have been made to forge closer links with Canada's transpolar neighbours—the Nordic countries (Denmark, Finland, Finland, Greenland, Iceland, Norway, and Sweden) and the Russian Federation—through such measures as the appointment in October 1994 of Mary May Simon, the founder of the Inuit Circumpolar Conference, as Canada's circumpolar ambassador, or the generally high level of activism of the Canadian government in regime construction in the Arctic.[17] However, the demographic realities of Canadian society make such linkages both limited and symbolic. From a Canadian perspective, such a limited neighbourhood has both benefits and disadvantages. Unlike most other small powers located next to great powers, Canada has no other neighbours to offset the preponderance of the United States. On the other hand, Canada has been able to forge a special relationship with the United States that few other countries living next to a great power have been able to match.

GEOSTRATEGIC LOCATION

A country's geographic location is absolutely invariant in the sense that its territorial limits are generally fixed. In that sense, a country's "neighbourhood"—the political communities on its borders with which it must deal on an ongoing basis—does not change much.

---

a particular responsibility to develop Arctic policy: Special Joint Committee, *Canada's Foreign Policy*, 45–46. Likewise, when Stephen Harper announced the construction of new icebreakers and a new deep-water port for the Arctic in July 2007, he claimed that these measures were necessary "because Canada's Arctic is central to our national identity as a northern nation. It is part of our history. And it represents the tremendous potential of our future." See http://pm.gc.ca/eng/media.asp?id=1742.

16 Quoted in James Eayrs, "The Cellophane Border: Reflections on Our Two Realities," *The Canadian*, May 22, 1976, 4.

17 See Oran R. Young, *Creating Regimes: Arctic Accords and International Governance* (Ithaca: Cornell University Press, 1998).

But a country's geostrategic location in global politics is more variable, shifting with time and the changing patterns of world politics. A survey of shifts in Canada's geostrategic location—and the effects this has had on policy—demonstrates this dynamic at work.

The "Long Peace"

From Confederation in 1867 until the Second World War (1939–1945), Canada was physically remote from the centre of the great power rivalries of Europe. Unlike small European states that were constantly threatened by their powerful neighbours, Canada never faced a serious national security problem, in large part because of its geographic location. Although the United States had twice attacked British North America—during the American revolution and in the War of 1812—the relationship between the United States and its neighbour to the north remained peaceful after 1867. In 1817, the Rush–Bagot agreement was put in place, limiting the deployment of naval vessels in the Great Lakes—one of the oldest arms control agreements. In the decades that followed, the British and the Americans gradually reduced their fortifications along the frontier, which gave rise to the idea of the world's longest "undefended border." (The border is in fact "defended," but by civilian rather than military agencies.)

To be sure, there were tensions in the Canada–United States relationship caused mainly by quarrels over the land border.[18] But in most cases, the difficulties were caused by factors not directly related to relations between Canada and the United States, but rather were caused either by tensions in British–American relations[19] or by nongovernmental actors.[20] The threats of an American diminished once the border between the two countries was clearly established, and particularly after the British and Americans managed to resolve most of their disputes with the signing of the Treaty of Washington in 1871.

Thus, after 1814, a "long peace" was slowly established between the two governments. A number of factors explain this. Certainly the existence of a kind of balance of power between Britain and the United States, in which British naval supremacy was counterbalanced

---

18 The three most prominent quarrels were the so-called Aroostook War between lumberjacks in Maine and New Brunswick between 1839 and 1842; President James K. Polk's sabre-rattling over the Oregon boundary to fulfil the promise of his campaign slogan—"Fifty-four forty or fight"—to put the American boundary at 54 degrees, 40 minutes of latitude (just north of Prince Rupert, B.C.); and the Alaska Boundary dispute, discussed further in Chapter 3.

19 Such as during the American civil war in the 1860s or over the border between Venezuela and British Guiana (now Guyana) in the late 1890s.

20 Prior to 1871 there were several cross-border incidents involving insurgents, rebels, and terrorists. After the 1837 rebellion in Upper Canada, William Lyon Mackenzie established a government-in-exile on Navy Island in the Niagara River that was being supplied by an American steamboat, the SS *Caroline*. In December 1837, a militia raiding party from Upper Canada crossed into the United States, seizing the *Caroline*, killing an American, setting fire to the ship, and sending it over the Falls. In October 1864, sympathizers of the Confederacy attacked St. Albans, a town in Vermont, from Canadian soil, killed one man, and wounded others. After the American civil war, Irish-American members of the Irish Republican Brotherhood, the Fenians, conducted terrorist attacks in Canada, apparently seeking to provoke an Anglo–American war that they believed would further the cause of Irish independence. On these episodes, see John Herd Thompson and Stephen J. Randall, *Canada and the United States: Ambivalent Allies*, 4th ed. (Montréal and Kingston: McGill-Queen's University Press, 2008), 38–39.

by American power on land, was one of these factors. The emergence of economic inter-dependence, reinforced by the cultural proximity between the two countries, also contributed to the reduction of tensions. Finally, the convergence of political values—particularly the fact that the United States and Canada were liberal democracies—probably allowed both governments to develop the kind of tolerance and mutual sympathy that encourages the renunciation of war as a means of resolving differences. In this sense, Canadian–American relations are an excellent example of the phenomenon of "democratic peace" articulated by liberal theorists of international relations.[21]

Although the two countries enjoyed a long period of peace during the nineteenth century, many Americans nonetheless dreamed of territorial expansion, an idea captured most clearly in the pithy phrase of an American editor, John Louis O'Sullivan. It was the fulfilment of America's "manifest destiny," he wrote in 1845, "to overspread the continent allotted by Providence for the free development of our yearly multiplying millions."[22] As the *Philadelphia Public Ledger* put it flamboyantly in 1853 (in a passage that has been much quoted since), the United States was bounded on the "East by sunrise, West by sunset, North by the Arctic Expedition and South as far as we darn please."[23] The allure of manifest destiny weakened steadily over the course of the nineteenth century, but the idea refused to die completely. In 1911, for example, the Speaker-Designate of the House of Representatives, Champ Clark, declared that "I hope to see the day when the American flag will float over every square foot of the British North–American possessions clear to the North Pole."[24] The idea continues to attract some Americans even in the contemporary era. For example, Pat Buchanan, an ultraconservative commentator and presidential candidate in 1992, 1996, and 2000, wrote in 1992 that "There is nothing wrong with Americans dreaming of a nation which, by the year 2000, encompasses the maritime and western provinces [and] the Northwest Territories all the way to the North Pole." (In 2002, he was still advocating that if Canada broke apart, the United States should pick up the pieces by offering statehood "should any breakaway Canadian province wish it," and was also suggesting that Greenland, which in his view "lacks the requisites of nationhood," should "eventually be formally annexed by the United States.")[25]

---

21 For a critical review of these different hypotheses, see Stéphane Roussel, *The North American Democratic Peace: Absence of War and Security Institution-Building in Canada–US Relations, 1867–1958* (Montréal and Kingston: McGill-Queen's University Press, 2004).

22 Quoted in George Brown Tindall and David E. Shi, *America: A Narrative History*, 2nd ed. (New York: W.W. Norton, 1989), 333.

23 Quoted in Aaron Sachs, *The Humboldt Current: Nineteenth-Century Exploration and the Roots of American Environmentalism* (Harmondsworth, U.K.: Penguin, 2007), 6; Walter L. Hixson, *The Myth of American Diplomacy: National Identity and U.S. Foreign Policy* (New Haven: Yale University Press, 2008), 72.

24 Quoted in J.L. Granatstein, "Free Trade Between Canada and the United States: The Issue That Will Not Go Away," in Royal Commission on the Economic Union and Development Prospects of Canada (Macdonald Commission), *Collected Research Studies*, vol. 29: *The Politics of Canada's Economic Relationship with the United States*, Denis Stairs and Gilbert R. Winham, eds. (Toronto: University of Toronto Press, 1985), 24.

25 Buchanan, quoted in *Toronto Star*, March 3, 1996; see also Patrick J. Buchanan, *A Republic, Not an Empire: Reclaiming America's Destiny*, 2nd ed. (Washington, DC: Regnery Publishing, 2002), 370.

If in the nineteenth century the United States government tended to do as it pleased to its south, it was singularly more cautious with its northern neighbour. The military might of Britain and the need to preserve good relations with London doubtlessly explains why American presidents no longer pursued the idea of trying to acquire British North America by force. Reflecting on two quarrels over territorial claims being made by the United States in 1844—over the Oregon territory in the northwest and over Texas in the southwest—Thomas Hart Benton, a Democratic senator from Missouri, asked in a United States Senate debate on the annexation of Texas that led to the Mexican–American war, "Would we take 2,000 miles of the Canadas in the same way? I presume not. And why not? Because Great Britain is powerful, and Mexico weak."[26] On those occasions when local transborder problems occurred that had the capacity to escalate into war, cooler heads always prevailed in Washington. The desire for good relations was reciprocated in London and Ottawa, eventually making the use of force unthinkable.[27]

Geostrategic Shifts and the "Kingston Dispensation" of 1938

From the end of the eighteenth century until the middle of the twentieth century, war between the great powers unfolded far from Canada. They engaged Canadians emotionally, particularly when Britain was involved, and Canadians fought—and died—in these conflicts, as they did during the Nile Expedition in Sudan in 1884–85, in the Boer War between 1899 and 1902, and the First World War from 1914 to 1918, all of which we examine in more detail in Chapter 5. But these wars never threatened Canada directly. If Canada had any strategic importance to the great powers of this era, it was in the country's geographic remoteness from the European vortex of world politics. Canada's principal utility was as a supplier to Britain of soldiers, material, and food secure from direct attack. "At present," Mackenzie King noted matter-of-factly in 1938, "the danger of attack upon Canada is minor in degree and second-hand in origin."[28]

The strategic importance of Canada, and the relative security afforded by its geographic isolation, changed dramatically with the outbreak of the Second World War. By the early summer of 1940, the threat that Canadians felt was palpable. Nazi Germany had invaded Denmark and Norway in April 1940 and France, Belgium, the Netherlands, and Luxembourg in May, and after several weeks of *Blitzkrieg* the Nazis had occupied much of western Europe to the Channel. The possibility of a successful Nazi invasion of England seemed very real; and the United States was committed to remaining officially neutral, even if President Franklin Delano Roosevelt was openly sympathetic to the cause of Britain and its allies. The Nazi victories in Europe caused a significant shift that occurred in strategic thinking in Canada.

---

26 *Three Speeches of the Honorable Thomas H. Benton* (New York: n.p., 1844), 22.

27 However, it was not until May 1931 that Defence Scheme No. 1, which planned for a war with the United States, was officially laid to rest and officers in the Department of National Defence were ordered to burn their copies of the Scheme. James Eayrs, *In Defence of Canada*, vol. 1: *From the Great War to the Great Depression* (Toronto: University of Toronto Press, 1964), 70–78.

28 Quoted in James Eayrs, "The Foreign Policy of Canada," in Joseph E. Black and Kenneth W. Thompson, eds., *Foreign Policies in a World of Change* (New York: Harper and Row, 1963), 675.

A decade before, close military cooperation with the United States would have been unthinkable: in 1927 the prime minister, Mackenzie King, had dismissed as "damn nonsense" the idea of sending a military attaché to Washington.[29] But a process of "geostrategic reorientation," as David Haglund termed it,[30] was under way, even if only slowly. By 1938, when the risk of war in Europe became more pressing, we can see the beginnings of North American defence cooperation. The basic principle was laid out in two short speeches given by Roosevelt and King in August of that year. While receiving an honorary degree at Queen's University in Kingston on August 18, 1938, Roosevelt referred to the Sudetenland crisis then seizing Europe. Calling North America "a strong citadel wherein civilization can flourish unimpaired," Roosevelt declared that "I give to you assurance that the people of the United States will not stand idly by if domination of Canadian soil is threatened by any other Empire."[31] For his part, King provided a comparable commitment at a weekend picnic in Woodbridge on August 20: "We, too, have our obligations as a good friendly neighbour, and one of these is to see that, at our own instance, our country is made as immune from attack or possible invasion as we can reasonably be expected to make it, and that, should the occasion ever arise, enemy forces should not be able to pursue their way, either by land, sea or air to the United States, across Canadian territory."[32]

Even though the Canadian part was given in Woodbridge, Michel Fortmann and David Haglund have termed this exchange of commitments the "Kingston Dispensation"—in other words an arrangement rather a formal undertaking.[33] From an American perspective, the Kingston Dispensation was a logical way of dealing with Canada's likely belligerency in an impending European war, since control of Canadian territory by a hostile power would have constituted a national security threat to the United States.

But the Dispensation also had important strategic consequences for Canada. First, it provided the country with more security than would be possible with just its own resources or even with the backing of Britain. Second, while the American assurance allowed some Canadian free-riding on defence expenditures, it did not exempt Canada entirely from having to contribute to defence. For Roosevelt's declaration contained an implicit threat: If Canadians were to prove incapable of providing for their own security, the United States would do it for them—whether Ottawa wanted it or not. This is the "defence against help" strategy originally articulated by Nils Ørvik in the early 1970s: Smaller states in global politics have an interest in maintaining a certain level

---

29 C.P. Stacey, *Canada and the Age of Conflict*, vol. 2: *1921–1948: The Mackenzie King Era* (Toronto: University of Toronto Press, 1981), 226.

30 David G. Haglund, "Le Canada dans l'entre-deux-guerres," *Études internationales* 31 (December 2000), 728.

31 The speech is reproduced in Roger Frank Swanson, *Canadian-American Summit Diplomacy, 1923–1973* (Toronto: McClelland & Stewart, 1975), 52–54; original typescript text available http://www.ibiblio.org/pha/7-2-188/188-09.html.

32 Jessie E. MacTaggart, "Adequate Defence, King Pledges," *Globe and Mail*, August 22, 1938, 1; also quoted in James Eayrs, *In Defence of Canada: Appeasement and Rearmament* (Toronto: University of Toronto Press, 1965), 183.

33 Michel Fortmann and David G. Haglund, "Canada and the Issue of Homeland Security: Does the 'Kingston Dispensation' Still Hold?," *Canadian Military Journal*, Spring 2002, 17–22.

of defence spending in order to avoid "unwanted help" from larger powers that might be threatened by low levels of defence preparedness of their smaller neighbours.[34]

However, according to the "defence against help" dynamic, the minimum that Canadians must devote to defence is essentially what the United States judges necessary. If the two governments do not share the same perception of the threat, the threshold desired by the United States may well be higher than the level that Canadians consider sufficient. Thus the government in Ottawa has to articulate security policies not only to deal with threats directed against Canada (if there are indeed threats there), but also those threats directed against the United States.[35]

Two years after the 1938 Kingston Dispensation, when France had been overrun by the Nazis and Britain seemed on the point of collapsing, Roosevelt invited King to Ogdensburg, New York, where the two leaders issued a joint statement agreeing to the creation of a formal mechanism of joint defence between Canada and the United States, the Permanent Joint Board on Defence (PJBD). This was followed in April 1941 by the Hyde Park Declaration, which smoothed economic cooperation between Canada and the United States in war material.[36] Even though these agreements did not contain any formal provisions of mutual assistance in the case of aggression, they formed the basis of a military alliance between the two countries.

The Cold War "Glacis," 1945–1991

The strategic shifts introduced during the Second World War had long-term effects. The sense of security encouraged by the distorting distances of Mercator's projection, and Canada's relative strategic unimportance, evaporated with changes in both the balance of power and military technology. With the emergence of the Soviet Union and the United States as rivals after 1945, Canada's geostrategic position shifted dramatically—from being an ocean east (or west) of major-power confrontations to being directly sandwiched between the two superpowers. And advances in military technology—notably the invention of nuclear weapons and the development of long-range delivery systems—heralded a new-found strategic importance for Canada as an American "glacis."[37]

---

34 Nils Ørvik, "Defence Against Help: A Strategy for Small States," *Survival* 15 (September/October 1973), 228–31; Ørvik, "The Basic Issue in Canadian National Security: Defence Against Help, Defence to Help Others," *Canadian Defence Quarterly* 11:1 (Summer 1981), 8–15. For an update, see Donald Barry and Duane Bratt, "Defense Against Help: Explaining Canada–U.S. Security Relations," *American Review of Canadian Studies* 38:1 (Spring, 2008), 63–89.

35 See Stéphane Roussel, "Pearl Harbor et le World Trade Center: Le Canada face aux États-Unis en période de crise," *Études internationales* 33:4 (décembre 2002), 667–95.

36 On these agreements, see Galen Roger Perras, *Franklin Roosevelt and the Origins of the Canadian–American Security Alliance, 1933–1945* (Westport, CT: Praeger, 1998), 76–78; Stacey, *Age of Conflict*, vol. 2, 311–12, 315–17; Roussel, *North American Democratic Peace*, 171–72.

37 In medieval Europe, a *glacis* was a slope built downward from a fortification designed to expose attackers to withering fire; water was poured on it so that the slope would freeze, making it even more difficult to navigate. In the Cold War, the term was used to describe those countries that formed a figurative "slope" to the two superpowers (Eastern Europe for the Soviet Union, Canada for the United States). See, for example, Stephen Clarkson, "Poor Prospects: 'The Rest of Canada' Under Continental Integration," in Kenneth McRoberts, *Beyond Quebec: Taking Stock of Canada* (Montréal and Kingston: McGill-Queen's University Press, 1995), 252.

The terms of the Kingston Dispensation continued to operate throughout the Cold War: the United States continued to protect Canada, though Canada was expected to do its part. After 1946, the United States military began to regard the Canadian North as a key sector for the defence of the North American continent and sought to plan against a Soviet transpolar attack. In the decade following the Second World War, American military planners wanted to ensure that surveillance and interception systems against Soviet bombers were located as close to the Soviet Union (and as far away from the American industrial heartland) as possible. The most appropriate solution was what the *Financial Post* referred to as an "Atomic Age Maginot Line"[38]—a network of radar stations and jet-interceptor bases across the Canadian and American north. Moreover, during the 1950s, American requirements grew increasingly more elaborate, with radar lines multiplying.

But Canada had neither the resources nor the will to erect this type of defence, which put Canadian policymakers in a dilemma. Neither King, nor Louis St. Laurent, who took over from him in 1948, were ready to dip into the treasury to finance such a project. At the same time, however, leaders in Ottawa understood that Canada had to satisfy some of the requirements formulated by the Americans for fear that the United States would unilaterally undertake the projects in the Canadian North that they judged essential for their safety. In other words, for Canada, it was as much (if not more) a question of sovereignty rather than security. The solution was a compromise: Canada assumed one-third of the costs of construction and maintenance of the Pinetree Line, built in 1951, and all of the costs of the Mid-Canada Line, built in 1954. But the expenses of the Distant Early Warning, or DEW, Line, built in 1954, were entirely paid for by the United States.[39]

The culmination of Canadian–American defence cooperation was the signature in May 1958 of the North American Air Defence Command (NORAD) agreement. NORAD *continentalized* air defence—in the sense that the territory of both the United States and Canada was considered a single territory to be defended against bomber attack, with the forces of each country combined into a single command.[40] Even after the development and deployment of intercontinental ballistic missiles (ICBMs), which could not be intercepted by jet fighters, NORAD remained integral to North American defence throughout the Cold War. The mission adapted as technology evolved, so that by the late 1970s, and the emergence of space-based detection systems, the United States proposed in 1981 to change NORAD's name to the North American *Aerospace* Defence Command.[41]

The argument here is not that "Geography dictates [NORAD]," as Norman Senior mistakenly put it in 1960.[42] Geography merely dictated that during the Cold War Canada was

38 Joseph T. Jockel, *No Boundaries Upstairs: Canada, the United States and the Origins of North American Air Defence, 1945–1958* (Vancouver: UBC Press, 1987), 24.

39 Shelagh D. Grant, *Sovereignty or Security? Government Policy in the Canadian North, 1936–1950* (Vancouver: UBC Press, 1994).

40 Jockel, *No Boundaries Upstairs;* Jon B. McLin, *Canada's Changing Defense Policy, 1957–1963: The Problems of a Middle Power in Alliance* (Toronto: Copp Clark Publishing Co., 1967), chap. 3.

41 Joseph T. Jockel, *Canada in NORAD, 1957–2007: A History* (Montréal and Kingston: McGill-Queen's University Press, 2007).

42 C. Norman Senior, "Some Political and Economic Aspects of the Unequal Partnership Between Canada and the U.S. in Matters of Defence," *Western Political Quarterly* 13 (September 1960), supplement, 72, quoted in John W. Warnock, *Partner to Behemoth: The Military Policy of a Satellite Canada* (Toronto: New Press, 1970), 136.

located physically between the two superpowers. Rather, it was politics that dictated the consequences of geographic location. First, Americans had to consider Canadian territory important to their defence, and to use this territory to create as much distance between themselves and the Soviet Union as possible. Second, politics explain the Canadian attachment to continental air defence: The vast majority of Canadians supported the alignment of their country with the United States in global affairs during this period. On the other hand, the vast majority of Canadians would not have tolerated the kind of massive defence expenditures necessary to provide the United States with sufficient assurance against attack by bombers. Nor would they have tolerated either doing nothing and watching as United States forces operated unilaterally in the North without Canadian permission, or allowing the United States access to the North to undertake these defence tasks on its own. In either case, Canadian sovereignty would have been intolerably violated.

Although NORAD attracted considerable criticism in Canada during the Cold War, this binational command probably made it possible to find a compromise that was acceptable to both Canada and the United States. NORAD brought Americans the security they sought, while providing Canadians with assurance that the United States would not violate their sovereignty to ensure their own defence. It also institutionalized a means for Canada to contribute to the formulation of continental defence and thus helped to legitimize full Canadian participation in a fundamentally unequal relationship. Moreover, NORAD did not impose the kind of heavy financial burden that would have been required for an entirely Canadian system of detection and interception.

NORAD's original terms provided for periodic renewal after ten years, and over the course of the Cold War the agreement was renewed five times (in 1968, 1973, 1975, 1980, and 1986). But Canadians did not have a great deal of room to manoeuvre. While the government could have withdrawn, the costs of doing so would have been high. The United States would have regarded a withdrawal during the Cold War era as an unfriendly act, with negative strategic implications. As Arnold Heeney, then the ambassador in Washington, put it in August 1959, "it is inconceivable that the United States will allow its defensive arrangements to be frustrated by our refusal to cooperate."[43] In this sense, geographic location imposed a considerable constraint on any Canadian government that might have wished to withdraw from continental air defence. As long as the United States government wanted some form of northern air defence, Canadians had the choice of participating—or facing unpalatable consequences.[44]

The Post-Cold War Era, 1991–2001

With the end of the Cold War, Canada's geostrategic "location" shifted considerably, eloquent testimony to the fact that even a seemingly permanent factor like geographical location is never an absolute invariant. The breakup of the Soviet Union in 1991, and the increasing integration of the Russian Federation into systems of global governance such as the Group of Seven (G7), led within three years to the dismantling and destruction of large numbers of nuclear weapons in both Russia and the United States and the eventual

---

43 Quoted in David Cox, "Canada and NORAD, 1958–1978: A Cautionary Retrospective," *Aurora Papers* 1 (Winter 1985), 43.

44 D.W. Middlemiss and J.J. Sokolsky, *Canadian Defence: Decisions and Determinants* (Toronto: Harcourt Brace Jovanovich, 1989), 149–57.

decision in Moscow and Washington to "de-target" each other: by 1994. Russian and American nuclear weapons were no longer programmed to attack each other. In such an environment, NORAD's original raison d'être had disappeared and Canadian territory no longer had the same strategic importance.

As a result, it was decided that the North Warning System would be downsized and many of Canada's CF-18 interceptors would be mothballed. Likewise, new tasks were added: in the 1991 renewal and NORAD was given responsibility for counter-narcotics surveillance.[45] But however reduced its role, NORAD was sustained by both governments during the ten years of the post–Cold War era for prudential reasons. As the 1994 white paper on defence noted, "The Government believes it is prudent to preserve the ability of Canada and the US to regenerate forces should a strategic threat to the continent arise in the future."[46]

Although NORAD changed its mission in the post–Cold War era, Canadian territory retained its geostrategic importance for at least one American weapons system. After the Strategic Defense Initiative (SDI)[47] championed by the administration of Ronald Reagan in the mid-1980s was abandoned, work on a more limited Ballistic Missile Defense (BMD) program continued in the late 1980s and early 1990s. Because some of the ground-based BMD weapons systems under development would be effective if they were placed on Canadian soil, the administration of Bill Clinton continued to hope that Canada would join the BMD program.

The Post-9/11 Era

The attacks of September 11, 2001 refocused attention on Canada's geostrategic importance. First, the risk of a new terrorist attack using the same means as those employed on 9/11 meant that NORAD patrols increased considerably in the months after that date; for a time at least, interception again became a priority.[48] Second, 9/11 galvanized the administration of George W. Bush into embracing an unabashed policy of preemptive attacks on security threats that was buttressed by a military strategy of "full spectrum dominance."[49] To this end, the Bush administration accelerated the work on BMD and authorized the

---

45 Hal P. Klepak, "The Impact of the International Narcotics Trade on Canada's Foreign and Security Policy," *International Journal* 49:1 (Winter 1993–94), 66–92.

46 Canada, Department of National Defence, *1994 Defence White Paper* (Ottawa: Minister of Supply and Services Canada, 1994), 23.

47 In its most lavish version, SDI was designed to cover the United States with an "astrodome defence" against nuclear attack by means of a space-based and ground-based defence system. SDI components would identify ICBMs as they left their silos; computers would then direct the fire of high-technology weapons systems such as hunter-killer satellites, space-based kinetic kill vehicles, particle beam accelerators, lasers, and electromagnetic rail guns to destroy missiles and their nuclear warheads as they passed through the various phases of their flight to their target. According to SDI enthusiasts, it was theoretically possible to destroy every independently targeted warhead in every bus of every ballistic missile launched in a strike against the United States; every bomber; every cruise missile; and even depressed-trajectory missiles fired from submarines offshore. By all accounts they were convinced that such a fantastic scheme, if put in place, would render nuclear weapons obsolete by making a nuclear attack impossible.

48 Joseph T. Jockel, "After the September Attacks: Four Questions About NORAD's Future," *Canadian Military Journal*, Spring 2002, 11–16.

49 United States, President, *The National Security Strategy of the United States*, September 2002, available http://www.globalsecurity.org/military/library/policy/national/nss-020920.pdf.

deployment of the first ground-based elements. The question was whether NORAD, with its monitoring and detection capabilities, was going to be involved in the antimissile system—which would have meant that Canada would participate too. Although Paul Martin had been in favour of Canada participating in the BMD program before he became prime minister, once in power he dithered on this issue, largely because his cabinet, the Liberal caucus, as well as public opinion—especially in Québec—was divided on this issue.[50] And when the Martin government finally made decisions on BMD, they appeared contradictory and unlikely to satisfy anyone. On the one hand, on August 5, 2004 the two governments announced an amendment to the agreement that would have allowed NORAD to provide early warning data (or Integrated Tactical Warning/Attack Assessment—ITW/AA) to the American-run ballistic missile command.[51] Because ITW/AA data was necessary for making the system work, Canada's agreement on the amendment meant that it was, ipso facto, "participating" in a ballistic missile defence system.

On the other hand, a mere six months later, Martin's foreign minister, Pierre Pettigrew, rose in the House of Commons to announce that Canada would not participate in the "operationalization" of the BMD program. He offered no reasoned justification for the decision, other than that it was not in Canadian interests. But he did not revoke the amendment of August 2004.[52] As a result, the Martin government's decisions meant that Canada was not participating in BMD; but via NORAD it was participating in BMD.

Lastly, 9/11 showed that the "Kingston Dispensation" remains as relevant as ever. Even though the nineteen terrorists who committed the attacks had all been legally admitted to the United States through nine different airports with documents issued to them by the U.S. government and had organized the attacks on American soil, rumours that they had entered the United States through Canada immediately began circulating after 9/11. Much to the chagrin of the Canadian embassy in Washington, they kept being repeated by such high-level American officials as Hillary Clinton, New York senator and later Barack Obama's secretary of state; John McCain, senator from Arizona and 2008 Republican presidential candidate; and Janet Napolitano, Obama's secretary of the Department of Homeland Security.[53] One of the reasons why the 9/11 rumour persisted was that in December 1999, a terrorist, Ahmed Ressam, had tried to make his way into the United States from Canada and had been arrested by American border officials in the state of Washington in a car with a trunk full of explosives that he was planning to use in an attack on Los Angeles International Airport.[54]

But the American concern with the security of their borders was a useful reminder of the responsibility articulated by Mackenzie King not to allow enemies of the United States

---

50 James Fergusson, "Shall We Dance? The Missile Defence Decision, NORAD Renewal, and the Future of Canada–US Defence Relations," *Canadian Military Journal* 6:2 (Summer 2005), 13–22.

51 Canada, Department of National Defence, "Canada and United States Amend NORAD Agreement," *News Release* NR 04.058, August 5, 2004.

52 Canada, Parliament, House of Commons, *Debates*, 38th Parl., 1st sess., edited Hansard 064, February 24, 2005, 12h00.

53 Doug Struck, "Canada Fights Myth It Was 9/11 Conduit," *Washington Post*, April 9, 2005, A20; "McCain Defends Napolitano, Insists 9/11 Perpetrators Came from Canada," CBC.ca, April 24, 2009.

54 Stewart Bell and Rohan Gunaratna, *Cold Terror: How Canada Nurtures and Exports Terrorism Around the World* (Toronto: John Wiley, 2007), 157–74.

to use Canadian territory to attack the United States. This principle, which had been applied to military forces during the Second World War and the Cold War, now applies to terrorists. Thus, in the months after 9/11, the Canadian government adopted new laws to fight terrorism, increased the spending on public safety, and concluded a number of agreements with the United States, particularly the "Smart Border" agreement of December 2001 that focused on increasing security at the borders. Since 2001, as we will see in Chapter 5, creating a "North American security perimeter" or a "North American security community" has been part of what Justin Massie characterizes as Canada's reactive response to 9/11.[55]

ECONOMIC STRUCTURE

For much of their history, Canadians were wedded to the benefits of comparative advantage within the "North Atlantic Triangle."[56] Such benefits consisted of exporting raw materials and agricultural produce and importing manufactured goods, first from Britain directly and then from the United States via indirect investment in branch plants located in Canada. A basic feature of Canada's economic structure is that since the repeal of the Corn Laws in 1846, the Canadian economy has never been wholly self-sufficient.

Instead, Canada has been and continues to be dependent on foreign trade for its well-being. A third of the country's gross domestic product (GDP) is generated by trade, and in particular exports. "The necessity of marketing this great surplus of commodities must always be the principal concern of Canadian foreign policy," wrote F.R. Scott in 1932.[57] So it had been, and would be. For a small country heavily dependent on trade, Rodney de C. Grey declared in 1981, "foreign policy should, in major part, be trade relations policy."[58] Roy MacLaren, Jean Chrétien's first minister for international trade, was even more succinct: for Canada, he said, "foreign policy *is* trade policy."[59] (Claire Turenne Sjolander, looking at Chrétien's international policy, preferred it the other way around: "trade policy is now the 'tail' that has begun to wag the foreign policy 'dog.'"[60])

Canada's trading patterns evolved in a particular way. Over the course of the twentieth century, the country's trade became progressively unbalanced, concentrated in one market,

55   Justin Massie, "Canada's (In)dependence in the North American Security Community: The Asymmetrical Norm of Common Fate," *American Review of Canadian Studies* 37:4 (Winter 2007), 493–516.

56   John Bartlet Brebner, *North Atlantic Triangle: The Interplay of Canada, the United States and Great Britain* (New York: Columbia University Press, 1945; rpt. Toronto: McClelland & Stewart, 1966); see also David G. Haglund, *The North Atlantic Triangle Revisited: Canadian Grand Strategy at Century's End* (Toronto: Canadian Institute of International Affairs, 2000).

57   F.R. Scott, "The Permanent Bases of Canadian Foreign Policy," *Foreign Affairs* 10 (1932), 627.

58   Quoted in Richard G. Lipsey, "Canada and the United States: The Economic Dimension," in Charles F. Doran and John H. Sigler, eds., *Canada and the United States: Enduring Friendship, Persistent Stress* (Englewood Cliffs, NJ: Prentice-Hall, 1985), 81.

59   Andrew Cohen, "Canada in the World: The Return of the National Interest," *Behind the Headlines* 52 (Summer 1995), 4.

60   Claire Turenne Sjolander, "International Trade as Foreign Policy: 'Anything for a Buck,'" in Gene Swimmer, ed., *How Ottawa Spends 1997–98* (Ottawa: Carleton University Press, 1998), 111–34, 113.

the United States. And in the process this made the Canada–United States trading relationship the largest and most complex in the world. In 1901, 53 percent of Canada's exports went to Britain, with 38 percent going to the United States; by 1939, 36 percent went to Britain and 41 percent went to the United States. By the mid-1950s, fully 60 percent of exports went to the United States; the British share had fallen dramatically to under 9 percent. By 1970, just under 70 percent of Canada's trade was with the United States; by 1985, that percentage had risen to over 75. By 1993, fully 80 percent of exports went to the United States, with all of western Europe accounting for just 7 percent. This dependence peaked in 2003, with 86 percent of Canadian exports going to the United States. Thereafter it decreased somewhat, dropping to 77.7 percent in 2008.[61] In short, over the course of the last century Canada grew not only dependent on external trade for its prosperity, but increasingly dependent on a single market to sustain it.

What implications does this economic structure have for the making of international policy in Canada? First, and most obviously, the political and security interests of the government in Ottawa will hinge on trade. As Gerald Helleiner told a parliamentary committee on foreign policy in 1985, "The first priority for a country like Canada, so dependent on the stability and predictability of the international economic system, must surely be, overwhelmingly, the stability and order of the international system. There can be no higher priority for Canadian foreign policy."[62] This interconnection between peace and economic growth has always been recognized by Canadian governments. It is this feature of Canada's condition, perhaps more than any other, that explains why governments in Ottawa have historically been so concerned with the maintenance of global peace and the avoidance of systemic war.

Second, the increasing concentration of Canada's trade with the United States creates extreme vulnerability. The government in Washington, like the governments of all countries, will seek to defend and advance the interests of the United States and those of its citizens. But the pursuit of self-interest by Americans has the capacity to inflict severe damage on the Canadian economy, as the Smoot-Hawley tariff of 1930 demonstrated. That measure, introduced into the United States Congress by Senator Reed Smoot and Representative Willis Hawley even before the stock market crash of 1929, was signed into law by President Herbert Hoover in June 1930. It provided for massive increases in the tariffs imposed by the United States on imported goods.[63] This American protectionism prompted both Mackenzie King and his Conservative successor, R.B. Bennett, to raise Canadian tariffs in retaliation. As a result, Canada's trade with the United States plummeted over the next three years, deepening the Depression and its effects on production,

---

61 Data from: Canada, Parliament, Special Joint Committee Reviewing Canadian Foreign Policy, *Canada's Foreign Policy: Principles and Priorities for the Future* (Ottawa, November 1994), 29; Brian W. Tomlin and Maureen Appel Molot, "Talking Trade: Perils of the North American Option," in Tomlin and Molot, eds., *Canada Among Nations 1986: Talking Trade* (Toronto: Lorimer, 1987), 11; Michael Hart, *A Trading Nation* (Vancouver: UBC Press, 2003), tables 4.5, 6.1, 9.1, 12.1; Canada, Department of Foreign Affairs and International Trade, Office of the Chief Economist, available http://www.international.ca.

62 Cited in Canada, Parliament, Special Joint Committee of the Senate and of the House of Commons on Canada's International Relations, *Independence and Internationalism* (Ottawa: June 1986), 12.

63 Gilbert R. Winham, "The Evolution of the Global Trade Regime," in John Ravenhill, ed., *Global Political Economy* (Oxford: Oxford University Press, 2008), 141–42; Stacey, *Age of Conflict*, vol. 2, 126–29; Peter Kasurak, "American Foreign Policy Officials and Canada, 1927–1941: A Look Through Bureaucratic Glasses," *International Journal* 32:3 (Summer 1977), 544–58.

jobs, and prosperity. By 1933, Bennett's government, backed by the Liberal opposition, responded to American protectionism as Canadian governments had in the past—and would again in the future: it sought a trade agreement with the United States.

Not all American protectionist measures are directed against Canada. Although it is the largest trading partner of the United States, Canada accounted for merely 17.6 percent of American trade flows in 2008.[64] American policymakers are, as a consequence, prone to subsume Canada in their wider efforts to encourage "fairer" trading practices by the European Union and Japan and create what they like to call a "level playing field" in international trade. Canada often gets "sideswiped" in the process. However, some policies embraced by the government in Washington are frequently aimed quite purposely at Canada, particularly those Canadian policy initiatives that damage American interests.

The willingness of the United States, and in particular the Congress, to defend American interests by imposing retaliatory and often punitive measures on Canadians is nicely illustrated by the case of border broadcasting in the 1970s,[65] the National Energy Program in the 1980s,[66] the *Sports Illustrated* dispute in the 1990s,[67] and the

---

64 United States Census Bureau, Foreign Trade Statistics, available http://www.census.gov/foreign-trade/ statistics/highlights/top/top0812yr.html.

65 In 1976, to promote support for Canadian television, the Trudeau government introduced legislation that made it impossible for Canadian firms advertising on American border stations to deduct these costs for income tax purposes. When revenues from Canadian advertisers dropped sharply, American television stations along the border pressed their members of Congress for relief. In 1977, when the United States Senate was considering amendments to the U.S. Income Tax Act, senators from border states successfully argued for retaliatory action by excluding convention expenses incurred in Canada as tax-deductible. Between 1978 and 1980, when a solution was finally agreed upon, it is estimated that the loss to Canada's tourist and convention industry had been $200 million, while the estimated value of advertising diverted from American border stations to Canadian networks had been just $20 million. Donald K. Alper and Robert L. Monahan, "Bill C-58 and the American Congress: The Politics of Retaliation," *Canadian Public Policy* 4 (Spring 1979), 184–95; Isaiah A. Litvak and Christopher J. Maule, "Bill C-58 and the Regulation of Periodicals in Canada," *International Journal* 36:1 (Winter 1980–81), 89.

66 In 1980, the Trudeau government moved to "Canadianize" the oil and gas industry under the National Energy Program, which imposed new taxes and levies, particularly on American-owned oil companies operating in Canada. Allan Gotlieb, Canada's ambassador to the United States, who was charged with selling the NEP to the Americans, wrote later that the NEP was "poorly conceived, poorly put together, poorly rationalized. . . . It was developed in secret . . . without regard to the international impact." It was, he concluded, "unsaleable." Allan Gotlieb, *The Washington Diaries, 1981–1989* (Toronto: McClelland & Stewart, 2006), 29. For the often heavy-handed response of the Reagan administration, see Stephen Clarkson, *Canada and the Reagan Challenge*, upd. ed. (Toronto: McClelland & Stewart, 1985), 71–81.

67 In 1993 *Sports Illustrated* decided to launch a Canadian edition. This would be a "split run" production: it would be printed in Canada, and thus qualify as a "Canadian" magazine for tax purposes, but would simply use all-American content. The Chrétien government, concerned that it would draw Canadian advertising revenue away from Canadian magazines, responded by imposing an excise tax of 80 percent on advertising revenue. In 1996, the Clinton administration took Canada to the World Trade Organization and won. The Chrétien government then introduced new legislation, C-55, that would ban Canadians from advertising in split runs. This prompted members of Congress to consider taking measures against Canadian steel—not surprising since the minister behind the Canadian legislation, Sheila Copps, was an MP for Hamilton, home of two major steel companies, Dofasco and

softwood lumber dispute, which persisted for nearly three decades before being resolved in 2006.[68]

The third consequence of Canada's economic sensitivity and vulnerability is that virtually all foreign policy issues become linked to Canadian–American relations. Decisions tend to be based on a calculation of the degree to which the issue—and the options being discussed—will impinge on the relationship with the United States. Policies on such diverse issues as human rights violations in Cuba, the acquisition of new helicopters for the Department of National Defence, or the Canadian mission in Afghanistan tend to be filtered through this Canadian–American lens. Such a calculus is hardly unique; all states must engage in it because the interests, power, and reach of the United States are pervasive. As Canada's ambassador in Washington, Charles Ritchie, noted of the American government to his diary in July 1963, "They are *everywhere*, into *everything*—a wedding in Nepal, a strike in British Guinea, the remotest Greek island, the farthest outpost of Donegal, the banks of the Limpopo. All countries' private and domestic affairs are of interest to the Americans."[69] But for Canada, the consequences of insensitivity to American concerns are greater than for any other state. Lester Pearson put it this way in July 1967 when explaining his government's position on the Vietnam war:

> This is not the over-riding consideration in determining our own policy, of course, but we can't ignore the fact that a first result of any open breach with the United States over Vietnam, which their Government considered to be unfair or unfriendly, would be more critical examination by Washington of certain special aspects of our relationship from which we, as well as they, get benefit . . . It is not a very comforting thought, but, in the economic sphere, when you have 60 per cent or so of your trade with one country, you are in a position of considerable economic dependence.[70]

Pearson's concern was not that a wrong move by Ottawa would bring about instant American retaliatory measures, crippling the Canadian economy. John W. Holmes has

---

Stelco. Sarah Armstrong, "Magazines, Culture Policy and Globalization: The Forced Retreat of the State?," *Canadian Public Policy* 26:3 (September 2000), 369–85; Keith Acheson and Christopher J. Maule, "No Bark, No Bite: The Mystery of Magazine Policy," *American Review of Canadian Studies* 31:3 (Autumn 2001), 467–82; Christopher Sands, "A Chance to End Culture Trade Conflict Between Canada and the United States," *American Review of Canadian Studies* 31:3 (Autumn 2001), 483–99; Patricia M. Goff, "Imagining Independence: At the Intersection of Cultural and Foreign Policies," in Brian Bow and Patrick Lennox, eds., *An Independent Foreign Policy for Canada? Challenges and Choices for the Future* (Toronto: University of Toronto Press, 2008), 185–206.

68 The United States government argues that the "stumpage fee" that some provincial governments in Canada charge companies to log Crown land constitutes an unfair subsidy and has, since the early 1980s, sought to change Canadian practice or penalize Canadian softwood producers in those provinces in which stumpage fees are charged. A good survey is to be found in Steven Kendall Holloway, *Canadian Foreign Policy: Defining the National Interest* (Toronto: Broadview Press, 2006), 212–15; for details, see Daowei Zhang, *The Softwood Lumber War: Politics, Economics, and the Long U.S.–Canadian Trade Dispute* (Washington: Resources for the Future Press, 2007).

69 Charles Ritchie, *Storm Signals: More Undiplomatic Diaries, 1962–1971* (Toronto: Macmillan, 1983), 53.

70 Quoted in John W. Holmes, *The Better Part of Valour: Essays on Canadian Diplomacy* (Toronto: McClelland & Stewart, 1970), 175.

argued that the result would be more subtle: "Whether [Canadians] like it or not—and they do not—they are vulnerable to American displeasure. This displeasure is not likely to take the form of punitive action or crude reprisal; Canadians would feel it rather in the drying up of the good will which restrains the United States from exploiting the economic and military power it has to do Canada damage."[71]

Little wonder, then, that Canadian officials frequently demonstrate considerable sensitivity to how their international policy decisions are likely to be received in Washington. On numerous occasions, Canadian policy has been determined not directly by the American government but by Canadian assessments that a divergent policy on an issue would not be worth the damage such divergence would likely do to Canadian–American relations. The case of the recognition of the People's Republic of China (PRC) provides a useful example. In 1949, the Communists under Mao Zedong seized control of China, forcing the Kuomintang (KMT) government of Chiang Kai-shek to flee to Taiwan. As of October 1, 1949, there were two governments, one in Taipei, the other in Beijing, both claiming to be the legal government of all China. Other countries had to decide which claim to recognize. For fully nineteen years after October 1, 1949, Canada recognized the KMT as the legal government of all China. This was not because the Canadian government liked the KMT; virtually all Canadian officials had little sympathy for the Chiang government, believing it to be inefficient and corrupt. Nor was it because Canadian officials believed in the wisdom of American policy toward the PRC; on the contrary: Washington's attempt to keep Beijing isolated in international affairs was seen in Ottawa as both mistaken and shortsighted. Nor was it because the United States was constantly threatening Canada with economic retaliation to keep Ottawa in line. It was simply that, while most Canadian officials wanted to recognize the PRC, they calculated that the matter was not important enough to warrant antagonizing the United States on what was in the 1950s and 1960s a very-high-stakes issue in American politics.[72]

However, there is nothing automatic about this calculus. On numerous occasions the Canadian government has decided that it was in Canada's interests to cross swords with the United States in public on issues of global policy and risk the negative consequences. John Diefenbaker did so during the Cuban missile crisis of 1962. Lester Pearson spoke out on Vietnam in 1965. Pierre Trudeau opposed the United States on a number of issues ranging from the bombing of Hanoi and Haiphong in December 1972 to the invasion of Grenada by American forces in October 1983. Brian Mulroney refused to participate in the Strategic Defense Initiative in 1985. Jean Chrétien crossed both Clinton and Bush on numerous occasions, most importantly on the American invasion of Iraq in 2003. Paul Martin refused to participate in the Ballistic Missile Defense program. And although Stephen Harper has not openly opposed the United States on global issues in the years he has been in power, he has not spoken out in support of the U.S.-led mission in Iraq or embraced BMD (even though as leader of the opposition he had spoken in favour of the war against Iraq in 2003 and had indicated his support for joining BMD).

---

71 Holmes, *The Better Part of Valour,* 177–78.

72 John W. Holmes, *The Shaping of Peace: Canada and the Search for World Order, 1943–1957,* vol. 2 (Toronto: University of Toronto Press, 1982), 130–42; Paul M. Evans and B. Michael Frolic, eds., *Reluctant Adversaries: Canada and the People's Republic of China, 1949–1970* (Toronto: University of Toronto Press, 1991).

On occasion the Canadian government will decide to support American policy despite misgivings. A good example was the response of the Mulroney government to the U.S. bombing of Libya in April 1986. These raids were carried out in response to several terrorist incidents in Europe linked directly to Libya's leader, Muammar al-Qaddafi. Despite criticism in the House of Commons from both the Liberals and the New Democrats about the impropriety of the attack, both the prime minister and Erik Neilsen, the minister of national defence, came out solidly behind the bombing, arguing that it was an appropriate response. Even though Canadian officials had serious concerns about the use of force by one of the superpowers against a smaller power, they were kept well hidden.

The reason for keeping quiet on this issue was simple. In the week that Reagan authorized the strike against Libya, the Finance Committee of the United States Senate was considering whether to approve the start of the Canada–United States free trade negotiations. On April 11, a number of senators had quite unexpectedly indicated that they were going to deny "fast track" approval of the negotiations, and indeed introduced a motion vetoing the proposal on April 16. The vote on this veto was delayed three times while frantic behind-the-scenes negotiations were conducted between the White House and Capitol Hill to secure a working majority on the committee. When the vote finally came on April 23, the veto failed to get a majority, allowing the negotiations to proceed. But it was close: The senators split 10–10 on whether to veto the negotiations. Given the timing of the attack on Libya, the Canadian government decided that prudence dictated overt support for the strike, not because this would gain Canada favours in Washington, but because if Canada had been critical of, or hesitant about, the attack, it might have been noticed by the senators and might have swayed their votes on the free trade issue.[73]

In sum, Canada's economic structures and location in the international political economy have a persistent impact on international policy. Moreover, there is a deep interconnection between economic structures on which the wealth of Canadians depend and the imperatives of the country's geostrategic location. Governments in Ottawa understand that while the neighbourhood has its benefits—a deep integration with the world's largest economy that provides considerable wealth for Canadians—there are also geostrategic expectations that come with that neighbourhood that push Canada in particular directions. Those imperatives are reinforced by the dynamics of the various international organizations to which the Canadian government belongs.

THE DYNAMICS OF GROUP MEMBERSHIP

Multilateral diplomacy, according to Tom Keating, "involves working with coalitions of states, primarily but not exclusively within formal associations or institutions, to achieve foreign policy objectives. It also implies a willingness to maintain solidarity with these coalitions and to maintain support for these institutions."[74] For many students of global politics, multilateralism is generally considered more advantageous than the alternatives—unilateralism (trying to achieve policy objectives by "going it alone") or bilateralism

---

73 G. Bruce Doern and Brian W. Tomlin, *Faith and Fear: The Free Trade Story* (Toronto: Stoddart, 1991), 35–39.

74 Tom Keating, *Canada and World Order: The Multilateralist Tradition in Canadian Foreign Policy,* 2nd ed. (Toronto: Oxford University Press, 2002), 4.

(through bilateral diplomacy).[75] Canada has been a committed multilateralist, a function of the dominance of the idea of internationalism, discussed in Chapter 5. While Canada's enthusiasm for multilateralism has given rise to the fanciful trope that "Canadians have multilateralism in their DNA,"[76] there can be no denying that Canada has been, as Robert Wolfe puts it, "a great joiner."[77] It is a member of a large number of international institutions and clubs and coalitions of states. Participation in these groupings of states constitute "relative invariants," constraining and impelling the Canadian government and in the process helping to shape international policy. We examine the different kinds of groups to which Canada belongs, looking at the degree of *openness* of association or institution, for openness will determine the kind of obligations that membership is likely to impose on the Canadian government.

International Institutions

The United Nations is the best example of an open international organization, since it is a universal organization. Any sovereign state can apply for membership provided that it promises to respect the United Nations Charter and it makes appropriate financial contributions. The same is true for the specialized agencies of the UN and a number of functional organizations, such as the International Court of Justice (ICJ), the World Trade Organization (WTO), the International Bank for Reconstruction and Development (IBRD), the International Labour Organization (ILO), World Health Organization (WHO), the Food and Agriculture Organization (FAO), and the like.

Other institutions are non-universal. Their membership is limited by some attribute, such as geography (the Organization of American States, the African Union, Asia-Pacific Economic Cooperation forum, South Pacific Forum); level of economic development (Organisation for Economic Co-operation and Development); general political orientation (the Non-Aligned Movement); language (Organisation internationale de la Francophonie); religion (Organisation of the Islamic Conference); or common history (the Commonwealth). These organizations are, from a Canadian perspective, open in the sense that they have governments of all sorts as members.

---

75 John Gerard Ruggie, "Multilateralism: Anatomy of an Institution," *International Organization* 46:3 (Summer 1992), 561–98; Joseph S. Nye, Jr., *The Paradox of American Power: Why the World's Only Superpower Can't Go It Alone* (London: Oxford University Press, 2002).

76 As Renato Ruggiero, director-general of the World Trade Organization, put it: "The Road Ahead: International Trade Policy in the Era of the WTO," address to the Fourth Sylvia Ostry Lecture, Ottawa, May 28, 1996, available http://www.wto.org/english/news_e/sprr_e/ottawa_e.htm. Likewise, Canada's ambassador to France noted that "our support for multilateralism . . . is so deep-seated that one could say it is part of our national DNA." See Claude Laverdure, "Key Issues of Canada's Foreign Policy," presentation at the International Colloquium of the Centre d'études canadiennes de Paris 3 Sorbonne, May 19, 2006, available http://www.international.gc.ca/canada-europa/France/actualites/discours_C_Laverdure_CEC_19_mai_2006-en.asp.

77 Robert Wolfe, "Canada's Adventures in Clubland: Trade Clubs and Political Influence," in Daudelin and Schwanen, eds., *Canada Among Nations 2007*, 181. On multilateralism, see Keating, *Canada and World Order*; David Black and Claire Turenne Sjolander, "Multilateralism Re-constituted and the Discourse of Canadian Foreign Policy," *Studies in Political Economy* 49 (Spring 1996), 7–36; and A. Claire Cutler and Mark W. Zacher, *Canadian Foreign Policy and International Economic Regimes* (Vancouver: UBC Press, 1992).

Canada is a member of all universal international organizations and home to two: the International Civil Aviation Organization (ICAO) and the Secretariat of the Convention on Biological Diversity, both located in Montréal. Canada is also a member of a number of open regional organizations, such as the OSCE, the Organization of American States (OAS), and the Asia-Pacific Economic Cooperation (APEC) forum, as well as the Organisation internationale de la Francophonie (OIF) and the Commonwealth. We will revisit these last two in Chapter 7.

It is difficult to make firm generalizations about how participation in this type of organization affects international policy in Canada. What we can conclude is that operating in such organizations does not impose any *generalized* set of obligations on Canadian governments. In the main, Canadian representatives to such organizations will tend to work with "friends" and not against them, sponsoring initiatives that favour friendly states and their perspectives. If Canadians have initiatives they want to press—such as the banning of antipersonnel landmines or an international convention on the rights of children—Canadian representatives will tend to seek out other likeminded countries to achieve common goals and convince skeptical or recalcitrant governments.

Most of the time, international organizations of this type do not make decisions that impose major obligations on Canada; Ottawa tends to accept the majority decisions of such organizations as binding on Canadian practice. In those cases when the UN Security Council imposes sanctions under Article 41 of the Charter, the government in Ottawa will generally introduce those sanctions into Canadian law by using the United Nations Act, 1985, which allows the government to impose them.[78] In rare cases, an international organization of which Canada is a member may seek to impose a specific obligation that the government in Ottawa has no desire to be bound by; in such cases, Ottawa will generally have no hesitation in simply not acting on that decision (as occurred when the United Nations Human Rights Committee found that Ontario's separate school system was in violation of Article 26 of the United Nations International Covenant on Civil and Political Rights since it funded Roman Catholic schools but not other faith-based schools[79]).

Clubs and Coalitions

Like open international organizations, clubs and coalitions of states come together to pursue a common purpose, but one is generally admitted only by invitation. Clubs and coalitions tend to be composed of "friends" or "likeminded" states. Sometimes they include governments that are not friends but are willing to temporarily put aside traditional differences in order to achieve an agreed-upon goal. Coalitions of this sort may be either highly organized and institutionalized or loose groupings. Canada belongs to a range of international

---

78 The act permits the government to make regulations to give effect to Security Council sanctions and to permit the government to punish violators by seizing their property, imposing fines of up to $100,000 or prison terms of up to ten years: http://laws.justice.gc.ca/PDF/Statute/U/U-2.pdf.

79 Arieh Hollis Waldman, who enrolled his two children in a private Jewish school in Toronto, contended that Ontario's refusal to extend public funding to all faith-based schools was discriminatory. Having exhausted all domestic legal remedies, he took the government of Canada to the United Nations Human Rights Committee in 1996. The Committee's 1999 decision in *Waldman v. Canada* is available at http://www1.umn.edu/humanrts/undocs/session67/view694.htm. Neither the federal nor the Ontario government chose to act on the Committee's decision.

coalitions that span all the concerns of international policy, and, like many countries, is persuaded by the idea that, as Lorraine Eden and Fen Osler Hampson put it, "clubs are trump."[80]

Canada belongs to the most important groups in the architecture of contemporary global governance. It was a member of the Group of Seven (G7), which became the G8 after Russia joined in 1997. This group was described by one senior Canadian official as "the most exclusive multilateral forum in the world."[81] Canada was also a founding member of the G-20, consisting of the finance ministers and central bank governors from 20 countries. The G-20 was established in 1999 in the aftermath of the Asian financial crisis of 1997; Canada's finance minister, Paul Martin, Jr. was its first chair. A G-20 Leaders' summit was convened after the global financial crisis of 2008; at the G-20 summit in Pittsburgh in September 2009, the leaders decided that the group would replace the G8 in 2010. Canada is also a member of the Financial Stability Forum, a group of eleven countries[82] whose finance ministers and central bank governors meet to monitor financial flows and discuss policy options, and its successor, the Financial Stability Board, whose has membership expanded to match that of the G-20. We examine these groups in more detail in Chapter 7.

Canada is also a member of key international coalitions and clubs focused on global trade. During the Tokyo and Uruguay Rounds of trade negotiations under the General Agreement on Tariffs and Trade (GATT), Canada was a member of the Quadrilateral Group of leading traders, commonly known as the Quad (the United States, Japan, the European Union, and Canada), or the Cairns Group of Fair Trading Nations, organized by Australia to press for greater liberalization of agricultural trade in the early days of the Uruguay Round of trade negotiations.[83] With the emergence of the World Trade Organization, the club scene shifted. The "old Quad" gave way to a "new Quad" (sometimes called the G-4): four governments diametrically opposed to each other on agricultural trade—the United States, the European Union, Brazil, and India. When the new Quad decided to invite other "interested parties" to the discussion on agriculture, Australia and Japan got the nod but Canada was not invited. This was largely because in global agricultural trading circles Canada's agricultural trade policy is so bizarre—the government in Ottawa pronounces itself to be in favour of liberalized trade in agriculture and in favour of maintaining protectionist barriers against agricultural imports at the same time[84]—that on

---

80 Lorraine Eden and Fen Osler Hampson, "Clubs are Trump: The Formation of International Regimes in the Absence of a Hegemon," J. Rogers Hollingsworth and Robert Boyer, eds., *Contemporary Capitalism: The Embeddedness of Institutions* (Cambridge: Cambridge University Press, 1999), 361–94.

81 J.H. Taylor, "Preparing for the Halifax Summit: Reflections on Past Summits," *Canadian Foreign Policy* 3 (Spring 1995), 46.

82 The members of the Financial Stability Board (1999–2009) were: Australia, Britain, Canada, France, Germany, Hong Kong Special Administrative Region, Italy, Japan, Netherlands, Singapore, and the United States.

83 Andrew F. Cooper, Richard A. Higgott, and Kim Richard Nossal, *Relocating Middle Powers: Australia and Canada in a Changing World Order* (Vancouver: UBC Press, 1993), chap. 3.

84 The key to understanding Canadian policy on global agricultural trade is to recognize that no government in Ottawa has been able to reconcile the contradictory interests of Canada's farmers. Wheat and beef farmers are incredibly efficient and thus favour the elimination of agricultural barriers; for

that particular issue Ottawa has lost credibility with all other players, protectionists and free traders alike, with the result that the minister is marginalized. However, as Wolfe demonstrates, the marginalization is limited to agricultural trade; in other spheres of policy, "Canada is still a valued player in many [WTO] clubs."[85]

In the area of development assistance, the key "club" for Canada has historically been the Colombo Plan, named after the city in Sri Lanka (then Ceylon) where foreign ministers from seven Commonwealth nations—Australia, Britain, Canada, India, New Zealand, Pakistan, and Sri Lanka—gathered in January 1950 to put in place a program for development. Other development assistance programs are administered through both the Commonwealth and the Organisation internationale de la Francophonie. Other clubs include the Development Assistance Committee (DAC), a committee of the Organisation for Economic Co-operation and Development (OECD) that coordinates contributions to development assistance institutions. Canada is also active in international financial institutions (IFIs) that provide funding for development assistance, such as the World Bank and the International Monetary Fund. The Canadian government is not only on the board of directors of these central IFIs, but also on the boards of all the regional development banks for Africa, Asia, the Caribbean, and the Inter-American Development Bank.

But the clubs can also be narrowly focused on an individual country. Many countries have "donor coordination groups" whose purpose is to align the various donations with the recipient government's priorities and harmonize the development activities to increase effectiveness. While the vast majority of these donor coordination groups operate without controversy, sometimes the donor coordination process can draw its members into active support for human-rights-violating regimes. For example, in 1967 the Netherlands invited a group of states and IFIs to form the Inter-Governmental Group on Indonesia (IGGI) to coordinate development assistance to Indonesia; this group met throughout the 1970s, a period when the Indonesian government under Suharto was engaging in massive human rights violations, including the widely reviled practice of transmigration, extrajudicial executions, and Indonesia's invasion of the Portuguese colony of East Timor in 1975.[86]

Some coalitions are military. In 1914, as part of the British Empire, Canada joined with other allies to oppose the Central powers—Germany, Austria-Hungary, and the Ottoman Empire. In 1939, this time as a sovereign state, it participated in what would become, in

---

a variety of reasons, including the size of family farms and decades of supply management price support, farmers in the dairy, egg, and poultry industries are only able to stay in business by maintaining protectionist barriers, particularly against imports from the United States. This fundamental difference plays itself out in political/electoral terms. The vast majority of wheat and beef producers are located in the west, while the vast majority of dairy and poultry farmers are concentrated in Ontario and Québec. Moreover, the overrepresentation of rural Canada, where just 2 percent of the population is employed in agriculture, means that, as Wolfe puts it, "politicians are tied in knots by the farm lobbies." Wolfe, "Adventures in Clubland," 193. See also Andrew F. Cooper, *In Between Countries: Australia, Canada, and the Search for Order in Agricultural Trade* (Montréal and Kingston: McGill-Queen's University Press, 1998), 65–76; Grace Skogstad, "Canadian Agricultural Trade Policy: Continuity Amidst Change," in Fen Osler Hampson, Michael Hart, and Martin Rudner, eds., *Canada Among Nations 1999: A Big League Player?* (Toronto: Oxford University Press, 1999), 73–90.

85 Wolfe, "Adventures in Clubland," 194.

86 For details, see Harold A. Crouch, *The Army and Politics in Indonesia*, rev. ed. (Ithaca: Cornell University Press, 1988).

1941, the Grand Alliance that gathered the United States, Britain, the Soviet Union, and an ever-increasing number of states against Nazi Germany and its allies. In 1950, Canadian soldiers fought in Korea with troops provided by more than thirty other states against North Korean forces supported by the Soviet Union and the People's Republic of China. This coalition, formed at the initiative of the United States (which also provided the majority of the troops), was legitimized by a resolution of the United Nations Security Council—passed when the Soviet Union, with its veto, was boycotting the Council—condemning the aggression against South Korea.[87]

The coalition put together by George H.W. Bush following the Iraqi elimination of the state of Kuwait in August 1990 resembled the one in Korea. Legitimized by a resolution of the UN Security Council, the operation involved more than thirty states. Some, like the United States, Britain, France, and Syria, contributed combat ground forces that eventually engaged the Iraqi army. Others, like Italy and Canada, contributed a mixture of ground units and naval and air forces. Many others contributed naval forces or medical units (Canada contributed three naval vessels, a squadron of CF-18 jet fighters, and a field hospital). Others still contributed material or financial assistance. Not all members of the coalition were friends, but each had its own reasons for wanting to see the Iraqis expelled and Kuwait restored,[88] and all explicitly or implicitly recognized the leading role of the United States.

All of these were military coalitions but not allied operations. Canada's alliance operations—Canada's contribution to the NATO bombing of Serbia in 1999 and participation in the multinational operation led by the United States to oust the Taliban government in Afghanistan following 9/11 and put in place a government more aligned with the West—will be examined in the next section.

Coalition membership can have important effects on Canadian policy, usually depending on the power of the other members of the coalition. When the other coalition members are less important, and the costs of crossing other coalition members not so high, the Canadian government has demonstrated a willingness to bear those costs. For example, in the case of the Cairns Group, one of the key reasons Ottawa was willing to disrupt that coalition, with its persistently ambivalent attitude toward agricultural trade, was that the cost of confronting Canadian farmers was far higher than the cost of enduring the ridicule of other Cairns Group members.

By contrast, when the other members of the coalition are more powerful or more important, the costs of defection are much higher. In the case of Indonesia, for example, the desire to be "on side" with the United States and its other allies in Southeast Asia, which had their own reasons for supporting Suharto as a bulwark against Soviet and Vietnamese expansion, prompted a succession of Canadian governments to overlook widespread human rights abuses by the government in Djakarta and to accept the invasion of East Timor.[89]

---

87 See Denis Stairs, *The Diplomacy of Constraint: Canada, the Korean War, and the United States* (Toronto: University of Toronto Press, 1974).

88 Andrew F. Cooper, Richard A. Higgott, and Kim Richard Nossal, "Bound to Follow? Leadership and Followership in the Gulf Conflict," *Political Science Quarterly* 106:3 (1991), 391–410.

89 Sharon Scharfe, *Complicity: Human Rights and Canadian Foreign Policy: The Case of East Timor* (Montréal: Black Rose Books, 1996); Kim Richard Nossal, "Les droits de la personne et la politique étrangère canadienne: le cas de l'Indonésie," *Études internationales* 11 (juin 1980), 223–38.

A similar dynamic can obtain in the case of military coalitions. During the Gulf conflict in 1991, all the members of the anti-Iraq coalition, including Canada, were tightly bound to the preferences of the United States. What had started off in August 1990 as a coalition to impose sanctions on Iraq and deter an Iraqi attack on Saudi Arabia—Operation Desert Shield—was turned quite unilaterally by the United States into an offensive coalition—Operation Desert Storm—as Bush decided to change the purpose of the coalition in October and November. But those smaller members of the coalition that had joined in the belief that the purpose would remain defensive and had little desire for a war against Iraq were stuck. Like a queasy roller coaster rider who has little desire to continue the ride, they had few choices but to hang on tightly until the end. They could have tried to get off the ride—by pulling their troops out of the coalition—but the diplomatic and political costs of doing so would have been exorbitant. In the event, it is hardly surprising that not a single coalition member withdrew after the purpose of the coalition was changed by the United States.[90]

Jean Chrétien's experience with the "coalition of the willing"[91] put together by George W. Bush in 2003 to invade Iraq demonstrates how coalition dynamics can shape Canada's international policy. Over the winter of 2002–2003, the Chrétien government decided that it would not rule out participating in the invasion of Iraq then being threatened by the United States. All members of the Canadian Forces (CF) who were engaged in exchanges with other armed forces were left where they were. As a result, in the lead-up to the final decision, Canada looked to be very much part of the American-led coalition. Members of the CF were deployed to U.S. Central Command headquarters in Florida to help plan the invasion, and were relocated with CENTCOM headquarters to Qatar just before the invasion. Approximately 100 Canadian officers were on secondment to American and British units that were readying to participate in the invasion; indeed, the most senior officer, BGen Walter Natynczyk, who went on to become Chief of the Defence Staff in 2008, was on exchange at a U.S. army headquarters in Kuwait, actively involved in the invasion planning. Moreover, a Canadian naval officer, Commodore Roger Girouard, assumed command of a multinational naval task force, TF 151, which would be "double-hatted"—in other words, it would support both Operation Enduring Freedom (the mission in Afghanistan) and Operation Iraqi Freedom (the invasion of Iraq).

However, as the time for decision drew closer, all of the costs of actually disrupting Canada's ongoing relationship with its coalition partners by withdrawing Canadian personnel loomed so large that they were all simply left in place by the government in Ottawa. The result was a huge irony. One the one hand, Chrétien announced just before the invasion that Canada would not participate in the coalition, to the cheers of his caucus and the general approval of public opinion. And the coalition dynamic kicked in: Chrétien's decision (and it was entirely his decision) proved very costly, wrecking an already poor relationship with Bush, as we will see in Chapter 7. On the other hand, the reality was that, as Janice Gross Stein and Eugene Lang note, "Canada's indirect contribution to the American war effort in Iraq—three ships and one hundred exchange officers—exceeded that of all but three other countries that were actually part of the coalition."[92]

---

90 Cooper, Higgott, and Nossal, *Relocating Middle Powers*, chap. 5.

91 This is a euphemism for military interventions that are conducted without the approval of the United Nations Security Council.

92 Janice Gross Stein and Eugene Lang, *The Unexpected War: Canada in Kandahar* (Toronto: Viking Canada, 2007), 90.

Alliances

Alliances constitute a special kind of international coalition deserving of separate consideration. An alliance is essentially an agreement between states that they will provide mutual assistance to one another in the event that they are attacked. Prior to the Second World War, alliances tended to be ad hoc and not deeply institutionalized. Since 1945, however, alliances tended to take increasingly complex institutional forms, with permanent structures designed to coordinate the security policies of their members.[93] Canada is a member of just one alliance, the North Atlantic Treaty, signed in April 1949, which in 1951 gave rise to an institution to manage and coordinate the alliance, the North Atlantic Treaty Organization (NATO). NATO, together with a number of bilateral agreements signed with the United States (but which do not constitute an alliance in the strict sense of the term), shape Canada's contemporary security policy.

The principal benefit an alliance provides for its members is much greater security. However, alliance membership imposes two major constraints on the international policy of its members. First, in return for the security benefits (benefits too costly or simply impossible for each ally to attain on its own), an agreement is made to absorb some of the costs of collective defence, putting financial resources, troops, military bases, and other facilities at the disposal of the alliance.

Second, each alliance member agrees not to take independent or unilateral action on issues of collective defence; alliance membership implies that on such questions, each state will consult its partners and will agree to coordinate defence policy with other allies. Respect for the principles of unity and solidarity is essential for maintaining the cohesion of any alliance, since division can easily undermine the collective effort and allow a potential adversary to gain advantage. Thus, over the course of the Cold War, the Western allies always sought to ensure that the Soviet Union was not able to provoke differences within NATO. To this end, the Atlantic Alliance created elaborate mechanisms for consulting, exchanging information, and harmonizing policy. To be sure, these processes were a function of the distribution of power among the allies. The United States, the largest and most influential member of NATO, has often been quite content to inform (and not "consult") its allies about its defence initiatives, even if they affected the security of the alliance as a whole, and then invoke the principle of solidarity to prod other members to support its lead. Such an approach would be unthinkable for other smaller allies like Canada, which generally were happy to express their views and then support the decisions adopted by the more powerful members of the alliance.

Canada was a founding member of the Atlantic Alliance, and every Canadian government has grappled with the intertwined benefits and obligations that come with membership. Strategically, Canada benefitted from the stability generated by this alliance during the Cold War. The Second World War had clearly demonstrated that Canada's prosperity was intimately linked to Europe; thus the Canadian government had an interest in European stability. Two problems faced Western policymakers in the late 1940s: first, how to deter the Soviet Union from doing to other European states what it had done in Czechoslovakia in February 1948—staging a coup and incorporating Czechoslovakia into the Soviet sphere; second, how to ensure that Germany would never again pose a threat to European peace and security. For governments in western Europe, and in Ottawa, there was a third concern: how

---

93 Stephen M. Walt, *The Origins of Alliances* (Ithaca: Cornell University Press, 1987), chaps. 1–2.

to ensure that the United States did not retreat into the kind of isolationism that had marked its policy after the First World War. A transatlantic alliance was seen in Ottawa as the best way to achieve all three goals,[94] which was a key reason why Canadian governments were such enthusiastic supporters of NATO during the first half of the Cold War.

But for the Canadians, NATO was always more than just a military alliance. Canadian officials in the late 1940s hoped that the military alliance would lay the foundation for a "North Atlantic community" of states.[95] Hence Ottawa pushed for the inclusion of an article in the Treaty of Washington that pledged the signatories to deepen economic linkages with each other. The result was Article 2 of the Treaty[96]—often dubbed the "Canadian article" because it was included in response to Canadian pressures for it.

In the event, however, Article 2 never developed as the Canadians hoped. Canada nonetheless derived certain diplomatic benefits from its NATO membership. First, the country benefitted by having what Canadian officials describe as a "seat at the table." In other words, the officials had access to the processes of multilateral decision-making about military strategy and alliance policy during the Cold War. Moreover, membership in NATO gave Canada the status of a country interested in European security, with the result that Canada is always consulted on such issues. Second, NATO also provided Canadians with a way of counterbalancing its relationship with the United States. By being part of a multilateral institution that included European states, Canadians hoped to create a "counterweight" and avoid having to deal with the Americans on a strictly bilateral basis when decisions about Canadian security had to be made.[97]

Surveys of public opinion during the Cold War suggest that Canadians tended to be aware of the advantages NATO membership afforded. "Atlanticism"—the idea that Canada and the United States enjoyed a special transoceanic bond with Europeans—became an important part of Canadian identity, particularly at the level of the political elite.[98] This

---

94 Best expressed in the Cold War saw, attributed to Lord Ismay, NATO's first secretary-general, that NATO's purpose was "to keep the Americans in, the Soviets out, and the Germans down."

95 For details, see Stéphane Roussel, "L'instant kantien: la contribution canadienne à la création de la "communauté nord-atlantique" (1947–1949)," in Greg Donaghy, ed., *Canada and the Cold War, 1943–1957* (Ottawa: Department of Foreign Affairs and International Trade, 1999), 119–156.

96 Article II of the North Atlantic Treaty reads: "The Parties will contribute toward the further development of peaceful and friendly international relations by strengthening their free institutions, by bringing about a better understanding of the principles upon which these institutions are founded, and by promoting conditions of stability and well-being. They will seek to eliminate conflict in their international economic policies and will encourage economic collaboration between any or all of them."

97 On counterbalancing and counterweights, see Michael Tucker, *Canadian Foreign Policy: Contemporary Issues and Themes* (Toronto: McGraw Hill Ryerson, 1980), 227–28; Roy Rempel, *Counterweights: The Failure of Canada's German and European Policy, 1955–1995* (Montréal and Kingston: McGill-Queen's University Press, 1996), 34–36. To be sure, the success of this "counterweight" strategy is difficult to evaluate, in large part because Washington tended to make a distinction between the defence of Europe and the defence of North America. Roussel, *North American Democratic Peace,* 204–209.

98 Paul Buteux, Michel Fortmann, and Pierre Martin, "Canada and the Expansion of NATO: A Study in Élite Attitudes and Public Opinion," in David Haglund, ed., *Will NATO Go East? The Debate over Enlarging the Atlantic Alliance* (Kingston: Queen's Centre for International Relations, 1996), 147–79; Kim Richard Nossal, "A European Nation? The Life and Times of Atlanticism in Canada," in John English and Norman Hillmer, eds., *Making a Difference? Canada's Foreign Policy in a Changing World Order* (Toronto: Lester Publishing, 1992), 79–102.

support explains why Canadians were generally willing to bear the costs of membership. These costs included permanently stationing tens of thousands of members of the Canadian armed forces in Germany between 1951 and 1991 (and all the associated expenditures involved in moving, educating, and supporting families of military personnel); it also included spending on military equipment so that Canada could effectively contribute to a war against the Soviet Union on Europe's Central Front if one happened to break out. As John Halstead noted, what Canada spent on NATO during these forty years was far less costly than returning to Europe to fight a third war.[99]

While NATO membership generated considerable debate in Canada during the Cold War, both in civil society[100] and within the state,[101] there can be little doubt that NATO enjoyed a generally high level of support among Canadians. It is for this reason that the alliance acted as an invariant in much the same way as the aerospace defence agreement with the United States: It was a given in every government's calculation. It constrained prime ministers considering withdrawal of Canada's troop commitment, such as Trudeau in the late 1960s or Mulroney in the mid-1980s.[102] Alliance considerations also drove much of how Canadians spent their defence dollars, maintaining an inventory of weapons systems, such as main battle tanks or artillery systems, that made little sense for the defence of Canada alone, outside the alliance context.[103]

The breach of the Berlin Wall in November 1989, the reunification of East and West Germany in October 1990, the end of the Warsaw Pact in July 1991, and the dismantling of the Soviet Union in December 1991 profoundly changed the European security situation. But the Atlantic Alliance, deprived of its original raison d'être, moved quickly to reinvent itself by embracing new missions. At summits in London in July 1990 and Rome in November 1991, NATO decided that in addition to collective defence and the maintenance of transatlantic links, it would support cooperative relations with its old adversaries. The North Atlantic Cooperation Council (NACC), created in 1991, and the Partnership for Peace (PfP), established in 1994, met this need. This new mission led to the expansion of

---

99 John G.H. Halstead, "Canada and NATO: Looking to the 90s," in Margaret O. MacMillan and David S. Sorenson, eds., *Canada and NATO: Uneasy Past, Uncertain Future* (Waterloo: University of Waterloo Press, 1990), 151–52.

100 For many observers, NATO was seen as an instrument of American domination, and there were a number of voices calling for a withdrawal, including the New Democratic Party. See, for example, Kenneth McNaught, "From Colony to Satellite," in Stephen Clarkson, ed., *An Independent Foreign Policy for Canada?* (Toronto: McClelland & Stewart, 1968), 173–83; and James M. Minifie, *Peacemaker or Powdermonkey: Canada's Role in a Revolutionary World* (Toronto: McClelland & Stewart, 1960).

101 Within the government there was a running debate over whether Canada should accept nuclear weapons. See Erika Simpson, *NATO and the Bomb: Canadian Defenders Confront Critics* (Montréal and Kingston: McGill-Queen's University Press, 2001).

102 On Trudeau, see J.L. Granatstein and Robert Bothwell, *Pirouette: Pierre Trudeau and Canadian Foreign Policy* (Toronto: University of Toronto Press, 1990), 3–29, and Bruce Thordarson, "Cutting Back on NATO, 1969," in Don Munton and John Kirton, eds., *Canadian Foreign Policy: Selected Cases* (Scarborough: Prentice-Hall Canada, 1992), 174–88; on Mulroney, see Joel J. Sokolsky, "Canadian Defence Policy: Coping with the Gap," in Brian W. Tomlin and Maureen Appel Molot, eds., *Canada Among Nations 1986: Talking Trade* (Toronto: Lorimer, 1987), 59–62.

103 Kim Richard Nossal, "Defending the 'Realm': Canadian Strategic Culture Revisited," *International Journal* 59:3 (Summer 2004), 503–520.

the alliance: three former members of the Warsaw Pact—Hungary, Poland, and the Czech Republic—were admitted in 1999, and in 2002 invitations were extended to seven new members: Bulgaria, Estonia, Latvia, Lithuania, Rumania, Slovakia, and Slovenia.

A second new function was crisis management in Europe. The collapse of Yugoslavia into civil war in 1991 eventually prompted NATO to intervene and help to restore order and maintain peace, first in Bosnia in 1995 and then in Kosovo in 1999. After the Dayton Accords of November 1995, a NATO-led Implementation Force (IFOR) was deployed, followed in December 1996 by a Stabilization Force (SFOR). NATO also intervened in the growing crisis in the Serbian province of Kosovo in 1998, which resulted in the bombing of Serbia by NATO forces from March to June 1999 and was followed by the occupation of Kosovo by the NATO-led Kosovo Force (KFOR).

A third new mission was embraced at the 2002 summit in Prague: NATO's involvement in the war against terrorism that evolved out of the invoking of Article 5, the collective defence provisions of the North Atlantic Treaty, following 9/11. The Taliban government of Afghanistan was overthrown by the Northern Alliance, an alliance of Afghani militias supported by the United States and its allies. When an international conference in Bonn in December 2001 put in place a new government, the International Security Assistance Force (ISAF) was also created as a UN-mandated "coalition of the willing" rather than a UN force. ISAF operated in tandem with the U.S. combat mission, Operation Enduring Freedom. While a large number of NATO members were involved in ISAF, it was not until August 2003 that NATO took over command of ISAF and expanded its operations throughout Afghanistan.

All these events had an impact on Canada. Despite the disappearance of the "Soviet threat," the Alliance continued to be one of the principal pillars of Canada's international policy. In addition to the continuing importance of maintaining solid transatlantic ties, Ottawa saw the potential of an expanded NATO as an institution that could coordinate crisis management and assist in the fight against terrorism. But as NATO evolved in the 1990s and early 2000s, the costs associated with membership did not diminish. Mulroney may have decided to withdraw Canadian troops from Europe as a cost-cutting measure in 1991, but it was not long before events conspired to bring them back. From 1992 to 1995, Canada maintained a force of more than 2000 soldiers in Croatia and Bosnia under the auspices of the United Nations Protection Force (UNPROFOR). The Canadian government decided to commit more than 1000 soldiers to IFOR and its successor, SFOR. Canada also contributed to the bombing of Serbia, with CF-18s flying some 600 missions, and deployed 1300 Canadian troops with KFOR in the summer of 1999.[104] Canada also contributed forces to the war in Afghanistan, deploying special forces to fight alongside American combat troops in the initial invasion and then to ISAF in 2003, and a battle group of 2800 troops to Kandahar under OEF and then NATO command in 2006.[105]

While all of these missions involved costs, both political and human, there is no sentiment within the government in Ottawa for changing the centrality of NATO to Canada's

---

104 Kim Richard Nossal and Stéphane Roussel, "Canada and the Kosovo War: The Happy Follower," in Pierre Martin and Mark R. Brawley, eds., *Alliance Politics, Kosovo, and NATO's War: Allied Force or Forced Allies?* (New York: Palgrave, 2000), 181–99.

105 Kim Richard Nossal, "No Exit: Canada and the 'War Without End' in Afghanistan," in Hans-Georg Ehrhart and Charles C. Pentland, eds., *The Afghanistan Challenge: Hard Realities and Strategic Choices* (Montréal and Kingston: McGill-Queen's University Press, 2009), 157–73.

international policy. It is not just that contemporary policymakers value the "seat at the table" as much as their Cold War predecessors; rather, those who make international policy for Canada remain convinced that NATO continues to play an important role in creating and maintaining a global order that serves the interests of Western states like Canada.

MATERIAL CAPABILITIES

The final factor that will affect the room for manoeuvring of those who make international policy in Canada are the material capabilities available to them. Most students of international relations recognize the importance of the material capabilities of a state's decision-makers, even if they do not agree on the precise role they play in determining outcomes. Material capabilities commonly mentioned include population; geography; GNP (both absolute and per capita); industrial capacity; technological innovation; natural resources (including food and raw materials); reserves of petroleum, gas, coal, and uranium; size of armed forces; military expenditures; and military preparedness.[106] Other authors, seeking to explain why some small states manage to exert influence without such material capability, have added certain resources that are more difficult to quantify: credibility, know-how, specialization in "niche" areas, or diplomatic activism.[107]

Canada has fewer capabilities relative to other states in the international system. While it occupies more land than any other state except the Russian Federation, and while it is generously endowed with natural resources, Canada's population, at 34 million, is small relative to other communities. Although it has one of the largest economies in the world—in 2009 it was ranked as the eleventh-largest economy by the International Monetary Fund, the World Bank, and the Central Intelligence Agency[108]—its industrial capacity is limited and specialized; employment is predominantly in the service sector and the economy as a whole is not only highly dependent on international intercourse but also highly sensitive to economic changes outside Canada's borders, particularly in the United States. The Canadian Forces are small, both relatively and absolutely—66,000 as of 2009—and not as well equipped as other armed forces.

As we will see below, this relative lack of material capability limits Canada's range of choice and scope of action. Not only does lack of capacity shape the Canadian government's foreign (and domestic) objectives, it also limits the tools of statecraft available to

---

106 Hans Morgenthau, *Politics Among Nations: The Struggle for Power and Peace* (New York: Alfred A. Knopf, 1948), 80ff; Klaus Knorr, *The Power of Nations: The Political Economy of International Relations* (New York: Basic Books, 1975); Michael Handel, *Weak States in the International System* (London: Taylor and Frances, 1981), 25; Kurt M. Campbell and Michael E. O'Hanlon, *Hard Power: The New Politics of National Security* (New York: Basic Books, 2006).

107 For example, Erling Bjøl, "The Power of the Weak," *Cooperation and Conflict* 3 (1968); Robert O. Keohane, "The Big Influence of Small Allies," *Foreign Policy* 1:2 (1971), 161–82; Ulf Lindell and Stefan Persson, "The Paradox of Weak State Power: A Research and Literature Overview," *Cooperation and Conflict* 21:2 (1986), 79–97.

108 International Monetary Fund, World Economic Outlook Database, April 2009; World Bank, World Development Indicators Database, July 1, 2009, available http://siteresources.worldbank.org/DATAS-TATISTICS/Resources/GDP.pdf; United States, Central Intelligence Agency, *The World Factbook*, available https://www.cia.gov/library/publications/the-world-factbook/index.html. These rankings are derived from gross domestic product on an official-exchange-rate basis; when GDP is calculated on a purchasing-power-parity (PPP) basis, Canada drops to thirteenth or fourteenth.

policymakers to achieve their objectives—or to rebuff the importunities of other states in the international system.

CONCLUSION

All of the elements discussed in this chapter can be considered invariants in the sense that they cannot be changed by even the most determined or ambitious government in Ottawa. No one can change Canada's geographic location, and thus all Canadian governments must grapple with whatever geostrategic consequences of geography the global politics of a particular era impose. But what might prevail in one era might not apply in another: The same geographic "facts" had very different meanings for policy in 1899, 1919, 1939, 1959, 1989 or 2009. The nature of the international system and the state of technology tends to determine the strategic importance of Canada's geography. Similarly, governments in Ottawa may try to tinker with Canada's economic structure, but the constraints of Canadian federalism, the depth of Canadian-American economic integration, and the nature of representative government all preclude ambitious restructuring that would alleviate Canadian dependence on and sensitivity to the global economy. Participation in international institutions, coalitions, and clubs is also a relative invariant, for memberships do not change rapidly or radically. Likewise, no government in Ottawa is able to change the fundaments of Canada's material capabilities: what changes there will be in the "elements of national power" and will come marginally, incrementally, and over the span of generations.

Thus, Canada's international policy objectives and the means used to attain these goals will be shaped by the unyielding constraints and imperatives imposed by geography, economic structure, Canada's international connections, and the capabilities of the country. Such conditions set considerable limits on what the government can do in foreign policy, they will frequently define what it must do, and more often than not they dictate how it may or must be done. However, these invariants serve as the parameters of decision—constraints, imperatives, and opportunities to be grappled with. The invariants themselves do not explain the government's ability or inability to achieve foreign policy goals, or its capacity (or lack thereof) to defend Canadian interests. Such ability is determined not by Canada's attributes, but by its power. It is to the contentious issue of Canada's power in global politics that we now turn.

CHAPTER 3

Power and Status: Canada's International Influence

Power lies at the heart of theorizing about making international policy, because governments, when they pursue policies beyond their borders, are confronted not only with the power of other states, but also with the limits of their own capacity. Power, as Hans J. Morgenthau put it succinctly, is the means to a country's ends.[1] In the anarchic environment of global politics, where there is no authority to arbitrate between states or force governments to comply with rules, only power makes it possible to achieve political goals. We implicitly recognize the connection between power and the capacity for control when we talk about countries in world politics in terms of their size: superpowers, great powers, middle powers, small powers, and so on.

Because of the importance of power, it is not surprising that it occupies a central place not only in the making of Canada's international policies, but also in the scholarly literature. Indeed, as Maureen Appel Molot has noted, students of Canada's external policies have tended to obsess over the concept of power, often ignoring other important issues.[2] The academic debate over Canada's power has a distinctly political character that touches on Canadian identity: by trying to determine what kind of power Canada was, Canadians were in fact seeking to determine their place and role in the international system. But this introspective focus on power tended to obscure the link between ends and means identified by Morgenthau.

The first part of this chapter examines the contending interpretations of Canada's power in the international hierarchy. We will show that these concepts led to the formulation of *theories* (assumptions and hypotheses with explanatory capabilities) and *normative positions* (policies that the government should follow) that are generally contradictory. These so-called "theories of Canadian foreign policy" have limited analytical utility, since they do not say much about Canada's real international influence. We thus use an alternative approach in the second part of the chapter and examine Canada's power and the methods available to the Canadian government to defend and promote its international interests. The third part focuses on the implementation of these methods by the Canadian government, in particular in the context of its relations with the United States.

IMAGES OF CANADA'S POWER

There are three broad images of Canada's power in the international system. Since the 1940s, Canada has traditionally been regarded as a "middle power," an image that was deeply connected with internationalism, examined in more detail in Chapter 5. The other images—Canada as a satellite or as a major or principal power—were elaborated later and mainly in response to the idea of Canada as a middle power.

---

1 Hans J. Morgenthau, *Politics Among Nations: The Struggle for Power and Peace*, 5th ed. (New York: Alfred A. Knopf, 1948, 1973), 27.

2 Maureen Appel Molot, "Where Do We, Should We, or Can We Sit? A Review of the Canadian Foreign Policy Literature," *International Journal of Canadian Studies* 1–2 (1990), 86.

Canada as Middle Power

We start with the dominant vision that Canadians—and others in the international system—have of Canada as a middle power. We examine the origins of the concept and the difficulties of actually defining what a middle power is, and look at the popularity of the idea before discussing the alternative images it spawned.

The Emergence of the Concept

It is often said that it was during the First World War, and in particular the battle for Vimy Ridge in April 1917—the first major victory of the Canadian Corps on the Western Front—that marked the birth of Canada as a nation.[3] In fact, the "birth" took somewhat longer and was a slower evolution into nationhood that extended over the years between the First and Second World Wars.

In the interwar era, one of the main preoccupations of the Canadian government was to be recognized by the international community as an independent entity in world politics—sovereign and distinct from Britain and the Empire. Thus Ottawa sought—and secured—a seat at the Paris peace conference of 1919, separate admission to the League of Nations, the ability to send Canadian diplomatic representatives abroad, and the ability to sign its own international treaties.[4] Eventually, Canada and the other self-governing dominions in the British Empire were granted sovereignty by the Statute of Westminster, 1931, discussed in more detail in Chapter 5. However, the question of Canada's rank in the international system did not seem important. Judging from the historical evidence, Canadian officials in the interwar period implicitly accepted the division of the international system into a simple dichotomous hierarchy. On top were the "great powers"; on the bottom were all other states, lumped together into what German scholars in the 1930s referred to as the *Nichtgrossmachten*—literally, the non–great powers. Loring Christie, an official in the Department of External Affairs, had no illusions about Canada's status. During the Ethiopian crisis of 1935, he wrote bluntly that Canada had little choice but to follow the great powers: "if the Great Powers start, you start; if they don't, you don't; where they go, you go; when they stop, you stop. The theory of our having a voice and control is eyewash."[5]

However, officials in Ottawa were sensitive to differences of status *within* the ranks of the smaller powers. For example, when the United States objected to Canada and the other self-governing dominions being given separate representation from Britain on the grounds that since they were members of the British Empire, it would be like giving Britain additional votes, the proposed exclusion did not sit well with any of the dominion prime ministers, prompting inevitable, if infelicitous, comparisons between their countries and other small powers. For example, Canada's prime minister, Sir Robert Borden, noted huffily that

---

3 C.P. Stacey, "Nationality: The Experience of Canada," *Historical Papers* 2:1 (1967), 11; see, however, Desmond Morton and J.L. Granatstein, *Marching to Armageddon: Canadians and the Great War, 1914–1919* (Toronto: Lester & Orpen Dennys, 1989), 260.

4 C.P. Stacey, *Canada and the Age of Conflict*, vol. 1: *1867–1921* (Toronto: Macmillan, 1977), chap. 9; and John Hilliker, *Canada's Department of External Affairs*, vol. 1: *The Early Years, 1909–1946* (Montréal and Kingston: McGill-Queen's University Press, 1990), 79–81.

5 Quoted in J.L. Granatstein, *The Ottawa Men: The Civil Service Mandarins, 1935–1957* (Toronto: Oxford University Press, 1982), 73.

"It is hardly to be anticipated that Canadians will consider that their country is suitably recognized by being placed on an equality with Siam and Hedjaz."[6] Likewise, when it was proposed that Canada's newly appointed representative to Washington be given a diplomatic rank below that of ambassador, Christie objected. "To rank him as Minister Resident or Chargé d'Affaires," he wrote, "would be to rank him below the agents of many comparatively insignificant Powers."[7]

The role played by Canada's armed forces in the Second World War contributed to the evolution of thinking about the country's position in the international hierarchy, almost as though what the Canadian Corps had started in Vimy in 1917 had been completed by those who fought at Hong Kong in 1941, Dieppe in 1942, and Normandy in 1944. Canada achieved international recognition as a state, and then, having secured sovereignty the government in Ottawa, was now keen to have the great powers recognize its sizable war effort— just over 1 million Canadians, about 10 percent of the population, served in the armed forces; 42,000 lost their lives—by giving Canada a seat in the decision-making councils of the alliance. In an eerie replay of Borden's complaints a generation earlier, King pressed the Canadian case to Winston Churchill, the British prime minister: "You will, I am sure, appreciate how difficult it would be for Canada, after enlisting nearly one million persons in her armed forces and trebling her national debt in order to assist in restoring peace, to accept a position of parity with the Dominican Republic or El Salvador."[8]

Britain and the United States initially rebuffed the Canadians with the same arguments that had been used at the peace conference after the First World War: If countries like Canada were given a seat at the table, other allies would also claim representation, making decision-making for the war effort cumbersome. In response, officials in Ottawa formulated the so-called "functional" principle of representation. Functionalism asserted that in those areas where a smaller state had both interest and expertise (in Canada's case, food and raw materials, for example), it should be regarded as a major power and given the right to be represented on the decision-making bodies in those areas. Accepted hesitantly by the United States and Britain, this principle allowed Canada to be represented in a variety of international forums in such areas as civil aviation, atomic energy, and international trade.[9]

---

6 Quoted in Stacey, *Canada and the Age of Conflict*, 248. Hedjaz was an independent kingdom in what is now Saudi Arabia; Siam was Thailand's name before 1939.

7 Canada, Department of External Affairs, *Documents on Canadian External Relations*, vol. 3: *1919–1925*, Lovell C. Clark, ed. (Ottawa: 1970), 7. Four ranks of diplomats were originally agreed to at the Congress of Vienna in 1815: ambassador extraordinary and plenipotentiary (whose mission was known as an embassy); envoy extraordinary and minister plenipotentiary (such missions were termed legations); minister resident; and chargé d'affaires. Contemporary diplomatic ranks include: high commissioner (used for representatives of a Commonwealth country posted to another Commonwealth country), commissioner, permanent delegate, permanent representative, head of mission, and head of delegation.

8 Quoted in James Eayrs, "Defining a New Place for Canada in the Hierarchy of World Powers," *International Perspectives* (May/June 1975), 7.

9 On the functional principle, see Adam Chapnick, *The Middle Power Project: Canada and the Founding of the United Nations* (Vancouver: UBC Press, 2005); also John W. Holmes, *The Shaping of Peace: Canada and the Search for World Order,* vol. 1 (Toronto: University of Toronto Press, 1979), 29–73; A.J. Miller, "The Functional Principle in Canada's External Relations," *International Journal* 35:2 (Spring 1980), 309–28.

Moreover, the efforts of Canada and countries of similar stature like Australia left its mark on the organization of the postwar international system.

Canada's contribution to the war also prompted many Canadians, both inside and outside government, to rethink their conception of their country's place in the international hierarchy. Lionel Gelber, writing in 1944, put it in these terms:

> Under the impact of war, Canada has moved up from her old status to a new stature. With her smaller population and lack of colonial possessions, she is not a major or world power like Britain, the United States or Russia. But with her natural wealth and human capacity she is not a minor power like Mexico or Sweden. She stands in between as a Britannic Power of medium rank. Henceforth in world politics, Canada must figure as a Middle Power.[10]

Canadian officials gradually abandoned their simplistic conception of a world divided between the great and the "non-great" powers in favour of a more discriminating division. Mackenzie King expressed this evolution when he told the House of Commons in 1944 that "The simple division of the world between great powers and the rest is unreal and even dangerous. The great powers are called by that name simply because they possess great power. The other states in the world possess power and therefore, the capacity to use it for the maintenance of peace."[11]

It was not until early 1945 that the term *middle power* was adopted by the government in Ottawa to describe Canada's rank (and even then, it was used tentatively with the prefix "so-called" frequently added). The appearance of this new concept was not the result of some abstract intellectual exercise by officials in the Department of External Affairs but more the result of a careful political calculus. The Canadian government did not like the proposals for a new international organization, the United Nations, that was being discussed by the "Big Four" (the United States, Britain, the Soviet Union, and China) at meetings held at Dumbarton Oaks, a mansion in the Georgetown suburb of Washington, D.C., from August to October 1944. Of considerable concern to Canada and other countries like Australia was the plan to have the new United Nations dominated by the great powers, giving only the Big Five (as the Four had by then become with the addition of France) permanent representation on the Security Council and the right of veto.

When the Dumbarton Oaks proposals were circulated for comment, the Canadians and Australians tried hard to secure better representation for middle powers. Lester Pearson, for example, called for "not only abandoning the fiction that [El] Salvador and Russia are equal on the World Security Council, but also abandoning the fiction that outside the group of four or five great powers, all other states must have an exactly equal position."[12] However, their arguments were not persuasive enough to overcome the belief that the

---

10 Lionel Gelber, "A Greater Canada Among the Nations," *Behind the Headlines* (1944), quoted in Peter C. Dobell, *Canada's Search for New Roles: Foreign Policy in the Trudeau Era* (Toronto: Oxford University Press, 1972), 2.

11 Quoted in R.A. MacKay, "The Canadian Doctrine of the Middle Powers," in Harvey L. Dyck and H. Peter Krosby, eds., *Empire and Nations: Essays in Honour of Frederic H. Soward* (Toronto: University of Toronto Press, 1969), 134.

12 Lester B. Pearson, *Words and Occasions* (Toronto: University of Toronto Press, 1970), 63; also John English, "'A Fine Romance': Canada and the United Nations, 1943–1957," in Greg Donaghy, ed., *Canada and the Cold War, 1943–1957* (Ottawa: Department of Foreign Affairs and International Trade, 1999), 73–89.

League of Nations had failed in part because the great powers had not been given appropriate powers. Thus, the United Nations Charter adopted at the conference held in San Francisco from April to June 1945 confirmed the oligarchic powers of the great powers.

Although the efforts of the Australians and Canadians were unsuccessful, the term remained. The concept of "middle power" was to be used to indicate Canada's place in the international system.

Defining the "Middle"

But what exactly was a middle power? While the idea has been used in international politics for centuries,[13] it is exceedingly difficult to define. Two broad approaches have traditionally been used. The first is the *positional* approach: Simply put, middle powers are those "in the middle." In the nineteenth century German scholars suggested that the *Mittelmächte* were those smaller states in the geographical or geostrategic "middle" between adversarial great powers. Alternatively, middle powers could be identified in a positivist empirical way by looking at the attributes of power in quantitative terms (population, gross national product, natural resources, military capability, etc.). Middle powers were thus those states whose indicators of size and power situated them in the "middle" between the great powers on the one hand and smaller states on the other.[14] But the positional definition is analytically problematic, because there is little agreement on what attributes should be used or how they should be interpreted. Because of this, determining the "middle" using a positional approach often becomes little more than an intuitive and impressionistic exercise: We just *know* that countries like Canada, Australia, Sweden, Brazil, and South Africa are middle powers simply because they are not states like the United States, the Russian Federation, or China on the one hand, but not states like Jamaica, Singapore, or Botswana on the other.

The second approach defines middle powers not by what they *are*, but what they *do*. In this view, middle powers pursue a particular style in foreign policy.[15] John W. Holmes called this kind of diplomacy "middlepowermanship" (coining the term as an ironic counter to the tendency of American officials to glowingly describe their diplomacy vis-à-vis the Soviet Union and China in the late 1950s and early 1960s as "brinkmanship.")[16]

---

13 Carsten Holbraad, *Middle Power in International Politics* (London: Macmillan, 1984); Jennifer M. Welsh, "Canada in the 21st Century: Beyond Dominion and Middle Power," *The Round Table* 93:376 (September 2004), 3.

14 For examples of this approach, see Peyton V. Lyon and Brian W. Tomlin, *Canada as an International Actor* (Toronto: Macmillan, 1979), 72; Laura Neack, "Empirical Observations on 'Middle State' Behavior at the Start of a New International System," *Pacific Focus* 7:1 (March 1992), 6–11; Jonathan H. Ping, *Middle Power Statecraft: Indonesia, Malaysia and the Asia-Pacific* (Aldershot: Ashgate, 2005), esp. chap. 3. Adam Chapnick calls this the *hierarchical* approach: "The Middle Power," *Canadian Foreign Policy* 7:2 (Winter 1999), 76–79.

15 Paul Painchaud, "Middlepowermanship as an Ideology," in J. King Gordon, ed., *Canada's Role as a Middle Power* (Toronto: Canadian Institute of International Affairs, 1966), 29–35.

16 John W. Holmes, "Is There a Future for Middlepowermanship?," in Gordon, ed., *Canada's Role as a Middle Power*, 13–28; for a discussion of this term, see Kim Richard Nossal, " 'Middlepowerhood' and 'Middlepowermanship' in Canadian Foreign Policy," in Nikola Hynek and David Bosold, eds., *Canada's Foreign and Security Policy: Soft and Hard Strategies of a Middle Power* (Toronto: Oxford University Press, 2010), 20–34.

Middlepowermanship was deeply connected to the internationalist approach to foreign policy pursued by Canada during the Cold War era, one of the dominant ideas about international policy we examine in Chapter 5. As we will see, internationalism was a set of ideas that encouraged countries to take an active and engaged approach to international politics as the best means to prevent a recurrence of systemic war. Certainly the officials who worked in the Department of External Affairs—such as Lester Pearson, Escott Reid, and John W. Holmes—favoured a resolutely activist middle-power diplomacy.

Middle-power diplomacy aims at reinforcing the stability of the international system, regarded as essential for prosperity and security. In concrete terms, this policy puts a premium on efforts to help resolve conflict, either through mediation, conciliation, or good offices, and an almost systematic participation in multilateral operations mounted by the international community intended to ensure peace. Of course, middle powers are not the only ones to engage in such diplomacy, but they tend to do it more systematically than any other category of states.[17]

Mediation between countries in conflict is one of the key elements of middle-power diplomacy. However, during the height of the Cold War era, Canada's mediatory diplomacy was not aimed at trying to mediate *between* the two rival blocs headed by the United States and the Soviet Union. Rather, Canada was a firmly committed member of the Western alliance, and much of Canada's mediatory diplomacy was directed at disputes *within* the Western bloc. Such intra-bloc diplomacy included the negotiation of a compromise over the Suez crisis in 1956, discussed further below; various (and mostly unsuccessful) attempts to restrain those foreign policy initiatives of the United States that policymakers in Ottawa feared might precipitate a third world war (such as the wars in Korea and Vietnam[18]); and the periodic divisions within the Commonwealth over racial domination in southern Africa.[19]

Now it is true that toward the end of the Cold War, some Canadians, including some Canadian political leaders, came to believe that Canada was really in the middle *between* the two blocs rather than a committed member of the West. For example, Pierre Elliott Trudeau often painted the Soviet Union and the United States as equally responsible for endangering world peace, with Canada cast as the good peacemaker located equidistant from the two superpowers. On at least one occasion he did this in a speech given in the United States itself (much to the chagrin of Canada's ambassador to the States, Allan

---

17 Charles-Philippe David and Stéphane Roussel, "Une espèce en voie de disparition? La politique de puissance moyenne du Canada après la Guerre froide," *International Journal* 52:1 (Winter 1996–7), 39–68.

18 Denis Stairs, *The Diplomacy of Constraint: Canada, the Korean War and the United States* (Toronto: University of Toronto Press, 1974), esp. chap. 4; Douglas A. Ross, *In the Interests of Peace: Canada and Vietnam, 1954–1973* (Toronto: University of Toronto Press, 1984); Robert Bothwell, "The Further Shore: Canada and Vietnam," *International Journal* 56:1 (Winter 2000–1), 89–114; Greg Donaghy, *Tolerant Allies: Canada and the United States, 1963–1968* (Montréal and Kingston: McGill-Queen's University Press, 2002), esp. 123–47.

19 Frank R. Hayes, "South Africa's Departure from the Commonwealth, 1960–61," *International History Review* 2 (July 1980), 453–84; and Hayes, "Canada, the Commonwealth and the Rhodesia Issue," in Kim Richard Nossal, ed., *An Acceptance of Paradox: Essays on Canadian Diplomacy in Honour of John W. Holmes* (Toronto: Canadian Institute of International Affairs, 1982); Linda Freeman, *The Ambiguous Champion: Canada and South Africa in the Trudeau and Mulroney Years* (Toronto: University of Toronto Press, 1997).

Gotlieb, whose job it was to try to undo the damage created by Trudeau's public proclamation of the moral equivalence of the two superpowers[20]). Toward the end of his time in
office, Trudeau did try to mediate between the rival blocs: His "peace initiative," undertaken in the winter of 1983–84, cast Canada firmly in the "middle" between the blocs.[21]
Certainly Trudeau's "last hurrah," as Granatstein and Bothwell called it, has tended to
reshape our memories of Canada's middle-power diplomacy during this period. For example, Jennifer Welsh wrote in 2004 that "During the frosty decades of the Cold War, the role
of a middle power seeking to find a niche between the United States on the one hand and
the Soviet Union on the other made a lot of sense for Canada."[22] In fact, it was really only
at the end of the Cold War era that some Canadians tried to locate Canada *between* the
superpowers.

The most important aspect of Canada's internationalist diplomacy during the Cold War
was its attempts to manage regional conflicts. Ottawa feared that local conflicts—"brush-
fire wars"—might degenerate and prompt the superpowers to intervene, and possibly
become the spark that would start a world war. The Canadian government was thus keen
to help reinforce international mechanisms for conflict management—particularly those
associated with the United Nations. As a result, Canada became a strong supporter of international peacekeeping and truce supervision. The Canadian government served on the
International Commission of Supervision and Control (ICSC) in Indochina from 1954
until 1973—and also served on the International Commission of Control and Supervision
(ICCS) established to supervise an American withdrawal from Vietnam after the Peace of
Paris of 1973.[23] Canada also participated in every UN peacekeeping mission from the Cold
War era down to 1988.[24]

Indeed, the very idea of the "Blue Helmets"—troops from various UN member states
interposed between belligerents—came from a Canadian initiative. During the Suez crisis
of 1956, the Canadian government was deeply concerned about the rupture in the Atlantic

---

20 Allan Gotlieb, *The Washington Diaries, 1981–1989* (Toronto: McClelland & Stewart, 2006), 61. J.L.
Granatstein and Robert Bothwell note that "Trudeau suffered from what his critics saw as an apparent unwillingness or inability to distinguish between the superpowers. [Yuri] Andropov's Russia was
infinitely worse than the United States, even [Ronald] Reagan's United States, but Trudeau often
seemed unable to make the distinction." Granatstein and Bothwell, *Pirouette: Pierre Trudeau and
Canadian Foreign Policy* (Toronto: University of Toronto Press, 1990), 375.

21 On Trudeau's peace initiative, see: Granatstein and Bothwell, *Pirouette*, 365–75; Ivan Head and Pierre
Trudeau, *The Canadian Way: Shaping Canadian Foreign Policy, 1968–1984* (Toronto: McClelland &
Stewart, 1995).

22 Welsh, "Beyond Dominion and Middle Power," 584.

23 Douglas A. Ross, *In the Interests of Peace: Canada and Vietnam, 1954–1973* (Toronto: University of
Toronto Press, 1984).

24 Joseph T. Jockel, *Canada and International Peacekeeping* (Toronto: Canadian Institute of Strategic
Studies, 1994); J.L. Granatstein, "Peacekeeping: Did Canada Make a Difference? And What
Difference did Peacekeeping Make to Canada?," in John English and Norman Hillmer, eds., *Making
a Difference? Canada's Foreign Policy in a Changing World Order* (Toronto: Lester Publishing,
1992); Patricia Fortier, "The Evolution of Peacekeeping," in Rob McRae and Don Hubert, eds.,
Human Security and the New Diplomacy: Protecting People, Promoting Peace (Montréal and
Kingston: McGill-Queen's University Press, 2001), 41–54.

alliance that had been caused by the invasion of Egypt by Britain, France, and Israel after the Suez Canal had been nationalized by the Egyptian government of Gamal Abdul Nasser. The European allies had purposely not told the United States about the invasion, hoping that Washington would accept the fait accompli. Instead, the administration of Dwight D. Eisenhower was furious, going as far as to threaten economic sanctions against Britain.[25] Lester Pearson, then Canada's foreign minister, seeking ways to allow the British and French to withdraw their forces, proposed a United Nations force to be sent to supervise a truce and the withdrawal of the invading troops.[26] Canada's successful mediation clearly contributed to the maintenance of peace and the stability of the international system—a contribution recognized when Pearson was awarded the Nobel Peace Prize in 1957.

Middlepowermanship in Question

Used only timidly in 1945, the notion of Canada as a middle power had by the mid-1970s become securely anchored in the vocabulary of both students and practitioners of Canadian foreign policy.[27] However, this image had not gone unchallenged. When Trudeau came to power in 1968, he made it clear that he thought that the idea of Canada as a middle power was passé. Canadians had to remind themselves, he said in April 1968, "that we're perhaps more the largest of the small powers than the smallest of the large powers. And this is a complete change, I think, from our mentality of 20 years ago."[28] Trudeau's rejection of middle-power status also meant a rejection of middlepowermanship and the various diplomatic roles associated with it. Rather, his emphasis in the late 1960s was on modesty and realism, which demanded that "we should not exaggerate our influence upon the course of world events."[29] It was thus not surprising that his government's foreign policy review, published in 1970, should predict that "Canada's 'traditional' middle-power role in the world seemed doomed to disappear."[30]

It was, however, a premature burial. The critical rhetoric was never reflected in a major reorientation of policy, and Canada continued to assume the roles associated with middle-power diplomacy. While Trudeau had come to office critical of peacekeeping, Canada joined six new peacekeeping missions during his prime ministership. Likewise, Trudeau's peace initiative of 1983–84 was firmly in the middle-power tradition of Lester Pearson.

---

25 United States, Department of State, *Foreign Relations of the United States, 1955–1957*, vol. 16: *Suez Crisis, July 26–December 31, 1956*, ed. John P. Glennon (Washington, DC: U.S. Government Printing Office, 1955–1957), 1038–1344.

26 Lester B. Pearson, *Mike: The Memoirs of the Rt. Hon. Lester B. Pearson, vol. 2: 1948–1957* (Toronto: University of Toronto Press, 1973), chaps. 10–11; John W. Holmes, *The Shaping of Peace: Canada and the Search for World Order, 1943–1957,* vol. 2 (Toronto: University of Toronto Press, 1982), 348–70.

27 See R.B. Byers, David Leyton-Brown, and Peyton V. Lyon, "The Canadian International Image Study," *International Journal* 32:3 (Summer 1977), 605–607.

28 Quoted in Bruce Thordarson, *Trudeau and Foreign Policy: A Study in Decision-Making* (Toronto: Oxford University Press, 1972), 69.

29 Quoted in Eayrs, "Defining a New Place for Canada," 7.

30 Canada, Secretary of State for External Affairs, *Foreign Policy for Canadians* (Ottawa: Information Canada, 1970), main booklet, 6; Peyton V. Lyon, "The Trudeau Doctrine," *International Journal* 26 (Winter 1970–1), 19–43.

Indeed, reporting on his peace mission to Parliament in February 1984, he referred to the need for a middle-power role in defusing the tensions between the superpowers.[31] And the term "middle power" would feature prominently in his foreign policy memoirs, written a decade after his departure from Ottawa.[32]

While the middle-power role associated with internationalism did not disappear after 1968, the term itself did. In the period 1984–1993, the Progressive Conservative government of Brian Mulroney carefully avoided any use of the term "middle power" to describe either Canada or its international policies, even though it remained firmly committed to the pursuit of middle-power diplomacy.[33] The attempts of both Mulroney and his external affairs minister, Joe Clark, to solve differences within the Commonwealth on the issue of apartheid in South Africa were firmly in the tradition of their predecessors. Similarly, Canada remained an active peacekeeper: During this period, Canadians were deployed to oversee the Soviet withdrawal from Afghanistan and the Iran–Iraq ceasefire; Canada contributed to the peace process in Central America; and Canadians saw service on new missions in Namibia, Cambodia, Somalia, the former Yugoslavia, Rwanda, and Haiti. Indeed, the Mulroney government defended its decision to use force against Iraq in essentially middle-power terms, even invoking the memory of a Liberal prime minister, Lester Pearson.[34]

Even though the conditions for middle-power activism seemed less than favourable in the aftermath of the Cold War,[35] the idea of Canada as a middle power persisted, as John Ravenhill has noted.[36] Indeed, when André Ouellet, Chrétien's first foreign affairs minister, announced the new government's foreign policy review in 1993, he said that "It's clear Canada's foreign policy must be reviewed in the context of [. . .] Canada's capacity, as a middle power, to play an important role at the United Nations."[37] And the

---

31 Canada, Parliament, House of Commons, *Debates*, 1983–84, 1211–16, February 9, 1984; rpt. C. David Crenna, ed., *Pierre Elliott Trudeau: Lifting the Shadow of War* (Edmonton: Hurtig Publishers, 1987), 106–110.

32 Head and Trudeau, *Canadian Way*, 7, 310–19; also Pierre Elliott Trudeau, *Memoirs* (Toronto: McClelland & Stewart, 1993), 329–41.

33 See the official statements of the government's international policies during this era: Secretary of State for External Affairs, *Competitiveness and Security: Directions for Canada's International Relations* (Ottawa: Supply and Services Canada, 1985); *Canada's International Relations: Response of the Government of Canada to the Report of the Special Joint Committee of the Senate and the House of Commons* (Ottawa: Supply and Services Canada, 1986).

34 Kim Richard Nossal, "Quantum Leaping: The Gulf Debate in Australia and Canada," in Michael McKinley, ed., *The Gulf War: Critical Perspectives* (Sydney: Allen and Unwin, 1994), 48–71; for an alternative argument that Canada made a "more-than-middlepower military contribution" to the Gulf War, see John Kirton, "Liberating Kuwait: Canada and the Persian Gulf War, 1990–91," in Don Munton and John Kirton, eds., *Canadian Foreign Policy: Selected Cases* (Scarborough: Prentice-Hall Canada, 1992), 392.

35 David and Roussel, "Une espèce en voie de disparition?"; Kim Richard Nossal, "Pinchpenny Diplomacy: The Decline of 'Good International Citizenship' in Canadian Foreign Policy," *International Journal* 54:1 (Winter 1998–9), 88–105.

36 John Ravenhill, "Cycles of Middle Power Activism: Constraint and Choice in Australian and Canadian Foreign Policies," *Australian Journal of International Affairs* 52:3 (November 1998), 321.

37 Quoted in Mark Neufeld, "Hegemony and Foreign Policy Analysis: The Case of Canada as a Middle Power," *Studies in Political Economy* 48 (1995), 102, n49.

Chrétien government pursued an active diplomacy intended to reinforce the stability of the international system: its activism to ban antipersonnel landmines and small arms, its efforts to create a United Nations rapid reaction force, its enthusiastic support for an International Criminal Court, and its signing of the Kyoto accords were all evidence of middle-power activism.[38]

By contrast, Paul Martin committed his government to what he termed a "new multilateralism," but explicitly rejected the middle-power label. "The traditional notion of Canada as a middle power," asserted the *International Policy Statement* released in April 2005, "is outdated and no longer captures the reality of how power is distributed in the 21st century." Indeed, in the opinion of the IPS, "Our old middle power identity imposes an unnecessary ceiling on what we can do and be in the world."[39] It was no coincidence that such views very much reflected the perspective of Jennifer Welsh, a Canadian professor of international relations at the University of Oxford. In 2004 she had penned an eloquent argument for a "new vision" for Canada's role in the world, suggesting that the country should embrace a new identity: that of a "model power."[40] In her view, "Canada's new identity crisis can be summed up like this: The middle power mantra is losing its punch."[41] When the book came to Martin's attention, he brought her in to assist in the drafting of the overview to the IPS. But Martin never got an opportunity to put in place the international policy articulated in the IPS; the Conservative Party of Canada won a minority in the January 2006 elections, and Stephen Harper was sworn in as prime minister on February 6, 2006.

Unlike every other newly elected prime minister since 1968, Harper did not initiate a foreign policy review when he came to office, and so since 2006 there has not been a rhetorical declaration of his international policy. But while many of his government's policies, not surprisingly, demonstrated substantial continuity from the changes introduced by Paul Martin,[42] in at least one area of international policy Harper differed from Martin: He openly resurrected the notions of Canada as a middle power and middle-power diplomacy. In a speech to the Council on Foreign Relations in New York in September 2007, Harper

---

38 Brian W. Tomlin, "On a Fast-Track to a Ban: The Canadian Policy Process," *Canadian Foreign Policy* 5:3 (Spring 1998), 15–20; Keith Krause, *Norm-Building in Security Spaces: The Emergence of the Light Weapons Problematic*, GERSI/REGIS Working Papers 11, Montréal, 2001, available http://depot.erudit.org/bitstream/000854dd/1/000257pp.pdf; James Fergusson and Barbara Levesque, "The Best Laid Plans: Canada's Proposal for a United Nations Rapid Reaction Capability," *International Journal* 52:1 (Winter 1996–7); Darryl Robinson, "The International Criminal Court," in McRae and Hubert, eds., *Human Security*, 170–77; Heather A. Smith, "Canada and Kyoto: Independence or Indifference?," in Brian Bow and Patrick Lennox, eds., *An Independent Foreign Policy for Canada? Challenges and Choices for the Future* (Toronto: University of Toronto Press, 2008), 207–21.

39 Canada, *Canada's International Policy Statement: A Role of Pride and Influence in the World*, overview booklet (Ottawa, Government of Canada, 2005), 2, 5.

40 Jennifer Welsh, *At Home in the World: Canada's Global Vision for the 21st Century* (Toronto: Harper-Collins Publishers, 2004); see also Welsh, "Reality and Canadian Foreign Policy," in Andrew F. Cooper and Dane Rowlands, eds., *Canada Among Nations 2005: Split Images* (Kingston and Montréal: McGill-Queen's University Press, 2005), 23–46.

41 Welsh, "Beyond Dominion and Middle Power," 587.

42 For example, Kim Richard Nossal, "Defense Policy and the Atmospherics of Canada–U.S. Relations: The Case of the Harper Conservatives," *American Review of Canadian Studies* 37:1 (Spring 2007), 23–34.

suggested that the United States needs middle powers like Canada, noting with approval that middle powers "step up to the plate to do their part . . . willing to assume responsibilities, seek practical, do-able solutions to problems and who have a voice and influence in global affairs because they lead, not by lecturing, but by example."[43]

Alternative Images of Canada's Power

While the image of Canada as a middle power has been, and continues to be, dominant in the discourse of international policy in Canada, there have been two other visions of Canadian power, one self-denigrating and the other self-flattering.

Over the course of the last century, some have argued that Canada has always been a dependency or satellite within the imperial orbit of imperial western powers—first within the British empire and then the American empire. In this view, Canada's colonial status was never in its essence affected by either the British North America Act of 1867 or the Statute of Westminster of 1931. Rather, the shifting nexus of global hegemony from Britain to the United States in the first half of the twentieth century drew Canada, as a subordinate state, with it. Because of the economic, ideological, and cultural linkages between Canada and the United States, which had been a consistent feature of life on the North American continent, the country was pulled into an emerging, even if informal, American empire.[44] In circular fashion, it was argued, Canada went from being an imperial dependency of Britain back to being an imperial dependency of the United States.[45] In short, what for some marked the emergence of a middle power in world politics was, for others, merely a transfer of dependent orbit.

Such a view has deep historical roots. In 1920, well before the impact of the shift in economic dependence from Britain to the United States had been felt, Archibald MacMechan lamented that Canada was little more than an American "vassal state," a theme repeated in 1946 by A.R.M. Lower, who described Canada as a "subordinate state," and declared that it was a "complete satellite of the United States."[46] After the Second World War, when Canadian–American integration increased dramatically, some authors rejected outright the idea that Canada was a middle power. James M. Minifie, for example, argued that the country's "close association with policies of military and economic imperialism makes Canada the choreboy of the Western world, [and] returns Canada from colony to satellite in three generations."[47] Those writing from a political economy perspective sought to analyze the

---

43 Office of the Prime Minister, Address to the Council on Foreign Relations, New York, September 25, 2007, available http://pm.gc.ca/eng/media.asp?id=1830.

44 John Hutcheson, *Dominance and Dependency: Liberalism and National Policies in the North Atlantic Triangle* (Toronto: McClelland & Stewart, 1978), 44–45.

45 Kenneth McNaught, "From Colony to Satellite," in Stephen Clarkson, ed., *An Independent Foreign Policy for Canada?* (Toronto: McClelland & Stewart, 1968), 177–78.

46 Quoted in Philip Resnick, "Canadian Defence Policy and the American Empire," in Ian Lumsden, ed., *Close the 49th Parallel Etc.: The Americanization of Canada* (Toronto: University of Toronto Press, 1970), 99.

47 James M. Minifie, *Peacemaker or Powdermonkey: Canada's Role in a Revolutionary World* (Toronto: McClelland & Stewart, 1960), 52; also John W. Warnock, *Partner to Behemoth: The Military Policy of a Satellite Canada* (Toronto: New Press, 1970).

implications of Canada's increasing economic integration with the United States.[48] Indeed, George Grant went further still: His analysis of the cultural, technological, socioeconomic, and hence political homogenization of North America led him to predict gloomily that "Canada's disappearance as a nation is a matter of necessity."[49]

In the 1980s, the foreign and domestic policy agenda of the Progressive Conservative government of Brian Mulroney gave fresh impetus to the perspective that Canada was being sucked into the American imperial orbit. Lawrence Martin, for example, argued that between 1984 and 1993 "border boy politicians whose mindsets were but American attenuations . . . closed down the Canadian dream."[50] Likewise, Marci McDonald sneeringly titled her book on Canadian–American relations during the Mulroney era *Yankee Doodle Dandy*, leaving readers in no doubt as to her views about the results of what she termed Mulroney's kowtowing to "corporate America" and fawning over American presidents.[51]

In the post-9/11 era, when the administration of George W. Bush embraced an assertive and robust policy of "full-spectrum dominance" and "preemptive war" and organized a coalition to invade Iraq, we saw a resurgence of the idea of American empire.[52] In Canada, there was a comparable resurgence of the idea that Canada was firmly planted within the American imperium. For example, Greg Albo argued in 2006 that the support of business and state elites in Canada for the new American imperial agenda made Canada "one of the Empire's strongest allies."[53] Stephen Clarkson, who in the late 1960s edited the iconic collection of the satellite perspective—*An Independent Foreign Policy for Canada?*—continued his exploration of Canada's dependent status in the context of North American integration.[54]

If there has been a long tradition of self-denigration, we have also seen the emergence of a tradition of seeing Canada not as a dependent satellite, nor as a middle power, but as a major power. In 1975, James Eayrs argued Canada's power had been affected by the oil crisis of 1973, by the growing importance of natural resources—particularly food and fuel—in world politics; and, finally, by the decline of the United States as a hegemonic

---

48 Walter Gordon, *A Choice for Canada: Independence or Colonial Status* (Toronto: McClelland & Stewart, 1966); Wallace Clement, "Continental Political Economy: An Assessment of the Relations Between Canada and the United States," *Canadian Review of American Studies* 10 (Spring 1979), 77–88.

49 George Grant, *Lament for a Nation: The Defeat of Canadian Nationalism* (Toronto: McClelland & Stewart, 1965), 280.

50 Lawrence Martin, *Pledge of Allegiance: The Americanization of Canada in the Mulroney Years* (Toronto: McClelland & Stewart, 1993), 272–73.

51 Marci McDonald, *Yankee Doodle Dandy: Brian Mulroney and the American Agenda* (Toronto: Stoddart, 1995).

52 William Odum and Robert Dujarric, *America's Inadvertent Empire* (New Haven: Yale University Press, 2005); Michael Cox, "The Empire's Back in Town: Or America's Imperial Temptation—Again," *Millennium* 32:1 (February 2003), 1–27.

53 Greg Albo, "Empire's Ally: Canadian Foreign Policy," *Canadian Dimension* 40:6 (November/December 2006); see also the contributions in George Melnyk, ed., *Canada and the New American Empire: War and Anti-War* (Calgary: University of Calgary Press, 2004).

54 Stephen Clarkson, *Does North America Exist? Governing the Continent After NAFTA and 9/11* (Toronto: University of Toronto Press, 2008). In the meantime, Brian Bow and Patrick Lennox argue that the historical parallels between the 1960s and the early 2000s warrant revisiting the debate from the late 1960s: see Brian Bow and Patrick Lennox, eds., *An Independent Foreign Policy for Canada? Challenges and Choices for the Future* (Toronto: University of Toronto Press, 2008).

power in world affairs, symbolized by its ignominious withdrawal from Vietnam in 1973. In his view, "Canada has almost sinfully bestowed upon it the sources of power," making the country a "foremost power foremost in the dictionary sense of 'most notable or prominent.' "[55] Eayrs's terminology was adopted by the editors of a 1977 collection of essays on Canadian foreign policy: Norman Hillmer and Garth Stevenson entitled their work *Foremost Nation*, arguing that the term "illustrates graphically the rapid changes which the world in general and Canadian foreign policy in particular have recently undergone. . . ."[56] Likewise, Peyton Lyon and Brian Tomlin examined indices of relative national power focusing on the military, economic, resource, and diplomatic capabilities, and discovered that in their overall index, Canada was ranked sixth in the international system. "Canada," they confidently asserted, "should now be regarded as a major power."[57]

David Dewitt and John Kirton developed the most unabashed perspective of Canada as a major power. The terminology of choice in their 1983 book was *principal* power. Such powers, they argued, are principal in three ways. First, they are states "that stand at the top of the international status ranking." Second, they "act as principals" in the international system, and not as the "agents" of other states. Finally, principal powers have "a principal role in establishing, specifying, and enforcing international order." In the shifting patterns of global politics, Canada's star was seen as rising. After 1968, Dewitt and Kirton declared, Canada was "an ascending principal power in an increasingly diffuse, nonhegemonic international system."[58]

The idea that Canada was a major, foremost, or principal power rested on the assumption that the United States was in decline in global politics. However, in the years after the end of the Cold War and the disappearance of the Soviet Union, the United States grew to dominate the international system to the point where Hubert Védrine, the French foreign minister from 1997 to 2002, invented a new word to describe American power—hyperpower.[59] But the vast gap that appeared between American and Canadian power made little difference to the willingness of some Canadians to continue to see Canada as more than a middle power. Thus, for example, in 2006 Stephen Harper spoke glowingly to audiences in both London and New York of Canada as an "emerging energy superpower."[60] John Kirton, writing in 2007, argued that Canada was "emerging as a modern major or principal power in the world."[61]

55 Eayrs, "Defining a New Place for Canada."

56 Hillmer and Stevenson, eds., *Foremost Nation*, 2.

57 Lyon and Tomlin, *Canada as an International Actor*, 72. Writing somewhat later, Laura Neack would come to a similar conclusion: "Empirical Observations," 5–21.

58 David B. Dewitt and John J. Kirton, *Canada as a Principal Power: A Study of Foreign Policy and International Relations* (Toronto: John Wiley and Sons, 1983), 38, 40.

59 Kim Richard Nossal, "Lonely Superpower or Unapologetic Hyperpower? Analyzing American Power in the Post–Cold War Era," paper delivered to South African Political Studies Association, Saldanha, Western Cape, June 29–July 2, 1999, available http://post.queensu.ca/~nossalk/papers/hyperpower.htm.

60 Office of the Prime Minister, address by the Prime Minister at the Canada–U.K. Chamber of Commerce, London, July 14, 2006, available http://pm.gc.ca/eng/media.asp?id=1247; address to the Economic Club of New York, New York, September 20, 2006, available http://pm.gc.ca/eng/media.asp?category=2&id=1327. For a discussion, see Duane Bratt, "Tools and Levers: Energy as an Instrument of Canadian Foreign Policy," in Robert Bothwell and Jean Daudlin, eds., *Canada Among Nations 2008: 100 Years of Canadian Foreign Policy* (Montréal and Kingston: McGill-Queen's University Press, 2009), 209–31.

61 John J. Kirton, *Canadian Foreign Policy in a Changing World* (Toronto: Thomson Nelson, 2007), 29; also 30, 80.

Assessing Images of Canada's Power: Normative Corollaries

Attempts to locate Canada in the international hierarchy offer a diffracted image of Canada's power. At one end of the spectrum, Canada is cast as a mere vassal state in international politics, tied to empires by economic linkages and military incapacity, forever the victim of foreign domination. At the other, Canada is cast as an emergent great power. Between these extremes are conceptions of Canada as the largest of the small or the smallest of the large—or simply "in the middle."

These divergent images are, however, inescapable, since it is impossible to quantify a state's power objectively. Any evaluation will always be subjective and thus deeply political. When we talk about Canada as a major power, a middle power, or a satellite, we are in effect referring to how Canadians—and foreigners—see Canada within the international hierarchy. In other words, discussions of Canada's power are the domain of *perceptions* rather than objective reality.

But the various images of Canada's international rank are not politically neutral; on the contrary, they have important normative consequences. For policymakers, such images frame discussions of international policy, shape political objectives, and guide policy behaviour. For example, the near-pathetic image of Canada as an American satellite almost certainly contributed to the Trudeau government's decision to adopt economic policies aimed at reducing Canadian dependence on the United States. These images can also be used to justify inaction. For example, Mackenzie King's eagerness to deny Canada's influence in the 1920s and 1930s can be seen as the careful calculation of a politician worried that any external engagement would threaten national unity and trigger the kind of electoral backlash experienced by the Conservatives following the conscription crisis of 1917–1918.

These can be used for a variety of political purposes. For example, Trudeau's questioning of the concept of middle power in the late 1960s was not simply the result of a hard analysis of Canada's relative power. On the contrary: because the foreign policy—and the formidable reputation—of his predecessor had been largely built on the concept of middle power, Trudeau opted for a more modest policy that allowed him to distance himself from Pearson. Likewise, when Chrétien claimed in 1994 that the prime minister of a country of 28 million people could not tell China, a country of 1.2 billion people, how to behave on human rights, this was little more than a justification for wanting to avoid having the thorny issue of human rights dampen the pursuit of a closer trade relationship with China.[62]

Determining a state's ranking in the international hierarchy is useful as a general guide to its status, or standing, in international politics. Of the three images of Canada's power we have examined, there can be little doubt that Canada enjoys the status of a middle power in contemporary global politics. Certainly it does not enjoy the status of a great, major, or even principal power, if only because it lacks the most important attribute needed for major-power status: the subjective recognition of other states. But neither is Canada

---

62 Speaking in 1994, Chrétien expressed doubts about Canada's ability to sway a country as large as the People's Republic of China: "I'm the Prime Minister of a country of 28 million people," he said. "[Jiang Zemin] is the President of a country with 1.2 billion people. I'm not allowed to tell the Premier of Saskatchewan or Quebec what to do. Am I supposed to tell the President of China what to do?," *Globe and Mail*, March 19, 1994; for a critique, see Bruce Gilley, "Reawakening Canada's China Policy," *Canadian Foreign Policy* 14:2 (Spring 2008), 121–30.

regarded as a marginal state, a country of no global consequence. This is why Canada sits somewhere in the middle, however vague this concept might be.

But even if one could establish a clear status-ranking for Canada, what would locating the country in the global hierarchy of states tell us about Canadian power? We suggest that for all of the utility of rankings in establishing status, they are not very useful for establishing a state's power. One difficulty in using the terms "major power," "middle power," and "minor power" is that they tend to distort not only the concept of power itself, but also a clear consideration of how power—or lack of it—affects the making of a state's international policy. To get a better sense of a state's power in global politics, we have to move beyond status and look to a complementary method of analyzing a state's power in the international system. The power analysis approach directs our attention not to generalized indication of status ranking but to the possession and exercise of power.

RETHINKING CANADA'S POWER: A POWER ANALYSIS APPROACH

Power analysis tries to grapple with the irony that a concept that is so central to politics and international relations remains so essentially contested.[63] It begins by discarding the idea that power can be assessed by looking at the "elements of national power"—population, territory, industrial and technological capacity, and military might—associated with Hans Morgenthau's definition cited at the beginning of this chapter and underpinning discussions of Canadian rank in international politics. Instead, a power analysis perspective sees power in *relational* terms rather than as resources that one possesses. For some, what David Baldwin termed the "power analysis revolution"[64] tries to establish what kind of relationship exists between actors or agents, usually phrased in terms of actor A, actor B, and action X. Thus, for example, Robert Dahl's famous formulation puts it succinctly: "A has power over B to the extent that he can get B to do something that B would not otherwise do."[65] Steven Lukes, by contrast, alerts us to the importance of the interests of the actors and the essential negativity of power: "A exercises power over B when A affects B in a manner contrary to B's interests."[66] For others, the relational definition must be broader than just actors A and B. Stefano Guzzini, among others, reminds us that actors and agents operate within broader structures of governance, dominance, and hegemony, and that *structural power* is of crucial importance in determining the effects of power.[67] Michael Barnett and Raymond Duvall

---

63 Michael Barnett and Raymond Duvall, "Power in International Politics," *International Organization* 59:1 (Winter 2005), 41.

64 David Baldwin, "Power and International Relations," in Walter Carlsnaes, Thomas Risse, and Beth A. Simmons, eds., *Handbook of International Relations* (London: SAGE, 2002), 178.

65 Robert A. Dahl, "The Concept of Power," in Roderick Bell, David V. Edwards, and R. Harrison Wagner, eds., *Political Power: A Reader in Theory and Research* (New York: Free Press, 1969), 80; Stanley Hoffmann, "Notes on the Elusiveness of Modern Power," *International Journal* 30:2 (Spring 1975), 188.

66 Steven Lukes, *Power: A Radical View*, 2nd ed. (London: Palgrave Macmillan, 2005), 30.

67 Stefano Guzzini, "The Use and Misuse of Power Analysis in International Theory," in Ronen Palan, ed., *Global Political Economy: Contemporary Theories* (London: Routledge, 2000), 54–67.

broaden the focus even further. Borrowing from the sociologist John Scott, they suggest that "In general terms, power is the production, in and through social relations, of effects that shape the capacities of actors to determine their circumstances and fate."[68]

In this view, the "elements of national power" are not irrelevant to the "production of effects," but power analysis rejects a common assumption that the possession by a state of certain attributes (military might, or technological or industrial ability) will give that state power.[69] But having or exercising power and having capabilities, or *power resources*, are not necessarily related. The "paradox of unrealized power" is that capabilities do not automatically confer power.[70] Likewise, a relative lack of power resources does not necessarily relegate one to powerlessness. During the Cold War era, both of the superpowers—and their adversaries—were to discover this: the United States in Vietnam and the Soviet Union in Afghanistan. Power analysis also rejects a second misconception that power resources are fungible—in other words, that capabilities can be easily "converted" into the ability to have one's interests prevail. Although some authors glibly speak of power as the currency of politics, it is not, as Baldwin points out,[71] at all like currency. Currency is highly fungible; indeed, its very purpose is to provide an effective means for exchange. Power resources in international politics, by contrast, are highly infungible. What State A uses to exercise power over State B in one area cannot simply be converted (as currency is) to exercise comparably successful power in another area—or against other actors. For example, a well-equipped armed force may be a most effective resource against State B's invasion of another state; it may prove entirely useless as a means of getting State B to cease subsidizing a protected industry or getting State C to vote against a resolution in the United Nations Security Council.

Using a power analysis perspective, we get a rather different view of Canada's power. If we see power as relational, and focus on the interests of different actors and agents in global politics, we can see the degree to which the government in Ottawa is able to achieve its international policy objectives and secure and advance Canada's interests, at least as they are defined by state officials. Power is the ability to shift the behaviour of others in ways that are conducive to Canadian interests (e.g., securing the release of a Canadian from a Saudi jail; getting the United States Congress to moderate "Buy American" legislation); the ability to deter others from acting in a manner contrary to Canadian interests (e.g., convincing the European Union not to impose a ban on Canadian fur or aluminum); or the ability to rebuff the importunities of other states to act in a manner judged to be inconsistent with Canadian interests (e.g., refusing the invitation of the United States to participate in the Ballistic Missile Defense scheme). It also concentrates our attention on the ability—or lack of it—to prevail in conflicts of interest over a huge range of issues that engage an equally huge range of actors in international politics: with insurgents in Kandahar province in

---

68 Barnett and Duvall, "Power," 42; see John Scott, *Power* (London: Polity Press, 2001), 1–2; also Scott's "map of power relations," 16.

69 For example, William C. Wohlforth, "The Stability of a Unipolar World," *International Security* 24:1 (Summer 1999), 5–41; John Mearsheimer, *The Tragedy of Great Power Politics* (New York: W.W. Norton, 2001).

70 David A. Baldwin, "Power Analysis and World Politics: New Trends Versus Old Tendencies," *World Politics* 31:2 (January 1979), 163ff.

71 David A. Baldwin, "Money and Power," *Journal of Politics* 33:3 (August 1971), 578–614.

Afghanistan over the future politics of that country; with European governments opposed to the Canadian seal hunt; with transnational criminal organizations engaged in drug running, money laundering, or human trafficking; with governments in Khartoum or Rangoon or Beijing over human rights—either particular human rights cases or human rights violations in general; with the government in Canberra over the use of phytosanitary measures to keep Canadian salmon out of the Australian market.

A power analysis approach also directs our attention to the degree to which the Canadian government exercises structural power, both generally and specifically. Generally, Canada's structural power will be exercised by its participation in, and support for, various international institutions that seek to create and maintain a particular global order. These would include international organizations whose primary purpose is global governance, including the United Nations, the Development Assistance Committee of the Organisation for Economic Co-operation and Development, the World Bank and the International Monetary Fund, and the International Criminal Court. But there are a range of other institutions that seek to impose a particular order. For example, the North Atlantic Treaty Organization, originally created as an alliance to protect Western countries against the Soviet Union, has expanded both its membership and its mission since the dismantling of the Soviet Union; it is now actively engaged in the establishment of order outside the geographic region of its members. For example, NATO militarily intervened in Kosovo in 1999, seizing it from Serbia and running it as a protectorate. Likewise, after the oust of the Taliban government in Afghanistan in 2001, NATO has been actively involved in Afghan politics, seeking to reinforce the power and authority of the government of Hamid Karzai through a range of activities, including training and equipping the Afghan security forces, fighting insurgents opposed to the post-Taliban order, and delivering development assistance.

Specifically, structural power is exercised by Canadian government support for (or opposition to) particular political forces in particular countries, since that support (or opposition) will contribute to particular outcomes. Seemingly innocuous or apparently apolitical transactions such as trade, development assistance, immigration, or even tourism will all have an impact on others, and will, in Barnett's and Duvall's words quoted above, "shape the capacities of actors to determine their circumstances and fate."

TECHNIQUES OF POWER AND INFLUENCE

Power in international politics is exercised by tools of statecraft that range on a continuum from violent and costly techniques such as force and punishment at one end to peaceful and costless ones such as persuasion at the other. These are the overt techniques; to them must be added those instances in which one actor is able to ensure that its interests prevail over those of another, not by *exercising* power but simply by *having* power. In cases of structural power, the powerful achieve their interests not by having to actually use such techniques as force or sanction, but rather because other actors, anticipating the outcome of challenging or crossing the powerful, will shape their behaviour to conform to the interests of the dominant state. This "rule of anticipated reaction" clouds the assessment of power considerably, for it is the possession rather than intention or overt use of power that causes behaviour.

The range of techniques used by the Canadian government to exercise power in the international system is limited. This stems from four interconnected factors: the lack of capacity, the lack of desire, the dominant domain and scope of Canada's foreign policy behaviour, and the nature of the foreign policy objectives traditionally evinced by decision-makers in Ottawa.

The Use of Force and the Canadian Military

One of the reasons force is so often confused with power is that in conflict, force remains the *ultima ratio*—the last resort. It is true that over the long sweep of history, a state's ability to prevail in a conflict has in the final analysis depended on its capacity to use military might. But force is a useful instrument of statecraft in only a few of the power relationships in international politics and for only a few states. Great powers, or those states with acute and imminent threats to their security, cannot ignore the consequences of relative military capabilities. In those circumstances, it would be useful—indeed necessary—to count soldiers, to enumerate the weapons of war, to assess those military intangibles such as will and morale, and to estimate what demographic, economic, and natural resources are available to sustain the application of force. For most other states, however, the ability to use force as an instrument of foreign policy will be less relevant.

Canada is often seen as an "unmilitary community": a "peaceable kingdom" that devotes little of its attention and even less of its wealth to its military forces.[72] However, as Desmond Morton has argued, "This is no accident. Canadians have come by their attitudes through the weight of historical experience."[73] It has now been almost 200 years since the War of 1812, when Canada was last invaded by another country's armed forces,[74] and one would have to go back to 1759 to find a case of prolonged military occupation. In Canadian history there is no traumatic event like the fall of France in 1940, the surprise attack on Pearl Harbor by Japan in December 1941, or the attacks of September 11, 2001.

Nonetheless, as Figure 3.1, on the next page, shows, this "peaceable kingdom" has been to war eight times since the beginning of the twentieth century in defence of Canada's interests and to project Canadian power, costing the lives of well over 100,000 Canadians and thousands more wounded, disabled, or traumatized.[75]

---

72 R.B. Byers, "The Canadian Military and the Use of Force: End of an Era?," *International Journal* 30:2 (Spring 1975), 289–90; Stéphane Roussel, "La culture stratégique d'un paisible royaume," in Roussel, eds., *Culture stratégique et politique de défense: L'expérience canadienne* (Montréal: Athéna, 2007), 7–11.

73 Desmond Morton, "Defending the Indefensible: Some Historical Perspectives on Canadian Defence, 1867–1987," *International Journal* 42:4 (Autumn 1987), 628.

74 Between 1866 and 1871, the Fenian Brotherhood, an Irish nationalist group founded in the United States; Fenians staged a number of armed attacks on Canada from American territory to pressure Britain to withdraw from Ireland.

75 In addition to those who died while in service to the Canadian state, a number of Canadians died while fighting wars overseas for other forces. Sixteen Canadians died on the Nile Expedition of 1884–85, discussed in Chapter 5. Approximately 1500 Canadians volunteered to fight in the Spanish Civil War (1936–1939), forming the Mackenzie-Papineau Battalion, named after the leaders of the 1837 uprisings in Canada. Over 700 of the "Mac-Paps" lost their lives. Likewise, a number of Canadians volunteered to serve with American forces during the Vietnam War (1965–1973); 121 were confirmed killed in action and seven remain missing in action.

FIGURE 3.1	Canada at War, 1899-2009

War	Number Killed*
Boer War (1899-1902)	270
First World War (1914-1918)	60,661
Russian Intervention (1918-1919)	6
Second World War (1939-1945)	42,042
Korean War (1950-1953)	312
Persian Gulf War (1991)	0
Bombing of Serbia (1999)	0
Afghanistan Mission (2001-present)	131 (as of September 2009)

*Does not include the 116 Canadians killed while in service on peacekeeping missions between 1950 and 2007.

In addition, the Canadian Forces (CF) have participated in numerous peacekeeping missions.[76] During the Cold War, deadly force was only rarely used by the CF; it was more frequently used against Canadians by others: over 80 Canadians died on peacekeeping missions between 1947 and 1993. In the post–Cold War period, when "second generation" peacekeeping emerged, more force was used. In the United Nations Operations in Somalia (UNOSOM), the militaries of a number of countries were deployed to forcibly bring an end to the Somali civil war; in effect, war broke out between the United Nations forces and Somalis, leading to an unprecedented number of deaths of peacekeepers and the deaths of numerous Somalis. Deadly force was also used by units of the Canadian Airborne Regiment deployed at Belet Huen for that mission (including the torture and killing of a Somali teenager, Shidane Arone, who had been caught trying to enter the Canadian compound).[77] In a little-publicized operation several months later, soldiers with the Princess Patricia's Canadian Light Infantry serving with the United Nations Protection Force (UNPROFOR) in the Former Republic of Yugoslavia in September 1993 engaged in a sustained firefight with a Croatian army unit that was seeking to prevent UN troops from entering a Serb area in the Medak Pocket being ethnically cleansed by Croatian forces. Four Canadians were wounded in the battle, with 27 Croatian fatalities.[78]

---

76 Alex Morrison, "Canada and Peacekeeping: A Time for Reanalysis?" in David B. Dewitt and David Leyton-Brown, eds., *Canada's International Security Policy* (Scarborough: Prentice-Hall Canada, 1995); Sean M. Maloney, *Canada and UN Peacekeeping: Cold War by Other Means* (Toronto: Vanwell Publishing, 2003).

77 David Bercuson, *Significant Incident: Canada's Army, the Airborne, and the Murder in Somalia* (Toronto: McClelland & Stewart, 1996). The "Somalia affair" would have far-reaching effects: criminal charges were laid, the Canadian Airborne Regiment was disbanded in disgrace in 1995, and a public inquiry led to the resignation of several senior officers of the CF.

78 David Pugliese, "Canada's Secret Battle," *Ottawa Citizen*, October 7, 1996, 6–7. By the time another journalist, Carol Off, retold the story, the "secret battle" had become a "secret war": *The Ghosts of Medak Pocket: The Story of Canada's Secret War* (Toronto: Random House Canada, 2004). Also see Lee Windsor, "Professionalism Under Fire: Canadian Implementation of the Medak Pocket Agreement, Croatia 1993," *The Army Doctrine and Training Bulletin* 4:3 (Fall 2001), 20–27. Partly because of the fallout from the "Somalia affair," this operation was totally ignored by the Chrétien government at the time; it was not until 2002 that the operation was recognized with a Commander-in-Chief unit commendation awarded by Governor General Adrienne Clarkson.

Why has the government in Ottawa been willing to put Canadians in harm's way, often in places far from Canadian soil, where Canada did not seem to have any particular interests? Unlike the great powers, which use their armed forces to *directly* promote or defend their interests—as Britain and France did in Suez in 1956; as the Soviet Union did when it invaded Hungary in 1956, Czechoslovakia in 1968, and Afghanistan in 1979; or as the United States did when it invaded Grenada in 1983, Panama in 1989, and Iraq in 2003— the Canadian government has always used the CF beyond Canada's borders as an *indirect* instrument of international policy: to defend or maintain a particular international order, and thus indirectly the security of Canada.[79] It is for this reason that the CF has always been used overseas in a *multilateral context*. In the Boer War and the First World War, Canadians fought as part of the British Empire. In the Second World War, Canada was part of an ad hoc alliance that gradually expanded into a broad multinational alliance, the Allies (who eventually called themselves the United Nations), which sought to defeat the Axis (Nazi Germany together with Germany's major partners, Japan and Italy, and its minor partners, Hungary, Romania, and Bulgaria). In Korea, the Persian Gulf, and the mission in Afghanistan, Canadian troops were part of multinational forces led by the United States and sanctioned by the United Nations. In both the intervention in Russia in 1918–19 and the bombing of Serbia in 1999, Canadian forces were part of a multilateral operation: the Russian intervention was a joint Allied operation involving British, American, and Japanese troops; Canada's participation in the Kosovo war was undertaken under the auspices of NATO.

In each case of the use of force, there will be particular considerations. In Chapter 5, for example, we will explore the degree to which Canadian participation in the Boer War and the Great War was deeply connected to ideas about the defence of the British Empire. In the Cold War period, Canada's contributions to expeditionary missions—both war-fighting in Korea and numerous peacekeeping missions—were not only a manifestation of Canada's embrace of internationalism after the Second World War, also explored in Chapter 5, but also a function of self-interested calculations of Canadian policymakers. In particular, by committing the CF to missions abroad, the government in Ottawa understood that it would secure Canada a "seat at the table" in international affairs. This was particularly true for the Canadian forces that were stationed in Europe from 1950 to the end of the Cold War as part of Canada's contribution to NATO.[80] In the post-9/11 era, a mix of motives prompted the Chrétien, Martin, and Harper governments to send Canadian forces to (and keep them in) Afghanistan, including: a desire to contribute to the United States–led "War on Terror"; a concern to solidify the control of the government of Hamid Karzai in Kabul and the broad multilateral Afghanistan Compact that backed it; a desire to support NATO; and a commitment to advancing development and human security in Afghanistan.[81]

---

79 Kim Richard Nossal, "Defending the 'Realm': Canadian Strategic Culture Revisited," *International Journal* 59:3 (Summer 2004), 503–520.

80 See Michel Fortmann, Albert Legault, and Stéphane Roussel, "De l'art de s'asseoir à la table: Le Canada et les négociations européennes sur l'*Arms Control* (1972–1986)," in Paul Létourneau, ed., *Le Canada et l'OTAN après quarante ans* (Québec: CQRI, 1992), 138–91.

81 These are the four "strong reasons" adduced by the Independent Panel on Canada's Future Role in Afghanistan chaired by John Manley: see their *Report* (Ottawa, 2008), 20–22, available online at http://dsp-psd.pwgsc.gc.ca/collection_2008/dfait-maeci/FR5-20-1-2008E.pdf. See also Janice Gross Stein and Eugene Lang, *The Unexpected War: Canada in Kandahar* (Toronto: Viking

Other roles played by the CF include sovereignty protection, disaster relief, and aid to the civil power. In particular, the threat of force was used by Canada in conflicts over fishing. In April 1988 Canada arrested a French vessel in the Gulf of St. Lawrence, prompting France to recall its ambassador from Ottawa and harass Canadian citizens at Parisian airports.[82] In December 1989, HMCS *Saguenay*, a Canadian destroyer, fired shots at the *Concordia*, an American scalloper caught fishing illegally in Canadian waters.[83] In March 1995, the CCGS *Cape Roger* fired shots across the bow of the *Estai*, a Spanish freezer-trawler operating in international waters, and arrested it for overfishing in the "nose" and "tail" of the Grand Banks in defiance of turbot quotas set by the North Atlantic Fisheries Organization.[84]

Protection of Canadian sovereignty in the Arctic is another mission of the CF.[85] It was ostensibly for this purpose that the Trudeau government purchased a small expensive fleet of long-range patrol aircraft in the mid-1970s,[86] and the Mulroney government proposed in 1987 the purchase of a small and even more expensive fleet of nuclear-propelled submarines. Although the submarines were designed for anti-submarine warfare (ASW) service with NATO in the North Atlantic, the purchase was justified in terms of monitoring foreign submarine traffic in the Arctic and asserting Canadian territorial claims over Arctic waters. This proposal, which would have cost $10 billion, was quietly allowed to die when no cabinet minister could ever articulate how a vessel operating under water could "show the flag" as successfully as a surface vessel.[87]

Sovereignty protection in the Arctic resurfaced in the 2000s because of the impact of global warming on the extent of multiyear ice in the Arctic. With more of the Northwest Passage ice-free than in the past, there would be not only more development of petroleum and minerals in the region, but also the expansion of commercial shipping, posing challenges to Canadian sovereignty.[88]

Canada, 2007). The multifaceted nature of the Afghanistan mission is clearly evident in Lee Windsor, David Charters, and Brent Wilson, *Kandahar Tour: The Turning Point in Canada's Afghan Mission* (Mississauga: John Wiley & Sons Canada, 2008).

82 Ted L. McDorman, "The Canada–France Maritime Boundary Case: Drawing a Line Around St. Pierre and Miquelon," *American Journal of International Law* 84:1 (January 1990), 164.

83 The *Concordia* chose to call the Canadian bluff: it did not stop after the warning shots were fired, but raced back toward American waters; the *Saguenay* did indeed stop firing and gave chase, but abandoned it when the scalloper crossed into US waters. James D. Kiras, "Maritime Command, National Missions, and Naval Identity," in Michael L. Hadley, Robert Neil Huebert, Rob Huebert, and Fred W. Crickard, eds., *A Nation's Navy: In Quest of Canadian Naval Identity* (Montréal and Kingston: McGill-Queen's University Press, 1996), 344.

84 Donald Barry, "The Canadian–European Union Turbot War," *International Journal* 53:2 (Spring 1998), 252–84.

85 Ken S. Coates, P. Whitney Lackenbauer, William R. Morrison, and Greg Poelzer, *Arctic Front: Defending Canada in the Far North* (Toronto: Thomas Allen, 2008).

86 Michael Tucker, *Canadian Foreign Policy: Contemporary Issues and Themes* (Toronto: McGraw-Hill Ryerson, 1980), chap. 5, 143–74.

87 Canada, Department of National Defence, *Challenge and Commitment: A Defence Policy for Canada* (Ottawa: June 1987), 23–24, 52–55; Nathaniel French Caldwell, Jr., "La souveraineté du Canada et le programme de sous-marins nucléaires," *Défense nationale* 47:3 (mars 1991), 83–91.

88 Andrea Charron, "The Northwest Passage: Is Canada's Sovereignty Floating Away?" *International Journal* 60:3 (Summer 2005), 831–48; see also the debate between two of Canada's foremost experts

The Arctic role of the CF also played an important part in the campaign leading up to the January 2006 general election. In December 2005, the leader of the Conservative Party, Stephen Harper, played the "Arctic card"[89] by promising that a Conservative government would construct a new military deep-water port in the Iqaluit region that would be home to 500 members of the Canadian Forces, open an army training centre in Cambridge Bay, establish a new 650-person airborne battalion for response anywhere in the Arctic, and expand the Canadian Rangers, the community-based defence force that provides a military presence in remote Arctic communities. He also promised that a Conservative government would purchase three heavy naval troop-carrying icebreakers, deploy a new Arctic sensor system for monitoring the movement of ships and submarines in Arctic waters, purchase new fixed-wing search-and-rescue aircraft to be based in Yellowknife, and upgrade existing Aurora aircraft for coastal surveillance.[90]

One of the functions of the CF is to provide disaster relief. Units have been deployed in Canada to fight floods in Saguenay in 1996 and Winnipeg in 1997, to assist in the ice storm in eastern Canada in 1998, and even help Toronto cope with a snowstorm in 1999. But there is also an international aspect. In 1994, the Chrétien government deployed an ambulance unit to Rwanda to provide humanitarian assistance to refugees beset by a cholera epidemic in the wake of the genocidal massacres; however, the field ambulance unit was not able to deploy fast enough and only arrived after the peak of the outbreak. The experience convinced the government in Ottawa to create a dedicated unit to be available for immediate deployment in the event of disaster. The Disaster Assistance Response Team (DART) was established in 1996, and can be deployed for relief missions up to 40 days. It has been deployed to Honduras after Hurricane Mitch in 1998, to Izmit, Turkey after an earthquake in August 1999, to Sri Lanka after the December 2004 tsunami, and to Muzaffarabad, Pakistan after an earthquake in October 2005.[91]

Finally, the Canadian military is also used to augment the power of the Canadian state domestically. Such "aid to the civil power"[92] has been exercised sporadically over Canada's

---

on the Arctic: Franklyn Griffiths, "The Shipping News: Canada's Arctic Sovereignty Not on Thinning Ice," *International Journal* 58:2 (Spring 2003), 257–82; Rob Huebert, "The Shipping News Part II: How Canada's Arctic Sovereignty Is on Thinning Ice," *International Journal* 58:3 (Summer 2003), 295–308.

89 In Canadian politics, the "Arctic card" is an attempt by politicians to appeal to the unique place the Arctic occupies in the nationalist imagination in English-speaking Canada. Political leaders understand that "standing up for Arctic sovereignty" (as Harper entitled his Winnipeg speech) is a surefire vote winner in English-speaking Canada.

90 Nossal, "Defense Policy," 28; Stéphane Roussel and François Perreault, "Le retour du Canada dans l'Arctique ou le parfait alignement des logiques stratégiques, politiques et idéologiques," in Miriam Fahmy, ed., *L'état du Québec 2009* (Montréal: Fides, 2008), 574–79; Elinor Sloan, "Canada's International Security Policy Under a Conservative Government," in Andrew F. Cooper and Dane Rowlands, eds., *Canada Among Nations 2006: Minorities and Priorities* (Montréal and Kingston: McGill-Queen's University Press, 2006), 155–56. The government's Arctic strategy was unveiled in July 2009: see Canada, *Canada's Northern Strategy: Our North, Our Heritage, Our Future* (Ottawa, July 2009), esp. 9–11.

91 Michael Rostek, "The Canadian Forces: A Cosmopolitan-Minded Military?" in Lorraine M. Elliott and Graeme Cheeseman, eds., *Forces for Good: Cosmopolitan Militaries in the Twenty-First Century* (Manchester: Manchester University Press, 2004), 207–18.

92 Desmond Morton, "'No More Disagreeable or Onerous Duty': Canadian and Military Aid to the Civil Power, Past, Present and Future," in Dewitt and Leyton-Brown, eds., *Canada's International Security Policy*, 129–152.

history. Soldiers were deployed to cope with protests that broke out after conscription was introduced: on April 1, 1918, soldiers fired on a crowd in Québec City, killing four. Troops were also used to break strikes, as they did in Winnipeg in 1919. In October 1970, troops were deployed in a number of Canadian cities after the Trudeau government invoked the War Measures Act to deal with the Front de Libération du Québec (FLQ), which had murdered a Québec cabinet minister and kidnapped a British diplomat.[93] The CF was also deployed during the Oka crisis of July–August 1990.[94]

Punishments and Threats: Sanctions and Coercion

When a state cannot or does not want to use force to ensure that its interests prevail, it can try to impose its will by the use of harmful measures—or threats of harm—targeted against others. Indeed, since the early twentieth century, sanctions have been seen as a preferred tool of statecraft, since these are measures "between words and wars"[95]—they are not as destructive as the use of force, but they have more impact than mere rhetoric. The use of sanctions proliferated after the end of the Cold War: the 1990s were called "the sanctions decade" because of the popularity of using this tool of statecraft, particularly by the United Nations.[96] While sanctions have become "smarter,"[97] there is still a major debate over whether sanctions "work"[98] and what kinds of effects they have.[99] Nonetheless, sanctions remain a popular policy option, particularly in cases of human rights violations.

Until the late 1970s, Canadian governments demonstrated a marked reluctance to employ international sanctions. In October 1935, Mackenzie King was shocked to learn

93 Marc Laurendeau, *Les Québécois violents: la violence politique, 1962–1972,* 3rd ed. (Montréal: Boréal, 1990).

94 In July 1990, a dispute between the Mohawk first nation at Kanesatake and the Québec town of Oka over the town's plans to expand a golf course on land regarded as sacred escalated when the provincial police, the Sûreté du Québec, intervened, resulting in the death of one police officer and prompting the neighbouring Mohawks at Kahnawake to blockade the Mercier bridge and several highways into Montréal. As the resulting massive traffic jams caused tensions to mount, the premier of Québec, Robert Bourassa, invoked the section of the National Defence Act that allows provincial governments to request the deployment of the Canadian Armed Forces in "aid to the civil power." A company of the Royal 22e Regiment (the Van Doos) was despatched, and over 2500 regular forces and reservists were put on alert. At the end of August, the Mohawks at Kahnawake lifted their blockade, and the Mohawks at Kanesatake abandoned their protest at the end of September. The town of Oka abandoned its planned golf-course expansion.

95 Peter Wallensteen and Carina Staibano, eds., *International Sanctions: Between Words and Wars and the Global System* (London: Routledge, 2005).

96 David Cortright and George A. Lopez, *The Sanctions Decade: Assessing UN Strategies in the 1990s* (Boulder: Lynne Rienner, 2000).

97 David Cortright and George A. Lopez, eds., *Smart Sanctions: Targeting Economic Statecraft* (Lanham, MD: Rowman and Littlefield, 2002).

98 Robert A. Pape, "Why Economic Sanctions Do Not Work," *International Security* 22:2 (Autumn 1997), 90–136; however, see Jean-Marc F. Blanchard and Norrin M. Ripsman, "Asking the Right Question: *When Do* Economic Sanctions Work Best?" *Security Studies* 9:1/2 (Autumn 1999), 219–53.

99 For example, Lori Buck, Nicole Gallant, and Kim Richard Nossal, "Sanctions as a Gendered Instrument of Statecraft: The Case of Iraq," *Review of International Studies* 24:1 (January 1998), 69–84.

that Canada's representative to the League of Nations, W.A. Riddell, had taken a personal initiative in proposing sanctions against Italy following its invasion of Ethiopia; worse, the proposed measure on oil was being widely referred to as "the Canadian sanction." Riddell had acted without instructions from the government and King, fearing that League sanctions against Italy might lead to war, quickly disavowed his initiative.[100]

During the Cold War era, Ottawa refused to participate in American-led trade sanctions against the People's Republic of China in the 1950s or Cuba in the 1960s and 1970s but did join an embargo on strategic goods to the Soviet Union being coordinated by the Western alliance. It joined in imposing United Nations sanctions against white minority regimes in Rhodesia and South Africa in the 1960s. While in general Ottawa preferred multilateral sanctions, it occasionally imposed sanctions unilaterally—the Trudeau government sanctioned India after New Delhi detonated a nuclear device in 1974, and the Clark government sanctioned Argentina in 1979 for the human rights abuses being committed by the military junta there.

The late 1970s marked a watershed in Canada's approach to sanctions. Beginning in 1979, the government imposed sanctions against a variety of states: against Vietnam after its invasion of Kampuchea in early 1979; against Iran following the seizure of the United States embassy in Tehran in 1979; against the Soviet Union after its invasion of Afghanistan in December of that year; against Poland after the imposition of martial law in December 1981; against Argentina following its invasion of the Falkland Islands in the spring of 1982; against the Soviet Union after Soviet fighters shot down a Korean Air Lines airliner in September 1983; against South Africa after the outbreak of violence in the fall of 1984; against China after the Beijing massacre in June 1989; against Iraq following the invasion of Kuwait in August 1990; against the former Yugoslavia after its collapse into civil war in 1991–92; and against Haiti after the military overthrew Jean-Bertrand Aristide following the 1991 elections.[101] Likewise, on numerous occasions Canada used its aid program as a sanction, suspending development assistance to such countries as Afghanistan, Cuba, El Salvador, Fiji, Guatemala, Indonesia, Libya, Peru, Suriname, Sri Lanka, and Uganda.[102] Ottawa also participated in the increasing use of sports sanctions in international politics during this era.[103]

In the post–Cold War era, the Canadian government was an active supporter of the expanding United Nations sanctions regime. However, reflecting an increasing concern for the ethics of international sanctions,[104] Ottawa joined in the move to make sanctions

---

100 Stacey, *Age of Conflict*, vol. 1, 180–88.

101 Kim Richard Nossal, *Rain Dancing: Sanctions in Canadian and Australian Foreign Policy* (Toronto: University of Toronto Press, 1994).

102 T.A. Keenleyside, "Development Assistance," in Robert O. Matthews and Cranford Pratt, eds., *Human Rights in Canadian Foreign Policy* (Montréal and Kingston: McGill-Queen's University Press, 1988), 187–208.

103 Donald Macintosh and Michael Hawes, with contributions from Donna Greenhorn and David Black, *Sport in Canadian Diplomacy* (Montréal and Kingston: McGill-Queen's University Press, 1994).

104 Thomas G. Weiss, David Cortright, George A. Lopez, and Larry Minear, eds., *Political Gain and Civilian Pain: The Humanitarian Impacts of Economic Sanctions* (Lanham, MD: Rowman and Littlefield, 1997); Joy Gordon, "A Peaceful, Silent, Deadly Remedy: The Ethics of International Sanctions, " *Ethics and International Affairs* (1999), 123–42.

"smarter": when Canada was elected to the Security Council in 1999 for a two-year term, Robert Fowler, Canada's permanent representative, worked to strengthen the sanctions over "conflict diamonds."[105]

In the post-9/11 era, the governments of Jean Chrétien, Paul Martin, and Stephen Harper all demonstrated an enthusiasm for sanctions of different sorts.[106] In that period, the United Nations Security Council was particularly active. By 2009, UN sanctions were in place against Al-Qaeda and the Taliban, Côte d'Ivoire, North Korea, Democratic Republic of the Congo, Iran, Iraq, Lebanon, Liberia, Sierra Leone, Somalia, and Sudan. The government in Ottawa implemented each of these UN sanctions regimes by invoking the United Nations Act, 1985, which is the legislative authority for the government in Ottawa to implement Security Council measures invoked under Article 41 of the UN Charter. In addition, however, the Harper government imposed its own sanctions against Belarus in December 2006, against Burma in December 2007, and against Zimbabwe in September 2008—all for deteriorating human rights conditions in those countries. Development assistance and diplomatic sanctions were also imposed after Hamas won the Palestinian Legislative Council elections of January 25, 2006. Because Hamas had been listed as a terrorist organization by the Chrétien government in November 2002,[107] the Hamas victory posed a thorny issue for the equally new Conservative government. When the new Hamas government was sworn in at the end of March 2006, the Harper government immediately cut all diplomatic contacts and suspended Canadian development assistance. The minister of foreign affairs, Peter MacKay, declared that there would be "not a red cent to Hamas."[108]

However popular sanctions are as a tool of Canadian statecraft, they tend to be imposed as punishments for acts of wrongdoing.[109] Thus, sanctions are rarely used against countries considered "friends"—even when they engage in behaviour substantially similar to that of other states subject to sanctions. When the United States invaded Grenada in October 1983, when a U.S. Navy vessel shot down an Iranian airliner in the Persian Gulf in July 1988, when American forces invaded Panama and overthrew the government of Manuel Noriega in December 1989, or when the United States invaded Iraq in 2003 without United Nations approval, the Canadian government never considered sanctions against the United States comparable to those imposed against the Soviet Union or Vietnam.

Using threats as a tool of statecraft is not unknown to Canadian foreign policymakers, but its application tends to be very limited. In cases wherein the targets of Canadian threats are highly dependent on Canada, this instrument tends to achieve its desired effect. As we

---

105 Paul Knox, "Canada at the UN: A Human Security Council?" in Maureen Appel Molot and Fen Osler Hampson, eds., *Canada Among Nations, 2000: Vanishing Borders* (Toronto: Oxford University Press, 2000), 309–310; Kim Richard Nossal, "Smarter, Sharper, Stronger? UN Sanctions and Conflict Diamonds in Angola," in Andrew F. Cooper and Ramesh Thakur, eds., *Enhancing Global Governance: Towards a New Diplomacy?* (Tokyo: United Nations University Press, 2002), 248–67.

106 For the current Canadian sanctions regimes, see http://www.international.gc.ca/sanctions.

107 For Public Safety Canada's "listed entities," see http://www.publicsafety.gc.ca/prg/ns/le/cle-eng.aspx.

108 http://www.cbc.ca/canada/story/2006/03/29/ottawa-hamas060329.html.

109 Kim Richard Nossal, "International Sanctions as International Punishment," *International Organization* 43:2 (Spring 1989), 301–22.

will see in Chapter 12, the federal government successfully coerced francophone African states in the late 1960s to halt a bid by the government of Québec for a greater degree of international recognition. None too subtly, Ottawa reminded these states that Québec City could hardly match the development assistance programs administered by the federal government.

But there are relatively few situations in which others are sufficiently dependent on Canada that they will bend to a threat of harm. To be sure, when Canada and the United States have a dispute, it is often suggested that Canada should use threats of retaliation as part of its strategy to secure Canadian interests. However, the Canadian government generally never uses retaliatory threats in its relations with the United States, simply because of the considerable power differential between the two countries. If a government in Ottawa used threats against the United States to achieve its objectives, it would have to reckon with the consequences should the threats of damage fail to deter or move the administration in Washington. When a threat fails, one has a choice: either back down or impose the threatened deprivation. Either way, in the context of the Canadian–American relationship, coercion is a mug's game. The United States has a huge capacity to absorb whatever privations Canada might visit on it, and, more importantly, it has a huge capacity to administer even more damaging blows in retaliation should a dispute escalate. Moreover, the higher the stakes for American interests, the more likely the government in Washington will use its substantial capabilities to protect those interests. A willingness to "play hardball," as policymakers in Washington call it, can easily—and quickly—replace the otherwise leavening condition of friendship between the two countries.

Diplomacy: The Art of Persuasion

Because of its limited capacities, its vulnerabilities, and its dominant relationship with the United States, the Canadian government's most potent technique in achieving its objectives is the use of influence. For a state with limited ability to use the techniques of power— force, sanctions, or coercion—the techniques of influence assume greater prominence. In the context of international politics, the art of persuading others to move to positions more congenial to one's interests is known as *diplomacy*. Canadian diplomacy is, not surprisingly, aimed at a wide variety of players on an array of issues: trying to persuade the Department of Homeland Security in the United States to change its policies on border restrictions; negotiating a free-trade agreement with the government of Colombia; trying to convince the Saudi government not to execute a Canadian teenager convicted of murder; rallying support among delegations at the United Nations General Assembly for changes in the wording of a resolution; trying to secure the agreement of the government of Israel to ban further settlement in the West Bank; trying to persuade other governments to vote for Canada in its bid for a seat on the Security Council.

Some diplomacy can be conducted by the prime minister at summit meetings, as we will see in Chapter 7. But much of a state's diplomacy has to be carried out by the foreign service—Canada's diplomatic representatives posted to other countries and to international organizations. A foreign service is not only an essential part of the apparatus of state, but also potentially one of the state's most useful assets in pursuing international policy.[110] It is

---

110 John W. Holmes, *Canada: A Middle-Aged Power* (Toronto: McClelland & Stewart, 1976), 44–53.

a power resource of considerable potency, as the record of Canadian diplomacy in the decade after the Second World War demonstrates. That era has come to be known as the "golden age of Canadian diplomacy."[111] Of course, such a lavish assessment reflects in large part the mythologizing that is an inevitable part of a country's history-making, but the hyperbole is not entirely unwarranted. During this period, the government was generally successful in achieving its foreign policy objectives and securing Canadian interests, particularly vis-à-vis the United States. There are a number of reasons for this. In part, it is because officials in this period recognized Canada's limitations internationally and framed their international objectives accordingly. In part it is because Canadian policymakers paid extraordinary attention to maintaining good relations with the United States. And in part it can also be attributed to the diplomatic skills of the external affairs minister, Lester Pearson, his diplomats in the Department of External Affairs, and the general support for diplomacy as a tool of Canadian statecraft provided by the political leadership in cabinet.

By contrast, the 1970s were characterized as an era of "frustrated designs" in Canadian foreign policy.[112] While the international context had changed somewhat from the 1950s, one of the reasons that so many of the initiatives undertaken by the Trudeau government failed was not simply because foreign policy objectives were often cast without regard to the constraints of power in that era, but also because the craft of Canadian diplomacy suffered considerably after 1968. As we will see in Chapter 9, diplomacy was publicly disparaged by the prime minister and his senior advisers throughout the 1970s and never nurtured as it was in the 1950s. Trudeau underestimated the extent to which a foreign service figures in the calculus of a state's power resources, and how those resources might be used to bring others closer to one's own interests.

In the 1990s, Canada's diplomacy took a hit of a different sort. In order to deal with the long-term consequences of two decades of budget deficits by the Mulroney Conservatives and Trudeau Liberals, the Chrétien government deeply cut the budgets of all departments involved in international policy. This had an immediate impact as the Department of Foreign Affairs and International Trade shrank and there were fewer foreign service officers to deploy to embassies and consulates abroad and fewer officers at DFAIT headquarters in the Lester B. Pearson Building in Ottawa to work on international dossiers. It was not at all coincidental that during this period of financial stringency, the minister of foreign affairs, Lloyd Axworthy, borrowed the idea of "soft power" from the work of American political scientist Joseph S. Nye, Jr. as an animating idea for Canadian international policy. Nye had conceived the term as part of a debate in American policy and academic circles in the late 1980s and early 1990s about whether the United States was a declining power in world politics. On one side were the "declinists" who saw the importance of military power declining as a factor in world politics. On the other side were scholars like Nye who argued that the declinists were wrong; that the United States was endowed with both "hard power" and "soft power"—which he defined as the ability to "get others to want what you want," or what he also called "co-optive power."[113]

---

111 For example, Andrew Cohen, *While Canada Slept: How We Lost Our Place in the World* (Toronto: McClelland & Stewart, 2003); see Adam Chapnick, "The Golden Age," *International Journal* 63:1 (Winter 2008–9), 205–21.

112 Tucker, *Canadian Foreign Policy*, ix.

113 Joseph S. Nye, Jr., *Bound to Lead: The Changing Nature of American Power* (New York: Basic Books, 1990).

Axworthy applied the term to Canadian statecraft, arguing that ideas were Canada's real strength in international policy, pointing to his successful campaign to ban antipersonnel landmines.[114] However, the underlying rationale for a "soft power" approach of "getting others to want what you want" was that it was perfect for a government that had slashed spending on all aspects of international policy, since it did not require much money to do it. All one needed was a few good ideas and others would "want what you want."[115]

The difficulty, of course, is that too often others are not persuaded by good ideas and simply refuse to "want what Canada wants." The United States, Russia, and China, for example, were not at all moved by Axworthy's idea about landmines. President Omar al-Bashir of Sudan was not persuaded by the "good idea" that the government in Khartoum should control the *janjaweed* militias who raped and slaughtered tens of thousands in Darfur. Groups like Al-Qaeda and Jemaah Islamiyah have little use for the "good ideas" of Western societies. The Pashtun insurgents in Afghanistan not only do not want what the Canadian government wants, but are committed to killing as many Canadian soldiers as they can and destroying as many of the "good works" of the Provincial Reconstruction Teams as possible. When the Kosovo Liberation Army successfully provoked Serbian forces into committing atrocities against the Kosovar Albanians in 1998 and 1999, even the best diplomacy was no substitute for "brute force."[116] In those circumstances, what one needs is not soft power, but power, period—that is, the means to prevail over others. And to do this, a state needs a full array of the instruments of power: a well-equipped military force and a well-maintained foreign service to press Canadian interests abroad in hundreds of different settings.

POWER AND CANADIAN–AMERICAN RELATIONS

Relations with the United States are a central preoccupation of Canada's international policy, to the point that there is a constant search for equilibrium between relations with the United States and relations with the rest of the world. But Canada's opportunities for exercising power in its relations with the U.S. are limited. Force is not an option; nor are economic sanctions. Coercion is a dangerous game to play with a state that has a great capacity for inflicting damage and a willingness to do so if pushed. Persuasion, it has been suggested, is the most effective instrument, both generally in Canada's relations with other states and specifically in the context of Canadian–American relations.

Canadians are often cynical about their country's relations with the United States. When there is a difference of opinion between the two countries, or when Washington wants Ottawa to adopt a policy unpopular in Canada—as was the case when the administration of George W. Bush tried to push the Paul Martin government into making a decision on

---

114 Brian W. Tomlin, "On a Fast-Track to a Ban: The Canadian Policy Process," *Canadian Foreign Policy* 5:3 (1998), 3–24.

115 Nossal, "Pinchpenny Diplomacy"; also Kim Richard Nossal, "Foreign Policy for Wimps," *Ottawa Citizen*, April 23, 1998, A19; and the minister's response: Lloyd Axworthy, "Why Soft Power Is the Right Policy for Canada," *Ottawa Citizen*, April 25, 1998, B6.

116 Wayne Nelles, "Canada's Human Security Agenda in Kosovo and Beyond: Military Intervention Versus Conflict Prevention," *International Journal* 52:3 (Summer 2002), 462.

Ballistic Missile Defense in 2004[117]—many Canadians almost instinctively assume that their government will simply bend to American power. Indeed, the trope that the prime minister is merely a "lap dog" of the American president is deeply embedded in Canadian political discourse.[118] But to what extent is this perspective justified? Is it possible for Canada to dissociate itself from American policy—or, better still, to influence it?

One does not have to accept the argument that Canada is a satellite of the United States to recognize that it must take into account certain disadvantages in its relationship with that country: its wealth is heavily dependent on the high degree of integration of the North American economy; its military activities, such as the mission in Afghanistan, occur in the context of international institutions such as NATO that are dominated by the U.S.; and its culture has been deeply permeated by American influences. Given this, it is no surprise that one should see the possibilities for Canadian influence as minimal or non-existent.

However, it is necessary to take a more nuanced approach to Canadian–American relations. For if one compares this "disparate dyad," as Naomi Black famously called it,[119] with any other relationship between a great power and a much weaker neighbour, many conclude that, over the broad sweep of history, Canadians do relatively well in negotiations with the United States.[120] But evaluating the Canada–United States relationship reveals contradictory points of view, some cynical and pessimistic, others reassuring and optimistic.[121]

On the one hand, one can readily point to cases where negotiations with the United States resulted in American interests prevailing over Canadian interests. Two historical examples—the Alaska Boundary award of 1903 and the acid rain dispute of the 1980s—illustrate the dynamic of dominance at work.

The Alaska Boundary dispute is usually summoned out of the historical closet to demonstrate how Canada was bullied by the United States—and sold out by the imperial government in London to boot—an interpretation that, as David G. Haglund has demonstrated, is

---

117 For a discussion of what he calls Canada's "participation/non-participation shuffle," see James Fergusson, "Shall We Dance? The Missile Defence Decision, NORAD Renewal, and the Future of Canada–US Defence Relations," *Canadian Military Journal* 6:2 (2005), 13–22.

118 Even former prime ministers have engaged in this: for example, in a speech to the Canadian Bar Association in Québec City in August 2008, Chrétien claimed that Harper was "le nouveau petit chien des États-Unis [the new lapdog of the United States]." Tracey Tyler, "Chrétien Blasts PM on China," *Toronto Star*, August 19, 2008.

119 Naomi Black, "Absorptive Systems Are Impossible: The Canadian–American Relationship as a Disparate Dyad," in Andrew Axline, James Hyndman, Peyton Lyon, and Maureen Appel Molot, eds., *Continental Community? Independence and Integration in North America* (Toronto: McClelland & Stewart, 1974), 92–110.

120 Robert O. Keohane and Joseph S. Nye, Jr., *Power and Interdependence: World Politics in Transition* (Boston: Little, Brown, 1977), chap. 7; Harald von Riekoff and Hanspeter Neuhold, eds., *Unequal Partners: A Comparative Analysis of Relations Between Austria and the Federal Republic of Germany and Between Canada and the United States* (Boulder: Westview, 1993); Stéphane Roussel, *The North American Democratic Peace* (Montréal and Kingston: McGill-Queen's University Press, 2004).

121 Stéphane Roussel, "Canada–U.S. Relations: Time for Cassandra?" *American Review of Canadian Studies* 30:2 (Summer 2000), 135–57.

pure Canadian nationalist mythology.[122] For our purposes here, however, the boundary award does provide a useful illustration of why a correct assessment of power is so important for negotiating with the United States. The dispute hinged on the interpretation of the words of an Anglo–Russian treaty of 1825 (a treaty inherited by the United States when it purchased Alaska from Russia in 1867). The treaty defined the boundary as a line not to exceed 10 marine leagues (about 55 kilometres) inland from a line "parallel to the sinuosities of the coast." The problem lay in the fjord-like geography of the American Panhandle, and in particular a deep inlet called Lynn Canal, at the head of which were two well-established American communities, Dyea (which was a thriving gold rush boomtown but is now abandoned) and Skagway. The Canadian government contended that the "sinuosities" meant drawing the line 10 leagues from the *mouths* of inlets such as Lynn Canal, assuring Canada access to the sea from the Yukon territory where gold had just been discovered; if the Canadian claim were accepted, Dyea and Skagway would become Canadian and parts of the Panhandle would become exclaves, separated from Alaska proper by strips of Canadian territory. For its part, the United States claimed that the line should be measured from the *heads* of the inlets, ensuring not only that Dyea and Skagway would remain American but also that the United States would control a continuous stretch of coastline from Alaska proper down the Panhandle. In this interpretation Canada would have no access to the sea north of the Dixon Entrance.

When American, British, and Canadian officials sat down to negotiate a settlement in the fall of 1898, the Americans proposed a compromise that would keep Skagway American but give Canada access to the sea. However, in what C.P. Stacey describes as "a mood of rather extravagant self-confidence,"[123] Sir Wilfrid Laurier decided to refuse anything less than the original claim. Nor did the Canadians accept any proposals being made to them by the British for arbitration or settlement, believing that time, and British imperial power, were on their side. It was a bad miscalculation. Theodore Roosevelt, who became president after William McKinley was assassinated in 1901, refused to accept the weak legal arguments being put forward by the Canadians, but he did propose that the case be arbitrated by a tribunal of three "impartial jurists of repute" from each side. In the end, the tribunal was not at all impartial. Roosevelt appointed three politicians, all of whom were committed to the American claim; moreover, the President's letter of instruction was clear: "there will of course be no compromise." On the British/Canadian side, the two Canadian members were just as deeply committed to the Canadian claim. The British chairman of the Canadian side was Lord Alverstone, the chief justice of England. And while Roosevelt warned that if there were any "captious objections" to the American claim, "I am going to send a brigade of American regulars up to Skagway and hold it by all the power and force of the United States," the threat was unnecessary: Lord Alverstone sided with the American members on the issue of the Lynn Canal.[124] However, as Haglund reminds us, Canadian nationalist mythology stops the story there. It does not mention that

---

122 David G. Haglund, "The TR Problem in Canada–US Relations," *London Journal of Canadian Studies* 23 (2007/08); also see David G. Haglund and Tudor Onea, "Victory Without Triumph: Theodore Roosevelt, Honour, and the Alaska Panhandle Boundary Dispute," *Diplomacy & Statecraft* 19:1 (March 2008), 20–41.

123 Stacey, *Age of Conflict*, vol. 1, 89.

124 Ibid., 86–99; also Donald Creighton, *Canada's First Century* (Toronto: Macmillan, 1970), 96–97.

the reason why Roosevelt proposed a tribunal was to give Canada a face-saving solution, and it does not relate how Alverstone achieved compromises for the Canadian side elsewhere in the Panhandle, including convincing the American side to abandon their claim to two large islands in the Portland Canal, making Roosevelt the first president in American history to preside over the territorial shrinkage of the United States during his term of office.[125]

On some issues, however, not even the finest diplomacy will prompt a change in Washington. A good example was the issue of acid rain, which bedevilled Canadian–American relations throughout the 1980s. Canada contended that emissions of sulphur dioxide and nitrous oxide from factories and power-generating plants as far away as the American Midwest were being transported long distances by prevailing winds and falling on Ontario, Québec, and the Maritimes as acidic precipitation, affecting lakes, rivers, sandstone buildings, and the maple sugar industry. For its part, the United States government argued that more research was needed to demonstrate the linkage between emissions in the Ohio valley and damage in eastern Canada. Over the course of a decade, four Canadian prime ministers grappled with the intractable: a United States government that resolutely refused to move, and indeed had little incentive to do so, given the entrenched regional, political, and economic interests at stake. In the early 1980s, the Trudeau government tried persuasion in a variety of forms: rational scientific argument, quiet diplomacy, stiff diplomatic notes of protest, impassioned entreaty. The Liberals became so frustrated that they even went so far as to try overt propaganda techniques, passing out leaflets to hapless American tourists accusing their country of fouling the Canadian environment and urging them to press for change when they got home.

When Brian Mulroney and the Progressive Conservatives came to power in 1984, the tone and mood in the Canadian–American relationship changed considerably—and with some initial success. Mulroney managed to achieve what Trudeau had not: an admission from Ronald Reagan at the Québec City summit in 1985 that Canada and the United States had a shared responsibility to preserve the environment. But that was as far as it went. Neither the president nor Congress subsequently moved to tackle the sources of acid rain with any seriousness. The frustration of the Conservative government mounted as it rediscovered the wheel, finding that little more could be done short of embracing options either unthinkable or immensely costly, such as Canadians paying for the installation of "scrubbers" at American utilities and factories.[126] In the end the Mulroney government decided to resort to the same kind of public diplomacy that had been embraced by the Trudeau government in the early 1980s. Ministers started giving vitriolic speeches denouncing acid rain; by the summer of 1988, propaganda was again being given to American tourists. The issue was only resolved when changes occurred in the United States itself: the Senate majority leader, Robert Byrd, from the coal-producing state of West Virginia, was replaced by Senator George Mitchell of Maine, which was also

---

125 Haglund, "TR Problem," 38.

126 The Coase Theorem, developed by economist Ronald Coase, suggests that as long as the United States did not have a legal obligation not to allow emissions from American sources from polluting Canada (and until 1990, it did not), one "efficient" option for the government of Canada would have been to absorb the costs of trying to make factories and power-generating plants in the United States cleaner. See Robert O. Keohane, *After Hegemony: Cooperation and Discord in the World Political Economy* (Princeton: Princeton University Press, 1984), 85ff.

affected by acid rain. Members of Congress from the southern states, which were being hit with increased air pollution from Mexico, changed their views; and the presidency shifted from Reagan to George H.W. Bush.[127]

On the other hand, while these historical cases are significant, they are far from representative. In general, the United States has avoided acting in a way that would damage the bonds of friendship between the two countries. That friendship is founded on convergent interests and common values, and the deep economic and cultural bonds between the two societies. But it is to some extent a function of a hard calculation of national interest. The United States has no interest in upsetting what has become a very predictable relationship with a northern neighbour unlikely to do serious harm to its interests. Consequently, only in very rare cases is the U.S. government inclined to force a showdown with Canada and use the full range of power resources at its disposal. As a result, the government in Ottawa has more room to manoeuvre in protecting Canada, despite the great difference of power.

On a purely tactical level, Canada does not lack assets in its relations with the United States. First, Ottawa can take advantage of Canada's relative insignificance in the eyes of policymakers in Washington. Canadian–American issues must compete for priority on the American foreign policy agenda with a range of global issues considered much more important in Washington. The attention of American foreign policymakers is necessarily diverted and dissipated.[128] Sometimes this works to Canada's advantage: not all Canadian policies that damage the interests of some Americans make it to the president's agenda. On other occasions, however, it becomes a problem when the Canadian government needs the intervention of the White House.

Second, American leaders are much more constrained in their relations with Canada than Canadians suppose. They are seldom willing to mobilize the immense means theoretically at their disposal to bend Ottawa to their will. Although some argue that Canada has to worry about American retaliation, in fact, as Brian Bow has demonstrated, the United States actually rarely uses "linkage politics," in which American annoyance about Canadian policy on one issue will result in tit-for-tat retaliation on another completely different issue. Far more important, in Bow's view, is what he aptly calls "grudge linkages": a president simply becomes so annoyed at a prime minister's policies that it affects the overall relationship.[129] This reflects the observation of Allan Gotlieb, Canada's ambassador to Washington in the 1980s, who notes that the United States might not engage in linkage, "but everything, broadly speaking, is linked."[130]

Third, the primarily pluralist character of the American political system and the sometimes erratic behaviour of the government resulting from this pluralism are both a disadvantage and an opportunity for Canadian leaders. The separation of powers that gives

---

127 The best survey of this dispute and its resolution is Don Munton and Geoffrey Castle, "Reducing Acid Rain, 1980s," in Munton and Kirton, eds., *Canadian Foreign Policy*, 376–78.

128 Edelgard Mahant and Graeme S. Mount, *Invisible and Inaudible in Washington: American Policies Toward Canada* (Vancouver: UBC Press, 1999).

129 Brian Bow, "Rethinking "Retaliation" in Canada–U.S. Relations," in Bow and Lennox, eds., *An Independent Foreign Policy for Canada?* 63–82.

130 Allan Gotlieb, "Foremost Partner: The Conduct of Canada–US Relations," in David Carment, Fen Osler Hampson, and Norman Hillmer, eds., *Canada Among Nations 2003: Coping with the American Colossus* (Toronto: Oxford University Press, 2003), 25.

Congress so much authority over American foreign policy often has a direct impact on decision-making in Washington—and thus on relations between the United States and other countries.[131] The world is still living with the legacies of the decision by the Senate in 1919 to refuse to ratify the Treaty of Versailles and join the League of Nations, keeping the United States out of global politics during the interwar period and thus, arguably, contributing to the outbreak of the Second World War. And all of the trading partners of the United States have experienced the contradictory tendencies in Washington where protectionists and free-trade enthusiasts can be found in both the executive branch and in Congress—at the same time.

Canadians often experience the effects of the impact of the separation of powers and the impact of Congress on American foreign policy. In 1979, Ottawa negotiated treaties on fisheries and boundaries on the east coast with the administration of Jimmy Carter. When the agreements were considered by the United States Senate, two senators, Claiborne Pell of Rhode Island and Edward Kennedy of Massachusetts, believed that the treaties did not sufficiently protect the interests of their constituents. These two senators were able to rally enough opposition among their 98 colleagues that the new administration of Ronald Reagan, knowing that the treaties would fail a ratification vote, withdrew them from consideration. The failure of the 1979 treaties prompted John W. Holmes to note testily that the United States "is increasingly incapable of conducting rational relations with any foreign country as the federal administration is bound and overruled by the captious actions of a Congress that is a law unto itself, disdainful even of international commitments."[132] But, as Gotlieb reminds us, this is the logical consequence of the independent power of members of Congress, where "each can have his own domestic and foreign policy."[133]

By the same token, however, the American system also presents Canada with opportunities for creative statecraft. The pluralism of policymaking in Washington mitigates concerted and united efforts by the United States to pursue a consistently hard line against Canada. While some Americans, both within and outside government, may be pressing for tougher measures against Canada on some issue, one will always be able to find other groups or bureaucratic/political actors to enlist as allies of Canadian interests within the policy process.[134] For example, during the long-running softwood lumber dispute, the American softwood lumber industry and their Congressional supporters always complained loudly about what they claimed was an unfairly subsidized price of Canadian softwood lumber; the government in Ottawa has always sought to enlist support from those Americans who have an interest in lower lumber prices, such as the housing industry and consumer associations (and their Congressional supporters).[135] A similar strategy

131 Kim Richard Nossal, "The Imperial Congress: The Separation of Powers and Canadian–American Relations," *International Journal* 44:4 (Autumn 1989), 863–83.

132 John W. Holmes, *Life with Uncle: The Canadian–American Relationship* (Toronto: University of Toronto Press, 1981), 61.

133 Gotlieb, *Washington Diaries,* 110.

134 Allan Gotlieb, *"I'll Be with You in a Minute, Mr. Ambassador': The Education of a Canadian Diplomat in Washington* (Toronto: University of Toronto Press, 1991), 79–115.

135 Daowei Zhang, *The Softwood Lumber War: Politics, Economics, and the Long U.S.–Canadian Trade Dispute* (Washington: Resources for the Future Press, 2007).

was pursued in environmental issues on the Canadian–American agenda, such as acid rain, and the Garrison Diversion and the Devils Lake issues.[136]

CONCLUSION

In the international system, no state is truly autonomous—in the sense that no state, not even the most powerful, is able to ensure its actions will accord with its preferences. This is particularly true for Canada: The government cannot do exactly as it pleases in international affairs. If it is to be effective—in other words, able to achieve its objectives—a state's international policies have to be crafted with careful attention to what is attainable. "Discretion in diplomacy," John W. Holmes has written, "is in the calculation of the issues at stake and the forces which can be mustered"[137]—and, of course, the forces that can be mustered against one by others.

Because of this, the question of capabilities assumes considerable importance. The main focus of Canada's international "power relationships" is the United States, not only because of the imperatives of neighbourhood and economic structure, but also because of the position of the United States as the dominant power in the contemporary international system. It is when the focus of an assessment of Canada's power is fixed on its dominant relationship that the utility of a "power analysis" approach rather than a "power image" approach becomes evident. The picture that emerges is not that of a "principal power"; rather, it is of a state that must always be sensitive to the preponderance of power on the North American continent. Power analysis also directs our attention to the importance of disparities in capability, of the importance of strategy and calculation of how to derive maximum advantage by a judicious use of the resources and techniques of power. Although there is a clear asymmetry of capabilities between Canada and the United States, Canada does not lack what power-analysts term *power resources*. But it cannot avoid the necessity of showing "how wit with small means may accomplish wonders where great force availeth not."[138]

---

136 The Garrison Diversion project was a massive irrigation scheme in North Dakota that would have pumped waters from the Mississippi River basin over the continental divide into Red River in the Hudson Bay basin system. Devils Lake, also in North Dakota, has been described as a giant pothole—it is a lake with no natural outlet that floods when precipitation and runoff exceeds the rate of evaporation. The solution was to construct an artificial outlet. But like the larger Garrison Diversion project of which it was a part, the outlet would mean that biota from the Missouri River basin would be introduced to the Red River. For the politics of these cases, see Kim Richard Nossal, "The Unmaking of Garrison: United States Politics and the Management of Canadian–American Boundary Waters," *Behind the Headlines* 37 (December 1978); and Kevin Ma, "Canada–US Relations and the Devils Lake Dispute," in Brian W. Tomlin, Norman Hillmer and Fen Osler Hampson, *Canada's International Policies: Agendas, Alternatives, and Politics* (Toronto: Oxford University Press, 2008), 317–31.

137 John W. Holmes, *The Better Part of Valour: Essays on Canadian Diplomacy* (Toronto: McClelland & Stewart, 1970), vii.

138 Quoted in Annette Baker Fox and William T.R. Fox, "Domestic Capabilities and Canadian Foreign Policy," *International Journal* 39:1 (Winter 1983–4), 25.

CHAPTER 4

Society and International Policy

Just as a country's international policy decisions are shaped by the external environment and the power it exercises in pursuit of its policy objectives, so too are the decisions of policymakers shaped by their domestic environment. Indeed, the relationship between the state and society is particularly important in a liberal democratic country like Canada, where the relationship between governors and the governed is shaped and conditioned by the normative principles of liberal democratic theory. These include the equality of all citizens, the consent to be governed, the supremacy or sovereignty of "the people," representative institutions of governance that provide for the public accountability of the governors, and the primacy of the constitution and the rule of law. In short, the precepts of democratic liberalism suggest that the behaviour of democratic governments *should* be affected and conditioned by the preferences of groups and citizens in society.

This chapter seeks to assess how and to what extent societal actors in Canada shape international policy in Canada. We are interested in the political behaviour of a range of actors and agents that are distinct from the state: citizens as individuals, firms, but also the various associations that comprise civil society. While Michael Edwards argues that trying to define "civil society" is like trying to nail jelly to a wall,[1] in this book we use the oft-quoted working definition of the Centre for Civil Society at the London School of Economics:

> Civil society refers to the arena of uncoerced collective action around shared interests, purposes and values. In theory, its institutional forms are distinct from those of the state, family and market, though in practice, the boundaries . . . are often complex, blurred and negotiated. . . . Civil societies are often populated by organizations such as registered charities, development non-governmental organizations, community groups, women's organizations, faith-based organizations, professional associations, trade unions, self-help groups, social movements, business associations, coalitions, and advocacy groups.[2]

First, we examine the interests that societal actors in Canada have in international policy. Our discussion is organized thematically in order to demonstrate how and why Canadians are interested in external policy. The second part of the chapter explores what impact societal actors have on international policy.

SOCIETAL INTERESTS

Public opinion polls consistently reveal that Canadians have a deep interest in global politics.[3] Indeed, their range of interests in international affairs is so rich and diverse that it would take a larger canvas than we have here to do them justice. While there are different ways to examine the interests and impact of society on foreign policy, we organize the discussion around three broad sets of interests: those of

---

1 Michael Edwards, *Civil Society*, rev. ed. (London: Polity Press, 2009), 4.

2 Centre for Civil Society, "What Is Civil Society?" April 23, 2009, available http://www.lse.ac.uk/collections/CCS/introduction/what_is_civil_society.htm.

3 See the persistently high levels of interest over a 20-year period reported in Pierre Martin and Michel Fortmann, "Support for International Involvement in Canadian Public Opinion after the Cold War," *Canadian Military Journal* 2:3 (Autumn 2001), fig. 1, 44. "The picture that emerged was one of a society in which the vast majority express an interest in international events . . . and expect their government to be actively engaged in finding solutions to international problems."

individuals in their ethnicity, which we use in a Weberian sense[4]; those of individuals in their egoistic material and physical well-being; and individuals' altruistic interests in giving expression to their empathy with the well-being of others.

Ethnic Interests

Canada, like Australia, New Zealand, South Africa, and the United States, is a political creation of émigré settlers who fashioned their new polity after their own image (rather than integrating into the existing political communities of the Aboriginal inhabitants they displaced and marginalized). Successive waves of immigration played a fundamental role in shaping the new settler society that would eventually become Canada. The process began with the first tenuous settlements of British, French, Dutch, and Swedes established in the late sixteenth and early seventeenth centuries. From 1600 to 1763, when all North Americans east of the Mississippi (save those on the islands of St-Pierre and Miquelon) became subjects of the British Crown, the other European sponsors of North American settlements were gradually eliminated as large-scale sources of immigrants. This was the result of successive British military victories—first against the Netherlands and Sweden and then against France. Of course, by the time of the Conquest, the size of the French-Canadian community was significant, but after that it grew very slowly. By contrast, the size of the English-Canadian community grew rapidly, swelled by waves of immigrants from the British Isles.

At the time of Confederation, the ethnic composition of Canada was fairly homogenous. The first census in 1871 revealed that exactly 60 percent of the new dominion's 3,485,761 citizens reported their origin as the United Kingdom (the largest group being from Ireland) and 31 percent as French-Canadian. The next-largest ethnic group were Germans, who made up 6 percent.[5] Patterns of immigration over the next century altered the mix of the population, but not the continued dominance of the two so-called "founding" groups. The continuous flow of immigrants from Britain was augmented by those who came from Asia to work the transcontinental railroad; by immigrants from northern, central, and eastern Europe who contributed to the expansion of the prairies in the first decades of the century; and by some Americans. The diversity in the immigrant pool increased after the Second World War and the huge dislocation caused by that conflict and the Cold War. In the late 1960s, with the liberalization of the rules governing immigration, Canada's ethnicity diversified further, with increased immigration from the Caribbean, Africa, the Middle East, the Indian subcontinent, and east Asia. Crises in international politics during the postwar period also had an effect. There were marked increases in immigration to Canada after the Hungarian revolt was crushed by the intervention of the Soviet Union in 1956; after the Soviet intervention in Czechoslovakia in

---

4 Max Weber argued that ethnic groups were "those human groups that entertain a subjective belief in their common descent because of similarities of physical type or of customs or both, or because of memories of colonization and migration; conversely, it does not matter whether or not an objective blood relationship exists." Richard Swedberg and Ola Agevall, *The Max Weber Dictionary: Key Words and Central Concepts* (Stanford: Stanford University Press, 2005), 91–92. This usage differs from colloquial use, which often conceives of an "ethnic group" as a subordinate group within a larger national community, often applied to groups of immigrants.

5 Figures from C.P. Stacey, *Canada and the Age of Conflict*, vol. 1: *1867–1921* (Toronto: Macmillan, 1977), 4–5.

1968; after Idi Amin Dada expelled Ugandans of Asian extraction in 1972; and after Vietnam expelled the Hoa—Vietnamese of Chinese extraction—in 1978 and 1979. Likewise, war, instability, and poverty also prompt movement. In the 1970s, immigration from Lebanon increased after the outbreak of civil war there; in the 1980s, migrants fled the wars in Central America; in the 1990s, large numbers left the civil wars that wracked the former Yugoslavia. Between 2001 and 2006, the top 10 countries of origin for immigrants were (in descending order of numbers) China, India, Philippines, Pakistan, the United States, South Korea, Romania, Iran, Britain, and Colombia.[6]

Because of the marginalization of First Nations in the process of European settlement, the fundamental cleavage in Canadian politics was historically between English-Canadians and French-Canadians. That historical duality and the ethnic diversity of subsequent waves of immigrants have both had an impact on Canadian foreign policy—but in different ways.

Historical Duality

As we will see in the next chapter, historically French-speaking and English-speaking Canadians had very different worldviews and very different conceptions about the appropriate role for their country in world politics. And each group projected its foreign policy interests largely on the basis of ethnicity. Canadians of English extraction manifested an often jingoistic concern for the British Empire of which they were a part, and for Britain, from whence they had come. One measure of this sentiment was the tendency to refer to Britain as the "Mother Country" in political discourse. French Canadians, by contrast, had little such emotional attachment to Britain, even less attachment to the Empire, and virtually no comparable emotional attachment to the idea that France was Canada's other "Mother Country." Having long before been abandoned by that "mother," French Canadians tended to define their foreign policy interests in primarily unhyphenated terms. Indeed, for most French Canadians, relations with English Canada—galvanized by such issues as Ontario's Regulation 17 that banned the teaching of French—loomed larger than foreign affairs.[7]

Importantly, neither side could accept the other's *Weltanschauung* as legitimate in the context of Canadian politics. As we will see in Chapter 5, it was not uncommon for English-Canadians to brand French-Canadian opposition to wars that did not involve Canadian interests directly as "treason." There was, as a consequence, constant uneasiness between the two groups. The chagrin of each with the other's view on world politics was reflected, often most virulently, in foreign affairs for a half-century from the Boer War until the end of the Second World War.

The culmination of these tensions between the two occurred over the issue of conscription during the First World War, a crisis comparable to the hanging of Louis Riel 30 years earlier. While English-speaking Canadians regarded conscription as both legitimate and essential, French-speaking Canadians had a different view. Contrary to popular belief in English

---

6 "Canada's Newcomers: Immigration Patterns," CBC News, December 4, 2007, available http://www.cbc.ca/news/background/immigration/patterns.html; also Elizabeth Riddell-Dixon, "Assessing the Impact of Recent Immigration Trends on Canadian Foreign Policy," in David Carment and David Bercuson, eds., *The World in Canada: Diaspora, Demography, and Domestic Politics* (Montréal and Kingston: McGill-Queen's University Press, 2008), 31–49.

7 Gérard Filteau, *Le Québec, le Canada et la guerre 1914–1918* (Montréal: Éditions de l'Aurore, 1977), 19–25.

Canada, Québécois, including the "nationalistes," were not opposed to Canada's participation in the Great War—provided that those who answered the call to arms were volunteers and were not being forced to fight overseas through conscription. Following the introduction of conscription, the seizure of a young man of military age by military police led to riots in Montréal and Québec City. Seven hundred soldiers from Toronto were deployed; on Easter Monday 1918, some troops trapped in a Québec City square by rioters opened fire on the crowd, killing four passersby and wounding numerous demonstrators.[8]

These events severely tested national unity. As we will see in the next chapter, William Lyon Mackenzie King, the prime minister for much of the interwar era, constantly sought to avoid finding himself in the same situation as Sir Robert Borden, the prime minister who introduced conscription. However, when King did face his own conscription crisis during the Second World War, the impact was not as traumatic, though it does permit us to see just how deep the divisions between the two language groups were.[9]

By the end of the Second World War, these divisions had begun to blur. In 1949, the new prime minister, Louis St. Laurent, could lead what he termed a "crusade" to convince the population, particularly those Québécois who were always mistrustful of overseas military engagements, that Canada should join the new Atlantic alliance then being negotiated.[10] While Québécois supported both the North Atlantic Treaty of 1949 and Canadian participation in international peacekeeping when it emerged in the 1950s,[11] the cleavage over military expeditions overseas would reappear on a number of occasions in the years after the Second World War: during the Korean War (1950–1953), over the 1991 Persian Gulf war, and over the mission in Afghanistan after 2001.[12] Only in the case of Canada's participation in the NATO intervention in Kosovo in 1999 would we see support for military action in Québec similar to that among English Canadians.[13]

---

8 Desmond Morton, *A Military History of Canada* (Toronto: McClelland & Stewart, 1999), 157.

9 Even before war had broken out in 1939, King had promised not to introduce conscription (a promise that proved handy in the defeat of Maurice Duplessis's Union Nationale by the provincial Liberals in the October 1939 election and equally handy in the reelection of the federal Liberals in the March 1940 federal elections). However, as the opposition Conservatives sought to make conscription an issue, King decided to try to take the issue off the agenda by holding a plebiscite that asked voters to release the federal government from its promise not to introduce conscription. In the vote, held in April 1942, 80 percent of English-speaking Canadians voted yes while 85 percent of French-speaking Quebeckers voted no. In the event, it was not until 1944 that King had to implement conscription; almost 13,000 conscripts were sent overseas. Of this number, 313 were wounded and 69 killed. C.P. Stacey, *Arms, Men and Government: The War Policies of Canada, 1939–1945* (Ottawa: Queen's Printer, 1970), 479.

10 James Eayrs, *In Defence of Canada*, vol. 4: *Growing Up Allied* (Toronto: University of Toronto Press, 1980), 51; C.P. Stacey, *Canada and the Age of Conflict: A History of Canadian External Policies*, vol. 2: *1921–1948: The Mackenzie King Era* (Toronto: University of Toronto Press, 1981), 416–7.

11 James Ian Gow, "Les Québécois, la guerre et la paix, 1945–1960," *Canadian Journal of Political Science* 3:1 (March 1970), 88–122.

12 Jean-Christophe Boucher and Stéphane Roussel, "From Afghanistan to 'Quebecistan': Quebec as the Pharmakon of Canadian Foreign and Defence Policy," in Jean Daudelin and Daniel Schwanen, eds., *Canada Among Nations 2007: What Room for Manoeuvre?* (Montréal and Kingston: McGill-Queen's University Press, 2008), 128–56.

13 Kim Richard Nossal and Stéphane Roussel, "Canada and the Kosovo War: The Happy Follower," in Pierre Martin and Mark R. Brawley, eds., *Alliance Politics, Kosovo, and NATO's War: Allied Force or Forced Allies?* (New York: Palgrave, 2000), 181–99.

Contemporary Diversity

Canada's original duality has been overlaid by the consequences of an expanded pool of immigrants that has resulted in a much more diverse population. Many recent immigrants, no less than the newly arrived English in the nineteenth century, have been prone to define their foreign policy interests in terms of ethnicity. These interests are diverse. More often than not, these groups are most concerned with the maintenance of good relations between their adopted nation and their original homeland, seeking such functional goals as the negotiation of trade agreements or direct flights between Canada and their countries.

But often the interests are overtly political. For example, one of the prime objectives of the Canada–Israel Committee, an umbrella group established by the Canadian Jewish Congress, B'nai B'rith and the Canadian Zionist Federation, is to achieve a sympathetic "tilt" in Canada's policies toward Israel and the conflict in the Middle East. Groups such as the Canadian Islamic Congress, the Canadian Arab Federation, and the Arab Palestine Association seek to achieve a rather different end. In this, Canada becomes what David Taras and David Goldberg have called a "domestic battleground"[14] in which the positions of protagonists in the Middle East are reproduced and replayed—albeit without the lethal violence—in Canada, not only against each other, but often involving the state.[15]

At times groups are propelled into the political arena in Canada by a major event in their former homeland. After the Beijing massacre of June 4, 1989, when hundreds were killed as soldiers began clearing Tiananmen Square of pro-democracy protestors who had been camped there, Canadians of Chinese descent and many of the 7000 students from China in Canada on student visas helped well-established groups like the Federation of Chinese Canadians and the Chinese Canadian National Council organize large public demonstrations across Canada in the days after the massacre.[16] In March 1999, when Canadian CF-18s started dropping bombs on targets in Serbia, large numbers of Serbian Canadians and their supporters turned out for protests across the country; the largest protests occurred in Toronto, where for two nights the protestors turned violent, throwing a Molotov cocktail into the U.S. Consulate on University Avenue, pelting the building with eggs, paint, stones, and bottles, breaking windows, and assaulting police officers and firefighters who arrived to put out the fire in the consulate.[17] In April and May 2009, as the Sri Lankan army seized control of territory held by the Tamil Tigers, surrounding their final military base, thousands of members of Canada's Tamil community started a series of protests, joining Tamils in other countries. In Ottawa, some 30,000 Tamils inaugurated

---

14 David Taras and David Goldberg, eds., *The Domestic Battleground: Canada and the Arab–Israeli Conflict* (Montréal and Kingston: McGill-Queen's University Press, 1989); also David Howard Goldberg, *Foreign Policy and Ethnic Interest Groups: American and Canadian Jews Lobby for Israel* (Westport, CT: Greenwood Press, 1990).

15 For example, the Canadian Arab Federation (http://www.caf.ca/HomePage.aspx) and B'nai B'rith (http://www.bnaibrith.ca) quarrelled over a series of issues. The dispute between the Canadian Arab Federation and the Conservative government of Stephen Harper is discussed below.

16 Among the more imaginative protests were the efforts of a group of students in Montréal. When the Chinese government set up a "hot line" to encourage people to turn in protestors, they dialled these numbers round the clock to keep the lines occupied. The sizeable long-distance bills from this operation were paid for by a Chinese-Canadian businessman.

17 "NATO Hits Serbs Harder; Toronto Protest Turns Ugly," *Globe and Mail*, March 26, 1999, A1, A19; "Third Night of Protests Passes Without Incident," *Globe and Mail*, March 27, 1999, A18.

a "nonstop" protest that closed much of the area around Parliament Hill for much of April. In Toronto, even larger protests closed down much of the downtown in May; on May 10, thousands of protestors swarmed the Gardiner Expressway, trapping thousands of motorists.[18]

Frequently, ethnic communities in Canada will be internally divided, reflecting the political divisions in their country of origin. In December 1982, when President Zia ul-Haq of Pakistan paid a visit to Ottawa, he was greeted by very different messages from Canadians of Pakistani origin. Some took out advertisements welcoming Zia, while others, such as the Council of Concerned Pakistanis Abroad, loudly protested the human rights violations by his regime.[19] Likewise, when Premier Li Peng of China paid an official visit to Canada in October 1995, he was greeted by angry advertisements from some groups of Chinese Canadians condemning his role in the Tiananmen massacre, while other Canadians of Chinese origin participated in the dinners held in his honour.

In other cases, the foreign policy interests expressed by ethnic communities will focus on long-standing desires for independence for their original homelands. At different times in history, members of the Armenian, Baltic, Palestinian, Sikh, Tamil, and Ukrainian communities in Canada were active in pressing the government in Ottawa to incorporate their concerns in Canada's relations with the "occupying" states. However, virtually every effort to secure Canadian government support for separatist causes has been unsuccessful, for Ottawa, with its eye firmly fixed on the souverainiste movement in Québec, and with the adage that those who live in glass houses do not throw stones firmly in mind, has steadfastly avoided giving any irredentist or separatist group comfort. Indeed, Pierre Elliott Trudeau managed to create a furore over his attempts to maintain a correct Canadian posture in the case of the Nigerian civil war. Asked by reporters about Canadian policy toward the break-away Nigerian state of Biafra, Trudeau quipped, "Where's Biafra?" While many commentators took this as Trudeau's indifference toward the plight of Biafrans, it was intended to convey the correct Canadian position that it did not recognize the breakaway state, not even to the point of the prime minister speaking its name.[20]

Likewise, during the Cold War era, Ukrainian Canadians tried vainly to move the government in Ottawa to recognize Ukraine as a country "occupied" by the Soviet Union, similar to the Baltic states of Estonia, Latvia, and Lithuania.[21] The Canadian government tended to be consistent in maintaining that Ukraine was an integral part of the Soviet Union. It was not until August 1991, following the coup d'état in the Soviet Union against Mikhail S. Gorbachev, that Brian Mulroney finally crossed what the *Globe and Mail*

---

18 "Frantic to Press Their Case, Tamils Swarm Gardiner," *Globe and Mail*, May 11, 2009, A1.

19 Elizabeth Riddell-Dixon, *The Domestic Mosaic: Domestic Groups and Canadian Foreign Policy* (Toronto: Canadian Institute of International Affairs, 1985), 3.

20 Trudeau admitted in his foreign policy memoirs that his quip was "unhelpful": Ivan Head and Pierre Elliott Trudeau, *The Canadian Way: Shaping Canada's Foreign Policy, 1968–1984* (Toronto: McClelland & Stewart, 1995), 103; J.L. Granatstein and Robert Bothwell, *Pirouette: Pierre Trudeau and Canadian Foreign Policy* (Toronto: University of Toronto Press, 1990), 277.

21 Samuel J. Nesdoly, "Changing Perspectives: The Ukrainian-Canadians' Role in Canadian–Soviet Relations," in Aloysius Balawyder, ed., *Canadian–Soviet Relations, 1939–1980* (Oakville, ON: Mosaic Press, 1981), 107–27; Roy Norton, "Ethnic Groups and Conservative Foreign Policy," in Nelson Michaud and Kim Richard Nossal, eds., *Diplomatic Departures: The Conservative Era in Canadian Foreign Policy, 1984–1993* (Vancouver: UBC Press, 2001), 241–59.

termed "a forbidden line"[22] and shifted decades of Canadian policy in one stroke. Mulroney promised that if the decision of the independence referendum scheduled for December 1, 1991 was positive, Canadian recognition of Ukraine would follow. And he was as good as his word: After the referendum Ottawa extended recognition to Ukraine and later moved to open a Canadian embassy in Kiev.[23]

In rare cases, the advocacy of ethnic groups in Canada on behalf of political causes in their homelands takes a lethal form. Indeed, the only major acts of terrorism and political assassination in Canada since the terrorist campaigns of the Front de libération du Québec (FLQ) in the 1960s have been committed by those associated with the quest for independence for Armenia and Khalistan. Armenian terrorists shot and seriously wounded a Turkish diplomat in April 1982 and assassinated the Turkish military attaché in August of that year. In March 1985, a group calling itself the Armenian Revolutionary Army attacked the Turkish embassy in Ottawa, killing a Canadian security guard.

The worst case of terrorism in Canada involved a double aircraft bombing by supporters of the creation of an independent Sikh state of Khalistan. On June 23, 1985, a bomb in a suitcase that had been checked through to Bombay on a Canadian Pacific Airlines flight from Vancouver exploded at Narita airport in Tokyo, killing two Japanese baggage handlers; almost simultaneously, Air India flight 182 from Toronto to London—which had connected with a flight from Vancouver—exploded over the north Atlantic, killing all 329 abroad, including 270 Canadians.[24]

Canada has also been used as a sanctuary or base of operations by foreign terrorists. In the 1990s, there were two high-profile cases of failed terrorist bomb plots in the United States that involved terrorists who had crossed the border from Canada. In July 1997, Gazi Ibrahim Abu Mezer, a Palestinian who had been admitted to Canada on a student visa and had crossed into the United States, was arrested when New York City police raided an apartment and found bombs, suicide vests, and evidence that Mezer and another Palestinian were planning a bomb attack on the New York subway system.[25] In December

---

22 Ross Howard, "Tit for Tat? Ottawa Crosses a Forbidden Line," *Globe and Mail*, August 31, 1991, D5.

23 Kim Richard Nossal, "The Politics of Circumspection: Canadian Policy Towards the Soviet Union, 1985–1991," *International Journal of Canadian Studies* 9 (Spring 1994), 27–45; Nelson Michaud and Kim Richard Nossal, "The Conservative Era in Canadian Foreign Policy, 1984–93," in Michaud and Nossal, eds., *Diplomatic Departures*, 20–21.

24 Stewart Bell, *Cold Terror: How Canada Nurtures and Exports Terrorism Around the World* (Toronto: John Wiley and Sons, 2007), 23–46. Inderjit Singh Reyat, of Duncan, B.C., was the only suspect convicted for the bombings; in 1991 he was found guilty of manslaughter in the Narita bombing and sentenced to ten years; in 2003 he was found guilty of manslaughter in the case of the Air India bombing, and sentenced to an additional five years. He was released in July 2008.

25 Mezer had tried to sneak into the United States three times through the woods along the Washington–British Columbia border. On the first two occasions, in June 1996, he was arrested and sent back to Canada. On the third occasion, in January 1997, Canada refused to take him back, and the U.S. Immigration and Naturalization Service moved to deport him from the United States. However, a friend posted bond and Mezer was released. He moved to Brooklyn, where he was planning a suicide attack when he was arrested. When the story came to light, there was such a furore that the U.S. Department of Justice conducted an investigation that revealed, inter alia, how easy it was to gain entry to Canada. United States, Department of Justice, Office of the Inspector General, *Bombs in Brooklyn: How the Two Illegal Aliens Arrested for Plotting to Bomb the New York Subway Entered and Remained in the United States*, March 1998, available http://www.usdoj.gov/oig/special/9803.

1999, Ahmed Ressam, an Algerian, was arrested at Port Angeles getting off the ferry from Victoria with nitroglycerin and timers in his car in an al-Qaeda plot to bomb Los Angeles International Airport on New Year's Eve.[26] After 9/11, and particularly after the 7/7 attacks in Britain in 2005, there was increased sensitivity to the threat of attacks from so-called "home-grown" terrorists—those who were raised in Canada but who had sympathies with Islamist terrorism. Over the summer of 2006, 18 Muslim men were arrested in Toronto and charged with terrorism offences.[27]

Egoistic Interests

An individual's egoistic interests are those concerned with their own material and physical well-being. In the context of international policy, such interests would include economic well-being and individual security—the relative freedom of the individual, as a member of the political community, from the fear of physical or economic threats to personal values emanating from outside the state.

Material or Economic Interests

As we noted in Chapter 2, much of Canada's wealth derives from the production and export of a wide range of raw materials, processed and manufactured goods, and services. The interest of individuals in their material well-being will prompt them to protect their economic interests. In international policy, this interest is persistently in evidence as Canadians seek to maximize their individual, corporate, organizational, class, and occupational well-being. The range of these economic interests is wide and varied, as can be seen by the following suggestive examples from three groups—business, organized labour, and agriculture.

The protection and advancement of the interests of business occur both at the level of the individual firm and at the associational level. Individual firms that are affected by international developments or by changes in government policy will seek to maximize their parochial economic interests through political demands made directly to the state. Such interests will range from macro concerns like Canada's negotiating position at the Doha Round of trade negotiations to micro concerns like negotiating special pre-clearance arrangements for its products.

Businesses also organize to press the collective interests of their particular industries. These groups will lobby government about concerns on defence policy and procurement, international trade policy, tariffs on imports, export promotion of the wide range of natural

---

26 It was discovered that Ressam had entered Canada on a forged French passport, but had applied for (and received) a valid Canadian passport under a false name. Bell, *Cold Terror*, 148–74. For a discussion of the wider implications of the Ressam case for Canada–U.S. relations, see David G. Haglund, "North American Cooperation in an Era of Homeland Security," *Orbis* 47:4 (Fall 2003), 675–91.

27 At the time of their arrest, news reports indicated that the members of the cell were planning to bomb the CN Tower, the Canadian Security Intelligence Service offices in Toronto, and the Toronto Stock Exchange; they were also planning to storm the Parliament buildings in Ottawa and try to behead Prime Minister Stephen Harper. While charges against seven of the "Toronto 18," as they came to be known, were eventually stayed, the others went to trial. By September 2009, one had been convicted and three others had pleaded guilty to various terrorism charges. For the uncontested statement of facts in the case against Saad Khalid, who pleaded guilty and was sentenced to 14 years in prison, see http://www.theglobeandmail.com/news/national/uncontested-statement-of-facts-in-khalid-case/article1275256.

resources and manufactured goods produced in Canada, and on such related matters as international industrial standards, intellectual property, Canada's labour policies, environmental protection, and international development assistance.

Of considerable importance are the umbrella groups that press not the interests of a particular industry or sector but those of business as a whole. These associations are all well endowed by their members, highly institutionalized, and permanently embedded fixtures of the policymaking scene in Ottawa.[28] The peak association is the Canadian Council of Chief Executives—formerly the Business Council on National Issues, which was active in the 1980s pressing for a free-trade agreement with the United States. The CCCE is a group of approximately 150 chief executive officers of leading firms with revenues of $800 billion whose mission is to shape the public policy agenda in such areas as fiscal, taxation, trade, competition, energy, environmental, education, and corporate governance policies. The president and CEO of the CCCE is John Manley, who was deputy prime minister under Jean Chrétien and served in a range of portfolios, including foreign affairs, industry, and finance. The CCCE played a key role in reshaping the North American integration agenda following 9/11, when increasing concern about terrorism caused the U.S. government to increase the difficulty of crossing the border, a process known as "thickening" the border or the "re-bordering" of North America.[29] Concerned about the impact on trade of longer wait times at the border, Thomas d'Aquino, then president of the CCCE, launched was called the North American Security and Prosperity Initiative. The initiative pushed for a "reinvention" of North American borders to create "a zone of cooperation encompassing the continent" that would allow North America to be "open to business but closed to terrorism"; the harmonization of regulatory frameworks; the negotiation of a resource security pact; the creation of a "North American defence community of sovereign nations"; and the creation of "specialized joint commissions" to implement these initiatives.[30] Other peak business groups include the Canadian Chamber of Commerce, whose mission includes advocacy and policy inputs on a range of issues. In 2008, the Chamber's reports included a report on the Canada–U.S. border and several submissions on such issues as immigration and global competition policy. In Québec, the Conseil du Patronat du Québec has a similar mission. Canadian Manufacturers & Exporters, or CME, was formed by a merger of the Canadian Manufacturers' Association and the Canadian Exporters Association in 1996; it works to improve competitiveness and expand exports. It maintains a representative in Washington who works with the Canadian embassy and other interest groups to lobby members of Congress and government departments on issues of concern. In 2009 CME lobbied hard against the "Buy American" provisions of the American Recovery and Reinvestment Act, the stimulus package adopted to deal with the global financial crisis of 2008. The Recovery Act's provisions excluded Canadian firms from bidding on state or municipal projects funded by this package, even though American firms would be free to bid on provincial or

---

28 John Kirton and Blair Dimock, "Domestic Access to Government in the Canadian Foreign Policy Process, 1968–1982," *International Journal* 39:1 (Winter 1983–4), 95; Riddell-Dixon, *Domestic Mosaic*, 8.

29 Thomas J. Biersteker, "The Rebordering of North America? Implications for Conceptualizing Borders After September 11," in Peter Andreas and Biersteker, eds., *The Rebordering of North America: Integration and Exclusion in a New Security Context* (New York: Routledge, 2003), 153–66.

30 Canadian Council of Chief Executives, *Security and Prosperity: Toward a New Canada–United States Partnership in North America*, January 2003, available http://www.ceocouncil.ca/en/publications/publications.php.

municipal projects funded by Canada's $40 billion stimulus package included in the budget of February 2009. This group established provincial divisions in 1919; the Québec division of CME is MEQ (Manufacturiers et exportateurs du Québec).

But the collective efforts of business are also occasionally more ad hoc. For example, in the national debate over the free-trade agreement in 1987 and 1988, a number of businesses and business groups formed an advocacy group for free trade—the Canadian Alliance for Trade and Job Opportunities—and recruited two prominent public figures, Peter Lougheed and Donald Macdonald, as co-chairs. Lougheed, a Progressive Conservative, was until November 1985 the premier of Alberta and a persistent supporter of free trade. Macdonald was a former Liberal cabinet minister and chair of the Royal Commission on the Economic Union and Development Prospects for Canada. As commissioner, he became convinced of the need for a free-trade agreement with the United States, and the commission's final report recommended that option. However, the report did not appear until September 1985—well after the 1984 election that brought Brian Mulroney to power, and after Mulroney had already embraced the idea. Macdonald, who had broken with the Liberal party over John Turner's rejection of a free-trade agreement, spent 18 months touring the country giving speeches in support of the pact (for which yeoman service Mulroney was to appoint him in August 1988 as Canada's high commissioner to London).

It is a useful reminder about how the political and economic environment can change over time to reflect the role of business interests in earlier debates on free trade with the United States. In both the 1891 and 1911 general elections, free trade—then called "reciprocity"—was the key issue, and on each occasion, those whose economic interests would have been negatively affected—primarily the manufacturers who were protected by the high tariff walls erected by Sir John A. Macdonald's National Policy—tried to generate anti-American feeling in Canada in order to defeat reciprocity. In 1891, the business community distributed propaganda with slogans such as "Keep Out the Wolves."[31] In 1911, the Liberal government of Sir Wilfrid Laurier, which had negotiated a free-trade agreement and fought an election on the issue, went down to defeat in a wave of anti-American sentiment generated in large part by the business community.

Organized labour in Canada also has international policy interests, but tends to define them primarily in the context of the well-being of union members.[32] Particular Canadian unions have pressed interests they wish to see advanced via international policy, both parochial (protection of jobs and industries, access to foreign markets) and global (promotion of free-trade unionism in other countries, entrenchment of international labour and environmental standards, and advancement of particular causes). While the involvement of most unions in international issues tends to be episodic and on occasion inflammatory,[33] some of the larger unions, such as the Canadian Auto Workers (CAW) or the Canadian Union of Public Employees, together with the labour movement's peak associations, the Canadian Labour Congress, and the Confédération

---

31 On the 1891 election, see Patricia K. Wood, "Defining 'Canadian': Anti-Americanism and Identity in Sir John A. Macdonald's Nationalism," *Journal of Canadian Studies* 36:2 (Summer 2001), 56; J.L. Granatstein, *Yankee Go Home? Canadians and Anti-Americanism* (Toronto: HarperCollins, 1996), 48–49.

32 Canadian labour groups and their interests are surveyed in Riddell-Dixon, *Domestic Mosaic*, 24–28.

33 For example, under the leadership of Sid Ryan, president of the Ontario division of the Canadian Union of Public Employees Ontario since 1992, CUPE Ontario voted in May 2006 to sanction Israel

des Syndicats Nationaux (CSN) in Québec, maintain international departments, take stands on global issues, and engage in international solidarity activities.

On occasion, internationalist goals will conflict with the economic interests of a labour organization's membership. Throughout the 1970s, the Canadian Labour Congress maintained a long-standing opposition to the liberalization of trade, advocating instead the maintenance of high duties and quotas designed to minimize the flow of textiles and shoes from the global South (though it tried to mitigate the protectionist nature of this position by arguing that because these products were produced by low-paid labour, importing them encouraged exploitation of workers in low-wage countries). In the 1980s, the CLC strongly opposed the free-trade initiative from its inception, fearing that one of the significant results of freer trade would be large-scale unemployment, particularly in branch-plant secondary manufacturing industries. However, with the entrenchment of free trade in North America in the 1990s and the rise of globalization in the 2000s, the position of the CLC has gone in a different direction. Following the lead of the CSN in Québec, the CLC embraced what Ian Robinson has called an "internationalist turn."[34] While the CLC continued to oppose anything that smacks of trade liberalization—including the North American Free Trade Agreement, the World Trade Organization, the Multilateral Agreement on Investment, the Free Trade Area of the Americas, and the Security and Prosperity Partnership—it embraced a more internationalist agenda that in its essence seeks to reform international institutions and their rules. This "turn" involved taking a more active role, engaging in political action such as opposing the Canada–Colombia free-trade agreement of 2009 and speaking out on such issues as the civil war in Sri Lanka or ethnic conflict in Kenya. The turn also saw the CLC mount its own Labour International Development Program, which runs projects in 26 countries in Africa, Asia, the Middle East, and Central and South America on a cost-shared basis with the Canadian International Development Agency (CIDA).[35]

Another important producer group with economic interests in foreign policy is agriculture.[36] However, the diversity of agricultural production means that the interests of this sector are not uniform. As we noted in Chapter 2, Canadian agricultural producers are

---

for what were described as Israel's "apartheid-like policies." In January 2009, CUPE Ontario called for any professor who was Israeli to be banned from Ontario universities unless they explicitly criticized Israel. The January 2, 2009 press release was quickly taken down from its website after a storm of protest erupted, including a rebuke by Paul Moist, CUPE's national president, and calls for Ryan's resignation by members of CUPE local 3902 at the University of Toronto. Ryan's campaign against Israel between 2006 and 2009 was widely condemned and criticized as both anti-Semitic and bigoted, with the eventual boycott resolution described by one critic as a "low point in the proud history of the Canadian labour movement's involvement in international affairs." See "CUPE Passes Milder Anti-Israel Resolution," *National Post*, February 23, 2009.

34 Ian Robinson, "The International Dimension of Labour Federation Economic Strategy in Canada and the United States, 1947–2000," in Jeffrey Harrod and Robert O'Brien, eds., *Global Unions? Theory and Strategies of Organized Labour in the Global Political Economy* (London: Routledge, 2002), 124.

35 Details of these activities are available http://canadianlabour.ca.

36 Grace Skogstad, *The Politics of Agricultural Policy-Making in Canada* (Toronto: University of Toronto Press, 1987); Theodore H. Cohn, "Canada and the Ongoing Impasse over Agricultural Protection," in Claire Cutler and Mark Zacher, eds., *Canadian Foreign Policy and International Economic Regimes* (Vancouver: UBC Press, 1992), 62–88; Andrew F. Cooper, *In Between Countries: Australia, Canada, and the Search for Order in Agricultural Trade* (Montréal and Kingston: McGill-Queen's University Press, 1998).

sharply divided into two groups. On the one hand, there are those, primarily but not exclusively in the west, who produce grains, oilseed, and beef. On the other hand, although the dairy, egg, and poultry industries operate across Canada, they are concentrated in Ontario and Québec. Despite this difference, all Canadian agricultural producers have been affected by the patterns of global politics.

Beginning in the early 1960s, a major shift in grain exports was initiated by the Progressive Conservative government of John Diefenbaker. Despite his propensity for anti-communist rhetoric[37] and his opposition expressed earlier in the 1950s to selling food to communist countries, Diefenbaker presided over a radical transformation in the pattern of grain exports. In February 1961, his government announced that it had signed a credit agreement for the sale of grain to the People's Republic of China, which was beset not only by the economic chaos caused by Mao Zedong's failed efforts to industrialize China rapidly—the "Great Leap Forward"—but also by three successive crop failures that produced massive famines across China. Exports to the PRC jumped from $8.7 million in 1960 to $147.4 million in 1962.[38] Likewise, the Soviet Union and Eastern Europe became an important, if unsteady, market for Canadian grains during this period. Over the period 1963 to 1979, an average of 20 percent of Canada's annual grain exports went to the Soviet Union and Eastern Europe.[39] By the late 1970s, Canada's dominance in these markets was unrivalled by the world's other major grain exporters, Argentina, Australia, and the United States.

However, the interests of Canadian farmers became heavily dependent on the state of great-power relations. The Canadian dominance in the China market in the 1960s was helped by the enmity between Beijing and Washington and by strong fears of the PRC in Canberra that kept Australia from selling wheat to China. But when relations between China and the West improved in the 1970s, both the United States and Australia began to compete aggressively in the China market. Likewise, the deterioration of East–West relations in the late 1970s culminated in an attempt to use grain exports as a technique of Western statecraft. This time another Progressive Conservative prime minister, Joe Clark, sought to stop any increase in grain exports to the Soviet Union by joining the partial grain embargo proposed by President Jimmy Carter in January 1980 following the Soviet invasion of Afghanistan. Fortunately for Canadian grain farmers, the embargo quickly fell apart as Americans, Australians, and Canadians watched Argentina expand its shipments to the Soviet Union tenfold. Moreover, Canadians watched Americans try to divert grains originally destined for the Soviet Union to China. By the end of 1980, both Australia and Canada had backed out of the embargo, and Ronald Reagan, who had promised American farmers that he would terminate the ban, had been elected president and brought the United States embargo to an end.[40]

---

37 John G. Diefenbaker, *One Canada: Memoirs of the Right Honourable John G. Diefenbaker*, vol. 2: *The Years of Achievement, 1956 to 1962* (Toronto: Macmillan, 1976), 108–10.

38 Patrick Kyba, "Alvin Hamilton and Sino–Canadian Relations," in Paul M. Evans and B. Michael Frolic, eds., *Reluctant Adversaries: Canada and the People's Republic of China, 1949–1970* (Toronto: University of Toronto Press, 1991), 169.

39 Carl H. McMillan, "Canada's Postwar Economic Relations with the USSR—An Appraisal," in Balawyder, ed., *Canadian–Soviet Relations*, 145, table 4.

40 Robert L. Paarlberg, "The 1980–81 US Grain Embargo: Consequences for the Participants," and John Kirton, "Economic Sanctions and Alliance Consultations: Canada, the United States and the Strains of 1979–82," both in David Leyton-Brown, ed., *The Utility of International Economic Sanctions* (London: Croom Helm, 1987).

Canada's farmers have also been affected by the evolution of the multilateral trading system and the efforts of the various rounds of trade talks—the Uruguay Round (1986–1994), and then the Doha Round that began in 2001 and that despite breaking down in 2008 is still technically ongoing. As noted above, Canada's farmers are deeply divided over the general trend toward the liberalization of global trade reflected not only in the negotiation of free-trade agreements with the United States and Mexico but also by efforts at a global level at the World Trade Organization. On the one hand, beef and grain farmers are internationally competitive; not surprisingly, these groups favour liberalizing the international market in agriculture as much as possible. On the other hand, the profitability of the dairy, egg, and poultry industries in Canada is largely sustained by a system of supply management that requires the maintenance of protectionist barriers, particularly against imports from the United States.

The differing interests of these two groups are well represented by industry associations. Groups like the Canadian Cattlemen's Association and its Foreign Trade Committee work to "eliminat[e] programs, measures and subsidies that distort world trade." For its part, the Grain Growers of Canada is a peak association of 13 associations and provincial councils that represent approximately 70,000 grain, pulse and oilseed farmers; it pushes for the elimination of export subsidies and reductions in "distorting domestic support."[41]

By contrast, the interests of the 23,500 farmers in the five industries that support (and are supported by) supply management—dairy farmers, producers of hatching eggs and of table eggs, chicken farmers, and turkey farmers—are represented by both provincial and national peak associations. The Dairy Farmers of Canada represents over 13,000 farms and is dedicated to opposing WTO measures that it claims would "devastate" Canada's dairy farms. The Egg Farmers of Canada and the Canadian Hatching Egg Producers represent the 1000 egg producers and the 300 producers of hatching eggs in Canada. Over 2800 chicken farmers and 500 turkey farmers are represented by the Chicken Farmers of Canada and the Turkey Farmers of Canada. In Québec, the Union des produceurs agricoles (l'UPA) is the peak agricultural association, while dairy, egg, and poultry farmers are represented by the Fédération des producteur de lait du Québec, Les Éleveurs de volailles du Québec, the Fédération des producteurs d'oeufs de consommation du Québec, and the Syndicat des producteurs d'oeufs d'incubation du Québec. All these groups are devoted to the maintenance of supply management, which is championed nationally and internationally by coalitions such as the SM5 (Supply Management 5) and the GO5 Coalition (for *Gestion de l'offre*, French for supply management). These coalitions lobby government at the federal and the provincial levels and at the World Trade Organization in Geneva.[42]

Interests in Security

Individuals also have an interest in security, which, in the context of international affairs, means safety from threats of harm emanating from other states. To be sure, over the past half-century our understanding of security has shifted from the traditional idea that security was purely about the military activities of the state, such as the causes of war, military strategy,

---

41 See http://www.cattle.ca/cca-foreign-trade-committee and http://www.ggc-pgc.ca.

42 The positions of these groups on global trade are available: http://www.dairygoodness.ca, http://www.eggs.ca, http://www.cbhema.com, http://www.chicken.ca, http://www.turkeyfarmersofcanada. ca, http://www.upa.qc.ca, and http://www.go5quebec.ca.

the impact of technology on war-fighting, and arms control. Even before the end of the Cold War, students of international relations were reconceptualizing what it meant to be secure in a world dominated by nuclear weapons.[43] During the decade-long post–Cold War era (1991–2001), the end of Soviet–American rivalry and increasing incidence of civil war gave rise to new and expanded understandings of security, with security being "adorned" with adjectives of different sorts: common, comprehensive, collective, cultural, environmental, and human security.[44] After 2001, the string of Islamist terrorist attacks that followed 9/11[45] convinced many that a "new age" had dawned in global politics,[46] spawning yet another renaissance in security studies.[47]

The way Canadians have conceived of security has evolved in a comparable fashion over the years. For much of their history, when Canadians have been concerned about their security, the focus tended to be on the issues of war and peace. It has only been recently that Canadians and their government have expanded the nature of the "threat."

As we noted briefly in the previous chapter, Canadians have rarely been threatened by military aggression. The last serious invasion occurred in 1812, and, by the end of the nineteenth century, the possibility of American invasion was exceedingly remote. And despite the propaganda employed by the government in Ottawa during the two world wars that painted the possibility of an invasion, Canadians never had to worry about anything more than episodic incursions by German U-boats in the waters of the St. Lawrence River. But if they were safe from foreign invasion, Canadians were nonetheless very much touched by the wars of the twentieth century and developed a fear and horror of war that on occasion would be expressed.

Given the gruesomeness of trench warfare and the huge number of Canadians killed, wounded, and permanently disabled in four years of fighting, it should not be surprising that a sizeable peace movement emerged in Canada in the 1920s.[48] In the House of Commons, J.S. Woodsworth and Agnes Macphail pressed the pacifist point of view, calling for the abolition of the Department of National Defence and attacking cadet training as "the most obnoxious part of our whole military establishment" because it created, as Macphail put it,

---

43 For example, R.B.J. Walker, "Security, Sovereignty, and the Challenge of World Politics," *Alternatives* 25 (1990), 3–27; Jessica Tuchman Mathews, "Redefining Security," *Foreign Affairs* 68:2 (Spring 1989), 162–88.

44 Barry Buzan, Ole Wæver, and Jaap de Wilde, *Security: A New Framework for Analysis* (Boulder: Lynne Rienner, 1998); Kim Richard Nossal, "The Adornment of 'Security' in Australia and Canada," *Australian Journal of International Affairs* 49:1 (May 1995), 33–47; on human security, see Roland Paris, "Human Security: Paradigm Shift or Hot Air?" *International Security* 26:2 (Fall 2001), 87–102.

45 Cities where major attacks against "Western" targets by groups claiming a connection to Al-Qaeda or radical Islamism have occurred include Bali (October 2002), Casablanca (May 2003), Riyadh (May 2003), Jakarta (August 2003, September 2004, and July 2009), Madrid (March 2004), London (July 2005), Bali (October 2005), Amman (November 2005), and Mumbai (July 2006 and November 2008).

46 For an excellent and sober reflection on the impact of 9/11, see Caroline Kennedy-Pipe and Nicholas Rengger, "Apocalypse Now? Continuities or Disjunctions in World Politics after 9/11," *International Affairs* 82:3 (May 2006), 539–52.

47 The literature on international security in the post-9/11 era is vast; the best guide for navigating the different approaches is Alan Collins, ed., *Contemporary Security Studies* (New York: Oxford University Press, 2007).

48 On the anti-militarism of this era, see James Eayrs, *In Defence of Canada*, vol. 1: *From the Great War to the Great Depression* (Toronto: University of Toronto Press, 1964), 104–119.

"a bombastic military spirit of toy soldierism."[49] The League of Nations Society in Canada pressed the cause of peace by a wide variety of public education activities, sponsoring speakers, distributing pamphlets and posters, even ensuring that high school instruction about the League was made compulsory in every province but Ontario and Quebec (where local school boards had to approve the use of Society materials).[50] The government in Ottawa was pressed to sign the Kellogg–Briand Pact of 1928, an agreement named after President Calvin Coolidge's secretary of state, Frank B. Kellogg, and Aristide Briand, the French foreign minister, that renounced war as an instrument of foreign policy.[51] And just as students at the University of Oxford declared that they would not fight "for King or country," so too did students debating at McGill University and the University of Toronto in 1934 pass resolutions in favour of pacifism.[52]

The appearance of nuclear weapons in 1945 period produced a different kind of insecurity. There were some Canadians who believed that the existence of such hugely destructive weapons, produced in increasing numbers over the course of the Cold War era, provided security through the dynamic of mutual assured destruction, or MAD.[53] For others, however, nuclear weapons offered no such assurances of safety. On the contrary: these weapons themselves generated a high degree of insecurity, nicely captured by a generation of popular movies: the understated fatalism of *On the Beach* in the 1950s, the nervous satire of *Dr. Strangelove* in the 1960s, and the more nightmarishly explicit movies of the early 1980s—*Testament*, *The Day After*, and *Threads*. Such insecurity was entirely understandable, for the logic of deterrence provided little comfort. By its very nature, deterrence could not be demonstrated, or guaranteed, to work.[54] There was also the fear that the system would break down and that nuclear war would "accidentally" break out as the result of either a technical malfunction or a local or regional crisis. And finally, for some there was simply the nagging feeling that deterrence could not last forever. The conclusion in the face of such insecurity (i.e., lack of safety) seemed obvious: Security could only be assured by the elimination of such weaponry.

During the Cold War, this sense of insecurity led numerous people in Canada and elsewhere to press for a fundamental change in how their safety was assured. There were three

---

49 Canada, Parliament, House of Commons, *Debates, 1926–1927*, April 9, 1927, 2193; "Training of Cadets Warmly Attacked by Woman Member," *Globe and Mail*, April 11, 1927, 2. Also see Mark Howard Moss, *Manliness and Militarism: Educating Young Boys in Ontario for War* (Toronto: University of Toronto Press, 2001), 141–42.

50 Donald Page, "The Institute's 'Popular Arm': The League of Nations Society in Canada," *International Journal* 33:1 (Winter 1977–8), 49.

51 Stacey, *Age of Conflict*, vol. 2, 97–103.

52 On February 9, 1933, merely days after Adolf Hitler came to power in Germany, the Oxford Union debated, and passed by a significant majority, the motion "That this House will in no circumstances fight for its King and Country." Canadian student activity is described in Eayrs, *In Defence of Canada*, vol. 1., 110–12.

53 According to the doctrine of mutual assured destruction, both the Soviet Union and the United States had enough nuclear weapons to destroy each other many times over (the so-called "overkill capacity"); and neither side could destroy the other through a surprise attack. Thus, because if either superpower launched a nuclear attack, both countries would be completely destroyed, both would be deterred from starting a war. That, at least, was the theory.

54 The most cogent argument we have seen on this matter is Leon Wieseltier, "When Deterrence Fails," *Foreign Affairs* 63:4 (Spring 1985), 827–47.

identifiable waves of pacifism in Canada. The first occurred in the late 1950s and faded after 1963 when the first nuclear arms control treaty was signed. The second was in the late 1960s, galvanized by the war in Vietnam. The third came in the early and mid-1980s, sparked by the aggressive line taken by the administration of Ronald Reagan.

In the first period, there were four leading "peace" organizations: the Canadian Committee for the Control of Radiation Hazards, later to become the Canadian Committee for Nuclear Disarmament (CCND); the Combined Universities Campaign for Nuclear Disarmament, both formed in 1959 and modelled after the Campaign for Nuclear Disarmament (CND) in Britain; the Voice of Women (VOW), created in 1960; and the Canadian Peace Research Institute, formed in 1961.[55] These groups pressed the Diefenbaker government to equip three weapons systems that Canada had purchased from the United States (Honest John surface-to-surface missiles, Bomarc surface-to-air missiles, and CF-104 Starfighters) with nuclear weapons.[56]

The second wave occurred in the late 1960s and the early 1970s, an outgrowth of the antiwar movement that swept through Western countries as a result of the escalation of the American involvement in the war in Vietnam. During this period, it was not just nuclear weapons that were the focus of protests, but the dominant position of the United States itself. Antiwar sentiment in Canada thus focused not only on nuclear weapons, but also on Canada's "satellite" status, which we examined in the previous chapter, and its subordinate position in NATO and NORAD, increasingly seen as institutions that tied Canada to American imperialism.[57] To be sure, the antiwar movement of the late 1960s was magnified by what Canadians were seeing south of the border during this period: the racial unrest that flared up in numerous American cities, student protests, and the widespread violence that seemed to be endemic to American society.

The third pacifist wave started in Europe in the late 1980s in response to the deployment of new weapons systems in Europe by the two superpowers. In 1975, the Soviet Union moved to try to eliminate NATO's superiority in intermediate-range ballistic missiles in the European theatre by deploying new SS-20 missiles, which had greater accuracy and longer range. To reassert NATO superiority, Western European governments urged the United States to deploy a new generation of missiles, Pershings and ground-launched cruise missiles, which would carry nuclear warheads. Huge demonstrations were held in Western Europe in the early 1980s to protest this plan. While Canadians were not affected by the Euromissile debate directly, there was an indirect impact: The United States Air Force wanted to be able to test air-launched cruise missiles (ALCMs) and their inertial guidance systems over territory comparable to the Soviet Union. While the missiles being tested would not carry nuclear warheads, there was considerable opposition to the tests

---

55 See Andrew Richter, *Avoiding Armageddon: Canadian Military Strategy and Nuclear Weapons, 1950–1963* (Vancouver: UBC Press, 2002); on the Voice of Women, see Ann Denholm Crosby, "Myths of Canada's Human Security Pursuits: Tales of Tool Boxes, Toy Chests, and Tickle Trunks," in Claire Turenne Sjolander, Heather A. Smith, and Deborah Stienstra, eds., *Feminist Perspectives on Canadian Foreign Policy* (Toronto: Oxford University Press, 2003), 91–94. For a discussion of disarmament diplomacy, see Albert Legault and Michel Fortmann, *A Diplomacy of Hope: Canada and Disarmament, 1945–1988* (Montréal and Kingston: McGill-Queen's University Press, 1992).

56 Jon B. McLin, *Canada's Changing Defense Policy, 1957–1963: The Problems of a Middle Power in Alliance* (Baltimore: Johns Hopkins University Press, 1967), chaps. 4 and 6; Peyton V. Lyon, *Canada in World Affairs*, vol. 12: *1961–1963* (Toronto: Oxford University Press, 1968), 76–222.

57 See the contributions to Stephen Clarkson, ed., *An Independent Foreign Policy for Canada?* (Toronto: McClelland & Stewart, 1968).

because of what were seen as the implications of helping the United States expand its nuclear arsenal.[58] Layered onto the concerns about the cruise was the announcement by Ronald Reagan in March 1983 that the United States was planning to pursue the Strategic Defense Initiative (SDI), immediately dubbed "Star Wars." Galvanized by a large number of advocacy and citizens groups concerned with peace, such as the Canadian Peace Alliance, Operation Dismantle, Project Ploughshares, and Science for Peace,[59] massive "Refuse the Cruise" and anti–Star Wars protests erupted across the country, with tens of thousands of Canadians engaging in street demonstrations, peace camps, and other political activities, and pushing the idea that Canada should become a neutral country.[60]

The peace movement, which had grown so dramatically in the 1980s, dissipated almost completely in the post–Cold War era. Antiwar protests did occur, sometimes on a massive scale. For example,in the weeks before the start of the Gulf War in January 1991, 150,000 protestors clogged the streets of Montréal.[61] In other cities there were demonstrations, candlelight vigils, and public protests featuring slogans imported from the United States— "No Blood for Oil"—and the refrain from John Lennon's "Give Peace a Chance." Since then there have been other antiwar protests, often to protest wars in other countries— against Canadian participation in the NATO bombing of Serbia in 1999, discussed above; against the U.S.-led invasion of Iraq in 2003; against Canadian policy toward the Lebanon war in 2006; and against the Sri Lankan attacks on the Tamil Tigers in 2009. But none has moved as many Canadians into political action as the peace movement did in the 1980s.

The Canadian mission in Afghanistan that began in 2001 galvanized a small but robust peace movement dedicated to bringing the mission to an end. As had occurred in the Gulf War of 1991, this movement also imported as their catch-cry an American protest slogan invented for the 2003 Iraq war—"Support our troops. Bring them home"—without any evident irony. The campaign to secure a Canadian withdrawal from Afghanistan was coordinated by several pan-Canadian advocacy groups such as the Canadian Peace Alliance, the Council for Canadians, and the Rideau Institute's "Ceasefire.ca" campaign. But the fact that so many members of the Canadian Armed Forces were dying in the Afghanistan mission had a persistently dampening effect on antiwar demonstrations.

It is true that the terrorist attacks of September 11, 2001 prompted fears that Canada would also be a target, particularly after Osama bin Laden, the leader of Al-Qaeda, the group that carried out the 9/11 attacks, specifically included Canada in a list of Western countries targeted for attack in a message broadcast on Al Jazeera in 2002.[62] But the fear was not as visceral as

---

58 John Clearwater, *"Just Dummies": Cruise Missile Testing in Canada* (Calgary: University of Calgary Press, 2006).

59 Riddell-Dixon, *Domestic Mosaic*, 59, estimates that in Toronto and Vancouver alone there were 250 active peace groups.

60 Although he was not associated with any peace group in particular, one of principal advocates of the neutralist project was the columnist Gwynne Dyer, who produced, with Tina Viljoen, a television series entitled *The Defence of Canada* (1986), which proposed a policy of neutrality comparable to that of Finland. See also Gwynne Dyer, "The Possibility of Canadian Neutrality," in Mel Hurtig, ed., *The True North Strong & Free?* (Vancouver: Gordon Soules Book Publishers, 1987), 123–32.

61 Claire-Andrée Cauchy, "La plus grosse manifestation de l'histoire du Québec," *Le Devoir*, February 17, 2003, A1.

62 "Bin Laden's message," BBC News World Service, November 12, 2002, available http://news.bbc.co.uk/2/hi/middle_east/2455845.stm.

that inspired by the possibility of a nuclear war in the 1980s. The security measures taken by the government in Ottawa after 9/11 were accepted, but not with enthusiasm, mainly because terrorism did not produce the same reaction in Canada as in the United States, where, as Frank Harvey has so cogently pointed out, insecurity and fear of another terrorist attack actually increased as more resources were devoted to homeland security.[63] It is this differential threat perception that explains why there was such tepid support among Canadians for the mission in Afghanistan, even though it was often presented as Canada's principal contribution to the global war on terror.[64] Indeed, for many Canadians, terrorism is seen as a phenomenon that is more effectively tackled by addressing issues of social justice and eliminating poverty than by using armed force. In this sense, the interests in security expressed by many Canadians seem to be more altruistic than egoistic, focusing as they do on the safety of others.

Altruistic Interests

Canadians have historically manifested an interest in the condition of peoples of other countries. We have already examined one manifestation of this—the tendency of groups to feel empathy toward their homelands. Here we focus on empathy of a different sort: interests that Canadians have in the well-being of others in the international system that do not involve ties of ethnicity or desire for material gain. Altruistic interests, like egoistic ones, can be divided into two general sets: those dealing with the material well-being of other individuals and those dealing with their security. These most commonly manifest as interests in international development and human rights.

Development

The concern of Canadians for international development springs most basically from recognition of "the fat cat status which Canada occupies in the community of nations," as John W. Holmes put it.[65] Confronted with evidence of human suffering in other parts of the world— from deprivation, hunger, malnutrition, or disease—the traditional inclination of Canadians, who in the main are wealthy, well-fed, and healthy compared to much of humankind, has been to attempt in some fashion to ameliorate the human condition elsewhere. Much of this inclination is the result of

> the intangible pressures of ethical values. However hard-pressed or insecure they feel economically, and however skeptical they may be of past efforts to alleviate the lot of the world's poor, most citizens of the rich countries are still unable to deny some basic humanitarian impulse, some motive of "human solidarity" or "international social justice" for wanting to end deprivation and suffering.[66]

---

63 Frank Harvey, *The Homeland Security Dilemma: Fear, Failure and the Future of American Security* (New York: Routledge, 2008).

64 See Kim Richard Nossal, "Rethinking the Security Imaginary: Canadian Security and the Case of Afghanistan," in Bruno Charbonneau and Wayne S. Cox, eds., *Locating Global Order: American Power and Canadian Security After 9/11* (Vancouver: UBC Press, forthcoming); Boucher and Roussel, "From Afghanistan to 'Quebecistan.'"

65 John W. Holmes, *Canada: A Middle-Aged Power* (Toronto: McClelland & Stewart, 1976), 293.

66 North–South Institute, *In the Canadian Interest? Third World Development in the 1980s* (Ottawa: North–South Institute, 1980), 27.

One should not overstate the nature of this interest. As Jean-Philippe Thérien and Alain Noël argue, there is a close relationship between Canada's development assistance policies and the institutions of the welfare state, and rises and declines in support for development assistance seem to be strongly linked to shifts in support for the welfare state.[67] Moreover, the interest of Canadians in development is not truly altruistic. The vast majority of Canadians, like other humans, are not altruistic in the true sense of that word toward anyone but kin. Most will respond to evidence of human suffering elsewhere with genuine empathy, but will not be moved to take concrete action. All too easily, the images of human suffering elsewhere are tuned out, the troubled feelings suppressed, and concern passes into either token action—or inaction.

However, numerous Canadians are interested in giving expression to their empathetic feelings. Often this takes a passive form, such as the high levels of support for the government's international development assistance programs in response to a pollster's question. But more frequently it takes an active form, as indicated by the large number of individuals who donate their time, money, and energies in attempts to alleviate suffering elsewhere and the numerous nongovernmental organizations (NGOs) and third-sector groups that exist to assist in international development, ranging from fundraising for development or humanitarian purposes to raising awareness of development issues to actually delivering development programs in the global South.[68] Each group has its own mandate. These include NGOs specifically devoted to development, mostly voluntary agencies, such as the Canadian University Service Overseas (CUSO) and its francophone branch, the Service universitaire canadien outre-mer (SUCO); Inter Pares; Oxfam-Canada and Oxfam-Québec; the Canadian branch of the United Nations International Children's Emergency Fund—UNICEF Canada; the Fondation Paul-Gérin-Lajoie; the World University Service of Canada; World Vision Canada; and the Young Men's Christian Association of Canada.

Other groups are also involved in development assistance. We have noted above that many of the larger unions in Canada maintain development assistance programs. The major churches have organizations specifically for the promotion of development, such as the Catholic Organization for Development and Peace, the Primate's World Relief and Development Fund of the Anglican Church, the Committee on the Church and International Affairs of the United Church, Presbyterian World Service and Development, Lutheran World Relief, and the Mennonite Central Committee.[69] Likewise, a number of women's groups have development programs: the Young Women's Christian Association of Canada, the National Council of Women, the Canadian Federation of Business and Professional Women's Clubs, and MATCH

67 Jean-Philippe Thérien and Alain Noël, "Welfare Institutions and Foreign Aid: Domestic Foundations of Canadian Foreign Policy," *Canadian Journal of Political Science* 27:3 (September 1994), 529–58.

68 Tim Brodhead and Cranford Pratt identify four subsets of NGOs: fundraising branches of international agencies; Canadian development and humanitarian fundraising agencies; nonprofit development agencies; and development education organizations: "Paying the Piper: CIDA and Canadian NGOs," in Cranford Pratt, ed., *Canadian International Development Assistance Policies: An Appraisal*, 2nd ed. (Montréal and Kingston: McGill-Queen's University Press, 1996), 88–90.

69 Bonnie Greene, *Canadian Churches and Foreign Policy* (Toronto: James Lorimer, 1990); Riddell-Dixon, *Domestic Mosaic*, 37–42.

International, a women's group that directly funds development projects initiated and implemented by women in the global South.[70]

This institutional proliferation has also given rise to a number of umbrella groups, including the Protestant Canadian Council of Churches and the Canadian Conference of Catholic Bishops. The key umbrella groups for voluntary agencies, the Canadian Council for International Cooperation and its Quebec organization, l'Association québécoise des organismes de coopération internationale, attempt to coordinate the efforts of their members.

Finally, the private sector has also made a contribution, mainly through partnerships between government, NGOs, and private actors. Canadian corporations, which have useful skills for economic development, make contributions to development assistance projects.[71] Some financial institutions, such as Développement international Desjardins or Vancity (Vancouver City Savings Credit Union), have created microcredit programs to assist small entrepreneurs in developing countries.[72]

The expression of empathetic interests can take various forms. The response of Canadians to the Ethiopian famine in the fall of 1984 and the Indian Ocean tsunami of December 2004 demonstrated the effect that human disasters can have: Huge numbers of Canadians donated money and goods to alleviate the effects of those disasters.[73] However, conclusions should be drawn from these cases with care, for the factors that led to an outpouring of concern in 1984 and 2004 were highly contingent and not easily reproducible. Certainly not every case of human suffering elsewhere in the world will elicit such a response from Canadians. On the contrary, the drought in Mozambique in 1985 that took over 100,000 lives, the 1991 famine in the Horn of Africa, the 1991 cyclone in Bangladesh that killed almost 140,000 people, or the 2003 earthquake in Bam, Iran that killed more than 43,000 people show us another pattern: While in each of these cases, the Canadian government contributed to the relief effort, these disasters did not engage Canadians in the same way.

---

70 Riddell-Dixon, *Domestic Mosaic*, 35–37.

71 Andrea Martinez, "The Telecommunications Equipment Market: Globalization or Selective Regionalization," *Canadian Journal of Communication* 21:2 (1996); Martin Rudner, "Le Canada et le monde en développement: l'aide et le commerce dans le cadre de la nouvelle politique étrangère canadienne," *Études internationales* 27:2 (juin 1996), 381–395.

72 Desjardins: http://www.did.qc.ca; Vancity's International Community Investment Deposit: http://www.vancity.com.

73 In 1984, after television crews "discovered" the famine in Ethiopia, the public response to these images in Canada as elsewhere was massive. Some private initiatives, such as the song "Tears Are Not Enough," which joined "We Are the World" on the charts, were high-profile. But most of the response was at the local level. The flow of donations was so unprecedented that NGOs and the government in Ottawa were hard-pressed to keep pace. In early November, Joe Clark, the external affairs minister, allocated $50 million to a special fund for Africa, promising that some would be used to match private donations; by April 1985, private donations had exceeded those funds by 300 percent. David R. Morrison, *Aid and Ebb Tide: A History of CIDA and Development Assistance* (Waterloo: Wilfrid Laurier University Press, 1998), 234–38. The response in the case of the tsunami that hit the countries around the Indian Ocean on December 26, 2004, killing almost 225,000 people and leaving more than 10 million homeless, was similar: governments, both federal and provincial, led the way in donations, but the public donated $230 million and the business community donated $36 million.

Human Rights

Canadians have also been prone to take an interest in human rights violations elsewhere in the world. As in the case of international development, the interest of Canadians in human rights is neither sustained nor widespread, but they have made a constant appearance in Canadian foreign policy. There were protests in Canada at the treatment of the Boers by the British during the South African War[74] and at the Armenian genocide by Turkish forces after 1915.[75] As the Axis powers expanded in the 1930s, Canadians protested the slaughter of Ethiopians by the invading Italian armies and the treatment of Jews in Nazi Germany. When the Japanese army seized the Chinese capital of Nanjing in 1937, an action that continues to be known as "the rape of Nanjing,"[76] the widespread reaction in Canada was outrage. Japan was Canada's fourth-largest market for exports, primarily strategic metals, and there were thus widespread calls for bans on trade. City councils debated official boycott measures, as did church congregations. Numerous groups, including many "patriotic associations" of Chinese Canadians, organized demonstrations, distributing pamphlets and the paraphernalia of protest such as boycott buttons. The voluntary boycott of Japanese goods, and even of stores owned or run by Japanese Canadians, proved popular.[77] While the protests were not successful—Canada kept trading with Japan until well into 1941—they are instructive. They illustrated not only the sympathy generated by the persecution of other peoples, but also the dilemma that will often haunt those interested in human rights—the choice between commercial interests and the defence of the oppressed.

Before 1945, this interest in the welfare of others tended not to focus on those whose rights were being violated by their own government, but when they were victims of a foreign power's aggression.[78] More often than not, the public seemed to accept implicitly what governments in this era embraced explicitly: that what happened inside a sovereign state, including how a government treated its citizens, was simply no one else's business.

The Second World War changed this. In 1945, the United Nations legitimized the conception of universal human rights, enshrining the idea in the Universal Declaration that was adopted in 1948. That, and the revelations of the full extent of the Holocaust and the fate of both Jews and other Europeans in Nazi death camps, served to change how Canadians have regarded human rights violations. Since then, how other governments treat their citizens has been a constant, if not widespread, focus of Canadian interests. At different times over the postwar period, human rights violations by a large number of countries have caught the attention of the Canadian public at large.[79]

---

74 Page, ed., *Imperialism and Canada*, ibid.

75 Stacey, *Age of Conflict*, vol. 1, 258.

76 The "Rape of Nanjing" was a six-week "orgy of crime" (as an international tribunal later put it)—a reported 150,000 male civilians were killed and some 25,000 women and girls were raped and murdered.

77 A.R.M. Lower, *Canada and the Far East—1940* (New York: Institute of Pacific Relations, 1941), 23–28.

78 To be sure, members of ethnic groups were prone to raise concerns about the treatment of their fellow citizens by their own government, as Ukrainians did in the late 1930s. See Nesdoly, "Changing Perspectives," 109–112.

79 Robert O. Matthews and Cranford Pratt, eds., *Human Rights in Canadian Foreign Policy* (Montréal and Kingston: McGill-Queen's University Press, 1988).

However, the public's interest tends to be both episodic and unsystematic. Some violations seem to drift in and out of the public consciousness. That was the case with South Africa. For the four decades apartheid was practised in South Africa, the Canadian public's interest in this issue tended to peak at crisis points—the Sharpeville massacre in April 1960, the Soweto uprising of 1977, and the unrest in the townships that began in the fall of 1984—but then die away.[80]

Likewise, some human rights violations draw attention, while others go unremarked by the public. One can contrast the killings around Beijing on the night of June 4, 1989—which transfixed the international community and sparked massive protests in Canada, as elsewhere[81]—with the genocide in Cambodia in the mid-1970s or the genocide in Rwanda in 1994. In those cases, interest in Canada was minimal. Canadians might have been shocked when they saw the artificially recreated scenes of slaughter in the films *The Killing Fields* or *Hotel Rwanda*, made a decade after the events on which they are based, but at the time, there was relatively little interest. When the minister of foreign affairs, André Ouellet, announced during the Rwandan genocide that "Canadians are shocked at these acts" and that "Canadians deplore the acts of barbarism,"[82] it was clear that he was speaking for "Canadians" only in a symbolic sense, for Canadians might have been horrified by the images they were seeing of those men, women, and children who were slaughtered, often at close range by machetes, but the horror did not spark collective anger comparable to that regarding Tiananmen.

Usually, attention is focused tightly only when some event involving the violator—like a visit by a leader or the outbreak of violence—jogs the collective memory and provides a focus, and a forum, for criticism. For example, there had been virtual silence in Canada on the human rights record of the government of General Suharto in Indonesia in the mid- and late 1970s, even though Amnesty International and the United States Congress had cited the government in Djakarta as one of the world's most persistent human rights violators, and even though Indonesia was engaged in an alleged campaign of repression in East Timor, which it had invaded in December 1975. However, when it was announced that Pierre Trudeau was to visit Indonesia in January 1983, a great deal of public criticism of both the Indonesian record and Canadian policy suddenly emerged.[83] And then it dropped off the agenda again (except for op-ed pieces that would invariably run on December 7, the anniversary of the invasion of East Timor)—until November 1997, when Suharto came to Vancouver to attend the Asia Pacific Economic Cooperation (APEC) forum. His presence galvanized sizeable student protests. The RCMP used pepper spray on protestors and a television cameraman—an episode that prompted the prime minister to quip, when he was asked about the incident, "For me, pepper, I put it on my plate."[84]

---

80 Linda Freeman, *The Ambiguous Champion: Canada and South Africa in the Trudeau and Mulroney Years* (Toronto: University of Toronto Press, 1997).

81 Kim Richard Nossal, *Rain Dancing: Sanctions in Canadian and Australian Foreign Policy* (Toronto: University of Toronto Press, 1994), chap. 8.

82 Department of Foreign Affairs, *Press Release* 69, April 8, 1994; CIDA, *Press Release* 94–15, May 2, 1994.

83 Sheldon E. Gordon, "The Canadian Government and Human Rights Abroad," *International Perspectives*, November/December 1983, 9.

84 W. Wesley Pue, ed., *Pepper in Our Eyes: The APEC Affair* (Vancouver: UBC Press, 2000). In his memoirs, Chrétien claimed that he made a joke about pepper because he didn't know about what had

A final indicator of the interest of Canadians in the human rights of others is a general willingness to accept as immigrants or refugees those whose rights have been violated by being displaced by political conflict. While prior to the Second World War the Canadian government sought to keep the door to European Jews fleeing Nazi persecution tightly closed,[85] there was a slow loosening of restrictions on immigration in the 1950s,[86] with the door opened to some political refugees. After the Hungarian revolution of 1956 was crushed by the Soviet Union, some 39,000 Hungarians made their way to Canada.[87] In 1972, when Idi Amin, Uganda's president, expelled 50,000 Ugandans of Asian origin, many of them rendered stateless, the Canadian government of Pierre Trudeau welcomed 7,000, many of whom settled with the assistance of local committees across Canada.[88] In the late 1970s when Vietnam was reunified after the war, the government in Hanoi outlawed private property and closed down private businesses, prompting hundreds of thousands of Hoa (Vietnamese who are ethnically Han Chinese) to try to leave Vietnam. In 1978 and 1979, the exodus turned into an expulsion, with the government in Hanoi charging an exit fee before the Hoa were put on leaky boats and cast into the South China Sea, where approximately 200,000 perished. The response of many ordinary Canadians to the plight of some 400,000 surviving "boat people" was to offer to sponsor families, with the result that between 1979 and 1982, over 50,000 Vietnamese settled in Canada.[89] The same response came during the war in Kosovo in 1999, when tens of thousands of Kosovar Albanians fled Serb repression into Albania and Macedonia, overwhelming them and prompting NATO to look for countries willing to lodge the refugees. The Canadian government received hundreds of offers from community agencies and families willing to lodge refugees (though the war was over and Kosovo was occupied by NATO before many of the offers could be acted on).

The picture of domestic interests painted here is of necessity limited. We have not examined the full range of interests that Canadians have been prone to express, nor all of the organizations and groups that exist to press collectively the foreign policy concerns of Canadians. However incomplete, the picture demonstrates that Canadians not only have a range of interests in global politics, but also a willingness to express them in a variety of political contexts. We now turn to a consideration of how the expression of these interests influences international policy in Canada.

---

happened at the protests and couldn't hear the question properly because everyone was shouting at him: see Jean Chrétien, *My Years as Prime Minister* (Toronto: Random House, 2008), 184–85. However, the video of the exchange between Chrétien and a guerrilla journalist and celebrity interviewer, Nardwuar the Human Serviette, who asked him the question at the press conference, is posted on YouTube and tells a rather different story: http://www.youtube.com/watch?v=yWf2LLaHkM0.

85 Irving M. Abella and Harold Martin Troper, *None Is Too Many: Canada and the Jews of Europe, 1933–1948* (Toronto: Lester & Orpen Dennys, 1982), ix: the title is taken from the response of an unidentified Canadian immigration officer in 1945 who was asked how many Jews would be admitted to Canada after the war.

86 For a discussion of the evolution of immigration policy after 1945, see Freda Hawkins, *Canada and Immigration*, 2nd ed. (Montréal and Kingston: McGill-Queen's University Press, 1988), 72–88.

87 Peter I. Hidas, "The Hungarian Refugee Student Movement of 1956–57 and Canada," *Canadian Ethnic Studies* 30:1 (1998), 19–49.

88 Peter C. Dobell, *Canada in World Affairs*, vol. 17: *1971–1973* (Toronto: Canadian Institute of International Affairs, 1985), 323–27.

89 Gerald E. Dirks, *Controversy and Complexity: Canadian Immigration Policy during the 1980s* (Montréal and Kingston: McGill-Queen's University Press, 1995), 66–69.

THE INFLUENCE OF SOCIETAL ACTORS

In a liberal democratic political system like Canada, there are two ways societal actors can affect international policy. They can try to influence the *policymaking environment*, determining the bounds within which the government has to operate. Using the terminology proposed by Denis Stairs,[90] societal actors can try to determine (or "set") the international policy agenda and the priorities (agenda-setting), or to specify the broad parameters of acceptable options (parameter-setting). But they can also try to influence the *decision-making process*, or, more precisely, the specific decisions, or policy choices, that the Canadian government takes in international affairs (policy-setting) or influence how those policy decisions are implemented (administration-setting).

Such a distinction between the process and the environment is, of course, somewhat artificial. In the real world of policymaking, neither government officials themselves nor those societal actors who press their demands on government think in these terms. However, drawing this analytical distinction allows us to probe the various ways individuals and civil society can influence international policy in Canada and to assess with greater accuracy society's impact on policy outcomes.

In the remainder of this chapter, we examine first how civil society can influence the government's international policy agenda. We then look at the more limited role of societal actors in the formulation and implementation of policy. An examination of the bounds and parameters that society places on decision-makers is examined in the next chapter.

The Policymaking Environment

Defining Canada's international policy agenda is the process of establishing which issues are deemed important enough by societal actors to warrant government attention and action. The state, to paraphrase Karl Marx, may make its own agenda but it cannot make it entirely as it pleases. There is little doubt that external events play a critical role in determining what Ottawa's international policy agenda will be. Some will be entirely expected and predictable, for Canada's involvement in global politics has its own seasonal rhythm. All of the major summits the prime minister attends are set on a regular basis, as we will see in Chapter 7: the Group of Twenty (G-20) summit; the annual meeting of heads of government of Asia-Pacific Economic Cooperation (APEC) forum members; the biennial Commonwealth Heads of Government Meetings; and summits of La Francophonie. In the spring there are annual NATO ministerial meetings and the appearance of the minister of foreign affairs at the annual meeting of the foreign ministers of the Association of Southeast Asian Nations (ASEAN). In the autumn, the minister of foreign affairs (or sometimes the prime minister) goes to New York for the annual session of the General Assembly, while the minister of finance will be in Washington for the annual meeting of the International Monetary Fund. Indeed some of these meetings even allow for extremely long-term planning, notably the turn that Canada took in hosting the G7/8 summit (Montebello in 1981, Toronto in 1988, Halifax in 1995, and Kananaskis in 2002), and the G-20 summit in Huntsville in 2010.

But some external occurrences will be entirely unforeseen: an invasion of one country by another, an assassination of a foreign leader, a massacre, a terrorist attack, the collapse of a major financial institution, the outbreak of a riot that can lead to repression

90 Denis Stairs, "Public Opinion and External Affairs: Reflections on the Domestication of Canadian Foreign Policy," *International Journal* 33:1 (Winter 1977–8), 128–49.

or revolution—such events will thrust themselves rudely and unexpectedly onto a government's agenda. Thus, when he came to power in February 2006, the government of Stephen Harper was not seeking thorny international policy issues to deal with. But there was no way he could avoid the issues thrust on his agenda once he was in power: the deteriorating situation in Afghanistan and the Israeli bombing of Lebanon.

The agenda may also be affected by civil society. Generally, the capacity of societal actors to put an issue on the agenda is dependent on the degree of societal support for that issue. However, securing such support is not always easy. The cause must have some resonance with public opinion and sufficiently interesting to attract the attention of the media. Moreover, the chances of catching the government's ear tend to be better if the issue can be grafted onto existing priorities, even if it has to be done somewhat artificially.

All the groups mentioned above are likely to press the government to put their concerns on its agenda. At times an item may make it to the agenda because it is pressed by a large ethnic group in Canada, and the government may be eager to respond. In the post–Cold War period, the Chrétien government embraced an activist and high-profile policy toward Haiti in February 1996, in large measure because a by-election was being held in the Montréal riding of Papineau-Saint-Michel, which has the highest concentration of voters of Haitian origin of any riding in Canada. The government ensured that Canada's Haitian connection enjoyed a special prominence in the very tight race between Pierre Pettigrew, whom Chrétien had appointed minister of state for international cooperation before he had won a seat in the House of Commons, and Daniel Turp, the souverainiste candidate for the Bloc Québécois. Pettigrew was dispatched to Port-au-Prince to attend the inauguration of René Préval as president; while there, Pettigrew made sure he announced that Canada was contributing $700,000 to the United Nations Children's Emergency Fund in Haiti. (On the other hand, 10 years later, the deteriorating situation in Haiti returned to haunt Pettigrew, who by that time had become the minister of foreign affairs in Paul Martin's cabinet, and certainly contributed the loss of his seat in the January 2006 elections to Vivian Barbot, a Canadian of Haitian origin who won the seat for the Bloc Québécois.)

Why are some issues of such concern to Canadians that they are thrust onto the agenda while others produce little or no reaction? Part of the explanation can be found in the discussion of interests in the first part of this chapter, and the recognition that many issues will not arouse concern because they do not touch the concrete interests of Canadians. But another part of the explanation lies in how the issues are structured for the public. Despite the rise of the internet and the increasing use of unmediated sources of information and opinion, it would appear that the traditional media, both print and electronic, continues to play an important role in structuring and shaping society's perceptions of issues and their relative importance.[91] Thus the choices made by editors and producers about which stories are important involve a dynamic process of trying to reflect on the one hand a judgement about what is "important" and on the other an educated guess about what they think their readers, listeners, or viewers will want to see. This calculus will always have political effects, because individuals tend to respond to cues about international affairs that they receive from the mass media.

---

91 For a balanced assessment of what Peter Preston calls the "utterly uncertain" impact of the internet on print media, see Bob Franklin, "The Future of Newspapers," and Peter Preston, "The Curse of Introversion," *Journalism Studies* 9:5 (October 2008), 630–49.

The media's role in shaping the news, in turn, has an impact on foreign policy, particularly on the foreign policy agenda.[92] As Denis Stairs has noted, while the media may not have an important influence on the substance of foreign policy, it has "a very significant impact on the day-to-day activities" of policymakers.[93] Politicians are sensitive to the international policy issues reported on the front pages of such newspapers as *Le Devoir* or the *Globe and Mail* or broadcast on the variety of electronic media, for any issue may be raised in the House of Commons during Question Period or at a press conference. This, in turn, makes the bureaucracy sensitive to the media's treatment of foreign issues, for it will be to the bureaucrats that politicians turn for appropriate response.

However, it should be noted that while the state may not be able to determine its own agenda, it still has considerable latitude in choosing how to deal with issues on that agenda. Indeed, governments are increasingly inclined to try to shape the agenda through consultation. Traditionally this was done through parliamentary institutions like standing committees, which we examine in more detail in Chapter 10. But during the Chrétien era, the government encouraged extra-parliamentary processes. In 1994, it inaugurated a National Forum on Canada's International Relations that was designed to provide groups in society for input in the process. In February 1996, Lloyd Axworthy, Chrétien's foreign minister, opened the issue of whether Canada should take on the leadership of the UN mission in Haiti to public discussion on the internet. In January 2003, the foreign affairs minister, Bill Graham, launched a huge pan-Canadian consultation entitled "Dialogue on Foreign Policy." It issued its final report in June,[94] just months before Paul Martin took over from Chrétien and launched his own foreign policy review.

These consultations offer, in theory at least, some advantages. They give civil society organizations a privileged platform and attract attention to issues that might otherwise remain in the shadows. They offer a forum for the consideration of ideas, concepts, or projects that ministers or their officials may find useful. Certainly Axworthy admitted having drawn inspiration from the National Forum series.[95]

But attempts by governments to put in place mechanisms that give the policy process the appearance of wide consultation with societal groups should be viewed with care. For mechanisms like this actually do little to enhance the democratization of Canadian foreign policy.[96] First, these mechanisms are designed for elites, not the broad mass of the citizenry. Such meetings provide an opportunity for the very homogenous group that makes up Canada's foreign-affairs elite to travel to Ottawa, be put up in a downtown hotel, and, over fine food and wine, be given an opportunity to discuss foreign policy and listen to

---

92 B.E. Burton, W.C. Soderlund, and T.A. Keenleyside, "The Press and Canadian Foreign Policy: A Re-examination Ten Years On," *Canadian Foreign Policy* 3 (Fall 1995), 51–69.

93 Denis Stairs, "The Press and Foreign Policy in Canada," *International Journal* 33:2 (Spring 1976), 238.

94 Bill Graham, "A Dialogue on Foreign Policy: Report to Canadians," June 2003, available http://www.foreign-policy-dialogue.ca/en/final_report/index.html.

95 Steven Lee, "Beyond Consultations: Public Contributions to Making Foreign Policy," in Fen Osler Hampson and Maureen Appel Molot, eds., *Canada Among Nations 1998: Leadership and Dialogue* (Ottawa: Carleton University Press, 1998), 65.

96 Kim Richard Nossal, "The Democratization of Canadian Foreign Policy: The Elusive Ideal," in Maxwell A. Cameron and Maureen Appel Molot, eds., *Canada Among Nations 1995: Democracy and Foreign Policy* (Ottawa: Carleton University Press, 1995), 29–43.

ministers give speeches. But the taxpaying *demos*—the "many" who foot the bill—are nowhere to be found at these meetings. Second, and more importantly, these mechanisms tend to do little more than reveal the wide range of opinion among Canadians on policy issues. But, for the government, this would be precisely the ideal outcome: confronted by a cacophony of advice on an issue, government officials are more able to rationalize *their* policy choices. Such a calculus was stated candidly by de Montigny Marchand, a deputy minister in the Department of External Affairs in the summer of 1983, at the height of the controversy over cruise missile testing:

> We can listen and we can accommodate, to some extent we can even manage certain contradictions, but we cannot avoid the overriding need for a policy which is a coherent synthesis of national interests and priorities. . . . There will be times when government exercises its leadership somewhat ahead of public opinion.[97]

While consultations present some advantages, their real purpose is to legitimize government initiatives while giving the process a "democratic" veneer that allows civil society to articulate their agenda priorities.

The Decision-Making Process

In principle at least, societal actors and interests could influence the making and implementation of international policy, as in some areas of domestic policy. The self-management of doctors and lawyers is one example of public policy being administered by private associations. In international policy, there are a few instances of this kind of administration-setting by groups and individuals outside the government.

The Management of International Policy

Involving societal actors in international or multilateral negotiations is one form of international policy administration. Since the 1970s, the government has routinely invited representatives of industries affected by international negotiations to join the Canadian delegations to these negotiations. Delegations to negotiations on fisheries, deep-sea mining, and tariffs featured regular participation by those whose concrete interests were going to be affected by the outcome of the talks. For example, the advisers to the Canadian negotiators on the East Coast maritime boundary with the United States included the president of the Nova Scotia Fishermen's Association, a fleet captain with National Sea Products, a skipper, a union representative, and a member of the Atlantic Fishing Vessel Owners' Association.[98]

By the late 1990s, this had become routine practice. The Canadian delegation to the World Trade Organization ministerial meeting in Seattle in 1999 consisted of 84 members, and outlining the membership in detail indicates the range of voices in these negotiations. A slight majority, 44, were drawn from the federal government: the minister of international

---

97 De Montigny Marchand, "Foreign Policy and Public Interest," *International Perspectives*, July/August 1983, 9.

98 See Stairs, "Public Opinion and External Affairs," 149; Stephen Greene and Thomas Keating, "Domestic Factors and Canada–United States Fisheries Relations," *Canadian Journal of Political Science* 13:4 (December 1980), 731–50; Elizabeth Riddell-Dixon, *Canada and the International Seabed: Domestic Determinants and External Constraints* (Montréal and Kingston: McGill-Queen's University Press, 1989); Gilbert R. Winham, "Bureaucratic Politics and Canadian Trade Negotiation," *International Journal* 34:1 (Winter 1978–9), 64–89.

trade, Pierre Pettigrew, the minister of agriculture and agri-food, Lyle Vanclief, and their deputy ministers; Canada's ambassador to the WTO, Sergio Marchi; and 39 officials from nine federal departments. The other 40 delegates included 26 observers (two senators and eight MPs from all parties, plus seven ministers and nine officials from the provinces and territories) and 14 "private-sector advisers." These included the chief executives of a number of the peak business associations we surveyed above: Nancy Hughes Antony of the Canadian Chamber of Commerce, Perrin Beatty of CME (Canadian Manufacturers & Exporters), Tom d'Aquino of the Business Council on National Issues (the forerunner of the Canadian Council of Chief Executives), Gérald Ponton of MEQ (Manufacturiers et exportateurs du Québec), Gilles Taillon of the Conseil du Patronat du Québec, and Lise Lachappelle, president of the l'Association canadienne des pâtes et papiers. Two labour leaders were included: Ken Georgetti, president of the Canadian Labour Congress, and Henri Massé, president of the Fédération des travailleurs et travailleuses du Québec. There were also representatives of the agricultural community, the cultural community, and two representatives of environmental organizations, including Elizabeth May, the leader of the Green Party, who at time was executive director of the Sierra Club. Two consultants rounded out the delegation.[99]

Another example of civil society affecting the shaping of policy was the role that the NGO community played in the efforts of Lloyd Axworthy, the minister of foreign affairs, to secure a global ban on antipersonnel landmines in 1996 and 1997. Axworthy managed to secure this treaty by what came to be known as the "Ottawa Process"—a process that saw the Canadian government cooperate closely with the NGO community, and the International Campaign to Ban Landmines (ICBL) in particular, to sidestep traditional multilateral diplomatic channels and in essence try to embarrass other mine-using governments like the United States into signing onto the ban with a "surprise challenge."[100] To be sure, the Ottawa Process proved a very effective way to get a treaty on landmines, and Jody Williams and the ICBL were awarded the Nobel Peace Prize in 1997. But involving the NGO community so deeply in the policy-implementation process came at a steep price. Not only did Axworthy's "surprise challenge" tactics ensure that never again would there be an "Ottawa Process" on any other issue (since friends and allies of Canada, having been burned once would be twice shy), but, by all accounts, some American officials, annoyed at being sandbagged by Axworthy, lobbied hard to ensure that his nomination for the 1997 Nobel Prize did not succeed, even though many believed he was clearly as deserving as Williams of the honour.[101]

---

99 Denis Stairs, "Foreign Policy Consultations in a Globalizing World: The Case of Canada, the WTO and the Shenanigans in Seattle," *Policy Matters* 1:8 (December 2000), 25–26.

100 Maxwell A. Cameron, Robert J. Lawson and Brian Tomlin, eds., *To Walk Without Fear: The Global Movement to Ban Landmines* (Toronto: Oxford University Press, 1998); Lloyd Axworthy, *Navigating a New World: Canada's Global Future* (Toronto: Vintage Canada, 2003), 126–55. For a more sober reassessment, see Adam Chapnick, "The Ottawa Process Revisited," *International Journal* 58:3 (Summer 2003), 281–293.

101 The deeply symbiotic relationship between Williams and Axworthy was critical to the achievement of a landmines ban. Without Williams and the ICBL, Axworthy would never have been able to pull off his highly undiplomatic "surprise challenge" to other governments that generated the impetus for a ban (for details, see Brian W. Tomlin, "On a Fast-Track to a Ban: The Canadian Policy Process," *Canadian Foreign Policy* 5:3 [Spring 1998], 15–20). But by the same token, without Axworthy and the diplomatic resources of the Canadian state, Williams and the ICBL would never have been able to achieve a global ban so quickly.

In some areas of international policy, nongovernmental organizations have traditionally played a more direct role in the implementation of international policy. In the case of development assistance, the agency responsible for administering this area of international policy—the Canadian International Development Agency (CIDA)—turned increasingly to nongovernmental organizations to implement development assistance programs. As Alison Van Rooy concluded, this trend "made CIDA dependent on NGOs' activity and expertise . . . and it is this dependence that has opened the door for NGO influence on policy."[102]

In at least one case, the government turned to the private sector to administer its relationship with a foreign state. Because Canada recognizes the People's Republic of China as the only legitimate government of China, it cannot deal with the government of the Republic of China on Taiwan—at least not without provoking a row with Beijing. However, the Canadian government, like other Western governments, wants to be able to deal with the government in Taipei not only because of the importance of Canada's trade with Taiwan, but also because Taiwan is a member of APEC, where it operates as "Chinese Taipei," a name that is sufficiently politically neutral that it is acceptable to the rival governments across the Formosa Strait. So in 1986 the Canadian government contracted with the Canadian Chamber of Commerce to open and run a Canadian Trade Office in Taipei. Foreign service officers from the Department of Foreign Affairs and International Trade are seconded to the CCC to run the office. However, it looks and operates like any other Canadian diplomatic mission abroad.[103]

But such examples tend to be the exception rather than the rule. In most areas of international policy, Canadian governments have zealously excluded participation by civil society actors in the actual administration of policies and programs. Instead, that task is carried out by a professional bureaucracy generally unaffected by societal actors. As Stairs notes, this is partly due to the traditional secrecy surrounding the actual implementation of external policy. The shrouds that cover the deliberations of Cabinet, and the privileged status of communications from other governments, make it difficult to delegate the tasks of administration to domestic groups. Then there is the nature of statecraft itself. The processes of diplomacy and negotiation, which lie at the core of a state's international activities, do not allow policymaking and policy implementation to be easily compartmentalized. In foreign affairs, the administration and the making of policy are, in a real sense, one and the same.

International Policy-Setting

Except in rare cases, attempts to convince the government to adopt a given position or to modify a decision that has already been made are generally unfruitful. This was the case with the protests against Japan in the fall of 1937 mentioned above. The government of Mackenzie King had numerous reasons not to involve Canada in the Far Eastern conflict— or in any other international conflict, for that matter, as we will see in the next chapter. Nor did King have want to cross the various groups in Canada that had a concrete interest in continuing to trade with Japan. As a result, he resolutely resisted public pressures for any form of action, arguing that Canada should take no action that would put it on one side or

---

102 Alison Van Rooy, "The Altruistic Lobbyists: The Influence of Non-governmental Organisations on Development Policy in Canada and Britain," PhD thesis, University of Oxford, 1994, quoted in Morrison, *Aid and Ebb Tide*, 442.

103 Paul M. Evans, "Canada and Taiwan: A Forty-Year Survey," *Transactions of the Royal Society of Canada*, series 1, vol. 1 (1990), 165–88.

the other in the Sino–Japanese conflict. Moreover, he said, while his government was interested in human welfare in "the Orient, Spain, or in any part of the world, it was particularly concerned with the welfare of the Canadian people."[104]

The issue of cruise missile testing in the early 1980s provides yet another illustration of this process at work. As we noted above, when it became known in 1982 that the government was planning to allow the United States Air Force to test the inertial guidance system of the air-launched cruise missile over Canada, a wave of public protest erupted. In the fall of 1982 and the spring of 1983, huge rallies were held across the country, pressing the government to "Refuse the cruise." In Vancouver alone, over 65,000 people joined the city's mayor in a march through the streets. Petitions and letters flooded into Ottawa. A makeshift "Peace Camp" was erected on Parliament Hill. Peace groups, scientists, church leaders, labour leaders, academics, and a variety of literary figures joined the opposition. The Canadian Conference of Catholic Bishops and the moderator of the United Church added their voices to the protest. The premier of Saskatchewan, Grant Devine, spoke out against testing over his province. Operation Dismantle threatened to take the federal government to court on the grounds that cruise testing constituted a threat to their right to life guaranteed under Section 7 of the Charter of Rights and Freedoms. Public opinion polls revealed that a majority of Canadians were opposed to cruise testing.[105] One member of Parliament, Paul McRae (Liberal: Thunder Bay–Atikokan), openly worried about the political consequences of such opposition. "Can anyone doubt," he wondered, "that [voters] will deal harshly with politicians who are not serious about arms control?"[106] (It might be noted that although McRae did not run in the next election in 1984, the Liberal candidate in Thunder Bay–Atikokan ran third.)

For all the clamour, however, the government held firm, refusing to alter its course. On May 9, 1983, Trudeau wrote an "open letter" to Canadians, defending the testing.[107] On June 14 the government used its majority in the House of Commons to vote down a motion by the New Democratic Party opposing cruise missile testing 213 to 34. The final decision was announced at the time the federal government traditionally reserves for announcing unpopular decisions: on a Friday in July, after Parliament had recessed for the summer.[108] The first tests began in March 1984.

The cruise missile issue demonstrates how and why the government can avert attempts by civil society to determine the content and orientation of policy. Governments are in the fortunate position of being able to hear what they want to hear on contentious foreign policy issues. They know that on any political issue, Canadians will rarely speak with one voice. And the public opinion polls—like the consultations discussed above—merely reinforce this view.

---

104 King to the House of Commons, February 11, 1938, quoted in Lower, *Canada and the Far East*, 31.

105 Adam Bromke and Kim Richard Nossal, "Tensions in Canada's Foreign Policy," *Foreign Affairs* 62 (Winter 1983–84), 341–42.

106 House of Commons, *Debates*, 1983, vol. 22, 25043, May 2, 1983.

107 The text of Trudeau's letter is reproduced in C. David Crenna, ed., *Pierre Elliott Trudeau: Lifting the Shadow of War* (Edmonton: Hurtig Publishers, 1987), 50–52.

108 Pauline Jewett, the NDP external affairs critic, called the timing "sleazy." *Globe and Mail*, July 16, 1983. On the well-established practice of making political announcements on a Friday, see David Taras, "Prime Ministers and the Media," in Leslie A. Pal and Taras, eds., *Prime Ministers and Premiers: Political Leadership and Public Policy in Canada* (Scarborough: Prentice-Hall Canada, 1988), 39.

Moreover, government officials can be relatively assured that they do not have to worry about the kind of electoral retribution that McRae fretted about during the cruise testing issue.

Electoral Politics and International Policy

In a democratic system, elections are generally considered the main means by which the citizenry can bend policymakers to their will. For this reason, it might be thought that politicians would keep a careful eye on public opinion surveys, listen more carefully to the voters as the next election approaches, and make policy decisions purely on the basis of electoral calculations. However obvious this principle may appear, it is not always followed, particularly in the area of international policy.[109] There are two reasons for this.

First, specific foreign policy issues do not lend themselves well to electoral retribution. Opposition to highly specific decisions, such as whether to sign a free-trade agreement with Colombia, will likely be diffused among the electorate and lack geographic concentration. Conversely, opposition to specific functional policy issues, such as the fishery or the closing of a military base, is likely to be so geographically concentrated that it will create regional rather than national electoral considerations. The same Burkean principles invoked by Marchand quoted above would apply no less to such cleavages.

Second, international issues are rarely a key issue at election time. The only elections that were dominated by debates over international policy issues were the elections of 1891, 1911, 1917, 1940, 1963, and 1988. In 1917 and 1940, the issue of conscription for overseas service dominated the elections. In 1963, the defence policy of John Diefenbaker's government was at issue. In 1891, 1911 and 1988, the elections focused on trade relations with the United States. Indeed, Canadian–American trade relations has been one issue that, along with the cleavage between English-speaking and French-speaking Canadians and the question of the degree of state intervention in the economy, is regular in Canadian elections.[110] And, not surprisingly, all three issues are fundamental to Canadian identity. Moreover, these three issues rarely emerge as separate electoral issues but tend to be intertwined.

International issues played a decisive role in all these elections. In 1891, as we noted above, the embrace of free trade, or "unrestricted reciprocity," as it was known then, by the Liberals under Laurier allowed Sir John A. Macdonald to play the nationalist card. He whipped up anti-American sentiment in English Canada by warning of the "impending danger" of annexation. He castigated the Liberal plan as "veiled treason" and suggested that because the editor of the *Globe*, a Liberal newspaper, was an annexationist, the proposal for reciprocity was tantamount to advocating union with the United States.[111] Likewise, the 1911 election is generally remembered as the rejection of the policy of free trade with the United States. But the vote was more than simply a rejection of the reciprocity treaty. Also at issue was Laurier's policy on Canada's contribution to the Royal Navy. One might certainly interpret the outcome in 1911 as a simple combination of these

---

109 Ivan Head, Trudeau's foreign policy adviser, admitted in 1977, "I very seldom give much thought to what we'll look like in the next election" when offering advice. Quoted in Don Munton and Dale H. Poel, "Electoral Accountability and Canadian Foreign Policy: The Case of Foreign Investment," *International Journal* 33:1 (Winter 1977–8), 219, n6.

110 Richard Johnston, André Blais, Henry E. Brady, and Jean Crête, *Letting the People Decide: Dynamics of a Canadian Election* (Montréal and Kingston: McGill-Queen's University Press, 1992), 6–7.

111 Wood, "Defining 'Canadian,'" 49–69.

issues, as Mackenzie King did, claiming that the Liberal defeat was the result of an "unholy alliance between the [Québec] Nationalists . . . and the Tories of the other provinces."[112] But these issues were also intimately linked to other differences driven by the dominant linguistic cleavage.

In 1917 and 1940, the English–French cleavage was clearly evident, with the Liberals under Laurier in 1917 and King in 1940 sweeping Québec as a result of their promises not to introduce conscription. The leader of the NDP in the 1960s, Tommy Douglas, described the 1963 election as a referendum on nuclear arms, and the fall of the Progressive Conservative government of John Diefenbaker is often seen as a rejection of his policy on this issue. But Diefenbaker's defeat was not simply because he refused to arm Honest John missiles and Starfighter jets with nuclear warheads. A number of other factors, including the collapse of support within the Cabinet itself, the state of the economy, and the deterioration of Diefenbaker's leadership qualities, contributed to his downfall.[113] Likewise, the issue of free trade dominated the 1988 election, often to the exclusion of other issues. However, even if the major parties, for strategic reasons, avoided raising the issue of the reintegration of Québec into the Constitution through the Meech Lake Accord that had been signed the year before, the linguistic cleavage and the personalities of the party leaders also played a role.[114]

But these elections are the exception—and even then we should keep in mind Ramsay Cook's observation that "To many electors in times past these foreign policy problems doubtless loomed less large than they have to later textbook writers."[115] The 40 general elections in Canada between 1867 and 2008 suggest that international policy is not an issue that will generate support, particularly in peacetime. In the winter election of 2005–2006, Paul Martin and the Liberal party tried to play the anti-American card by linking the leader of the Conservative Party of Canada, Stephen Harper, with George W. Bush, who was exceedingly unpopular in Canada. In the end, however, the tactic of startling voters into abandoning the Conservatives did not produce any significant gains in the polls (though it did arouse the ire of the American ambassador in Ottawa, who gave a speech in the middle of the campaign suggesting that everyone "tone it down"[116]).

CONCLUSION

For purposes of clarity, we have made a distinction between the policymaking *process* and the policymaking *environment*. Societal actors do not have a great deal of influence on the process of making international policy in Canada. Individuals and civil society can engage in considerable activity to try to influence the specific policy decisions taken by government, but, at the end of the day, their real influence is marginal. They have a little more latitude in the management and implementation of policy, but this has been a relatively recent phenomenon and difficult to measure. And even on this level, the state retains its prerogative to insist

---

112 Quoted in Stacey, *Age of Conflict*, vol. 1, 147.

113 Lyon, *Canada in World Affairs,* 176–222.

114 See the analysis in Johnston et al., *Letting the People Decide,* 212–44.

115 Ramsay Cook, "Foreign Policy and the Election," *International Journal* 18:2 (Summer 1963), 374.

116 See Chapter 7.

that the implementation of policy is the responsibility of the bureaucracy. In short, in the area of international policy, the state of Canada is "relatively autonomous." Policy reflects what policymakers define as in the *national* interest rather than the interest of a particular group, class, or region.

However, the state does not exercise the same control over the policymaking *environment*. This chapter demonstrates how in some circumstances civil society can and does determine what issues the government must deal with on its agenda. In addition, societal influence is evident at another level—defining parameters of policy. At this most general level, society can in theory define the bounds of acceptable policy actions. As Denis Stairs notes, parameter-setting establishes "certain limits on what the policy-makers are actually able to do—able, that is, within the range of what they regard as acceptable, or tolerable, political and other costs. Such opinions [of societal actors] can serve, in short, to confine the policy community's range of politically workable choices."[117] The constraints imposed are essentially negative in nature: They serve to rule out certain options rather than insist on particular courses of action. Moreover, the parameters of "acceptable behaviour" established by society will be exceedingly broad. Because of this latitude, it is unlikely that government officials will be *unanimously* agreed on a course of action that falls outside the range of acceptable behaviour.

It is at this level that society has the most potent influence on the state's foreign policy behaviour. The next chapter is devoted to an examination of parameter-setting in practice, demonstrating how societal actors set the boundaries of acceptable policy behaviour and what their impact has been on international policy in Canada over the past century.

---

117 Denis Stairs, "Public Opinion and External Affairs: Reflections on the Domestication of Canadian Foreign Policy," *International Journal* 33:1 (Winter 1977–8), 131, n6.

CHAPTER 5

Dominant Ideas in International Policy

The influence of civil society on the conduct of international policy is especially noticeable in the definition of the parameters of policy—in other words, the boundaries or limits of acceptable policy options. In this chapter, we explore the role of ideas in this process of parameter-setting. Every era is, in effect, marked by broad currents of ideas that dominate debates and reflections on international policy and Canada's place in world politics. All of the ideas, values, postulates, metaphors, and concepts we use to discuss international policy we will designate here as "dominant ideas."

IDEAS, CULTURE, AND INTERNATIONAL RELATIONS

In every political community, certain preferences, beliefs, attitudes, and values will be dominant—in the sense that they are held by a majority of the members of the community. This patchwork of ideas will, however, vary dramatically from one epoch to another. Consider how in the first half of the nineteenth century the idea of slavery was considered perfectly legitimate in the southern States. But today, 150 years after the end of the Civil War, one would never hear a politician in the American South trying to seek election by promising a return to slavery. Ideas determine what is legitimate and illegitimate, what is just and unjust, and what is acceptable and unacceptable. Societies develop sets of ideas to govern all manner of social relations: between parents and children, between buyers and sellers, between citizens and governments, and between citizens themselves. Moreover, this applies equally to relations *between* political communities: The choices of foreign policymakers are framed and determined by ideas that are dominant at a particular time.

It is true that for much of the past 50 years, international relations theory has not placed much importance on the role of ideas. Rather, mainstream IR theories during the Cold War era—realism, structural realism, neoliberalism, and neomarxism—employed materialist and rationalist assumptions about the world; this, combined with positivist methodologies that looked only at that which can be observed, quantified and measured, ensured the marginalization of ideational approaches to global politics. In this theoretical perspective, ideas were regarded as fixed and determined purely by the material environment. Thus, for example, realists argued that states were guided solely by a search for power, and that whatever values leaders might have were to be subordinated in the cold, rational pursuit of power. In this view, any other choice was seen as "irrational" and thus counterproductive, if not dangerous.

Since the end of the Cold War, we have seen the growing popularity of constructivist theory, which accords considerable importance to the world of ideas. The international relations literature now abounds in research on ideational variables, such as political discourse, norms, identity, perceptions, understanding, beliefs, values, ethics, morality, and the importance of historical experience. After a long fixation on the material environment, IR scholars were rediscovering the importance of intellectual and sociocultural factors. In particular, the concept of culture, so long neglected by international relations literature, returned to the study of international policy in a major way.[1]

---

1 For example, Alexander Wendt, "Anarchy Is What States Make of It: the Social Construction of Power Politics," *International Organization* 46:2 (Spring 1992); Audie Klotz, *Norms in International Relations: The Struggle Against Apartheid* (Ithaca: Cornell University Press, 1995); Yosef Lapid and Friedrich Kratochwil, eds., *The Return of Culture and Identity in IR Theory* (Boulder: Lynne Rienner, 1996); Alexander Wendt, *Social Theory of International Politics* (Cambridge: Cambridge University Press, 1999). For a good overview, see Jeffrey T. Checkel, "Social Constructivisms in Global and European Politics: A Review Essay," *Review of International Studies* 30:2 (2004): 229–44.

Strategic culture is a coherent and relatively permanent system of ideas (beliefs, perceptions, analogies, metaphors, and symbols about the present and the past) that is more or less coherent and logical.[2] It shapes the way actors perceive the world around them and indeed, in turn, may shape their policy preferences. A state's strategic culture, it has been argued, acts like a "selector," encouraging policymakers to consider only those policy options that fit with their strategic notions, eliminating others out of hand.[3] By definition, a culture is widely embraced within a society and can endure for long periods of time. We can speak of a distinct "American strategic culture" during the Cold War that was shaped by the Japanese surprise attack on Pearl Harbor in December 1941, and the perceived need to deter the Soviet Union by the accumulation of a huge nuclear arsenal so that it could not do to the United States what Japan had done. This was a view that was accepted unconditionally by the vast majority of Western policymakers. Those who did not accept this dominant perspective, and sought the renunciation of war and nuclear weapons, were dismissed at best as naïve dreamers or at worst as dangerous and irresponsible.

In this chapter, we explore *dominant ideas* about international policy that shaped the ways Canadians have conceived of their relations with the rest of the world.[4] We should also indicate what this chapter is *not* about. Its purpose is not to examine, as Denis Stairs has done,[5] how political culture affects Canada's international policy. Nor do we want to look at the characteristics of strategic culture in Canada, as David Haglund has done.[6] Nor are we concerned to demonstrate the deep attachment of Canadians to ideologies such as liberalism[7] or nationalism and its close relation, anti-Americanism,[8] and the effect that

2 This definition is inspired by the work of Alastair Iain Johnston, Peter J. Katzenstein, and critics like Michael Desch. See Johnston, "Thinking About Strategic Culture," *International Security* 19 (Spring 1995), 32–64; Katzenstein, ed., *The Culture of National Security: Norms and Identity in World Politics* (New York: Columbia University Press, 1996); Desch, "Culture Clash: Assessing the Importance of Ideas in Security Studies," *International Security* 23 (Summer 1998), 141–70. An excellent overview is provided in David Haglund, "What Good Is Strategic Culture? A Modest Defence of an Immodest Concept," *International Journal* 59:3 (Summer 2004), 479–502.

3 Stéphane Roussel and David Morin, "Les multiples incarnations de la culture stratégique et les débats qu'elles suscitent," in Stéphane Roussel, ed., *Culture stratégique et politique de défense: l'expérience canadienne* (Montréal: Athéna, 2007), 17–42.

4 For a discussion of dominant ideas in Canadian public policymaking, see G. Bruce Doern and Richard Phidd, *Canadian Public Policy: Ideas, Structure and Process* (Toronto: Methuen, 1983), 54–59.

5 Denis Stairs, "The Political Culture of Canadian Foreign Policy," *Canadian Journal of Political Science* 15:4 (December 1982), 667–90.

6 David G. Haglund, *The North Atlantic Triangle Revisited: Canadian Grand Strategy at Century's End* (Toronto: Canadian Institute of International Affairs, 2000).

7 Stéphane Roussel, "L'instant kantien: la contribution canadienne à la creation de la 'communauté nord-atlantique,' Ottawa (1947–1949)," in Greg Donaghy, ed., *Canada and the Cold War, 1943–1957* (Ottawa: Department of Foreign Affairs and International Trade, 1999), 119–56; available http://www.dfait.gc.ca/department/~history/coldwar_section05-en.asp.

8 John W. Holmes, "Nationalism in Canadian Foreign Policy," in Peter Russell, ed., *Nationalism in Canada* (Toronto: McGraw-Hill Ryerson, 1966), 203–206; J.L. Granatstein, *Yankee Go Home? Canadians and Anti-Americanism* (Toronto: HarperCollins, 1996); Kim Richard Nossal, "A Thermostatic Dynamic? Electoral Outcomes and Anti-Americanism in Canada," in Richard A. Higgott and Ivona Malbašić, eds., *The Political Consequences of Anti-Americanism* (London: Routledge, 2008), 129–41.

these ideologies have had on government policy. Rather, we concentrate on the dominant ideas that shaped the ways Canadians have conceived of their relations with the rest of the world.

Studying dominant ideas poses some difficulties. First, by their very nature, dominant ideas are both intangible and latent: Even if one can claim that they exist, it is difficult to *demonstrate* that they exist, for the simple reason that they are generally not expressed; and they are not expressed because, being dominant, they are so rarely challenged. For example, public opinion surveys show that the majority of the population is in favour of Canada's membership in the United Nations—an outgrowth, as we will see below, of a commitment to internationalism. But this support is rarely expressed actively; rather, it only appears when a pollster's question prompts the response. To test the depth of the support of Canadians for the UN, the government would need to propose that Canada withdraw. Of course, no government in Ottawa has ever proposed such an option that would allow us to test this idea.

The second difficulty is an apparently contradictory and paradoxical characteristic of dominant ideas. While ideas persist over time, they are not static or immutable. On the one hand, there is little doubt that ideas are persistent. The beliefs, metaphors, analogies, and doctrines that are associated with a particular vision of the world tend to survive the conditions that gave birth to them. Even if they no longer appear appropriate, they continue to exert an influence on policy, generally until a crisis or a major transformation in the internal or external environments produces a real alternative. Thus, Pierre Elliott Trudeau came to power in 1968 announcing the death of Canada as a middle power—and of internationalism—but this idea remained quite alive, in large part because the conditions were not ripe for the emergence of a new dominant idea.

However, the persistent quality of ideas does not mean that they cannot or do not change. On the contrary: Ideas evolve, change, and are sometimes replaced by very different ideas. Sometimes the evolution is slow and at times almost imperceptible, as policymakers try to reassess changes both in the global system and in society. But sometimes the change in ideas is exceedingly rapid, particularly following profound upheavals in the human condition: major wars, economic collapse, or natural disasters. In such circumstances, ideas that might be dominant at one time may be entirely inappropriate for a government faced with a radically changed environment, explaining why decision-makers in Ottawa can be confronted with similar situations at different times in history, but the interplay of dominant ideas at the time will prompt them to pursue very different policies.

While *domestic* political, economic, and sociocultural factors play a major role in this evolutionary process, it is the *external* environment that tends to trigger shifts in ideas. Thus, the upheavals caused by both of the world wars, the end of the Cold War, or the events of September 11, 2001 help explain the transition from one set of ideas to another. Each of these events provided Canadians with an opportunity to reevaluate their country's place in the world. Indeed, this chapter's organization reflects the importance of external factors, since each of the ideas that have been dominant in the history of Canada's external relations is associated with a particular period in the evolution of the international system: the interwar, Cold War, post–Cold War, and post-9/11 eras.

While shifts in ideas tend to be triggered by major events, it is important to recognize that ideas do not appear and disappear in a stroke. Instead, they follow a long cycle of emergence, prevalence, and decline, so that two sets of ideas can coexist, one in decline and the other emerging. The almost imperceptible nature of this cycle, combined with the latency of dominant ideas, makes it difficult for the analyst to identify ideas, particularly in periods of rise and decline. Likewise, it is impossible to know if an emerging idea will become dominant.

A third and final difficulty lies in the notion of dominance itself. When we speak of dominance, we are implying that an idea is *widely* embraced by both the political elite and the citizenry, not that it is *unanimously* held by everyone. There always were, and always will be, dissenting voices that question and criticize dominant ideas—and often propose alternative ones. During the Cold War, the peace movement always questioned certain policies associated with internationalism, such as strong support for NATO. Indeed, each of the dominant ideas we explore in this chapter generated its own antithesis. The inevitable clash between a dominant idea and its antithesis is what makes the process so political.

The often contending ideas about international policy focus on how the government should fashion Canada's relations with the rest of the world. We can identify three sets of values, beliefs, and operational principles over the course of the twentieth century. *Imperialism*, dominant in the years before the First World War, was a mixture of sentimental, economic, and legal attachment to the British Empire. *Isolationism*, which arose after the First World War, held that Canada's national interests were best served by a policy on noninvolvement in world affairs and by avoiding international obligations. While isolationism is often associated with American foreign policy during the interwar period, it was also embraced by many Canadians, albeit with Canadian characteristics. *Internationalism*, the antithesis of isolationism, rests on the assumption that the national interests are better served when one plays an active role in world politics, particularly when one contributes to the establishment and maintenance of international order. Indeed, internationalism put a premium on accepting more responsibilities and obligations. This idea was dominant throughout the Cold War era, and has demonstrated considerable durability in the new environment created by the disappearance of socialism in Eastern Europe and the dismantling of the Soviet Union between 1989 and 1991. The end of the Cold War allowed the emergence of new ideas, such as the concept of human security or regionalism, but the true rival of internationalism appears to be the idea of *continentalism*. This idea, which has a long history in Canadian politics but emerged during the free-trade debate in the late 1980s, defines Canada's interests as deeply connected to the United States.

BEFORE THE GREAT WAR: IMPERIALISM

Great empires, as a form of political organization that gathered different nations together under a metropolis, gradually disappeared over the course of the twentieth century as the nation-state spread over the globe. However, in the nineteenth century, empires were not only seen as legitimate, but were the dominant form of political organization. Moreover, many felt that the imperial form of government could encompass both the principles of self-determination *and* the maintenance of a centralized political unit that spanned continents and acted as a unified political and economic actor in global politics.

The idea of imperialism was central to how all Canadians in the latter part of the nineteenth century were obliged to conceive of their country's relations with the world. Canada was but one unit within a larger political and economic organization, the British Empire. It was the first part of the Empire to be made a self-governing "dominion," a status that eventually included Australia, New Zealand, South Africa, Newfoundland, and, in 1922, the Irish Free State. Canada and the other dominions might have been

FIGURE 5.1	Four Dominant Ideas

Imperialism
Premises
- Canada is a member of the British Empire.
- Canadians belong to the same civilization as Britons.
- Canada's security is best assured by its membership in the Empire.

Prescriptions
- Canada should support the Empire.
- Canada should contribute to the security of the Empire as a whole.
- Canada should avoid international obligations that risk weakening its links with the Empire.

Era of Dominance
- Prior to the First World War

Isolationism
Premises
- Canada is an independent state.
- International obligations are likely to force Canada to get involved in overseas wars against its will.
- Canada (and the United States) pursue different, and morally superior, foreign policy than European states.

Prescriptions
- Canada should remain on the sidelines of international conflicts.
- Canada should refuse international obligations.
- International policy should never put national unity at risk.
- Canada should distance itself from Britain.

Era of Dominance
- Between the two world wars (1919–1939)

Internationalism
Premises
- Canada as a middle power with global interests to promote
- Liberal values should guide international policy.
- Canada is a member of large international groups.

Prescriptions
- Canada should take responsibility for creating and maintaining international order.
- Canada should be an active member of international institutions.
- International law should take primacy.
- Canada should champion global peace, acting as a mediator, or bridge-builder, in international conflicts.
- Canada should seek independence and distinctive policies from the United States and seek counterweights to American power.

Era of Dominance
- Cold War era (1945–1991)

Continentalism
Premises
- The United States is Canada's most important partner in nearly all areas of policy.
- Canada's prosperity depends on maintaining secure access to the American market.

Prescriptions
- Priority should be placed on establishing institutions for managing trade with the United States.
- Canada should ensure that its weaknesses do not threaten the security of the United States.
- Canada should support the international policies of the United States.

Era of Dominance
- Post-9/11 era?

self-governing in matters of domestic policy, but on matters of foreign policy they were in theory, though not always in practice, subject to the authority of the imperial government in London. In Canada, as elsewhere in the Empire, formal political allegiance was therefore always dual: Loyalty to Crown and Canada as a separate political community went hand-in-hand with loyalty to Crown and Empire.

For many Canadians, loyalty to Empire went well beyond such a legal-formal allegiance to the Crown. It was also a matter of sentiment: the emotionalism of attachment to *patria*—fatherland, or native land—though Canadians from Britain seemed to prefer the more maternal appellation, "Mother Country." But the pride in and love for Britain and things British so evident in English Canadians was not simply patriotism. Nor, it is important to recognize, can we regard such sentiments as nationalism, for those imbued with an attachment to Empire also tended to be strong Canadian nationalists.[9] Rather, imperialism was "love of Empire" (with a capital E). This emotional attachment took different forms. In some guises it was marked by the same evangelical spirit of Rudyard Kipling's "white man's burden"; sometimes it was an overtly racist attachment to the Anglo-Saxon people, often with an anti-French Canadian flavour. Sometimes it expressed itself as an attachment to the political ideology and institutions of British governance, often expressed as a rejection of dominant political practices in the United States.[10] It was often militaristic and bellicose in the populist tradition of British jingoism. In others still the attachment was an outgrowth of the deep religious schisms that cleaved the dominion. In effect, imperialism was a mixture of all these elements rather than being any single one.

Imperialism as a dominant idea in Canadian foreign policy enjoyed a remarkably speedy rise, reaching its height at the time of the Boer War of 1899–1902. Even as late as the mid-1880s, imperialism did not enjoy sufficient popularity to affect Canadian policy. In 1884, the imperial government in London, fighting an insurgency by the Mahdi in Sudan, sent General Charles "Pasha" Gordon to evacuate Khartoum. When Gordon and his expedition were besieged by the Mahdi's forces, the British prime minister, William Gladstone, dispatched a relief expedition up the Nile. The commander of the expedition recruited 396 Canadian voyageurs to help navigate the white water of the Nile cataracts. All but six members of the Canadian Voyageur Contingent were hired by the imperial government as civilian noncombatants—at British, not Canadian, expense.[11] It was not until January 1885 that the relief force arrived in Khartoum, but it was too late. Two days earlier, the Mahdi's forces had seized the city and killed Gordon. A wave of shock washed across the Empire, prompting the Australian colonies to offer to send contingents to fight the insurgency. But Macdonald did not feel impelled to join. "Why should we waste money and men in this wretched business?" he wrote to the Canadian high commissioner in London, grumbling that he had no desire to sacrifice Canadians "to get Gladstone and Co. out of the hole they have plunged themselves into by their own imbecillity [sic]."[12]

9 Carl Berger, *The Sense of Power: Studies in the Ideas of Canadian Imperialism, 1867–1914* (Toronto: University of Toronto Press, 1970), 259–65; also.

10 S.F. Wise and Robert Craig Brown, *Canada Views the United States: Nineteenth Century Political Attitudes* (Seattle: University of Washington Press, 1967); Granatstein, *Yankee Go Home?* 15–16.

11 C.P. Stacey, "Canada and the Nile Expedition of 1884–85," *Canadian Historical Review* 33:4 (1952), 319–40. Sixteen of the Nile Voyageurs died in service overseas.

12 C.P. Stacey, *Canada and the Age of Conflict: A History of Canadian External Policies,* vol. 1: 1867–1921 (Toronto: Macmillan, 1977), 41–44.

By the turn of the century, however, imperialism had swept across English Canada. In part, increasing Canadian attachment to imperialism reflected an increasing jingoism in the "Mother Country" during this era. In part it was fuelled by the celebration throughout the Empire of Queen Victoria's Diamond Jubilee in 1897. But behind what John W. Holmes whimsically called "the hallucinations of Jubilee imperialism"[13] lay serious ideas for the institutionalization of the Empire. In the view of the Imperial Federation League and its successors, the British Empire League and the Round Table movement, the Empire could be fashioned into a multinational federation comprising the various self-governing dominions and underwritten by liberal-democratic principles and the institutions of responsible government. They proposed the establishment of a representative government, elected by the many subjects of the Sovereign beyond the seas, with the authority to make decisions for the Empire as a whole but responsible to the voters of the Empire.[14] Such an idea, however, always foundered on the rocks of the contradictions implicit in the imperial arrangement: The British had little desire to share political authority over *their* affairs with either the self-governing "colonials" or with those peoples commonly regarded as incapable of governing themselves, much less Britons.

While the proposals for a federative empire might have implied the creation of a global economic unit, in fact for Canadians imperialism was always a political rather than an economic idea. To be sure, in the eighteenth and early nineteenth centuries, the Empire had been a singular economic unit, united by mercantilist laws and policies that kept foreign products out of imperial markets and ensured that the products of the various parts of the Empire enjoyed a competitive advantage, often as a result of imperial laws that prohibited colonial possessions from trading outside the Empire. And under this mercantilist system, some Canadians had prospered. However, by the middle of the nineteenth century, the imperial government in London had progressively abandoned mercantilist policies in favour of free trade, forcing Canadians to begin to look for markets elsewhere. From that point on, Canada's trade with the United States began to grow as its trade with the Empire declined. As a result, imperialism might have bound Canadians to Britain, but commercial links increasingly tied Canada to the United States.[15]

However, at the political and military level, imperialism carried considerable normative weight with English Canadians for much of the nineteenth century and into the twentieth century. While it is possible to argue that the "long peace" in North America actually owed its existence to a variety of other factors,[16] many Canadians—particularly English-speaking Canadians—believed it was Canada's membership in the Empire and British military power

---

13 As an example, Holmes cites the paean penned by a Nova Scotia poet: "Hail our great Queen in her regalia/One foot in Canada, the other in Australia." Holmes, "Nationalism in Canadian Foreign Policy," 206 and n3.

14 Carl Berger, *The Sense of Power: Studies in the Ideas of Canadian Imperialism, 1867–1914* (Toronto: University of Toronto Press, 1970), 120–27; James Eayrs, "The Round Table Movement in Canada, 1909–1920," *Canadian Historical Review* 38 (March 1957), rpt. Carl Berger et al., *Imperial Relations in the Age of Laurier* (Toronto: University of Toronto Press, 1969), 61–80.

15 Michael Hart, *A Trading Nation: Canadian Trade Policy from Colonialism to Globalization* (Vancouver: UBC Press, 2002), 25–44.

16 Stéphane Roussel, *The North American Democratic Peace: Absence of War and Security Institution-Building in Canada-US Relations, 1867–1958* (Montréal and Kingston: McGill-Queen's University Press, 2004), 111–17.

that guaranteed Canadian security and prevented the expanding United States from swallowing Canada. At the same time, the security guarantee involved a comparable calculation: If the Empire protected Canada, Canadians had to contribute to the defence of the Empire. This logic underwrote the willingness of many Canadians to contribute forces to the Boer War (1899–1902) and the First World War from 1914 to 1918, and to support the Royal Navy as it was expanded in the first decade of the twentieth century.

Finally, imperialism demanded that Canadians should avoid doing anything that would threaten links with Britain and Empire. Thus, in August 1940, when it appeared that Britain might be defeated by Nazi Germany, Prime Minister Mackenzie King met with President Franklin D. Roosevelt at Ogdensburg, New York, to create the Permanent Joint Board on Defence, the first Canada–U.S. defence institution. But while King was motivated by a desire to tie the neutral United States more closely to the British side in the war,[17] imperial-minded Canadians had a very different interpretation: This move smacked of abandoning the Mother Country and taking shelter under the American defence umbrella. When Arthur Meighen, a Conservative senator who had been prime minister briefly in the 1920s, learned about the meeting of King and Roosevelt at Ogdensburg, he wrote to Richard Hanson, the leader of the Conservative opposition: "Really I lost my breakfast when I read the account this morning and gazed on the disgusting picture of these potentates posing in the very middle of the blackest crisis of this Empire."[18]

Even at its zenith, imperialism as a dominant idea ran into two obstacles. First, it did not sit easily with Canada's dualistic nature. The paradoxical demands of loyalty to Canada and Empire might have been easy for those Canadians of British extraction to manage. But such divided loyalty was more difficult for French Canadians. As Henri Bourassa put it in 1917:

> French-Canadians are loyal to Great Britain and friendly to France; but they do not acknowledge to either country what, in every land, is considered the most exclusively national duty: the obligations to bear arms and fight. The only trouble with the French-Canadians is that they remain the only true "unhyphenated" Canadians. Under the sway of British Imperialism, Canadians of British origin have become quite unsettled as to their allegiance. The French-Canadians have remained, and want to remain, exclusively Canadian.[19]

To be sure, there was a commitment among the dominant elites of French-Canadian society to membership in the Empire. In particular, the hierarchy of the Roman Catholic Church played an important role in legitimizing the imperial connection. "Loyalty for the children of the Church of Christ is not a matter of sentiment," Louis-Nazaire Bégin, the archbishop of Québec, wrote to the faithful in Montréal in 1900, "it is a serious and strict duty of conscience, derived from a sacred principle." Indeed, Monseigneur Bégin felt compelled to add (for this was written during the Boer War), "it would be impossible to find a succession of men, who have been more loyal than the bishops, the clergy of Quebec."[20]

---

17 J.L. Granatstein. *How Britain's Weakness Forced Canada into the Arms of the United States* (Toronto: University of Toronto Press, 1989), 27.

18 Quoted in J.L. Granatstein, "The Conservative Party and the Ogdensburg Agreement," *International Journal* 22:1 (Winter 1966–67), 74.

19 Joseph Levitt, ed., *Henri Bourassa on Imperialism and Biculturalism, 1900–1918* (Toronto: Copp Clark, 1970), 174.

20 Robert J.D. Page, ed., *Imperialism and Canada, 1895–1903* (Toronto: Holt, Rinehart and Winston, 1972), 75.

But, as Bourassa implied, such sentiments represented a very different emotional response to the relationship with Britain. The clergy might have been loyal, but it was less out of love of Empire and more to protect a particular social order.

Imperialism concealed a second contradiction: Membership in the Empire was inconsistent with a desire for self-government, a desire shared by English-speaking and French-speaking Canadians alike. But neither the Canadian government nor the Canadian people had any formal say in the most important decision that a community can make: the decision to go to war. As Bourassa said in 1912, "The seven millions of people in Canada have less voice, in law and in fact, in the ruling of th[e] Empire, than one single sweeper in the streets of Liverpool. . . . [H]e at least has one vote to give for or against the administration of that Empire."[21]

As long as the Empire—and therefore Canada—was at peace, these contradictions did not pose a problem. But in times of war, they burst into the open. The first time Canadians were forced to confront their divergent attitudes toward defending the Empire was during the Boer War—a conflict in which the interests being defended were so remote that they did not actually affect Canada or Canadians. The conflict had its roots in the South African gold rush of the 1880s, when British migrants to the quasi-independent South African republic of Transvaal quickly outnumbered the Dutch settlers, or Afrikaaners. Paul Kruger, president of Transvaal, responded by effectively disenfranchising all *Uitlanders* ("outlanders," or foreigners). The imperial government in London purposely escalated tensions with Transvaal in 1898 and 1899, prompting Kruger to issue an ultimatum that led to the outbreak of war on October 12, 1899. The imperial government in London asked the self-governing colonies of the Empire to contribute forces. This time, the prime minister, Sir Wilfrid Laurier, was not able to take the view that Macdonald had taken on the insurgency in Sudan just 14 years previously. This time, the reaction in Canada to the outbreak of war was intense. The mood was feverishly jingoistic, with young men flocking to recruiting centres to volunteer their services for the imperial cause. That mood had been whipped up, as Carman Miller argues, by the English-language press, which enthusiastically plumped for military action. The Montréal *Star* sent some 6000 prepaid telegrams to prominent Canadians asking what their view of Canada's "duty" was, and published an entirely manipulated sample of the replies. The vast majority of the letters published expressed support for war, with only a few opposing, mostly from individuals with French-Canadian names. However, the editors had carefully pruned the replies received, negative and positive, from both English and French Canadians, in order to produce the appearance of overwhelming support.[22] In private, considerable pressure was put on the prime minister. John Willison, editor of *The Globe*, a Liberal newspaper, pleaded with Laurier that the government's choice was simple: "either send troops or get out of office."[23] A government MP, Henri Bourassa, who dared to criticize the imperial government for its war policies in South Africa, was hissed in Parliament and called a traitor in the press.[24] Among French Canadians, emotions also ran high, with

---

21 Levitt, ed., Bourassa on Imperialism, 64.

22 Carman Miller, *Painting the Map Red: Canada and the South African War, 1899–1902* (Montréal and Kingston: McGill-Queen's University Press, 1993); Page, ed., *Imperialism and Canada*, 61–91.

23 Quoted in Stacey, *Age of Conflict*, 59.

24 Bourassa's writings and speeches on the South African war are reproduced in Levitt, ed., *Bourassa on Imperialism*, 35–43.

violent street demonstrations and symbolic desecrations of the Union Jack. In the end, Laurier bowed to pressure and reluctantly dispatched a Canadian contingent to South Africa. But the differences exposed by the Boer War provided a foretaste of the far more profound effects that the Great War would have on Canadian society 15 years later.

The sentimental attachment to the British Empire explains, in part, the willingness of many Canadians to go to war in August 1914. It is true that the declaration of war on Germany was issued by King George V on the advice of his ministers in London, not in Ottawa. Canadians had no say in the matter, just as Bourassa had said in 1912. When Britain was at war, all of the Empire was, ipso facto, at war. But for the vast majority of English Canadians, such legalities were quite irrelevant. Had they been consulted, the outcome would have been the same—willing participation on the side of the Mother Country. For French Canadians, by contrast, there was no such automatic identification of their interests in fighting in the war that had broken out in Europe.

The actual process of fighting this war fully exposed the internal contradictions of imperialism. For this was a war unlike any other in human experience. Within months, the belligerents had entrenched themselves in a vast front that stretched from Switzerland to the English Channel, lobbing artillery shells as fast as they could be produced and engaging in numerous and bloody attempts to break through the opposing lines. Much of the fighting achieved little, but the human and material costs were massive. And therein lay the problem for the self-governing dominions like Canada: The government in London expected the various parts of the Empire to contribute their young men and their wealth for the successful prosecution of the war, but the dominions, supposedly self-governing, had no control over the conduct of the war. As David Lloyd George, the British prime minister, admitted in December 1916, the dominions "have made enormous sacrifices, but we have held no conference with them as to either the objects of the war, or the methods of carrying it out. They hardly feel that they have been consulted."[25] Increasingly, as the number of casualties grew, the enthusiasm that had been so marked in the fall of 1914 waned. The Unionist coalition government under Sir Robert Borden was to discover this in the elections that were held in December 1917. While the Unionists won a clear majority, the popular vote, particularly among civilians, demonstrated significant areas of dissension in Ontario, Quebec, and the Maritimes.

The length and nature of the war had another effect. By the end of 1916, trench warfare had largely exhausted the supply of volunteers. Borden had to decide whether to reduce the Canadian contribution to the war or to maintain it by imposing conscription. French-speaking Canadians, who generally did not feel the same emotional commitment that had spurred voluntary recruitments in English Canada, had little interest in being forced to fight what was widely seen as an "English" war; indeed, Ernest Lapointe, the Liberal MP for Kamouraska, told the House of Commons in 1917 that had Lower Canada known that one day its citizens would be conscripted to fight in an imperial army, it would never have agreed to enter Confederation.[26] Francophone Quebeckers visited their anger on the Conservatives in the elections of December 1917—and in every subsequent election until the end of the 1950s. Of course, for many English Canadians, this was merely

25 Quoted in Donald Creighton, *Canada's First Century* (Toronto: Macmillan, 1970), 145.

26 Cited in John MacFarlane, *Ernest Lapointe and Quebec's Influence on Canadian Foreign Policy* (Toronto: University of Toronto Press, 1999), 21.

more evidence of perfidy, treason, and the abandonment of the Mother Country in its hour of need. The rancorous division between English and French Canadians erupted in sectarian violence, particularly in Québec over the Easter weekend of 1918. In short, the First World War not only put considerable strain on the relationship between the Empire and the Canadian government, it also exposed fundamental cleavages within the country.

Canadian participation in the First World War not only caused a considerable decline in enthusiasm for imperialism, but also the emergence of isolationism, a different set of ideas about how Canada should engage the world. However, before we examine isolationism, we need to look at another idea that had an important impact on Canada's international policies during the period between the two world wars—*autonomism*. This was the name given to the idea that Canada should assume control of *all* elements of policy, domestic and external, from Britain. (It was not called *independence*—though that is what it was—because independence from Britain was what the Americans had sought, and that is not the route that Canadians wanted to follow.[27]) Autonomism was a logical outgrowth of the autonomy in domestic policy achieved with Confederation in 1867, and while many Canadians had advocated autonomism before 1914, its acceptance was greatly catalyzed by the Great War. It was manifested in Borden's insistence on more effective consultation in the conduct of the war; separate representation for Canada at the peace conference; and separate Canadian membership in the League of Nations, the new international organization created by the Peace of Versailles. That such initiatives did not arouse the vitriol of imperialists was indicative of the shifts occurring in the public mood at the time.

Indeed, it was these new demands by the dominion governments, particularly the governments of Canada and South Africa, that transformed the Empire into the Commonwealth. It was clear that the *de facto* rights of sovereign statehood being exercised by the dominions did not mesh with their continued *de jure* constitutional subordination to the imperial government in London. At a succession of conferences in the 1920s, the Empire was negotiated out of existence. In 1926, the Imperial Conference agreed with the conclusion of the inter-imperial relations committee, chaired by the Earl of Balfour, that the dominions

> are autonomous Communities within the British Empire, equal in status, in no way subordinate one to another in any aspect of their domestic or external affairs, though united by a common allegiance to the Crown, and freely associated, as members of the British Commonwealth of Nations.[28]

The conference also agreed to alter the role of the governor general in the dominions. While originally the governor general was the representative of the imperial government, the Imperial Conference of 1926 recommended that henceforth the governor general was solely the representative of the Crown in the dominion, and that official channels of communications between a dominion government and the government in London be conducted on a government-to-government basis. After the Imperial Conference in 1930 clarified how the governor general was to be appointed, these recommendations were enshrined in legislation—"An Act to give effect to certain resolutions passed by Imperial Conferences

---

27 Adam Chapnick, "Running in Circles: The Canadian Independence Debate in History," in Brian Bow and Patrick Lennox, eds., *An Independent Foreign Policy for Canada? Challenges and Choices for the Future* (Toronto: University of Toronto Press, 2008), 25–40.

28 G.P. de T. Glazebrook, *A History of Canadian External Relations*, rev. ed., vol. 2: *In the Empire and the World, 1914–1939* (Toronto: McClelland & Stewart, 1966), 90–91.

held in the years 1926 and 1930"—that was approved by the British parliament and given Royal Assent on December 11, 1931. However, the act that brought the British Empire to an end is better known by its short title, the Statute of Westminster 1931.[29]

It should be noted that the growing autonomism of the 1920s did not suddenly eliminate the love of Empire that had fuelled the enthusiasm for war in 1914. Imperialist sentiment lingered, particularly in British Columbia, southern Ontario, and the Maritimes. The daily press both reflected this sentiment and helped to keep it alive.[30] Thus, by the end of the 1930s, there was still a clear attachment to Britain, the legal and constitutional freedom won in the Statute of Westminster notwithstanding. For this reason, supporting Britain in the Second World War was never in question for the majority of Canadians. As J.L. Granatstein and Robert Bothwell put it, "support for Britain was first a moral duty, and a political duty, if it was at all, a long way after. Canadian autonomy once achieved turned out to be like free will: it existed to enhance the righteous choice." They quote Stephen Leacock, writing on this subject in the summer of 1939: "If you were to ask any Canadian, 'Do you have to go to war if England does?' he'd answer at once, 'Oh, no.' If you then asked, 'Would you go to war if England does?' he'd answer 'Oh, yes.' And if you asked 'Why?' he would say, reflectively, 'Well, you see, we'd have to.'"[31]

The degree to which this attachment to Britain lingered well after the Second World War can be seen in the case of the Suez crisis of 1956. In response to the nationalization of the Suez Canal by Egyptian president Gamal Abdel Nasser in July, Israel launched a military attack on Egypt on October 29, 1956. This was followed by British and French attacks beginning on October 31, which caused a deep rift between Washington and its two major European allies. This split caused great consternation in Ottawa. As Prime Minister Louis St. Laurent wrote to Sir Anthony Eden, the British prime minister, on October 31, Anglo-American cooperation was crucial for peace and security: "It would be a tragedy beyond repair if it were now to disappear, or even to be weakened. It is hard for a Canadian to think of any consideration—other than national survival or safety—as more important."[32] At the United Nations, Lester Pearson, Canada's foreign minister, tried to negotiate a compromise solution and managed to secure agreement to a number of resolutions that would put a United Nations Emergency Force between the combatants.[33] But in the process, the Canadians found themselves voting against Britain and France on a number

---

29 Available http://www.statutelaw.gov.uk/documents/1931/4/ukpga/c4.

30 For example, the *Evening Telegram* of Toronto remained a consistent champion of the Empire throughout the interwar period, eagerly attacking anything that smacked of anti-imperialism: see Donald Page, "The Institute's 'Popular' Arm: The League of Nations Society in Canada," *International Journal* 33 (Winter 1977–8), 39–40 and Stacey, *Age of Conflict*, vol. 2: *1921–1948: The Mackenzie King Era* (Toronto: University of Toronto Press, 1981), 186.

31 Stephen Leacock, "Canada and the Monarchy," *The Atlantic* (June 1939), 735–744, quoted in J.L. Granatstein and Robert Bothwell, "'A Self-evident National Duty': Canadian Foreign Policy, 1935–1939," in Granatstein, ed., *Canadian Foreign Policy: Historical Readings* (Toronto: Copp Clark Pitman, 1986), 125–44.

32 St. Laurent to Eden, Ottawa, October 31, 1956, *Documents on Canadian External Relations*, vol. 22: *1956–1957 (Part 1)* (Ottawa: Minister of Public Works and Government Services Canada, 1999).

33 The literature on Pearson and the Suez crisis is considerable. John English, *The Worldly Years: The Life of Lester Pearson,* vol. 2: *1949–1972* (Toronto: Alfred A. Knopf Canada, 1992), esp. 107ff; for a more journalistic account, John Melady, *Pearson's Prize: Canada and the Suez Crisis* (Toronto: Dundurn

of occasions. Moreover, in an emergency debate in the House of Commons, St. Laurent claimed to be "scandalized" by what he sarcastically referred to as "the supermen of Europe." Pearson, for his part, claimed that Canada was not "a colonial chore-boy running around shouting 'Ready, aye, ready.'"[34]

Pearson's choice of words was not accidental. In Canadian politics, the phrase "Ready, aye, ready" signified support for Empire, most famously associated with the Chanak crisis of 1922. In the summer of that year, the Turkish nationalist army under Kemal Atatürk defeated the Greek army in western Anatolia and turned northward to the Dardanelles, which had been declared a neutral zone by the Treaty of Sèvres, and defended by a small British garrison at Çanakkale (or Chanak). Deciding to stand firm, the British prime minister, Lloyd George, threatened the Turks with war, at the same time asking the dominions to contribute troops to the cause. To bolster the imperial government's position, the request to the dominions was given to the press.[35] Unfortunately for Lloyd George, newspapers moved information more quickly than government telegrams: Both the Australian and Canadian prime ministers heard about London's request from the newspapers before they received the official request. Mackenzie King was distinctly displeased, and his government decided to turn down the imperial request.

Meighen, then leader of the opposition Conservatives, criticized King's refusal, claiming that "When Britain's message came, then Canada should have said: 'Ready, aye, ready; we stand by you.'"[36] But this phrase was often used—by both Liberals and Conservatives. Laurier, then the leader of the opposition Liberals, had used them in August 1914 in support of the declaration of war against Germany: "When the call comes," Laurier had stated, "our answer goes at once, and it goes in the classical language of the British answer to the call to duty: 'Ready, aye, ready.'"[37] In turn, Laurier was but echoing Sir George E. Foster, a Conservative MP, who in 1896 had said to the House of Commons: "It is the right and duty of Britain herself and of every dependency that belongs to her to be ready, aye, ready as well as steady in its sentiments of loyalty and devotion for the Empire as a whole."[38] However, Meighen was widely criticized for his advocacy of sending troops to Chanak, and the phrase "ready, aye, ready" assumed a pejorative connotation and was always associated thereafter with the Conservatives' tendency to put Britain and Empire ahead of Canadian interests. When Pearson used it in 1956, everyone understood that he

---

Press, 2006). For Pearson's own account, see Mike: *The Memoirs of the Rt. Hon. Lester B. Pearson,* vol. 2: *1948–1957* (Toronto: University of Toronto Press, 1973), chaps. 10–11. On Canada and Suez, see John W. Holmes, *The Shaping of Peace: Canada and the Search for World Order, 1943–1957,* vol. 2 (Toronto: University of Toronto Press, 1982), 348–70; a short overview is provided in Robert W. Reford, "Peacekeeping at Suez, 1956," in Don Munton and John Kirton, eds., *Canadian Foreign Policy: Selected Cases* (Scarborough: Prentice-Hall Canada, 1992), 58–77.

34 James Eayrs, *Canada in World Affairs*, vol. 9: *October 1955 to June 1957* (Toronto: Oxford University Press, 1959), 188.

35 Inbal A. Rose, *Conservatism and Foreign Policy During the Lloyd George Coalition, 1918–1922* (London: Routledge, 1999), 228–53.

36 Stacey, *Age of Conflict*, vol. 2, 30.

37 Canada, Parliament, House of Commons, *Debates*, 12th Parl., 4th sess., Special War Session, August 19, 1914, 10; quoted in Stacey, *Age of Conflict*, vol. 1, 176.

38 House of Commons, *Debates*, 7th Parl., 6th sess., January 16, 1896, 157.

was taking a dig at all those who still thought in terms of defining Canadian policy according to British interests.

The failure of the St. Laurent government to support Britain over Suez did not sit well with many English Canadians. As Robert Bothwell put it, "What Pearson saw as a rescue operation for a declining British power was seen by many Canadians as a betrayal of Canada's great friend and ally."[39] The *Globe and Mail* ran a series of editorials denouncing the government. Howard Green, a Conservative MP who was to become foreign minister under John Diefenbaker in 1959, attacked St. Laurent for criticizing "our two mother countries" and "knifing our best friends in the back."[40] Even Meighen emerged briefly from retirement to give an updated version of his celebrated speech from 34 years earlier.[41] The issue was raised in the election campaign of 1957. On a number of occasions, Diefenbaker discovered that he could draw a favourable response, particularly in Ontario and the Maritimes, by criticizing Canadian policy on Suez.

The Suez crisis of 1956 was the last time "support for Britain" was a major issue in Canadian foreign policy. Pro-British sentiment persisted, but by the 1960s Britain had ceased to hold special importance for Canadians. While one can sometimes hear still echoes of those links to Empire in contemporary Canadian politics, as Cara Spittal has demonstrated,[42] there is little doubt that by the 1970s the imperialist idea itself was well and truly dead.

BETWEEN THE WARS: ISOLATIONISM

Autonomism is rarely remembered as a dominant idea, in large part because it became obsolete so fast, a victim of its own success. With the Statute of Westminster, Canada acquired all the legal rights of a sovereign state and only needed to exercise them. However, it was in the context of a more independent foreign policy for Canada that isolationism emerged as a dominant idea in the evolution of international policy.

Isolationism as practised by Canadians during the years between the two world wars was in many respects inspired by an American dominant idea. Since 1789, isolationism had been firmly embedded in the practice of American foreign policy. It had two primary normative tenets: Do not become involved in European power politics; and do not enter into what Thomas Jefferson called "entangling alliances" that would suck the young republic into the maelstrom of international relations and rob it of its independence.[43] Isolationism was so

---

39 Robert Bothwell, "Canada's Moment: Lester Pearson, Canada, and the World," in Norman Hillmer, ed., *Lester Pearson: The Unlikely Gladiator* (Montréal and Kingston: McGill-Queen's University Press, 1999), 27.

40 Peter Stursberg, *Lester Pearson and the American Dilemma* (Toronto: Doubleday Canada, 1980), 156–57.

41 Quoted in Eayrs, *Canada in World Affairs*, 188, 50n.

42 Cara Spittal, "The Transatlantic Romance of the North Atlantic Triangle: Narratives of Autonomy and Empire in Canadian Foreign Relations," in Robert Bothwell and Jean Daudelin, eds., *Canada Among Nations 2008: 100 Years of Canadian Foreign Policy* (Montréal and Kingston: McGill-Queen's University Press, 2009), 317–42.

43 Alexander de Conde, *Entangling Alliance* (Durham: Duke University Press, 1958).

strongly rooted in American political culture that it was with little surprise that after the First World War the Americans turned their back on European politics and refused to ratify the Treaty of Versailles or join the new League of Nations.

The isolationism that appeared in Canada between 1919 and 1939 had some surface commonalities with the ideas in vogue in the United States, but there were deep differences.[44] It is true some Canadians had negative views of European politics: Laurier told the Imperial Conference in 1911 that "All the nations of Europe today, in my humble estimation, have gone, if I may say so, quite mad."[45] But there was simply no tradition in Canada of avoiding European politics or being "entangled" with European powers.

If Americans returned to isolationism *despite* their brief participation in the First World War, Canadians embraced isolationism *because* of that war. The human costs of four years of fighting on the Western Front were gruesome for all participants. For Canada, with its small population, the toll was particularly grim. In 1916, Canada's population was approximately 8 million. Over 619,000 Canadians, 446,000 of them volunteers, served with the forces. For the 425,000 who served in Europe, casualties were high: Fully 60,661 Canadians, nearly 1 percent of the entire population, were killed. Of those who survived, 34,000 needed artificial limbs and 60,000 received disability pensions.[46]

The carnage encouraged Canadians to withdraw from world politics and to embrace instead the basic tenet of American isolationism: a deep resentment of European politics. The connection was made explicitly during a debate on the Treaty of Versailles in September 1919 by C.G. "Chubby" Power, a Liberal MP from Quebec: "Our policy for the next hundred years should be that laid down by George Washington absolute renunciation of interference in European affairs. I believe the people of Canada will approve of this policy, namely, to let Europe be the arbiter of its own destiny while we in Canada [turn] our energies to our own affairs.[47] The tone could be savage: "It was European policy, European statesmanship, European ambition, that drenched the world with blood," N.W. Rowell, Canada's representative to the League of Nations, bluntly told the first meeting of the League in 1920. "Fifty thousand [sic] Canadians under the soil of France and Flanders is what Canada has paid for European statesmanship trying to settle European problems."[48]

For many Canadians, the new League of Nations was a major concern. While Canadians enjoyed the prestige that came with being a member of this international organization, there

---

44 On the attributes of Canadian isolationism, see the work of David G. Haglund: "Le Canada dans l'entre-deux-guerres," *Études internationales* 31:4 (December 2000), 727–43; and "Are *We* the Isolationists?" *International Journal* 58:1 (Winter 2002–3), 1–23.

45 Quoted in Stacey, *Age of Conflict*, vol. 1, 141. Such political opposites as Laurier and Bourassa often referred to Europe as the "vortex of militarism": on Laurier, see Desmond Morton, *Canada and War: A Military and Political History* (Toronto: Butterworths, 1981), 50; on Bourassa, see Levitt, *Bourassa on Imperialism*, 48, 53.

46 Figures from Morton, *Canada and War*, 82, 86; Stacey, *Age of Conflict*, vol. 1, 192, 235.

47 House of Commons, *Debates*, 13th Parl, 3rd sess., 1919, vol. 1, 230, September 11, 1919.

48 Quoted in James Eayrs, "'A Low Dishonest Decade': Aspects of Canadian External Policy, 1931–1939," in Hugh L. Keenleyside et al., *The Growth of Canadian Policies in External Affairs* (Durham: Duke University Press, 1960), 61. See also James Eayrs, *In Defence of Canada*, vol. 1: *From the Great War to the Great Depression* (Toronto: University of Toronto Press, 1964), 6.

was deep concern over the collective security provisions. Article X of the Covenant of the League read:

> The Members of the League undertake to respect and preserve against external aggression the territorial integrity and existing political independence of all Members of the League. In case of any such aggression or in case of any threat or danger of such aggression the Council shall advise upon the means by which this obligation shall be fulfilled.

In other words, if collective security was to work, Article X carried with it the obligation to declare war on an aggressor. This was seen as a means by which Canada could be drawn back into the vortex. Few Canadians were as blunt (or as rude) as William E. Borah, a Republican senator from Idaho and a leading isolationist in the United States Congress, who dismissed the League as "the gathered scum of the nations organized into a conglomerate international police force."[49] But the fear that League membership would drag North America into another European war was shared by Canadians. As the Liberal MP from Témiscouata, C.A. Gauvreau, put it to the House of Commons: "I see in the League of Nations a source of trouble, of entanglements and international dangers the more to be apprehended because there are in Europe so many sore and bleeding wounds not yet healed up."[50] More than one speaker in the debate on the Versailles treaty sounded the theme raised by Lucien Cannon (Liberal: Dorchester): "I am not in favour of England ruling this country, but I would rather be ruled by England than by Geneva."[51]

Far from the conflicts of Europe, North Americans had a very different view of the collective security provisions of the League of Nations. North Americans had long abandoned the use of force in their relations with each other[52] and widely believed in what can be called "North Americanism" or "exceptionalism"—the idea that North Americans were different than Europeans, particularly in how they resolved conflicts.[53] For this reason, many North Americans thought that collective security was like an insurance policy that functioned only to the advantage of Europeans. Indeed, that was exactly the metaphor used by the government leader in the Senate, Raoul Dandurand, when he was Canada's representative at the League Assembly in 1924:

> May I be permitted to add that in this association of Mutual Insurance against fire, the risks assumed by the different States are not equal? We [Canadians] live in a fire-proof house, far from inflammable materials. A vast ocean separates us from Europe.[54]

---

49 Quoted in Thomas N. Guinsburg, *The Pursuit of Isolationism in the United States Senate from Versailles to Pearl Harbor* (New York: Garland Publishing, 1982), 32.

50 House of Commons, *Debates*, 13th Parl, 3rd sess., 1919, vol. 1, 146–47, September 9, 1919.

51 Quoted in Richard Veatch, *Canada and the League of Nations* (Toronto: University of Toronto Press, 1975), 29.

52 Roussel, *North American Democratic Peace*; Sean Shore, "No Fences Make Good Neighbors: The Development of the Canadian–American Security Community, 1871–1940," in Emanuel Adler and Michael Barnett, eds., *Security Communities* (Cambridge: Cambridge University Press, 1998), 333–67.

53 Donald Barry, "The Politics of 'Exceptionalism': Canada and the United States as a Distinctive International Relationship," *Dalhousie Review* 60 (Spring 1980), 114–37.

54 "The Geneva Protocol (Dandurand, 2 October 1924)," in Walter A. Riddell, ed., *Documents on Canadian Foreign Policy, 1917–1939* (Toronto: Oxford University Press, 1962), 462–65.

While Dandurand was not an isolationist,[55] he was expressing the belief of many Canadians during this period that it was unlikely that Canadians would ever need the help of Europeans but very likely that Canadians would be called on to fight wars in Europe.

While the influence of isolationism could be seen across Canada, it was particularly noticeable among French Canadians, partly because of their indifference to the British Empire, but also because they had been quite literally cut off from France since 1763. P.B. Waite has argued that this led francophones to define themselves as a North American, not a European people—a sentiment nicely reflected in an editorial in *Le Devoir* in 1938, which declared: "Laissons l'Europe à ses heurts d'idées, à ses chocs de régimes, à ses querelles racistes. Enracinons-nous au sol d'Amérique."[56] Léon Mercier Gouin, a lawyer and the son and grandson of two former Québec premiers, suggested at a 1937 conference on Canadian foreign policy that "French Canadians are in favour of isolation in one form or another. . . . From this it follows that we do not intend to have Canada become one of the policemen of the world. 'Charity begins at home,' and our internal problems are quite enough for us."[57]

Those "internal problems" included not only the huge rift that had emerged between Canada's two language communities over foreign affairs, but also, as Robert Bothwell reminds us, the sharp economic divisions of class and income that had appeared at the end of the Great War.[58] Thus, the international policies of the Canadian government in the interwar period were framed by a desire to avoid reopening the wounds of 1917 and to promote reconciliation and economic development. In other words, unlike isolationism in the United States, Canadian isolationism was a policy designed to promote national unity.

Isolationism as it was practised in Canada during the interwar period also differed from American isolationism on another level. For Canadians, staying out of European quarrels was a useful way of asserting the autonomy recently achieved from Britain. Indeed, in the 1920s and 1930s many in the government in London openly doubted whether Canada would come to Britain's aid if another conflict were to break out in Europe.[59] This desire to reinforce Canada's autonomy also explains another paradoxical difference. Unlike

---

55 See Stéphane Paquin, "Raoul Dandurand: porte-parole de la conscience universelle," in Greg Donaghy and Kim Richard Nossal, eds., *Architects and Innovators: Building the Department of Foreign Affairs and International Trade, 1909–2009* (Montréal and Kingston: McGill-Queen's University Press, 2009).

56 "Leave Europe to their clash of ideas, their conflicts between regimes, their racial quarrels. Let us plant ourselves firmly in the soil of America," quoted in P.B. Waite, "French-Canadian Isolationism and English Canada: An Elliptical Foreign Policy, 1935–1939," *Journal of Canadian Studies* 18:2 (Summer 1983), 141.

57 Quoted in Robert Bothwell and Norman Hillmer, eds., *The In-Between Time: Canadian External Policy in the 1930s* (Toronto: Copp Clark, 1975), 20.

58 Robert Bothwell, "The Canadian Isolationist Tradition," *International Journal* 54:1 (Winter 1998–9), 76–88.

59 See Gregory A. Johnson and David A. Lenarcic, "The Decade of Transition: The North Atlantic Triangle in the 1920s," and B.J.C. McKercher, "World Power and Isolationism: The North Atlantic Triangle and the Crises of the 1930s," both in B.J.C. McKercher and Lawrence Aronsen, eds., *The North Atlantic Triangle in a Changing World: Anglo-American-Canadian Relations, 1902–1956* (Toronto: University of Toronto Press, 1996), 81–109, 110–46.

Americans, whose isolationism prompted them to refuse to join the League of Nations, Canadians eagerly embraced their membership in this new international organization, even while they remained deeply distrustful about the obligations that came with that membership. The explanation of this apparent contradiction—welcoming membership in the League but not the obligations that came with it—is that Canadians, and their leaders, regarded membership in the League as an invaluable symbol of Canadian autonomy that gave Canadians a voice and an opportunity to assert an independent identity on the world stage. As a result, there was never any sentiment, within the government or the public, for remaining outside the League like the Americans. And when in 1934 a Conservative senator introduced a motion to have Canada withdraw from the League, he was openly disavowed by his leader, Prime Minister R.B. Bennett; no other member of Parliament spoke in favour of the motion, which was handily voted down.[60]

By the late 1930s, with the rise of Nazi Germany under Adolf Hitler, the prospect of another war loomed larger. There were still some isolationist voices. Frank Underhill, a professor of history at the University of Toronto who was one of the founders of the Co-operative Commonwealth Federation (CCF), the predecessor of the New Democratic Party (NDP), continued to preach isolationism: Canadians, he argued, should "like Ulysses and his men, sail past the European siren, our ears stuffed with tax-bills [from the last war]."[61] Likewise, *L'Action nationale*, a nationalist Québec newspaper, editorialized that "Notre mot d'ordre est net. Pas un homme, pas un sou, pas un fusil, pas une cartouche pour les guerres de l'Angleterre."[62] Even the undersecretary of state for external affairs, O.D. Skelton, believed that "It is probable that those opposed to participation in British wars now constitute a majority of people in Canada."[63]

Skelton was to be proved wrong about majority opinion. When German troops invaded Poland on September 1, 1939, the vast majority of Canadians abandoned their isolationist sentiments. Parliament was convened and officially approved a declaration of war against Germany that King George VI announced on September 10—one week after the British declaration of war. The vote in Parliament suggested that the country went into the Second World War relatively united. J.S. Woodsworth, the leader of the CCF, voiced his objections, but the rest of his party did not oppose the war. Three Québécois nationalist MPs expressed disapproval, but other Québec MPs appeared to be satisfied by the government's promise not to introduce conscription. While there was little enthusiasm for the war in Québec, Québécois nonetheless enlisted in larger numbers than in 1914–18. And while the King government's decision in the autumn of 1944 to renege on its earlier promise and introduce conscription aroused considerable passions in Québec, there were none of the violent confrontations that had marked the introduction of conscription in the First World War. It is also important to note that there was very little enthusiasm for war in English Canada either. Certainly there was none of the jingoistic zeal that had greeted the outbreak of war in 1914; the memories of that war were still too fresh.

---

60 Stacey, *Age of Conflict*, vol. 2, 164–65.

61 Quoted in ibid., 232.

62 Quoted in Waite, "French-Canadian Isolationism," 136.

63 Quoted in Norman Hillmer, "The Anglo-Canadian Neurosis: The Case of O.D. Skelton," in Peter Lyon, ed., *Britain and Canada: Survey of a Changing Relationship* (London: Frank Cass, 1976), 77–78.

Canada's pursuit throughout the Cold War of a policy of internationalism, which we discuss in the next section, might suggest that the Second World War marked the end of isolationism. But as the case of imperialism suggests, ideas often linger a long time before disappearing. This was certainly the case with isolationism, an idea that the historian C.P. Stacey once described as a "tough weed."[64] In the 1990s, the uncertainties that accompanied the end of the Cold War and the effort to put the federal government's finances in order combined to create favourable conditions for the reappearance of what for many scholars looked like isolationism.[65] While the government of Jean Chrétien may not have described Canada as a "fireproof house" in the 1990s, it certainly behaved as though Canada did not need to be as engaged as in the past. The government cut the budgets of all the departments involved in international policy—the Department of Foreign Affairs and International Trade, the Department of National Defence, and the Canadian International Development Agency—and scaled back international involvements.[66] However, it is clear that the Canadian public continued to support international engagement by their government. From support for the NATO mission in Kosovo in the spring of 1999 to pressure on the government for more robust involvement in Darfur, we can clearly see that for the public in the 1990s and in the first decade of the twenty-first century, the mood in Canada was not at all what it had been after the Great War.

THE COLD WAR ERA: INTERNATIONALISM

Internationalism is, in many respects, the antithesis of isolation. If isolationism believes in the rightness of acting unilaterally in international politics, of not devoting resources and energy to build and maintain international order, and of mistrusting international institutions, internationalism is a doctrine that supports an active engagement in international conflict and a commitment to global organizations charged with maintaining peace.

Well over 60 million people were killed in the Second World War, a mere generation after a war that was supposed to be "the war to end all wars." More than 42,000 Canadians were killed between 1939 and 1945. But unlike the First World War, which caused Canadians to turn inward, this cataclysm transformed Canadian ideas about the proper relationship between their country and the rest of the world, propelling the country outward to be actively engaged in global politics.

Internationalist ideas were driven by both a strategic calculation and a moral concern. First, internationalism rested on a simple strategic premise: the idea that peace is indivisible.

---

64 C.P. Stacey, "From Meighen to King: The Reversal of Canadian External Policies, 1921–1923," *Transactions of the Royal Society of Canada*, series IV, vol. 7, 1969, 246.

65 Joseph T. Jockel and Joel J. Sokolsky, "Dandurand Revisited: Rethinking Canada's Defence in an Unstable World," *International Journal* 48:2 (Spring 1993), 380–401; Jean-François Rioux and Robin Hay, "Canadian Foreign Policy: From Internationalism to Isolationism," and Douglas A. Ross, "Canada's Functionalism Isolationism and the Future of Weapons of Mass Destruction," both in *International Journal* 54:1 (Winter 1998–9), 57–75, 120–42.

66 Kim Richard Nossal, "Pinchpenny Diplomacy: The Decline of 'Good International Citizenship' in Canadian Foreign Policy," *International Journal* 54:1 (Winter 1998–9), 88–105; Andrew Cohen, *While Canada Slept: How We Lost Our Place in the World* (Toronto: McClelland & Stewart, 2003); Tom Keating, "A Passive Internationalist: Jean Chrétien and Canadian Foreign Policy," in Lois Harder and Steve Patten, eds., *The Chrétien Legacy: Politics and Public Policy in Canada* (Montréal and Kingston: McGill-Queen's University Press, 2006), 124–41.

In other words, the fate of any one state and the peace of the international system as a whole are deeply interconnected. In this view, the outbreak of war in a seemingly distant part of the globe can plunge the whole system into conflict. Physical distance from great-power rivalries is not necessarily a guarantee that one will be able to avoid involvement. Technological developments and increasing interdependence between societies made inclinations to withdraw from international engagement illusory if not dangerous. In short, the concept of the "fireproof house" was obsolete. But internationalism was also driven by moral concerns. Canadian policymakers were genuinely concerned about the problem of war and peace. The horror and destruction of the Second World War, together with the atrocities perpetrated by totalitarian regimes, created in many policymakers an ethical concern for extending principles like justice, freedom, and democracy to the international level. Internationalism thus rose from this desire to contribute to the construction of a more peaceful and just world.

Internationalism is characterized by five elements. First, it puts a premium on the notion of *responsibility*: Each state with an interest in avoiding war must take a constructive part in the management of conflicts that will inevitably arise in global politics. Second, *multilateralism* is essential for defusing the clashes of interests that can lead to war. States should be prepared to forego the advantages of acting unilaterally in international politics in the larger interests of establishing and maintaining order within the community of states. Third, participation in *international institutions* is a cardinal principle, for institutionalization promotes multilateralism and dampens the unilateral impulse. Fourth, support for institutions must be given concrete expression by a willingness to enter into *formal commitments* to use national resources for the system as a whole—directly connected to the functionalism examined in Chapter 3. Finally, the stability of the global system must also be assisted by the *reinforcement of, and respect for, international law*.

Internationalism is sometimes described as "liberal"—for two reasons. Some use it because this approach was initially formulated and implemented by Liberal governments, particularly the government of Louis St. Laurent. But the adjective is also used because internationalism takes as its starting point the application of political liberalism to global politics. Not only is internationalism founded on liberal values (such as peace, freedom, justice, and democracy), but the means to promote it are inspired by some of the key tenets of liberal philosophy: individual rights, equality, rule of law, transparent systems of governance, and the management of economic exchange. Moreover, because the majority of Canadians value these principles, internationalism generates considerable consensus.

Internationalism also played a role similar to isolationism: It promoted a sense of Canadian identity at the national and the international levels.[67] Since the liberal values on which internationalist ideas are based reflect an idealistic vision of international relations, it is possible for Canada to distinguish itself from the great powers that prefer a more "realistic" approach to global politics. Canadians can thus more easily claim to be following a policy that is distinct from the United States, and to assume roles that Americans cannot or do not want to play, such as mediator or peacekeeper. Moreover, being able to

---

67 Stéphane Roussel and Chantal Robichaud, "L'État post-moderne par excellence? Internationalisme et promotion de l'identité internationale du Canada," *Études internationales* 35:1 (March 2004), 149–70.

participate in multilateral institutions provides Canada with a counterweight to the influence of the United States.[68]

Finally, it should be noted that this definition of internationalism cast Canada as an *aligned* member of the Western camp in global politics during the Cold War. In other words, internationalism as it was practised by Canadians was different from the kind of internationalism of a neutral state like Sweden. Rather, Canadian internationalism was framed within the context of the rivalries between the superpowers that emerged before the Second World War was even over. Military alignment with the United States and western Europe against the Soviet Union and participation in the multilateral and institutional manifestations of that alignment, such as NATO, must be seen as integral to this dominant idea.

According to Donald Creighton, the war brought about a "diplomatic revolution" in Canada.[69] The rapid expansion of the government as a result of the war brought a number of new players with new ideas to Ottawa. In 1946, Louis St. Laurent became the secretary of state for external affairs, or foreign minister; in 1948, he became the leader of the Liberal party and thus prime minister. St. Laurent's deputy was Lester B. Pearson, who in 1946 was appointed the undersecretary of state for external affairs—as the deputy minister of the Department of External Affairs was called before 1993. When St. Laurent became the prime minister, he appointed Pearson as his foreign minister and found him a safe Liberal seat in which to run for election to the House of Commons. However, a number of other senior civil servants, such as Dana Wilgress, Norman Robertson, Hume Wrong, and Escott Reid, also contributed to the reformulation of Canada's international policies during this period.[70]

Pearson and St. Laurent were avowed internationalists. Pearson had served in London and Geneva in the late 1930s, where he had watched King's cautious interwar foreign policy "with impatience."[71] By November 1938, he was questioning his own isolationist tendencies. In a letter to External Affairs, he wondered, "would our complete isolation from European events (if such a thing were possible) save us from the effect of a British defeat; and, even if it did, could we stand by and watch the triumph of Nazism?"[72] By 1942, he was publicly urging the abandonment of isolationism:

> In 1919 we were only interested in the road back. We know where that led. We must now keep our eyes on the road ahead. This time we must maintain, for the organization and application of the peace, the spirit and forms of international co-operation which we are forging in the heat and flames of war.[73]

---

68 On counterweights in Canadian foreign policy, see David Haglund and Stéphane Roussel, "Escott Reid, the North Atlantic Treaty, and Canadian Strategic Culture," in Greg Donaghy and Stéphane Roussel, eds., *Escott Reid, Diplomat & Scholar* (Montréal and Kingston: McGill-Queen's University Press, 2004), 44–66.

69 The title of chap. 7 in Donald Creighton, *The Forked Road: Canada, 1939–1957* (Toronto: McClelland & Stewart, 1976).

70 For a discussion of the senior civil servants during this period, see J.L. Granatstein, *The Ottawa Men: The Civil Service Mandarins, 1935–1957* (Toronto: Oxford University Press, 1982).

71 L.B. Pearson, "Forty Years On: Reflections on Our Foreign Policy," *International Journal* 22:3 (Summer 1967), 357.

72 Quoted in John English, *Shadow of Heaven: The Life of Lester Pearson*, vol. 1: *1897–1948* (Toronto: Lester & Orpen Dennys, 1989), 201–202.

73 Lester B. Pearson, *Words and Occasions* (Toronto: University of Toronto Press, 1970), 55.

Pearson's precepts of internationalism—responsibility, multilateralism, commitment, and international institutions—sprang from "his preoccupation with peaceful methods of resolving conflict."[74] As he wrote in his memoirs, "Everything I learned during the war confirmed and strengthened my view as a Canadian that our foreign policy must not be timid or fearful of commitments but activist in accepting international responsibilities."[75]

St. Laurent's attachment to such ideas was just as strong. In October 1945, in the debate on joining the United Nations, he argued that "Canada is prepared to take whatever risk may be involved in joining this organization, because the other risk, that of not having an international organization, is something of such consequence that one dare hardly envisage it."[76] Four months after King appointed him to the external affairs portfolio, St. Laurent delivered what has come to be regarded as the classic statement of postwar Canadian internationalism. In the Gray Lecture at the University of Toronto in January 1947, he outlined the five principles on which Canadian foreign policy was to be based: national unity, political liberty, the rule of law in international affairs, the values of a Christian civilization, and the acceptance of international responsibility.[77] Importantly, two of these principles—the rule of law and the acceptance of responsibility—broke sharply with Canada's interwar diplomacy.

Changes in Canadian policy in the five years after the war were no less significant than changes in attitude. Internationalism in practice would bring policies unthinkable a generation earlier: a strong and durable commitment to the creation of a new organization that had a mandate to keep global peace; the pursuit of defence cooperation with the United States in peacetime (formally achieved with a joint declaration in 1947); support for a multiracial Commonwealth after the independence of India, Pakistan, and Ceylon (now Sri Lanka) in 1947[78]; enthusiastic support for the creation of a peacetime alliance that would involve the unprecedented stationing of Canadian troops on active service abroad[79]; and participation in the Korean War in 1950.[80]

It should be noted that the internationalism of the postwar period was not the result of public opinion. The government was not compelled to embrace an activist role for Canada in the United Nations in the way that Laurier had been compelled to join the South African war, or that King had been deterred from pursuing an activist role in the League of Nations. Rather, if there was a "revolution," it was a "top down" movement, often featuring ideas

---

74 Denis Stairs, "Present in Moderation: Lester Pearson and the Craft of Diplomacy," *International Journal* 29:1 (Winter 1973–4), 145.

75 *Mike: The Memoirs of the Rt. Hon. Lester B. Pearson*, vol. 1: *1897–1948* (Toronto: University of Toronto Press, 1972), 283.

76 Dale C. Thomson, *Louis St. Laurent: Canadian* (Toronto: Macmillan, 1967), 176.

77 The Gray lecture is reprinted in R.A. Mackay, ed., *Canadian Foreign Policy, 1945–1954: Selected Speeches and Documents* (Toronto: McClelland & Stewart, 1970), 388–99; also in Granatstein, ed., *Canadian Foreign Policy: Historical Readings*, 25–33.

78 Holmes, *Shaping of Peace*, vol. 2, chap. 8; James Eayrs, *In Defence of Canada*, vol. 3: *Peacemaking and Deterrence* (Toronto: University of Toronto Press, 1972), chap. 4.

79 Holmes, *Shaping of Peace*, vol. 2, 98–122; the text of the North Atlantic Treaty is reprinted in Mackay, ed., *Canadian Foreign Policy, 1945–1954*, 192–95.

80 Denis Stairs, *The Diplomacy of Constraint: Canada, the Korean War and the United States* (Toronto: University of Toronto Press, 1974).

conceived by government officials themselves. For example, Escott Reid, a senior official in External Affairs, was at the centre of Canadian policymaking on the new United Nations and was one of the first Canadian officials to propose the creation of a formal alliance of Western countries (what eventually became the Atlantic alliance through the North Atlantic Treaty of 1949); and it was Reid, with Pearson, who thought of the importance of nonmilitary cooperation between the members of the alliance (what eventually became Article 2 of the North Atlantic Treaty).[81] Those policymakers who still clung to isolationist ideas, such as Prime Minister Mackenzie King, were forced to yield to the enthusiasms of the new generation, who in numerous speeches sought to convince the Canadian public of the benefits of internationalist engagement.[82]

Their efforts bore fruit. Canada's internationalist commitments caused little opposition. When the UN Charter was voted on by Parliament, only five MPs, all from Québec, voted against it. Only two votes were cast against the North Atlantic Treaty in 1949, again from Québec, where distrust of international military commitments was still fuelled by the memory of the conscription crisis of 1942–1944. And in 1950, the outbreak of the Korean War brought not bitter division but a measure of consensus. English-language newspapers were fully behind participation; indeed, the government was criticized for not doing enough. Initially the French-language press was noncommittal, caught in what Denis Stairs called the cross-pressures arising from "a conflict between a traditional commitment to isolationism on the one hand, and a hostility to communism on the other."[83] But by the time St. Laurent announced in August the government's intention to send ground forces, only *Le Devoir* and the *Montréal Matin* opposed participation, with most French-language newspapers approving the dispatch of troops.[84] In Parliament, there was similar bipartisan support, leading the *Ottawa Journal* to remark that "It would have seemed a strange debate to Laurier and Borden and Meighen. . . . There was the Canadian Parliament begging its executive ministers to send ships or troops or planes to fight in a far-off mountainous land where no Canadians are and whose economic interest to Canada is less than that of Smiths Falls."[85]

Internationalism, John Holmes has written, "was almost a religion in the decade after the Second World War."[86] The hold of its orthodoxy proved exceedingly durable. Over the course of the Cold War era, Canada participated in the majority of peacekeeping missions organized by the United Nations; Canadian leaders undertook personal initiatives to resolve interstate conflict, such as Pearson's diplomacy over the Suez crisis in 1956, for which he was awarded the Nobel Prize for Peace; and the idea of Canadian activism on behalf of the larger community of states as a normative good was increasingly entrenched in Canadian political culture.

---

81 See Haglund and Roussel, "Escott Reid"; also Escott Reid, *Time of Fear and Hope: The Making of the North Atlantic Treaty, 1947–1949* (Toronto: McClelland & Stewart, 1977).

82 James Eayrs, *In Defence of Canada*, vol. 4: *Growing Up Allied* (Toronto: University of Toronto Press, 1980), 51.

83 Stairs, *Diplomacy of Constraint,* 58.

84 J.I. Gow, "Les Québécois, la guerre et la paix, 1945–1960," *Canadian Journal of Political Science* 3:1 (March 1970), 88–122, esp. 98, table 4.

85 Stairs, *Diplomacy of Constraint,* 55–57.

86 Holmes, *Shaping of Peace*, vol. 2, 119.

However, the fervour of that first decade waned as the opportunities for Canada to put its internationalist ideals into practice diminished. The world of the 1960s was different from the early 1950s. The process of decolonization had given birth to new hotbeds of tension, complicating the task of the United Nations. The countries of western Europe had recovered from their wartime devastation, putting new strains on the Atlantic alliance as they redefined their role; Canada, which had been a central actor at the creation of NATO, found itself increasingly marginalized, stripped of influence. The rise of China as an autonomous major power had altered the global balance of power. And detente between the United States and the Soviet Union had lessened tensions between the two superpowers, limiting the possibilities of mediatory diplomacy. In short, if internationalist religiosity is measured purely by activism in peacekeeping and mediatory diplomacy, by the late 1960s, Canadians were lapsed internationalists.

Pierre Elliott Trudeau, who came to power in 1968 openly critical of the internationalist orthodoxy, tried to deliver the coup de grâce. "There comes a time for renewal," boldly declared the foreign policy review published by his government in 1970.[87] The Trudeau review called into question many of the traditional manifestations of internationalism, including the relevance of United Nations peacekeeping, Canada's role in international affairs, and even the commitment to the North Atlantic Treaty Organization (NATO).

However, looking at the Trudeau review and its aftermath offers important lessons about the degree to which ideas can survive even prime ministerial assaults and enjoy a long and healthy life. During Trudeau's long tenure as prime minister, the institutions created between 1945 and 1950, particularly the United Nations and the Atlantic alliance, remained at the heart of Canada's international policies. Likewise, internationalist policies, such as peacekeeping, development assistance, and initiatives to protect human rights and promote disarmament,[88] remained popular. And despite his cavalier criticisms of internationalism of the late 1960s, Trudeau never abandoned the basic principles of this dominant idea; indeed, his "peace initiative" of 1983–84 was firmly within an internationalist framework that none of his predecessors would have disavowed. In short, Trudeau's continued embrace of internationalism underscores the degree to which public support for this dominant idea remained quite consistent for well over a generation, from "Pearsonian internationalism" of the 1950s to the "constructive internationalism" (also called "new internationalism") of the Mulroney government in the late 1980s.[89]

Another measure of the enduring appeal of a dominant idea in foreign policy is how the electorate responds to political parties that explicitly advocate an alternative idea. In the late 1960s, the New Democratic Party (NDP) and the Parti Québécois (PQ) adopted a policy that explicitly rejected internationalism and embraced neutralism, promising to withdraw

87 Canada, Secretary of State for External Affairs, *Foreign Policy for Canadians*, main booklet (Ottawa: Information Canada, 1970) 8.

88 Robert O. Matthews and Cranford Pratt, eds., *Human Rights in Canadian Foreign Policy* (Montréal and Kingston: McGill-Queen's University Press, 1988); Albert Legault and Michel Fortmann, *A Diplomacy of Hope: Canada and Disarmament, 1945–1988* (Montréal and Kingston: McGill-Queen's University Press, 1992).

89 Canada, Parliament, Special Joint Committee of the Senate and of the House of Commons on Canada's International Relations, *Independence and Internationalism* (Ottawa, June 1986), 137–40; see also Joe Clark, "Canada's New Internationalism," in John W. Holmes and John Kirton, eds., *Canada and the New Internationalism* (Toronto: Canadian Institute of International Affairs, 1988).

from NATO and NORAD. Given that polls consistently demonstrated that 85 percent of Canadians rejected neutralism, this was a plank in the party's platform that cost the NDP votes for more than 20 years. To be sure, the party's parliamentary leadership, recognizing this, often tried to soften the neutralist plank, but the party's militant base always insisted on retaining it.

For its part, the Parti Québécois learned more quickly. After it had won the November 1976 provincial election and prepared to present the voters of Québec with a proposal for withdrawal from the Canadian federation, the PQ sought to make its proposed foreign policy as attractive as possible. Between 1977 and 1979, the PQ leadership undertook a lengthy—and ultimately successful—campaign to convince the hardliners within the party to give up the neutralist platform that had been a staple of the PQ's foreign policy since 1969. As a result, the 1979 white paper on sovereignty-association embraced a foreign policy blueprint for an independent Québec that was deeply Pearsonian and internationalist: military alignment with the West, including membership in NATO and NORAD; membership in the UN, La Francophonie, and even the Commonwealth; and diplomatic activism. Moreover, at the federal level, the Bloc Québécois reflects the same strong commitment to internationalism.[90]

In short, despite questions being raised about its health, internationalism continued alive and well. The principles associated with this dominant idea continued to impose on policymakers. If the governments of Jean Chrétien, Paul Martin, and Stephen Harper no longer used the word "internationalist" to describe their foreign policies, there is little doubt that basic internationalist principles (responsibility, multilateralism, engagement, international institutions, and the rule of law) undergird Canada's international policies. Indeed, some have argued that the period of 1945–1957—sometimes called the "golden age" of Canadian foreign policy—should serve as a permanent inspiration for Canada's international relations,[91] almost as though there was, as John W. Holmes entitled one his books, "no other way."[92]

THE POST–COLD WAR ERA: IDEAS IN FLUX

Major global or national upheavals or cataclysms inevitably cause a shift in dominant ideas as new ideas emerge that reflect the new environment. Thus, the trauma of the First World War gave rise to isolationism, and the global disruptions of the Great Depression and the Second World War prompted the emergence of internationalist ideas. The end of the Cold War might have prompted a reevaluation of the main trends of Canada's international policies—and the possible emergence of new dominant ideas. Certainly internationalism

---

90 Stéphane Roussel and Charles-Alexandre Théorêt, "A 'Distinct Strategy'? The Use of Canadian Strategic Culture by the Sovereignist Movement in Québec, 1968–1996," *International Journal* 59:3 (Summer 2004), 557–77; also Roussel and Théorêt, "Defence Policy Distorted by the Sovereignist Prism? The Bloc Québécois on Security and Defence Questions (1990–2005)," in David Carment and David Bercuson, eds., *The World in Canada: Diaspora, Demography, and Domestic Politics* (Montréal and Kingston: McGill-Queen's University Press, 2008), 169–88.

91 For example, Cohen, *While Canada Slept.*

92 John W. Holmes, ed., *No Other Way: Canada and International Security Institutions* (Toronto: University of Toronto Press, 1986).

and the concept of middle power, formulated in the context of a bipolar world that had disappeared, no longer seemed an appropriate guide to policy. However, this is not what occurred. During the post–Cold War era—the decade from the end of the Soviet Union in 1991 until the attacks of September 11, 2001—a number of ideas about Canadian international policy were in contention.

There were several reasons for this. First, in 1991 there was no cataclysm comparable to those of 1914 or 1939. Rather, the Cold War ended through a relatively slow process that began with the emergence of Mikhail Gorbachev as general secretary of the Communist Party of the Soviet Union in 1985 and his pursuit of the twin policies of *perestroika* (restructuring) and *glasnost* (openness); the progressive collapse of Soviet and communist power in the pro-Soviet regimes of Eastern Europe in 1989, culminating most famously by the breaching of the Berlin Wall in November; the declarations of independence by some of the republics of the Soviet Union in 1990 and 1991; and the final collapse of the Soviet regime itself after the coup of August 1991 that led to the dissolution of the Soviet Union in December 1991. However momentous these events were, they did not cause any radical transformation in Canadian perceptions about their relations with the world. Second, the precise shape of the evolving international system and the threats remained fuzzy, at least until the 9/11 attacks. As the white paper on defence of 1994 stated, the defining feature of international politics during this period was uncertainty: "Canada faces an unpredictable and fragmented world, one in which conflict, repression and upheaval exist alongside peace, democracy and relative prosperity."[93] Finally, it was during this period that funding for all aspects of Canada's international policy—diplomacy, defence, and development assistance—was cut deeply as the Chrétien government struggled to control the federal deficit that had ballooned after 20 years of deficit spending by the Trudeau and Mulroney governments. This limited the resources the government was able to invest in international engagement during this era.

In many respects, internationalist ideas were still quite evident in Canadian opinion, as Don Munton has clearly shown.[94] They were also reflected in policy during this era. Brian Mulroney was enthusiastic about the new era in Russian–American relations, marked by the cooperation of the superpowers at the time of the Gulf War of 1991, and strongly supported the more muscular initiatives of the United States in subsequent years. In fact, a number of the diplomatic initiatives of the Progressive Conservative government were clearly in the tradition of middle-power internationalism, particularly those focused on management of regional conflicts and arms control.[95] Indeed, the concept of "cooperative security," enunciated by Mulroney's secretary of state for external affairs, Joe Clark, in September 1990, was a clear attempt to adapt the basic principles of internationalism

---

93 Canada Department of National Defence, *1994 Defence White Paper* (Ottawa: Minister of Supply and Services, 1994), chap. 1.

94 For example, Don Munton, "Whither Internationalism?" *International Journal* 58:1 (Winter 2002–3), 155–80.

95 Andrew F. Cooper, Richard A. Higgott, and Kim Richard Nossal, *Relocating Middle Powers: Australia and Canada in a Changing World Order* (Vancouver: UBC Press, 1993); Michel Fortmann and Manon Tessier, "The Conservative Approach to International Peacekeeping," in Nelson Michaud and Kim Richard Nossal, eds., *Diplomatic Departures: The Conservative Era in Canadian Foreign Policy, 1984–1993* (Vancouver: UBC Press, 2001), 113–27.

(responsibility and multilateralism) to the new global environment.[96] The foreign policy of the Liberal government of Jean Chrétien after 1993 also featured middle-power diplomacy: Canada continued to support a variety of international institutions and continued to contribute to the multilateral forces deployed to Bosnia, Kosovo, and East Timor (now Timor-Leste).

However, the Mulroney and Chrétien governments pursued policies that represented a retreat from the fundamentals of internationalism. Mulroney brought home the Canadian Forces that had been stationed in Germany since 1951 as part of Canada's NATO commitments. In September 1993, he recalled Canada's peacekeeping forces stationed in Cyprus, bringing to an end a 29-year commitment to UNFICYP. For its part, the Chrétien government may have maintained Canada's contribution to peacekeeping, but it had little of the enthusiasm for the job exhibited by its predecessors. Rather, it demonstrated caution, resisting when other NATO allies wanted to use air strikes in Bosnia in 1994. And while Canada participated in the NATO peacekeeping forces in Bosnia (IFOR and SFOR) established by the Dayton Accords of November 1995, it did so with considerable reluctance and with 1000 troops, far fewer than the 4000 troops that its other NATO partners had hoped for.

Instead, in the 1990s the Chrétien government pursued what might be thought of as a policy of "internationalism lite"—pushing the *rhetorical* envelope of international engagement while not actually *doing* very much. Lloyd Axworthy, who was minister of foreign affairs from 1996 until he left politics in 2000, articulated what can be regarded as a radical vision for Canada's international relations. He openly disparaged the pursuit of "naked self-interest" in global politics, arguing instead that because Canadians were "on the road to global citizenship," they preferred to articulate ideas of a global "common good."[97] Indeed, Paul Heinbecker, one of Axworthy's senior advisers in the Department of Foreign Affairs and International Trade who served as Canada's ambassador and permanent representative to the United Nations, dismissed the very idea of the national interest: "Canadians are moved by humanitarian impulse, not by the cold-blooded or rational calculations of realpolitik. . . . Principles are often more important than power to Canadians."[98]

Certainly Axworthy encouraged Canadians to rethink those principles. When he came to office in 1996, he explicitly rejected the dominant fixation with the *state* as the traditional object of security. He championed the notion of "human security"—the idea that the proper focus of security policy should be on *people* rather than on *states*, arguing that Canada should be willing "to take risks on behalf of victims of war in far-flung places."[99] As Tomlin, Hillmer, and Hampson demonstrate, that concept emerged out of the shifts in

---

96 David Dewitt, "Common, Comprehensive and Cooperative Security," *Pacific Review* 7:1 (1994), 1–15; Kim Richard Nossal, "Seeing Things? The Adornment of 'Security' in Canada and Australia," *Australian Journal of International Affairs* 49:1 (May 1995), 33–47.

97 Lloyd Axworthy, *Navigating a New World: Canada's Global Future* (Toronto: Random House Canada, 2003), 1–5.

98 J.L. Granatstein, "The Importance of Being Less Earnest: Promoting Canada's National Interests Through Tighter Ties with the U.S.," *Benefactors Lecture 2003* (Toronto, C.D. Howe Institute, 2003), 12, available http://www.cdhowe.org/pdf/benefactors_lecture_2003.pdf.

99 Lloyd Axworthy, "Canada and Human Security: The Need for Leadership," *International Journal* 52:2 (Spring 1997), 183–196; also Lloyd Axworthy, "Civilians in War: 100 Years After The Hague Peace Conference," in Department of Foreign Affairs and International Trade, *Statements and Speeches*, 99/48 (New York: September 24, 1999).

ideas and agendas of the post–Cold War era.[100] Human security was not only formally enshrined in Canadian policy,[101] but Axworthy also put the idea into action. He was the prime mover behind a global ban on anti-personnel landmines and pressed for global action on children affected by war.[102] Human security was used to justify Canadian participation in the bombing of Serbia in early in 1999 and in the intervention in East Timor later that year.[103] It was reflected in the increased emphasis on the role of women in Canada's development assistance policies.[104] Under Axworthy, the Canadian government also sponsored the International Commission on Intervention and State Sovereignty (ICISS), a blue-ribbon panel of experts to examine the notion of national sovereignty and how it could be fitted to the requirements of human security.[105]

Axworthy's embrace of this concept generated considerable interest (and a huge literature[106]). Although human security is in itself a useful idea that has generated considerable debate in IR, its application in the context of Canadian policy was limited. Francis J. Furtado has concluded that it "never became the animating concept of Canadian

---

100 Brian W. Tomlin, Norman Hillmer, and Fen Osler Hampson, *Canada's International Policies: Agendas, Alternatives and Politics* (Toronto: Oxford University Press, 2008), 202–29.

101 Canada, 1999, Department of Foreign Affairs and International Trade, *Human Security: Safety for People in a Changing World* (Ottawa: April 1999). This document was quickly removed from the DFAIT website after Axworthy resigned in 2000; today it can only be found at http://www.summit-americas.org/Canada/HumanSecurity-english.htm.

102 See Brian W. Tomlin, "On a Fast-Track to a Ban: The Canadian Policy Process," *Canadian Foreign Policy* 5:3 (1998), 3–24; Axworthy, *Navigating a New World*, 126–55; Carmen Sorger and Eric Hoskins, "Protecting the Most Vulnerable: War-Affected Children," in Rob McRae and Don Hubert, eds., *Human Security and the New Diplomacy: Protecting People, Promoting Peace* (Montréal and Kingston: McGill-Queen's University Press, 2001), 134–51.

103 Axworthy, *Navigating a New World*, 177–99; Kim Richard Nossal and Stéphane Roussel, "Canada and the Kosovo War: The Happy Follower," in Pierre Martin and Mark R. Brawley, eds., *Alliance Politics, Kosovo, and NATO's War: Allied Force or Forced Allies?* (New York: Palgrave, 2000), 181–99; T.S. Hataley and Kim Richard Nossal, "The Limits of the Human Security Agenda: The Case of Canada's Response to the Timor Crisis," *Global Change, Peace and Security* 16:1 (2004), 5–17.

104 Edna Keeble and Heather Smith. "Institutions, Ideas, Women and Gender: New Directions in Canadian Foreign Policy," *Journal of Canadian Studies* 35:4 (2001), 130–41.

105 Ramesh C. Thakur, Andrew F. Cooper, and John English, eds., *International Commissions and the Power of Ideas* (Tokyo: United Nations University Press, 2005); Jennifer Welsh, "From Right to Responsibility: Humanitarian Intervention and International Society," *Global Governance* 8:4 (2002), 503–21.

106 Robin J. Hay, "Present at the Creation? Human Security and Canadian Foreign Policy in the Twenty-First Century," in Fen Osler Hampson, Michael Hart, and Martin Rudner, eds., *Canada Among Nations 1999: A Big League Player?* (Toronto: Oxford University Press, 1999), 215–32; Peter Stoett, *Human and Global Security: An Exploration of Terms* (Toronto: University of Toronto Press, 1999); George MacLean, "Instituting and Projecting Human Security: A Canadian Perspective," *Australian Journal of International Affairs* 54:3 (2000), 269–76; Roland Paris, "Human Security: Paradigm Shift or Hot Air?" *International Security* 26:2 (2001), 87–102; Rosalind Irwin, ed., *Ethics and Security in Canadian Foreign Policy* (Vancouver: UBC Press, 2001); Prosper Bernard, Jr., "Canada and Human Security: From the Axworthy Doctrine to Middle Power Internationalism," *American Review of Canadian Studies* 36:2 (Summer 2006), 233–61; and David Bosold and Wilfried von Bredow, "Human Security: A Radical or Rhetorical Shift in Canada's Foreign Policy?" *International Journal* 61:4 (Autumn 2006), 829–44.

policy,"[107] much less a dominant idea. In large part this was because unlike other dominant ideas about international policy explored in this chapter, human security was not so much an animating idea about how Canada should engage global politics as it became a *domestic political* strategy for managing the large gulf between rhetoric and reality. For, as numerous analysts have noted,[108] it was precisely during this period that Canada actually did less on the world stage than it had the past. Despite the government's rhetoric about how much Canada contributed to global politics, the huge reduction in spending on international policy in the 1990s meant that fewer Canadian peacekeepers were deployed overseas, fewer Canadian development assistance dollars were being spent, and fewer Canadian diplomats were being sent to foreign capitals. An emphasis on rhetoric rather than action followed naturally; during periods of budget cutbacks, when little money is made available for international engagement, rhetoric is often the only alternative. Ironically, the less the Canadian government did on the international stage, the more important internationalism became as what Hector Mackenzie terms the "central myth" in Canadian self-perceptions by the end of the twentieth century, with the stories of Canada's earlier exploits on the international stage told and retold as an "inspirational tale."[109] But, as Denis Stairs acidly reminds us, "The spinning of tales—tales not false, perhaps, but certainly canted—becomes an increasingly valued and admired art as the policy establishment struggles to bridge the gap between what well-intentioned Canadians think and what the government really is doing."[110] However, because these rhetorical flourishes proved to be highly popular with Canadians, what can be called "ear candy"[111] became the preferred substitute for policy as ministers engaged in what Stairs called "inflated and self-serving rhetoric [that was] clearly designed to appeal to the preferences and prejudices of a population indoctrinated by its own myths."[112]

By contrast, regionalism was an idea about Canada's approach to international politics comparable to the other ideas surveyed in this chapter. This idea suggests that rather than looking at international relations from a *world* or *global* perspective, one should look at

---

107 Francis J. Furtado, "Human Security: Did It Live? Has It Died? Does It Matter?" *International Journal* 63:2 (Spring 2008), 420.

108 Fen Hampson and Dean Oliver, "Pulpit Diplomacy: A Critical Assessment of the Axworthy Doctrine," *International Journal* 53:3 (Summer 1998), 379–406; Kim Richard Nossal, "Pinchpenny Diplomacy: The Decline of 'Good International Citizenship' in Canadian Foreign Policy," *International Journal* 54:1 (Winter 1998–9), 28–47; Cohen, *While Canada Slept*; Allan Gotlieb, "Romanticism and Realism in Canada's Foreign Policy, *Benefactors Lecture 2004* (Toronto: C.D. Howe Institute, 2004), available http://www.cdhowe.org/pdf/benefactors_lecture_2004.pdf.

109 Hector Mackenzie, "Canada's Nationalist Internationalism: From the League of Nations to the United Nations," in Norman Hillmer and Adam Chapnick, eds., *Canadas of the Mind: The Making and Unmaking of Canadian Nationalisms in the Twentieth Century* (Montréal and Kingston: McGill-Queen's University Press, 2007), 90–91.

110 Denis Stairs, "Challenges and Opportunities for Canadian Foreign Policy in the Paul Martin Era," *International Journal* 58:4 (Autumn 2003), 489–90.

111 For a discussion of this dynamic, see Kim Richard Nossal, "Ear Candy: Canadian Policy Toward Humanitarian Intervention and Atrocity Crimes in Darfur," *International Journal* 60:4 (Autumn 2005), 1017–32.

112 Stairs, "Challenges and Opportunities," 503.

region as the proper focus of a country's international politics, with attention given to international relationships, particularly economic relations, within the region.[113] In this perspective, each region of the globe has particular features that are shaped in part by geographic proximity and in part by efforts of elites of states within those regions to create the *idea* of region. These features include the political (the links, conflicts, and power relations between the states in that region), the institutional (the organizations developed for security and economic exchange within the region), and the cultural and historical ties. Regionalism has both a normative and an analytical dimension: For some, looking at regions allows one to better understand contemporary world order; for others, regions are where a state's international policy should be focused.

The popularity of regionalism (both as a guide for international policy and as a way of analyzing world politics) was closely related to the development of international institutions that emerged to oversee the process of regional integration, in particular in Europe. In the late 1950s and early 1960s, the focus was on western Europe and the development of pan-European institutions. In the late 1980s and early 1990s, not only was European integration deepened by the creation of the European Union, but similar efforts to foster regional integration were occurring in both the Asia-Pacific, with such institutions as the Asia-Pacific Economic Cooperation (APEC) forum, and in North America with the signing of the Canada–United States Free Trade Agreement that came into force in January 1989, and then the North American Free Trade Agreement (NAFTA), which came into force in January 1994. Regional initiatives were also taking place in Latin America and Africa. In short, by the mid-1990s, it very much looked as though the world was being reorganized around a number of large regional economic blocs.

There can be little doubt that, beginning in the mid-1980s, Canadians and their government were affected by this broader movement. It is true that one might interpret the creation of a "North Atlantic community" of the sort that St. Laurent, Pearson, and Reid championed in the late 1940s as a form of regionalism, just as the Canada–U.S. free-trade agreement of the late 1980s might be seen as a form of North American regionalism. But the "new regionalism," at least as it was widely interpreted in Canada, implicitly called into question these traditional axes, as though they had little to offer Canada, and instead called for the development of new horizons. Increasingly the fostering of relations with regions other than North America was seen as a way of diversifying Canada's international policies and thus avoiding an overly restrictive partnership with the United States. Three different groups vied for dominance in what David Haglund called "a lively geopolitical jamboree"[114]: those who argued for a continuation of traditional ties with the Atlantic community; those who advocated a closer relationship with the Asia-Pacific; and those who argued for greater integration of the Western hemisphere as Canada's region.

For analysts like Michael Hart, the evolving international system in the late 1980s left Canada little choice but to confront its regional future. Hart's proposition was simple: "Over the years, Canadians have made a cult out of seeking to be a European nation, an Atlantic nation, a Pacific nation, and even an Arctic nation—anything but what we are, a

---

113 An excellent overview of regionalism in world politics and the vast literature it has spawned is provided by Rick Fawn, "'Regions' and Their Study: Wherefrom, What For, and Whereto?" *Review of International Studies* 35:S1 (February 2009), 5–34.

114 David G. Haglund, "Brebner's *North Atlantic Triangle* at Sixty: A Retrospective Look at a Retrospective Book," *London Journal of Canadian Studies* 20 (2004/2005), 129.

nation of the Americas."[115] And in his view, the Canadian government was beginning to find its vocation as a nation of the Americas. In 1989, the Mulroney government joined the Organization of American States (OAS) as a full member, with Joe Clark, the external affairs minister, proclaiming that "For too long, Canadians have seen this hemisphere as our house; it is now time to make it our home."[116] Likewise, over the course of the 1990s, the Liberal government of Jean Chrétien supported the idea of transforming the trilateral free-trade area with the United States and Mexico into an even larger regional project. In December 1994, President Bill Clinton called a Summit of the Americas in Miami, gathering the heads of government of all countries in the Western hemisphere except Cuba to launch the Free Trade Area of the Americas (FTAA); the Canadian government was the FTAA's most enthusiastic supporter.[117]

However, while Canada may have discovered its vocation as a nation of the Americas, the idea of regionalism has proved elusive. Certainly the creation of a regional North American community has been impossible for the three NAFTA partners.[118] It should thus not be surprising that even before 9/11, enthusiasts of a hemispherically defined regionalism should find that their momentum was being slowed by numerous obstacles: the difficulty of transcending the deep wellsprings of protectionism in the United States Congress, the growing protests of the anti-globalization movement, and the distrust of American hegemony in many countries in the Western hemisphere. However, the attacks of September 11 and the resulting "re-borderization"[119] of the United States effectively brought the FTAA process to a standstill—and with it ideas about region.

THE POST-9/11 ERA: THE CONTINENTALIST TURN?

Unlike the end of the Cold War, which unfolded slowly and relatively peacefully over a period of three years, the Al-Qaeda attacks of the morning of September 11, 2001 represented the kind of singular transformative event that tends to have a profound effect on ideas about world politics. In the United States in particular, the attacks heightened fears about American insecurity and accelerated a reconsideration of the border with Canada.

While the Canada–U.S. border was never actually closed on September 11, the alert level was raised to its highest, meaning that anything and anyone crossing the border into the

---

115 Michael Hart, "Canada Discovers Its Vocation as a Nation of the Americas," in Fen Osler Hampson and Christopher J. Maule, eds., *Canada Among Nations, 1990–91: After the Cold War* (Ottawa: Carleton University Press, 1991), 83.

116 Quoted in Maxwell A. Cameron, "Canada and Latin America," in Hampson and Maule, eds., *Canada Among Nations, 1990–91*, 111; Gordon Mace, "Explaining Canada's Decision to Join the OAS," in Michaud and Nossal, *Diplomatic Departures*, 142–59.

117 Gordon Mace, "The FTAA Stalemate: Implications for Canadian Foreign Policy," in Isabel Studer and Carol Wise, eds., *Requiem or Revival? The Promise of North American Integration* (Washington: Brookings Institution, 2007), 108–123.

118 Ann Capling and Kim Richard Nossal, "The Contradictions of Regionalism in North America," *Review of International Studies* 35:S1 (February 2009), 147–67.

119 This refers to the various security measures that the United States government put in place after 9/11 to make it much more difficult for people and goods to enter the United States: see Thomas J. Biersteker, "The Rebordering of North America? Implications for Conceptualizing Borders After September 11," in Peter Andreas and Biersteker, eds., *The Rebordering of North America: Integration and Exclusion in a New Security Context* (New York: Routledge, 2003), 153–66.

United States was subjected to such intense scrutiny that, in the days after 9/11, lineups of trucks stretched for more than 30 kilometres down highways leading into the U.S., with reported cross-border waits of up to 12 hours. These delays caused millions of dollars in losses for companies on both sides of the border that had become used to just-in-time supply chains. The automotive sector was hit particularly hard, with some plants remaining closed as a result of parts shortages caused by border delays.[120] The new tighter border regime was entrenched by the creation of a mammoth bureaucracy, the Department of Homeland Security, with a new primary mission: preventing terrorists and terrorist weapons from entering the United States. The Uniting and Strengthening America by Providing Appropriate Tools Required to Intercept and Obstruct Terrorism (USA PATRIOT) Act, rushed through Congress in October 2001, provided broad powers to regulate and control borders (and much else besides); in the same month, the number of officers along the U.S.–Canadian border was tripled. As Thomas Courchene noted, after 9/11 the United States was no longer interested in an open border: "if the movement of persons, vehicles, and goods across the border compromises US security, then the border arrangements will be altered in ways that will serve to guarantee homeland security."[121] The American ambassador in Canada, Paul Cellucci, put it bluntly: In the post-9/11 world, "security trumps trade."[122]

This sudden alteration in Canadian–American relations brought about by 9/11 and the American reaction prompted the rediscovery of an idea that has had a long history in Canada but had never been dominant: continentalism.[123] In Canadian political history, continentalism connotes the idea that Canada, as the historian Allan Smith has put it, can only be understood as a part of a North American continental system.[124] In Smith's view, continentalism is a broadly capacious idea. For some it means simply that Canada's location makes it "an American nation," largely indistinguishable from its southern neighbour in terms of culture, norms, ideas, and practices. For others, continentalism is the process by which Canadians have been able to live on the same continent as the United States and nonetheless forge a separate and distinct country and keep the expansionism of the United States at bay. For others still, continentalism is purely normative, encouraging the view that Canada's interests are best served by policies that seek closer cooperation and economic integration with the United States. For others, continentalism means *continentalization*, or the creation of systems of management or governance that essentially erase the border between Canada and the United States.[125]

---

120 Capling and Nossal, "Contradictions of Regionalism," 156.

121 Thomas Courchene, "FTA at 15, NAFTA at 10: A Canadian Perspective on North American Integration," *North American Journal of Economics and Finance* 14 (2003), 275.

122 Joseph Brean and Sheldon Alberts, "US Loses Faith in Canada," *National Post*, March 26, 2003; Paul Cellucci, *Unquiet Diplomacy* (Toronto: Key Porter Books, 2005), 131–46.

123 For different perspectives on continentalism, see J.L. Granatstein and Norman Hillmer, *For Better or For Worse: Canada and the United States to the 1990s* (Toronto: Copp Clark Pitman, 1990). For a review, see Reginald C. Stuart, "Continentalism Revisited: Recent Narratives on the History of Canadian–American Relations," *Diplomatic History* 18:3 (July 1994), 405–414.

124 Allan Smith, *Canada: An American Nation?* (Montréal and Kingston: McGill-Queen's University Press, 1994), 4.

125 Stephen Clarkson, *Uncle Sam and Us: Globalization, Neoconservatism, and the Canadian State* (Toronto: University of Toronto Press, 2002).

Continentalism also has a deeply pejorative connotation in Canada as a result of some who have appropriated the word to imply that those who subscribe to such ideas are either anti-Canadian sellouts to American interests or are seeking the destruction of the Canadian nation through annexation or union with the United States. By contrast, we suggest that continentalism and Canadian nationalism are not incompatible; rather, that continentalism can best be understood as a set of ideas about how to advance Canada's interests by shaping the country's relations with the United States and the world. Continentalism suggests that the United States is Canada's most important partner, both economically and geopolitically. Because Canada's prosperity depends on maintaining secure access to the American market, priority should be placed on establishing institutions for managing trade with the U.S. Likewise, continentalism implies that Canadians should be sensitive to the security needs of Americans, and, where appropriate, should generally support the international policies of the government in Washington. Denis Stairs nicely captured the essence of the position when he wrote that "There is only one imperative in Canadian foreign policy. That imperative is the maintenance of a politically amicable—and hence economically effective—working relationship with the United States."[126]

Over the course of the twentieth century, we saw considerable continentalization in Canadian and American activities and there have been numerous continentalists in Canada over the years, but it was not until the beginning of the twenty-first century that we began to see continentalism—as we have defined it—emerge as an idea that is more broadly acceptable than it has ever been. The evolution of Canada over the twentieth century cannot be understood unless we look at the degree to which Canadians have been integrated into American culture and the American economy. Likewise, the pace of continentalization accelerated after the Second World War, ranging from defence to economic production. For example, defence integration, beginning in the 1940s, reached its apogee with the NORAD agreement of 1957, which treated the air defence of North America on a continental basis; likewise, the 1958 Defence Production Sharing Arrangements continentalized defence procurement, allowing Canadian and American firms to bid on defence contracts on either side of the border. Since the early 1960s, the electricity grid has been continentalized, with standards set by the North American Electricity Reliability Council (NERC). The 1965 Auto Pact continentalized the production of autos and auto parts, allowing the Big Three auto manufacturers to rationalize their production on a continent-wide basis.

Despite this continentalization, however, the dominant approach to the United States during the Cold War era was framed by Canada's commitment to internationalism. Canadian–American economic relations were marked by a reliance on multilateral institutions like the General Agreement on Tariffs and Trade (GATT), various protectionist measures designed to keep the economy as "Canadianized" as possible, and a persistent refusal to consider encouraging closer economic integration with the United States. This was very much in keeping with the precepts of internationalism and its focus on multilateralism. However, despite this, and despite efforts of the federal government to diversify the country's trade, Canada's reliance on the U.S. continued to build over the course of the century, accelerated by the huge wealth generated by the Auto Pact in the late 1960s and early 1970s. The "Nixon shocks" of

---

126 Denis Stairs, "Canada in the New Economic Environment," CANCAPS Paper 4 (July 1994), cited in Stéphane Roussel, "'Honey, Are You Still Mad at Me? I've Changed, You Know . . .': Canada–US Relations in a Post-Saddam/Post-Chrétien Era," *International Journal* 58:4 (Autumn 2003), 581.

August 1971—when the United States imposed a 10 percent surcharge on all imports—
rattled the government in Ottawa but did not change its fundamental orientation: In 1972, in
its "options" exercise, the Trudeau government explicitly rejected the option of closer economic integration with the United States in favour of the "Third Option," the diversification
of the economy to reduce Canada's dependence on trade with the United States.[127]

The beginnings of the turn to continentalism came out of the economic turmoil of the
1970s that was caused by external challenges like the Nixon shocks of 1971, the oil crises
of 1973 and 1979, and increasing American protectionism, but also domestic policy
choices that sought to manage the consequences of rampant inflation, high unemployment,
and huge variations in commodity prices through demand-side Keynesian measures such
as stimulative budgets. The severe recession of the early 1980s, exacerbated by the increasing number of protectionist measures adopted by the United States that affected Canadian
trade, prompted a rethinking of the traditional attitude of Canadians toward economic relations with the United States. As we saw in the previous chapter, most Canadian politicians
believed that it had been an iron law of Canadian politics since Laurier's Liberals went
down to defeat in the 1911 elections that free trade with the United States was a recipe for
electoral defeat; however, in 1985, Brian Mulroney, who had come to office in 1984 having promised never to consider free trade with the United States, changed his mind. Acting
on the advice of not only his own officials but also of a royal commission that had been
appointed by Trudeau in his final year in office, Mulroney's government embraced the idea
of a comprehensive trade agreement with the United States. The negotiation of this agreement in 1987, and the reelection of the Conservatives in the 1988 election, meant that, in
Brian W. Tomlin's memorable phrase, Canadians were "leaving the past behind."[128] The
Canada–U.S. Free Trade Agreement that came into force in January 1989—and the trilateral free-trade agreement between Canada, the United States, and Mexico that began in
January 1994—are the results of this.

Just as the Auto Pact of 1965 had produced a large increase in Canadian wealth in the
late 1960s, so too did these free-trade agreements. In the process, the integration of the
Canadian and American economies was accelerated and deepened, although the result was
not true interdependence. Rather, the mutual dependence worked quite asymmetrically:
Canadians in the aggregate remained far more dependent for their wealth on access to the
American market than Americans were dependent on Canada.[129]

It was this increased dependence on the United States over the course of the 1990s that
made the attacks of 9/11 so problematic for Canadians. The subsequent "thickening" of the
U.S. border posed a potential threat to the well-being of Canadians—but not because of the
costs of delays at the border. Rather, there was a fear that American operations with supply chains outside the United States would relocate those chains *behind* American borders

---

127 For the best accounts of the Trudeau period in Canada's trade policy, see Michael Hart, *A Trading
Nation: Canadian Trade Policy from Colonialism to Globalization* (Vancouver: UBC Press, 2003),
269–307, and J.L. Granatstein and Robert Bothwell, *Pirouette: Pierre Trudeau and Canadian Foreign
Policy* (Toronto: University of Toronto Press, 1990), 158–77.

128 Brian W. Tomlin, "Leaving the Past Behind: The Free Trade Initiative Assessed," in Michaud and
Nossal, *Diplomatic Departures*, 45–58.

129 The most perceptive discussion on the nature of interdependence remains David A. Baldwin,
"Interdependence and Power: A Conceptual Analysis," *International Organization* 34:4 (Autumn
1980), 471–506.

rather than face possible disruptions to just-in-time supply caused by the oppressive hand of a Department of Homeland Security that was more concerned with security than trade.

To be sure, in the months after 9/11, the Chrétien government tried to negotiate what was called a "Smart Border" (a border "smart" enough to keep legitimate movements of people and goods flowing across the line while stopping terrorists) with the United States. In December 2001, the two governments signed a declaration that agreed that public security and economic security are not mutually exclusive objectives, and adopted a 30-point "action plan" designed to smooth both the "secure flow of people" and the "secure flow of goods."[130]

But for many this was merely a stopgap measure; instead, what was needed was a radical shift in the Canadian–American relationship. The preferred proposed solutions advanced by academics, think tanks, and business groups was to deepen economic integration in a way that would address American concerns about security. Wendy Dobson, a professor of management at the University of Toronto and a former associate deputy minister in Canada's Department of Finance, argued that what was needed was a "Big Idea" that would capture the attention of an American government transfixed by threats to security. She proposed that Canada strike a "strategic bargain" with the United States that would try to deal with American security concerns in return for reducing the impediments to trade and the movement of people.[131] For others, the "Big Idea" involved the creation of a customs union, a common market, or a North American community that would allow Canada and the United States to create a common "security perimeter" behind which unrestricted trade could take place.[132] In January 2003, the Canadian Council of Chief Executives (CCCE), a peak organization of CEOs from approximately 150 corporations, launched the North American Security and Prosperity Initiative. The CCCE pressed for a "reinvention" of North American borders to create "a zone of cooperation encompassing the continent" that would allow North America to be "open to business but closed to terrorism."[133]

To what extent has this renewed embrace of continentalism shaped Canada's international policy in the post-9/11 era? There is little doubt that the government of Jean Chrétien struggled hard against the rise of continentalist pressures. The idea of a "security perimeter," for example, was consistently rejected; indeed, the Chrétien government refused to even use the term.[134] Likewise, reading—and reflecting—a broad strand of public opinion, Chrétien

---

130 Canada–U.S. Smart Border Declaration, December 12, 2001, available http://www.dfait-maeci.gc.ca/anti-terrorism/declaration-en.asp and http://www.dfait-maeci.gc.ca/anti-terrorism/actionplan-en.asp.

131 Wendy Dobson, "Shaping the Future of the North American Economic Space: A Framework for Action," *The Border Papers: C.D. Howe Institute Commentary 162* (Toronto: C.D. Howe Institute, April 2002), available http://www.cdhowe.org/pdf/commentary_162.pdf.

132 On different kinds of union, see Axel Huelsemeyer, "Toward Deeper North American Integration: A Customs Union?" *Canadian–American Public Policy* 59 (October 2004); also Hugh Segal, "North American Community: A Prospect to Excite and Inspire," *Inroads: A Journal of Opinion* 13 (2003), available http://www.inroadsjournal.ca/archives/inroads13/toc13.htm; Gotlieb, "Romanticism and Realism," esp. 40.

133 Canadian Council of Chief Executives, *Security and Prosperity: Toward a New Canada-United States Partnership in North America*, January 2003, available http://www.ceocouncil.ca/en/publications/publications.php.

134 Stéphane Roussel, "Sécurité, souveraineté ou prospérité? Le Canada et le périmètre de sécurité nord américain," *Policy Options* 23:3 (April 2002), 19–26.

refused to support the "coalition of the willing" put together by President George W. Bush for the American-led invasion of Iraq in March 2003. On the contrary: Chrétien encouraged anti-Bush and anti-American sentiment in Canada.[135]

But it is a measure of the changed circumstances that Chrétien's approach to relations with the United States was purposely abandoned by Paul Martin when he assumed the prime ministership in December 2003. Martin embraced the CCCE proposal of a "North American Security and Prosperity Initiative," which was taken by the Canadian, American, and Mexican governments and reshaped into the Security and Prosperity Partnership (SPP). The SPP was launched at a meeting of Martin, Bush, and President Vicente Fox of Mexico—or, as they were dubbed by the media, the "Three Amigos"—in March 2005. But the SPP, which created a series of bilateral and trilateral working groups of bureaucrats, soon lost steam. Indeed, Roland Paris, a professor at the University of Ottawa who was one of the Canadian bureaucrats who worked on the creation of the SPP, bitingly dismissed it as little more than "mind-numbing lists of mostly piddling initiatives."[136] Moreover, after the election of Barack Obama as president in 2008, there was no further reference to the "Three Amigos." The best indication of the current state of the SPP is websites: The Canadian and American SPP websites are devoted to the last leaders' summit held in April 2008; the Mexican government does not even bother maintaining a separate site: the Mexican URL for the SPP (http://www.aspan.gob.mx) now simply redirects to the president's home page.

While the SPP might have lost steam, there is little doubt that those who argue that Canada's international policies should be shaped with the idea that the United States is Canada's most important partner are now more dominant in Canadian discourse than at any time in the past. But it is not clear that it has supplanted internationalism as the dominant idea of the early twenty-first century.

CONCLUSION

Imperialism, isolationism, internationalism, and continentalism have dominated public debate about Canada's international policies for the past hundred years. These ideas act as constraints on policymakers by fixing the parameters of decision and by reducing the range of practical policy options. Leaders who ignore dominant ideas take a considerable political risk: The Laurier government could not have remained indifferent during the Boer War any more than the Chrétien government, exactly one hundred years later, could have closed its eyes to the violence being visited on Kosovar Albanians. Three concluding observations can be made about the impact of dominant ideas.

First, the transience of dominant ideas tends to be slow and at times almost imperceptible. Ideas do not appear and disappear in a stroke; instead, they are in a constant state of flux, some in decline, some ascending. Thus there will be periods when an idea in decline

---

135 Kim Richard Nossal, "A Thermostatic Dynamic? Electoral Outcomes and Anti-Americanism in Canada," in Richard A. Higgott and Ivona Malbašić, eds., *The Political Consequences of Anti-Americanism* (London: Routledge, 2008), 129–41.

136 Roland Paris, "A Trilateral Mishmash," *Globe and Mail*, February 26, 2007. The work of the SPP reported on the official websites (http://www.spp.gov, http://www.spp-psp.gc.ca/eic/site/spp-psp.nsf/Intro) confirms Paris's description.

coexists with one that is ascending. Indeed, politicians and bureaucrats often find it difficult to assess the degree to which an idea will linger in the population. Is an idea that seems to be emerging just a flash in the pan, or is it a real rupture with the past? Clear analysis is particularly difficult because two sets of ideas can easily coexist without the contradictions being too apparent. The Mulroney government was clearly inspired by continentalism—not only signing a free-trade agreement with the United States but also generally supporting the government in Washington. At the same time, however, its relations with the rest of the world seemed more marked much by internationalism. One can see the same ambivalence in the *International Policy Statement* published by the Martin government in 2005.

Second, the ideas dominant in society and those dominant within the government need not coincide. While the isolationism of the early 1920s is an example of coincidence, at times the government may be ahead of public opinion as it was in the case of autonomism during the First World War and in the early 1920s. At times, it may lag behind. For example, Mackenzie King had been so affected by the issue of conscription that in March 1948, when the government decided to commit Canada to an Atlantic alliance, he was overcome with fear that this would eventually lead to yet another conscription crisis: "I found myself perspiring from sheer anxiety."[137]

Finally, state officials will not hesitate to take the lead in giving impetus to dominant ideas in society and to use their authority to legitimize some ideas over others. Such was the case with the pursuit of autonomism by Borden and King, the pursuit of internationalism by St. Laurent and Pearson, and the pursuit of ideas about human security by Lloyd Axworthy. But their success will largely depend on how receptive Canadians are. To be well received, a new idea must, at the very least, be in harmony with the fundamental values, the preoccupations, and the recent experience of Canadian society. Perhaps this explains why continentalism has such difficulty commanding consensus among Canadians: This vision of the world does not sit easily with Canadians' need to reinforce their national identity and distinguish themselves from the United States. Indeed, harmony with the dominant values in Canadian society might well explain the longevity of internationalism that continues to dominate discussions of Canada's international policies.

---

137 Quoted in Eayrs, *In Defence of Canada*, vol. 4, 38.

PART 2

Actors and Processes

The first part of the book examined the parameters of policymaking—how domestic and global politics constrain and impel those who make international policy in Canada. The second part of the book examines the decision-makers. Four distinct sets of policymakers are examined: Cabinet ministers, including the prime minister and other ministers who have responsibilities for international policy; the international policy bureaucracy; legislators in the Senate and the House of Commons; and the provincial governments.

We begin with an examination of the prime minister and his or her preeminence in shaping international policy in Canada. In practice this means looking at a number of prime ministers: Robert L. Borden and Mackenzie King before the Second World War, and Pierre Elliott Trudeau, Brian Mulroney, Jean Chrétien, Paul Martin, and Stephen Harper in the contemporary era. Such preeminence springs in part from the wide-ranging powers associated with the position, particularly the power to structure the Cabinet, the senior civil service, and, in the context of international policy, ambassadorships.

In the latter part of the twentieth century, the head of government was increasingly propelled into prominence in international affairs because of the tendency to conduct international diplomacy by summit meeting. A separate chapter is devoted to summit diplomacy, because this forum for statecraft affords a prime minister an unparallelled opportunity to influence the making of international policy. Summit diplomacy has grown rapidly. Thirty years ago, it was largely up to prime ministers to determine how busy to make their international schedules, for the only regular multilateral summit meeting was the Commonwealth meeting. By contrast, today, a prime minister's international schedule is jammed: the G-20 summit, North American Leaders' Summits, the Summit of the Americas, the Commonwealth Heads of Government Meeting, the summit of La Francophone, and the Asia-Pacific Economic Cooperation summit, not to mention other special summit meetings. In this chapter we also look at summit diplomacy between the Canadian prime minister and the U.S. president.

We then turn to the other ministers who are involved in foreign policymaking. We look at the key ministers, the minister of foreign affairs and the minister of national defence. We look at the evolution of the external affairs portfolio from the days when it was held by the prime minister to the present. We also examine the evolution of other portfolios to serve foreign policy interests, including a separate minister for international trade, a minister of international cooperation, and junior ministers of state, who are in the ministry but do not sit in cabinet.

The bureaucracy that has been put in place for the making and implementation of international policy in Canada grew out of a growing need for the new self-governing dominion to conduct its own international affairs separately from the imperial government in London. In 1909, a Department of External Affairs was created—"external" because some of the "affairs" dealt with Britain and the other members of the Empire, and they were hardly "foreign." That organization would grow rapidly after 1945, as the Canadian government expanded the range and scope of its international activities. How the Canadian government organized its agencies to conduct foreign affairs is explored, ending with the emergence of the "3D" approach of the early 2000s, where a "whole-of-government" approach seeks to bring diplomacy, defence, and development together in a synergistic way. The influence of the bureaucracy on the making of international policy is explored in this chapter, including an assessment of how and why the bureaucracy exerts an influence.

In a parliamentary democracy, Parliament should be a potent influence on policymaking. In the case of foreign affairs in Canada, however, members of Parliament who are not ministers in Cabinet have limited influence on the policy process. We look at the roles of the Senate and of members of the House of Commons. The Standing Committee on Foreign Affairs and International Development of the House of Commons plays a special role in making foreign policy, for it is at the committee level that considerable influence can be exercised. An examination of the political party system and the impact of party on foreign policy completes this chapter.

The last two chapters of the book focus on the provinces and international policy. Canada is a federation like no other in the international system, for the Constitution Acts, 1867–1982, do not assign competence over all foreign affairs to either the federal or the provincial governments. Thus, provincial governments are free to conduct international relations in their sphere of competence as laid out in the original British North America Act, 1867 (renamed in 1982 the Constitution Act, 1867). We examine the different interests that propel Canada's provincial governments into the international system to pursue *paradiplomacy* (diplomacy conducted *alongside* the diplomacy of sovereign states).

Most of the time, the paradiplomacy of the provinces does not cause friction with the federal government. In the case of Québec, however, paradiplomacy is pursued as part of the efforts of the government in Québec City to project a sense of Québec's identity as a nation distinct within Canada. This "paradiplomatie identitaire," as it is known in Québec, has historically posed political problems with the federal government in Ottawa when the souverainiste Parti Québécois has been in power in Québec City and has pursued *protodiplomacy*—in other words, international activities designed to secure sovereignty for Québec in international politics. This chapter also looks at the role other countries have played in the politics of Québec's international activities.

CHAPTER 6

The Prime Minister and International Policy

Who makes international policy in Canada? The simplest answer is that the conduct of Canada's international policies is the prerogative of the Crown. However, the role of the Crown cannot be fully understood without referring to the nature of the contemporary international system on the one hand and the evolution of Canadian political institutions on the other. The Crown's responsibility for conducting Canada's external relations is partly a consequence of the doctrine of sovereignty, the essential organizing feature of contemporary international politics. The idea—and the practice—of sovereignty implies that there is one supreme political authority for each one of the political communities in the international system. In the monarchical system, which was the dominant form of political organization in Europe in the seventeenth and eighteenth centuries, a single individual was invested with supreme authority: the sovereign.[1] Thus it was the Crown who conducted relations with other sovereigns, sent ambassadors, negotiated treaties, and declared war. While the absolute power of the sovereign began to erode after the seventeenth century in favour of representative government, the prerogative powers of the Crown in foreign affairs remained largely unchanged and unaffected by the growing power of Parliament.

These political structures were reproduced in Canada during the six decades of slow evolution to statehood between 1867 and 1931, when Canada acquired sovereign statehood as a result of the Statute of Westminster. Today, Canada's head of state—Queen Elizabeth II, represented by the Governor General—is thus vested with the formal constitutional authority to make all those decisions that shape the country's role in world politics. As in Britain, the powers to negotiate and ratify treaties with other sovereign powers, to conduct diplomatic relations, and to wage war are all part of the royal prerogative. However, this authority is purely symbolic and must be interpreted in the context of Canadian parliamentary government. In Canada, as in Britain, the actual decision-making power in international policy is no longer exercised by the sovereign, but by the prime minister and cabinet, even though the symbols of that earlier era remain. Thus the cabinet determines Canada's objectives in international affairs and the means to try to achieve them. But the decisions of cabinet are all taken in the name of the Crown. Likewise, Canada's diplomatic representatives are still sent to other countries as representatives of Elizabeth II as Queen of Canada. This is why, for example, members of the Commonwealth send "high commissioners" to each other's capitals rather than ambassadors. In the formal rituals of contemporary international politics, ambassadors are only sent from one sovereign to another, presenting their "credentials" as formal indications of their status. This poses a problem in the case of countries that use the British sovereign as head of state (such as Australia, Britain, Canada, Jamaica, New Zealand, and about a dozen other states) and want to exchange diplomatic representatives with each other. In those cases, the Queen would be in the bizarre situation of presenting credentials to herself. Therefore, diplomats formally represent the government rather than the sovereign and are given the diplomatic rank of "high commissioners,"[2] which has the status equivalent to an ambassador. Even

---

1 Alan James, *Sovereign Statehood: The Basis of International Society* (London: Allen and Unwin, 1986); Stephen Krasner, *Sovereignty: Organized Hypocrisy* (Princeton: Princeton University Press, 1999). For a historical and critical analysis, see Jens Bartelson, *A Genealogy of Sovereignty* (Cambridge: Cambridge University Press, 1995).

2 Until 1926, the official representative of the imperial government in London in dominion capitals was the Governor General. In 1926, dominions were given the option of having the Governor General be the Crown's representative

those members of the Commonwealth that do not recognize the Crown as their head of state (although all recognize her as head of the Commonwealth, that being a condition of membership) have adopted the practice of terming diplomatic representatives to one another high commissioner.

However anachronistic the symbols of governance in Canada might appear to be, they explain why international policy is properly the responsibility of the political executive alone. It explains why the other institutions of governance, notably the legislature and the judiciary, have little role in the shaping of external policy, and why our focus must inescapably be on the Cabinet, and in particular on that central core of ministers most heavily involved in making international policy. Depending on the issue, that circle may include the minister of foreign affairs, the minister of national defence, the minister of finance, the minister for international trade, the minister of international development, and junior ministers of state. But on important issues, the prime minister will likely be at the centre.

THE PREEMINENCE OF THE PRIME MINISTER

According to British parliamentary tradition, the prime minister is a member of a collegial collective, and thus *primus inter pares*—first among equals. However, as Donald J. Savoie reminds us, in Canada "there is no longer any *inter* or *pares*"—the Canadian prime minister "has no outer limits defining his political authority within the government."[3] Moreover, the concentration of power in the hands of the prime minister has been reinforced by the pattern of prime ministerial tenure in Canada. Most prime ministers have served for either very brief periods or are sustained in power by the voters for long periods. While Sir Charles Tupper, Arthur Meighen, Joe Clark, John Turner, and Kim Campbell held the office briefly, Sir John A. Macdonald, Sir Wilfrid Laurier, W.L. Mackenzie King, and Pierre Elliott Trudeau served as prime minister for over a decade and a half. Jean Chrétien celebrated his tenth year in office a month before he retired, while Robert L. Borden, Louis St. Laurent, and Brian Mulroney each occupied the prime ministership for nine years. Such longevity had an inexorable impact on prime ministerial power. While these prime ministers were, as Robert Craig Brown suggests, very much creatures of their parties,[4] they nonetheless grew to dominate cabinet, caucus, and party. It is not coincidental that political scientists and historians tend to define distinct eras in Canada's international affairs that correspond to the tenure of prime ministers, since each prime minister has been inclined toward international activity and each has left a particular mark on the country's international policy, as the following brief sketches suggest.

---

rather than the representative of the British government. Instead, London would dispatch its own diplomatic representatives, which were high commissioners. H. Duncan Hall, *Commonwealth: A History of the British Commonwealth of Nations* (London: Van Nostrand Reinhold, 1971), 593–605.

3 Donald J. Savoie, *Governing from the Centre: The Concentration of Power in Canadian Politics* (Toronto: University of Toronto Press, 1999), chap. 4, 108.

4 Robert Craig Brown, "Fishwives, Plutocrats, Sirens and Other Curious Creatures: Some Questions about Political Leadership in Canada," in Leslie A. Pal and David Taras, eds., *Prime Ministers and Premiers: Political Leadership and Public Policy in Canada* (Scarborough: Prentice-Hall Canada, 1988), 29.

Robert L. Borden (1911–1920)

The Conservatives under Robert Borden came to power in 1911 as the result of the international policy issues that dominated the September election that year: the unease of English-speaking Canadians at the Reciprocity Agreement with the United States that had been negotiated by the Liberal government of Sir Wilfrid Laurier, and the equal unease of French-speaking Canadians about the Laurier government's plans for a Canadian navy. He arrived in the prime minister's office without much in the way of a foreign policy agenda—other than a sense of wanting to stop the tendencies toward continentalism evident under Laurier and a general sense of support for the Empire, although he believed that dominions like Canada should have a voice in the making of imperial defence policy.

Borden's nine years as prime minister illustrate the degree to which the prime minister can come to dominate international policy, for the key decisions that shaped Canada's external policy after the outbreak of war in 1914 were essentially his alone. First, he was responsible for pressing for a greater independent voice for Canada, not only within the Empire but also in the international system as a whole. He was pushed into this by the exigencies of fighting a war in which the self-governing dominion governments provided soldiers for the trenches but were given no say in war decisions by the imperial government and were not even provided with information by the government in London. Annoyed at having to gather his information from the daily press, Sir Robert (as he had become in June 1914) began to press the imperial government for a greater voice for Canada. But when he arrived in London, he was given the runaround by the imperial bureaucracy, leading him to threaten the imperial government that unless he were given the information "which is due to me as Prime Minister of Canada, I shall not advise my countrymen to put further effort into the winning of the War."[5] David Lloyd George, the minister of munitions, managed to mollify Borden, but only temporarily, since the imperial government continued to determine war policy unilaterally, periodically calling on the dominions for more men to fill the trenches of the Western Front. When he was informed by the colonial secretary in 1915 that there was no way to give the dominions a greater role in imperial decision-making, Borden responded:

> It can hardly be expected that we shall put 400,000 or 500,000 men in the field and willingly accept the position of having no more voice and receiving no more consideration than if we were toy automata. Any person cherishing such an expectation harbours an unfortunate and even dangerous delusion. Is this war being waged by the United Kingdom alone or is it a war waged by the whole Empire?[6]

When Lloyd George became British prime minister in December 1916, he sought to give the dominions a greater voice by creating an Imperial War Cabinet, which was intended to make decisions about the war. While it never achieved its original purpose, it did give Borden an opportunity to press for a more independent voice for Canada. As he confided to his diary in December 1918, "I am beginning to feel that in the end and perhaps sooner than later, Canada must assume full sovereignty."[7] Thus, by the end of the

---

5 Gaddis Smith, "Canadian External Affairs During World War I," in Hugh L. Keenleyside et al., *The Growth of Canadian Policies in External Affairs* (Durham: Duke University Press, 1960), 41.

6 Quoted in C.P. Stacey, *Canada and the Age of Conflict: A History of Canadian External Policies,* vol. 1: *1867–1921* (Toronto: Macmillan, 1977), 192.

7 Quoted in Smith, "External Affairs During World War I," 57.

war, he was arguing for separate Canadian representation at the peace conference and for separate membership in the League of Nations.

But Borden's frequent visits to Britain during the war also provided him with the opportunity to make another key decision that would shape both domestic politics and international policy for years to come. In his new year's address for 1916, Borden announced that Canada's troop commitment to the war would be raised to 500,000 soldiers—a huge contribution for a country of 8 million people. But given the decline in voluntary enlistments throughout 1916, there was only one way to meet this commitment: conscription. Borden announced to his cabinet in May 1917 that he was introducing conscription, even though, as he admitted to his diary, his Québec ministers warned that conscription would "kill them politically and the party for 25 years."[8] In the event, they underestimated the political impact of Borden's unilateral decision on conscription by more than half a century.

William Lyon Mackenzie King (1921–1926, 1926–1930, 1935–1948)

Of all Canadian prime ministers, William Lyon Mackenzie King served the longest: 7828 days, or almost 22 years. He led the Liberal party into seven elections and lost only one, in 1930 (though he did go down to personal defeat in his own riding twice, in the 1925 and 1945 elections). King's longevity in power is best explained by his essential pragmatism. Conscious of the political impact of Borden's decisions, he was always exceedingly careful to ensure that his international policies did not provoke Canada's sociolinguistic cleavages and deprive the Liberal party's hold on power. To that end, King pursued a cautious foreign policy that sought to avoid the kind of international commitments that might draw Canada into another war. For this reason, King rejected efforts by the imperial government in London to draw Canada and the other dominions into an "imperial" foreign policy—as we saw in the case of the Chanak crisis of 1922, discussed in Chapter 5.

King also took care to limit Canada's obligations to the League of Nations. His argument was consistent throughout the interwar period: Before Canada could agree to any League action, the matter would have to be put to Parliament.[9] As we will see in Chapter 10, the "Parliament will decide" formula was ingenious politically, but completely specious in formal constitutional terms since it is the executive, not Parliament, which has the authority to make international policy decisions. But it allowed King to avoid having to face a possible repetition of the divisions engendered by the First World War. For King, the lesson was always clear: Avoid the fate of Borden's Conservatives by avoiding the wars that would give rise to the need for conscription. Even during the Second World War, King was still worrying about conscription. If his government had to introduce conscription for overseas duty, he said in 1944, "the Liberal party would be completely destroyed, and not only immediately but for [an] indefinite time to come."[10]

---

8 Quoted in Stacey, *Age of Conflict,* vol. 1, 218; Desmond Morton, *A Military History of Canada* (Toronto: McClelland & Stewart, 1999), 151–58.

9 Richard Veatch, *Canada and the League of Nations* (Toronto: University of Toronto Press, 1975).

10 Quoted in Stacey, *Arms, Men and Governments: The War Policies of Canada, 1939–1945* (Ottawa: Information Canada, 1970), 446.

As we saw in Chapter 5, the Second World War convinced most senior officials in Ottawa that isolationism was an inappropriate policy. To be sure, King was able to survive two conscription crises in 1942 and 1944—partly by embracing and avoiding conscription at the same time, a policy encapsulated in his famous slogan "Not necessarily conscription but conscription if necessary."[11] But he never lost his mistrust of international military engagements. Thus, he was not at all enthusiastic about the support of his foreign minister, Louis St. Laurent, for a new alliance, this time directed against the Soviet Union. In January 1948, the British prime minister, Clement Attlee, officially invited Canada to take part in the talks that would eventually lead to the Atlantic Alliance. Lester Pearson, the undersecretary of state for external affairs, was tasked with convincing King not to refuse the British invitation. Pearson was successful, but, he confided to a colleague, "it was the worst struggle I've ever had."[12]

In his study of "the Mackenzie King era," the historian C.P. Stacey stresses the "overmastering importance" of the prime minister in making Canadian international policies in the 1920s and 1930s. Canada's policies were, he argued, "essentially the personal policies of the man who held that office."[13] Stacey's assessment is supported by those who witnessed this preeminence in practice. Pearson, who became prime minister in 1963, wrote after attending cabinet meetings: "it's enlightening to notice Mr King's absolute ascendency [sic] over & complete domination of his colleagues."[14]

Pierre Elliott Trudeau (1968–1979, 1980–1984)

When Pierre Elliott Trudeau assumed leadership of the Liberal party in April 1968, he was determined to recast Canada's role in world affairs. A little over a month later, he announced that there would be a "severe reassessment" of foreign policy.[15] Trudeau's criticisms of existing policy were wide-ranging and fundamental, and fixed firmly on the policies pursued by his predecessor, Lester Pearson.[16] First, he argued, Canadian foreign policy had not kept abreast of changes in the external environment. Policies that were designed

---

11 As J.L. Granatstein put it, King's famous phrase was "a precise statement of his policy." The national plebiscite in 1942 had given him the right to introduce conscription, but given Québec's continued opposition, King would refuse to implement it unless it was necessary to win the war. And, as Granatstein reminds us, King believed that introducing conscription would not be necessary in order to win the war. See Robert Bothwell, *Canada and Quebec: One Country, Two Histories*, rev. ed. (Vancouver: UBC Press, 1998), 75–76.

12 Quoted in Escott Reid, "Birth of the North Atlantic Alliance," *International Journal* 22:3 (Summer 1967), 428.

13 C.P. Stacey, *Canada and the Age of Conflict: A History of Canadian External Policies*, vol. 2: *1921–1948: The Mackenzie King Era* (Toronto: University of Toronto Press, 1981), ix; also R. Barry Farrell, *The Making of Canadian Foreign Policy* (Scarborough: Prentice-Hall Canada, 1969), 10–11.

14 Quoted in James Eayrs, *In Defence of Canada*, vol. 3: *Peacemaking and Deterrence* (Toronto: University of Toronto Press, 1972), 7.

15 Denis Stairs, "Reviewing Foreign Policy, 1968–70," in Don Munton and John Kirton, eds., *Canadian Foreign Policy: Selected Cases* (Scarborough: Prentice-Hall Canada, 1992), 174–204.

16 In his foreign policy memoirs, Trudeau denied that he was criticizing Pearson: Ivan Head and Pierre Trudeau, *The Canadian Way: Shaping Canadian Foreign Policy, 1968–1984* (Toronto: McClelland & Stewart, 1995), 7.

for the tense years of tight bipolarity—the commitments to the North Atlantic Treaty Organization (NATO) and the North American Air Defence (NORAD) agreement—were no longer appropriate in an era of relaxed tensions and growing multipolarity. For Trudeau, foreign policy was too determined by defence policy. Second, it was argued that the stress placed on the search for peace and order in the international system—typified by attachment to the United Nations and UN-sponsored peacekeeping missions—meant that Canadian interests were being neglected by decision-makers too concerned about the country's role in the world. In particular, the prime minister objected to the kind of middlepowermanship practised in the 1950s and 1960s, shrugging it off dismissively as "helpful fixing." In short, Trudeau held that Canadian foreign policy no longer served the national interest. Third, he believed that the external affairs minister and his department played too important a role in making international policy, with too little involvement by others who had a legitimate interest in the process. Armed with such objections, Trudeau set about trying to remould both the process and the substance of foreign policy.[17]

Over the next two years, his government undertook a review of foreign and defence policy. The defence review focused on the issue of the troops that Canada had had stationed in Europe as part of its NATO commitment since 1950. These forces symbolized everything Trudeau believed to be problematic about Canada's international policies: the internationalist diplomacy of St. Laurent and Pearson; the dependence on the United States, which dominated the Atlantic Alliance; and the dominance of defence policy. Trudeau wanted to withdraw Canada's forces from Europe and reduce the size of the armed forces. When his cabinet eventually discussed the issue in March 1969, he told his assembled ministers, who were split on whether Canada should bring home its troops stationed in Europe, that if Cabinet could not reach a decision, "we will bloody well start over again. We may be laughed at—but we will eventually reach an acceptable position." As Paul Hellyer, one of his cabinet ministers and a former minister of national defence, wrote in his diary, what Trudeau really meant was "acceptable to him."[18]

The "acceptable" position, announced in April 1969, was that Canada cut its troop commitments to NATO by half. The results of the foreign policy review were published in June 1970. Its French title, *Politique étrangère au service des Canadiens*, conveys the essence of the change with greater clarity than the more ambiguous *Foreign Policy for Canadians*[19]: It called for a narrower definition of interest in foreign policy, focusing instead on economic growth, combating pollution, defending sovereignty, and seeking to expand the range of international relationships to offset the dominance of the United States. The 1971 white paper on defence went in the same direction, ranking NATO and peacekeeping as less important than the protection of Canadian territory.[20] The 1968–1970

---

17 On the reviews, see J.L. Granatstein and Robert Bothwell, *Pirouette: Pierre Trudeau and Canadian Foreign Policy* (Toronto: University of Toronto Press, 1990), 3–35; Bruce Thordarson, *Trudeau and Foreign Policy: A Study in Decision-Making* (Toronto: Oxford University Press, 1972); Thordarson, "Posture and Policy: Leadership in Canada's External Affairs," *International Journal* 31:3 (Autumn 1976).

18 Quoted in J.L. Granatstein and Robert Bothwell, *Pirouette: Pierre Trudeau and Canadian Foreign Policy* (Toronto: University of Toronto Press, 1990), 23.

19 Canada, Secretary of State for External Affairs, *Foreign Policy for Canadians* (Ottawa: Information Canada, 1970).

20 Canada, Department of National Defence, *Defence in the 70s* (Ottawa: Information Canada, 1971).

review process illustrates nicely prime ministerial preeminence. The results of the review, called the "Trudeau Doctrine" by Peyton Lyon,[21] were very much a reflection of Trudeau's views. As J.L. Granatstein and Robert Bothwell conclude, "Without any doubt, Canadian foreign policy was now Pierre Trudeau's to direct."[22]

Having recorded his ideas about foreign policy for posterity, however, Trudeau spent the rest of his long tenure as prime minister ignoring, contradicting, or reversing the main tenets of the foreign policy paper. By 1984, he would have discovered, by turns, the utility of Canada's military alignment with the United States, the usefulness of the Atlantic alliance, the benefits of peacekeeping, and the wisdom of diplomatic activism. Despite his desire to leave his mark in international affairs,[23] his government's foreign policy was to continue to manifest many of the elements of Pearsonian internationalism, and the prime minister himself was to play an active role in summit diplomacy, from his mediatory efforts at the Commonwealth meeting in Singapore in 1971 to his peace mission in the winter of 1983–84.

From 1968 to 1984, Canada's international policies were cast in the image of the individual who sat in the prime minister's chair: punctuated by impressive initiatives, sudden policy reversals, a spirited independence, and occasional lack of respect (such as his performing a pirouette behind the Queen's back). The era was marked by thorny relations between Trudeau and American presidents. On the tape-recordings Richard Nixon made of his conversations in the White House, he referred to "that asshole Trudeau," calling him a "clever son of a bitch."[24] Nor did Trudeau and Ronald Reagan get on well, in large measure because Trudeau had little patience for Reagan. For example, Mark MacGuigan, Canada's foreign minister from 1980 to 1982, related that at two summits in 1982, Trudeau "constantly contradicted, refuted and needled Reagan," a performance that he thought "bordered on the self-indulgent."[25] And Trudeau was quite willing to thumb his nose at Washington on a range of issues, from the National Energy Program (NEP)[26] to fostering warm relations with states like Cuba.[27] However, his prime ministership was also marked

---

21 Peyton V. Lyon, "The Trudeau Doctrine," *International Journal* 26:1 (Winter 1970–1), 19–43.

22 Granatstein and Bothwell, *Pirouette*, 35.

23 Christina McCall and Stephen Clarkson, *Trudeau and Our Times*, vol. 2: *The Heroic Delusion* (Toronto: McClelland & Stewart, 1994), 342.

24 Lee-Anne Goodman, "Profanity and Paranoia on Record in the Oval Office," *Globe and Mail*, March 31, 2009.

25 Allan Gotlieb, *The Washington Diaries, 1981–1989* (Toronto: McClelland & Stewart, 2006), 66; also Mark MacGuigan, *An Inside Look at External Affairs During the Trudeau Years: The Memoirs of Mark MacGuigan*, ed. P. Whitney Lackenbauer (Calgary: University of Calgary Press, 2002), 17, 121–24.

26 The NEP was designed to insulate Canadians, particularly in the eastern provinces, from high oil prices on the global market by redistributing revenues from the Canadian oil market in order to keep Canadian oil prices below world market prices. The NEP also had provisions that affected foreign investors: It discriminated against foreign-owned energy companies and gave the federal government power to appropriate retroactively a 25 percent interest in any oil or gas discovered in lands owned in Canada's north. G. Bruce Doern and Glen B. Toner, *The Politics of Energy: The Development and Implementation of the NEP* (Toronto: Methuen, 1985).

27 In particular Trudeau's trip to Cuba in February 1976, which took place shortly after Cuban troops had been flown to Angola by the Soviet Union to intervene in a civil war there; Trudeau's sympathies for Castro were openly on display, prompting a negative reaction in Washington: see http://archives. cbc.ca/politics/prime_ministers/clips/13244.

by the pursuit of ideas (such as the protection of human rights and the environment) and a number of challenges (notably economic relations with the United States). His numerous, if sporadic, personal initiatives in international politics were marked by a personal enthusiasm and commitment that allowed him to define goals, even if he was not always able to achieve the outcomes desired.

Studying the Trudeau era allows us not only to reflect on the prime minister's influence on international policy, but also to consider the limits of that influence. On the one hand, there is little doubt Trudeau shaped Canada's foreign policy, both in form and, to a lesser extent, in substance. This influence was above all manifested in the many ideas and initiatives he embraced that were designed to break with the past. But ideas and initiatives alone cannot trump the structural constraints imposed by geography, economics, and politics. As we noted in Chapter 2, these constraints bind leaders and limit their options, and so it is not particularly surprising that over his long years in office Trudeau never managed to reshape the fundamentals of Canada's international policy. In particular, he was unable to alter the patterns of Canada–United States economic relations, since over his long years in office, Canada's trade with—and thus dependence on—the United States simply kept growing despite considerable efforts by his government. Moreover, his efforts to change the country's international policies provoked its own reaction within the political realm, as many Canadians reacted with disfavour to his international initiatives.[28]

Brian Mulroney (1984–1993)

It is paradoxical that one of Trudeau's most bitter failures—the Third Option, a policy designed to reverse the trend toward the continentalization of the Canadian economy—paved the way for what will undoubtedly be regarded as the greatest triumph of his successor, Brian Mulroney: free trade with the United States. After Mulroney was elected leader of the Progressive Conservatives in 1983, he set out to "refurbish" the relationship with the United States that had steadily deteriorated since the Liberals returned to office in 1980. As opposition leader in 1983–84, Mulroney adopted a simple pro-American, anti-Soviet posture. For example, while Trudeau characterized the shootdown of Korean Air Lines flight 007 in September 1983 by Soviet fighters as an accident, Mulroney called it an act of cold-blooded murder. When the United States invaded Grenada in October 1983, the Conservatives distanced themselves from the Trudeau government's criticism of the invasion. In his public speeches, Mulroney started to articulate the themes that would dominate the 1984 election campaign: Canada under a Conservative government would be a "better ally, a super ally" of what Mulroney claimed were the country's "four traditional allies"—the United States, Britain, France, and Israel. (Canada in fact does not have an alliance with Israel, but it can be assumed that Israel was simply added to the list in a crass attempt to woo Jewish voters.) A Conservative government, Mulroney promised, would

---

28 See Michel Fortmann and Martin Larose, "Une contre-culture stratégique en émergence? Pierre Elliott Trudeau, les intellectuels canadiens et la révision de la politique de défense libérale à l'égard de l'OTAN (1968–1969)," in Stéphane Roussel, ed., *Culture stratégique et politique de défense: L'expérience canadienne* (Montréal: Athéna, 2007).

stop being so critical of United States policy and would give Washington the benefit of the doubt. Canada under the Conservatives would also spend more on defence. Finally, he promised to take a firmer line with the Soviet Union.

In the federal election of September 4, 1984, the Progressive Conservatives under Brian Mulroney took 211 seats, the largest majority in Canadian history. Mulroney was sworn in on September 17, determined, as Trudeau had been, to change the foreign policy inherited from his predecessor, in particular Canadian–American relations. Between 1980 and 1984, relations between the two countries had deteriorated over a series of disputes involving the NEP, acid rain, and questions of international security.

Once in power, Mulroney put his own stamp not only on the decision-making process, but also on the substance of policy.[29] However, he quickly abandoned many of the pre-conceived and simplistic ideas about international policy he had brought to the prime minister's office. Over the nine years he was in power, Mulroney was, in practice, neither as pro-American nor as anti-Soviet as his rhetoric in opposition had suggested—or as the Liberal opposition sought to paint him. Toward the Soviet Union, he maintained a measured tone. While he pressed the Soviet government on human rights and remained skeptical about the reforms being introduced by Mikhail S. Gorbachev, he also developed a relationship with Moscow that grew progressively more cordial, particularly after the disintegration of the Soviet Union in 1991.[30]

In Canadian–American relations, Mulroney was far from a "super ally." While he did support a number of initiatives of the United States, notably the bombing of Libya in 1986, the invasion of Panama in 1989, and the use of force against Iraq in 1990–91, Mulroney frequently distanced his government from Washington's policies in Central America, the Middle East, Southeast Asia, and South Africa. In the case of Cuba, the Conservative government was considerably more strident in its opposition to American policy than the previous Liberal government had been. For example, Mulroney enacted the Foreign Extraterritorial Measures Act, 1985, an unprecedented piece of legislation that made it illegal for firms operating in Canada to comply with United States attempts to destabilize the Cuban government of Fidel Castro.[31] In defence policy, Mulroney refused to lend Canadian legitimacy to the Strategic Defense Initiative.[32] And although the government embraced a long list of new weapons systems in its white paper on defence in 1987, in fact Mulroney presided over a progressive downsizing of Canada's military establishment and overseas

---

29 Nelson Michaud and Kim Richard Nossal, eds., *Diplomatic Departures: The Conservative Era in Canadian Foreign Policy, 1984–1993* (Vancouver: UBC Press, 2001); John Kirton, "The Foreign Policy Decision Process," in Maureen Appel Molot and Brian W. Tomlin, eds., *Canada Among Nations 1985: The Conservative Agenda* (Toronto: James Lorimer, 1986), 25–45.

30 Kim Richard Nossal, "The Politics of Circumspection: Canadian Policy Towards the Soviet Union, 1985–1991," *International Journal of Canadian Studies* 9 (Spring 1994), 27–45.

31 Maxwell A. Cameron, "Canada and Latin America," in Fen Osler Hampson and Christopher J. Maule, eds., Canada Among Nations *1990–91: After the Cold War* (Ottawa: Carleton University Press, 1991), 111.

32 Adam Bromke and Kim Richard Nossal, "A Turning Point in Canada–United States Relations," *Foreign Affairs* 66 (Fall 1987), 150–69.

commitments to its allies.[33] By the time he left office in 1993, Canada had withdrawn its forces from Europe, ending its most visible form of commitment to its NATO allies.[34]

But it was in the area of Canadian–American relations that Mulroney left his major mark, through the Canada–United States Free Trade Agreement of 1988 and the North American Free Trade Agreement of 1993. Mulroney had come to power opposed to free trade, but changed his mind in 1985, partly because a royal commission that had been appointed by Trudeau in 1983 recommended that Canada take a "leap of faith" and seek a comprehensive free-trade agreement with the United States.[35] Given the deeply entrenched opposition to free trade with the United States in Canada, it required a comparable leap of faith for Mulroney to change his mind about the issue, negotiate an agreement with Washington, and present it to a deeply divided electorate in the 1988 election. However, the Conservative victory in 1988 opened the door for the expansion of free trade in North America. Mexico, seeing the success of the Canadian initiative, approached the United States to negotiate its own free-trade agreement. The Canadian government, fearful of the consequences of a separate agreement, pressed successfully to have the Mexican–American negotiations trilateralized to include Canada. Both the agreements constitute a durable and substantial legacy of Mulroney's time in office.

Another clear example of Mulroney's personal impact on foreign policy was the case of South Africa. Mulroney had not demonstrated any interest in apartheid prior to the renewed outbreak of unrest in the townships in the southern summer of 1984; he had been content to follow the Trudeau government's policy of avoiding imposing sanctions.[36] But following the declaration of a state of emergency by South Africa in 1985, Mulroney enthusiastically embraced a sanctionist policy, in the process directly confronting the anti-sanctionist approach favoured not only by the Reagan administration but also by the British government of Margaret Thatcher.[37]

Mulroney also took a leadership role on a number of dossiers in global environmental policy, including ozone depletion and climate change. In 1987, the Canadian government

---

33 Norrin M. Ripsman, "Big Eyes and Empty Pockets: The Two Phases of Conservative Defence Policy," in Michaud and Nossal, eds., *Diplomatic Departures*, 100–27.

34 Kim Richard Nossal, "A European Nation? The Life and Times of Atlanticism in Canada," in John English and Norman Hillmer, eds., *Making a Difference? Canada's Foreign Policy in a Changing World Order* (Toronto: Lester Publishing, 1992), 79–102; Stéphane Roussel, "Amère Amérique . . . L'OTAN et l'intérêt national du Canada," *Canadian Defence Quarterly* 22 (March 1993), 35–42.

35 The Royal Commission on the Economic Union and Development Prospects for Canada under the direction of Donald S. Macdonald, a former Liberal finance minister, was appointed by Trudeau in 1983, and reported in 1985: see Gregory J. Inwood, *Continentalizing Canada: The Politics and Legacy of the MacDonald Royal Commission* (Toronto: University of Toronto Press, 2005).

36 T.A. Keenleyside, "Canada–South Africa Commercial Relations, 1977–1982: Business as Usual?" *Canadian Journal of African Studies* 17:3 (1983), 449–67.

37 Kim Richard Nossal, *Rain Dancing: Sanctions in Canadian and Australian Foreign Policy* (Toronto: University of Toronto Press, 1994), chap. 5; Linda Freeman, *The Ambiguous Champion: Canada and South Africa in the Trudeau and Mulroney Years* (Toronto: University of Toronto Press, 1997); David R. Black, "How Exceptional? Reassessing the Mulroney Government's Anti-apartheid 'Crusade,'" in Michaud and Nossal, eds., *Diplomatic Departures*, 173–193.

strongly supported the Montréal Protocol designed to address the depletion of the ozone layer. Mulroney supported the recommendations of the Bruntland Commission and embraced the language of sustainable development. The government also established a $3 billion Green Plan to fund environmental research. At the United Nations Conference on Environment and Development (UNCED) in Rio de Janeiro, held in June 1992, the Canadian government put forward a number of initiatives for international standards. Mulroney was the first leader to sign the UN Framework Convention on Climate Change (FCCC) in 1992.[38] (In April 2006, *Corporate Knights* magazine honoured Mulroney as the "greenest prime minister in Canadian history."[39])

In short, by the time he resigned as prime minister in June 1993, Mulroney was demonstrating what every prime minister had before him: a desire and a capacity to dominate the process of foreign policy decision-making. Like Trudeau, he came to office with a definite set of ideas about changing foreign policy. And while some criticized Mulroney for "running his own foreign policy," as Andrew Cohen put it,[40] Barbara McDougall, Mulroney's external affairs minister observed that:

> No one should be surprised—or offended—that Prime Minister Mulroney shaped his government's foreign policy. That's what heads of government *do*. François Mitterrand, Boris Yeltsin, Mikhail Gorbachev, Margaret Thatcher, Anwar Sadat, Menachem Begin—does anyone honestly think that their visions . . . were designed by desk officers?[41]

Jean Chrétien (1993–2003)

The approach to international policy taken by Jean Chrétien, who came to power in November 1993, followed a well-established pattern. As leader of the opposition, he had been highly critical of some of the international policy decisions of the Mulroney Conservatives. As head of government, he immediately sought to distance himself from his predecessor and impose his own stamp on international policy.

For example, Chrétien had criticized the EH-101 as a "Cadillac" helicopter; his very first decision was to cancel the program (even though it cost over $473 million in cancellation fees[42]). He had criticized Mulroney for spending $3.5 million to refit an Airbus A-310 Polaris for prime ministerial travels, a kind of Canadian equivalent of the "Air Force One" Boeing 747 used by presidents of the United States for their travels. Calling it a "flying Taj Mahal," he refused to fly on the Polaris, which remained grounded, and instead

---

38 Heather A. Smith, "Shades of Grey in Canada's Greening During the Mulroney Era," in Michaud and Nossal, eds., *Diplomatic Departures*, 71–83.

39 "Mulroney Praised for His Green Record as PM," CTV.ca, April 20, 2006; see also http://www.corporateknights.ca/web-stories/298-brian-mulroney-greenest-pm.html.

40 Andrew Cohen, "The Diplomats Make a Comeback," *Globe and Mail*, November 19, 1994, D1–D2.

41 Barbara McDougall, "How We Handled Foreign Policy," *Globe and Mail*, December 9, 1994.

42 Andrew Richter, "Forty Years of Neglect, Indifference and Apathy: The Relentless Decline of Canada's Armed Forces," in Patrick James, Nelson Michaud and Marc J. O'Reilly, eds., *Handbook of Canadian Foreign Policy* (Lexington Books, 2006), 51–82, 62.

used one of the fleet of Challenger executive jets operated by the Canadian Armed Forces.[43] Rather, Chrétien took to talking about his "Chevrolet" foreign policy.[44]

Likewise, Mulroney had been criticized for being too close to the United States,[45] and Chrétien sought at all costs to avoid projecting the same image.[46] As a result, in the first years of his nine years in office, he only met Bill Clinton in the context of multilateral meetings—at the Seattle meeting of the Asia Pacific Economic Cooperation (APEC) forum in November 1993 or at the NATO summit in January 1994. Indeed it was not until February 1995, 15 months after Chrétien became prime minister, that Clinton visited Canada for a bilateral meeting, and not until 1997 that Chrétien went to the United States on a bilateral visit. Nonetheless, as we will see below, Chrétien and Clinton developed a close friendship. In contrast, relations with the United States deteriorated considerably when George W. Bush arrived in the White House in January 2001.

Between 1993 and 2003, Chrétien demonstrated: a willingness and a capacity to shape international policy. Often policy decisions were framed by him alone. For example, he became involved personally in the rescue mission for refugees in Zaire in late 1996, maintaining hands-on control of the day-to-day management of the Canadian initiative.[47] Likewise, the commitment under the Kyoto accords for reducing Canada's greenhouse gas emissions to 6 percent below 1990 levels was essentially decided by Chrétien without consulting cabinet; the minus-6 figure was arrived at quite arbitrarily: Chrétien pulled this number out of thin air and phoned Canada's negotiators at Kyoto, ordering them to

---

43 In his memoirs, Chrétien acknowledges that when his Challenger was parked at Seattle airport between the 747s used by other leaders, "I realized for the first time that I might have gone a bit overboard as Opposition leader in criticizing Brian Mulroney's imperial style, which turned out to be quite modest compared to that of most heads of government." Jean Chrétien, *My Years as Prime Minister* (Toronto: Alfred A. Knopf Canada, 2007), 86.

44 Tom Keating, "A Passive Internationalist: Jean Chrétien and Canadian Foreign Policy," in Lois Harder and Steve Patten, eds., *The Chrétien Legacy: Politics and Public Policy in Canada* (Montréal and Kingston: McGill-Queen's University Press, 2006), 130.

45 For example, Lawrence Martin, *Pledge of Allegiance: The Americanization of Canada in the Mulroney Years* (Toronto: McClelland and Stewart, 1993), 272, called him a "border-boy politician"; Marci McDonald, *Yankee Doodle Dandy: Brian Mulroney and the American Agenda* (Toronto: Stoddart, 1995), 4, referred to him as "Washington's lapdog."

46 Fen Osler Hampson and Maureen Appel Molot, "Does the 49th Parallel Matter Any More?" in Maureen Appel Molot and Fen Osler Hampson, eds., *Canada Among Nations 2000: Vanishing Borders* (Ottawa: Carleton University Press, 2000), 18.

47 After the Rwandan genocide of 1994, hundreds of thousands of Hutus, including many Interahamwe *génocidaires*, fled into eastern Zaire following the victory of the Tutsis. In early 1996, Interahamwe Hutus, aided by Zairian forces, attacked Tutsis in eastern Zaire, bringing the Rwandan army into the conflict and catching large numbers of refugees between the belligerents. The United Nations secretary-general called for the creation of a multinational force to protect civilians. When the United States indicated its willingness to have Canada play a leading role, Chrétien was crucial in talking to other world leaders and putting together a diverse multinational force over the weekend of 9–10 November. However, the multinational force quickly fell apart as a number of governments, including the Clinton administration, grew increasingly concerned about becoming involved in a larger war; by the middle of December the crisis resolved itself as the refugees that were to be rescued returned to Rwanda themselves. For the account of the Great Lakes initiative by Chrétien's foreign affairs adviser, see James Bartleman, *Rollercoaster: My Hectic Years as Jean Chrétien's Diplomatic Advisor, 1994–1998* (Toronto: McClelland & Stewart, 2005), 171–204. See also Andrew Cooper and Ian Taylor, "'Made in Africa' versus 'Out of Africa': Comparing South Africa's Non-leadership with Canada's Leadership in the 1996

present it as Canada's number.[48] Chrétien also put his personal stamp on the most difficult decision of his three mandates: his refusal in March 2003 to join the coalition put together by the United States to invade Iraq and overthrow the regime of Saddam Hussein.[49]

But his legacy was more diffuse than Trudeau's or Mulroney's. As Donald Savoie has noted, Chrétien's forte in international policy, as in another areas of policy, was his pragmatism. In Savoie's view, Chrétien actually had very little longer-term influence on Canada's role in the world, simply because he saw policy not in strategic terms, but as little more than a series of thorny files to be successfully managed. "En gros, sa stratégie en ce domaine était d'en avoir aucune."[50]

Paul Martin (2003–2006)

Paul Martin did not enjoy a long mandate as prime minister. He took over from Jean Chrétien as leader of the Liberal party in November 2003, and as prime minister in December. He called an election for June 2004, after which his Liberal government was reduced to a minority. In the election of 23 January 2006, the Conservative Party of Canada under Stephen Harper won a minority. Nonetheless, Martin's 26 months in office were marked by intense activity in international policy.

Unlike some prime ministers who come to office without interest or experience in international policy, Martin arrived at 24 Sussex Drive with long experience in the area gained as the minister of finance in Chrétien's government. As he said when he turned down Chrétien's offer of the foreign affairs portfolio after the November 2000 election: "I am probably doing more in terms of foreign policy right now at Finance than I could do as minister of foreign affairs."[51]

But like other prime ministers, Martin sought to put his own stamp on international policy. He did this in a number of ways. First, as we will see in Chapter 9, he reorganized government. On the day he took office, December 12, 2003, he moved to split the Department of Foreign Affairs and International Trade into two separate departments. He also created a new department, Public Safety and Emergency Preparedness Canada (today just called Public Safety Canada),[52] that brought together a number of agencies involved

---

Crisis in Eastern Zaire," *Commonwealth and Comparative Politics* 39:1 (March 2001), 23–41, and Sean M. Maloney, "Helpful Fixer or Hired Gun: Why Canada Goes Overseas," *Policy Options* (January/ February 2001), 59–65.

48 For the story of how Chrétien personally selected Canada's Kyoto commitment, unilaterally changing the number agreed to by the provinces and the federal cabinet, see Jeffrey Simpson, Mark Jaccard and Nic Rivers, *Hot Air: Meeting Canada's Climate Change Challenge* (Toronto: McClelland & Stewart, 2007), 33–41. Perhaps not surprisingly, a rather different story appears in Chrétien's memoirs: see *My Years as Prime Minister*, 385.

49 Donald Barry, "Chrétien, Bush, and the War in Iraq," *American Review of Canadian Studies* 35:2 (Summer 2005), 215–45.

50 Donald J. Savoie, "Chrétien: la politique, une question de pouvoir," *Policy Options* 24:6 (June–July 2003), 85: "Basically, his strategy in this area [of policy] was to have no strategy."

51 Paul Martin, *Hell or High Water: My Life in and out of Politics* (Toronto: McClelland & Stewart, 2008), 228.

52 Its formal name under the 2005 legislation is the Department of Public Safety and Emergency Preparedness; its French name, *Ministère de la Sécurité publique et de la Protection civile*, differs significantly from its English name.

in national security, including the Canada Border Services Agency, the Royal Canadian Mounted Police, and the Canadian Security and Intelligence Service, as well as agencies responsible for the federal prison system, the National Parole Board and Correctional Service Canada. This new agency, often compared to the new Department of Homeland Security created in the United States after the attacks of 9/11, sought to refocus the attention of the federal government on national security.[53] This reorganization of domestic security would find its counterpart in the reorganization of the Canadian Forces, as the prime minister approved the creation of Canada Command, an integrated command for homeland defence, broadly similar to NORTHCOM, the new Northern Command created by the United States after 9/11.[54] Finally, Martin also created "Canada Corps"—an institutionalized state-supported agency to send young Canadians to "places in the world that need them" to assist in good governance, democratization, and development.[55]

Martin also sought to put his stamp on international policy by publishing a foreign policy review. Like previous reviews of Canadian foreign policy,[56] the Martin review was intended to distance him from his predecessor. But unlike previous reviews, *Canada's International Policy Statement*, released in April 2005, was intended to be a comprehensive statement of international policy. It was the equivalent of four policy statements, on foreign policy, defence, international trade, and development assistance, and attempted to integrate the main activities of the principal agencies that manage Canada's day-to-day relations with the rest of the world.[57]

In international affairs, Martin pursued several priorities. As a former minister of finance, his first priority was to maintain Canada's prosperity and economic competitiveness. He sought in particular to minimize the shocks for the Canadian economy of events such as terrorist attacks, pandemics, or financial crises in the emergent economies. He had particular interest in the architecture of global governance and pushed hard for the creation of a new global forum that would bring together the heads of government of the 20 most important economies.[58] His interest in global governance also prompted him to embrace

---

53 The Martin government also released a "national security policy" in 2004; for a discussion, see Edna Keeble, "Defining Canadian Security: Continuities and Discontinuities," *American Review of Canadian Studies* 35:1 (Spring 2005), 1–23.

54 For details, see Elinor C. Sloan, *Security and Defence in the Terrorist Era: Canada and North America* (Montréal and Kingston: McGill-Queen's University Press, 2005), chap. 5.

55 The Canada Corps idea emerged in early 2004, making its appearance in the 2004 budget and the Speech from the Throne in October, and touted in the *International Policy Statement* of 2005. Eventually located within CIDA, it made its official debut in the Ukrainian presidential elections of December 2004 and monitored elections in a number of other countries before being reorganized as the Office for Democratic Governance in 2007.

56 David Malone, "Foreign Policy Reviews Reconsidered," *International Journal* 56:4 (Autumn 2001), 555–78; William Hogg, "Plus Ça Change: Continuity, Change and Culture in Foreign Policy White Papers," *International Journal* 59 (Summer 2004), 521–36; also the contributions in *Études internationales* 37:1 (March 2006), "Les livres blancs et les politiques étrangères: pratiques comparées," ed. Nelson Michaud, 5–138.

57 Government of Canada, *Canada's International Policy Statement: A Role of Pride and Influence in the World*, overview booklet (Ottawa: Government of Canada, 2005), archived online by Library and Archives Canada (http://www.collectionscanada.gc.ca).

58 Paul Martin, "Verbatim: Une politique qui rendra sa place au Canada sur la scène internationale," *Policy Options* 25:6 (June/July 2004), 5–8.

new ideas about state sovereignty, and particularly the "responsibility to protect" (or R2P) agenda embraced by the United Nations in 2005.[59] Another priority was to repair the relationship with the United States that had been seriously mismanaged in the final years of the Chrétien government.

In each case, however, Martin found it difficult to put his ideas into practice. His idea for a new architecture that would bring the leaders of the 20 largest economies together—what he called the "L20"[60]—was several years ahead of its time: it was not until the financial crisis of 2008 that a new G-20 architecture was embraced, as we will see in Chapter 7.

In the case of R2P, Martin found himself caught by the gap that was emerging between the rhetoric of humanitarian intervention and the realities of global politics. At the very time that Martin was pressing his "responsibilities agenda," atrocity crimes were being committed against the Fur people in the Darfur region of Sudan by government-backed militias known as the *janjaweed*, killing thousands of people and driving hundreds of thousands more into refugee camps across the border in Chad. While the administration of George W. Bush labelled the campaign against the Fur as a genocide, governments all over the world, including Martin's, demonstrated a manifest unwillingness to accept any "responsibility" to "protect" the Fur against the predations of their own government.[61]

Finally, although Martin had come to power promising to improve Canadian–American relations, he found that appealing to the deep strain of anti-Americanism in the electorate was too tempting. Although he made some initial moves to improve the relationship, his government's policy on the issue of Canada's involvement in the United States Ballistic Missile Defense (BMD) program soured the mood considerably. Although Martin came to office in favour of Canadian participation in BMD, he chose to avoid making a decision on the issue throughout 2004. The tipping point came during a visit by George Bush to Canada in November and December 2004. As he put it later, he was "infuriated" by the public pressure that Bush put on him during this visit.[62] In February, without giving the Bush administration any advance warning or offering any reasoned justification for the decision, the Martin government abruptly announced that it would not join BMD, saying only that it was "not in Canada's interests." The United States government was not pleased: The U.S. ambassador, Paul Cellucci, claimed to be "perplexed" by the decision; the U.S. secretary of state, Condoleezza Rice, immediately postponed a planned trip to Canada.[63]

---

59 Alex J. Bellamy, *Responsibility to Protect* (London: Polity, 2009); Marie-Joëlle Zahar, "Intervention, Prevention, and the 'Responsibility to Protect': Considerations for Canadian Foreign Policy," *International Journal* 60:3 (Summer 2005), 723–34.

60 For details, see John English, Ramesh Chandra Thakur, Andrew Fenton Cooper, *Reforming from the Top: A Leaders' 20 Summit* (Tokyo: United Nations University Press, 2005).

61 Kim Richard Nossal, "Ear Candy: Canadian Policy Toward Humanitarian Intervention and Atrocity Crimes in Darfur," *International Journal* 60:4 (Autumn 2005), 1017–32.

62 American and Canadian officials had agreed beforehand that Bush would not raise BMD publicly in order to avoid embarrassing Martin on this thorny issue. However, in a speech in Halifax on December 1, 2004, Bush inserted a sentence, "I hope we'll also move forward on ballistic missile defense cooperation to protect the next generation of Canadians and Americans from the threats we know will arise," that violated that agreement. On Martin's reaction, see *Hell or High Water*, 387–88.

63 "Rice May Postpone Visit to Canada," *Globe and Mail*, March 1, 2005, A4.

By the end of 2005, however, Martin was clearly unconcerned about the atmospherics of the relationship. In the middle of the 2005–06 election campaign, he openly and publicly criticized the Bush administration for its refusal to sign on to the Kyoto accords; and in a move designed to signal to voters his distance from Bush, Martin went out of his way to arrange a special photo opportunity with Bill Clinton, who remained very popular in Canada.[64] Moreover, the Liberal party election campaign openly tried to appeal to the deep strain of anti-Americanism in Canada by painting Stephen Harper and the Conservatives as patsies of George W. Bush.[65]

Paul Martin demonstrates how an individual interested in international issues can, in a relatively short amount of time, make his mark in international policy by promoting new ideas. In this respect, Martin's period as prime minister resembled the first years of the governments of Louis St. Laurent and Pierre Elliott Trudeau. However, Martin's prime ministership also illustrates that ideas, no matter how good or original, are seldom sufficient to change policy in a durable way. Martin never really recovered from the sponsorship scandal bequeathed him by Chrétien.[66] Moreover, the election campaigns of 2004 and especially 2005–2006 showed that even considerable activity on the international level is not always translated into electoral benefits.

Stephen Harper (2006–)

Given the portraits of the prime ministers presented above, it will come as no surprise that Stephen Harper sought to assert his preeminence in international policy after the Conservative Party of Canada achieved a minority in the January 2006 election. It is clear that in his first mandate (2006–08), Harper saw international policy through the lens of domestic politics—as one of the ways that the Conservatives might unseat the Liberals as Canada's "natural governing party" (as the party was often called by pundits)[67]. Thus,

---

64 *Globe and Mail*, Toronto, December 9, 2005.

65 Kim Richard Nossal, "A Thermostatic Dynamic? Electoral Outcomes and Anti-Americanism in Canada," in Richard A. Higgott and Ivona Malbašić, eds., *The Political Consequences of Anti-Americanism* (London: Routledge, 2008), 129–41.

66 In the aftermath of the 1995 referendum in Québec, the federal government initiated an ad campaign in Québec to raise the awareness of Québécois about the federal government. Investigations by the Auditor-General, Sheila Fraser, and by a commission of inquiry headed by Justice John Gomery discovered that the sponsorship program was riddled with corruption: Funds were awarded to friends of Liberals in Québec who did not do the work billed or who funnelled funds back to the Liberal party. Indeed, Chrétien purposely timed his departure from politics to ensure that Martin would have to deal with the fallout from the corruption. For a discussion that places the scandal in broader perspective, see David A. Good, *The Politics of Public Money: Spenders, Guardians, Priority Setters, and Financial Watchdogs Inside the Canadian Government* (Toronto: University of Toronto Press, 2007).

67 The term was first used in discussions of British politics in the 1970s (e.g., Alan Watkins, "The State of the Labour Party," *The Political Quarterly* 43:4 [October 1972], 411). In Canada, it was first used by academics—for example, Edwin R. Black, "Turning Canadian Politics Inside Out," *The Political Quarterly* 51:2 (April 1980), 141—but then gained wide currency in Canadian politics in the 1980s and 1990s.

Harper methodically set about pursuing international policies that he judged would maximize electoral support for the Conservatives.

An initial priority was the Canadian–American relationship. As noted above, Liberal attack ads in the waning days of the 2005–06 election campaign had painted Harper as being in favour of the war in Iraq and claimed that a Harper victory "will put a smile on George W. Bush's face"; the ad ended "Well, at least someone will be happy, eh?"[68] But while Harper moved to improve the tone of the relationship with George W. Bush, he did not embrace policies designed to evoke happiness in Washington. Indeed, even before he was sworn in as prime minister, Harper sharply rebuked the American ambassador to Canada, David Wilkins, over Arctic sovereignty.[69] In not a single speech after he came to office did Harper offer a word of support for the American mission in Iraq. And he made no move to reverse Martin's decision on BMD, even though he, like Martin, had come to office in favour of Canadian participation in the BMD program.

A second priority was the mission in Afghanistan. In July 2005, the Martin government had agreed to redeploy the approximately 2000 Canadian troops assigned to the NATO-led International Security Assistance Force (ISAF) in Kabul, where they had been serving since August 2003, to the American-led Operation Enduring Freedom in the Kandahar region. The arrival of the main contingent of Canadians in the Kandahar region in February 2006 coincided not only with the arrival of the Conservative government, but also with the expansion of the Taliban insurgency in southern Afghanistan and the importation of insurgent tactics from Iraq, including roadside improvised explosive devices (IEDs) and suicide bombing attacks. The first Canadian combat death from hostile fire came within a month, and the number of deaths mounted steadily. While Canada's mission in Afghanistan was inherited by the Conservative government, Harper very much sought to manage the domestic politics of the mission, as we will see in Chapter 10.[70]

Other international policy initiatives clearly designed to win favour among the electorate included giving the government of Québec a formal role in a United Nations body, UNESCO, discussed further in Chapter 12.[71] This agreement can be seen as the international policy counterpart to the historic resolution in the House of Commons in November 2006 that recognized the Québécois as a nation—part of a very conscious campaign to improve Conservative fortunes in Québec. Likewise, the Conservative government's policies on the Middle East—particularly its sanctions against Hamas in March 2006, its more robust support for Israel during the Lebanon war in July 2006, and its boycott of the

---

68 All the Liberal attack ads from the 2005–06 campaign are archived at http://www.ctv.ca/servlet/ArticleNews/story/CTVNews/20060103/ELXN_liberal_attackads_060110/20060110.

69 Two days after the election, Wilkins was asked about the Arctic at a Q&A after a public lecture. He responded by restating the long-standing American claim that the waters of the Arctic archipelago constituted an international strait. Harper criticized the ambassador and reasserted the long-standing Canadian claim that Arctic waters were internal Canadian waters. "Harper Rebukes US Envoy over Arctic Dispute," *Globe and Mail*, January 27, 2006.

70 Kim Richard Nossal, "No Exit: Canada and the 'War Without End' in Afghanistan," in Hans-Georg Ehrhart and Charles C. Pentland, eds., *NATO and the International Engagement in Afghanistan* (Toronto: Oxford University Press, 2009), 157–73.

71 "Prime Minister Harper and Premier Charest Sign Historic Agreement Establishing a Formal Role for Québec in UNESCO," May 5, 2006, available http://pm.gc.ca/eng/media.asp?id=1151.

Durban Review Conference of 2009[72]—were embraced partly for the support these were believed to produce, not only among Jewish voters, but among other Canadians besides.

If Harper followed a well-trodden path in asserting preeminence in international policy, he was unlike his predecessors in seeking to impose tight personal control on all aspects of the policy process as part of his efforts to transform electoral politics. The unanimity of observers of Harper's prime ministerial style is striking: for example, assessing Harper's first three months in power, Paul Wells concluded that "Harper was at the centre of his government's policy direction and, especially, its communication philosophy. He would never be shy about stepping in to countermand a minister at a key moment."[73] John Kirton reports that Harper insisted on having the Prime Minister's Office "pre-approve" the political activities of both ministers and backbenchers.[74] John J. Noble suggested that Harper "has set the tone and the policy priorities in every aspect of his government."[75] One small measure of this desire for control was that the prime minister routinely made all the government's policy announcements himself, leaving ministers, as Jeffrey Simpson and Brian Laghi put it, "to stand behind him nodding like Bobblehead dolls"[76]

THE SOURCES OF PREEMINENCE

What accounts for preeminence in international policy? While every prime minister exhibits different patterns of dominance, we suggest that there are two general sources of preeminence. The first springs from the multiplicity of political functions a prime minister acquires when called on by the Governor General to form a government. First, in Canada, the prime minister controls the appointment process that shapes the government. Second, prime ministers also assume a wide range of responsibilities that propel them into the international system. In this chapter, we look at the power of appointment; in the next chapter we examine the impact of summit diplomacy on Canada's international policy.

The Power of Appointment

In Canada, the prime minister is the head of the government; its chief spokesperson, in and outside Parliament; the chair of Cabinet; and head of the parliamentary caucus and the

---

72 The United Nations World Conference Against Racism, Racial Discrimination, Xenophobia and Related Intolerance was held in Durban, South Africa, from August 31 to September 7, 2001. This conference was dominated by attacks on Israel, and when it was announced that a Durban review conference ("Durban II") was going to be held in Geneva in 2009, the Harper government announced on January 23, 2008 that it would not participate in what Jason Kenney, secretary of state for multiculturalism and Canadian identity, termed a "circus of intolerance." Gil Troy, "A Durban Review Diary," *Policy Options* (June 2009), 58–62.

73 Paul Wells, "Harper's First 100 Days: Taking Charge," *Policy Options*, November 2006, 84.

74 John Kirton, "Harper's 'Made in Canada' Global Leadership," in Andrew F. Cooper and Dane Rowlands, eds., *Canada Among Nations 2006: Minorities and Priorities* (Montréal and Kingston: McGill-Queen's University Press, 2007), 55, n5.

75 John J. Noble, "PMO/PCO/DFAIT: Serving the Prime Minister's Foreign Policy Agenda," in Jean Daudlin and Daniel Schwanen, eds., *Canada Among Nations 2007: What Room for Manoeuvre?* (Montréal and Kingston: McGill-Queen's University Press, 2008), 38–65, 59.

76 Jeffrey Simpson and Brian Laghi, "Incremental Man," *Globe and Mail*, October 4, 2008.

extra-parliamentary party. In these multiple roles, the prime minister determines the very shape of the government.

First, the prime minister controls the fates of everyone in the governing party. He or she decides who will be in cabinet, and in particular who will occupy the key international portfolios: the minister of foreign affairs, the minister of international trade, the minister of national defence, the minister responsible for development assistance, and junior ministers of state given particular international responsibilities. As Paul Gecelovsky notes, prime ministerial authority in international policy is entrenched through the issuing of mandate letters to cabinet appointees; these letters can constrain the bounds of a minister's mandate.[77] Such power to appoint gives every prime minister potent means to extract compliance from ministers, as Jean Chrétien once revealed. He was engaged in some last-minute negotiations over NAFTA with Bill Clinton, being conducted through the U.S. ambassador in Ottawa, James Blanchard. Blanchard asked Chrétien what would happen if the trade minister did not agree to what he and Clinton were negotiating. Chrétien replied, "Then I will have a new trade minister the following morning."[78]

Such control extends to the prime minister's parliamentary caucus. Because in Canada a party leader must sign the nomination papers of every candidate the party runs in elections, the leader has the final say power over who runs under the party's banner—and who does not. All party leaders have had occasion to use this power. For example, in November 2004, Carolyn Parrish, a Toronto-area MP who had a record of anti-American statements, appeared on the satirical show *This Hour Has 22 Minutes* and stomped on a George W. Bush doll as a joke, prompting Paul Martin to demand a meeting with her. Parrish said to a reporter that if the prime minister thought he could shut her up, he "could go to hell." Martin expelled her from the Liberal caucus hours after her comment was reported in the press. While she continued to sit as an independent, her efforts to be readmitted to the Liberal caucus were rejected by Martin; in the absence of a Liberal endorsement, she chose not to contest the 2006 election.[79] But at times just the threat will be enough: For example, in late 2006 Stephen Harper warned members of his parliamentary caucus not to discuss controversial budget cuts that he was introducing: "If I hear anyone speaking about them, you will have a very short political career."[80]

Second, the prime minister is responsible for appointing individuals to key bureaucratic positions. The clerk of the Privy Council, the most senior civil servant and the bureaucratic head of the Privy Council Office (PCO), must be selected. In consultation with the clerk, the prime minister must appoint deputy ministers for government departments; advisers in such key central agencies as the Prime Minister's Office (PMO) and the PCO; members of a burgeoning number of federal agencies, boards, and commissions; and

---

77 Paul Gecelovsky, "Of Legacies and Lightning Bolts: The Prime Minister and Canadian Foreign Policy," in Duane Bratt and Christopher J. Kukucha, eds., *Readings in Canadian Foreign Policy* (Toronto: Oxford University Press, 2007), 202.

78 Edward Greenspon and Anthony Wilson-Smith, *Double Vision: The Inside Story of the Liberals in Power* (Toronto: Doubleday, 1996), 48; Savoie, 108; Chrétien reports a slightly different response in his memoirs: Chrétien, *My Years as Prime Minister*, 85. For Paul Martin's account of how he "got quit" by Chrétien, see *Hell or High Water*, 235–36.

79 Ray Conologue, "Loose Cannon," *Saturday Night* (March 2005), 48–53.

80 Quoted in Simpson and Laghi, "Incremental Man."

ambassadors to foreign capitals, including deputy ministers of departments and Canadian ambassadors abroad.

The *duty* to appoint means that no prime minister can avoid those personnel decisions that so relentlessly shape an administration. By the same token, however, the *prerogative* to appoint gives the prime minister a potent means of imposing policy preferences on those admitted to government. A prime minister's appointments are critical to the process of policymaking, domestic and foreign. In deciding who will occupy international policymaking positions, the prime minister determines the kind of advice on foreign affairs the government will receive; the quality of bureaucratic and ministerial talent that can be brought to bear to support successful Canadian statecraft; the nature of the interplay among the individuals in the senior reaches of the state upon whom the prime minister must ultimately depend; and the nature and quality of the representation of Canadian interests abroad.

CONCLUSION

All prime ministers seem to want to put their stamp on Canada's international policy—even if they have little interest in foreign policy when they come to power. Most prime ministers tend to be critical of the foreign policy of their predecessors, though when their predecessors are from the same political party, they are more prudent in their criticism. Thus, St. Laurent, Trudeau, and Martin tended to be measured in their criticisms of King, Pearson, and Chrétien even while keeping their distance. By contrast, Diefenbaker, Pearson, Mulroney, Chrétien, and Harper did not hesitate to criticize the policies of their predecessors, all of whom belonged to rival political parties. And the power associated with the office of prime minister in Canada makes it possible for the policymaker at the apex to modify, sometimes dramatically, the main trends of international policy, because the prime minister can name his own team of ministers and senior officials to carry out the changes he or she wants.

One other factor propels prime ministers into the international realm, a factor that inevitably has an impact on Canada's international policy. That factor is summit diplomacy, which we look at in the next chapter.

CHAPTER 7

The Prime Minister and Summit Diplomacy

The management of a state's foreign policy is generally left to the diplomats and bureaucrats in the foreign ministry. These professionals represent their state's leaders in other capitals, dealing with foreign leaders on behalf of their government. On numerous occasions, however, the leaders themselves will want to deal directly with each other, eliminating the intermediary role of diplomats. The responsibility for attending international summit meetings and greeting dignitaries visiting Canada from abroad cannot be delegated to others—at least not without causing offence. As Stephen Harper frankly admitted in July 2006, "One of the biggest surprises I've had in this job has been the degree to which foreign policy has really taken a lot of my time."[1] Likewise, all Canadian prime ministers eventually discover that the "glitterati effect"—in which coolness accrues to those who are "seen" with the rich and famous—has an international equivalent: Being "seen" with other world leaders, particularly the leaders of the great powers, has definite domestic political benefits.

Diplomacy at the summit is not a new phenomenon in global politics. Throughout history, leaders of states have sought to negotiate directly with one another, particularly at the end of major conflicts. The enduring general peace of nineteenth-century Europe was created at a meeting of reigning monarchs and princes who met at the Congress of Vienna during the winter of 1814–15. And at Versailles in 1919, heads of government gathered to try to find a solution to the problem of war. Likewise, the meetings of Winston Churchill, Franklin Delano Roosevelt, and Joseph Stalin at Potsdam and Yalta during the Second World War laid the foundations for the new international order after 1945; indeed, it was during this period that the term "summit" was used to describe this kind of diplomacy.[2] While "summit diplomacy" was a new term to describe an old practice, until the Second World War, summit meetings were highly unusual and rare occurrences in world politics. After 1945, however, summitry became increasingly common.[3]

CONTEMPORARY SUMMIT DIPLOMACY

Today, the calendars of most world leaders revolve around a series of summit meetings, some special one-time affairs, others institutionalized and recurrent. Many of the summits have become not only deeply institutionalized but also highly regularized. The Group of Twenty (G-20) summit, a group of the nineteen largest economies in the world plus the European Union, occurs annually, as does the meeting of the Asia-Pacific Economic Cooperation (APEC) forum. Both the Commonwealth Heads of Government Meetings (CHOGM) and the Sommet of the Organisation internationale de la Francophonie (OIF) are held biannually. Some "regular" summit meetings meet only irregularly, such as the North Atlantic Treaty Organization heads of government meeting.

---

1 Graham Fraser, "A Change in Emphasis," *Toronto Star*, July 22, 2006.

2 Roger Frank Swanson, *Canadian–American Summit Diplomacy, 1923–1973* (Toronto: McClelland & Stewart, 1975), 2.

3 At the end of the nineteenth century, there were only one or two international conferences attended by official government representatives; today there are more than 9000 international meetings each year. Stéphane Paquin, *La nouvelle économie internationale* (Paris: Armand Colin, 2008), 92.

Some summits are intended to be special one-time meetings, such as the fiftieth anniversary of the founding of the United Nations in October 1995[4] or the UN Millennium Summit held in September 2000. Other summits are intended to be one-time meetings but give birth to a new cycle of meetings. For example, the Organization for Security and Cooperation in Europe (OSCE), a regional security organization of fifty-six states that bills itself as stretching from Vancouver to Vladivostok, began as an ad hoc conference. In 1973, all the countries of Europe, together with Canada and the United States, met in Helsinki to discuss ways of improving East–West relations; thirty-five leaders were present to sign the Helsinki Final Act in 1975. That was also the case with the Summit of the Americas, which was convened by President Bill Clinton in 1994 to discuss expanding hemispheric free trade. There was sufficient interest that follow-up summits were held in Santiago de Chile in April 1998, Québec City in 2001, Mar del Plata, Argentina, in November 2005, and Port of Spain, Trinidad and Tobago, in April 2009—though the focus of these summits is no longer on hemispheric free trade.

Likewise, after the collapse of the financial system in the fall of 2008, a summit of the leaders of the world's twenty most systemically important economies was held in Washington in November of that year. The group countries invited to Washington was based on the Group of Twenty (G-20) group of finance ministers and central-bank governors that was convened after the Asian financial crisis of 1997–98. Follow-up G-20 Leaders' summits were held in London in April 2009 and in Pittsburgh in September 2009. As we will discuss momentarily, at Pittsburgh the leaders decided that the G-20 would replace the Group of Eight (G8) industrialized countries as the most important summit for global governance.[5]

THE PRIME MINISTER'S SUMMIT CALENDAR

In addition to being expected to attend these multilateral summits, the Canadian prime minister is also involved in trilateral summits with the presidents of the United States and Mexico. The prime minister conducts wide-ranging bilateral summitry with foreign leaders both in Canada and abroad. Of these bilateral summits, the most important are the meetings the prime minister holds with the president of the United States. Sometimes these bilateral meetings are held when the two leaders gather for a summit with the Mexican president; at other times, the president and prime minister will meet together on a separate state visit.

When a leader's summit is convened, Canada must be represented at the highest level, propelling the prime minister into the international realm. And because Canada is a member of so many international organizations, the prime minister's annual calendar is increasingly crowded with summit meetings. As Figure 7.1 indicates, in 2008 and 2009, Stephen Harper had to attend fifteen multilateral leaders' summits and hosted Barack Obama, president of the United States, for a summit meeting in Ottawa in February 2009.

Not only does such a demanding schedule require a considerable personal commitment by the prime minister; but also, because most of these summits are highly scripted, a huge amount of bureaucratic energy is devoted to his involvement in their planning and

---

4 This meeting was captured in an unprecedented photograph of most of the world's leaders: available http://www0.un.org/UN50/UNHQ-Photos/50th-2.gif.

5 John English, Ramesh Thakur, and Andrew Cooper, eds., *Reforming from the Top: A Leaders' 20 Summit* (New York: United Nations University Press, 2005); Peter I. Hajnal, *The G8 System and the G-20: Evolution, Role and Documentation* (Aldershot, UK: Ashgate, 2007).

FIGURE 7.1	Stephen Harper's Summit Calendar, 2008–2009

	Location	Date
North American Leaders' Summit	New Orleans	April 21-22, 2008
G8 Summit	Hokkaido Toyako, Japan	July 7-9, 2008
Canada-EU Summit	Québec City	October 17, 2008
Organisation internationale de la Francophonie	Québec City	October 17-19, 2008
G-20 Leaders' Meeting	Washington	November 14-15, 2008
Asia-Pacific Economic Cooperation Forum	Lima, Peru	November 22-23, 2008
Summit with Barack Obama	Ottawa	February 19, 2009
G-20 Leaders' Meeting	London	April 1-2, 2009
NATO Summit Kehl, Germany	Strasbourg, France	April 3-4, 2009
Summit of the Americas and Tobago	Port of Spain, Trinidad	April 17-19, 2009
Canada-EU Summit	Prague	May 6, 2009
G8 Summit	L'Aquila, Italy	July 8-10, 2009
North American Leaders' Summit	Mexico	August 8-11, 2009
G-20 Leaders' Meeting	Pittsburgh	September 24-25, 2009
Asia-Pacific Economic Cooperation Forum	Singapore	November 14-15, 2009
Commonwealth Heads of Government	Port of Spain, Trinidad and Tobago	November 27-29, 2009

In addition, Harper travelled overseas in May 2008 for meetings in Paris, Bonn, Rome, and London with his European G8 counterparts, and in June 2009 to participate in the commemoration of the sixty-fifth anniversary of the D-Day landings. During this period he also held bilateral meetings with heads of government or state in Ottawa or in other capitals and conducted bilateral meetings at multilateral summits. Full details of the prime minister's calendar are available online at http://pm.gc.ca/eng under "Media Centre."

organization. For example, Canadian government officials attended over eighty preparatory meetings called by the Italian government to plan and organize the G8 meeting it hosted in L'Aquila in July 2009. Moreover, summitry becomes particularly difficult when there is a minority government, since the government must ensure that it can retain the confidence of the House of Commons in the absence of the prime minister and other ministers (this usually involves inviting opposition critics to the summit to "pair" with the absent minister).

We now turn to the regular summits on the prime minister's summit calendar.

The Group of Twenty (G-20) Summit

The most important summit meeting on the prime minister's agenda is the annual meeting of the G-20, which brings together the leaders of the world's nineteen largest economies, with the European Union as the twentieth member: Argentina, Australia, Brazil, Canada,

China, France, Germany, India, Indonesia, Italy, Japan, Mexico, South Korea, Russia, Saudi Arabia, South Africa, Turkey, United Kingdom, and the United States, plus the European Union. This summit evolved from the G7, a group of seven major industrialized countries (the United States, Japan, Britain, Germany, France, Italy, and Canada, together with the European Union as a regular member), that became the G8 in 1997 when the Russian Federation was admitted.

Although this annual summit is now a major event attracting thousands of delegates, members of the media, and protestors, it had exceedingly modest beginnings. In November 1975, Valéry Giscard d'Estaing, the president of France, invited the leaders of five other industrialized countries—the United States, Japan, Britain, Germany, and Italy—to the Château de Rambouillet outside Paris to prepare for the Conference on International Economic Cooperation between countries of the North and the South, which was to be held that December.

In contemporary global politics, whoever gets to issue the invitations to summits gets to determine who sits at the table. And the French government, who issued the invitations to the Rambouillet summit, chose not to invite Canada, even though the Trudeau government made a pitch for an invitation. The French argued that Canada was merely an economic appendage of the United States, and that therefore separate representation was unnecessary. Moreover, if Canada were invited, Belgium and the Netherlands would then have a claim, making the summit too large. While the government in Ottawa complained about being excluded,[6] and while some of the other invitees were sympathetic, no one insisted that Canada be there.

The Rambouillet summit was sufficiently successful that the participants agreed to hold another meeting in 1976, hosted by the United States. It was thus President Gerald Ford who was issuing the invitations. Over French objections, he extended one to Pierre Trudeau—on the grounds that the meeting was being held in the Western hemisphere and because of the ties between Canada and the United States. When the summit was held the following year, the British not only invited the European Communities (the forerunner of the European Union) but invited Canada back. According to one observer, Trudeau's performance at the Puerto Rico summit had impressed the other heads of government.[7] After 1977, both the EU and Canada were considered permanent members, and Canada hosted five G7/G8 summits: Montebello, Québec (1981), Toronto (1988), Halifax (1995), and Kananaskis, Alberta (2002).

Following the Puerto Rico summit, the G7 summit became increasingly institutionalized. While the summit never developed the quintessential stamp of international institutionalization—the establishment of a permanent secretariat with a secretary-general—most aspects of the meetings have become highly regularized. Early on, for example, it was agreed that the locale of each year's meeting would be rotated among the members and that the host would chair the meetings. In 1997, the G7 became the G8, when the Russian Federation, which had been attending as an invited guest, was given full membership, and hosted its first summit at St. Petersburg in 2006. As Figure 7.2 shows, by the time the G8

---

6 "We have the economic position in the world to justify our attendance," Allan J. MacEachen, the external affairs minister, plaintively told the House of Commons two weeks before the summit. Canada, Parliament, House of Commons, *Debates*, November 3, 1975.

7 Alex I. Inglis, "Economic Summitry Reaches Time of Testing in London," *International Perspectives* (September/October 1977), 33.

FIGURE 7.2	G6/G7/G8 Summit Rotations, 1975–2010		
Location	**Country**	**Host**	**Year**
Rambouillet	France	Valéry Giscard d'Estaing	1975
Puerto Rico	United States	Gerald Ford	1976
London	United Kingdom	James Callaghan	1977
Bonn	Germany	Helmut Schmidt	1978
Tokyo	Japan	Masayoshi Ohira	1979
Venice	Italy	Francesco Cossiga	1980
Montebello	Canada	Pierre Elliott Trudeau	1981
Versailles	France	François Mitterrand	1982
Williamsburg	United States	Ronald Reagan	1983
London	United Kingdom	Margaret Thatcher	1984
Bonn	Germany	Helmut Kohl	1985
Tokyo	Japan	Yasuhiro Nakasone	1986
Venice	Italy	Amintore Fanani	1987
Toronto	Canada	Brian Mulroney	1988
Paris	France	François Mitterrand	1989
Houston	United States	George H.W. Bush	1990
London	United Kingdom	John Major	1991
Munich	Germany	Helmut Kohl	1992
Tokyo	Japan	Kiichi Miyazawa	1993
Naples	Italy	Silvio Berlusconi	1994
Halifax	Canada	Jean Chrétien	1995
Lyon	France	Jacques Chirac	1996
Denver	United States	Bill Clinton	1997
Birmingham	United Kingdom	Tony Blair	1998
Cologne	Germany	Gerhard Schröder	1999
Kyushu-Okinawa	Japan	Yoshiro Mori	2000
Genoa	Italy	Silvio Berlusconi	2001
Kananaskis	Canada	Jean Chrétien	2002
Evian-les-Bains	France	Jacques Chirac	2003
Sea Island	United States	George W. Bush	2004
Gleneagles	United Kingdom	Tony Blair	2005
St Petersburg	Russian Federation	Vladimir Putin	2006
Heiligendamm	Germany	Angela Merkel	2007
Toyako	Japan	Yasuo Fukuda	2008
L'Aquila	Italy	Silvio Berlusconi	2009
Huntsville	Canada	Stephen Harper	2010*

* G8 summit originally scheduled to be hosted by Canada; Canada and South Korea will co-host G-20 summit.

For more information, see the G8 Information Centre, University of Toronto, http://www.g7.utoronto.ca/summit.

was replaced by the G-20 at the 2010 Huntsville summit hosted by Canada, the G8 had gone through five rotations. Since the G-20 replaced the G8 at the end of a rotation, a new and different rotation for the G-20 will emerge in the years after 2010.

Each of the G-20 leaders has a personal representative whose responsibility it is to plan the summit. These representatives—or "sherpas," as they are colloquially known (after the indispensable guides to another kind of summit)—engage in extensive planning and negotiation prior to each meeting, thrashing out what issues will (and will not) be on the agenda, and even working on a draft of the final communiqué, often months before the actual meeting. While sherpas come from different government departments, they have always had a foreign affairs connection and have always been very senior officials, such as the ambassador for multilateral trade negotiations, Canada's ambassador in the United States, Canada's permanent representative to the United Nations, or the deputy minister of the Department of Foreign Affairs and International Trade.

At the outset, the purpose of the G7 summit was to focus on issues of the global economy, energy, and North–South relations. However, discussion was not limited to these problems, for the leaders were unwilling to forgo the opportunity to exchange views on political and security questions. At the 1978 Bonn meetings, for example, the summit discussed aircraft hijacking; at Venice in 1980 and Versailles in 1982, the summit discussions revealed the extent of the split in the West over sanctions against the Soviet Union. At Venice in June 1987, the issue of sanctions arose yet again, though this time the focus was South Africa.

By the early 1990s, with the end of the Cold War, the topics discussed at the summit shifted considerably. No longer was the focus of security discussions fixed on the Soviet Union; instead, the leaders tended to focus on security threats in the post–Cold War era, including failed and failing states, the security of nuclear weapons, transnational crime, and money laundering. Other topics included health, the environment, infectious decisions, and forest management, which were discussed at the Denver summit. The security situation in the Balkans was often on the agenda during the 1990s. The 1999 summit in Cologne devoted considerable attention to the war then underway in Kosovo. In the years after 2001, the agenda was dominated by the global war on terror.

With the rise of India and China as emerging economies, however, the G8 came under increasing criticism. Some argued that it was overly Eurocentric: Not only were four of the leaders from western Europe (Britain, France, Germany and Italy), but the European Union was represented by both the head of government of the EU member that held the presidency of the European Union and the president of the European Commission. Others argued that the G8 was insufficiently representative of the world's economies. The first reaction of the group was to invite other governments and international organizations to the summit to attend "outreach" and "dialogue" sessions. At Hokkaido Toyako in 2008, for example, the Japanese prime minister invited the heads of government of the Group of Five largest emerging economies (Brazil, China, India, Mexico, and South Africa) to attend a meeting that was known as the G8+5; in addition, the prime minister of Australia and the presidents of Indonesia and South Korea were invited because they, together with Brazil, China, India, Mexico, and South Africa, along with the G8 make up the seventeen-member Major Economies Forum on Energy and Climate Change (MEF). For an African outreach session, South Africa, along with the leaders of the African Union, plus Algeria, Ethiopia, Ghana, Nigeria, Senegal, and Tanzania, were invited. In addition, the secretary-general of the United Nations, Ban Ki-moon, and the heads of the International Atomic

Agency, the International Energy Agency, and the Commonwealth of Independent States were invited.

Such moves did not satisfy the critics. At a meeting in Pretoria hosted by South African President Thabo Mbeki in October 2007, Luis Inacio Lula Da Silva, the president of Brazil, was blunt about the G8's outreach efforts: "It is useless for us to be invited for dessert at the powerful countries' banquet."[8] Some of the other G8 leaders themselves, such as Angela Merkel, the chancellor of Germany, and Nicholas Sarkosy, the president of France, pressed for expansion of the forum. In Canada, by contrast, there were mixed views. While Gordon Smith, a former deputy minister of foreign affairs, urged expanding the summit,[9] the Canadian government itself was notably silent on the issue. Some officials in Ottawa worried that a major change in the summit architecture could as easily result in a smaller summit meeting, with the smallest G8 members, Canada and Italy, dropped from a new forum. In the event, Canada's place was secure: In September 2009, at the G-20 Leaders' Summit in Pittsburgh, the leaders agreed that the G-20 would replace the G8 as the world's major economic forum, beginning with a summit co-hosted by Canada and South Korea in Huntsville, Ontario, in June 2010.

For the leader of a state like Canada, participation in this summit offers both opportunities and imperatives. It affords a prime minister an entrée to high-level discussions on a wide range of global economic and political questions. And it provides an arena in which to attempt to affect the course of great power diplomacy. Trudeau, Mulroney, Chrétien, and Harper all made full use of this opportunity, albeit with mixed results. The unanimous agreement on hijacking grew out of an idea by Trudeau, worked through with support from the Japanese prime minister. At the Montebello summit, which he hosted in 1981, Trudeau tried unsuccessfully to make North–South issues the focal point of the meetings to swing support for new initiatives in that area. In 1987, at the Venice summit, Mulroney tried to ensure that the issue of apartheid would be included in the final communiqué—again without success. In the summit he hosted at Kananaskis in 2002, Chrétien sought to ensure that the issue of security and the struggle against terrorism did not capture all the attention of the summit and pushed for the adoption of a development plan for Africa, New Partnership for African Development (NEPAD).[10] At the 2006 St Petersburg summit, John Kirton noted that Stephen Harper pushed for greater energy security, focusing on Russia's surplus capacity in oil and gas.[11]

At the same time, summit participation imposes obligations that constrain freedom of action. As in all multilateral institutions, there is an expectation that each participant will cooperate to achieve commonly-agreed-upon goals. While the consensus reached at these summit meetings does not have the force of law, decisions taken have exerted considerable

---

8 Paul Simao, "Summit Pushes Louder Voice for Poor," *The Star*, Johannesburg, October 17, 2007.

9 Gordon Smith, "Time to Get With It, G8—Admit, Second Class' Guests," *Globe and Mail,* July 14, 2009, A13.

10 For a assessment of Canada's diplomacy at Kananaskis, see John Kirton, "Canada as a Principal Summit Power: G7/8 Concert Diplomacy from Halifax 1995 to Kananaskis 2002," in Norman Hillmer and Maureen Appel Molot, eds., *Canada Among Nations 2002: A Fading Power* (Toronto: Oxford University Press, 2002), 209–32. On Canada and NEPAD, see David Black, "Canada and Africa: Activist Aspirations in Straitened Circumstances," in Ian Taylor and Paul Williams, eds., *Africa in International Politics: External Involvement on the Continent* (London: Routledge, 2004), 236–54.

11 See John Kirton, *Canadian Foreign Policy in a Changing World* (Toronto: Thomson Nelson, 2007), 198.

influence on domestic policies. For example, much of the G7 summit in Bonn in 1978 was devoted to reductions in government expenditure as a means of affecting the global economy. Following his return from Bonn, Trudeau announced an immediate cut in federal government spending. Within a month, $3.7 billion in spending cuts, ranging across the spectrum of government programs, had been announced.[12] As one senior official noted, the "communiqués provided,mutual reinforcement' which helped leaders resist domestic pressures in their own countries."[13]

For thirty-three years, membership in the G7/G8 provided the Canadian government with a seat at what was called "the most exclusive multilateral forum in the world."[14] With the emergence of the G-20 as the central forum for global governance in 2010, the Canadian prime minister remains at the centre, but is now one of a much larger group of voices around that table.

The Commonwealth

The Commonwealth of Nations is a loose association of independent countries that were part of, or had links to, the British Empire. The Commonwealth Heads of Government Meetings (CHOGM, pronounced *CHOG-um*) are held biennially, with different members hosting the summit. Canada has hosted the CHOGM twice: in Ottawa in 1973 and in Vancouver in 1987.

The Commonwealth summit is the oldest international meeting to which the Canadian prime minister is invited. The meetings had their origins in the halcyon days of Empire, and have undergone a slow evolution in name and function that reflects the changing nature of the membership over the past century. The first Colonial Conference was called in 1887 to discuss Imperial defence, telegraphs, and postal services. This meeting was not exactly "diplomacy at the summit": it was presided over by the colonial secretary, not the British prime minister, and Canada was represented not by Sir John A. Macdonald, the prime minister, but by Sir Alexander Campbell, the lieutenant governor of Ontario, and Sanford Fleming, the surveyor of the Canadian Pacific Railway; nor was this a meeting of equals, for only Britain was sovereign and only Canada was a self-governing dominion.[15] Further Colonial Conferences were in 1894, 1897, 1902, and 1907. After 1907, the name was changed to Imperial Conference, to reflect the achievement of self-governing status by two more dominions, Australia in 1901 and New Zealand in 1907. It was also agreed that the British prime minister would chair the meetings rather than the colonial secretary.

It is ironic that the Imperial Conferences proved to be the vehicle for the eventual transformation of Empire. At the meetings held after the First World War, dominion prime ministers sought an opportunity to address both the constitutional and policy issues of their relations with Britain. They used the conferences to rebuff British pressures for coordination in matters of defence and to press for an end to formal authority over their foreign policies.

---

12 Robert D. Putnam and Nicholas Bayne, *Hanging Together: The Seven-Power Summits* (Cambridge, MA: Harvard University Press, 1984), 67–99.

13 Allan Gotlieb, then the undersecretary of state for external affairs, quoted in *International Canada* (April 1981), 87–88.

14 J.H. Taylor, "Preparing for the Halifax Summit: Reflections on Past Summits," *Canadian Foreign Policy* 3 (Spring 1995), 46.

15 C.P. Stacey, *Canada and the Age of Conflict: A History of Canadian External Policies*, vol. 1: *1867–1921* (Toronto: Macmillan, 1977), 44–46.

Indeed, it was at the 1926 meeting, as we saw in Chapter 5, that the prime ministers agreed to autonomy for the dominions in external policy, laying the foundation for the Statute of Westminster in 1931—and the subsequent emergence of the modern Commonwealth.[16]

The Imperial Conferences gave way in the 1940s to "Prime Ministers' Conferences," the first of which was held in 1944. By the time the prime ministers gathered in January 1951, two of the seven dominions that had attended the last Imperial Conference in 1937 were no longer participating: in 1949 Newfoundland had joined Canada and in the same year Ireland had declared itself a republic and left the Commonwealth. But the club had three new members: when the British colonial possessions in the Indian subcontinent gained independence in 1947 and 1948, three—India, Pakistan, and Ceylon (now called Sri Lanka)—joined the Commonwealth; only Burma (today called Myanmar by its government), where anti-British sentiment in the late 1940s was much more intense, chose not to pursue Commonwealth membership. India, Pakistan and Ceylon radically transformed the association of what were often called the "white dominions."[17] But the change was not only racial; it was also constitutional. Wanting to break with the British Raj symbolically as well as literally, India became a republic, with a president as the head of state, rather than the other dominions, which were all "united by a common allegiance to the Crown" (as the Statute of Westminster has it). However, the government in New Delhi wanted to retain its association with the Commonwealth. Under the so-called "London formula," negotiated in 1948 and 1949, it was agreed that India would be welcome to remain as a member of the Commonwealth on the understanding that although there was no formal tie to the British Crown, the sovereign would be recognized as the Head of the Commonwealth.[18]

This formula set the stage for the rapid growth of the Commonwealth during the waves of decolonization of the 1950s and 1960s.[19] By the time that the Prime Ministers' Meeting was held in London in January 1969, the membership had grown to twenty-nine, with members from six continents. However, by that time, not all members of the Commonwealth had a Westminster form of parliamentary government. A number had presidential systems of government, and some heads of government had been brought to power by military coups, and thus had distinctly unparliamentary forms of government. The leaders decided that not only would they begin to hold meetings in different member countries, but that they would rename their summit the Commonwealth Heads of Government Meeting. When the 2009 CHOGM met in Port of Spain, Trinidad and Tobago, the Commonwealth had fifty-three members.[20]

---

16 G.P. de T. Glazebrook, *A History of Canadian External Relations*, vol. 2: *In the Empire and the World, 1914–1939* (Toronto: McClelland & Stewart, 1966), chaps. 16 and 17.

17 On the evolution of the multiracial Commonwealth, see John W. Holmes, *The Shaping of Peace: Canada and the Search for World Order, 1943–1957*, vol. 2 (Toronto: University of Toronto Press, 1982), 167–72.

18 James Eayrs, *In Defence of Canada*, vol. 3: *Peacemaking and Deterrence* (Toronto: University of Toronto Press, 1972), 236–56.

19 James Eayrs, *Northern Approaches: Canada and the Search for Peace* (Toronto: Macmillan of Canada, 1961), 74–100; Margaret Doxey, "Canada and the Evolution of the Modern Commonwealth," *Behind the Headlines* 40 (November 1982).

20 One member, Fiji, was partially suspended in December 2006 after the coup d'état and then fully suspended on September 1, 2009, after the military government refused to commit to hold elections; Zimbabwe quit the Commonwealth in December 2003 after having been suspended for human rights violations in March 2002.

Canadian prime ministers from Borden to Harper have had occasion to use the informality of these meetings to engage in international negotiation without the constraints of Cabinet, Parliament, or the bureaucracy. This tendency was more pronounced before 1946, when the prime minister was, by statute, also the secretary of state for external affairs. For example, at the 1921 Imperial Conference, Arthur Meighen strongly opposed the renewal of the Anglo–Japanese alliance, which was favoured by Britain and the Pacific dominions but opposed by the United States. Meighen's opposition, which was being voiced without the knowledge of his cabinet, provoked a split in the empire and altered the Conference's position on the question of renewal.[21]

Meighen's case is not unusual. Prime ministers were prone to make policy simply by their active participation in the meetings. King's mediatory diplomacy at the 1926 Imperial Conference helped formalize the independence of Canada and the other self-governing dominions. At the 1932 Imperial Economic Conference in Ottawa, R.B. Bennett was so rude and aggressive toward the British delegation that it affected the course of Anglo–Canadian trade negotiations. At the 1937 Imperial Conference, King insisted that the final communiqué contained nothing that might smack of a commitment to collective security under the League of Nations.[22]

After the Second World War, Canadian policymakers increasingly began to regard the Commonwealth as a unique international institution that might be useful in maintaining international order.[23] Indeed it was at these meetings that prime ministerial initiatives helped to entrench Canada's reputation as a mediator in international affairs. For a succession of prime ministers played a part in preventing the cleavages inherent in the association from developing into irreparable ruptures. This was particularly true on the issue of white minority rule in southern Africa. Canadian prime ministers consistently sought to keep the association from breaking apart over the institutionalized racism in South Africa and Rhodesia (as Zimbabwe was known prior to 1979). At the 1961 meetings that led to South Africa's departure from the Commonwealth, John Diefenbaker proposed a compromise on the issue of South African membership that helped mitigate the split along racial lines that were developing between the African and Asian members on the one hand and Britain, Australia, and New Zealand on the other.[24] At the Prime Ministers' Meetings in the mid-1960s, Lester B. Pearson tried to find acceptable middle ground between Britain and the black African states on the question of Rhodesia following Ian Smith's Unilateral

21 Stacey, *Age of Conflict*, vol. 1, 340–48; James Eayrs, *In Defence of Canada*, vol. 1: *From the Great War to the Great Depression* (Toronto: University of Toronto Press, 1964), 18–20.

22 For accounts of these meetings, see C.P. Stacey, *Canada and the Age of Conflict: A History of Canadian External Policies*, vol. 2: *1921–1948: The Mackenzie King Era* (Toronto: University of Toronto Press, 1981), 142–44; James Eayrs, *In Defence of Canada*, vol. 2: *Appeasement and Rearmament* (Toronto: University of Toronto Press, 1965), 53–60.

23 Tom Keating, *Canada and World Order: The Multilateralist Tradition in Canadian Foreign Policy*, 2nd ed. (Toronto: Oxford University Press, 2002), 115–16.

24 Frank R. Hayes, "South Africa's Departure from the Commonwealth, 1960–61," *International History Review 2* (July 1980), 453–84; also see the perspective of Diefenbaker's liaison officer from *External Affairs: H. Basil Robinson, Diefenbaker's World: A Populist in Foreign Affairs* (Toronto: University of Toronto Press, 1989), 127, 174–89.

Declaration of Independence in 1965.[25] Although, as we have seen, Trudeau came to power openly skeptical of mediatory diplomacy, he found himself playing just such a role at the Commonwealth conference in Singapore in 1971 over the issue of British arms sales to South Africa.[26] Brian Mulroney carried forward this tradition in the 1980s when the issue of apartheid dominated the CHOGM agenda at Nassau in 1985 and Vancouver in 1987. Mulroney, among others, challenged the British prime minister, Margaret Thatcher, in her bid to keep the Commonwealth from endorsing strong economic sanctions against South Africa. Indeed, at the Vancouver meetings, Mulroney had a heated dispute with Thatcher that prompted British officials to try to discredit the Canadian position.[27] Eventually, however, apartheid was dismantled and Nelson Mandela was elected president of a new multiracial regime. South Africa was readmitted in 1994 and hosted the 1999 CHOGM in Durban.

The Commonwealth meetings do not always deal with issues that are central to Canada's international policy concerns. But, as David Black reminds us, "the Commonwealth offers a rare forum in which Canada is unambiguously important."[28] Partly for this reason, prime ministers have traditionally regarded this unusual association of nations as sufficiently important that they will structure their calendars around these biennial meetings, despite the amount of time they take—in Trudeau's time, eight working days was the norm[29]—and despite the jet lag involved in transoceanic travel. Indeed, only twice has a Canadian prime minister chosen not to attend a CHOGM: Kim Campbell decided that since she was in the middle of a federal election campaign, it would be prudent to miss the meetings in Limassol, Cyprus, in October 1993; Paul Martin chose not to attend the CHOGM in La Valette, Malta, in November 2005 because a first ministers' conference had also been scheduled for those dates.

The meetings are intended to provide a forum for talks between leaders on a variety of often contentious global topics. However, they are held in a retreat-like setting, and the stress is therefore on informality. Chrétien's reflections on his five CHOGMs reveal clearly his view of the utility of these meetings: "It is incredibly useful to have leaders meet face-to-face, without their officials or advisers. No audience or cameras to impress. We meet, not as big shots, lawyers, or professional diplomats. But as human beings, sharing common values, committed to finding common ground. We look each other in the eye. We speak unvarnished truths. We tell a joke or story to break the tension. Trust and purpose

---

25 Frank R. Hayes, "Canada, the Commonwealth and the Rhodesia Issue," in Kim Richard Nossal, ed., *An Acceptance of Paradox: Essays on Canadian Diplomacy in Honour of John W. Holmes* (Toronto: Canadian Institute of International Affairs, 1982), 141–73; Arthur E. Blanchette, ed., *Canadian Foreign Policy, 1955–1965* (Toronto: McClelland & Stewart, 1977), 302–308.

26 Clarence G. Redekop, "Trudeau at Singapore: The Commonwealth and Arms Sales to South Africa," in Nossal, ed., *Acceptance of Paradox,* 174–95; for Trudeau's accounts, see Ivan Head and Pierre Trudeau, *The Canadian Way: Shaping Canadian Foreign Policy, 1968–1984* (Toronto: McClelland & Stewart, 1995), 107–115.

27 Linda Freeman, *The Ambiguous Champion: Canada and South Africa in the Trudeau and Mulroney Years* (Toronto: University of Toronto Press, 1997), 207.

28 Quoted in Keating, *Canada and World Order,* 180.

29 Head and Trudeau, *The Canadian Way,* 97.

are forged."[30] But the meetings have not only been regarded by prime ministers as an effective way to get to know fifty other leaders from different parts of the world. Canadian prime ministers have also tended to recognize the importance of this unusual association for the maintenance of a broader international order. Because of the principles on which it is based, and because of the very diversity of its members, the Commonwealth continues to offer a forum that allows leaders to exchange views and to try to find grounds for agreement on delicate and thorny issues, particularly those issues involving North and South.[31]

La Francophonie

The French geographer Onésime Reclus first invented the term "francophonie" in 1880 to define those who used French in their interactions with other, but it would not be until 1986 that the first Sommet de la Francophonie would be held in Paris.[32] This meeting brought together the leaders of forty-one governments with a French connection in their present or past, including Vietnam and Egypt.

The idea of a summit for "La Francophonie" was not new: In the late 1950s, the idea of a summit of French-speaking countries had been considered. But the government in Paris, beginning with Charles de Gaulle and the presidents who succeeded him, did not see the utility in creating a French-speaking equivalent of the Commonwealth Heads of Government Meetings. Paris was content to maintain its relations with its former colonies bilaterally or regionally, so that "French power and influence could be employed with maximum effect."[33]

But if a summit of leaders was not possible, a number of leaders of former French colonies or protectorates from the colonial era—particularly Léopold Sédar Senghor of Senegal, Habib Bourguiba of Tunisia, and Hamani Diori of Niger—wanted an institutional forum for maintaining links with the metropole in cultural and linguistic affairs. The roots of La Francophonie thus lie in the conferences and institutions created in the 1960s that brought together ministers and other representatives of French-speaking countries. In 1960, a conference of ministers of education of French-speaking countries was established (Conférence des ministres de l'Éducation nationale). The following year, the Association des universités partiellement ou entièrement de langue française was created in Montréal. L'Association internationale des parlementaires de langue française followed in 1967, and a conference for minister of youth and sports, Conférence des ministres de la Jeunesse et des Sports, was established in 1969.[34]

---

30 Jean Chrétien, "Making Progress Through Multilateralism," *Commonwealth Lecture 2004,* London, March 30, 2004.

31 Louis A. Delvoie, "The Commonwealth in Canadian Foreign Policy," *The Round Table: The Commonwealth Journal of International Affairs* 78:310 (1989), 137–43.

32 Xavier Deniau, *La Francophonie* (Paris: Presses universitaires de France, 2001).

33 John Kirton, "Shaping the Global Order: Canada and the Francophone and Commonwealth Summits of 1987," *Behind the Headlines* 44 (June 1987), 4.

34 Stéphane Paquin, "La relation triangulaire Québec-Ottawa-Paris et l'avènement de l'Organisation internationale de la Francophonie (1965–2005)," *Guerres mondiales et conflits contemporains* 223 (2006), 157–181. However, these were not the first francophone initiatives: The Union internationale des journalistes et de la presse de langue française was formed in 1950.

While the establishment of these functional institutions created few political waves in Canada, the creation of the first intergovernmental organization of La Francophonie, l'Agence de coopération culturelle et technique (ACCT, Agency for Cultural and Technical Assistance) in March 1970 coincided with the changes produced by the Quiet Revolution in Québec.[35] While in the early 1960s the federal government had generally supported Québec's involvement in these functional institutions, its attitude started to change with the articulation of the Gérin-Lajoie doctrine of 1965, discussed in more detail in Chapter 12, which asserted that the government of Québec should become an international actor in areas of provincial jurisdiction.

The federal position hardened when Pierre Elliott Trudeau assumed the prime ministership in 1968. Trudeau believed that foreign policy should serve the national interest of all Canadians and particularly that it should serve the interests of national unity. Indeed, many African leaders grew exasperated by the difficulties posed by the Québec–Canada problem for the creation of the ACCT; the Senegalese minister for international cooperation went so far as to threaten to leave Canada out of the project: "Il n'est pas acceptable que ce soit un État fédératif à majorité anglophone qui nous empêche de créer une agence francophone. À la rigueur, nous nous passerons d'eux."[36] The victory of the Parti Québécois in the November 1976 provincial elections and the hardening in federal–provincial relations that followed made it even more difficult to establish a summit for La Francophonie.[37]

In June 1982, however, the newly elected president of France, François Mitterrand, expressed his interest in creating an international organization for La Francophonie, and put his foreign affairs adviser, Régis Debray, in charge of the file in January 1983. Debray met Trudeau in Ottawa and then Jacques-Yvan Morin, Québec's deputy prime minister, in Québec City. To address the difficulties posed by the Canadian and Québec positions, Debray suggested a compromise for a francophone summit. There would be two segments: The first would be a summit only for heads of governments of sovereign states; the second, focusing on more technical matters, would be for all heads of governments, including those of Canadian provinces. Debray believed that this solution would not only interest Québec and other Canadian provinces, but also Wallonia in Belgium. However, this proposal was unacceptable to the PQ government. Québec was already a participating government in the ACCT, sharing an equal status with the federal Canadian government. Debray's compromise would have diminished that status and instead would have put Québec at the same secondary level as the other Canadian provinces. So the project broke down as the PQ launched an intensive lobbying effort in Paris to be recognized as an equal participant in the summit.

---

35 René Durocher, "L'ouverture du Québec sur le monde extérieur, 1960–1966," in Robert Comeau, ed. *Jean Lesage et l'éveil d'une nation: les débuts de la Révolution tranquille* (Sillery: Presses de l'Université du Québec, 1989), 108ff; on the Quiet Revolution, see Paul-André Linteau, René Durocher, Jean-Claude Robert, and François Ricard, *Québec Since 1930*, trans. Robert Chodos and Ellen Garmaise (Toronto: James Lorimer, 1991).

36 "It is not acceptable that it should be a federation with an anglophone majority that is preventing us from creating a francophone organization. If necessary, we will do it without them." Louis Sabourin, "An Agency's Painful Birth," *International Perspectives* (January/February 1972), 25–30.

37 Louise Beaudoin, "Origines et développement du rôle international du gouvernement du Québec sur la scène internationale," in Paul Painchaud, ed., *Le Canada et le Québec sur la scène internationale* (Sainte-Foy: Presse de l'Université du Québec, 1977), 441–70; André Patry, *Le Québec dans le monde* (Montréal: Leméac, 1980); and Dale C. Thomson, *Vive le Québec libre* (Toronto: Denau, 1988).

After Brian Mulroney and the Progressive Conservatives won the September 1984 election, there was a significant change.[38] Mulroney wanted to break with the hard-line attitude of the federal Liberals. When Laurent Fabius, the French prime minister, visited Ottawa and Québec in November 1984, there were none of the problems that had marked the triangular France–Québec–Canada relationship in the past. On the contrary: In a marked departure, Mulroney declared in front of the French prime minister that he saw nothing wrong with Québec and France enjoying direct and privileged relations with each other.

Mulroney also resurrected with Fabius the idea of a francophone summit. Finding the French government receptive, he negotiated an agreement with Paris on Québec's participation, and, just days after René Lévesque resigned as leader of the Parti Québécois in October 1985, he signed an agreement with the new premier, Pierre-Marc Johnson, outlining the conditions under which the provincial government could participate in a summit. Under this agreement, Québec agreed to participate under the designation "Canada Québec" along with the government of New Brunswick, which would attend as "Canada Nouveau-Brunswick." Part of the Debray compromise was resurrected in this agreement: When global political and economic issues were under discussion, only the federal government could make interventions; on issues relating to development and cooperation, all of the delegations from Canada—the federal government, Canada Québec, and Canada Nouveau-Brunswick—could participate. It should be stressed, however, that over time this distinction between the parts of the summit became less obvious.

The first francophone summit of leaders was held at Versailles, outside Paris, in February 1986. For the first time, two provincial premiers—Robert Bourassa, whose Liberals had replaced the PQ in the Québec elections of November 1985, and Richard Hatfield of New Brunswick—attended an international summit as virtually equal participants with the federal head of government. Moreover, Bourassa's participation at Versailles made it possible for Québec to play a more important role than envisaged in the initial agreement. As Gil Rémillard, Bourassa's minister of international relations, noted, the Québec delegation positioned itself so that Québec would be the host of the next summit.[39]

After the Québec summit in 1987, the Conférence des Chefs d'État et de gouvernement des pays ayant le français en partage (Conference of Heads of State and Government of Countries Sharing French)[40] met every two years. With the increasing institutionalization of the summit, La Francophonie itself institutionalized. It acquired a secretary general (the first was Boutros Boutros-Ghali, the former secretary general of the United Nations), a secretariat, and a charter. The ACCT was replaced by the Agence intergouvernementale de la Francophonie (AIF) in 1995, and in 1998 a ministerial meeting in Bucharest decided to adopt the name Organisation internationale de la Francophonie (OIF). Its headquarters

---

38 Luc Bernier, "Mulroney's International, Beau Risque': The Golden Age of Québec's Foreign Policy," in Nelson Michaud and Kim Richard Nossal, eds., *Diplomatic Departures: The Conservative Era in Canadian Foreign Policy, 1984–1993* (Vancouver: UBC Press, 2001), 128–41.

39 Gil Rémillard, "La doctrine Gérin-Lajoie au coeur de l'évolution du federalism canadien," in Stéphane Paquin, ed., *Les relations internationales du Québec depuis la doctrine Gérin-Lajoie (1965–2005): le prolongement externe des compétences internes* (Sainte-Foy, QC: Presses Université Laval, 2006), 258–59.

40 Initially it was styled Conférence des chefs d'État ayant en commun l'usage de français ("having the use of French in common"); the present name emerged after the Paris summit in 1991.

is located in Paris and is supported by the Agence universitaire de la Francophonie (AUF), the television channel TV5, Université Senghor, and the Association internationale des maires francophones (AIMF). The OIF also counts on the support of a consultative group, the Assemblée parlementaire de la Francophonie (APF). It cooperates with numerous other international organizations, including the UN, the Commonwealth, the Arab League, and the African Union.

And the OIF has grown well beyond the forty-one leaders who gathered at Versailles in 1986: It now has fifty-three full members, three associate members, and fourteen observers. Besides Québec and New Brunswick, the only non-sovereign government represented is the Communauté française de Belgique. Together, these governments represent approximately a quarter of the members of the UN and a third of the members of the World Trade Organization. Two of the members of the OIF are G8 members, and one, France, has a veto in the UN Security Council.

Like the Commonwealth Heads of Government Meetings, the summits of La Francophonie afford Canadian prime ministers an opportunity to pursue foreign policy concerns in a multilateral setting. For example, Mulroney explicitly used these summits to press his interests in human rights and environmental protection, raising these issues at Dakar in 1989.[41] At Cotonou, Benin in December 1995, Chrétien tried to continue to reinforce the political nature of the summit, pressing the view that La Francophonie could have played a more decisive role during the genocide in Rwanda in 1994. But much of the attention was fixed on the transformation of the ACCT and human rights violations in Nigeria, particularly the execution of Ken Saro-Wiwa, which divided the summit between those governments, like France and Canada, that wanted La Francophonie to take a strong stand, and those West African states that were concerned about damaging their relations with Nigeria, a dominant actor in the politics of the region.[42]

Occasionally, such political discussions create friction among the three delegations from Canada. Technically, the two provincial premiers are supposed to limit their interventions only to matters that fall within provincial jurisdiction, and technically, the provincial delegations never have to vote on issues and expose differences that might exist with the federal position. But this does not mean that there will not be differences of view. At the Bucharest summit in 2006, for example, Egypt proposed a resolution on the war in Lebanon that expressed sympathy for the "tragedy" of Lebanese victims of Israeli bombing, and called for a "total suspension of hostilities." While a majority of the summit members, particularly France, supported Egypt, Stephen Harper, backed by Switzerland, strongly reacted against this resolution, because it did not recognize the existence of civilian victims on the Israeli side. Jean Charest, the Québec premier, whose position was closer to that of France, played an intermediary role by proposing a suspension of the debate when the tone got too heated. Jacques Chirac, the president of France, was furious. At a press conference, he revealed the dynamics of the meeting: "Honnêtement, il y avait une très très très grande majorité, qui y était favorable. Le Canada y était hostile."[43] Because of that opposition, he said, it was necessary to find a solution so that no one lost

---

41 *Globe and Mail,* May 25, 1989.

42 *Globe and Mail*, December 2 and 4, 1995.

43 "Honestly, there was a huge majority in favour of [the resolution]. Canada was opposed to it."

face. At the final press conference, Chirac's coldness toward Harper was obvious, while he joked with Charest, who had taken part in the discussion of the final compromise with the French foreign minister, Philippe Douste-Blazy.[44]

Although it started as an organization that dealt with essentially technical issues, the OIF has become more and more political, involving itself in issues such as human rights, peacekeeping, democratization, election monitoring, and culture and globalization. Thus, for example, La Francophonie played an important role in pressing the issue of cultural diversity.[45] At the fifth summit, held in Mauritius in 1993, the leaders adopted a resolution supporting the idea of a cultural exception in multilateral trade negotiations. Since the Beirut summit of 2002 the issue of cultural diversity has been prominent on the OIF agenda.

Presidents and Prime Ministers

Because the relationship with the United States is the most important element of Canada's international policy, the prime minister is responsible for maintaining close relations with the American president. Since the brief meeting between Mackenzie King and Calvin Coolidge in Washington in November 1927, prime ministers have sought to establish a personal relationship with their American counterpart. Indeed, it is notable that with just two exceptions,[46] every prime minister from R.B. Bennett to Stephen Harper has met the president within six months of taking office, and every American president from Franklin Delano Roosevelt to Barack Obama has met with the Canadian prime minister shortly after their inauguration.[47] The increased use of multilateral summit diplomacy has increased the number of bilateral meetings: For example, Bill Clinton met three Canadian prime ministers in the months after his inauguration in 1993, all at multilateral summits: Brian Mulroney in April at the Russian–American summit in Vancouver organized by the prime minister; Kim Campbell at the G7 summit in Tokyo in July; and Jean Chrétien at the Asia-Pacific Economic Cooperation (APEC) summit in Seattle in December.

Canadian–American summits have been held in a variety of contexts and settings: at multilateral summits or at purely ceremonial affairs, including state funerals (although substantive business is not usually conducted on such occasions). Often the emphasis is on informality. For example, Mulroney met George H.W. Bush in 1990 at the president's

---

44 Christian Rioux, "Sommet de la Francophonie: Harper provoque un coup de théâtre," *Le Devoir*, October 1, 2006.

45 In the context of contemporary international relations, cultural diversity is the desire to maintain a thriving local culture, often in the face of the homogenizing influences of contemporary globalization. In policy terms, cultural diversity asserts that it is right and proper for governments to be able to act to protect local language and culture, and sees efforts of multilateral trade agreements to dismantle such protections as wrong. See Keith Acheson and Christopher Maule, "Convention on Cultural Diversity," *Journal of Cultural Economics* 28:4 (November 2004), 243–56; for the position of the Québec government, see http://www.mri.gouv.qc.ca/en/grands_dossiers/diversite_culturelle/index.asp.

46 Pierre Trudeau did not meet Lyndon Johnson when their terms of office overlapped in 1968. In the summer of 1984, Ronald Reagan invited John Turner to participate in the 25th anniversary celebration of the St. Lawrence Seaway, but Turner turned the invitation down.

47 Swanson, *Canadian–American Summit Diplomacy*, table 9, 22 for the meetings down to 1973.

summer cottage at Kennebunkport in Maine. As Bush recalled it, "He and Mila brought the kids, and there was no formality. There were no Marines or Mounties around. We had a good, easy time. And we could argue and talk frankly."[48]

Sometimes summit diplomacy has been conducted over a game of golf. Louis St. Laurent played with Dwight D. Eisenhower in the 1950s, and Jean Chrétien played numerous rounds of golf with Bill Clinton during their time in office in the 1990s, including making time during the Halifax G8 summit in 1995 and the APEC summit in Vancouver in 1997.[49] St. Laurent noted, tongue in cheek, that

> a game of golf was about the best way to have an international conference because you are getting off the go-cart quite frequently for only a couple of minutes but for time enough to reflect on what has been said and to reflect on what is going to be said when you get back on[50]

By contrast, Paul Martin was to discover that riding around with the president in a vehicle was not necessarily the best forum for conducting negotiations. In March 2005, Bush invited Martin and Vicente Fox, the president of Mexico, to his ranch at Crawford, Texas, and the president took the other leaders for a tour of the ranch in his pickup truck, with their aides following in a Secret Service vehicle. Without their advisers present, Martin thought it would be an appropriate time to press Bush on an American plan to conduct oil drilling in an Arctic wildlife refuge that bordered Yukon: "in the informal atmosphere of the truck ride, I was a little blunter and less diplomatic than usual. And Bush's response was equally blunt and unyielding." What Martin did not know was that the entire conversation was not private at all, but had been relayed to the Secret Service vehicle, where the leaders' aides were listening to the undiplomatic exchange.[51]

Until 1985, there was no planned predictability to these bilateral summits; they simply occurred, when either the need or the opportunity arose. When Mulroney became prime minister, however, he sought to regularize them. His first summit with Reagan in Canada was held in Québec City on March 18, 1985, and immediately dubbed the "Shamrock Summit," not only because it was held on St. Patrick's Day but also because both Reagan and Mulroney had made a great deal of their common Irish background. At a gala held on the evening of March 18, the president and prime minister treated the audience to a rendition of "When Irish Eyes are Smiling." For the remainder of the Mulroney years, the presidential summit became an annual affair, usually held in March or April.

When Chrétien came to power, however, bilateral summits with the president were no longer held on a regular basis. It was ironic in view of the very friendly relationship that he had developed with Bill Clinton over the 1990s that Chrétien came to power in 1993 promising he would not seek the same kind of "chummy" relations with the American president that Mulroney had enjoyed with Ronald Reagan and George H.W. Bush. He had no desire to go fishing with the American president, he liked to tell audiences on the

48 Quoted in Lawrence Martin, *Pledge of Allegiance: The Americanization of Canada in the Mulroney Years* (Toronto: McClelland & Stewart, 1993), 218.

49 Jean Chrétien, "Tales from the Nineteenth Hole," *My Years as Prime Minister* (Toronto: Alfred A. Knopf Canada, 2007), 192–98.

50 Quoted in Swanson, *Canadian–American Summit Diplomacy*, 161.

51 Paul Martin, *Hell or High Water: My Life in and out of Politics* (Toronto: McClelland & Stewart, 2008), 372–73.

campaign trail in 1993, "because I don't want to be the fish."[52] As a matter of policy, Chrétien sought to distance himself from such open displays of affection.[53] Thus, it was not until February 1995 that Clinton paid an official visit to Canada, addressed the House of Commons, and had his first bilateral summit with Chrétien. And although the two leaders developed a good personal relationship, Chrétien and Clinton kept their bilateral summitry purposely ad hoc. This continued after Clinton left office in 2001. During the Bush administration from 2001 to 2009, Chrétien, Martin and Harper met frequently with the American president, but there was no return to the practice of holding regular bilateral summits.

However, in 2005 a new regular annual summit was added to the prime ministerial agenda. In March 2005, Bush, Martin, and Fox met in Waco, Texas, and formalized a new trilateral agreement, the Security and Prosperity Partnership (SPP), discussed in Chapter 5. This first meeting was dubbed the "Three Amigos" summit, but it quickly became institutionalized: Bush, Fox, and the newly elected Stephen Harper gathered for a North American Leaders' Summit in Cancún in March 2006; Bush, Harper, and the newly elected Felipe Calderón Hinojosa met in Montebello in August 2007 and in New Orleans in April 2008, and Harper, Calderón, and the newly elected Barack Obama met in Mexico in August 2009.

These summits have a variety of purposes. First, they can be primarily ceremonial. The signing of an international agreement, the opening of a park, or the dedication of a bridge all provide an opportunity to engage in the rhetoric of neighbourhood. Most Canadians and some Americans are only too familiar with the repertoire of transborder clichés. After more a hundred summit meetings since 1927, speech-writers are hard pressed to come up with fresh ways of saying the same thing about the friendship between the two countries. But such rhetoric, while cloying, is a necessary part of Canadian–American relations. It provides an opportunity for public assurances by those at the summit that the world's most complex international relationship continues to function smoothly. Likewise, what John Holmes has called "the blandishments of hands-across-the-border oratory"[54] also provides assurances to Canadians that the United States remains disinclined to treat its northern neighbour as great powers have traditionally dealt with small states on their borders.[55]

Second, summit meetings can also be the setting for major policy decisions. For example, before the Second World War there were no formal defence cooperation linkages between Canada and the United States. Until then, Canada's only security guarantee came from Britain. But in the summer of 1940, Britain seemed on the verge of being invaded by Nazi Germany. King decided to turn to the United States. He and Roosevelt enjoyed a close

52 Chrétien, *My Years as Prime Minister,* 87.

53 See, for example, James Bartleman, *Rollercoaster: My Hectic Years as Jean Chrétien's Diplomatic Adviser, 1994–1998* (Toronto: McClelland & Stewart, 2005), 137.

54 John W. Holmes, *Life with Uncle: The Canadian–American Relationship* (Toronto: University of Toronto Press, 1981), 4.

55 Stéphane Roussel, *The North American Democratic Peace: Absence of War and Security Institution-Building in Canada–US Relations, 1867–1958* (Montréal and Kingston: McGill-Queen's University Press, 2004).

and friendly relationship and they met in the little town of Ogdensburg in upstate New York on August 17 and 18. Without any ceremony, they created the Permanent Joint Board on Defence (PJBD), a senior-level committee of Canadian and American military and diplomatic officials who advise both governments on continental defence. This very informal meeting marked a turning point in Canadian defence policy, signalling that Canada was counting on the United States rather than Britain for its security.[56] This was followed shortly by another summit that consolidated Canada's continental defence orientation. In 1940–41, Canada was experiencing a mounting balance-of-payments problem with the United States. King took up the matter with Roosevelt at a meeting at the president's Hyde Park estate in April 1941. After a brief chat, they issued the Hyde Park Declaration. Under this agreement, the United States agreed to purchase $200 to $300 million in defence equipment from Canada to relieve the deficit.[57] In the long term, this decision was to lead to the integration of the Canadian defence industry with that of the United States. Both the Ogdensburg Agreement and the Hyde Park Declaration demonstrate the capacity of the prime minister to take the country in a very new policy direction by a simple informal meeting with the American president.

Third, summits are also useful for clearing problems in the relationship that have proved resistant to resolution at lower levels. The best example of a prime minister using a summit meeting with a president to solve a contentious issue was Mulroney's meeting with Reagan in March 1987. Canada and the United States were quarrelling over Canada's long-standing claim to sovereignty over the Northwest Passage in the Arctic, a claim that had been reiterated after the voyage of the United States Coast Guard (USCG) icebreaker, *Polar Sea*, through the Passage in the summer of 1985. Canada's claim was that it had sovereignty over Arctic waters that lay within Canadian territorial limits; for its part, the United States claimed that some of those waters constituted an international strait—the Northwest Passage—and thus under international law were not fully subject to national sovereignty. Washington's opposition was fuelled in part by fear of setting a precedent. If the United States agreed to exempt Canada in the Arctic, other countries would use the exemption as a precedent to press for control over international straits that fell within their territorial waters. As a consequence, there was strong opposition within the American government to any kind of concession to Canada, particularly from the Department of State, the Joint Chiefs of Staff, the Pentagon, the U.S. Navy and the USCG. The negotiations between the two sides quickly became deadlocked.[58]

---

56 J.L. Granatstein, "Mackenzie King and Canada at Ogdensburg, August 1940," in Joel J. Sokolsky and Joseph T. Jockel, eds., *Fifty Years of Canada–United States Defense Cooperation* (Lewiston, NY: Edwin Mellen Press, 1993).

57 J.W. Pickersgill, ed., *The Mackenzie King Record*, vol. 1: *1939–1944* (Toronto: University of Toronto Press, 1960), 202. On the Hyde Park declaration: C.P. Stacey, *Arms, Men and Governments: The War Policies of Canada, 1939–1945* (Ottawa: Information Canada, 1970), 489; R.D. Cuff and J.L. Granatstein, "The Hyde Park Declaration, 1941: Origins and Significance," in Cuff and Granatstein, *Canadian–American Relations in Wartime* (Toronto: Hakkert, 1975); text of the declaration reprinted in Swanson, *Canadian–American Summit Diplomacy*, 78–79.

58 Franklyn Griffiths, ed., *Politics of the Northwest Passage* (Montréal and Kingston: McGill-Queen's University Press, 1987); Andrea Charron, "The Northwest Passage: Is Canada's Sovereignty Floating Away?" *International Journal* 60:3 (Summer 2005), 831–48.

In April 1987, Reagan visited Ottawa for the Shamrock III summit. At a meeting in the prime minister's office, Mulroney showed Reagan a globe and explained the Canadian position on the Arctic. Reagan was surprised to learn that many of the Arctic islands were permanently connected by ice—a key element in the Canadian claim: "That looks a little different than the maps they showed me on the plane coming into Ottawa," he admitted. On his way into lunch at 24 Sussex, Reagan took Frank Carlucci, his national security adviser, aside and told him that "I think we ought to do something for Brian" on the issues on the agenda—the Northwest Passage, acid rain, and free trade. Carlucci demurred, saying that the American positions on these issues were well established. After lunch, the American delegation had a private meeting in the sitting room to discuss their positions. Again it was proposed that something should be done to accommodate Mulroney, and again Carlucci argued against changing the American position. He recalled: "It was the only time I saw Ronald Reagan lose his temper. He turned and said,,You do it.'"[59] With this presidential directive, the deadlock was broken. While still nervous about precedents, the United States side eventually signed an agreement under which transit through the Northwest Passage by USCG icebreakers would only be undertaken with the consent of the Canadian government, a key concession formalized by the Arctic Cooperation Agreement of January 11, 1988. The role of Mulroney's personal diplomacy was, by all accounts, critical in obtaining what Canada's ambassador to the United States at the time, Allan Gotlieb, termed "an important concession."[60]

While summit meetings have often been used for this purpose,[61] there is, as Roger Frank Swanson suggests, a downside to using summits this way. If negotiations are carried to the summit and an impasse is reached, "there is no higher political authority to invoke."[62] In these cases, both sides have to wait for a change in leadership on either side of the border or for a change in policy circumstances before trying again. This is one of

---

59 Ronald Reagan Oral History Project, Interview with Frank Carlucci, 28 August 2001, 45–46, available http://web1.millercenter.org/poh/transcripts/ohp_2001_0828_carlucci.pdf; an account of the meeting was subsequently published by the project's research director, Jeffrey L. Chidester: "Friendship Has Its Benefits," *Toronto Star*, February 2, 2006. See also Christopher Kirkey, "Smoothing Troubled Waters: The 1988 Canada–United States Arctic Cooperation Agreement," *International Journal* 50 (Spring 1995), 412–13; and Brian Mulroney, *Memoirs* (Toronto: McClelland & Stewart, 2007), 494–500.

60 Allan Gotlieb, *"I'll Be with You in a Minute, Mr. Ambassador"*: The Education of a Canadian Diplomat in Washington (Toronto: University of Toronto Press, 1991), 114. Colin Powell, Reagan's national security adviser, later claimed that that he was always afraid when either Margaret Thatcher or Brian Mulroney called Reagan, because "they could get the president to do anything they wanted." Quoted in Mulroney, *Memoirs*, 500.

61 For example, at his meeting with Jimmy Carter in February 1977, Trudeau discussed the Garrison Diversion Unit, an irrigation and flood control scheme in North Dakota that threatened to pollute the Red River flowing into Manitoba, convincing Carter to put the scheme on his "hit list" of water projects to be cancelled. Kim Richard Nossal, "The Unmaking of Garrison: United States Politics and the Management of Canadian–American Boundary Waters," *Behind the Headlines* 37 (November 1978). Likewise, in a number of meetings in 1999, Chrétien and Clinton intervened personally to advance discussions on a number of dossiers that were bedeviling the relationship, including the Helms-Burton law, Pacific salmon fishery, softwood lumber, and the *Sports Illustrated* issue. For details, see Stéphane Roussel, "Canada–US Relations: Time for Cassandra?" *American Review of Canadian Studies* 30:2 (Summer 2000), 135–57.

62 Swanson, *Canadian–American Summit Diplomacy,* 14.

the reasons why some bilateral issues in the Canadian–American relationship can linger for years (as in the case of acid rain[63]) or even decades (as in the case of softwood lumber[64] or the Beaufort Sea boundary dispute[65]).

As in all summit diplomacy, how the president and prime minister get on with each other matters. Some leaders enjoy a good personal relationship: King and Roosevelt developed a friendship over their long years in office; Mulroney got on well with Reagan, but he developed a particularly close and personal friendship with Reagan's successor, George H.W. Bush. Sometimes a friendship develops unexpectedly. Given that Chrétien came to power promising not to develop the same kind of friendship that had marked Mulroney's time in power, it is ironic that he and Clinton should have become such good friends. As Clinton noted in his memoirs, "Chrétien would become one of my best friends among world leaders, a strong ally, confidant, and frequent golfing partner."[66] The two leaders often spoke by phone, and, just as Reagan was inclined to do Mulroney a favour, as we saw above, so too was Clinton. During the 1995 referendum debate, Clinton offered to use his authority as president to speak on the issue, as we will see in Chapter 12. In 1999, Clinton again accepted Chrétien's request to speak at an international conference on federalism at Mont Tremblant, delivering a speech that implicitly criticized the souverainiste project in Québec.[67]

But some prime ministers and presidents have not enjoyed a good relationship. For example, John G. Diefenbaker and John F. Kennedy did not get on.[68] According to his biographer,

---

63 Don Munton and Geoffrey Castle, "Reducing Acid Rain, 1980s," in Munton and John Kirton, eds., *Canadian Foreign Policy: Selected Cases* (Scarborough: Prentice-Hall Canada, 1992), 367–81.

64 Steven Kendall Holloway, *Canadian Foreign Policy: Defining the National Interest* (Toronto: Broadview Press, 2006), 212–15; Daowei Zhang, *The Softwood Lumber War: Politics, Economics, and the Long U.S.–Canadian Trade Dispute* (Washington: RFF Press, 2007).

65 In international law, the maritime boundary between countries is normally a line drawn at a 90-degree angle to the line of the coast, extending 200 nautical miles (about 370 kilometres) out into the ocean. However, the 1825 convention between Russia and Britain that established the boundary between Alaska and British North American territories agreed that the boundary line in the south would run along the summit of the mountain chain that ran along the coast until the 141st meridian, and then would run north along the 141st meridian (in the words of the original treaty, which was written in French, the language of diplomacy in the early 1800s), "dans son [sic] prolongation jusqu'à la Mer Glaciale [i.e., Beaufort Sea]." Canada claims that the "jusqu'à" meant that the *maritime* boundary should extend along the 141st meridian out into the ocean rather than just to the coast. In 1977, the United States claimed that the "jusqu'à" meant just to the coast, and that the maritime boundary should be drawn in the usual manner in international law; that is, at a 90-degree angle to the coast (which runs in a southeasterly direction at that point). These different interpretations create a wedge-shaped area of disputed ocean that has never been resolved even though oil and gas drilling rights on the continental shelf are affected by the rival claims. David H. Gray, "Canada's Unresolved Maritime Boundaries," *IBRU Boundary and Security Bulletin* (Durham, UK: International Boundaries Research Unit, Durham University, August 1997), 63–65.

66 Bill Clinton, *My Life*, vol. 2: *The Presidential Years* (Toronto: Random House Canada, 2005), 238.

67 Chrétien, *My Years as Prime Minister*, 195–96; Graham Fraser, "Liberal Continuities: Jean Chrétien's Foreign Policy, 1993–2003," in David Carment, Fen Osler Hampson and Norman Hillmer, eds., *Canada Among Nations 2004: Setting Priorities Straight* (Montréal and Kingston: McGill-Queen's University Press, 2005), 175.

68 For a good overview, see John Herd Thompson and Stephen J. Randall, *Canada and the United States: Ambivalent Allies* (Montréal and Kingston: McGill-Queen's University Press, 1994), 214–28.

Kennedy thought Diefenbaker "insincere and did not like or trust him."[69] For his part, Diefenbaker thought that Kennedy was brash and arrogant, particularly after an American briefing note was discovered in a wastepaper basket in the prime minister's office. Entitled "What we want from the Ottawa trip," the memo urged the president to "push" the Diefenbaker on a number of foreign policy issues. Diefenbaker's External Affairs liaison at the time, Basil Robinson, recalls that the prime minister believed that the memo "personified the attitude of the Americans: they thought nothing of pushing Canada around."[70]

Moreover, Diefenbaker developed a penchant for distinctly anti-American and undiplomatic behaviour. During the election campaign in the spring of 1962, Pearson, then the leader of the Liberal opposition, was invited to a White House ceremony for Nobel Prize winners and was photographed with Kennedy. Believing the president was deliberately trying to bring down his government by giving Pearson publicity, Diefenbaker dressed down the United States ambassador to Ottawa for an hour and a half and threatened to make public the American memo (for instead of following standard diplomatic practice of copying such a document and returning it to the United States embassy, the prime minister had kept the original).

The Kennedy administration was willing to be equally undiplomatic. When Diefenbaker announced publicly to the House of Commons his own interpretation of secret negotiations between Canada and the United States on the nuclear weapons question, the State Department in Washington issued a public press release challenging the prime minister's interpretation. Even Charles Ritchie, the Canadian ambassador in Washington, and no great fan of Diefenbaker, thought the "heavy-handed and overbearing action of the State Department . . . intolerable."[71]

The poor personal relationship between president and prime minister was reflected in sharp divisions over such critical policy issues as nuclear weapons, policy toward Cuba after Fidel Castro seized power, and the Cuban missile crisis.[72] Moreover, the poor personal relationship was felt at the official level, as Ritchie discovered: "[Kennedy's] reception of me, while perfectly civil, was, I thought, distinctly cool, and I came away with the impression that this reflected his attitude towards the Canadian government and particularly towards Mr Diefenbaker."[73]

By contrast, Lester B. Pearson, who came to power in 1963 promising to improve relations with the United States, enjoyed good relations with Kennedy and, initially at least, with Lyndon B. Johnson, who assumed the presidency in November 1963 after Kennedy was assassinated. But Pearson demonstrated how fragile the interpersonal relationship between president and prime minister can be when he decided to speak out on American policy toward Vietnam.[74] The Johnson administration had begun bombing North Vietnam

69 Quoted in Peyton Lyon, *Canada in World Affairs*, vol. 12: *1961–1963* (Toronto: Oxford University Press, 1968), 493.

70 Robinson, *Diefenbaker's World*, 206; also Lyon, *Canada in World Affairs*, 496–502.

71 Charles Ritchie, *Storm Signals: More Undiplomatic Diaries, 1962–1971* (Toronto: Macmillan, 1983), 32.

72 Jocelyn Ghent Mallet and Don Munton, "Confronting Kennedy and the Missiles in Cuba, 1962," in Munton and Kirton, eds., *Canadian Foreign Policy*, 78–100.

73 Ritchie, *Storm Signals*, 6; also 23–24.

74 Greg Donaghy, *Tolerant Allies: Canada and the United States, 1963–1968* (Montréal and Kingston: McGill-Queen's University Press, 2002), 128–31; John English, "Speaking Out on Vietnam, 1965," in Munton and Kirton, eds., *Canadian Foreign Policy*, 135–52.

in response to North Vietnamese incursions in the South, and Pearson had told close friends that not only did he think the air strikes "obscene," he also felt compelled to make an effort to alter Johnson's policies. The opportunity came when he was given a peace award by Temple University in Philadelphia on April 2, 1965: In his acceptance speech, Pearson suggested that the United States should halt the bombing and negotiate with North Vietnam. Johnson was, to put it mildly, furious. At a meeting with Pearson at Camp David the day after the speech, Johnson lost his temper.[75] He criticized the prime minister, loudly and loutishly, for having ignored a key diplomatic norm that demands that government leaders do not go criticizing the policies of other governments while on their soil—or, as Johnson put it, "pissing on my rug."[76] From then until 1968, when both leaders retired, there would no longer be a personal relationship between them. Moreover, according to one of Johnson's aides, William Bundy, Johnson's anger over the speech "seriously impair[ed] the relationship" as a whole.[77]

But the Temple University speech reveals another lesson about personal chemistry and the relationship as a whole. While the speech may have wrecked the personal relationship between the president and the prime minister, it had no impact on the Auto Pact, which was considered by Congress in 1965. As Dimitry Anastakis reminds us, "for all of the not inconsiderable fallout from that incident, Johnson never once wavered in his determination to see the auto pact passed by the U.S. Congress."[78] Indeed, Johnson devoted considerable presidential capital on arm-twisting on Capitol Hill for a trade agreement that, while beneficial for American auto makers, was overall far more beneficial for Canada. The juxtaposition of the furious anger over the Temple University speech and the presidential campaign for the Auto Pact illustrates the degree to which the personal relationship does not necessarily have negative impacts on all aspects of the relationship.

Conflict over the Vietnam War also eventually damaged the relationship between Pierre Trudeau and Richard Nixon. In January 1973 the Canadian House of Commons approved a resolution "deploring" the bombing of Hanoi and Haiphong that had been authorized by Nixon to force the North Vietnamese back to the negotiating table. Nixon's decision had been greeted by widespread criticism in Canada. For his part, Trudeau suggested to

---

75 See Lawrence Martin's graphic account in *The Presidents and the Prime Ministers: Washington and Ottawa Face to Face: The Myth of Bilateral Bliss, 1867–1982* (Toronto: Doubleday, 1982), 2, which claims that Johnson took Pearson out on a patio after lunch and "grabbed him by the shirt collar, twisted it and lifted the shaken prime minister by the neck." It makes a great story, but the laws of physics suggest that Martin dreamed this version of events up: Even assuming LBJ was strong enough to lift a heavyset man like Pearson, there is no way that someone of Pearson's weight could be lifted up by the flimsy fabric of a twisted shirt collar—at least not without suffering a severe and perhaps fatal injury. Charles Ritchie, the Canadian ambassador, who was watching the two leaders on the patio through a window, offers a less fanciful account in *Storm Signals*, 80–83.

76 This, at least, is what the folklore of Canadian foreign policy claims that Johnson said, though no one can agree on precisely how it was phrased: for differing versions, see Norman Hillmer and J.L. Granatstein, *For Better or for Worse: Canada and the United States to the 1990s* (Toronto: Copp Clark Pitman, 1991), 231; Herd and Thompson, *Ambivalent Allies*, 234; Stephen Clarkson, *Uncle Sam and Us: Globalization, Neoconservatism, and the Canadian State* (Toronto: University of Toronto Press, 2002), 383; and Donaghy, *Tolerant Allies*, 130.

77 Cited in English, "Speaking Out on Vietnam," 146.

78 Dimitry Anastakis, *Auto Pact: Creating a Borderless North American Auto Industry, 1960–1971* (Toronto: University of Toronto Press, 2005), 14.

reporters that "the bombing was the wrong way to bring the war to an end." The New Democratic Party (NDP), which held the balance of power in the twenty-ninth Parliament that had been elected in October 1972, indicated that when Parliament opened in January 1973 they would introduce a resolution "condemning" the United States—even though by that time Nixon had called off the attacks. Trudeau wanted to avoid a parliamentary quarrel over this issue, so the Liberal government introduced its own motion that contained the diplomatically softer word "deploring," which could command NDP support. The parliamentary resolution requested "all parties" to "refrain from acts of a warlike nature," and specifically asked the United States not to resume bombing Hanoi and Haiphong.[79]

Nixon was exceedingly angry at Trudeau, interpreting the resolution as an unfriendly and hostile gesture. For its pains, Canada was added to what was known as the Nixon administration's "shit list"[80] of countries not entirely friendly to the United States, such as Sweden. Such an honour had implications for the wider relationship, however. Unlike Johnson, Nixon was disinclined to do anything that would have been beneficial for Canada in his remaining nineteen months in power. The Canadian ambassador, Marcel Cadieux, was given the cold shoulder by administration officials; American bureaucrats had to meet their Canadian counterparts informally rather than at their offices. In short, all other areas of the relationship were infected by the president's anger.

Relations between George W. Bush and the three Canadian prime ministers who held office between 2001 and 2009 provide a further illustration of how the chemistry between the prime minister and the president can affect the overall relationship. Even before the presidential election of 2000 that brought Bush to power, several small incidents soured the relationship with Jean Chrétien before it began. During the campaign, Rick Mercer, a comedian from the satirical show *This Hour Has 22 Minutes*, played a joke on Bush. Posing as a journalist in a crowded scrum at a campaign rally in Michigan, Mercer told Bush that the Canadian prime minister, "Jean Poutine," had endorsed him. Bush, who had been criticized for not knowing the names of some foreign leaders, responded: "I appreciate his strong statement" and said that he was looking forward to being able to "work closely together."[81] More serious were comments attributed to Raymond Chrétien, a nephew of the prime minister who had been an associate undersecretary of state for external affairs from 1988 to 1991 and had been appointed as ambassador to Belgium by Brian Mulroney in 1991 before being appointed by his uncle as Canada's ambassador to the United States in 1994. In a candid talk to senior Canadian government officials in Ottawa in June 2000, Raymond Chrétien spoke about the two candidates then vying for the presidency: "We know Vice President [Al] Gore, he knows us; he's a friend of Canada. . . .

---

79 Douglas A. Ross, *In The Interests of Peace: Canada and Vietnam, 1954–73* (Toronto: University of Toronto Press, 1984), 342–43; also Dobell, *Canada in World Affairs*, 401–403.

80 J.L. Granatstein and Robert Bothwell, *Pirouette: Pierre Trudeau and Canadian Foreign Policy* (Toronto: University of Toronto Press, 1990), 54.

81 Audio available at http://www.democracynow.org/2000/3/7/g_w_bush_endorsed_by_imaginary. Bush self-deprecatingly acknowledged his blooper during his 2004 visit to Canada. In a speech in Halifax, he claimed that he had one regret about his visit to Canada: "There's a prominent citizen who endorsed me in the 2000 election, and I wanted a chance to finally thank him for that endorsement. I was hoping to meet Jean Poutine." See "Remarks by President Bush at Pier 21," Halifax, December 1, 2004, available   http://ottawa.usembassy.gov/content/content.asp?section=can_usa&document=bush_visit2004_pier21.

Governor Bush, on the other hand, doesn't know us as much. . . . When he thinks of borders, he thinks of Mexico, not of Canada."[82] While it might have been a factual statement, as Jean Chrétien asserts in his nephew's defence in his memoirs,[83] there is little doubt that it was interpreted by some as a preference for Gore over Bush.

Things did not get better after the inauguration, in particular when Bush made his first official visit to Mexico rather than to Canada, breaking with tradition. Awkwardness, if not impoliteness, increasingly marked the relationship. What many saw as Chrétien's cold and uncaring reaction following the attacks of September 11, 2001;[84] Bush's failure to include any mention of Canada in his speech to Congress after 9/11;[85] the president's apparent indifference to the "friendly fire" deaths of Canadian soldiers in Afghanistan killed by an attack by American F-16 jet fighters in April 2002;[86] Chrétien's speech on the anniversary of 9/11, which might be read as blaming the United States for those attacks;[87] the relative indifference of the prime minister when one of his senior advisers described Bush as a "moron" in November 2002.[88] The most serious crisis occurred in March 2003, when the prime minister, without following diplomatic protocol and informing Bush in advance, announced to the House of Commons that Canada would not be joining the international coalition organized by the United States to invade Iraq. The sight of the cheering Liberal MPs around Chrétien rising in a standing ovation received significant play on American networks and prompted Bush to cancel a planned visit to Canada in May 2003.[89]

---

82 *New York Times*, June 2, 2000.

83 Chrétien, *My Years as Prime Minister*, 288–89.

84 Eddie Goldenberg, Chrétien's senior policy adviser, suggests that after 9/11 Chrétien appeared to be uncaring because he "was always uncomfortable with public displays of emotion," and did not want to be seen as trying to score political points by visiting Ground Zero as many world leaders were doing. Eddie Goldenberg, *The Way It Works: Inside Ottawa* (Toronto: McClelland & Stewart, 2006), 263. See also Chrétien, *My Years as Prime Minister*, 292–97.

85 George W. Bush, "Address to a Joint Session of Congress and the American People," Washington, September 20, 2001; available http://georgewbush-whitehouse.archives.gov/news/releases/2001/09/20010920–8.html. Andrew Cohen, "Canadian–American Relations: Does Canada Matter in Washington? Does It Matter If Canada Doesn't Matter?" in Hillmer and Molot, eds., *Canada Among Nations 2002*, 34–48.

86 On April 17, 2002, four soldiers of the 3rd Battalion, Princess Patricia's Canadian Light Infantry (3 PPCLI), were killed by a bomb dropped on a group of Canadian troops by an American F-16 fighter at Tarnak Farm near Kandahar City. The pilot had ignored an order to "hold fire," for which he was eventually disciplined: Michael Friscolanti, *Friendly Fire: The Untold Story of the US Bombing That Killed Four Canadian Soldiers in Afghanistan* (Mississauga: John Wiley & Sons, 2005).

87 Shawn McCarthy, "PM Says U.S. Attitude Helped Fuel Sept. 11," *Globe and Mail*, September 12, 2002; http://www.ctv.ca/special/sept11/hubs/canadian/mccarthy01.html.

88 Chrétien's director of communications, Françoise Ducros, was watching Bush make a speech at a NATO summit in Prague on November 20, 2002. In front of reporters, Ducros said of Bush: "What a moron." The prime minister did not condemn the comment, instead saying that Bush "is not a moron at all." Only after American networks began relentlessly playing the story was Ducros finally forced to resign. "Canadian Official Called Bush, A Moron,'" *CBC News*, November 26, 2002; available http://www.cbc.ca/stories/2002/11/21/moron021121.

89 Stéphane Roussel, "'Honey, Are You Still Mad at Me? I've Changed You Know. . . .' Canada–US Relations in a Post-Saddam/Post-Chrétien Era," *International Journal* 63:4 (Autumn 2003), 575.

As relations between the two leaders deteriorated, other facets of the relationship were also marked by conflict. Trade disputes multiplied, including quarrels over wheat and then beef after the discovery of a case of mad cow disease; the reactivation of the never-ending softwood lumber dispute; and deregulation of energy distribution in the United States. Security issues, which after 9/11 consumed the Bush administration, also contributed to souring Canadian–American relations. At the multilateral level, the almost systematic refusal of the Bush administration to support the key multilateral treaties concluded during the 1990s—the Kyoto accords on greenhouse gas emissions, the International Criminal Court, the global ban on antipersonnel land mines—also created a further irritant in the relationship.

As we saw in the previous chapter, Paul Martin came to power in 2003 determined to improve Canada–US relations; there was, however, only a temporary improvement. The trade disputes still lingered; the Martin government found itself caught in the fallout from the Maher Arar rendition;[90] and, as we saw in the previous chapter, the decision not to participate in the Ballistic Missile Defense scheme soured the relationship. By the end of his time in power, Martin's criticisms of the United States became so frequent that the American ambassador to Canada, David Wilkins, admonished Martin, without mentioning the prime minister by name, to "tone it down." In a speech delivered in the middle of the Canadian election, Wilkins noted that "It may be smart election-year politics to thump your chest and criticize your friend and your number one trading partner constantly. . . . But it is a slippery slope . . . and all of us should hope that it doesn't have a long-term impact on the relationship."[91]

Like Brian Mulroney in 1984, Stephen Harper campaigned on the promise of an improvement in Canadian–American relations. At their first face-to-face meeting at the trilateral summit of Canada, the United States, and Mexico in Cancún on March 31, 2006, Harper and Bush agreed to revitalize the softwood lumber talks, and within a month the two countries had a seven-year renewable agreement that both sides claimed would bring the long-running dispute to an end.[92] In this instance, the relationship they established at

---

90 In September 2002, Maher Arar, a Syrian-born Canadian, travelled from Tunis to Canada. While he was on a layover in New York, he was detained by the United States Immigration and Naturalization Service on the basis of information provided to them by the Royal Canadian Mounted Police. Suspected of having links to Al-Qaeda, Arar was flown by the United States to Syria, where he was tortured. When the Syrian security apparatus could find nothing to connect him to any terrorist activity, they released him in October 2003. Paul Martin inherited the dossier and appointed a commission of inquiry headed by Dennis O'Connor, associate chief justice of Ontario. The O'Connor commission reported in September 2006, exonerating Arar and implicitly criticizing the RCMP for its involvement in Arar's extraordinary rendition to Syria. In January 2007, Stephen Harper formally apologized to Arar and his family for the role of the Canadian government in his rendition in 2002 and 2003, and awarded him a settlement of $11.5 million.

91 "Beyond the Blame Game: Re-evaluating and Re-assessing the U.S.–Canada Relationship," remarks by U.S. Ambassador to Canada David H. Wilkins, The Canadian Club, Ottawa, December 13, 2005; available http://ottawa.usembassy.gov/content/content.asp?section=embconsul&document=wilkins_121305.

92 "PM Strikes Deal with U.S. to End Lumber Dispute," CTV.ca, April 27, 2006. Details of the agreement are available at http://www.international.gc.ca/controls-controles/softwood-bois_oeuvre/other-autres/agreement-accord.aspx. For an overview, see Geoffrey E. Hale, " 'Getting Down to Business': Rebuilding Canada–U.S. Relations Under the Harper Government," in G. Bruce Doern, ed., *How Ottawa Spends, 2007–2008: The Harper Conservatives—Climate of Change* (Montréal and Kingston: McGill-Queen's University Press, 2007), 74–76.

the March summit was credited for Bush's willingness to expend some presidential political capital in April securing support from the U.S. lumber industry. But Michael Hart reminds us that Harper's change of policy was also an important factor. When Harper took office, Hart notes, he "reshape[d] the contours of Canada–US relations and pointed them in a more constructive direction. His government's ability to take the constantly boiling pot of softwood lumber off the front burner provided an important indicator of the effectiveness of this approach."[93]

Surveying the different relationships between presidents and prime ministers, what can we conclude about the impact of personal relations between the two leaders on the conduct of the broader relationship? Lawrence Martin argued that the two leaders "set the guiding tone, the leading temperament. If there is genuine warmth between them, there is usually the same between the countries."[94] On closer inspection, however, what we find is that "good chemistry" between the president and prime minister might on occasion have a positive effect on particular policy issues—as in the case of Arctic sovereignty in 1987 or the agreement on softwood lumber in 2006—but this dynamic is neither automatic nor does it affect the full range of relations between the two countries. Thus, for all of the good chemistry between leaders like Trudeau and Carter, Mulroney and Reagan, or Chrétien and Clinton, bilateral issues between the two countries continued to irritate the relationship during their time in office. In short, while presidents and prime ministers might enjoy a good personal relationship, this has little impact on their roles as leaders of their respective countries and the political imperatives that come with their respective offices. A good personal relationship merely makes the clash of interests a little less rancorous, and on occasion will help smooth conflicts.

By contrast, "bad chemistry" almost always has a negative impact on the relationship; Johnson's willingness to work to get the Auto Pact through Congress in 1965 while remaining deeply angry at Pearson was unusual. In particular, bad feelings between the leaders has a trickle-down effect on relations between Canadian and American officials at lower levels, which may also have a negative impact on policy. Officials will often sense the sour mood of the leader and this occasionally leads to foot-dragging and allowing small quarrels that might otherwise have been settled with a little good will to fester.

But one should draw conclusions with care, since the causal link between the personal relations of the two leaders and the state of the relationship is difficult to establish. The overall Canadian–American relationship is the product of numerous factors—economic, cultural, and political. The health of the economy is another key variable, since a recession inevitably causes a rise in protectionist sentiment in the United States, which has a direct effect on trade with Canada. Likewise, domestic politics (such as the relationship between the president and the Congress, or between Ottawa and Québec) can also affect relations,

---

93 Michael Hart, *From Pride to Influence: Towards a New Canadian Foreign Policy* (Vancouver: UBC Press, 2008), 270–71.

94 Lawrence Martin, *The Presidents and the Prime Ministers* (Toronto: Doubleday, 1982), 7. For other discussions, see Dwight N. Mason, "US–Canada Defence Relations: A View from Washington," in David Carment, Fen Osler Hampson, and Norman Hillmer, eds., *Canada Among Nations 2003: Coping with the American Colossus* (Toronto: Oxford University Press, 2003), 135–55; John J. Noble, "Canada–US Relations in the Post-Iraq-War Era: Stop the Drift Towards Irrelevance," *Policy Options* (May 2003), 19–24; and J. L. Granatstein, "The Importance of Being Less Earnest: Promoting Canada's National Interests Through Tighter Ties with the U.S.," *Benefactors' Lecture, 2003* (Toronto: C. D. Howe Institute, 2003), esp. 19–27; available http://www.cdhowe.org/pdf/benefactors_lecture_2003.pdf.

in a positive or negative way. In short, while the nature of the relationship between the president and the prime minister is certainly a factor to consider in analyzing Canadian–American relations, it is not the only one that counts.

CONCLUSION

Summitry—with the president, other leaders of the G-20, the Commonwealth, La Francophonie, NATO, or the many other summits that are now a pervasive feature of international policy—provides the prime minister with a unique opportunity for diplomacy that is, by definition, very personal. No other member of the political executive enjoys such access to the summit: that prerogative belongs to the head of government alone. After his first Commonwealth meeting in London in January 1969, Mitchell Sharp, Trudeau's first secretary of state for external affairs, realized, as he told Trudeau afterward, "that one of us was superfluous and I knew which one."[95] Joe Clark, Mulroney's external affairs minister, was no less self-effacing: "Summits are for heads of government, and it is idle for a foreign minister to resent them."[96] Moreover, even if a prime minister were disinclined to take advantage of the opportunities offered by summitry—and few are—a subordinate could not be sent as a substitute "without appearing to insult other national leaders."[97]

Participation is also personal in the sense that at a summit the prime minister is very much alone. However large an entourage of cabinet colleagues, senior bureaucrats, ambassadors, personal advisers, aides, and "handlers" prime ministers may bring with them, or however well they have been briefed or coached by their officials, much of the outcome will be determined by personal performance and personal relations with their opposite numbers.

Summitry combines with the authority of the office itself and the power of appointment to shape a prime minister's dominance of the policy process. Prime ministers do not—indeed they could not—take a personal hand in those many daily decisions and actions that constitute Canada's international behaviour. Their preeminence is manifested in the general policy direction the government takes as a whole.

But preeminence does not imply complete autonomy. While prime ministers are able to exert dominance in the policy process, they are not able to do exactly as they wish in international policy. The prime minister, as the head of a democratic responsible government of a small state in international politics, is bound and constrained by relations with colleagues in cabinet; by the bureaucracy, the parliament, and the provinces; by the polity; and by the often-unforgiving nature of the international system itself. But prime ministers are not, to use Borden's phrase, toy automata, responding in mechanistic and deterministic fashion to the forces of international, domestic, and governmental politics. Their personal qualities and idiosyncrasies, their moods and emotions, cannot be dismissed as unimportant, for in diplomacy, in which words are actions, such traits invariably bear on policy outcomes. Rather, assessing the prime minister's impact on foreign policy involves a balance: recognizing the importance of individual factors without losing sight of the broader structural constraints, domestic and global, under which any prime minister operates.

---

95 Mitchell Sharp, *Which Reminds Me A Memoir* (Toronto: University of Toronto Press, 1994), 200, 218.

96 Joe Clark, "The PM and SSEA: Comment," *International Journal* 50:1 (Winter 1994–5), 215.

97 Richard Rose, "British Government: The Job at the Top," in Richard Rose and Ezra N. Suleiman, eds., *Presidents and Prime Ministers* (Washington: American Enterprise Institute, 1980), 36.

CHAPTER 8

Widening the Circle: Other Ministers

Prime ministers tend to be the central figures in the development of many aspects of Canada's international policy—determining priorities, shaping their administrations through the process of appointment, and engaging in policymaking at summit meetings. But while the prime minister is a dominant figure in all aspects of Canadian policy, we must remember that other members of the Cabinet may be drawn into the policymaking process, often (but not always) at the decision-making stage and almost always at policy-implementation stage. How wide the circle is will vary according to the issue on the agenda. The issue may draw in the ministers of public safety, agriculture and agri-food, transport, fisheries, and so on. Certainly the minister of finance and the president of the treasury board—who are ex–officio members of all cabinet committees—will play an important role in shaping all policy decisions that involve spending, for their control of the purse strings can have a determining effect on policy outcomes.

However, there will be certain ministers who will almost always be involved in issues that touch on international policy. The purpose of this chapter is to survey the ministers primarily involved in the making international policies. This circle includes the minister of foreign affairs, the minister of national defence, the minister of international trade, the minister responsible for development assistance, the minister responsible for La Francophonie, and ministers of state for particular regions or issues. As we will see, these ministers have had different titles depending on the prime minister or the era.

THE KEY MINISTERS

The two ministers at the core of Canada's international policies have traditionally been the foreign minister, who is responsible for managing Canada's relations with other countries and has statutory responsibility for Canada's development assistance programs, and the minister of national defence, who is responsible for the Canadian Forces (CF), defence policy writ large, and particularly those aspects of Canada's international policy that involve the CF, such as involvement in expeditionary wars, international coalitions, international peacekeeping, arms control, protection of territory, or territorial waters. Between them, these ministers are responsible for well over $20 billion in annual spending, the largest items in the federal government's discretionary budget.

The Minister of Foreign Affairs

For many years, the portfolio that has statutory authority for the conduct of Canada's foreign relations was known formally as the *secretary of state for external affairs* (or, more colloquially, the *external affairs minister*). The rather stylized name of this portfolio is derived from its origins. As we will see in the next chapter, when a separate government department was created to handle Canada's relations with the outside world in 1909, responsibility for the new department was given to the secretary of state for Canada, the minister responsible for communications between the dominion and the imperial government in London. The secretary of state was responsible for the new Department of External Affairs until 1912, when a new position, the secretary of state for external affairs, was created, with responsibility for the Department of External Affairs was transferred to the prime minister (the secretary of state's department continued to exist until 1993, when it was abolished).[1] The "external" in the title of the portfolio needs brief explanation. While most other countries had ministers of "foreign affairs," that title was deemed inappropriate for the new department because in 1909 the "affairs" involved not only "foreign" countries like the United States, but also Britain and other parts of the Empire—and these countries were not considered "foreign" at all. By contrast, "external affairs" nicely captured relations with both foreigners and other governments in the Empire. This designation was adopted by a number of other members of the Commonwealth, including India and Australia, and even today is reflected in the name of Britain's foreign ministry, which is known as the Foreign and Commonwealth Office (FCO). But over the course of the twentieth century, as the "foreignness" of Britain in Canada slowly but steadily increased, the designation "external" was considered less and less appropriate. Australia, for example, dropped "external affairs" in favour of "foreign affairs" in 1970. When Prime Minister Jean Chrétien was sworn in as prime minister in November 1993, he decided to change the name of the portfolio to "minister of foreign affairs."[2]

From 1912 until 1946, the prime minister was also by law the secretary of state for external affairs. It was a role Prime Minister Mackenzie King held on to firmly. When Ernest Lapointe, his Québec lieutenant, expressed a desire to be given the portfolio after the October 1935 elections, King worried that "that English speaking Canada would not welcome his having control of External Affairs, during a European war that increasingly seemed imminent."[3] So the prime minister fobbed him off: "I said to Lapointe I thought I had better take on External Affairs for a time at least, because of the war situation."[4] "For a time" turned into eleven years, long after Lapointe's death in 1941. Only after the Second World War, which brought a hugely expanded role for the state in both domestic and international policy, was it becoming clear to King that he could no longer handle what by then had become a major portfolio in addition to the press of other prime ministerial duties. In September 1946, he passed the external affairs portfolio to Louis St. Laurent.

The minister of foreign affairs is above all responsible for relations between the Canadian government and other states. If bureaucrats are responsible for the day-to-day smooth running of good relations with other governments, the minister is responsible for directing the most delicate dossiers. By his decisions and statements, he sets the position of the Canadian government on international questions. But from time to time, the minister is also charged with defining the broad orientations, central concepts, and future priorities of Canada's international policy. These ideas, which constitute the directions that a minister wants to imprint on the activities of the bureaucracy, can be expressed in a variety of ways.

---

1 John Hilliker, *Canada's Department of External Affairs*, vol. 1: *The Early Years, 1909–1946* (Montréal and Kingston: McGill-Queen's University Press, 1990). The department of the secretary of state for Canada continued to exist and was given various responsibilities that were not assigned to an existing department. The portfolio was abolished in 1993 when Chrétien reorganized the government.

2 Technically the name of the department and its minister was not changed until May 13, 1995, when legislation formally changing the name came into force.

3 Quoted in John MacFarlane, *Ernest Lapointe and Québec's Influence on Canadian Foreign Policy* (Toronto: University of Toronto Press, 1999), 79.

4 Quoted in C.P. Stacey, *Canada and the Age of Conflict*, vol. 2: *1921–1948: The Mackenzie King Era* (Toronto: University of Toronto Press, 1981), 168.

For example, Louis St. Laurent laid down five priorities for Canadian foreign policy in a speech given at the University of Toronto in 1947.[5] Mitchell Sharp, external affairs minister from 1968 until 1974, announced the new policy of economic diversification for Canada (the "Third Option") in an issue of *International Perspectives*, a journal.[6] In 1990, Joe Clark, Brian Mulroney's secretary of state for external affairs, used the podium of the United Nations General Assembly to outline his vision of cooperative security.[7] For his part, Lloyd Axworthy promoted his ideas on human security by publishing a number of articles in scholarly journals.[8] Curiously—and quite unlike the case with defence policy, discussed below—the foreign policy reviews conducted after Brian Mulroney, Jean Chrétien, and Paul Martin came to office were put out by the government as a whole rather than by the foreign minister.[9] And even the 1970 review *Foreign Policy for Canadians*, which was issued by the secretary of state for external affairs, almost entirely reflected the thinking of Prime Minister Pierre Elliott Trudeau.

This illustrates one of the problems with the foreign affairs portfolio. Of all the positions in cabinet, there is no other portfolio likelier to produce conflict with the prime minister. It is true that a prime minister who maintains an interest in economic issues may quarrel with cabinet members charged with those portfolios. However, international policy is particularly susceptible to dissension. This is because of the structure of the policy area itself. The business of a state's international policy is such that there is a need for both the prime minister and the foreign minister to "share the territory" of international policy, as John Hilliker and Don Barry put it.[10] On the one hand, foreign policy forces the prime minister into taking a personal and active role in policy development that does not occur in other policy areas. In international policy, the prime minister is expected to take the lead in developing policy positions, both at the level of grand strategy and at the more micro level of tactics, and is expected to play a personal role as the key representative of the state—at international summits, in official visits to other states, and in acting as host to

---

5 Louis St. Laurent, "The Foundation of Canadian Policy in World Affairs (Gray Foundation Lectureship)," in Canada, Department of External Affairs, *Statements and Speeches* 47/2, Toronto, January 13, 1947. In this speech, St. Laurent identified five priorities for foreign policy: national unity, political liberty, rule of law, human values, and the importance of acceptance of international responsibilities. The speech is reproduced in R.A. Mackay, ed., *Canadian Foreign Policy, 1945–1954: Selected Speeches and Documents* (Toronto: McClelland & Stewart, 1970), 388–99; also in Granatstein, ed., *Canadian Foreign Policy: Historical Readings*, 25–33.

6 Mitchell Sharp, "Canadian–U.S. Relations: Options for the Future," *International Perspectives*, special issue, Autumn 1972.

7 Department of External Affairs, "Notes for an Address by the Secretary of State for External Affairs, the Right Honourable Joe Clark, to the 45th Session of the United Nations General Assembly," *Declaration* 90–55, New York, September 26, 1990, 12.

8 Lloyd Axworthy, "Canada and Human Security: The Need for Leadership," *International Journal* 52:2 (Spring 1997), 183–96; "Entre mondialisation et multipolarité: pour une politique étrangère du Canada globale et humaine," *Études internationales* 28:1 (March 1997), 105–21.

9 *Canada's International Relations: Response of the Government of Canada to the Report of the Special Joint Committee of the Senate and the House of Commons* (Ottawa: Supply and Services Canada, 1986); *Canada in the World* (Ottawa, 1995); *Canada's International Policy Statement: A Role of Pride and Influence in the World* (Ottawa, Government of Canada, 2005).

10 John Hilliker and Donald Barry, "The PM and the SSEA in Canada's Foreign Policy: Sharing the Territory, 1946–1968," *International Journal* 50:1 (Winter 1994–5), 162–88.

visiting foreign leaders. This permits the prime minister to develop personal relations with other world leaders that develop without the involvement of subordinates. Finally, international policy offers a prime minister an opportunity to acquire prestige that is politically useful back home.

The problem is that the foreign affairs portfolio requires precisely the same of a foreign minister. Foreign ministers are no less able to avoid the need to participate personally in summit diplomacy and the diplomacy of official visits, and they are no less able to avoid the necessity of crafting strategic and tactical policy responses to the often unpredictable challenges a state confronts in the international system.

In Canada, the relationship between the foreign affairs minister and the prime minister has often reflected these structural tensions. In at least one case, the relationship was distinctly unhappy: Mackenzie King, who had spent all of his years in power exercising the prerogatives of both portfolios himself. As a consequence, he spent his last years as prime minister chafing at the international policies being pursued by St. Laurent.[11] In the years after King's passing, by contrast, the relationship was much closer. But this in large part reflected the links between the Liberal party and personnel in the Department of External Affairs. Lester B. Pearson was the undersecretary of state for external affairs—as the deputy minister of the department was called before 1993—when St. Laurent became prime minister in 1948. He recruited Pearson into his cabinet as external affairs minister, finding Pearson a safe Liberal seat for easy election into the House of Commons. As Pearson later recounted in his memoirs, St. Laurent had implicit trust in him: "'Don't worry,' he told me. 'Do what is best. Do the right thing, and I'll back you.'"[12] In 1958, Pearson succeeded St. Laurent as leader of the Liberal party, and in 1963 he became prime minister after the Liberals won the elections that year. As his external minister, he appointed Paul Martin, Sr. While Pearson and Martin were not as close as Pearson and St. Laurent had been, a number of Pearson's old colleagues from the Department of External Affairs were in the upper reaches of the bureaucracy during his prime ministership. Thus from 1948 to 1957, and from 1963 to 1968, the links between the prime minister and External Affairs were unusually close.

This pattern was temporarily interrupted during the Progressive Conservative government of John G. Diefenbaker from 1957 to 1963. Diefenbaker was hesitant to give responsibility for external policy to his cabinet colleagues. "I have followed the tradition of the United Kingdom," he claimed, "that the Prime Minister must take a particular interest in that field of national activity on which [the] safety of the state so highly depends."[13] Of all prime ministers after King, only Diefenbaker chose to hold the external affairs post himself—for the first three months of his mandate, and then for another three months after his first external affairs minister, Sidney Smith, died quite unexpectedly in March 1959. But even when Smith was given the external affairs portfolio, Diefenbaker could not resist seeking to keep control. A few moments after being sworn in, Smith was asked by reporters to outline his

---

11 James Eayrs, *The Art of the Possible: Government and Foreign Policy in Canada* (Toronto: University of Toronto Press, 1960), 25.

12 Quoted in Eayrs, *Art of the Possible*, 26. On the close relationship between St. Laurent and Pearson, see Bruce Thordarson, "Posture and Policy: Leadership in Canada's External Affairs," *International Journal* 31:4 (Autumn 1976), 679.

13 Quoted in W.A. Matheson, *The Prime Minister and the Cabinet* (Toronto: Methuen, 1976), 161.

opinions on Canadian policy over Suez. When it became apparent that Smith favoured the approach taken by the defeated St. Laurent government, Diefenbaker cut in, contradicting his new minister. "This initial reprimand," James Eayrs has argued, "set the tone of their relationship."[14] (By contrast, when Diefenbaker appointed Howard Green, an old friend, to succeed Smith, the relationship was more harmonious. Certainly Diefenbaker left Green to pursue his special interest in disarmament while the prime minister focused on other aspects of international policy.)

After 1968, the close relationship between the prime minister and the Department ended. In addition, the relationship between the bureaucracy and the external affairs minister was never as close as it had been in the immediate post-1945 period; none of those who served as foreign minister after 1968 had a relationship with the bureaucracy comparable to their predecessors (other than Clark, who had been prime minister[15]). At first blush this might seem to be the result of the number of ministers who served in this position after 1968. A glance at the list of those who have held the position of foreign minister (Figure 8.1 on page 210) seems to indicate that ministers were cycled quickly through the external affairs portfolio. While Canada had only five foreign ministers between 1946 and 1968 (excluding the two periods when Diefenbaker was his own secretary of state for external affairs), nine ministers held the position in the Trudeau/Mulroney era (1968–1993), leading one former diplomat to argue that this "procession of ministers" had a deleterious effect on morale in the Department of External Affairs.[16] The "procession" accelerated after 1993: Nine ministers held the position in the sixteen years between 1993 and 2009.

In fact, while the *average* length of tenure for the portfolio fell from 4.4 years in the 1946–68 period to 2.5 years in the period between 1968 and the appointment of Lawrence Cannon in October 2008, what is striking is that the *pattern* of tenure remained remarkably similar to the earlier period. If one excludes the three short-lived governments of Joe Clark, John Turner, and Kim Campbell, the tenure of foreign affairs ministers from 1968 to 2000 looks remarkably similar to that in the 1946–1968 period. Both were marked by long-serving ministers: Pearson held the portfolio for nine years, from 1948 to 1957; Howard Green served for four years, from 1959 to 1963; Paul Martin served from 1963 to 1968; Mitchell Sharp served for six years (a period, as he notes in his memoirs, longer than any other external affairs minister up to that point with the exception of Pearson);[17] Clark held the external affairs portfolio for seven years before he was appointed minister for constitutional affairs in 1991; and Lloyd Axworthy held the post for almost five years. In the post-9/11 era, by contrast, seven ministers rotated through the portfolio between 2002 and 2009, mostly because of the minority governments of Paul Martin and Stephen Harper.

What did change after 1968 was the relationship between the prime minister and the external affairs minister.[18] Until then, there had been a general willingness to share the

---

14 Eayrs, *Art of the Possible,* 26–27.

15 David Cox, "Leadership Change and Innovation in Canadian Foreign Policy: The 1979 Progressive Conservative Government," *International Journal* 37:3 (Autumn 1982).

16 Arthur Andrew, *The Rise and Fall of a Middle Power: Canadian Diplomacy from King to Mulroney* (Toronto: James Lorimer, 1993), 143–44.

17 Mitchell Sharp, *Which Reminds Me A Memoir* (Toronto: University of Toronto Press, 1994), 164.

18 Kim Richard Nossal, "The PM and the SSEA in Canada's Foreign Policy: Dividing the Territory, 1968–1993," *International Journal* 50:1 (Winter 1994–5), 189–208.

| FIGURE 8.1 | Canada's Foreign Ministers, 1909–2009 |

Secretary of State for External Affairs

Charles Murphy	Liberal	June 1, 1909–Oct. 6, 1911
William Roche	Conservative	Oct. 10, 1911–Mar. 31, 1912
Sir Robert Borden*	Conservative	Apr. 1, 1912–July 9, 1920
Arthur Meighen*	Conservative	July 10, 1920–Dec. 28, 1921
William Lyon Mackenzie King*	Liberal	Dec. 29, 1921–Jun. 28, 1926
Arthur Meighen*	Conservative	June 29, 1926–Sep. 24, 1926
William Lyon Mackenzie King*	Liberal	Sep. 25, 1926–Aug. 6, 1930
R.B. Bennett*	Conservative	Aug. 7, 1930–Oct. 22, 1935
William Lyon Mackenzie King*	Liberal	Oct. 23, 1935–Sep. 3, 1946
Louis St. Laurent	Liberal	Sep. 4, 1946–Sep. 9, 1948
Lester B. Pearson	Liberal	Sep. 10, 1948–June 20, 1957
John G. Diefenbaker*	Progressive Conservative	June 21, 1957–Sep. 12, 1957
Sidney Smith	Progressive Conservative	Sep. 13, 1957–Mar. 17, 1959
John G. Diefenbaker (acting)*	Progressive Conservative	Mar. 19, 1959–June 3, 1959
Howard Green	Progressive Conservative	June 4, 1959–Apr. 21, 1963
Paul Martin, Sr.	Liberal	Apr. 22, 1963–Apr. 19, 1968
Mitchell Sharp	Liberal	Apr. 20, 1968–Aug. 7, 1974
Allan MacEachen	Liberal	Aug. 8, 1974–Sep. 13, 1976
Donald Jamieson	Liberal	Sep. 14, 1976–June 3, 1979
Flora MacDonald	Progressive Conservative	June 4, 1979–Mar. 2, 1980
Mark MacGuigan	Liberal	Mar. 3, 1980–Sep. 9, 1982
Allan MacEachen	Liberal	Sep. 10, 1982–June 29, 1984
Jean Chrétien	Liberal	June 30, 1984–Sep. 16, 1984
Joe Clark	Progressive Conservative	Sep. 17, 1984–Apr. 20, 1991
Barbara McDougall	Progressive Conservative	Apr. 21, 1991–June 24, 1993
Perrin Beatty	Progressive Conservative	June 25, 1993–Nov. 3, 1993

Minister of Foreign Affairs

André Ouellet**	Liberal	Nov. 4, 1993–Jan. 24, 1996
Lloyd Axworthy	Liberal	Jan. 25, 1996–Oct. 16, 2000
John Manley	Liberal	Oct. 17, 2000–Jan. 15, 2002
Bill Graham	Liberal	Jan. 16, 2002–July 19, 2004
Pierre S. Pettigrew	Liberal	July 20, 2004–Feb. 5, 2006
Peter MacKay	Conservative Party of Canada	Feb. 6, 2006–Aug. 13, 2007
Maxime Bernier	Conservative Party of Canada	Aug. 14, 2007–May 26, 2008
David Emerson (acting)	Conservative Party of Canada	May 27, 2008–Oct. 29, 2008
Lawrence Cannon	Conservative Party of Canada	Oct. 30, 2008–present

*Post was held by the prime minister; from 1912 to 1946, the prime minister was secretary of state for external affairs by law.

**Although he went by the new title from November 1993, technically Ouellet was secretary of state for external affairs from November 4, 1993 until May 12, 1995, when the legislation changing the portfolio's name went into force.

same policy "territory"; with the arrival of the Trudeau government, what emerged was an increasing tendency to "divide" it. A rudimentary division of labour emerged in each case, with the prime minister assuming a particular dossier close to his interests. Thus, at different times during his tenure, Trudeau pursued issues in international policy that particularly interested him: the administrative reform of the Department of External Affairs, arms control (notably his interest in what he called "nuclear suffocation," the reduction of the number of nuclear weapons), and the North–South issue.

This process was intensified under Mulroney. In the first years of his mandate, Mulroney was particularly interested in relations with the United States and the issue of apartheid in South Africa. With the end of the Cold War, he followed the evolving structures of the international system, but tended not to take the sort of sporadic initiatives that were the hallmark of Trudeau's involvement in foreign policy, though the 1991 push for "good governance" was an exception. Both of his external affairs ministers, Clark and McDougall, had greater latitude to pursue their particular interests in international policy.[19]

Such a rudimentary division of labour meant that generally the dossiers covered by prime minister and external affairs minister did not come into close contact. There were occasions when Mulroney and Clark openly disagreed. For example, in March 1988, Mulroney explicitly disavowed Clark's criticism of Israel over its human rights violations.[20] But on the whole the relationship between Mulroney and Clark evolved in a manner designed to minimize friction. Indeed, the only dossier they "shared" was Canada's South African policy. Both were involved in the implementation of that policy, Mulroney in a variety of summits, and Clark as the co-chair of a Commonwealth committee of foreign ministers.[21]

The sharing of tasks continued under Chrétien. The prime minister took primary responsibility for summit diplomacy and the various high-profile "Team Canada" trade missions that were the mark of his initial years in power. Because the number of dossiers Chrétien covered was more limited, both André Ouellet and Lloyd Axworthy were able to pursue their own international interests more easily, such as the issue of the land-mines ban, which Ouellet started and Axworthy finished, or developing the human security agenda.[22] But the prime minister always retained key decisions in his own hands, such as the setting of Canada's Kyoto targets in 1997 or the decision not to participate in the invasion of Iraq in 2003.

We noted in Chapter 6 the tendency of Stephen Harper to exercise tight control over all areas of policy. Not surprisingly, this centralizing tendency manifested in the relations between the prime minister and the various foreign ministers who served in his cabinet,

---

19 Harald von Riekhoff, "The Structure of Foreign Policy Decision Making and Management," in Brian W. Tomlin and Maureen Appel Molot, eds., *Canada Among Nations 1986: Talking Trade* (Toronto: James Lorimer, 1987), 22.

20 David H. Goldberg and David Taras, "Collision Course: Joe Clark, Canadian Jews, and the Palestinian Uprising," in Taras and Goldberg, eds., *The Domestic Battleground: Canada and the Arab–Israeli Conflict* (Montréal and Kingston: McGill-Queen's University Press, 1989), 207–23.

21 Linda Freeman, *The Ambiguous Champion: Canada and South Africa in the Trudeau and Mulroney Years* (Toronto: University of Toronto Press, 1997); Kim Richard Nossal, "Canadian Sanctions Against South Africa: Explaining the Mulroney Initiatives, 1985–86," *Journal of Canadian Studies* 25 (Winter 1990–91), 17–33.

22 Lloyd Axworthy, *Navigating a New World: Canada's Global Future* (Toronto: Vintage Canada, 2003).

with the prime minister taking the lead on important dossiers such as the mission in Afghanistan, the support of Israel during the war in Lebanon in 2006, or the issue of human rights in China.

In short, the policy "territory" and the policy autonomy of the foreign minister has tended to shrink over the years. Donald Savoie argued that one of the factors that explains this tendency—a factor that has an impact on all members of Cabinet—is the increasing concentration of power at the centre, particularly in the prime minister's "departments"— the Privy Council Office (PCO) and the Prime Minister's Office (PMO). In international policy, the PCO provides the prime minister with a source of information and advice that is independent of the advice and information available to the foreign affairs minister through the Department of Foreign Affairs and International Trade.

In the days of St. Laurent and Pearson, the external affairs portfolio was prestigious and much sought after. Indeed, until 1968, the portfolio had been seen as a stepping-stone to the prime ministership. Both St. Laurent and Pearson had achieved the leadership of party, and hence the prime ministership, from the external affairs portfolio; Pearson reckoned that his work in the external affairs portfolio and his Nobel Peace Prize in 1957 contributed heavily to his leadership victory.[23] Now it may have been nothing more than happenstance that two Liberal prime ministers in a row came to that position from External Affairs, but it contributed to the view that the portfolio was a way of increasing national recognition for activity on the international stage. When Paul Martin, Sr. launched his candidacy for the Liberal leadership in 1968, he was no doubt hoping to follow in St. Laurent's and Pearson's footsteps.

When Martin was defeated by Trudeau, this effectively ended the "tradition," such as it was. Since then, only one foreign affairs minister, Jean Chrétien, has made the move down Sussex Drive from No. 125, where the headquarters of the Department of Foreign Affairs and International Trade are located, to No. 24—and Chrétien's achievement of the party leadership in 1990 and his subsequent victory in the 1993 election had nothing to do with his brief stint as external affairs minister during John Turner's brief prime ministership in the summer of 1984.

But the portfolio lost none of its lustre. Writing his memoirs in 1993, Sharp could still describe external affairs as "the most attractive portfolio" in the Canadian cabinet: "It has prestige, challenge, some glamour (at least when travelling abroad), and seldom involves the kinds of problems that are routinely faced by, for example, the ministers of finance and health and welfare, with responsibilities for making decisions affecting the pocketbooks of Canadians."[24] Indeed, it is precisely because of its attractiveness that since 1968 appointment to it has been increasingly used for overtly partisan political purposes. The foreign affairs portfolio—and, for the opposition parties, the foreign affairs critic's dossier—has been increasingly regarded either as a reward for supporters or as a useful portfolio to assign to rivals.

There are numerous examples of the use of the portfolio as a reward. Sharp's early support for Trudeau's leadership bid in 1968 ensured that he was given his choice of portfolios. Trudeau appointed MacEachen to the external affairs portfolio in 1974 as a reward for his

---

23 Lester B. Pearson, *Mike: The Memoirs of the Rt. Hon. Lester B. Pearson*, vol. 3: *1957–1968* (Toronto: University of Toronto Press, 1974), 28.

24 Sharp, *Which Reminds Me*, 225.

service as House Leader during the 1972–74 minority government. Flora MacDonald, who threw her support to Joe Clark during the 1976 leadership campaign, was given External Affairs in 1979. Mulroney rewarded Sinclair Stevens for his support of the bid to oust Clark in 1983 by giving him the job of external affairs critic. In return for his support at the June 1990 leadership convention, Jean Chrétien gave Lloyd Axworthy the critic's dossier, and the foreign affairs portfolio itself in January 1996. Kim Campbell made Perrin Beatty external affairs minister in 1993 after his support for her successful leadership bid.

The portfolio has also been a useful means of mollifying defeated rivals for the party leadership. Prime ministers understand that there are considerable benefits to giving a political rival the prestigious foreign affairs portfolio: Not only does the minister of foreign affairs have to spend a fair amount of time outside Canada, he or she is unlikely to garner the political spotlight because of summitry and the relatively low profile of foreign policy in national politics. After he defeated Claude Wagner for the Progressive Conservative leadership in 1976, Clark appointed Wagner the external affairs critic. Turner gave the portfolio to Chrétien in the summer of 1984. And, having ousted Clark in a nasty leadership battle in 1983, Mulroney appointed Clark as his external affairs minister in September 1984. When Paul Martin, Jr. increasingly challenged Chrétien for the leadership of the Liberal party in the late 1990s, Chrétien also tried to use the portfolio to deflect the pressure, offering it to Martin after the November 2000 elections (an offer that Martin, no doubt well aware of why he was being offered the job, declined).[25] Likewise, when the Progressive Conservative party under Peter MacKay and the Canadian Alliance under Stephen Harper decided to merge as the Conservative Party of Canada in 2003, both leaders contested the leadership of the new party. After winning the 2006 election, Harper offered MacKay the foreign affairs portfolio.

After 1968, the portfolio also became increasingly onerous. The foreign affairs minister is not only technically responsible for the conduct of the full range of foreign relations, but is also responsible for two large departments: the Department of Foreign Affairs and International Trade and the Canadian International Development Agency (CIDA). In addition, the foreign minister must represent Canada in numerous sub-summit meetings.

The Minister of National Defence

The minister of national defence has a complex relationship with the minister of foreign affairs. On the one hand, the minister of national defence is by no means subordinate to the minister of foreign affairs. On the other hand, the Canadian Armed Forces are primarily an instrument of Canada's international policy, and thus create a need for National Defence to adjust to the policy objectives embraced by Foreign Affairs. The two ministers often encounter difficulties coordinating their respective policies.[26] For example, in the early 1960s, the quarrels within the cabinet of John G. Diefenbaker between the external affairs minister, Howard Green, and the minister of national defence, Douglas Harkness, over the

---

25 Paul Martin, *Hell or High Water: My Life in and out of Politics* (Toronto: McClelland & Stewart, 2008), 228.

26 It is useful to compare two perspectives on the problem of coordination, offered a quarter-century apart: Alasdair MacLaren, "Canada Needs to Reconcile Foreign and Defence Policies," *International Perspectives* (March/April 1977), 22–24; and David King, "We Need a Romanow Commission for Defence and Foreign Policy," *Policy Options* 23:3 (April 2002), 11–12.

acquisition of nuclear weapons remain an instructive example of this problem.[27] Likewise, when in the 1990s Lloyd Axworthy embraced the idea of human security, examined in Chapter 5, little thought was given to defining precisely what role the CAF would play in the implementation of this policy; the two ministers of national defence during this period, Doug Young and Art Eggleton, were not consulted. With each department pursuing their own understanding of "security," a coherent policy never emerged.

Like the foreign minister, the defence minister is from time to time given the responsibility of defining the broad elements of Canadian defence policy, normally published as white papers—in other words, formal statements of government policy.[28] Since 1947, six white papers on Canadian defence policy have been published, and, unlike the case with foreign policy reviews, often under the name of the minister.[29] Often these documents will be the occasion for proposing major new orientations in defence policy, and often, as we will see below, these new directions will be so ambitious that it proves difficult, if not impossible, to implement them.

The defence portfolio predates the creation of a minister for external affairs by some forty years. The first minister of militia and defence, as the portfolio was called from 1867 to 1922, was Sir George Étienne Cartier, one of the Fathers of Confederation. Cartier had expressly asked Sir John A. Macdonald that he be appointed to this post, not only because he considered it one of the more prestigious, but also because he believed that the militia could be a way to cement the unity of the young dominion.[30]

Cartier's faith and optimism proved unfounded. To be sure, in theory, the defence portfolio should be one of the most important in a country's government. Not only is the defence minister responsible for one of the core functions of any state—its protection—but the defence department and the armed forces normally loom large in purely material terms. Defence usually consumes a large portion of any government's annual budget, even in periods of downsizing or retrenchment, and the defence department and the armed forces are invariably one of the largest employers. Moreover, in most countries, the portfolio provides political visibility, particularly in periods of international crisis.

But in Canadian politics, this position is far from being as prestigious as it is in most other countries, in large part because Canadians, insulated from threats of foreign invasion for two centuries, have always regarded military affairs as of secondary importance. While DND and the CF have large budgets relative to other government departments, the position is not regarded as attractive and has generally not been a springboard to higher office. Of the 65 individuals who occupied this post between 1867 and 2009, just one, Kim Campbell, went on to become prime minister. Even more than the foreign minister, defence ministers do not remain long on the job, serving an average of 2.2 years (1.5 years since 1968).

---

27 Albert Legault and Michel Fortmann, *A Diplomacy of Hope: Canada and Disarmament, 1945–1988* (Montréal and Kingston: McGill-Queen's University Press, 1992), esp. chap. 1.

28 Audrey Doerr, "The Role of White Papers," in G. Bruce Doern and Peter Aucoin, eds., *The Structures of Policy Making in Canada* (Toronto: Macmillan, 1971), 197–200.

29 The first five are reproduced in Douglas L. Bland, *Canada's National Defence,* vol. 1: *Defence Policy* (Kingston, School of Policy Studies, Queen's University, 1997); the sixth is Canada, *A Role of Pride and Influence in the World: Canada's International Policy Statement,* defence booklet (Ottawa: April 2005).

30 Desmond Morton, *A Military History of Canada* (Toronto: McClelland & Stewart, 1999), 90.

One of the reasons for the speed with which ministers tend to move through the defence portfolio is its general unattractiveness. Historically, defence ministers in Canada have had to spend their time in office trying square a circle known as the "commitment-capability gap."[31] The "gap" is created when the cabinet gives the Canadian military a large number of policy tasks but then does not provide the resources necessary to perform them. Ministers of national defence have historically had to try to manage the shrinking of the military and its resources in times of peace or budgetary austerity, or trying to reform a generally very conservative military establishment.

To be sure, some individuals have dealt with these challenges brilliantly. These would include Frederick W. Borden, who occupied the portfolio from 1896 to 1911, called the most important peacetime minister in Canadian history by Desmond Morton;[32] Brooke Claxton, minister from 1946 to 1954, who presided over the reduction of the Canadian armed forces after the Second World War and then the rearmament of Canada at the beginning of the Cold War; and Paul Hellyer (1963–1967), who unified the different services of the armed forces. However, these are the exceptions.

Not only is the need to manage the commitment-capability gap disagreeable, but the job often requires dealing with crises or taking responsibility for unpopular policies. Even seasoned politicians have seen their political careers dashed by this portfolio. In November 1944, James Ralston—Canada's longest-serving defence minister, serving from 1926 to 1930 and from 1940 to 1944—was forced to resign by Mackenzie King because of Ralston's strong support for conscription for overseas service. His successor, A.G.L. McNaughton, an experienced military officer, was also brought down by the conscription issue. When McNaughton changed his mind about conscription, he could not get elected to the House of Commons and resigned in July 1945. In the 1980s, Perrin Beatty pushed an ambitious and costly defence white paper through cabinet, but was then shuffled to the health portfolio by Brian Mulroney in order to permit his successor to abandon the costly projects.[33] In the 1990s, David Collenette and Doug Young had to devote a considerable amount of their attention to the series of scandals that followed the mission to Somalia in 1993. In the 2000s, Stephen Harper's first minister of national defence, Gordon O'Connor, a former general in the CAF, spent much of his time trying to explain the Afghanistan mission to Canadians; when the results of public opinion polls showed no sign of shifting from the tepid support, O'Connor was shuffled out of the defence portfolio to national revenue.

Another reason for the short tenure of defence ministers in Canada is that a fair number have had their time in the portfolio cut short by factors that had little to do with defence policy. In 1985, Robert Coates had to resign after visiting a strip club while on a trip to Germany. Kim Campbell held the portfolio briefly before being catapulted into the party leadership (and then losing not only her own seat but also all but two Progressive Conservative seats in the 1993 elections). In 1996, David Collenette was caught up in the Somalia scandal and resigned from Cabinet. His successor, Doug Young, went down to

---

31 Louis F. Nastro and Kim Richard Nossal, "The Commitment–Capability Gap: Implications for Canadian Foreign Policy in the Post–Cold War Era," *Canadian Defence Quarterly* 27 (Autumn 1997), 19–22.

32 Morton, *Military History of Canada*, 166.

33 Norrin M. Ripsman, "Big Eyes and Empty Pockets: The Two Phases of Conservative Defence Policy," in Nelson Michaud and Kim Richard Nossal, eds., *Diplomatic Departures: The Conservative Era in Canadian Foreign Policy, 1984–1993* (Vancouver: UBC Press, 2001), 100–27.

defeat in the 1997 elections, one of only two Liberal cabinet ministers to suffer such a fate. Art Eggleton, who replaced him, had to resign in 2002 when it was discovered that a defence contract had been given to an ex-lover. His place was taken by John McCallum, who held the post for less than two years before he was caught in the rivalry between Jean Chrétien and Paul Martin, and was demoted to Veterans Affairs by Martin when he became prime minister in December 2003. David Pratt, Martin's defence minister, was in the position for less than six months when he was defeated in the June 2004 elections. Bill Graham, who succeeded Pratt, was himself thrown out of office when the Liberals lost the January 2006 elections.

As in the case of the foreign affairs portfolio, responsibility for different aspects of defence policy have often been shared among different ministers, generally but not exclusively in times of war. Thus, during the First World War, the government included a minister of overseas military forces, and between 1910 and 1922, responsibility for the Canadian navy was given to the minister of the naval service. During the Second World War, ministers of national defence for air, naval service, and national war service were put in place. Moreover, each of these ministers had an associate minister to assist them. While these positions were abolished at the end of the war, the position of associate minister of national defence was reactivated in 1953. It was, however, frequently left vacant before being finally abandoned by Stephen Harper in 2006.

Despite Cartier's hopes, this portfolio turned into a solid anglophone bastion. Prior to the First World War, four francophones held the position, but between 1896 and 1967, the portfolio was held exclusively by anglophones, a reflection of the deep divisions engendered by the Boer War and the First World War. Lester Pearson appointed Léo Cadieux to the portfolio in 1967; since then, only three francophones—Gilles Lamontagne, Jean-Jacques Blais, and Marcel Masse—have held it. It is also a male bastion: Only one woman, Kim Campbell, has served as defence minister. Of the nine associate ministers, three were francophones and one, Mary Collins, was a woman.

OTHER MINISTERS

After 1968, the growth in the scope and range of Canada's international affairs placed an increasing strain on the capacity of the external affairs minister to discharge these numerous responsibilities. However, simply appointing more ministers to deal with them was not possible because of the conventions of cabinet structure in Canada down to 1993. In Australia and Britain, a distinction is made between the "ministry" (which includes all ministers of the Crown responsible for government departments) and the "cabinet"—the ultimate decision-making body—which does not include all those in the ministry. In Canada, by contrast, convention until 1993 dictated that all ministers of the Crown sat in Cabinet.

This convention did not pose a major problem in the first century of Canada's existence, since the apparatus of state was not highly developed. But the expansion of the state, particularly in the 1960s, posed a problem. If each department or agency were assigned a separate minister, and if each minister were given a seat at the cabinet table, the cabinet would swell to unmanageable proportions. This convention therefore encouraged the growth in the 1970s of huge and sprawling agencies (such as the Ministry of Transport, responsible for a wide range of policy issue areas) or "twinned" departments (Health and Welfare, Employment and Immigration, or Energy, Mines and Resources). It also encouraged assigning ministers responsibility for a number of departments and agencies.

From 1945 to 1968, the secretary of state for external affairs did not have to share responsibility for Canada's international relations with anyone but the prime minister. The predominance of security issues and the close links between the prime minister and the external affairs minister encouraged this. However, as Andrew Cooper has argued, after 1968 several factors necessitated profound adjustments in the ministerial control of international policy: the arrival of Trudeau in power, shifts in the foreign policy preoccupations of Canadians from security to questions of social justice, development assistance and the economy, and increasing debates over national unity.[34]

The evolution was remarkable and was reflected in the composition of the cabinet. In the late 1960s, the external affairs minister only had to consult cabinet colleagues on those areas that had an international dimension—Finance, National Defence, Transport, Agriculture, Immigration, and so on. Twenty-five years later, by contrast, the foreign affairs minister did not only have to cooperate on policy with those colleagues, but also had to take account of newcomers whose portfolios impacted directly on issues that were traditionally the bailiwick of the Department of External Affairs. Thus, for example, in the Chrétien cabinet, responsibility for international policy was fragmented among several ministers. Besides the minister of foreign affairs, who played the most important role, several other ministers were active in this policy sphere: the minister responsible for La Francophonie, the international trade minister, the international cooperation minister, and the secretaries of state for the Asia-Pacific, Latin America, the Middle East, and international financial institutions.

What happened to prompt such a change? After 1968, certain policy areas assumed an increasing importance and thus required more sustained attention—notably La Francophonie, development assistance, and trade. This led to the creation, during the 1970s and 1980s, of new structures of ministerial responsibility. However, as this occurred, it gave rise to almost insoluble problems of coordination, leaving the impression that the external affairs portfolio was constantly being reformed.

The Minister for La Francophonie

One of the enduring tensions in Canadian politics has been the linguistic cleavage between anglophones and francophones. Law, convention, and policy have only been partly successful in bridging the gulf between the two communities, as the persistence of the national question in Québec shows. Before 1968, one of the important conventions in Canadian politics was the idea that prime ministers and party leaders had "lieutenants"—senior members of the party who could communicate (in both a figurative and literal sense) with the "other" linguistic community. The two francophone prime ministers prior to 1968—Laurier and St. Laurent—were both fluent in English, but both had lieutenants to smooth their relations with English Canada. In the case of anglophone prime ministers, not all were able to communicate with francophone Canadians in their own language. Most needed a francophone in a very basic way—to overcome their inability to speak and listen to several million Canadians. For example, Mackenzie King's Québec lieutenant was Ernest Lapointe, who served in that role from 1924 until his death in 1941, first as minister of fisheries and then minister of justice. Lapointe was one of those rare francophone

---

34 Andrew Cooper, "Trying to Get It Right: The Foreign Ministry and Organizational Change in Canada," in Brian Hocking, ed., *Foreign Ministries: Change and Adaptation* (London: Macmillan, 1998), 40–58.

Québécois, along with Raoul Dandurand and Louis St. Laurent, who played a significant role in Canada's international relations prior to the 1960s.[35] Prime ministerial unilingualism effectively came to an end in 1968: Trudeau and Mulroney were completely at ease in both official languages; Chrétien, Martin, and Harper had no difficulty communicating fluently in the other official language. Even those anglophones who were prime minister only briefly—Clark, Turner, and Campbell—spoke French.

In international policy, the problem of language arrived late. Prior to the 1960s, Canada's relations were predominantly with the anglophone world—with Britain and the United States—and neither Laurier nor St. Laurent had problems communicating with their British, Commonwealth, or American counterparts. So too the Department of External Affairs was a predominantly anglophone bureaucracy, where the few francophones wrote their memos and dispatches—even to one another—in English.

The anglophone dominance was to change after 1960. Externally, the rapid collapse of the French colonial empire had led to a sudden burgeoning of francophone states in the international system. Domestically, successive governments in Ottawa, catalyzed not only by the Quiet Revolution in Québec but also by a sustained campaign by *Le Devoir*, sought to give greater expression to Canada's linguistic and cultural duality by strengthening ties with this group of states, known as La Francophonie.[36] This diversification *did* pose a linguistic and cultural problem. Between 1909 and 1970, only two francophones held the position of external affairs minister: St. Laurent between 1946 and 1948 and Paul Martin, Sr. between 1963 and 1968. The 11 secretaries of state for external affairs who held the portfolio in these years were all anglophones (although a number were able to speak French).

The response to the increased need for a minister who was fluent in French was strictly ad hoc. When duties in French had to be performed, a francophone minister was called on. In 1971, Gérard Pelletier, the secretary of state, headed the Canadian delegation to the meetings of l'Agence de coopération culturelle et technique (ACCT); he would be called on again for this role in 1973, though by this time he was minister of communications. In 1972, Pelletier travelled to Bordeaux to open a school of international management. In 1975, Jean Marchand, a minister without portfolio, headed the delegation to the fourth meeting of l'Agence. When a highway being built with CIDA funds was ready to be opened in Niger in 1976, Jean-Pierre Goyer, the minister of supply and services, did the honours.

After the victory of the Parti Québécois in November 1976, the Trudeau government decided to confer a more official status on what had in effect become a francophone lieutenant for the external affairs minister. In May 1977, Goyer was appointed as "special adviser" to the external affairs minister in the area of "international francophone affairs." The arrangement was maintained during the Clark government in 1979: Martial Asselin, who was responsible for development assistance, assumed that role.

The post was formally institutionalized in January 1982, when Trudeau reorganized the machinery of government and appointed Pierre De Bané as the minister of state (external

35 MacFarlane, *Lapointe.*

36 Gilles Lalande, "La Francophonie et la politique étrangère du Canada," in Paul Painchaud, ed., *De Mackenzie King à Pierre Trudeau: Quarante ans de diplomatie canadienne (1945–1985)* (Québec: Les Presses de l'Université Laval, 1989), 217–48; Jean-Philippe Thérien, "Co-operation and Conflict in la Francophonie," *International Journal* 48:2 (Summer 1993), 492–526.

relations) to "assist" the secretary of state for external affairs "in the conduct of international relations." Charles Lapointe and Jean-Luc Pepin served as ministers of state (external relations) before the portfolio was given full ministerial status in December 1983 as the minister for external relations.

During the Mulroney years, from 1984 to 1993, the minister for external relations was generally the minister responsible for development assistance, discussed below. Responsibility for La Francophonie was given to senior ministers: first Lucien Bouchard and then, after he left the Progressive Conservatives in 1990 to form the Bloc Québécois, the responsibility was passed to Marcel Masse, the minister of communications. It was only in the cabinet shuffle of April 1991, when Masse was appointed as the minister of national defence, that the minister for external relations, Monique Landry, assumed responsibility for La Francophonie.

When André Ouellet was appointed as the minister of foreign affairs in November 1993, the external relations portfolio was left vacant.[37] In 1995, the name of the portfolio was changed to the minister for international cooperation, though the responsibility for La Francophonie was still associated with this new portfolio. In August 1999, a separate designation as minister for La Francophonie was created. Since then, the portfolio has had several names: secretary of state (Francophonie), minister of state (Francophonie); and under the Harper government, it is minister for La Francophonie.

Since 1982, the post has been occupied by a dozen different ministers. Four have been women: Monique Landry and Monique Vézina held the position in the latter years of the Mulroney government; Diane Marleau from 1997 to 1999 in the Chrétien years; and Josée Verner during the Harper government. And while all of those who have served as ministers responsible for La Francophonie were francophones, they were not necessarily from Québec: three of the last seven were from other provinces: Don Boudria and Diane Marleau were franco-Ontarians, and Ronald Duhamel was from Saint-Boniface in Manitoba.

It should be noted that the position of minister for La Francophonie has never been anything other than a second (or even third) portfolio. For example, Josée Verner, Harper's minister for La Francophonie, was also the minister of intergovernmental affairs and the president of the Queen's Privy Council for Canada. While the position was held by senior ministers in the Mulroney period, in most cases, the portfolio was often used as a way of increasing the number of francophones around the cabinet table or as a testing ground for promising backbenchers for other cabinet positions. In general, however, the minister responsible for La Francophonie has only had a limited influence on the formulation of international policy.

The Minister of International Cooperation

At the same time that language was becoming more problematic in foreign policy, other questions were raised about the issue of ministerial responsibility for the Canadian International Development Agency (CIDA). Created in 1968, CIDA was headed by a president, a rank equivalent to deputy minister, who reported to the secretary of state for external affairs. In the late 1970s, there were suggestions that CIDA should be given departmental status,

---

37 The minister for external relations had also been left vacant when Chrétien was appointed as external affairs minister in Turner's government in the summer of 1984, and when Perrin Beatty, who was bilingual, held the external affairs portfolio during Campbell's government in 1993.

with its own minister. Not only would the external affairs minister's workload be considerably reduced, but more importantly, it was argued, development assistance policy would receive different treatment around the cabinet table if there were a minister wholly responsible for CIDA.

The idea was tried by Joe Clark in 1979: Senator Martial Asselin, who had served in Diefenbaker's cabinet in the early 1960s, was made the minister of state responsible for CIDA (and also performed francophone duties for Flora MacDonald, as we noted above). However, this appointment must be seen in the context of the operation of the "federal principle" of Cabinet-making in Canada, the minimum requirement of which is that each province be represented in Cabinet. Clark had just two members of the House of Commons to draw on from Québec, and so sought to increase that province's representation in Cabinet by drawing on members of the Senate (a technique also used in the 1970s by the Liberals, by the Liberals in the 1990s, and the Conservatives in the 2000s). The experiment was as short-lived as the Clark government. CIDA was returned to the external affairs minister after the return of the Liberals in February 1980, and there it would stay until the election of the Mulroney government in 1984.

During the Mulroney period, the minister for external relations was appointed to "assist" the external affairs minister. Thus some responsibility for CIDA was exercised by the external relations minister, although the precise relationship between Clark, as the external affairs minister, and the two external relations ministers, Monique Vézina and Monique Landry, was never clearly articulated. In 1987, the House of Commons Standing Committee on External Affairs and International Trade, chaired by William Winegard, argued that the time had come to do away with the external relations portfolio and appoint a minister for international development whose mandate would be exclusively the "political management" of both CIDA and Canada's development assistance programs.[38] The government came part of the way: In March 1988, it announced that Landry would indeed be delegated more authority over CIDA, a process that, as Andrew Cooper argued, paradoxically contributed to a *reduction* in CIDA's institutional autonomy because it encouraged the "senior" minister, Joe Clark, to exercise tighter control over the "junior" minister.[39]

When Chrétien came to power in 1993, he appointed André Ouellet as foreign minister, but left the external relations portfolio vacant. During his two years in office, Ouellet was the minister for both DFAIT and CIDA, though in 1995, legislation was passed changing the name of the still-vacant position of minister for external relations to minister for international cooperation. In the cabinet shuffle of 25 January 1996 that saw Lloyd Axworthy appointed foreign minister, Pierre Pettigrew was appointed to the newly created post of minister for international cooperation. However, it would appear that Pettigrew's main role was to be Axworthy's "francophone lieutenant."

Thereafter, however, the responsibilities of the minister for international cooperation and the minister for La Francophonie were not as tightly bound as in the earlier period. Some incumbents were given both responsibilities. During the Chrétien years, for example,

---

38 Canada, Parliament, House of Commons, Standing Committee on External Affairs and International Trade, *For Whose Benefit? Report of SCEAIT on Canada's Official Development Assistance Policies and Programs* (Ottawa: May 1987), 114–17; David R. Morrison, *Aid and Ebb Tide: A History of CIDA and Development Assistance* (Waterloo: Wilfrid Laurier University Press, 1998), 277–80.

39 Andrew F. Cooper, *Canadian Foreign Policy: Old Habits and New Directions* (Scarborough: Prentice-Hall Canada, 1997), 232.

Don Boudria and Diane Marleau were both charged with assisting the foreign minister in the area of development assistance and providing support for La Francophonie, while Maria Minna and Susan Whelan concentrated on development assistance alone. During the Martin government, Aileen Carroll focused purely on development assistance; the minister responsible for La Francophonie was Jacques Saada, who held a new portfolio created by Martin, minister of the Economic Development Agency of Canada for the regions of Québec. In the Harper era, Josée Verner, the minister for international cooperation between February 2006 and August 2007, was both responsible for development assistance and the minister responsible for La Francophonie. However, when Verner was moved to intergovernmental affairs and president of the Privy Council in the cabinet shuffle of August 2007, she took her responsibility for La Francophonie with her, leaving Bev Oda to focus purely on development assistance as minister for international cooperation.

Of all the ministerial posts dealing with international policy, the international cooperation portfolio (and its external relations precursor) is the one occupied mostly by women. Eight of the 11 ministers who have occupied this portfolio since 1983—and all six appointees since 1997—have been women. While some might celebrate this as progress in the accessibility of women to cabinet-level positions, we need to put this in perspective. First, like the minister for La Francophonie, the minister for international cooperation is a portfolio of distinctly second rank. Second, the fact that this post in particular was given to women and that comparable progress was not seen in other portfolios tends to perpetuate a kind of gendered division of roles at the highest levels of the state. Portfolios that dealt with conflict (such as national defence, discussed below) were given almost exclusively to men, while portfolios dealing with cooperation were reserved almost exclusively for women and were less prestigious, less influential, and less likely to lead to promotion in Cabinet.[40]

The lack of influence of the minister of international cooperation was explicitly targeted in a 2007 report on the failure of Canadian aid policy in Africa by the Standing Senate Committee on Foreign Affairs and International Trade, chaired by Hugh Segal. Noting with some considerable understatement that "traditionally the minister responsible for CIDA has not been a high profile member of the Cabinet," the report echoed the Winegard committee's report from twenty years earlier and called for the appointment of a senior minister for CIDA who had "clout."[41]

The Minister of International Trade

Historically, international trade has always been crucial to Canada's wealth. Yet this importance has never been reflected in the structures of the Canadian government. For most of Canada's history, responsibility for trade policy was shared among three departments:

---

[40] Of the eight ministers for international cooperation since the portfolio was created in 1996, only one, Pierre Pettigrew, went on to higher positions: after a short stint as Axworthy's francophone lieutenant in 1996, Chrétien appointed him minister of human resources development and then minister of international trade from 1999 to 2003. He went on to serve in the Martin cabinet as minister of health, minister of intergovernmental affairs, and minister for official languages before being named minister of foreign affairs in July 2004.

[41] Canada, Parliament, Standing Senate Committee on Foreign Affairs and International Trade, *Overcoming 40 Years of Failure: A New Road Map for Sub-Saharan Africa* (Ottawa, February 2007), 94.

External Affairs, Finance, and Trade and Commerce. The promotion of external trade fell to the Trade Commissioner Service, which was housed in a "twinned" department—the Department of Trade and Commerce—that was responsible for both the promotion of external trade and domestic commerce (and, after 1969, when the Industry portfolio was merged with Trade and Commerce, industrial development). By the late 1970s, the Department of Industry, Trade and Commerce (IT&C) was responsible for a wide array of policy areas, such as tourism, business development, international trade policy, export promotion, international marketing, and domestic industrial design.

Throughout the 1970s the government in Ottawa struggled with attempts to create an "industrial policy" for Canada and at the same time sought—without success—to diversify the patterns of Canada's international trade. There was little consideration given to the creation of a separate bureaucratic structure with its own minister and the capacity for centralized coordination of international economic policy. In part, this was because of the nature of Canadian federalism, with jurisdiction over economic issues shared between the provinces and the central government, and in part because of the political bureaucratic strength of the existing departments in Ottawa that loosely shared responsibility for international economic policy. Nonetheless, by the early 1980s, marked by recession and increasing protectionism in the United States, the necessity of major bureaucratic reform became evident.

The Clark government was the first to experiment with giving international trade its own minister. Michael Wilson was appointed to assist the minister of industry, trade, and commerce in the area of international trade. Wilson was given the title minister of state for international trade. When Trudeau and the Liberals were returned to power in February 1980, the experiment was continued: Ed Lumley was named as the minister of state (trade) to assist the minister of industry, trade, and commerce.

In January 1982, Trudeau reorganized the major economic departments of government. As we will see in the next chapter, the foreign policy bureaucracy was also included in this reorganization. There were changes at the ministerial level as well. The trade side of Industry, Trade and Commerce was amalgamated into the Department of External Affairs, which was now presided over by the secretary of state for external affairs. However, rather than add further responsibilities to the external affairs minister, a minister of state (international trade) was appointed to assist the external affairs minister in the trade area. In 1983, the portfolio was renamed yet again, to the minister for international trade. That position continues to the present.

When the international trade portfolio first evolved in the late 1970s and early 1980s, it was considered a subordinate position, reflected not only in the subordinate title "minister of state" and then minister *for* (rather than minister *of*), but also in the language of the Orders-in-Council and the legislation that assigned to the incumbent the role of "assisting" more senior ministers. However, the portfolio quickly acquired a greater importance once the decision was made to seek a free-trade agreement with the United States: in June 1986, Pat Carney, a senior minister, was appointed to the portfolio and given the responsibility of managing the free-trade negotiations. Since then, those who have occupied this portfolio have generally been influential and senior members of the governing party: John Crosbie (1988–1991), Michael Wilson (1991–1993), Arthur Eggleton (1996–1997), Pierre Pettigrew (1999–2003), Jim Peterson (2003–2006), and Stockwell Day, who was appointed to the portfolio in October 2008.

Ministers of State

On November 4, 1993, Prime Minister Jean Chrétien announced his new cabinet, and at the same time announced a major reorganization of the Canadian cabinet structure that embraced the practice well-established in countries such as Britain and Australia of distinguishing between the *ministry* and the *cabinet*. Chrétien appointed a ministry of 30: 22 of those ministers would be members of the cabinet; eight other ministers were appointed as members of the ministry and thus bound by the principle of collective responsibility but were not members of the cabinet. The new positions were styled "secretary of state."[42]

This reorganization had an impact in the foreign affairs portfolio. Three of the eight secretaries of state were positions relating to international policy. To assist the minister of foreign affairs, Raymond Chan was appointed secretary of state (Asia-Pacific), and Christine Stewart was named secretary of state (Latin America and Africa). To assist the minister of finance, Douglas Peters was appointed secretary of state (international financial institutions). In 2002, a third regional position was created: Gar Knutson was appointed as secretary of state (Central and Eastern Europe and Middle East).

The practice of naming secretaries of state was abandoned by Paul Martin when he came to office in December 2003. Not only was the old style—minister of state—reintroduced, but Martin included had a ministry of equivalent size: 39; a large number of ministers of state were included, but the only one who had international policy responsibilities was Gar Knutson, named minister of state (new and emerging markets) and assigned to assist the minister of international trade. When Stephen Harper appointed his cabinet in 2006, he brought back the practice introduced by Chrétien: as of 2009, his cabinet had 27 ministers and his ministry included the full ministers and 11 ministers of state, some of whom were styled "secretary of state." After the 2008 election, Harper abandoned the secretary of state designation in favour of minister of state. One of these was a foreign affairs portfolio: Peter Kent was appointed minister of state of foreign affairs (Americas).[43]

The secretaries of state and ministers of state performed many of those functions that would normally have been done by the minister. In particular, those with regional responsibilities often travelled to different parts of the world to represent the minister of foreign affairs, and thus in that sense gave the minister the ability to be in several places at once. They gave speeches outlining Canadian policy in those regions. They worked with the Standing Committee on Foreign Affairs and International Trade of the House of Commons when explored issues fell into their regional bailiwicks. Within Canada, they were responsible for dealing with domestic groups that had an interest in Canadian relations with the region.

CABINET INVOLVEMENT IN INTERNATIONAL POLICY

In theory, cabinet is a group of ministers who collectively decide policy for the Canadian state. As an institution, the cabinet derives its importance and legitimacy from the fact that its members are broadly representative of the country as a whole, even if they might have

---

42 Legally, each secretary of state was appointed as "minister of state to assist," since legislation was never introduced to create this position.

43 In addition, there were two cabinet ministers who were also ministers of state: Jean-Pierre Blackburn was minister of national revenue and was also minister of state (agriculture); Marjory LeBreton was government leader in the Senate and also minister of state (seniors).

very diverse points of view, depending on their portfolios, the region of the country they represent, and their own political orientations. However, in the case of international policy, it is difficult to ascertain to what extent practice has mirrored theory. In the first place, it is clear that the major policy decisions that have confronted Canadian governments over the past century have been put before cabinet for discussion and resolution. In such cases, cabinet ministers deliberated. To what extent the outcome of decisions was influenced by individual members is difficult to know—in part because of the shrouds of cabinet secrecy, and in part because of the discretion that politicians have shown when they write their memoirs.

Second, there are a number of occasions when important issues of international policy have been decisioned without discussion by the full cabinet. In the summer of 1957, John G. Diefenbaker, who at the time was also external affairs minister, approved the signing of the NORAD agreement on the advice of George Pearkes, his minister of national defence, and the chairman of the chiefs of staff, General Charles Foulkes[44]; during the Cuban missile crisis, Diefenbaker made numerous decisions without informing his cabinet colleagues.[45] Pearson and his external affairs minister, Paul Martin, Sr., frequently would make foreign policy decisions on their own and inform their cabinet colleagues ex post facto, much to the chagrin of at least one of their number, Pierre Elliott Trudeau.[46]

Indeed, it was Trudeau's experience in the Pearson cabinet that prompted him to reform the cabinet structure in the late 1960s. These reforms were designed to promote more active cabinet deliberation on all policy issues. Issues were to be dealt with by cabinet committees that were empowered to take autonomous decisions, which were then circulated to all ministers. Only if there were objections would an issue be discussed in the weekly plenary cabinet meeting. Thus, throughout the Trudeau years, a cabinet committee on foreign policy and defence was responsible for discussing foreign policy decisions. Mulroney began by eliminating the cabinet committee on foreign policy and defence, but only temporarily: a year later, a committee was reestablished.[47] When Chrétien came to office in 1993 and reduced the number of cabinet committees from 15 to just four, the cabinet committee on foreign affairs did not survive. However, after the attacks of 9/11, a new ad hoc cabinet committee on public security and anti-terrorism was created. Chaired by John Manley, first as foreign minister and then as deputy prime minister, the committee included the president of the Privy Council, the solicitor general, and the ministers of national defence, finance, immigration, justice, transport, customs, and revenue.

The cabinet committee structure introduced by Stephen Harper in 2006 created eight committees, several of which deal with international policy. These included priorities and

---

44 Jon B. McLin, *Canada's Changing Defense Policy, 1957–1963* (Toronto: Copp Clark, 1967), 43–46.

45 Peyton V. Lyon, *Canada in World Affairs*, vol. 12: *1961–1963* (Toronto: Oxford University Press, 1968), 32–47, esp. 37, n55.

46 Bruce Thordarson, *Trudeau and Foreign Policy: A Study in Decision-Making* (Toronto: Oxford University Press, 1972).

47 For the fall and rise of the cabinet committee on foreign policy and defence, see John Kirton, "The Foreign Policy Decision Process," in Maureen Appel Molot and Brian W. Tomlin, eds., *Canada Among Nations 1985: The Conservative Agenda* (Toronto: James Lorimer, 1986), 25–46.

planning, operations, foreign affairs and security, environment and energy security, and the cabinet committee on Afghanistan. Two had explicitly international mandates. The cabinet committee on foreign affairs coordinated all aspects of international policy: foreign affairs, international development, defence, and public and national security. It was chaired by the minister of national defence, Peter MacKay, and included the minister of international cooperation, Bev Oda; the minister of veterans affairs, Gregory Thompson; the minister of foreign affairs, Lawrence Cannon; the minister of justice, Rob Nicholson; and the minister of public safety, Peter Van Loan. In addition, Gail Shea, minister of fisheries and oceans; Rob Merrifield, the minister of state (transport); Peter Kent, the minister of state of foreign affairs (Americas); and Gordon O'Connor, a minister of state who had been minister of national defence, served on the committee. The other committee with international policy responsibilities was the cabinet committee on Afghanistan, which was established in order to coordinate all aspects of Canada's mission in Afghanistan. It was chaired by the minister of international trade, Stockwell Day, with the minister of international cooperation as vice-chair, and also included the foreign minister, the defence minister, and the minister of public safety, Peter Van Loan.

A cabinet committee system is designed to encourage collegial participation in foreign policymaking. In practice, however, the very nature of international policy makes decision-making exercised once a week difficult. There are occasions when international negotiations will not wait and when decisions on tactics must be made quickly. Most important international events require a quick response from Ottawa, usually precluding the possibility of calling the cabinet together. Certainly that was the case in the days following Iraq's invasion of Kuwait in August 1990. The key ministers were away from Ottawa, and by the time they could be called back to the capital for a cabinet meeting, Mulroney had flown to Washington for a meeting with Bush and over dinner pledged Canada's support for the multilateral coalition being organized by the president.[48] Likewise, as we saw in Chapter 6, when Jean Chrétien needed to respond to the news that the United States had decided to revise its Kyoto targets on greenhouse gas emissions, an immediate decision was required.

Moreover, foreign policy decisions, particularly in the area of trade and development assistance, are frequently marked by considerable technical detail. Ministers, already hard pressed to fulfil the responsibilities of their own portfolios, are unlikely to find the time necessary to master the intricacies of another minister's portfolio. Deference to the responsible minister's recommendations follows naturally. Finally, ministers quickly discover how their "collegial involvement" in another minister's portfolio frequently breeds "interference" by other ministers in their own department's affairs. They quickly realize that the most effective way to protect their department's policy "turf" is to resist the temptation to tread into another minister's bailiwick. It is for these reasons that the prime minister or the ministers directly responsible are likely to exert the most influence in major decisions affecting Canadian foreign policy.

---

48 Andrew F. Cooper, Richard A. Higgott, and Kim Richard Nossal, *Relocating Middle Powers: Australia and Canada in a Changing World Order* (Vancouver: University of British Columbia Press, 1993), 128.

CONCLUSION

In 2010, the decision-making structures for international policy had evolved considerably from the days in the 1920s when Mackenzie King could make foreign policy by scrawling "I agree" on a memorandum from his undersecretary of state for external affairs. The circle of ministerial decision widened as the volume, scope, and complexity of the business of international policy widened, and as the state grew in size and complexity to meet these demands. However, there are limits to such expansion. The imperatives of summitry and the importance of personal involvement in diplomacy are no less important today than they were in the 1920s. For all of the increased institutionalization and bureaucratization, the importance of those at the apex of the decision-making system has not diminished markedly.

CHAPTER 9

The International Policy Bureaucracy

As we have seen in the previous chapters, the authority to make international policy resides in the hands of the prime minister and other ministers in cabinet. However, the process of decision-making will always be affected by those agencies of the state created to implement political decisions. But bureaucracies do more than merely implement decisions and administer programs. A bureaucracy's functions include the provision of policy information and advice to elected leaders, and therein lies a source of potent influence over the shaping of policy decisions. The purpose of this chapter is to examine the international policy bureaucracy and its impact on policymaking.

The "international policy bureaucracy" in Canada defies easy identification. Usually, one department can claim to be the pivotal point for advising on and implementing a country's international policy—the foreign ministry. We must therefore begin with the Department of Foreign Affairs and International Trade. But it should be remembered that there are few government agencies whose programs or activities do not have at least peripheral international ramifications. Over 30 federal departments, agencies, or Crown corporations have jurisdiction over policy issues with an international focus; in addition, as we will see in Chapters 11 and 12, many provinces have developed bureaucracies for the conduct of their own international activities.

ORGANIZING FOR FOREIGN AFFAIRS

"A foreign office," James Eayrs has written, "while not necessarily a frill of government, is an optional part of the state apparatus."[1] At least one Canadian prime minister has agreed: in 1980, Pierre Elliott Trudeau asserted that "Traditional concepts of foreign service have diminished relevance in an era of instantaneous, world–wide communications, in which there is increasing reliance on personal contacts between senior members of governments, and in which international relations are concerned with progressively more complex and technical questions."[2]

There is little doubt that, as Trudeau stated, technology has changed how diplomacy is practised, but it certainly has not changed the purpose of diplomacy, nor reduced its utility. Nor has the massive increase in the summit diplomacy discussed in Chapter 7 eliminated the need for a professional foreign service to conduct diplomatic relations when the heads of government have returned to their capitals. And, judging by the pervasiveness of the institution, few governments in contemporary world politics have regarded a foreign ministry as an "optional" agency. On the contrary: Virtually every government has created an agency whose officials are responsible for six key functions: representing the state abroad; providing information, intelligence, and assessments of politics in other countries; providing advice to political leaders on international policy; conducting negotiations with other governments; providing services to citizens abroad; and advancing the interests of their state in the international system.

The primary task of diplomacy is to achieve a state's international policy goals by peaceful means. Whether the objectives are parochial (securing concessions in a trade treaty) or wide-ranging (avoiding

---

1 James Eayrs, "Canada: the Department of External Affairs," in Zara Steiner, ed., *The Times Survey of Foreign Ministries of the World* (London: Times Books, 1982), 96.

2 Trudeau, in his letter of instruction to Pamela McDougall establishing the Royal Commission on Conditions of Foreign Service, August 28, 1980; reprinted in Canada, Royal Commission on Conditions of Foreign Service, *Report* (Ottawa, 1981), viii.

the outbreak of systemic war), diplomacy will be an indispensable tool to achieve them. A government needs negotiators and interlocutors who have the skill to move others to positions closer to its own interests by a judicious mix of coercion, inducement, and persuasion. Indeed, for states such as Canada, with limited capabilities, a dependence on persuasion means that a foreign service will be one of the most potent power resources to achieve its objectives. On those issues over which smaller states have little control—systemic peace or war, or relations between the great powers—diplomacy assumes a special importance. The art of facilitating dialogue between the great powers, of defusing tension, and of encouraging calm, moderation, and compromise, is all too often the only means at the disposal of a non-great power. And such efforts are impossible without a professional organization that can act continuously to give expression to both the broad and narrow interests of a state.

In Canada, the necessity of such an agency emerged only slowly. From 1867 onward, there was a steady growth in the bureaucracy devoted to international policy. Four broad periods can be identified. The first extended from Confederation to the establishment of the Department of External Affairs in 1909. The second covered the first three decades of the department, characterized, until the Second World War, by a certain modesty. The third period mirrors what is often called the "golden age of Canadian foreign policy"—from 1945 until the mid-1960s, a period marked by rapid and continuous expansion. The final period began with the election of Pierre Elliott Trudeau in 1968—it was marked by a continuing series of departmental reorganizations that continue today, more than forty years after they began.

The Early Years: 1867–1909

When the new Canadian government was organized in 1867, a foreign ministry was not considered a frill; it was not even contemplated. British and Canadians alike regarded the international policy of the Empire as indivisible. The new dominion might be self-governing, but only in matters of domestic and local politics. Because global policies of the Empire were made by the Imperial authorities, responsibility for the conduct of Canada's relations with the world rested with the government in London. Such an arrangement was acceptable to both the British and Canadians—at least at the outset.[3] Wishing neither full independence nor complete colonial subordination, Canadians were prepared to live with the ambiguity of what Sir Richard Cartwright called Canada's "tadpole sort of existence."[4] Moreover, there were distinct advantages to be gained from "drawing on British prestige and powers of enforcement, at no cost to Canada."[5]

However, the necessity of establishing separate diplomatic relations ended up prevailing. On matters that necessitated communication with other states and a physical presence abroad (such as attracting immigrants; settling boundaries, fisheries, and trade issues with the United States; or promoting trade with Europe), the government in Ottawa found itself drawn into diplomatic relations. The formal process was cumbersome, because the Empire

---

3 G.P. de T. Glazebrook, *A History of Canadian External Relations*, rev. ed., vol. 1: *The Formative Years to 1914* (Toronto: McClelland & Stewart Limited, 1966), 85.

4 Quoted in H. Gordon Skilling, *Canadian Representation Abroad: From Agency to Embassy* (Toronto: Ryerson, 1945), 186.

5 John Hilliker, *Canada's Department of External Affairs*, vol. 1: *The Early Years, 1909–1946* (Montréal and Kingston: McGill-Queen's University Press, 1990), 17.

was considered a single and indivisible sovereign. If the Canadian government wished to communicate with the United States, for example, the cabinet would have to route correspondence through the British governor general in Ottawa, who would then send it to London where it would be processed through the Colonial Office and then the Foreign Office, which would then send it to the British ambassador in Washington for presentation to the United States Department of State. To be sure, there were modifications to this in practice. The British, having little wish to handle the day-to-day practicalities of Canadian trade, allowed Ottawa to conduct its own commercial diplomacy. Trade negotiations "came to be direct in all but form, and the Canadians associated in them corresponded directly with the prime minister."[6]

In the beginning, Canadian officials were sent abroad to increase immigration into what was then a largely empty country and to increase trade. In 1868, the Dominion Agency for Emigration was opened in London, and in the 1870s, no fewer than 12 Immigration Offices were established from Antwerp to Worcester. Likewise, the requisites of trade prompted the opening of a worldwide network of trade commissions, and by 1907, 12 offices had been established abroad. "Commercial agents"—they were renamed "trade commissioners" in 1907—were located in Sydney, Cape Town, Mexico City, Yokohama, and a number of European and American cities by the turn of the century.[7] In 1880, a high commissioner was appointed to London, and, two years later, the federal government asked Hector Fabre, who was the Québec government's agent in Paris, to act in a similar capacity for Ottawa. While these officials were agents of the Canadian state abroad, they were not diplomats in anything but the most superficial sense. They were not accorded diplomatic status; nor, importantly, were they representatives of a sovereign government with an independent international personality, capable of conducting an independent foreign policy.

Canada's experience in this period demonstrates why Eayrs's claim that "Any government could conduct its foreign affairs without a ministry created expressly for that purpose" is so problematic. A state's leaders, Eayrs argues, "could rely instead upon their own resources and those of their staffs to supervise and coordinate departments of trade, defence, immigration, agriculture, fisheries and any others doing the country's business abroad, resorting again to their own resources to attend to any residue that might show up as 'foreign policy' pure if not so simple."[8] Perhaps Eayrs had these formative years in mind, for this is precisely how Canada conducted its foreign relations until the First World War. The emphasis was on "ad hocery." Relations with other states were carried on by different cabinet ministers and senior officials depending on the issue; portfolios did not always determine which minister would be involved. For example, when the Liberal government of Sir Wilfrid Laurier wanted to impose restrictions on immigration from Japan, it sent the postmaster general, Rodolphe Lemieux, and the undersecretary of state, Joseph Pope, to Tokyo in 1907 to negotiate with the Japanese government.[9]

---

6 Glazebrook, *Canadian External Relations*, vol. 1, 201.

7 O. Mary Hill, *Canada's Salesman to the World: The Department of Trade and Commerce, 1892–1939* (Montréal and Kingston: McGill-Queen's University Press, 1977); also Royal Commission on Conditions of Foreign Service, *Report*, table FST-2, 95–105.

8 Eayrs, "Canada: External Affairs," 96.

9 Hilliker, *Canada's Department of External Affairs*, vol. 1, 27; see also James Eayrs, "The Origins of Canada's Department of External Affairs," *Canadian Journal of Economics and Political Science* 25 (May 1959), 114–5.

Indeed, at times foreign relations were conducted by individuals who were not even in government: George Brown, proprietor of the Toronto *Globe*, negotiated a draft treaty with the United States in 1874; Sanford Fleming, the surveyor of the Canadian Pacific Railway, represented Canada at the 1887 Colonial Conference in London.[10] Nor was there a centralized system of record-keeping, so that correspondence on a variety of international subjects was scattered among different departments in Ottawa. Pope, conducting emigration talks in Japan in 1907, complained that if it had not been for the records kept by the British embassy in Tokyo, Canada's negotiating position with the Japanese government would have been untenable.[11]

This system survived until the turn of the century. "The machinery creaked," Glazebrook observed, "but on the whole it served the purpose."[12] However, it became increasingly clear that it was a less than efficient way of conducting foreign relations. For example, the high commission in London served as a base for officials from six different departments but there was no centralized control. "You will readily recognize," the high commissioner, Sir George Perley, wrote to Prime Minister Robert Borden in 1914, "that the situation is not conducive to good business and often produces overlapping and is very awkward."[13]

Modest Beginnings: 1909–1939

While this system had evolved because of the need to maintain imperial unity, the British, who had to carry much of the administrative load of Canada's foreign relations, came to be less than satisfied with the arrangement. Earl Grey, one of the few Governors General sent to Ottawa by Britain who took an interest in Canada's relations with other countries, made the creation of a Canadian department responsible for the conduct of foreign affairs one of his objectives.[14] Some officials in Ottawa were less than taken with such enthusiasms. Mackenzie King, at the time a senior official, confided to his diary that "The truth is His Ex. is getting into too many things"; for his part, Sir Wilfrid Laurier, the prime minister, "wished Earl Grey would mind his own business."[15] However, Grey pressed on. In 1908, he complained to the colonial secretary in London that negotiations with the United States were not proceeding smoothly because of the "chaotic conditions of the Administration here *qua* External Affairs. There is no Department, no official through whose hands all matters dealing with external affairs must go. Consequently there is no record, no continuity, no method, no consistency." He concluded by offering his opinions on Ottawa's bureaucratic expertise in international affairs at that time: "We have only three. One drinks at times, the other has a difficulty in expressing his thoughts and the third is the Under Secretary of State, Pope—a really first class official."[16]

---

10 C.P. Stacey, *Canada and the Age of Conflict: A History of Canadian External Policies*, vol. 1: *1867–1921* (Toronto: Macmillan of Canada, 1977), 30–1 and 45.

11 Eayrs, "Origins of External Affairs," 114–5.

12 Glazebrook, *Canadian External Relations*, vol. 1., 84.

13 Canada, Department of External Affairs, *Documents on Canadian External Relations*, vol. 1: *1909–1918* (Ottawa, 1967), 18.

14 Hilliker, *Canada's Department of External Affairs*, vol. 1, 32.

15 Eayrs, "Origins of External Affairs," 116, n22.

16 Eayrs, "Origins of External Affairs," 117.

Joseph Pope had been involved in Canada's international relations since the early 1880s and was a leading proponent in Ottawa of a separate foreign ministry for Canada. But it was not until Grey and James Bryce, the British ambassador in Washington, had added their voices to Pope's that Laurier agreed to create a foreign ministry. The new Department of External Affairs (DEA) was created by statute in 1909; as we saw in the previous chapter, the word "external" was chosen because the "affairs" related as much to Britain and to the various parts of the Empire as they did to other states, and these were not "foreign" countries. Pope was appointed as the department's deputy minister (his official title was undersecretary of state for external affairs), and, with a budget of $14,950, two clerks, a secretary, and temporary offices over a barber shop in the Trafalgar Building at the corner of Bank and Queen streets, he began a 16-year superintendency over the new department.[17] At first DEA was put under the authority of the secretary of state—Charles Murphy, and then William J. Roche—but Pope regularly bypassed his minister and dealt directly with the prime minister. In 1912, at the urging of Grey, the newly elected prime minister, Robert Borden, introduced legislation that made the prime minister the secretary of state for external affairs by law.[18]

The department's modest resources did not change much until the outbreak of the Second World War. When Pope retired in 1925, the prime minister, Mackenzie King, appointed O.D. Skelton, a professor of political science and dean of arts at Queen's University, as undersecretary. Skelton, in turn, recruited what J.L. Granatstein has termed "an extraordinary crew of well-educated and well-trained young officers,"[19] among them Hugh Keenleyside, Lester B. Pearson, Hume Wrong, and Norman Robertson. (By the 1950s, these "young officers" had transformed DEA and the Canadian foreign service into what one British diplomat would praise as "an elite organization of high quality.")[20]

In the interwar years, External Affairs had such a small staff that it did not need an organization chart; instead the officers were assigned tasks on an ad hoc basis. Officials in the East Block of the Parliament buildings, where External had moved after the prime minister took the department over in 1912, were given "dockets" to cover as the need arose. For example, at one point early in his career, Pearson's caseload included dockets on lighthouses in the Red Sea, aviation licences in Canada and Switzerland, international tariffs on cement, and the protection of young female artists travelling abroad.[21] This way of organizing the department's work was maintained throughout the interwar years.

It was during this period that Canada's representation abroad starting growing. The trade commissioner service continued to expand: more than 50 Canadian trade offices abroad were opened between 1907 and 1939. However, only three diplomatic missions

---

17 James Eayrs, *The Art of the Possible: Government and Foreign Policy in Canada* (Toronto: University of Toronto Press, 1961), 66.

18 Hilliker, *Canada's Department of External Affairs*, vol. 1, 58–59; Eayrs, "Origins of External Affairs," 119–21; *Documents on Canadian External Relations*, vol. 1, 12.

19 J.L. Granatstein, *A Man of Influence: Norman A. Robertson and Canadian Statecraft, 1929–68* (Toronto: Deneau Publishers, 1981), 33.

20 Lord Garner, "Comments on Report on Conditions of Foreign Service," *International Journal* 37:3 (Summer 1982), 390.

21 See Hugh L. Keenleyside, *Memoirs of Hugh L. Keenleyside*, vol. 1: *Hammer the Golden Day* (Toronto: McClelland & Stewart, 1981), 233.

were opened after the Imperial Conference of 1926 that allowed the self-governing dominions to conduct separate diplomatic relations. In February 1927, Vincent Massey became
Canada's first diplomatic representative to the United States, although with the relatively
low rank of minister, not ambassador; in 1928, the office in Paris was given diplomatic status; and in 1929, a mission was opened in Tokyo.[22] In addition, W.A. Riddell was
appointed the Canadian Advisory Officer to the League of Nations in December 1924. Two
missions were opened after the Depression: in December 1938, Canadian diplomats were
sent to Belgium and the Netherlands.

Expansion: 1939–1968

The outbreak of the Second World War in September 1939 forced the Canadian government to reconsider its approach to international relations. Diplomatic posts were opened in
those states considered important to the war effort: Australia, New Zealand, South Africa,
and Ireland. Within three years, diplomatic relations had been established with allied gov-
ernments-in-exile in London; with Argentina, Brazil, Chile, China, and the Soviet Union;
and with Newfoundland (which was a British possession before it joined Canada in
1949).[23] The wartime expansion of the foreign service was matched by a growth of staff in
Ottawa, as the small contingent from the interwar years was augmented by temporary
wartime appointments, mainly drawn from the universities.

The expansion continued after the war. Canada's commitment to internationalism led
the government to join more than 200 international organizations, virtually all of them
requiring a Canadian representative. The expansion of Canadian representation abroad was
also accelerated by decolonization in the 1950s and 1960s, which increased the number of
sovereign states in the international system. The commitment to internationalist engagement prompted the government in Ottawa to look favourably on opening diplomatic relations with many of the newly independent states. The numbers suggest the scale of the
increase: in 1945, Canada maintained 22 diplomatic missions abroad; by 1970, this number had grown to 101. While there were 67 members of the foreign service in 1946, by
1970, that number had grown to 725.[24]

Another measure of growth was the increasing complexity of the department, requiring more orthodox methods of bureaucratic organization. By 1945, the internal organization of the department was marked by institutionalized divisions responsible for
diverse aspects of DEA's work. There were three "political" divisions, four functional
divisions (legal, treaty, economic, information), and an administrative section.[25] Over
the next twenty-five years, those eight divisions would grow, by fission and conjugation,

---

22 Hilliker, *Canada's Department of External Affairs*, vol. 1, chap. 7; Stacey, *Age of Conflict*, vol. 1,
311–17; Skilling, *Canadian Representation Abroad*, chap. 5, 236–37.

23 Department of External Affairs, *Documents on Canadian External Relations*, vol. 6: *1936–1939*,
John A. Munro, ed. (Ottawa, 1972); ibid., vol. 7: *1939–1941, Part 1*, David R. Murray, ed. (Ottawa,
1974); Skilling, *Canadian Representation Abroad*, 249–54.

24 Department of External Affairs, *Annual Report 1970* (Ottawa: 1971).

25 The political divisions were unimaginatively titled Political I, II, and III. Political I was responsible
for international organizations; Political II for the Commonwealth, Europe, Africa, and the Middle
East; and Political III for the United States, Latin America, and the Far East.

to 71 administrative, managerial, functional, and geographic units.[26] Indeed, by the late 1960s, External Affairs had grown so large that it had spilled out of the East Block on Parliament Hill into a dozen office buildings dotted around downtown Ottawa. Eventually, in 1973, the department moved into its present home, the Lester B. Pearson Building, on Sussex Drive.

Down to the late 1960s, the bureaucratic organization for Canada's international policy relations reflected a continuing division of bureaucratic labour. External Affairs was responsible for Canada's diplomacy, diplomatic relations with other states, and representing Canada in international organizations. The Department of Trade and Commerce continued to manage the promotion of external trade, expanding further its global network of offices encouraging trade opportunities.[27] Controlling the movement of people into Canada initially fell under the domain of the Department of Mines and Resources. After 1950, it was the responsibility of Citizenship and Immigration, and finally, in 1966, an expanded Manpower and Immigration.[28] Finance was constantly involved, not only in the evaluation and approval of government spending on Canada's new commitments, but also in international monetary affairs.[29]

Responsibility for international security policy fell to several agencies. The Department of National Defence and Canada's armed forces were responsible for Canada's "defence," broadly conceived. This included the twin commitments to the North Atlantic Treaty Organization (NATO) and the North American Air Defence command (NORAD), the growing commitment to international peacekeeping and truce supervision, and maritime and Arctic security.[30]

A new bureaucracy evolved to administer a related aspect of Canada's international security policy. No sooner had the Second World War ended than Canadians were introduced to the world of espionage. On September 6, 1945, Igor Gouzenko, a cypher clerk at the Soviet embassy in Ottawa, defected, bringing with him evidence of the existence of large-scale espionage activities being conducted by the Soviet Union and directed at Canada's atomic research.[31] Catalyzed by evidence of Soviet espionage, the Royal Canadian

---

26   For a visual comparison, see the organization charts for 1952 and 1968 reproduced in Hilliker and Barry, *Canada's Department of External Affairs*, 414–415.

27   Glen Williams, *Not For Export: Towards a Political Economy of Canada's Arrested Industrialization* (Toronto: McClelland & Stewart Limited, 1983), 157–61; Michael Hart, *A Trading Nation: Canadian Trade Policy from Colonialism to* (Vancouver: UBC Press, 2003).

28   Freda Hawkins, *Canada and Immigration: Public Policy and Public Concern* (Montréal: McGill-Queen's University Press, 1972), 237–65.

29   A.F.W. Plumptre, *Three Decades of Decision: Canada and the World Monetary System, 1944–1975* (Toronto: McClelland & Stewart, 1977).

30   See James Eayrs, *In Defence of Canada*, vol. 1: *From the Great War to the Great Depression* (Toronto: University of Toronto Press, 1964), vol. 2: *Appeasement and Rearmament* (Toronto: University of Toronto Press, 1965); postwar roles are discussed in vol. 3: *Peacemaking and Deterrence* (Toronto: University of Toronto Press, 1972) and vol. 4: *Growing Up Allied* (Toronto: University of Toronto Press, 1980). D.W. Middlemiss and J.J. Sokolsky, *Canadian Defence: Decisions and Determinants* (Toronto: Harcourt Brace Jovanovich, 1989); David B. Dewitt and David Leyton-Brown, eds., *Canada's International Security Policy* (Scarborough, ON: Prentice-Hall Canada, 1995)

31   For a good overview, see Denis Smith, *Diplomacy of Fear: Canada and the Cold War, 1941–1948* (Toronto: University of Toronto Press, 1988), 94–109. For primary materials, see J.W. Pickersgill and

Mounted Police (RCMP) rapidly developed an intelligence, countersubversion, and counterespionage capacity. Unlike the agencies of other powers,[32] the RCMP Security Service was not an "offensive" intelligence agency: It conducted no covert operations outside Canada. But its domestic operations were an integral part of Canada's external alignments.[33] It eventually evolved into a separate agency, the Canadian Security Intelligence Service (CSIS).[34] Linked to this development was the evolution of a capacity to collect signals intelligence. In collaboration with the United States, Britain, Australia, and New Zealand, a unit of the National Research Council—with the ambiguous name "Examination Unit"— was given the task of intercepting Soviet communications. This unit evolved into the Communications Branch of NRC and then, in 1975, into the Communications Security Establishment, a bureau so secret that the government refused to even acknowledge its existence until 1983.[35] Similarly, the demands of the Cold War prompted the Canadian Broadcasting Corporation to create an International Service, whose mission included propaganda activities in Eastern Europe.[36]

Another new bureaucracy developed to administer the development assistance program inaugurated under the Colombo Plan in 1950, discussed in Chapter 2. At first, the foreign aid program was administered by the International Economic and Technical Co-operation Division (IETCD) of the Department of Trade and Commerce, created in 1951. IETCD's growth throughout the 1950s mirrored the increasing complexity of the development assistance program. In 1960, it was taken out of Trade and Commerce and given a separate existence as the External Aid Office. Headed by an official from External Affairs, the EAO was a "semi-autonomous" agency, reporting to the external affairs minister.[37]

By the end of the 1960s, a complex apparatus for the conduct of international policy had developed. In a generation, the bureaucratic landscape had changed dramatically. The Department of External Affairs had undergone a massive transformation, growing in size

---

D.F. Forster, *The Mackenzie King Record,* vol. 3: *1945–1946* (Toronto: University of Toronto Press, 1970), chap. 2; Robert Bothwell and J.L. Granatstein, eds., *The Gouzenko Transcripts: The Evidence Presented to the Kellock-Taschereau Royal Commission of 1946* (Ottawa: Deneau, 1982).

32 Such as the Central Intelligence Agency (CIA) in the United States, Britain's Secret Intelligence Service (or MI6), the Direction générale de la sécurité extérieure (DGSE) in France, or the SVR (Sluzhba Vneshney Razvedki, Foreign Intelligence Service) in the Russian Federation or the KGB (Komitet Gosudarstvennoye Bezopastnosti, Committee for State Security) in the former Soviet Union.

33 John Sawatsky, *Men in the Shadows: The RCMP Security Service* (Toronto: Doubleday Canada, 1980).

34 Canada, Commission of Inquiry Concerning Certain Activities of the Royal Canadian Mounted Police, *Second Report,* vol. 1: *Freedom and Security Under the Law* (Ottawa: August, 1981), 62–63; John Sawatsky, *Men in the Shadows: The RCMP Security Service* (Toronto: Doubleday Canada, 1980).

35 Stuart Farson, "Accountable and Prepared? Reorganizing Canada's Intelligence Community for the 21st Century," *Canadian Foreign Policy* 1 (Fall 1993), 48.

36 Hilliker and Barry, *Canada's Department of External Affairs,* vol. 2, 73–74.

37 David R. Morrison, *Aid and Ebb Tide: A History of CIDA and Development Assistance* (Waterloo, ON: Wilfrid Laurier University Press, 1998), 27–56; also Keith Spicer, *A Samaritan State? External Aid in Canada's Foreign Policy* (Toronto: University of Toronto Press, 1966).

and complexity: between 1962 and 1967, the department had grown by 50 percent.[38] Likewise, the departments responsible for the oldest external functions of the Canadian state—trade and immigration—had expanded their operations. Old bureaus with new international policy mandates and new agencies created to administer new external policy missions crowded the field.

Ironically, by the late 1960s, the bureaucracy responsible for Canada's international policy had come to resemble the early years. Numerous agencies were involved in the formulation and execution of different aspects of foreign policy. Not only did External Affairs, Trade and Commerce, and Manpower and Immigration each maintain a separate foreign service, but federal programs were also being delivered by numerous other departments represented abroad. In 1969, 1030 officials from 19 federal agencies served in missions abroad, not including Canadian Forces personnel serving in Europe or the United States.[39] While a number of interdepartmental committees tried to coordinate the efforts of these agencies, and while External Affairs exercised a broad leadership role, in the main each department went about its business within its own policy sphere largely resistant to central coordinative tendencies.[40]

The Trudeau Years: 1968–1984

In the year before Pierre Elliott Trudeau was elected as leader of the Liberal party, he had served in Lester Pearson's cabinet and had increasingly chafed at what he believed was an untidy and poorly organized state apparatus. When he assumed the prime ministership in 1968, Trudeau was determined to change the system. This proved to be a Sisyphean task: The next fifteen years were marked by what Denis Stairs has called the Trudeau government's "relentless preoccupation . . . with refining the administrative machine"[41] in hopes of eliminating the untidiness. Throughout this period, the prime minister and his officials in the Privy Council Office and the Prime Minister's Office tinkered with Canada's international policy bureaucracy in order to bring an end to what was seen as bureaucratic disorder bred by two decades of growth and diversification.

The Denigration of External Affairs, 1968–1970

Trudeau's first target was the special position of the Department of External Affairs. The department had always enjoyed a close relationship with the prime minister. This was partly because, until 1946, the prime minister was also the external affairs minister. But it was also because of the idiosyncratic pattern of recruitment to the cabinet after 1946 that maintained a link between the department and the prime minister. Louis St. Laurent moved from being external affairs minister to the prime ministership in 1948, while at the same

---

38 Hilliker and Barry, *Canada's Department of External Affairs*, vol. 2, 359–60.

39 Peter C. Dobell, "The Management of a Foreign Policy for Canadians," *International Journal* 26:1 (Winter 1970–1), 206.

40 Michael D. Henderson, "La gestion des politiques internationales du gouvernement fédéral," in Paul Painchaud, ed., *Le Canada et le Québec sur la scène internationale* (Québec: Presses de l'Université du Québec, 1977), 86–87.

41 Denis Stairs, "The Political Culture of Canadian Foreign Policy," *Canadian Journal of Political Science* 15:4 (December 1982), 688.

time Pearson was recruited from the bureaucracy to run as a Liberal in a byelection and, once elected, was appointed the external affairs minister. In 1958, Pearson became Liberal leader, and in 1963, prime minister. In addition, the department saw itself—and indeed was seen—as an elite corps within the civil service, retaining its own examinations, recruitment practices, and training.[42] All these factors had given External a primacy of place within the federal bureaucracy in the post-1945 period.

By contrast, Trudeau had no such connection to External Affairs, and indeed left in little doubt his distance from the department. In a television interview in January 1969, he expressed a view that would recur throughout his tenure: the notion that diplomacy is atavistic and that therefore the department responsible for diplomacy is, if not irrelevant, then certainly of secondary importance. "I think the whole concept of diplomacy today is a little bit outmoded," he said. "I believe it all goes back to the early days of the telegraph when you needed a dispatch to know what was happening in country A, whereas now most of the time you can read it in a good newspaper."[43] Eleven years later, Trudeau, by then one of the longest-serving Western leaders, was to voice similar doubts about "a concept of diplomatic practice grounded in an age which has disappeared and which, in any case, predates Canadian experience. Traditional concepts of foreign service have diminished relevance [today]. . . . I am not sure that our approach to foreign service adequately reflects this new era."[44]

This attitude led the Trudeau government to reduce the budget of the Department of External Affairs and often reject the policy advice offered by its bureaucrats.[45] In 1968, Trudeau had accepted the recommendations of External Affairs officials on how Canada should respond to the Nigerian civil war: Canada, the prime minister was advised, could, and should do nothing about the secessionist state of Biafra. This advice was grounded in the well-established diplomatic practice of noninterference in the internal affairs of other states, a practice particularly pertinent in Canada's case, given not only the desires for independence in Québec, but also French interference in Canadian politics, which we will examine in more detail in Chapter 12. However, External Affairs did not foresee that the public would be swayed more by the starvation of Biafrans than adherence to cardinal dictums of interstate relations. The Trudeau government was, as a consequence, subjected to considerable domestic criticism. "Biafra was our Bay of Pigs," one External Affairs official said, referring to the failed invasion of Cuba in 1961 that had been urged on President John F. Kennedy by the CIA, leading the president to distrust whatever advice was proffered by the agency afterward.[46] Indeed, after Biafra, DEA's advice was treated with considerable skepticism by Trudeau and many members of his cabinet;

---

42 See Marcel Cadieux, *The Canadian Diplomat*, trans. Archibald Day (Toronto: University of Toronto Press, 1963).

44 Letter, Trudeau to Pamela McDougall, August 28, 1980: Royal Commission on Conditions of Foreign Service, *Report*.

43 Quoted in Dobell, "Management of Foreign Policy," 202; also Bruce Thordarson, *Trudeau and Foreign Policy: A Study in Decision-Making* (Toronto: Oxford University Press, 1972), 91–92.

45 Peyton Lyon, "A Review of the Review," *Journal of Canadian Studies* 5 (May 1970), 34–47.

46 Thordarson, *Trudeau and Foreign Policy*, 150, n59. On Biafra, see Donald Barry, "Interest Groups and the Foreign Policy Process: The Case of Biafra," in A. Paul Pross, ed., *Pressure Group Behaviour in Canadian Politics* (Toronto: McGraw-Hill Ryerson, 1975), 118–23, 134–43.

certainly the department's recommendations no longer received the kind of easy acceptance by ministers so common in the years after 1945. For example, advice on Canada's commitment to NATO[47] and on the question of sovereignty in the Arctic went unheeded. The department's drafts of the foreign policy review paper were repeatedly rejected by ministers on the grounds that they were inadequate.

Two of Trudeau's appointments underscored the prime minister's distance from External Affairs. Ivan Head, a former foreign service officer himself, was installed in the Prime Minister's Office, first as Trudeau's legislative assistant, then as special assistant on international affairs. According to Jim Coutts, a former aide to Trudeau, Trudeau and Head got on well because "Trudeau found External Affairs smug and precious and distrusted the department, and in Head he found someone who disliked the department [even] more. . . ."[48] From 1968 until his appointment as president of the International Development Research Centre in 1977, Head played a key role in such foreign policy issues as the Nigerian civil war, the NATO decision of 1969, and Canadian policies toward the Arctic.[49] He also accompanied Trudeau on foreign trips and often acted as the prime minister's personal representative to other leaders. (This was at the time when Henry Kissinger, Richard Nixon's national security adviser, tended to exclude the State Department from a role in the formulation of foreign policy. A comparison between Kissinger and Head was inevitable.)[50] In the Privy Council Office, Michael Pitfield, a long-time personal friend of Trudeau, was deputy secretary (plans). According to J.L. Granatstein and Robert Bothwell, Pitfield "despised External Affairs' elitist pretensions," and "participated cheerfully in efforts to cut the department down."[51] His influence over the foreign policy process was to increase substantially when he became clerk of the Privy Council in 1975.[52]

The overt denigration of External Affairs did not last long. By 1971, Peter Dobell notes, "greater harmony" between Cabinet and the department prevailed.[53] Trudeau stopped making off-the-cuff-comments about Canada's diplomats, the budget had been restored, and the department's policy recommendations were no longer greeted with distrust by Cabinet. However, External's position had been completely changed: Its dominance over international

---

47 Michel Fortmann and Martin Larose, "An Emerging Counterculture? Pierre Elliott Trudeau, Canadian Intellectuals and the Revision of Liberal Defence Policy concerning NATO, 1968–1969," *International Journal* 49:3 (Summer 2004), 537–556.

48 Quoted in John English, "Two Heads Are Better Than One: Ivan Head, Pierre Trudeau, and Canadian Foreign Policy," in Greg Donaghy and Kim Richard Nossal, eds., *Architects and Innovators: Building the Department of Foreign Affairs and International Trade, 1909–2009* (Montréal and Kingston: McGill-Queen's University Press, 2009).

49 For Head's recollections of these events, see Ivan Head and Pierre Trudeau, *The Canadian Way: Shaping Canada's Foreign Policy, 1968–1984* (Toronto: McClelland & Stewart, 1995).

50 Indeed, when Head died in 2004, he was remembered as "The Kissinger of Canada": Ron Csillag, "Ivan Head: The Kissinger of Canada, 1930–2004," *Globe and Mail*, November 6, 2004, S9.

51 J.L. Granatstein and Robert Bothwell, *Pirouette: Pierre Trudeau and Canadian Foreign Policy* (Toronto: University of Toronto Press, 1990), 228.

52 Christina McCall and Stephen Clarkson, *Trudeau and Our Times*, vol. 2: *The Heroic Delusion* (Toronto: McClelland & Stewart, 1994), chap. 10.

53 Peter C. Dobell, *Canada's Search for New Roles: Foreign Policy in the Trudeau Era* (Toronto: Oxford University Press, 1972), 21.

policy and the close relationship with the political leadership it had enjoyed from its inception in 1909 had ended. As an in-house study admitted, it had become an ordinary department, and needed "to compete for [the prime minister's] attention in the quality of advice it offers and the effectiveness of the services it performs."[54]

New Process, New Players

The shift in External's position was accelerated by the rise of new bureaucratic players in international policy and new processes put in place by the prime minister. No longer were international issues dealt with by the departments of external affairs and national defence, with the bureaucrats able to present their ministers with their recommendations on an issue and secure quick agreement after the minister telephoned the prime minister. Issues were now subject to discussion by interdepartmental committees to ensure that the domestic ramifications of external behaviour (and external ramifications of domestic interests) received full discussion. Decisions were subjected to careful and institutionalized coordination to ensure that foreign policy behaviour fell within the government's policy and spending priorities.[55]

Moreover, as the foreign policy agenda became increasingly dominated by economic and functional issues, those departments into whose bailiwicks such concerns fell took a more active role in international policy. The development of international bureaucratic capabilities followed naturally. Expanded "international" divisions were created in departments like Agriculture; Communications; Consumer and Corporate Affairs; Justice; Energy, Mines and Resources; Environment; Fisheries and Oceans; Labour; National Revenue; Regional Economic Expansion; and Supply and Services.

Among the new bureaucratic players was an agency for the management of international development. In 1968, the External Aid Office was renamed: "aid," with its overtones of charity, was replaced with "development assistance." The new Canadian International Development Agency (CIDA) was headed by a president, a rank equivalent to deputy minister, who reported to the secretary of state for external affairs. However, like the External Aid Office before it, CIDA was a "non-statutory" agency—in other words, it was not created by legislation but merely by Order-in-Council. Indeed, as David Morrison notes, "the actual legal basis for CIDA could hardly have been vaguer."[56] As a result, at times CIDA was able to enjoy a relatively autonomous relationship with other agencies, depending on who was serving as president.

As interdepartmental discussions of international policy issues increased, there was greater need for coordination. Authority for foreign policy coordination was given to three central agencies: the Prime Minister's Office, the Privy Council Office, and the Treasury Board Secretariat.[57] Two of these agencies, the TBS and the PCO, developed an

---

54 A.S. McGill, *The Role of the Department of External Affairs in the Government of Canada,* vol. 3 (Ottawa, June 1976), 42.

55 Bruce Thordarson, "Posture and Policy: Leadership in Canada's External Affairs," *International Journal* 31:4 (Autumn 1976); on the new "rational" processes put in place by Trudeau, see G. Bruce Doern and Peter Aucoin, eds., *The Structures of Policy-Making in Canada* (Toronto: Macmillan, 1971), chaps. 2 and 3.

56 Morrison, *Aid and Ebb Tide,* 63.

57 Colin Campbell and George Szablowski, *The Superbureaucrats: Structure and Behaviour in Central Agencies* (Toronto: Macmillan, 1979).

institutionalized expertise that enabled them to get involved in international issues. The Defence, External and Cultural Affairs division of the Program Branch of the TBS and the External Policy and Defence Secretariat of the PCO were both active in the coordination of foreign policy in the 1970s. Within the PMO, there was no comparable institutionalization: The key figure was the prime minister's special assistant on international affairs. With Head's departure in 1977, the position was institutionalized in the Privy Council Office as the assistant secretary to Cabinet for foreign and defence policy.

The PCO also exercised its influence in another important way: Officials in the Machinery of Government Secretariat and the clerk of the Privy Council worked on what was commonly seen as a machine in need of fine tuning. Between 1970 and 1983, the international policy bureaucracy underwent four reorganizations, generating both cynicism and demoralization within the bureaucracy.[58] While each time the terminology used was different, the end was the same: to resolve the inherent untidiness of making international policy.

Four Reorganizations, 1970–1983

The first signs of bureaucratic reform appeared in 1970, with the Trudeau government's foreign policy review. "To meet the challenges of the coming decades," *Foreign Policy for Canadians* declared grandly, "the Government needs a strong and flexible organization for carrying out its reshaped foreign policy. . . . The Government has decided that there should be maximum integration in its foreign operations that will effectively contribute to the achievement of national objectives."[59] While some interpreted this as heralding the end of the foreign office and its absorption by the trade commissioner service,[60] in fact integration involved an attempt to coordinate different aspects of international policy across departments. To achieve this, an Interdepartmental Committee on External Relations (ICER) was created. The membership included key senior officials: the clerk of the Privy Council, the secretary of the Treasury Board, the president of CIDA, and the deputy ministers of Manpower and Immigration, of Industry, Trade and Commerce, and of Public Works. The undersecretary of state for external affairs chaired ICER, but External Affairs had no authority to manage the external operations of the different departments. Without clear lines of authority, ICER failed as a mechanism of coordination. By the mid-1970s, ICER had been allowed quietly to slip into disuse.[61]

---

58 According to the undersecretary of state for external affairs, Gordon Osbaldeston, a 1900-year-old Roman quotation enjoyed wide circulation in External Affairs during this period: "We trained hard, but it seemed that every time we were beginning to form up into teams, we would be reorganized. I was to learn that later in life we tend to meet any new situation by reorganizing, and a wonderful method it can be for creating the illusion of progress while producing confusion, inefficiency and demoralization." Gordon Osbaldeston, "Reorganizing Canada's Department of External Affairs," *International Journal* 37:3 (Summer 1982), 464–65.

59 Canada, Secretary of State for External Affairs, *Foreign Policy for Canadians*, main booklet (Ottawa, 1970), 39.

60 For example, James Eayrs, *Diplomacy and Its Discontents* (Toronto: University of Toronto Press, 1971), 39.

61 W.M. Dobell, "Interdepartmental Management in External Affairs," *Canadian Public Administration* 21:1 (Spring 1978), 83–102.

The second reorganization occurred in 1977, when Allan Gotlieb was appointed under-secretary of state for external affairs. Gotlieb set about to try to reposition the Department of External Affairs within the Ottawa bureaucracy and to restore its central role in the making of international policy, or, as Granatstein and Bothwell put it, "to get External Affairs plugged in once more."[62] Gotlieb's blueprint for External Affairs was articulated in a speech he gave at the University of Toronto in February 1979. Noting that the department "seemed to lack a clear and distinct idea of its role . . . in the wake of substantial changes in the international and domestic environments which had occurred in the 1970s," Gotlieb proposed a new role for External Affairs: External Affairs should become a central agency, and like other central agencies, such as the Privy Council Office, the Prime Minister's Office, the Treasury Board Secretariat, and the Department of Finance, engage in a broad coordinating role across government, advising Cabinet as a whole on a range of foreign policy issues rather than running programs.[63]

The third reorganization was designed to help create a "new" Department of External Affairs: to consolidate the foreign service, bringing together those civil servants from External Affairs, International Trade and Commerce, Immigration, and other government departments who served abroad. Consolidation was introduced after the Liberals were returned in the February 1980 elections. Under consolidation, all the senior officials serving abroad in the Department of External Affairs, of Industry, Trade and Commerce (IT&C, as it had become in 1969), and of Employment and Immigration (E&I) were to be integrated into External Affairs. From this pool were drawn the heads of posts for Canada's missions around the world. The idea behind this scheme was to allow posts abroad to operate more efficiently by streamlining the authority of the head of post. Instead of having to coordinate the activities of officials at a mission abroad who were receiving instructions from DEA, CIDA, IT&C, and E&I in Ottawa, the head of post would have authority over all staff, regardless of their function.[64]

Consolidation proved to be but a prelude. The Canadian economy continued to be buffeted by the economic dislocations that had been set in train by the Nixon shocks of 1971 that effectively ended the Bretton Woods system and imposed a 10 percent import surcharge, dramatically affecting Canadian interests. The Trudeau government had tried, through the Third Option, to foster economic growth within Canada, but without success. When Trudeau returned to power in 1980, his government tried once again, through measures such as the National Energy Program, to grapple with the consequences of high interest rates and recession. One part of that process involved reorganizing the federal government to provide Canada with a more effective way to formulate economic policy, both internal and external. As Ernie Keenes put it, the "reorganization of the Canadian state followed . . . the rhythms of the international political economy."[65]

---

62 Granatstein and Bothwell, *Pirouette*, 29.

63 Allan Gotlieb, *Canadian Diplomacy in the 1980s: Leadership and Service* (Toronto: Centre for International Studies, University of Toronto, 1979).

64 Jack Maybee, "Foreign Service Consolidation," *International Perspectives* (July/August 1980), 17–20.

65 Ernie Keenes, "Rearranging the Deck Chairs: A Political Economy Approach to Foreign Policy Management in Canada," *Canadian Public Administration* 35:3 (Autumn 1992), 381–401.

On January 12, 1982, the prime minister restructured the government. All departments with an economic mandate were affected. A new central agency, the Ministry of State for Economic and Regional Development, replaced the Ministry of State for Economic Development; the Department of Regional Economic Expansion and the "industry" side of the Department of Industry, Trade and Commerce were replaced by a Department of Regional Industrial Expansion. The "trade" side of IT&C, including those parts of the Trade Commissioner Service not included in consolidation as well as the Export Development Corporation and the Canadian Commercial Corporation, were all merged into the Department of External Affairs.[66] (Only CIDA was left unscathed, although officials hinted that its turn would come.)

The internal organization of the new department was similar to the tripartite ministerial structure discussed in the previous chapter. In addition to the undersecretary of state for external affairs, there was a deputy minister (foreign policy) and a deputy minister (international trade). The deputy ministers presided over two "wings" of the department, a "political wing" and a "trade wing." Policy planning, management, and personnel reported directly to the undersecretary. Parallel structures were created on both wings of the department.

By November 1982, it was obvious that the reorganization was not working. The small and cohesive Trade Commissioner Service was complaining of being "overwhelmed" by "antediluvian" bureaucratic procedures in External. The diplomats, faced with an influx of trade officials, lost traditional perks like private offices. A large organization was made even larger, leading to problems with morale. It was, in short, "a large bureaucratic mess."[67] In the winter of 1982–83, Trudeau rotated his senior mandarins. Pitfield was appointed to the Senate, while Osbaldeston moved from External to be the clerk of the Privy Council. External was given to Marcel Massé, who had been Joe Clark's clerk but had been shuffled to the presidency of CIDA to make room for Pitfield in 1980. Massé moved quickly to reorganize the department. In July 1983, the organizational structure introduced by Pitfield was scrapped. Gone were the team management approach and the parallel wings of the department. In their place was a more traditional way of organizing a foreign ministry, with five geographic branches—Asia and the Pacific, Africa and the Middle East, Latin America and the Caribbean, Europe, and the United States—each headed by an assistant undersecretary. Each branch was subdivided into at least three operating divisions (trade development, political relations, and programs).

When Trudeau retired from politics in 1984, the legacy of his fifteen years spent trying to create the perfect governmental structure was slim; there was little evidence that the international affairs bureaucracy functioned in a more rational way or fulfilled its policy responsibilities any better than in the past. The Grail-like quest for the perfect bureaucratic machine was conducted by administrative theorists such as Pitfield who tended to see international policy primarily as an engine for domestic economic growth, and the foreign service as merely a vehicle for "program delivery." Diplomats and their rituals were

---

66 Kim Richard Nossal, "Contending Explanations for the Amalgamation of External Affairs," in Donald Story, ed., *The Canadian Foreign Service in Transition* (Toronto: Scholars' Press, 1993), 37–58.

67 James Rusk, "New Face on External Gets Lifted Again," *Globe and Mail*, July 12, 1983, 10; James Rusk, "Straightening Out Merger Mess First Major Challenge for Massé," *Globe and Mail*, November 3, 1982, 9.

mocked as arcane and irrelevant. That was the reason the Department of External Affairs and its methods were questioned during this period.

From External Affairs to Foreign Affairs: 1984–1993

Many of the changes introduced during the Trudeau years proved to be short-lived. After the Progressive Conservatives under Brian Mulroney came to power in September 1984, there was less emphasis on machinery and more on policy. In 1985, the coordinating role of the PCO shifted considerably and a new undersecretary of state for external affairs, James ("Si") Taylor, a career diplomat, was appointed. Taylor, more concerned with the substance of foreign policy than merely with its management, assumed the more traditional role of the undersecretary—that of the government's chief adviser on foreign policy.[68]

During the Mulroney years, External Affairs and International Trade Canada (EAITC), as it was called under its new "applied title,"[69] continued to struggle with bureaucratic "turf" issues as other departments pursued their international policy mandates. EAITC's attempts to establish its primacy over all aspects of international policy produced mixed results. It lost control of the most important foreign policy area, the negotiation of a free-trade agreement with the United States. To guide the process of negotiating that agreement, the Mulroney government decided to create a separate agency. Usually, international negotiations on trade would be conducted by External Affairs and International Trade Canada, but Cabinet decided this issue was too important to be left to one department. Instead, a Trade Negotiations Office (TNO) under a chief negotiator, Simon Reisman, was created. It was to be staffed by officials seconded from other agencies of government like Regional Industrial Expansion, Finance, External Affairs, and the PCO, with some drawn from outside the bureaucracy.[70] While Reisman had the rank of ambassador and was nominally a deputy in EAITC, and while the TNO was nominally an administrative unit of External Affairs, the reality was that the TNO was an autonomous organization, with Reisman reporting directly to the prime minister.[71] This experiment was not altogether successful. As Doern and Tomlin put it, the TNO tended to demonstrate "an aggressive confidence that frequently made relations with other departments tense."[72] This was exacerbated by

---

68 Harald von Riekhoff, "The Structure of Foreign Policy Decision Making and Management," in Brian W. Tomlin and Maureen Appel Molot, eds., *Canada Among Nations 1986: Talking Trade* (Toronto: James Lorimer, 1987), 23.

69 The Canadian government has a unique form of nomenclature for its departments and agencies. Legally, all federal departments and agencies have formal statutory names in the style common to nearly every modern Weberian state: for example, the Department of X, or the Ministry of State for Y. However, federal departments and agencies also have "applied titles" that drop the "Department of" or "Ministry of State for" and add "Canada"—as in Revenue Canada, Supply and Services Canada, etc. External Affairs and International Trade Canada was given its applied title as of June 28, 1989.

70 David Leyton-Brown, "The Political Economy of Canada–U.S. Relations," in Tomlin and Molot, eds., *Canada Among Nations 1986*, 149–68.

71 Michael Hart, with Bill Dymond and Colin Robertson, *Decision at Midnight: Inside the Canada–US Free-Trade Negotiations* (Vancouver: UBC Press, 1994), 123–27.

72 G. Bruce Doern and Brian W. Tomlin, *Faith and Fear: The Free Trade Story* (Toronto: Stoddart, 1991), 286.

Reisman himself: By all accounts Reisman had a prickly personality and simply did not get on well with a variety of other players, including Patricia Carney, the trade minister, or Sylvia Ostry, who had been seconded from EAITC to oversee Canada's negotiating position in the Uruguay Round of multilateral trade negotiations.

While Mulroney was not inclined to denigrate the functions of diplomats as Trudeau did, there were fissures between the political leadership and the international policy bureaucracy between 1984 and 1993. First, Mulroney created serious morale problems as a result of his willingness to use diplomatic appointments for patronage purposes. All prime ministers have made non-career appointments, and some diplomatic posts, such as the high commissioner in London, have usually been reserved for patronage (or, in the euphemism preferred by officials in Ottawa, "politically inspired") appointments. But Mulroney made more patronage appointments to the foreign service during his time in office than his predecessors: 36 appointments in nine years, as against 15 in fifteen years made by Trudeau and 5 in five years made by Pearson.[73] To be sure, some were very well received, notably his appointment of Stephen Lewis, former leader of the Ontario New Democratic Party, as permanent representative to the United Nations, and Dennis McDermott, former president of the Canadian Labour Congress, as ambassador to Ireland. However, Mulroney was also inclined to use the foreign service as "the personal Senate of Brian Mulroney," as the Professional Association of Foreign Service Officers (PAFSO) put it.[74] Numerous friends and partisan supporters were appointed to a variety of diplomatic posts:[75] Patrick McAdam, Roy McMurtry, Donald Macdonald, and Fred Eaton to London; Ian MacDonald to Washington; Lucien Bouchard to Paris; Jean Drapeau to UNESCO; Norman Spector to Israel; Robert de Cotret to the World Bank; and Donald Cameron to Boston.

The most telling example of the gap that had appeared between ministers and the mandarins in the Pearson Building was the al-Mashat affair that followed the Gulf War.[76] In January 1991, Mohammed al-Mashat, the Iraqi ambassador to the United States, and thus the prime apologist for Saddam Hussein's invasion of Kuwait, sought to defect to Canada. His application was fast-tracked through EAITC and a security clearance was provided by the Canadian Security Intelligence Service (CSIS) within 24 hours. The associate undersecretary of state for external affairs, Raymond Chrétien, a 25-year veteran foreign service officer (and nephew of Jean Chrétien), sent his minister, Joe Clark, a memo bringing the al-Mashat case to his attention. The memo was given to Clark's chief of staff, David Daubney, who did not realize its importance and thus did not pass it on to Clark. Believing that the minister had been apprised, External Affairs granted al-Mashat landed immigrant status.

---

73 Andrew Cohen, "The Diplomats Make a Comeback," *Globe and Mail*, November 19, 1994, D1–D2.

74 O.P. Dwivedi and James Iain Gow, *From Bureaucracy to Public Management: The Administrative Culture of the Government of Canada* (Toronto: University of Toronto Press, 1999), 107.

75 For a history of patronage appointments in Canadian politics from Sir John A. Macdonald to Brian Mulroney, see Jeffrey Simpson, *Spoils of Power: The Politics of Patronage* (Toronto: Harper & Collins, 1988).

76 The following is drawn from the account of S.L. Sutherland, "The Al-Mashat Affair: Administrative Accountability in Parliamentary Institutions," *Canadian Public Administration* 34:4 (Winter 1991), 573–603.

However, when the story of al-Mashat's expedited entry into Canada broke, the Mulroney government immediately distanced itself from the decision, claiming that ministers had not been involved. Abandoning the well-established norm of Westminster parliamentary government that requires that ministers take responsibility for the actions of their civil servants, the Mulroney government publicly blamed Chrétien and Daubney for not informing the minister. During an investigation was conducted by the House of Commons Standing Committee on External Affairs and International Trade in late May and early June 1991, Chrétien in particular was roundly criticized by a number of witnesses, including Clark; de Montigny Marchand, the undersecretary of state for external affairs and Chrétien's immediate superior; and Paul Tellier, the clerk of the Privy Council.

As Sharon Sutherland has rightly argued, the al-Mashat affair had serious longer-term implications for the principle of ministerial responsibility in Canada.[77] However, it also had shorter-term implications for External Affairs. Raymond Chrétien was shunted out of Ottawa with a posting to Brussels. While Marchand had participated in the public humiliation of Chrétien, Mulroney quickly replaced him with Reid Morden. Put in the broader context of Mulroney's use of the foreign service as a source of patronage appointments, it is hardly surprising that the al-Mashat affairs deepened the crisis of morale in the department.

Finally, during Mulroney's tenure as prime minister, the international policy bureaucracy was again faced with budget cuts, although the reductions in the late 1980s and early 1990s were much harsher than those in the late 1960s. An obvious place to begin budget-trimming was the global network of Canadian diplomatic missions. In 1986, it was decided to close missions in each region, and the assistant deputy minister for each region was asked for his or her nominees. While seven missions were identified, actually closing them proved much harder. For example, when the proposal to close the mission in Helsinki became known, the Finnish community in Canada organized a vocal public relations campaign to convince EAITC to keep the mission, a campaign that was ultimately successful.[78] This budget-cutting became even more difficult after 1991, when the government was under pressure to expand Canadian representation abroad to all of the new countries that achieved independence in the wake of the collapses of both Yugoslavia and the Soviet Union between 1990 and 1992.

As a result, External Affairs sought other ways of trimming costs abroad, such as sharing consular services with Australia. Under the August 1989 Canada–Australia Consular Sharing Agreement, the two countries agreed to share consular services, taking advantage of the fact that both countries tended to concentrate their external representation in different regions of the world. Under the agreement, Australia provided consular services to Canadians in a number of countries in the Pacific; for its part, Canada agreed to provide services to Australians in selected countries in Africa, Latin America, and Europe. In 1993, the two countries took the process one step further, agreeing to co-locate in some missions. As a result, the Australian High Commission in Barbados moved into the premises of the Canadian High Commission in Bridgetown, Barbados, and a Canadian officer began working out of the Australian chancery in Phnom Penh, Cambodia.

---

77 Sutherland, "Al-Mashat Affair," 601–603; also "Ministerial Responsibility Left Wounded in Mashat Skirmish," *bout de papier* 8 (Fall 1991), 30.

78 John G. Kneale, "The Department and the Country," *bout de papier* 8 (Summer 1991), 13.

A turning point for international policy came with the February 1992 budget. The government closed the Canadian Institute for International Peace and Security (CIIPS), which had been created by the Trudeau government after the peace initiative of 1983–84.[79] Canada's peacekeeping operations were reoriented and Canada withdrew from the UN operation in Cyprus, where it had served since 1964. Canada's NATO bases in Europe were closed. Spending on Official Development Assistance (ODA) was cut, and, as we will see below, radically altered. And External Affairs was again reorganized.

In this reorganization, the undersecretary of state for external affairs, Reid Morden, announced that the department would be going "back to basics"—focusing only on political and economic affairs and eliminating overlap. This required transferring some roles to other departments. External's immigration function was moved to Employment and Immigration Canada; responsibility for international expositions was moved to Communications Canada; international sports was transferred to Fitness and Amateur Sport; and cultural and academic programs were moved to the Canada Council (a measure that was subsequently defeated in the Senate). As Evan Potter has argued, the "back to basics" shift effectively brought the "central agency" role of External to an end.[80]

But in one policy area, External Affairs extended its power after the 1992 budget. As noted above, the reorganization in 1982 did not touch CIDA, with the result that the issue of the purpose of CIDA's programs was not addressed. Should CIDA's programs be designed to further the wider goals of international development—such as providing assistance to the poorest countries of the world—or the narrower goals of Canadian foreign policy, such as supporting trade and exports in relatively prosperous Asian countries such as Indonesia and China? After Marcel Massé was reappointed president of CIDA in 1989, the tension in the relationship between CIDA and EAITC intensified as Massé sought to more policy autonomy for CIDA. By the same token, External Affairs tried just as hard to seize control of CIDA's budget and policy. In 1991, matters came to a head after Clark, who as secretary of state for external affairs was the minister responsible for both EAITC and CIDA, was made minister of constitutional affairs and Barbara McDougall was appointed external affairs minister. While Clark had always sought to preserve a degree of autonomy for CIDA, McDougall was not so inclined. For the 1991–92 budget, the cabinet decided to put funding for both ODA and assistance to the former Soviet Union and Eastern Europe into one budget envelope. The International Assistance Envelope (IAE) was controlled by External Affairs, which sought to shift large amounts of development assistance funds to spending on projects designed to assist countries in Central and Eastern Europe make the transition to democracy. This led to a showdown, the sudden ouster of Massé, and the leaking of an External Affairs memo in January 1993 that revealed the extent of EAITC's designs on CIDA.[81]

---

79 For the story of CIIPS, see Geoffrey Pearson and Nancy Gordon, "Shooting Oneself in the Head: The Demise of CIIPS," in Fen Osler Hampson and Christopher J. Maule, eds., *Canada Among Nations 1993–94: Global Jeopardy* (Ottawa: Carleton University Press, 1993), 57–81.

80 Evan Potter, "A Question of Relevance: Canada's Foreign Policy and Foreign Service in the 1990s," in Hampson and Maule, eds., *Canada Among Nations 1993–94*, 48–51.

81 Cranford Pratt, "Humane Internationalism and Canadian Development Assistance Policies," in Pratt, ed., *Canadian International Development Assistance Policies: An Appraisal* (Montréal and Kingston: McGill-Queen's University Press, 1994), 356–63.

When the new Liberal government of Jean Chrétien took power in November 1993, a number of changes occurred in the international policy bureaucracy. Chrétien took the symbolic step of changing the name of Canada's foreign ministry. The applied title was dropped, along with the venerable term "External," on the grounds that this no longer fitted Canada's circumstances. Instead, it was to be the Department of Foreign Affairs and International Trade (DFAIT). In the struggle between Foreign Affairs and CIDA, the Chrétien government came down on the side of DFAIT and completed the subordination of CIDA.[82] By 1994, it seemed that the diplomats, as Andrew Cohen put it, were making a comeback.[83]

A Further Decline: 1994–2006

But, as Cohen himself would demonstrate so clearly in his 2003 best-selling book on Canadian foreign policy, *While Canada Slept*, the comeback was only temporary.[84] As the Chrétien government embraced deficit reduction as one of its key priorities, all government departments involved in international affairs were hit hard by expenditure reductions. DFAIT shrank in size over the course of the 1990s. As Cohen notes, its budget was cut 25 percent and 980 positions, or 13 percent of its employees, were eliminated.[85] By 2001, the size of the department had been reduced to 1900 foreign service officers, 2800 non-rotational officers in Canada, and 4600 locally engaged personnel in foreign missions.[86]

And yet, the policy demands on the department increased dramatically during this period. Because the number of independent countries did not diminish, there were always good reasons to expand the number of diplomatic posts maintained by Canada, and so while some embassies abroad were closed, many more were opened. The activities of the Canadian government in international organizations increased as new organizations such as the International Criminal Court were created and negotiations in the institutions of global governance increased and became more complex. We should not forget that the number of Canadians travelling abroad during this period expanded, and when citizens travel abroad, they frequently need consular services provided by their government. Finally, as Denis Stairs has noted, DFAIT was required to engage in more consultations with the Canadian public and nongovernmental organizations.[87] Moreover, as the department was forced to try to "do more with less," morale sagged dramatically: fully one-half of the officers who had joined the department after 1990 had resigned by 2001.[88]

---

82 Cranford Pratt, "Development Assistance and Canadian Foreign Policy: Where We Are Now," *Canadian Foreign Policy* 2:3 (Winter 1994–95), 77–85.

83 Andrew Cohen, "The Diplomats Make a Comeback," *Globe and Mail*, November 19, 1994, D1–D2.

84 Andrew Cohen, *While Canada Slept: How We Lost Our Place in the World* (Toronto: McClelland & Stewart, 2003).

85 Cohen, *While Canada Slept*, 137.

86 Department of Foreign Affairs and International Trade, *2000–2001 Estimates*, pt. 3, 8.

87 Denis Stairs, "The Making of Hard Choices in Canadian Foreign Policy," in David Carment, Fen Osler Hampson, and Norman Hillmer, eds., *Canada Among Nations 2004: Setting Priorities Straight* (Montréal and Kingston: McGill-Queen's University Press, 2004), 168.

88 Daryl Copeland, "The Axworthy Years: Canadian Foreign Policy in the Era of Diminished Capacity," in Fen Osler Hampson, Norman Hillmer, and Maureen Appel Molot, eds., *Canada Among Nations 2001: The Axworthy Legacy* (Toronto: Oxford University Press, 2001), 168.

The pressure on DFAIT accelerated in the post-9/11 period, when a new emphasis was placed on the so-called "3D" approach to foreign policy: integrating the contributions of diplomacy, development, and defence in initiatives such as the Canadian mission to Afghanistan. In 2003 and 2004, DFAIT increasingly worked with CIDA and the Department of National Defence to coordinate activities abroad, particularly in Canada's growing mission in Afghanistan.[89] However, this increasing focus on the integration of the activities of the three departments abroad was interrupted by the decision of the new prime minister, Paul Martin, to pull DFAIT apart. On December 12, 2003, the day he became prime minister, Martin suddenly announced that the Department of Foreign Affairs and International Trade would be divided into two separate departments again, bringing to an end twenty-one years of fusion. He made this announcement without any prior discussion, or consultation with affected industry groups such as the Canadian Manufacturers and Exporters (CME). Nor was any explanation offered. The divorce was just imposed by prime ministerial fiat.

It did not last long. Although the Martin government split the department using an Order-in-Council, the legislation to give the two new departments their new formal mandates was never passed. By the time that legislation was ready to be considered by Parliament, the 2004 election had reduced the Liberals to a minority government. Moreover, there was growing criticism of the idea of splitting the department from academics, journalists, and former bureaucrats. Even the CME declared that they were quite happy with the combined department. When Bills C-31 and C-32 were introduced, this criticism was seized on by the opposition parties in Parliament. On February 15, 2005, on second reading, the three opposition parties in the House of Commons combined to defeat the government bill—the first time since 1925 that a government bill was defeated on second reading. When the Martin government insisted on pressing on with its plan, the Standing Committee on Foreign Affairs and International Trade, which was dominated by the opposition parties, protested the divorce by reducing the Estimates for the department by a single symbolic dollar.[90]

The International Policy Bureaucracy Today

After the Conservative Party of Canada under Stephen Harper won a minority in the January 2006 elections, the bureaucratic landscape did not much alter. When the Conservatives took power in February 2006, it was already decided that, as one Conservative put it, "we would not get involved in a complicated rejigging of the machinery of government . . . basically for the reason that if you start to reorganize the machinery of government, you kiss your productivity goodbye for the next two years as everyone figures out who reports to whom."[91]

---

89 Douglas L. Bland and Sean M. Maloney, *Campaigns for International Security: Canada's Defence Policy at the Turn of the Century* (Montréal and Kingston: McGill-Queen's University Press, 2004); David S. McDonough, "The Paradox of Afghanistan: Stability Operations and the Renewal of Canada's International Security Policy?" *International Journal* 62:3 (Summer 2007), 620–42.

90 Gerald Schmitz and James Lee, "Split Images and Serial Affairs: Reviews, Reorganizations, and Parliamentary Roles," in Andrew F. Cooper and Dane Rowlands, eds., *Canada Among Nations 2005: Split Images* (Montréal and Kingston: McGill-Queen's University Press, 2005), 245–70.

91 Quoted in Paul Wells, *Right Side Up: The Fall of Paul Martin and the Rise of Stephen Harper's New Conservatism* (Toronto: McClelland & Stewart, 2006), 283.

However, one of its first acts was to abandon the divorce by cancelling Martin's Order-in-Council of December 12, 2003. And although on April 1, 2006, the "new" Department of Foreign Affairs and International Trade was officially relaunched,[92] a few after-effects of the Martin divorce can still be felt, notably the relocation of the "trade" side of DFAIT out of the Pearson Building at 125 Sussex into the old Ottawa city hall, located next door at 111 Sussex. Harper also confirmed the continuing responsibility of the Department of Foreign Affairs and International Trade for the coordination of the international policy agenda.

But if the Department of Foreign Affairs and International Trade has been given the central role for the coordination of international policy that it enjoyed for much of the twentieth century, the bureaucratic landscape remains as crowded with those agencies with responsibility for key elements of Canada's international policy: at the centre, the clerk of the privy council, the foreign and defence policy adviser to the prime minister, located in the Privy Council Office;[93] the Department of National Defence and the Canadian Armed Forces; the Canadian International Development Agency, which underwent a major reorganization in 2007;[94] the Department of Finance and Treasury Board Secretariat, responsible not only for setting the budgets of the line departments but also for administering Canada's relations with international financial institutions; and Public Safety Canada, with its various agencies involved in national security, including the Canada Border Services Agency, the Royal Canadian Mounted Police, and the Canadian Security Intelligence Service.

THE INFLUENCE OF THE BUREAUCRACY

How influential is the bureaucracy in the making of Canada's international policy? The question touches on a key problem of contemporary governance: the degree to which the agencies created to advise political leaders, implement their policies, and administer their programs have come to dominate the policy process at the expense of the autonomy of the elected representatives.

Ministers and Mandarins

One should begin by making a distinction between the *influence* of permanent officials and their *power* to transform their own policy preferences into state practice. "Civil servants do not make policy, all rumour to the contrary notwithstanding," Mitchell Sharp declared in 1958. "That is the prerogative of the elected representative of the people. But in this day

---

92 Sarah McGregor, "Fewer Cabinet Seats but More Committees," *Embassy: Canada's Foreign Policy Newsweekly* 98:5 (April 2006), 1, 14.

93 The assistant secretary to the cabinet for foreign and defence policy was renamed diplomatic adviser during the Chrétien years, and renamed yet again as the foreign and defence policy adviser to the prime minister during the Martin and Harper years. See John J. Noble, "PMO/PCO/DFAIT: Serving the Prime Minister's Foreign Policy Agenda," in Jean Daudlin and Schwanen, eds., *Canada Among Nations 2007: What Room for Manoeuvre?* (Montréal and Kingston: McGill-Queen's University Press, 2007), 40; 60, n3.

94 Ian Smillie, "Foreign Aid and Canadian Purpose: Influence and Policy in Canada's International Development Agency," in Robert Bothwell and Jean Daudlin, eds., *Canada Among Nations 2008: 100 Years of Canadian Foreign Policy* (Montréal and Kingston: McGill-Queen's University Press, 2009), 183–208.

and age civil servants do have a profound influence on the making of policy."[95] Such was the perspective of a former deputy minister of trade and commerce who had just resigned from the civil service. In 1963, Sharp returned to the Department of Trade and Commerce, this time as its minister; in 1968, he was appointed Trudeau's first secretary of state for external affairs. But his views did not change much. In 1981, no longer in cabinet (though as northern pipeline commissioner, still in government), Sharp reiterated his view that public servants "wield great influence," attributing this to his belief that "Government is, in fact, a specialized affair which cannot be run successfully by amateurs without professional advice and professional execution. With rare exceptions, in a parliamentary system politicians are amateurs in any field of government administration." But, he added, it depended on the minister to assert the prerogative of authority that was explicitly recognized by both senior officials and ministers. "I understood the functions of my departmental advisers," he asserted. "I consulted them daily. . . . I asked them questions and listened to their answers. Sometimes I agreed; and sometimes I didn't. In the end I made my decisions and they carried them out."[96]

However, that was not the experience of one of Sharp's successors. Flora MacDonald was Joe Clark's external affairs minister in 1979–80. Following the defeat of the Clark government, MacDonald publicly criticized the senior bureaucrats in External Affairs. In a widely publicized account,[97] she charged that she was manipulated by her bureaucrats, lamenting the "entrapment devices" of her officials: "The unnecessarily long and numerous memos . . . the crisis corridor-decisions I was confronted with—here is the situation (breathless pause), let us have your instructions." She complained of the "one-dimensional opinions put forward in memos" and of being deprived of "the luxury of multiple-choice options on matters of major import." It is easy to note that there are, of course, ways of coping with such ploys. As Sharp reminded MacDonald none too subtly in a rejoinder, "it was our own fault for letting the system get out of hand."[98]

But ministers will sometimes be unwilling or unable to propose policy directions for officialdom to oppose. The politicians may instead abdicate responsibility for policy formulation to officials and become, in Douglas Hartle's words, "toothless tigers who gum the policy proposals of the senior bureaucracy."[99] Hartle, a former deputy secretary in the Treasury Board Secretariat, was well acquainted with the relationships between ministers and their mandarins. The problem of allowing officials to formulate policy proposals that are then passed "on the nod" is by no means new. Mackenzie King was no toothless tiger, but he too discovered the extent of his dependence for advice on Skelton when the latter died suddenly in 1941. "I have been tremendously at fault," King recorded in his diary after

---

95 Quoted in John Porter, *The Vertical Mosaic: An Analysis of Social Class and Power in Canada* (Toronto: University of Toronto Press, 1965), 427–28.

96 Mitchell Sharp, "The Role of the Mandarins," *Policy Options*, May/June 1981, 43.

97 MacDonald delivered the initial address to the annual meetings of the Canadian Political Science Association in June 1980; revised versions were published in *Policy Options* and as "Cutting Through the Chains," *Globe and Mail*, November 7, 1980, 7.

98 Sharp, "Role of the Mandarins," 44.

99 Douglas G. Hartle, "Techniques and Processes of Administration," *Canadian Public Administration* 19:1 (Spring 1976), 32.

Skelton's funeral, "in not concentrating more on work and perhaps mastering more myself, and trusting too greatly to the outside aides. . . . I was glad to have [Skelton] as a guide, but there are times when [his influence] was almost too strongly exerted to the extent of unduly influencing Government policy."[100]

But King found it hard to take his own advice. In the post-1945 period, he grew more dubious about the appropriateness of expanding Canada's external relations. Yet his reservations remained hidden, recorded only in his diary. In December 1947, for example, he wrote that Pearson, then undersecretary of state for external affairs, "with his youth and inexperience and influenced by the persuasion of others around him, had been anxious to have Canada's External Affairs figure prominently in world affairs and has really directed affairs from New York when he should have been in Ottawa, and without any real control by Ministers of the Crown."[101] John W. Holmes, who was an official in the Department of External Affairs at the time, concludes that on the question of general foreign policy directions in the immediate postwar period, External Affairs was "on the whole, well out in front of government." But, Holmes adds, "it would be a mistake to see this as a simple struggle between utopian officials and unimaginative politicians. . . . In this case, [the bureaucracy] provided an appropriate kind of leadership by formulating goals and schemes to attract the support of cabinet."[102] Is this an instance of public servants "unduly influencing Government policy," as King put it?

On some occasions, we can see such influence at work. One of the first decisions that the Progressive Conservative government of John G. Diefenbaker had to take when it came to office in 1957 after more than two decades in opposition was whether to approve the North American Air Defence (NORAD) command that had been negotiated between Canada and the United States. General Charles Foulkes, chairman of the chiefs of staff committee, presented the NORAD decision to the prime minister as a mere formality, and the new prime minister approved it without realizing the full implications of the agreement. Diefenbaker's hasty approval plunged his government into the first of what would be a number of political crises over defence issues. And while it is an extreme case, this episode shows how senior officials may acquire power over their political masters.[103]

The NORAD episode also illustrates that senior officials like Foulkes will always have conceptions of the "national interest" that are shaped by their individual and bureaucratic ideas about the public good, their desire to maintain the health of the organization to which they are attached, and their own career ambitions. Their view of what should be done, needless to say, might—or might not—be in accord with the individual or collective views of the elected representatives, who, quite understandably, have a different set of personal, political, and organizational imperatives. When there is a gap, ministers may impose their views; officials may only try to persuade their political overlords, for theirs is not to impose.

---

100 Quoted in Porter, *Vertical Mosaic*, 429.

101 J.W. Pickersgill and D.F. Forster, *The Mackenzie King Record*, vol. 4: *1947–1948* (Toronto: University of Toronto Press, 1970), 135–36.

102 John W. Holmes, *The Shaping of Peace: Canada and the Search for World Order, 1943–1957*, vol. 1 (Toronto: University of Toronto Press, 1979), 297–98.

103 Joseph T. Jockel, "The Military Establishments and the Creation of NORAD," *American Review of Canadian Studies* 12:3 (Fall 1982), 1–16.

If officials do engage in persuasion, however, they have a number of advantages over ministers, the most important of which is a virtual monopoly over information and analysis of that information. In foreign policy, this is all the more significant, for most of the intelligence that informs bureaucratic recommendations on policy is kept shrouded by the state under the veils of secrecy—a practice usually justified as necessary either for national security or for the success of interstate negotiations. As a result, politicians rarely have alternative sources of analysis that can claim to be as authoritative. Some have tried. As we saw above, Pierre Trudeau appointed Ivan Head to provide him with advice that differed dramatically from the advice from the bureaucracy. Flora MacDonald also sought advice from outside the bureaucracy. But if these outside sources do not have access to both the information and expertise of the bureaucracy, depending on their advice can be problematic.

For example, Clark's decision to move the Canadian embassy in Israel from Tel Aviv to Jerusalem in 1979 was in large part predicated on the analysis tendered by a Toronto lawyer who confidently predicted that while the Arab states might protest the move vigorously, they would take no substantive action against Canada.[104] One of the reasons why the Mulroney government had been so embarrassed by the al-Mashat affair was that Clark's chief of staff in the spring of 1991 was a political appointee with little experience in international affairs. David Daubney, a former Conservative MP who had been defeated in the 1988 elections, admitted to a parliamentary inquiry into the affair that he had not given Clark the memo about al-Mashat because he did not appreciate its significance. After all, he said, he was not a professional foreign service officer and therefore could not be expected to understand the significance of an Iraqi diplomat's defection during the Gulf conflict.[105]

Likewise, when Paul Martin wanted a fresh perspective for the international policy review that had been under way since 2003, he turned to a professor at the University of Oxford to assist in the writing of the document that was to highlight the review. Jennifer Welsh had just written a best-selling book on Canada's international affairs,[106] and Martin believed she could assist in bringing a fresh outside perspective to the kind of vision he wanted to articulate for Canada's foreign policy. While, as Allan Gotlieb has noted,[107] Welsh's involvement in the process helped to give some coherence to the International Policy Statement, her involvement caused considerable friction within the Ottawa bureaucracy, whose perspectives did not always mesh easily with the more visionary views of either Welsh or the prime minister himself. At the very least, Martin's decision to involve Welsh ended up leading to considerable delays in the eventual publication of the International Policy Statement as the disagreements between the various individuals contributing to the document had to be worked out. In the end, the IPS was not published until

---

104 George Takach, "Moving the Embassy to Jerusalem, 1979," in Don Munton and John Kirton, eds., *Canadian Foreign Policy: Selected Cases* (Scarborough, ON: Prentice-Hall Canada, 1992), 273–85; Norrin M. Ripsman and Jean-Marc F. Blanchard, "Lightning Rods Rather Than Light Switches: Arab Economic Sanctions Against Canada in 1979," *Canadian Journal of Political Science* 35:1 (March 2002), 151–74.

105 Sutherland, "Al-Mashat Affair," 590.

106 Jennifer Welsh, *At Home in the World: Canada's Global Vision for the 21st Century* (Toronto: HarperCollins, 2004).

107 Allan Gotlieb, "The Three Prophets of Foreign Policy," *Globe and Mail*, May 11, 2006, A19.

April 2005,[108] just months before Martin and the Liberals went down to defeat and the IPS was dispatched into the archives by the Conservative government of Stephen Harper.

While we can readily recognize the sources of bureaucratic power, we must also recognize that this power tends to be mitigated by the beliefs of individual civil servants themselves about the formal structure of political authority. Not only does this leaven what would otherwise develop into undisguised abuses of authority, it also allows effective ministers to exercise prerogatives that are properly theirs.[109] From this perspective, it is clear that the consensus in External Affairs on the most appropriate policy for Canada in the post-1945 period was an example of "civil service policy." For his part, the prime minister had his doubts. To his diary, King expressed annoyance at "the idea which has been growing up in E.A. [External Affairs] that these advisers are the men who are to settle everything and Ministers or P.M.'s only to be second."[110] Yet there is no evidence to suggest that the officials who spawned those policies—Pearson, Norman Robertson, Hume Wrong, and Escott Reid—did not recognize that they might propose, but ministers dispose. On the contrary: These senior officials had to work hard to secure ministerial approval for their policy preferences.

Assessing Bureaucratic Influence

In general, the bureaucracy has the least influence over the setting of Canada's broad international policy objectives, for, in theory at least, it falls to the political leadership to decide general objectives for the state in global politics. This is a responsibility recognized by all players in the policy game, politician and bureaucrat alike. Political leaders in Canada have tended to want to lay out general, long-term objectives in international policy at the outset of their mandates.

On the diplomatic side, Louis St. Laurent provided an outline of objectives in the Gray Lecture in 1947, shortly before he took over from Mackenzie King; Trudeau did the same in the foreign policy papers published in 1970; in 1985, the Mulroney government issued a "green paper" on foreign policy and in 1986 a detailed response to a parliamentary report on Canada's international relations; the government of Jean Chrétien issued a government statement on foreign policy in 1994, as did Paul Martin in 2005.[111] (By contrast, the government of Stephen Harper purposely did not engage in an international policy review in order to differentiate itself from the Chrétien/Martin governments.)

Likewise, on the defence side, white papers on defence have been published after a new prime minister takes office. In the same year that St. Laurent was outlining his vision for

---

108 Canada, *A Role of Pride and Influence in the World: Canada's International Policy Statement*, overview booklet (Ottawa: April 2005).

109 Michael M. Atkinson and Kim Richard Nossal, "Bureaucratic Politics and the New Fighter Aircraft Decisions," *Canadian Public Administration* 24:4 (Winter 1981), 531–62.

110 Quoted in Granatstein, *Man of Influence*, 107–108.

111 Excerpts from the Gray Lecture and the 1985 green paper reprinted in J.L. Granatstein, ed., *Canadian Foreign Policy: Historical Readings* (Toronto: Copp Clark Pitman, 1986); Secretary of State for External Affairs, *Canada's International Relations: Response of the Government of Canada to the Report of the Special Joint Committee of the Senate and the House of Commons* (Ottawa: December 1986) and Canada, *Canada in the World: Government Statement* (Ottawa: 1994); Canada, *A Role of Pride and Influence in the World: Canada's International Policy Statement*, overview booklet (Ottawa: April 2005).

Canada's diplomacy, the minister of national defence, Brooke Claxton, was publishing Canada's first postwar defence white paper. Paul Hellyer brought out the 1964 defence white paper shortly after the return of the Liberals to power under Pearson. After Trudeau became prime minister, the 1970 foreign policy review was followed by the 1971 defence white paper under Donald Macdonald. The Mulroney government took three years to produce a defence white paper; it was finally published in 1987 under Perrin Beatty. David Collenette was Jean Chrétien's first defence minister and he put out a defence white paper in 1994. Paul Martin's defence minister, Bill Graham, oversaw the "defence" contribution to the 2005 International Policy Statement. And in May 2008, Stephen Harper and his defence minister, Peter MacKay, unveiled the Canada First Defence Strategy.

Although all governments since 1968 have embraced "grand" decisions about Canada's international policy objectives, the day-to-day realities of statecraft tend to make it difficult to implement broad schemes. As William Hogg has noted, white papers and other major statements on international policy are little more than "snapshots in time" that cannot do much more than describe the national and international contexts of the period in which they are written.[112] Perhaps it is for this reason that at the bureaucratic level there is considerable resistance to such exercises. Charles Ritchie, who served as Canada's permanent representative to the UN, as ambassador in Washington, and as high commissioner in London, confided to his diary that he saw policy "as the tortuous approach to an ill-defined objective. All-out decisions, unqualified statements, irreconcilable antagonisms are foreign to my nature and to my training."[113] Allan Gotlieb, who was undersecretary of state for external affairs from 1977 to 1981 and ambassador to Washington from 1981 to 1989, wrote in 2004 that governments "should not try to conceptualize or package our foreign policy in value-wrapped formulations about Canada's place in the world." Rather, he preferred Lester Pearson's approach: When asked to define Canada's international policy, Pearson was reported to have said, "Ask me at the end of the year, and when I look back at what Canada has done, I'll tell you what our foreign policy is."[114] Pearson's son, Geoffrey, reflected his father's perspective. "As a general rule," he wrote in 1977, "governments do not *plan* foreign policy." Geoffrey Pearson had just finished a stint as director of the Policy Analysis Group, the division of External Affairs charged with developing long term policy objectives.[115] "Planning," he continued, "suggests clear objectives, identifiable means of reaching them, and some control of the environment in which one is operating. These conditions are not often present in world politics."[116]

---

112 William Hogg, "Plus Ça Change: Continuity, Change and Culture in Foreign Policy White Papers," *International Journal* 49:3 (Summer 2004), 536.

113 Charles Ritchie, *Diplomatic Passport: More Undiplomatic Diaries, 1946–1962* (Toronto: Macmillan, 1981), 56.

114 Allan Gotlieb, "Romanticism and Realism in Canada's Foreign Policy," *Benefactors Lecture 2004* (Toronto: C.D. Howe Institute, 2004), 31; http://www.cdhowe.org/pdf/benefactors_lecture_2004.pdf.

115 On planning international policy in Canada, see Daniel Madar and Denis Stairs, "Alone on Killer's Row: The Policy Analysis Group and the Department of External Affairs," *International Journal* 32:4 (Autumn 1977), 727ff; Howard Balloch and David Angell, "Foreign Policy Planning and Coordination in Canada: The Policy Planning Staff at External Affairs," *Canadian Public Administration* 35:4 (Winter 1992), 449–63.

116 G.A.H. Pearson, "Order Out of Chaos? Some Reflections on Foreign-Policy Planning in Canada," *International Journal* 32:3 (Autumn 1977), 756.

It is because laying out meaningful international policy objectives at the broadest levels is so difficult that ministers and their mandarins are prone to concentrate on the day-to-day problems of Canadian diplomacy—the "little" decisions. How will the Canadian delegation vote on a resolution before the UN General Assembly? How should a *note verbale* to the Chinese foreign ministry be worded? Should Canada send peacekeepers to a country split by civil war? How should the Canadian embassy in Washington respond to a bill being introduced into the United States Congress that threatens Canadian steel manufacturers? What kinds of allocations should be made for a rural development scheme in the Sahel? Should the prime minister respond personally to a case of human rights violations, or let the minister of foreign affairs take the lead? Such are the daily decisions that confront those who make international policy in Canada. Put up to ministers, and often approved on the nod, these are essentially bureaucratic decisions in the sense that officials, armed with the authority bestowed by expertise, can define tactics on behalf of elected leaders who are constrained by their own human limitations. The minister who would try to personally supervise every aspect of the vast range of Canada's international relations, or who would try to micromanage all the actions that are taken daily on Canada's behalf in the international system, would fast become swamped in a heavy sea of communications.

It is at this level, therefore, that the bureaucracy is likely to exert the most influence on the process. Expertise, access to information, and the ability to draw on the accumulated organizational "wisdom" of the executive departments makes the bureaucrat an obvious source of advice for the minister who, having defined an end, must seek the means to achieve it. The dependence of ministers on their civil servants for advice on the essentially technical tactics of statecraft provides those who tender that advice with potent influence.

CONCLUSION

The control the prime minister exercises over international policy comes from the power of appointment, the imperatives of summit diplomacy, and the prime minister's ability to determine the main priorities of government. The impact of ministers on policy results from their ability to define the broad outlines of their ministry, the dossiers over which they have responsibility, and the prestige of the office. The influence of civil servants can be seen at the other end of the spectrum—on the "little" decisions that define so much of what Canada does in the world. The agencies that were put in place during the twentieth century to provide advice to political leaders have come, therefore, to exert a growing influence on the process of foreign policy. The expertise and access to information and knowledge make officials an indispensable source of advice to a minister who, having decided on objectives, must then determine how to achieve them.

CHAPTER 10

The Role of Parliament

Parliament occupies what Gerald Schmitz and James Lee have called a paradoxical place in the making of international policy in Canada.[1] The paradox is that while according to the theory of parliamentary supremacy, Parliament is supposed to occupy a central place in Canadian politics, in fact members of Parliament (MPs) play a highly marginal role in the formation of Canada's international policies. Control over the formulation and implementation of foreign policy remains firmly vested in the hands of the political executive in Cabinet. "A foreign policy decision is a cabinet decision," James Eayrs wrote in 1961, and so it remains today.[2] Although responsible to Parliament, ministers of the Crown have, by convention and practice, relegated to the legislature a distinctly secondary role. Indeed, some would go further and deny that Parliament has even a modicum of influence over international policy. Roy Rempel, who spent four years on Parliament Hill as a foreign and defence policy adviser, leaves in no doubt his view: The subtitle of his memoir is *An Insider's Account of the Irrelevance of Parliament in the Making of Canadian Foreign and Defence Policy*.[3] The purpose of this chapter is to explore the nature of Parliament's contribution to international policy in Canada and to identify the reasons it is as marginalized as it is.

LIMITED POWERS, LIMITED INFLUENCE?

It would be hard to deny the common academic view that Parliament plays only a limited role in the making of international policy in Canada. There are a number of reasons for the limited influence of the Canadian legislature.

First, the nature of foreign policy is such that it provides MPs with relatively few opportunities to engage in the task for which legislators are most noted—lawmaking. Legislation on international policy does not often come before members of Parliament, although there are some notable exceptions. For example, the government tends to use legislation to organize the bureaucracy for the conduct of international policy. In 1909, as we saw in Chapter 9, the government of Sir Wilfrid Laurier introduced the External Affairs Act to create a Canadian foreign ministry; in 1982, the government of Pierre Elliott Trudeau used legislation to amalgamate External Affairs with the trade promotion functions of the Department of Industry, Trade and Commerce; and in 2005, the Liberal government of Paul Martin tried unsuccessfully to use legislation to split the Department of Foreign Affairs and International Trade (as it had become in 1993) back into two separate departments—a failure we will discuss below. (It should be added, however, that legislation is not always necessary for government organization. As we noted in the previous chapter, Canada's bureaucracy for delivering international development assistance was created by a series of Orders-in-Council.)

---

1 Gerald Schmitz and James Lee, "Split Images and Serial Affairs: Reviews, Reorganizations, and Parliamentary Roles," in Andrew Fenton Cooper and Dane Rowlands, eds., *Canada Among Nations 2005: Split Images* (Toronto: Oxford University Press, 2005), 245.

2 James Eayrs, *The Art of the Possible: Government and Foreign Policy in Canada* (Toronto: University of Toronto Press, 1961), 103. For a more recent assessment, see John English, "The Member of Parliament and Foreign Policy," in Fen Osler Hampson and Maureen Appel Molot, eds., *Canada Among Nations 1998: Leadership and Dialogue* (Ottawa: Carleton University Press, 1998), 69–80.

3 Roy Rempel, *The Chatter Box: An Insider's Account of the Irrelevance of Parliament in the Making of Canadian Foreign and Defence Policy* (Toronto: Breakout Educational Network, 2002).

Likewise, when the Canadian government signs an international treaty, it may need to implement it by introducing or amending domestic legislation. Thus, Bill C-130 was introduced in 1988 to implement the free-trade agreement with the United States, and Bill C-53, the Settlement of International Investment Disputes Act, was introduced in the House of Commons in March 2007 in order to implement the Convention on the Settlement of Investment Disputes between States and Nationals of other States, which Canada had signed on December 15, 2006. Not all international agreements, however, need to be implemented by legislation. Standing rules give the government "blanket authority" to negotiate and implement agreements on a number of issues, such as double taxation, social security arrangements, extradition agreements, or agreements to transfer offenders from other states to serve their time in Canadian prisons.

Finally, some international initiatives require legislation, particularly in the economic, environmental, and resource issue areas. When the Trudeau government wanted to assert Canadian sovereignty in the Arctic in 1970, it introduced the Arctic Waters Pollution Prevention bill.[4] When the Liberal government of Jean Chrétien got into a quarrel with the United States in 1996 over the efforts of the Clinton administration to extend American law extraterritorially into Canada, it amended legislation that had been introduced by the Progressive Conservative government of Brian Mulroney in 1984—the Foreign Extraterritorial Measures Act, 1985—by dramatically increasing fines for anyone in Canada who obeyed foreign legislation.[5]

A second reason for the lack of a legislative role in international policy decision-making is that Cabinet has been unwilling to grant Parliament significant decision-making powers in this area of policy. When Paul Martin, Sr., Lester Pearson's external affairs minister, wrote in 1969 that legislators "can discuss, but they cannot make, foreign policy,"[6] he was reflecting a half-century of executive dominance over the policy-making process.

It is true that prime ministers from Wilfrid Laurier to Stephen Harper have proclaimed that, on matters of foreign policy, it would be Parliament that would make the decisions. Laurier was the first to use the "Parliament will decide" formula. In a House of Commons debate on the Naval Service bill in February 1910, he said:

> If England is at war we are at war and are liable to attack. I do not say that we shall always be attacked, neither do I say that we would take part in all the wars of England. That is a matter that must be determined by circumstances, upon which the Canadian parliament will have to pronounce and will have to decide.[7]

---

4 Franklyn Griffiths, ed., *Politics of the Northwest Passage* (Montréal and Kingston: McGill-Queen's University Press, 1987); John Kirton and Don Munton, "The *Manhattan* Voyages, 1969–70," in Munton and Kirton, *Canadian Foreign Policy: Selected Cases* (Scarborough: Prentice-Hall Canada, 1992), 205–26.

5 Kim Richard Nossal, "'Without Regard for the Interests of Others': Canada and American Unilateralism in the Post–Cold War Era," *American Review of Canadian Studies* 27:2 (Summer 1997), 179–97.

6 Paul Martin, "The Role of the Canadian Parliament in the Formulation of Foreign Policy," *The Parliamentarian* 50 (October 1969), 259.

7 Quoted in C.P. Stacey, *Canada and the Age of Conflict: A History of Canadian External Policies*, vol. 1: *1867–1921* (Toronto: Macmillan, 1977), 135.

Mackenzie King invoked the formula over the Chanak crisis of 1922. Facing a request from the Imperial government in London for Canadian troops, King was able to deflect the request by insisting that such an issue would have to be debated by Parliament.[8] Seventy years later, Chrétien would echo King's Chanak diplomacy when faced with requests for commitments of Canadian troops to peacekeeping missions in the former Yugoslavia. In 1995, not really wanting to join what would become the NATO Implementation Force (IFOR) in Bosnia, Chrétien demurred: "Before we make a decision, we will go to the House of Commons."[9] Likewise, when the Harper government was facing increasing calls from the opposition parties to withdraw from Canada's combat mission in Afghanistan in the fall of 2007, Harper appointed a blue-ribbon panel chaired by a former Liberal deputy prime minister, John Manley, to examine Canada's options in Afghanistan and advise Parliament: "I have no doubt," Harper said, "they will examine the issues honestly, fairly, and expertly, and offer wise, impartial counsel that will help Parliamentarians and all Canadians choose the right course for Canada in Afghanistan."[10]

But when prime ministers say "Parliament will decide" issues of international policy, they do not actually mean it, for prime ministers have always jealously guarded the prerogative to decide such matters. What they *really* use this formula for is as a refuge from unwanted foreign requests or from uncomfortable domestic political circumstances.

The third reason Parliament has such a slim impact on policy is because historically relatively few politicians developed an expertise in international issues. To be sure, it is difficult to measure precisely how much interest the average parliamentarian has in international issues. A study undertaken by Douglas Bland shows that while many MPs have a considerable interest in defence questions, they find it difficult to find the information necessary for them to develop expertise in this area.[11] Moreover, in any Parliament, there will always be those who have a well-developed expertise in international affairs and who tend to be highly active on matters of international policy. For example, Bill Graham (Liberal: Rosedale), first elected in 1993, was a professor of international law. Appointed chair of the Standing Committee on Foreign Affairs and International Trade in 1995, he was appointed to the cabinet by Chrétien in January 2002, taking over from John Manley as foreign minister, before becoming minister of national defence in the second Martin cabinet (2004–2006). Likewise, Pierre Pettigrew (Liberal: Papineau), who replaced Graham as foreign minister in 2004, was always interested in international trade. Daniel Turp (Bloc Québécois: Beauharnois-Salaberry), who served in the House of Commons from 1997 to 2000, was also a professor of international law at the Université de Montréal. Turp was one of the most active opposition MPs during the Kosovo war in 1999, persistently pursuing the government on the international legal aspects of NATO's operations in the Balkans. He also tried on a number of occasions to secure approval of legislation that would require Parliament to approve international treaties (he was more successful in convincing his colleagues in the Assemblée nationale du Québec

---

8 James Eayrs, *In Defence of Canada*, vol. 1: *From the Great War to the Great Depression* (Toronto: University of Toronto Press, 1964), 78–80.

9 *Globe and Mail*, October 20, 1995.

10 "Prime Minister Harper Announces Independent Advisory Panel on Afghan Mission," October 12, 2007, available http://pm.gc.ca/eng/media.asp?id=1853.

11 Douglas L. Bland, "Parliament's Duty to Defend Canada," *Canadian Military Review* 1:4 (Winter 2000–2001), 35–44.

of the wisdom of such legislation: As we will see in Chapter 12, in 2002, the Québec legislature passed such legislation for international agreements signed by the Québec government.)

However, these are the exceptions. Most parliamentarians tend to have a parochial outlook that keeps their gaze fixed on domestic issues. Such parochialism is at once reinforced and reinforcing in circular fashion. "Let us conciliate Quebec and Ontario before we start conciliating Roumania and Ukrania," an MP told the House in 1923.[12] Such a view has found persistent expression. In 1994, Janko Peric, (Liberal: Cambridge), who himself was born in Croatia, argued that instead of sending Canadian soldiers to keep warring factions in the former Yugoslavia apart, Canadians should put themselves first. "The reality," he said, "is that we are here and they are there."[13] Such parochialism makes it difficult for ordinary parliamentarians to usurp the longstanding prerogatives of the executive in the shaping of external policy.

This is not to suggest that Parliament does not have a role in international policy. Rather, because parliamentarians do not have the *power* to shape foreign policy, they can only have an impact on the policy process, as Eayrs has noted, by influencing the decision-makers.[14] Such influence is exerted both formally and informally. To exercise this influence, they can use not only their status as a "watchdog" over the executive, but also the visibility that accompanies their position. They have a number of opportunities to intervene in the policy process: in the Senate or the House of Commons, in parliamentary committees, in caucus meetings, or in press conferences. They enjoy a privileged access to ministers and senior civil servants. In short, members of Parliament have the ability to help shape the process of making international policy. Whether they do so, however, is another matter, and so we must examine the nature and extent of parliamentary influence on international policy.

THE SENATE

Canada's upper house was originally designed to provide each of the country's regions (or "divisions") with some representation in federal institutions and provide what Sir John A. Macdonald called "the sober second-thought in legislation." But because the British North America Act, 1867, granted the power to name senators to the Governor General—and thus in practice the prime minister of the day—the Senate quickly turned into the country's foremost pork barrel. Every prime minister from Macdonald to Harper has used the Senate to provide friends and party supporters with a sweet patronage appointment that in 2009 carried a basic salary of $130,400 per year and is tenable until the age of 75.

Because it has been so consistently used for patronage, the two functions envisaged by the Fathers of Confederation for the Senate never evolved. Indeed, the upper house never acquired an important political role in Canada. Well might Sir George Foster, Sir Robert Borden's minister of trade and commerce who had represented Canada at the Versailles peace conference, remark on his appointment in 1921 that "I have today signed my warrant of political death. How colourless the Senate—the entering gate to coming extinction."[15]

---

12 Quoted in Eayrs, *Art of the Possible*, 113.

13 Interview in *Hamilton Spectator*, February 5, 1994.

14 Eayrs, *Art of the Possible*, 103.

15 Cited in W. Stewart Wallace, *The Memoirs of the Rt. Hon. Sir George Foster* (Toronto: Macmillan, 1933), 207.

However, David C. Docherty suggests that while Canadians sneer at the Senate and treat it "like a strange relative, best not talked about,"[16] we should remember that it does have influence on politics in Canada, including foreign policy: It can approve or reject legislation, it debates issues of public interest, and it undertakes inquiries on important issues.

The Senate can suggest amendments to legislation, just as it can reject bills passed by the House of Commons. However, this tends to occur only on those rare occasions when the upper house is controlled by the opposition party. Thus, for example, in 1913, the Liberal opposition, which had a majority in the Senate, voted down the naval bill of Robert Borden's Conservative government. And in the spring of 1992, both Liberal and Conservative senators voted down Bill C-93, legislation introduced by the Mulroney government to transfer international cultural programs to the Canada Council.

The Senate can stall legislation emanating from the House of Commons. For example, in July 1988, John Turner, leader of the Liberal opposition, sought to force a general election by instructing the Liberal majority in the upper house, most of them appointed by Trudeau, to vote against Bill C-130, the free-trade legislation. But because the legitimacy of the Senate as a "representative" institution has been completely eroded by its use as an instrument for patronage, Turner's ploy was widely denounced, by both supporters and opponents of the free-trade agreement.[17] Indeed, the Liberal who chaired the Senate Foreign Affairs committee, George van Roggen, chose to resign as chair rather than vote against Bill C-130 on Turner's instructions.

Where can senators try to exercise their influence on international policy? Not on the floor of the Senate, where debate is usually perfunctory and questions about foreign affairs that are put to the government leader during the few minutes that pass for Question Period are invariably met with the standard answer that inquiries of the government have to be made before a proper response can be given.

Rather, senators seek to exercise influence on the various standing and special committees of the Senate, whose principal task is to carry out inquiries into specific issues. The committees and subcommittees can vary from one parliamentary session to another, depending on the priorities of the government. Thus, for example, since the Committee on External Relations was established in March 1938, there has always been a committee on foreign affairs—since 2006, it has been called the Standing Committee on Foreign Affairs and International Trade—but there has not always been a committee on national defence. Sometimes there has been a separate standing committee, sometimes a special committee, and sometimes as a subcommittee of the foreign affairs committee. Abolished in the 1990s, it was recreated in May 2001 as the Standing Committee on National Security and Defence.

Since 1960, the Senate has evolved an important investigatory role—conducting in-depth inquiries into different aspects of policy in Canada.[18] In international policy, Senate committees have examined a wide array of policy issues. For example, throughout the 1980s, the

---

16 David C. Docherty, "The Canadian Senate: Chamber of Sober Reflection or Loony Cousin Best Not Talked About," *Journal of Legislative Studies* 8:3 (2002), 27–48.

17 Peter C. Newman, "An Exercise in Liberal Arrogance," *Maclean's*, August 8, 1988, 29; Diane Francis, "A Job for the Hacks and Bagmen," *Maclean's*, August 15, 1988, 9.

18 Colin Campbell, *The Canadian Senate: A Lobby from Within* (Toronto: Macmillan of Canada, 1978), 10.

subcommittee on defence undertook a series of studies on the Canadian Forces (CF).[19] It was also in the 1960s that the Senate began contributing to the foreign policy reviews that generally followed changes in prime minister. Trudeau's decision in 1968 to conduct an extensive review of foreign policy provided the committee with the impetus to undertake its own review of selected aspects of external policy. Likewise, senators were members of special joint committees of Parliament that conducted reviews of foreign policy for the Mulroney government in 1985 and 1986 and for the Chrétien government in 1994.[20]

Senate investigations invariably provide a solid contribution to the discussion of international policy. The committee reports feature meticulous research based on testimony from numerous expert witnesses. Moreover, the reports tend to be more reflective, more critical, and less partisan, simply because senators do not have to face reelection and cannot be punished by prime ministers the way members of the House of Commons can. On occasion, Senate committees will float trial balloons, making the kind of unusual or audacious recommendations that would be impossible for their colleagues in the House of Commons, who have to be more sensitive to the moods of public opinion or to the tendency of prime ministers to punish those who step outside the tight controls established by the political centre discussed in Chapter 6.

Senate committee investigations have varying impacts on international policy. In some cases, Senate reports may contribute to shifts in thinking about a particular issue. For example, the Foreign Affairs committee's 1978 report on Canadian–American trade relations concluded that the government should "consider seriously the option of bilateral free trade with the United States." The committee then spent the next three-and-a-half years exploring the feasibility of that option, concluding in its final report in 1982 that Canada had more to gain than it had to lose by negotiating a general, across-the-board free-trade agreement.[21] The Trudeau government chose not to embrace that advice; instead it focused on trying to liberalize trade at the Tokyo Round of the General Agreement on Tariffs and Trade talks in Geneva and explore sectoral free trade with the United States. But the Senate committee made an important contribution to the shift in thinking about free trade that occurred in Canada in the mid 1980s, particularly the positive report of the Royal Commission on the Economic Union and Development Prospects for Canada (the Macdonald Commission). The Senate committee added to the process of legitimizing the free-trade idea (and, by the same token, delegitimizing the notion that free trade would spell the end of the country).[22]

---

19 Canada, Parliament, Senate, Standing Committee on Foreign Affairs, Sub-Committee on National Defence, *Manpower in the Canadian Armed Forces* (Ottawa: January 1982); *Canada's Maritime Defence* (Ottawa: May 1983); *Canada's Territorial Air Defence* (Ottawa: January 1985); *Canada's Land Forces* (Ottawa: October 1989). See R.P. Pattee and Paul G. Thomas, "The Senate and Defence Policy: Subcommittee Report on Canada's Maritime Defence," in David Taras, ed., *Parliament and Canadian Foreign Policy* (Toronto: Canadian Institute of International Affairs, 1985), 101–119.

20 Parliament, Special Joint Committee on Canada's External Relations, *Independence and Internationalism: Report of the Special Joint Committee on Canada's External Relations* (Ottawa: 1986); Special Joint Committee of the Senate and the House of Commons Reviewing Canadian Foreign Policy, *Canada's Foreign Policy: Principles and Priorities for the Future* (Ottawa: November 1994).

21 Standing Committee on Foreign Affairs, *Canada–United States Relations*, vol. 2 (Ottawa: 1982), 124; vol. 3, passim.

22 G. Bruce Doern and Brian W. Tomlin, *Faith and Fear: The Free Trade Story* (Toronto: Stoddart, 1991); Tomlin, "Leaving the Past Behind: The Free Trade Initiative Assessed," in Nelson Michaud and

We can see a similar dynamic in the area of defence and security. Senate committees have been more inclined to take conservative positions on defence and have been one of the more robust champions of increased defence spending, criticizing the spending cuts imposed on the Department of National Defence in the 1970s, 1980s, and 1990s. After 9/11 in particular, pressure from the Senate for a reversal of the long-term secular reduction of spending on the CF grew more insistent, buttressed by three reports issued in rapid succession in 2002.[23] It can be argued that the pressure of the Senate committee under the leadership of Colin Kenny contributed to the substantial increases in spending introduced by Martin after he assumed the leadership of the Liberal party and the prime ministership from Chrétien in 2003.

By the same token, however, governments may brusquely reject the recommendations of Senate committees and even try to punish senators for taking positions the government finds embarrassing. For example, in February 2007, the Standing Senate Committee on Foreign Affairs and International Trade, chaired by Senator Hugh Segal, published a devastating critique of global development assistance to Africa. Gathering testimony from over 400 witnesses, the committee concluded that ordinary Africans had been completely failed by both their own leadership and the international community, including Canada. The Committee went so far as to suggest that the government should conduct an immediate review of the Canadian International Development Agency to determine whether CIDA should be abolished because the agency was "ineffective, costly, and overly bureaucratic."[24] Not only did the government studiously ignore the report, but Segal was forced to resign as chair of the committee by the Conservative leadership.[25]

Often the government simply remains indifferent to the efforts of the Senate to contribute to the development of policy. One reason for such indifference is the very nature of parliamentary surveillance: Ex post facto investigations are essentially reactive, responding to developments elsewhere. For example, the 1993 study on peacekeeping followed the radical transformation of peacekeeping roles in the post–Cold War era.[26] Trailing government policy in such a fashion gave the committee considerable capacity to suggest modifications to established policy; its capacity for taking the lead was more limited.[27]

Kim Richard Nossal, eds., *Diplomatic Departures: The Conservative Era in Canadian Foreign Policy, 1984–1993* (Vancouver: UBC Press, 2001), 45–58.

23 Standing Senate Committee on National Security and Defence, *Canadian Security and Military Preparedness* (Ottawa: February 2002); *Defence of North America: A Canadian Responsibility* (Ottawa: September 2002); *For an Extra $130 Bucks . . . Update on Canada's Military Financial Crisis* (Ottawa: November 2002).

24 Standing Senate Committee on Foreign Affairs and International Trade, *Overcoming 40 Years of Failure: A New Road Map for Sub-Saharan Africa* (Ottawa: February 2007), available http://www.parl.gc.ca/39/1/parlbus/commbus/senate/com-e/fore-e/rep-e/repafrifeb07-e.pdf.

25 "Hugh Segal Turfed from Helm of Senate Committee," CTV.ca, February 17, 2007.

26 Standing Senate Committee on Foreign Affairs, *Meeting New Challenges: Canada's Response to a New Generation of Peacekeeping* (Ottawa: February 1993).

27 W.M. Dobell, "Parliament's Foreign Policy Committees," in Taras, ed., *Parliament and Canadian Foreign Policy*, 29–34.

THE HOUSE OF COMMONS

The lower house has greater political visibility than the Senate, and generally the members of the House of Commons are considered to be more important than senators. There are three reasons for this. First, MPs enjoy more legitimacy than senators, since they are elected rather than appointed for patronage reasons. Second, it is from the ranks of MPs that the prime minister draws the vast majority of the cabinet. Third, it is the members of the House of Commons who determine who will form the government by giving or denying their vote of support to the individual who is called on by the Governor General to form a government.

That, at least, is the theory; the practice is rather different. The potentially enormous power of ordinary MPs to make and unmake governments is deeply constrained by a number of factors, the most important of which is party discipline. All MPs, but particularly on the government side, are expected to vote precisely as the party leadership demands (except in the rare case of "free votes," where the MP is permitted to vote with his or her conscience on an issue). While we see party discipline operating in all parliamentary systems, in Canada it takes a particularly pernicious form, as we saw in Chapter 6, entrenching the central power of the prime minister. Paradoxically, the more democratic way in which party leaders are selected in Canada diminishes democracy by giving party leaders overweening power. The fact that Canadian party leaders are selected by conventions, not by the party's parliamentary caucus, gives them the kind of autonomy—and power—that their counterparts in Britain or Australia simply do not enjoy. In London and Canberra, party leaders must always be wary that their parliamentary caucuses do not revolt and decide to remove them from power. In Canada, we have only seen one instance of a caucus coup in the recent past: In December 2008, Stéphane Dion, the Liberal leader of the opposition, was unceremoniously pushed from office (though, like Margaret Thatcher in Britain and Simon Crean and Mark Latham in Australia, he was given an opportunity to fall on his sword gracefully and resign).

The power that springs from leadership selection is entrenched by two other powers: the right to expel MPs from caucus and the related power to grant or deny an individual the right to run for the party in election. Thus party leaders have the ability to impose the ultimate punishment on those who sit behind them in the House: banishment to one of the desks, far away from the Speaker up by the curtains, that are reserved for independents; or refusal to allow an individual to run for election under the banner of the party. While some MPs have been able to survive expulsion—John Nunziata managed to win one election in the Toronto riding of York South–Weston as an independent after he was expelled from the Liberal caucus by Chrétien in 1996—more often than not excommunication will put an immediate end to an individual's political career. Given such power vested in the hands of party leaders, it is hardly surprising that MPs have so little autonomy and thus so little impact on the policymaking process.

While MPs may not *make* foreign policy decisions, members of the House of Commons who are not members of Cabinet nonetheless exert an influence in an indirect way by fulfilling three important political functions: the representation, legitimation, and educative functions.[28]

---

28 R.B. Byers, "Perceptions of Parliamentary Surveillance of the Executive: The Case of Canadian Defence Policy," *Canadian Journal of Political Science* 5 (June 1972), 234.

Speaking for Voters: The Representative Function

In a parliamentary democracy, representative government implies both the periodic accountability of the representatives to the represented through the electoral system and a continuing responsiveness to the demands and interests of constituents. The House of Commons is where this representative function occurs as MPs seek to present the interests of their constituents. How MPs do this depends on which side of the speaker they sit. Opposition members tend to use the openness of the floor of the House, where parliamentary rules allow MPs to draw public attention to constituents' concerns. They can make statements, ask questions during Question Period, lay petitions from their constituents before the House, and participate in a variety of debates—from debates on legislation, "take-note" debates on matters of national concern, or during adjournment debates (known colloquially as "the late show").

Government members, by contrast, have no less interest in communicating the concerns of constituents to ministers in Cabinet, but most are prone to keep this process hidden from public view when doing so might embarrass the government. The imperatives of party discipline and the ambitions of backbenchers themselves combine to put a premium on the use of private channels for those who sit on the government side. Thus, for example, in the winter of 2004–2005, when the Martin government was considering whether to join the Ballistic Missile Defense (BMD) program being constructed by the United States,[29] Liberal MPs sought to impress on Martin the depth of opposition to BMD being expressed by their constituents. While the opposition to BMD in Québec was almost unanimous—and hence Martin's eventual decision in February 2005 not to participate in BMD was widely attributed to that province[30]—in fact many Liberal MPs in other parts of the country were just as passionate in representing the opposition of their constituents, though many tended to do so more privately.

On most foreign policy issues, representing public concerns is problematic. Local issues, or some issues in Canadian–American relations such as softwood lumber, will inevitably prompt MPs to press these concerns in the House.[31] But as we noted in Chapter 4, most international policy issues remain sufficiently peripheral to the majority of Canadians that they do not seek to translate their interests into concrete political action. Where there is heightened interest in an issue, it tends to be geographically diffused, creating few imperatives for members of Parliament whose electoral bailiwicks are by nature and design geographically localized.

Creating Legitimacy: The Legitimation Function

The House of Commons draws most of its influence from its legitimacy as the only political institution elected by the country as a whole, thus able to speak in the name of the political community. The Commons confers legitimacy on the prime minister and the cabinet simply by sustaining the governing party in office. In foreign affairs, however, legitimacy

---

29 James Fergusson, "Shall We Dance? The Missile Defence Decision, NORAD Renewal, and the Future of Canada–US Defence Relations," *Canadian Military Journal* 6:2 (Summer 2005), 13–22.

30 On Québec opinion on BMD and how to interpret it, see Pierre Martin, "All Québec's Fault, Again? Québec Public Opinion and Canada's Rejection of Missile Defence," *Policy Options* (May 2006), 41–44.

31 Don Munton and Dale H. Poel, "Electoral Accountability and Canadian Foreign Policy: The Case of Foreign Investment," *International Journal* 33 (Winter 1977–8), esp. 220–22.

is conferred in a more episodic and indirect way, since so many decisions are taken by the executive without reference to, or debate in, the House. MPs express confidence in the executive through periodic votes, including formal votes of confidence, and, more indirectly, by a continued willingness to approve the annual departmental estimates necessary to allow the government to function in the international sphere.

Governments also use votes, motions, and resolutions in Parliament on potentially controversial foreign policy issues to create legitimacy for the course of action they have chosen, even when they do not need parliamentary approval.[32] MPs approved Canada's membership in the United Nations in 1945 and the North Atlantic Treaty in 1949. Likewise, the government of Brian Mulroney introduced a motion endorsing the free-trade initiative on March 17, 1987, even though no formal parliamentary approval for these negotiations was needed.

Such efforts to create legitimacy are particularly important when it involves the most important decision that a political community can take: to go to war. Unlike the United States, where only the Congress is authorized to declare war, there is no need for the executive in Canada to seek the approval of Parliament. All that is required is an Order-in-Council requesting that the monarch issue a declaration of war. And, until 1950, the government could put Canada's armed forces on active duty whenever it decided that there was an emergency. Neither a formal declaration of war nor the deployment of Canada's armed forces require parliamentary debate or approval; the executive alone has the authority to do this.

However, while Laurier committed Canadian troops to fight the Boer War in 1899 without any involvement by Parliament, subsequent governments were rather less willing to take this delicate and important decision without the legitimacy of parliamentary approval. Thus, in August 1914, Canada was placed in a state of war when King George V issued the formal proclamation that the British Empire was at war with Germany. The Canadian parliament was prorogued for the summer and the Imperial decision was implemented by a series of Orders-in-Council issued by the Canadian government. However, Borden recalled Parliament and two weeks later the House of Commons approved of the government's policy, albeit ex post facto.

By the time that Nazi Germany attacked Poland on September 1, 1939, prompting Britain to declare war, Canada was a sovereign state. Although Parliament was prorogued for the summer, King recalled the MPs and in a Speech from the Throne outlined the government's intention to declare war on Germany. There was no formal motion approving the declaration. Rather, MPs were told that a vote to approve the address in reply to the Speech from the Throne would be considered approval for a declaration of war. On September 9, the address in reply was approved, with only four MPs, including three Québec nationalists, dissenting from the motion. The next day King George VI, as king of Canada, issued a formal declaration of war against Germany. A similar procedure was used in July 1940 against Italy, although this time the motion explicitly called for Parliament to approve a declaration of war.

By contrast, in July 1950, the government of Louis St. Laurent committed Canadian forces to the defence of South Korea after North Korea's invasion, shortly after the House of Commons had prorogued for the summer. When Parliament returned in August 1950,

---

32 Peter C. Dobell, *Canada in World Affairs*, vol. 17: *1971–1973* (Toronto: Canadian Institute of International Affairs, 1985), 395.

however, that decision was not debated. Indeed, when the prime minister was asked if there would be resolution approving the use of force in Korea, St. Laurent was blunt:

> No, sir; that would be something which has never been done. The government announces to parliament what its policy is, and asks parliament for the ways and means to carry it out. It is for that reason that we have our appropriation bill. If parliament does not authorize the ways and means to carry out the policy, it cannot be carried out.[33]

Nonetheless, in the fall of 1950, partly in response to the Korean War deployment, the National Defence Act was amended to require the government to recall Parliament within 10 days of putting troops on active service. (However, as critics of the legislation noted at the time, Section 32 says nothing at all about what Parliament is to do once it is so recalled other than "meet and sit"!)

In August 1990, Brian Mulroney ordered the dispatch of three naval vessels and then a squadron of CF-18 jet fighters to the Persian Gulf to participate in an international coalition that had been formed after the Iraqi invasion of Kuwait on August 2, 1990. As in the case of the Korean War, the House of Commons had risen for its summer break and was not due to reconvene until September 24. However, Mulroney had little desire to recall Parliament: He was reluctant to subject the government's handling of the Oka crisis (discussed in Chapter 3) to parliamentary debate. It was not until October 23, 1990—long after the Oka barricades had been dismantled—that the Commons approved the deployment to the Gulf.

A similar political calculation lay behind the motion introduced by the Harper minority government in May 2006 that the House of Commons extend Canada's military mission to Afghanistan until 2009. While Canadian troops had been deployed to Afghanistan shortly after 9/11 without the explicit approval of Parliament, the motion to extend the mission was designed by Harper to remove Afghanistan as a potential election issue; a further resolution in 2008, extending the mission to 2011, removed Afghanistan as an election issue in the 2008 elections.[34]

The executive can, of course, be deprived of authority by a vote of non-confidence, either if the government party is in a minority position in the House or if the government's own backbench revolts. While minority governments have occurred with some regularity, confidence in the government has been withdrawn formally only five times. Arthur Meighen in 1926, John Diefenbaker in 1963, Trudeau in 1974, Clark in 1979, and Martin in 2005 were all forced to seek dissolution, though the non-confidence in 1974 should be treated differently, since the Trudeau government wanted to go to the electorate and engineered its own defeat. Only once has confidence in the government been withheld on an issue that might be broadly construed as falling within the foreign policy sphere. In February 1963, the Diefenbaker government was brought down on the question of its handling of defence policy.[35] We return to the particular problems of minority governments below.

---

33 House of Commons, *Debates*, 21st Parl., 3rd sess., September 8, 1950, p. 495, quoted in Michel Rossignol, "Parliament, the *National Defence Act*, and the Decision to Participate," Background Paper BP-303 (Ottawa: Parliamentary Research Branch, Library of Parliament, August 1992).

34 David Rudd, "Afghanistan, Darfur and the Great (Unexpected) Debate over Canada's Military Role in the World," *Policy Options* 27:5 (June 2006), 53–57; Kim Richard Nossal, "No Exit: Canada and the 'War Without End' in Afghanistan," in Hans-Georg Ehrhart and Charles C. Pentland, eds., *NATO and the International Engagement in Afghanistan* (Toronto: Oxford University Press, 2009).

35 Peyton V. Lyon, *Canada in World Affairs, 1961–1963* (Toronto: University of Toronto Press, 1968), 176–92.

Likewise, the incidence of large-scale backbench revolts in the House of Commons is rare. On matters of external policy, it has occurred only over the issue of conscription (in 1944, 34 Liberals from Québec voted against the King government's conscription legislation). Canadian governments have been fortunate (from their perspective at least) to have sitting behind them in the House a placid group of MPs with a healthy regard for party discipline. Moreover, when dissidence occurs, it usually involves only a few MPs. For example, a small group of Liberal backbenchers opposed the Trudeau government on the issue of the cruise missile in June 1983; another group of Liberals opposed the Chrétien government on the same issue in 1994.[36] During the first *intifada* uprising in the territories occupied by Israel after 1987, a small pro-Arab group emerged in the Progressive Conservative caucus to oppose the more pro-Israeli perspective of Prime Minister Mulroney.[37] However, it is necessary to keep in mind that these exceptions confirm the rule: On the implementation of foreign policy, MPs have little say.

Speaking to Voters: The Educative Function

In theory, discussion of international policy in the House of Commons might be educative in two senses: It might "educate" MPs themselves, by increasing their knowledge, expertise, and understanding of an issue; or it might "educate" the public and develop public opinion on an issue. In practice, very little of the former occurs; the only "education" that results from such activities as Question Period and parliamentary debates is that of the attentive public.

Question Period is often held up as a means by which the opposition parties can draw public attention to foreign policy issues by seeking to elicit from ministers an indication of the government's position on those issues. As Roy Rempel has noted, this part of the House's business has become deeply politicized. Largely because it is the only part of parliamentary proceedings well covered by the media, Question Period is often marked by undignified shouting matches, with all participants trying to produce a sound bite that will make it onto the evening news. Opposition MPs ask questions with exaggerated and feigned outrage, government MPs try to shout down the opposition, and ministers try hard to avoid answering questions put to them.[38] However, these brief exchanges, when broadcast on the evening news, can have important policy impacts.[39]

Debates in the House of Commons provide some opportunity for education in international affairs. However, debates also provide an opportunity for MPs to engage in most of the other functions noted above. The House of Commons has traditionally limited full-scale debates over foreign policy to major issues in Canadian foreign policy. Over the years, debates have been held on questions of war—as we have seen—and peace, and also key transitions such as the Free Trade Agreement with the United States.

---

36 D.W. Middlemiss and J.J. Sokolsky, *Canadian Defence: Decisions and Determinants* (Toronto: Harcourt Brace Jovanovich, 1989), 52–53; also House of Commons, *Debates*, 35th Parl., 1st sess., February 3, 1994, 888–89.

37 David H. Goldberg and David Taras, "Collision Course: Joe Clark, Canadian Jews, and the Palestinian Uprising," in Taras and Goldberg, eds., *The Domestic Battleground: Canada and the Arab–Israeli Conflict* (Montréal and Kingston: McGill-Queen's University Press, 1989), 209–210.

38 Rempel, *Chatterbox*, 181–83.

39 See Donald J. Savoie, *Governing from the Centre: The Concentration of Power in Canadian Politics* (Toronto: University of Toronto Press, 1999), 94–96.

One such symbolic occasion was the achievement by Sir Robert Borden of equal status as a separate actor in international politics, symbolized by Canadian membership in the League of Nations. Borden submitted the Treaty of Versailles for approval to the House of Commons on September 2, 1919. A lively debate over the Treaty ensued, one that involved a large number of speakers and demonstrated the range of opinion about Canada's proper role in world affairs.[40]

However, Sir Robert Borden's successors in the interwar period found various reasons for stifling parliamentary discussion of international affairs. Neither King nor R.B. Bennett was much disposed to promote parliamentary debate on foreign policy, frequently grounding their justification in the argument that discussion of international events unfolding in Europe and the Far East might upset the delicate balance of world power.[41] It was a not uncommon argument. Paul Martin, Sr., Pearson's external affairs minister, wrote in 1969 that "Over-participation on the part of Parliament tends to hinder diplomacy. The public discussion of delicate international negotiations could well lead to detrimental consequences for the country and even for the world."[42] Likewise, in May 1995, when Bosnian Serbs captured a number of Canadian peacekeepers in Pale, Chrétien resisted calls by the opposition Bloc Québécois and Reform for a parliamentary debate, arguing that discussion in the House would weaken the hands of officials negotiating with the Bosnian Serbs. "It is better to be cool," Chrétien said.[43]

But in general, governments understand the symbolic importance of parliamentary debates on foreign policy. After the Second World War, Louis St. Laurent attempted to foster more debate in the House when he assumed the External Affairs portfolio in 1946. The following year, he used consideration of the estimates of the Department of External Affairs to present a full report on Canada's international activities to the House, triggering an extensive debate on foreign policy.[44] Thereafter, when the House went into Committee of Supply for consideration of the External Affairs estimates, it became practice to have the external affairs minister brief interested MPs on Canadian foreign policy. This practice, continued by Pearson, was not always seen to be successful. Pearson complained to MPs in 1950 that "I have pleaded for more interest in external affairs in the House of Commons to empty benches and empty press gallery seats. . . . Possibly we ourselves, in the House of Commons, are somewhat to blame for the lack of interest."[45] A quarter of a century later, with his years as foreign minister, leader of the opposition, and prime minister behind him, Pearson was to note in his memoirs that "much of the debating seemed artificial, a kind of play-acting. The words were for the record, not uttered in the hope that they would change the mind of anyone. . . . [I]t often seemed that to talk in the House was not relevant or important enough to be given priority over other and graver business of government."[46]

---

40 Stacey, *Age of Conflict*, 289–94.

41 Eayrs, *Art of the Possible*, 108.

42 Martin, "Role of the Canadian Parliament," 259.

43 Jeff Sallot, "Why Ottawa's Keeping Its Cool," *Globe and Mail*, June 6, 1995, A6.

44 R. Barry Farrell, *The Making of Canadian Foreign Policy* (Scarborough: Prentice-Hall Canada, 1969), 146–47.

45 Quoted in Eayrs, *Art of the Possible*, 112.

46 *Mike: The Memoirs of the Rt. Hon. Lester B. Pearson*, vol. 2: *1948–1957*, John A. Munro and Alex I. Inglis, eds. (Toronto: University of Toronto Press, 1973), 12.

Nonetheless, debates on foreign affairs continued to be held when the estimates were considered, supplemented by the practice of having ministers make Government Statements on motions, with opposition members allowed to comment. While Government Statements were not really debates, they nonetheless provided an opportunity for exchanges of views on international affairs.

These practices ceased in 1969. The parliamentary reforms introduced by Trudeau in that year abolished the Committee of Supply; instead, the government's main estimates were automatically referred to various standing committees. As a result, discussion of international policy fell off sharply. "We did not get a chance to discuss foreign affairs," John Diefenbaker complained to the House in 1974, referring to the previous six years. "Foreign affairs during that period were as foreign as the constitution of Timbuktu."[47] The former prime minister's awkward analogy did not much move the government. It was not until December 1977 that the Trudeau government sponsored its first full-scale debate on external relations.[48] Even then, there was not a marked increase in the years thereafter and the practice of making Government Statements on motions fell into disuse.

The situation changed after September 1984 with the election of the Progressive Conservatives under Mulroney. The Conservatives were more inclined to use the House of Commons to announce and discuss foreign policy matters. Announcements on Arctic sovereignty, apartheid in South Africa, free-trade negotiations with the United States, Soviet–American arms control talks, Namibian independence, or the withdrawal of peacekeepers from Cyprus were all made in the Commons.

A number of debates were held on foreign policy issues. An emergency debate was held after the Beijing massacre in June 1989. The Commons debated the evolving Gulf crisis three times in the fall of 1990. As the January 15, 1991, deadline imposed by the Security Council for Iraq's withdrawal from Kuwait approached, the Commons held an unprecedented three-day debate on Canadian involvement in the conflict. The House was still debating the issue when the war broke out, but MPs decided to continue the debate, which in the end engaged 128 speakers and went on for so long past the January 18 deadline originally set by the Government House Leader that Hansard formally recorded that 34 hours of debate as occurring on a single day.[49]

Despite this record, the Conservatives were frequently criticized by the Liberal party in the election campaign of 1993 for their "undemocratic" foreign policy. The Liberals charged that the Mulroney government refused to consult Parliament on foreign policy issues and promised that they would bring more foreign policy issues to the Commons and allow MPs to debate major international agreements.[50]

The Liberal promise reflected a concern about the number of important decisions that the Conservatives made without consulting Parliament. In August 1990, after a visit to the White House, Mulroney agreed to commit Canadian troops to the international coalition

---

47 House of Commons, *Debates*, 30th Parl., 1st sess., vol. 1, October 3, 1974, 81.

48 House of Commons, *Debates*, 30th Parl., 3rd sess., vol. 2, December 19–20, 1977, 1993–2027, 2045–57.

49 Kim Richard Nossal, "Quantum Leaping: The Gulf Debate in Australia and Canada," in Michael McKinley, ed., *The Gulf War: Critical Perspectives* (Sydney: Allen and Unwin, 1994), 48–71.

50 Lloyd Axworthy, "Canadian Foreign Policy: A Liberal Party Perspective," *Canadian Foreign Policy* 1 (Winter 1992–93), 14.

that President George H.W. Bush was organizing.[51] Likewise, most of the decisions that committed Canadian troops to the large number of "second generation" peacekeeping missions (and thus could place troops in a combat situation) were also made without consulting Parliament: the UN Transitional Authority in Cambodia (UNTAC), created in February 1992; the UN Protection Force (UNPROFOR) in the former Yugoslavia, also created in February 1992; the UN Operation in Somalia (UNOSOM), authorized in April 1992; and UNPROFOR II, created in November 1992.[52]

Given the Liberal promise, it is perhaps not surprising that one of the first items of business in the new parliament after Chrétien took office in November 1993 was a debate on the issue of Canada's contribution to peacekeeping in Bosnia. A common theme sounded by many of the speakers in that first debate was that such debates were a refreshing change from the Mulroney years, an "opening up" of the policy process to parliamentary input. Indeed, many speakers during this debate praised the Chrétien government for having foreign policy debate and complained that there had been *no* debates on foreign policy *at all* during the Mulroney era,[53] a distortion of the record that was more a function of the deep unpopularity of the former prime minister than anything else.[54]

Between 1994 and 2008, numerous debates on foreign and defence issues took place in the Commons. The successive wars in the Balkans and in Afghanistan often caused sharp discussions. In 1994 and 1995, the Reform Party asked, on several occasions, that Canadian troops be withdrawn from Bosnia, where their safety was endangered. In 1999, during the Kosovo war, Canadian participation in NATO operations against Serb forces caused debates as impassioned as those that had occurred during the Gulf War eight years earlier. On three separate occasions—in May 2006, April 2007, and March 2008—the House of Commons held lengthy debates on Canada's mission in Afghanistan.[55]

Although more time has been spent discussing foreign affairs in the House of Commons under Mulroney, Chrétien, Martin, and Harper than during the Trudeau years, there is still a limit to how far governments or MPs can go: as Peter Dobell has noted, "Competition for the limited time available in the House of Commons is so intense that only the most controversial foreign policy issues will make it onto the agenda." Instead, suggests Dobell, parliamentary committees provide a more effective opportunity for the consideration of foreign policy.[56]

---

51 Andrew F. Cooper, Richard A. Higgott, and Kim Richard Nossal, *Relocating Middle Powers: Australia and Canada in a Changing World Order* (Vancouver: University of British Columbia Press, 1993), chap. 5.

52 Nicholas Gammer, *From Peacekeeping to Peacemaking: Canada's Response to the Yugoslav Crisis* (Montréal and Kingston: McGill-Queen's University Press, 2001); Michel Fortmann and Manon Tessier, "The Conservative Approach to International Peacekeeping," in Michaud and Nossal, eds., *Diplomatic Departures*, 113–27.

53 For example, Jesse Flis, parliamentary secretary to André Ouellet, the minister of foreign affairs: House of Commons, *Debates*, 35th Parl., 1st sess., January 25, 1994, unrev., 134, 282.

54 For an assessment, see Kim Richard Nossal, "Opening Up the Policy Process: Does Party Make a Difference?," in Michaud and Nossal, eds., *Diplomatic Departures*, 276–89.

55 Nossal, "No Exit."

56 Peter Dobell, response to Kim Richard Nossal, "The Democratization of Canadian Foreign Policy?," *Canadian Foreign Policy* 1 (Fall 1993): 105.

Commons Committees

Of the many standing, special, and joint committees of the House, the Standing Committee on Foreign Affairs and International Trade is considered one of the more prestigious. One attraction is doubtless the subject matter. According to some MPs, however, another attraction is that membership on this committee affords backbenchers unequalled opportunity for foreign travel—on committee investigations, to meetings of interparliamentary associations, or as members of government delegations to international conferences or organizations.

The foreign affairs committee does provide MPs with an opportunity, however limited, to enhance their knowledge of foreign policy, to sharpen their views on international issues, and to engage in policy development. MPs can question ministers and their officials, interview expert witnesses, and pursue investigations in Canada and abroad in an atmosphere far less partisan than on the floor of the House. They gain in the process a familiarity with the diverse issues of foreign policy, a function that has been part of the committee's raison d'être since the Second World War.

The committee has gone through several incarnations. What is now the Standing Committee on Foreign Affairs and International Trade technically began with the thirty-fifth Parliament in January 1994. Its progenitors, however, go back to 1924. In March of that year, King moved to create a Standing Committee on Industrial and International Relations.[57] Such an unlikely combination was attributable to King's desire to refer decisions of the International Labour Organization, whose conventions posed a thorny problem for the federal government (since labour matters fall under the jurisdiction of the provincial governments), to this committee. Thus the committee's work on external relations during the interwar period was limited to an ILO draft convention on hours of work, a plan to use university scholarships as a means of promoting peace, and the question of employment of Chinese and Indian seamen on Canadian ships. The committee did not meet after 1936, although it remained a standing committee of the house.

With the end of the Second World War, a separate Standing Committee on External Affairs was created in September 1945.[58] But old habits died hard. The first items sent by the King government to the new committee were two ILO conventions dating from the 1930s. Obviously not much stimulated by its investigation into the 1932 ILO Convention on the Protection against Accidents of Workers Employed in Loading or Unloading Ships, the committee's first report to the House recommended that "it be empowered to consider matters connected with external affairs and report from time to time any suggestion or recommendation deemed advisable."[59]

While the government's first reaction was to deny the request (Louis St. Laurent, the acting external affairs minister, worried that such wide-ranging powers "would lead to a very serious disturbance of the order of business"),[60] eventually King gave in, and in May 1946 the

57 Eayrs, *Art of the Possible,* 118.

58 House of Commons, *Debates,* 20th Parl., 1st sess., vol. 1, September 12, 1945, 109; September 18, 1945, 244.

59 House of Commons, Standing Committee on External Affairs, *Minutes of Evidence and Proceedings,* 20th Parl., 1st sess., #1, iii–vi, #5, iv.

60 House of Commons, *Debates,* 20th Parl., 1st sess., vol. 2, November 16, 1945, 2182–83.

committee began consideration of the estimates of the Departmental of External Affairs.[61] Until the reforms of 1968 that provided for the automatic referral of departmental estimates to the appropriate standing committee of the House, the external affairs committee alone was freed from the constraint of having to wait for an explicit reference from the House.

It was, as a result, one of the more active Commons committees. In 1968, it became the Standing Committee on External Affairs and National Defence, and its activity increased even further as a result of the reforms introduced by the Trudeau government. One measure of its activity was the increased use of subcommittees. For example, there was a regular sub-committee on international development assistance, reflecting not only the growing importance of this facet of external policy but also the increasing inability of the whole committee to deal adequately with this issue as well as matters of defence and broader issues of foreign policy. Sometimes subcommittees were organized on a regional basis, as was the subcommittee on Canada's relations with Latin America and the Caribbean in the early 1980s.[62] Subcommittees were also important catalysts for detailed studies on issues ranging from United Nations peacekeeping to Canadian–American relations.[63] In February 1986, the Mulroney government, judging that defence questions should receive special attention, split the committee in two and gave each new committee an additional responsibility. The Standing Committee on External Affairs and International Trade was joined by a new defence committee, which also assumed responsibility for veterans' affairs.

While serving on these committees undoubtedly had a positive effect on the expertise of MPs, it is clear that the committees did not have a substantive influence on the direction of policy, at least judging by the number of times that the government accepted committee recommendations that diverged from its own policy preferences. The 1970 report on Canada–United States relations, for example, was more nationalistic in its position on foreign ownership and American cultural dominance than was the Trudeau cabinet at the time.[64] In 1987, the Standing Committee on External Affairs and International Trade, chaired by William Winegard, issued a report critical of many aspects of the government's international development assistance policies. While some of the committee's recommendations were accepted by the government, others, including its recommendation to reduce the level of tied aid, were not.[65] In short, members of the committee have shown no disinclination to disagree with the government over the years. By the same token, however, the government has not shown any disinclination to ignore unpalatable recommendations served up by the committee.

61 Standing Committee on External Affairs, *Minutes*, 20th parl., 2nd sess., #1.

62 John R. Walker, "Foreign Policy Formulation—A Parliamentary Breakthrough," *International Perspectives*, May/June 1982, 10–12.

63 Don Page, "The Standing Committee on External Affairs, 1945 to 1983—Who Participates When?" in Taras, ed., *Parliament and Canadian Foreign Policy*, 40–65.

64 House of Commons, Standing Committee on External Affairs and National Defence, *11th Report* (Ottawa, 1970).

65 House of Commons, Standing Committee on External Affairs and International Trade, *For Whose Benefit?* (Ottawa, May 1987); David R. Morrison, "Canada and North–South Conflict," in Maureen Appel Molot and Brian W. Tomlin, eds., *Canada Among Nations 1987: A World of Conflict* (Toronto: James Lorimer, 1988), 136–58; also Morrison, "Evaluating Development Assistance, 1987," in Munton and Kirton, eds., *Canadian Foreign Policy*, 349–66.

The government, for its part, has on occasion used the committee for its own ends. A telling example would be the persistent use of the committee to legitimate its decisions on the question of renewal of the NORAD agreement with the United States. The agreement came up for reconsideration six times between 1968 and the early 1990s—in 1973, 1975, 1980, 1981, 1986, and 1991—and six times the committee was charged with providing a recommendation to the government. However, there is little doubt that on each occasion, the government had no intention of recasting its fundamental commitment to a system of joint air defence with the United States, regardless of the recommendations of the committee. Indeed, before the committee even began its first set of investigations in March 1973, the minister of national defence, James Richardson, said that if Canada's role in NORAD did change, it would be as a result of decisions taken in the United States, not because Ottawa foresaw a change.[66]

When the agreement came up for renewal again in 1975, the situation had not changed. Negotiations were already under way with the United States when the reference was handed down to the committee, and it was clear to the members that they were not in a position to recommend anything but renewal if they wanted their recommendations to be accepted. "Your mind appears to be made up," Allan McKinnon, the Progressive Conservative defence critic, complained to Richardson.[67] And so it was: The government renewed the agreement, this time for five years. When the committee again had the NORAD agreement referred to them by the Trudeau government in 1980, and by the Mulroney government in 1985, on each occasion it recommended renewal.[68]

For the 1991 renewal, the government referred the issue to the Standing Committee on External Affairs and International Trade rather than the defence committee, because the decision was regarded as a diplomatic rather than a military question. With the end of the Cold War, however, members of the committee were more hesitant about the raison d'être of the aerospace command. In April 1991, the committee voted for the renewal of the treaty for two years by just one vote. While the United States wanted a 10-year renewal, the Mulroney government rejected the committee's recommendation and renewed the treaty for five years.[69] It is clear, given the government's persistent commitment to NORAD over the years, that it sent the issue to the standing committee not for advice but to legitimate its own decisions. (The subsequent renewals in 1996 and 2001 did not attract much attention from MPs, and in 2006, the Harper government decided to bring the periodic renewals to an end. On May 8, 2006, the House approved making the NORAD agreement permanent.)[70]

At times, however, the government does not even use the standing committee for consideration of foreign policy matters by MPs. When Trudeau renewed his interest in North–South

66 *Globe and Mail*, February 6 and 7, 1973.

67 Quoted in Michael Tucker, *Canadian Foreign Policy: Contemporary Issues and Themes* (Toronto: McGraw-Hill Ryerson, 1980), 50.

68 Douglas A. Ross, "American Nuclear Revisionism, Canadian Strategic Interests, and the Renewal of NORAD," *Behind the Headlines* 39 (April 1982); Ross, "Canada and the Strategic Defense Initiative: Managing Strategic Doctrinal Incompatibilities," in Lauren McKinsey and Kim Richard Nossal, eds., *America's Alliances and Canadian–American Relations* (Toronto: Summerhill Press, 1988).

69 Government of Canada, *News Release* 96, April 19, 1991; also the discussion in Canada, Department of National Defence, *1994 Defence White Paper* (Ottawa, 1994), 23.

70 House of Commons, *Debates*, 39th Parl., 1st sess., May 8, 2006.

problems in 1980,[71] the government chose not to have the issue examined by the standing committee or by one of its subcommittees. Instead the cabinet created a special parliamentary committee. The Parliamentary Task Force on North–South Relations was one of five special panels established in May 1980 on different policy issues. Like the other task forces, the North–South panel was small, had a specific mandate, a nine-month reporting deadline, and was designed to maintain as high a public profile as possible.[72]

Likewise, when foreign policy was reviewed in 1985 and 1994, the Mulroney and Chrétien governments both sought to increase public awareness for their foreign policy reviews by creating special joint committees of MPs and senators.[73] And, in 2003, when the new minister of foreign affairs, Bill Graham, wanted to reshape foreign policy, he established a series of "dialogues" on foreign policy with citizens, bypassing the Commons committee he had chaired for so long. It is hardly surprising that many students of Canadian international policy conclude that the work of the standing committee does not always have an effect.[74]

Although on these occasions the intention was to focus public and parliamentary attention on key issues by establishing new structures of parliamentary input, it might be noted that in bypassing the standing committees, the government was in effect commenting on the utility of the existing structures for investigation, debate, and advice.

POLITICAL PARTIES AND INTERNATIONAL POLICY

Canada's parliament has been dominated by two major political parties, the Liberals and the Conservatives. Over the years, a number of other smaller parties have managed to elect MPs to the House of Commons: the New Democratic Party (formerly called the Co-operative Commonwealth Federation), the Bloc Québécois, and the Canadian Alliance (which began life in the 1980s as the Reform Party and merged with the Progressive Conservatives in 2003 to become the Conservative Party of Canada). Some small parties, like the Social Credit Party and its Québec wing, the Ralliement créditiste, disappeared.

The parties in the House of Commons contribute to the formation of international policy in a context that is highly partisan. The MPs from the majority party support the position of the governing party, whether by conviction or by obligation; the MPs on the opposition benches must, evidently, oppose.

The Opposition Opposes

One of the principal purposes of the opposition is to draw the attention of the media and the general public to what it considers the errors or gaffes of the government. In the 1980s, a group of particularly disrespectful MPs on the Liberal benches, known as the

---

71 Kim Richard Nossal, "Personal Diplomacy and National Behaviour: Trudeau's North–South Initiatives and Canadian Development Assistance Policies," *Dalhousie Review* 62 (Summer 1982), 278–91.

72 House of Commons, *Debates*, 32nd Parl., 1st sess., vol. 2, May 23, 1980, 1356–57; also House of Commons, Parliamentary Task Force on North–South Relations, *Report to the House of Commons on the Relations Between Developed and Developing Countries* (Ottawa, 1980).

73 Special Joint Committee on Canada's International Relations, Independence and Internationalism; Special Joint Committee Reviewing Canadian Foreign Policy, Canada's Foreign Policy; Special Joint Committee on Canada's Defence Committee, *Security in a Changing World* (Ottawa: October 1994).

74 English, "Member of Parliament," 77–79; Bland, "Parliament's Duty," 38–39.

"Rat Pack,"[75] took delight in barraging the Mulroney government with criticism and engaging in distinctly un-parliamentary behaviour. During Chrétien's first government, the incisive interventions of Lucien Bouchard, the first leader of the Bloc Québécois, were particularly dreaded by Liberal ministers.

Opposition MPs sometimes have a difficult task. They lack the research resources that are routinely available to those on the government side, particularly if they are a third party or, worse, not recognized as an official party. However, they also have certain assets. For example, they do not have to put their policy positions into practice—at least in the immediate term—and thus they can say almost anything without having to worry about the consequences. In 1994, for example, the Bloc Québécois issued a dissenting report on national defence that recommended that NORAD be transformed into a "military alliance" and expanded in order to provide "new members" with political and economic stability—revealing that the Bloc simply had no understanding of the joint military command.[76] Opposition parties also have the luxury of being able to change their positions on a whim: During the debate on the Gulf War of 1991, the Liberal leader, Jean Chrétien, vilified the Mulroney government for its commitment of Canadian troops to the international coalition, and then quite suddenly decided to support the Canadian commitment once war had broken out. And obviously, when opposition parties are elected to power, their positions not only solidify, they also become much more realistic. Thus, the aggressive opposition of the Liberals to North American free trade suddenly grew quite blurry after they won the 1993 election.

Opposition also occurs *within* political parties. After Trudeau's resignation in 1984, the Liberals had difficulty putting forward a coherent line on foreign policy matters. During the 1984 elections, Chrétien, then Prime Minister John Turner's external affairs minister, joined the party's president, Iona Campagnola, and a number of other Liberal candidates in embracing a nuclear freeze despite Turner's opposition.[77] After he was replaced by Chrétien as Liberal leader in June 1990, Turner found an opportunity to return the favour. When Chrétien stood in the House and spoke out against the Mulroney government's policy of deploying troops in the Gulf War, Turner made a special trip from Toronto[78] to speak in the debate and methodically picked apart all the arguments of his erstwhile colleagues.[79] Not even when Chrétien

---

75 The "Rat Pack" included Don Boudria, Sheila Copps, John Nunziata, and Brian Tobin, all of whom assumed positions of responsibility in Chrétien's government; *Globe and Mail*, March 9, 1987.

76 Special Joint Committee Reviewing Canadian Foreign Policy, *Canada's Foreign Policy: Dissenting Opinions and Appendices* (Ottawa: November 1994): see the Bloc's dissenting report, 1–26; for an elaboration, see David G. Haglund and Stéphane Roussel, "It's a Long Road from Fort Greely to Chicoutimi: Quebec Sovereignty and the Issue of Missile Defense," *Contemporary Strategy* 27:4 (July 2008), 361–75. Stéphane Roussel and Charles-Alexandre Théorêt, "Defence Policy Distorted by the Sovereignist Prism? The Bloc Québécois on Security and Defence Questions (1990–2005)," in David Carment and David Bercuson, eds., *The World In Canada: Diaspora, Demography, and Domestic Politics* (Montréal and Kingston: McGill-Queen's University Press, 2008), 169–188.

77 John Kirton, "Managing Canadian Foreign Policy," in Brian W. Tomlin and Maureen Molot, eds., *Canada Among Nations 1984: A Time of Transition* (Toronto: James Lorimer, 1985), 20–21.

78 After he was replaced as leader, Turner returned to practise law in Toronto, but did not immediately resign his seat in the Commons. Technically he continued to represent the riding of Vancouver Quadra until the 1993 elections, making periodic appearances in the House to avoid being sanctioned for absenteeism.

79 House of Commons, *Debates*, 34th Parl., January 16, 1991, 17132–34.

formed the government after the 1993 election did splits within the caucus dissipate: When his government had to decide whether to continue cruise missile testing, many of the Liberal MPs who had so vociferously opposed testing in the 1980s were still in the House.

That the opposition opposes is a normal, if not necessary, part of democracy. However, for much of Canada's history, there has been significant agreement on many aspects of international policy among Canadian parliamentarians. Down to 1993, Liberals and Conservatives had similar ideas about the broad strategic directions for the country, however much they may have differed on the means.[80] By contrast, there was little agreement on economic and trade policy, where a deep divide separated the parties.

Strategic Consensus

During the interwar years (1919–1939) and the Cold War era (1945–1991), there was a clear convergence between the Liberals and Progressive Conservatives on Canada's basic alignment in international affairs. Although they might have disagreed over particular policies, both parties always saw Canada as one of the Western democracies. In August 1914, as in September 1939, both parties favoured going to war on the side of the British. And when the Cold War emerged after the Second World War, neither party questioned Canada's membership in the Western camp. There might have been some debate over whether London or Washington should be regarded as the true leader of the Western coalition, but there was no question about Canada's participation in this coalition.

Between 1945 and 1990, there was very little change in this fundamental alignment as a country committed to Western security.[81] It is true that Trudeau came to power in 1968 not fully convinced of this consensus: He questioned the hard line vis-à-vis the Soviet Union and socialist countries like China and Cuba and wanted to withdraw the Canadian forces stationed in Europe as part of NATO. But Trudeau eventually came around to a more traditional internationalist position by the mid-1970s.[82]

Only the Co-operative Commonwealth Federation and its successor, the New Democratic Party, stood out as the voice in Parliament that historically offered both ends and means differing substantively from those of the major parties. The CCF's leader, J.S. Woodsworth, as discussed in Chapter 5, was a persistent exponent of pacifism in the interwar years, even opposing Canadian participation in the Second World War. This view was mirrored in the postwar period by the CCF and its successor. In particular, the NDP pledge to withdraw from the North Atlantic Treaty Organization and NORAD, which was a plank of the party's platform between 1969 and 1988, starkly set it apart from the other mainstream parties.

---

80 Robert A. Spencer, "Parliament and Foreign Policy 1960," *International Journal* 15 (Autumn 1960); Garth Stevenson, "Foreign Policy," in Conrad Winn and J. McMenemy, eds., *Political Parties in Canada* (Toronto: McGraw-Hill Ryerson, 1976); Neil Nevitte and Roger Gibbins, "Foreign Policy Debates and Sleeping Dogs: All Quiet on the Parliamentary Front," *Canadian Public Policy* 12:3 (1986), 401–12.

81 Myriam Gervais and Stéphane Roussel, "De la sécurité de l'État à celle de l'individu: l'évolution du concept de sécurité au Canada (1990–1996)," *Études internationales* 29:1 (March 1998), 28–29.

82 The best survey of Trudeau's approach to foreign policy is J.L. Granatstein and Robert Bothwell, *Pirouette: Pierre Trudeau and Canadian Foreign Policy* (Toronto: University of Toronto Press, 1990).

In short, despite some episodic shifts, there was consensus on the general strategic directions for Canada during the course of the Cold War. It was only after the 1993 elections, as we will see below, that this strategic consensus dissipated.

Divergence over Trade Policy

By contrast, since Confederation the two major parties have systematically adopted divergent positions on trade policy and economic relations with the United States.[83] On the issue of Canada's location in the changing international political economy, there was little consensus. Canada's economic relationship with the United States has proved to be a source of deep division between the Liberals and Conservatives over the course of the twentieth century. However, the parties have shifted their positions over the decades. At the beginning of the century, it was a Liberal government that proposed a free-trade agreement with the United States; it was vociferously opposed by the Conservatives under Borden, who defeated Laurier in the 1911 elections. Likewise, it was a Liberal government that encouraged increasing economic integration with the United States in the decade after the war. The Progressive Conservatives under John Diefenbaker regarded this with considerable concern, pledging in 1957 that a PC government would pursue a policy of seeking greater economic independence from the United States, a policy that eventually developed decidedly anti-American aspects.

But in the 1960s there was a turn, and the parties changed places. By the 1970s, the Liberal party embraced the economic nationalist position, seeking to lessen Canada's economic dependence on the United States.[84] And by the early 1980s, it was the Progressive Conservatives who were the pro-American party, castigating the Liberals for their anti-Americanism, declaring Canada "open for business," and eventually embracing free trade, first with the United States alone, and then with Mexico and the United States in a North American accord. As Brian W. Tomlin has noted, by embracing free trade, the Conservatives were "leaving the past behind."[85] But it was also what Thompson and Randall have called the "ultimate irony" of Canadian politics: "the Tories, named out of the legacy of an American Revolution rejected in 1776, embraced the United States with an ardor never before experienced by the Canadian body politic."[86] For their part, the Liberals in 1988 denounced the Canada–United States free-trade agreement even more vociferously than had Borden's Conservatives in 1911 and pledged to rip it up if elected. Needless to say, however, when the Liberals were elected in 1993, they did not abandon the agreement, which had by then expanded to include Mexico. The economic realities of the close integration of the

---

83 Michael Hart, *A Trading Nation: Canadian Trade Policy from Colonialism to Globalization* (Vancouver: UBC Press, 2002).

84 Kim Richard Nossal, "Economic Nationalism and Continental Integration: Assumptions, Arguments and Advocacies," in *The Collected Research Studies/The Royal Commission on the Economic Union and Development Prospects for Canada*, vol. 29: *The Politics of Canada's Economic Relationship with the United States*, Denis Stairs and Gilbert R. Winham, eds. (Ottawa: Supply and Services Canada, 1985), 55–94.

85 Tomlin, "Leaving the Past Behind."

86 John Herd Thompson and Stephen J. Randall, *Canada and the United States: Ambivalent Allies*, 3rd ed. (Montréal and Kingston: McGill-Queen's University Press, 2002), 7.

Canadian and American economies were too strong. But the debate over free trade revealed two approaches to Canada's international policy: between internationalists, who favour a diversification of Canada's political and economic relations, and continentalists, who have promoted closer relations with the United States.

The Contemporary Party System and International Policy

The general elections of October 1993 radically altered the political landscape in Canada. While the Liberals won a majority, the election almost wiped the Progressive Conservatives out as a national party. While the PCs won 16 percent of the popular vote across the country, their vote split everywhere, producing a dramatic and historic defeat. The party held 155 seats at dissolution, but only two PCs were returned; the party lost official party status in the House of Commons; and Prime Minister Kim Campbell and all of her ministers except Jean Charest lost their seats. The NDP did not fare much better. Its vote collapsed, particularly in Ontario. Only nine members, all from the west, were elected, and the party also lost its official status in the House.

Two regionally based parties emerged in the election. The Bloc Québécois, formed under the leadership of Lucien Bouchard after the collapse of the Meech Lake constitutional accord in 1990, ran candidates in all Québec ridings on a souverainiste platform and won 49 percent of the popular vote in the province and 54 seats in the Commons, two more than the Reform party. Thus Bouchard was in the ironic position of being both the Leader of the Opposition in the federal legislature and the chief advocate of the breakup of the Canadian state. Reform, which had only one MP at dissolution, won 52 seats, capturing over 50 percent of the popular vote in British Columbia and Alberta and winning 46 of the 58 seats in those provinces. While Reform won only one of the 99 seats in Ontario, its candidates ran second in many ridings in that province.

This transformation in the political landscape also had a number of effects on Canada's international policy. Most importantly, whatever consensus might have existed between the major parties disappeared with the eclipse of the Progressive Conservatives after the 1993 election. Neither the Bloc nor Reform shared the new Liberal government's assumptions about foreign affairs,[87] seen most immediately in the dissenting reports that the new parties issued as part of the 1994 foreign policy review.[88] Over the course of the 1990s, the two regional parties diverged on numerous international issues.[89] The Bloc advocated intervention in the Bosnian conflict—its leader, Lucien Bouchard, even referred to Canadian peacekeepers as "our" soldiers[90]—and supported Canadian federal policy on the

---

[87] Michel Fortmann et Gordon Mace, "Le Bloc Québécois et la politique étrangère canadienne," *Canadian Foreign Policy* 1 (Fall 1993), 109–112; Stéphane Roussel, "Une culture stratégique en évolution," in Stéphane Paquin (in collaboration with Louise Beaudoin), eds., *Histoire des relations internationales du Québec* (Montréal: VLB, 2006), 278–87.

[88] Special Joint Committee Reviewing Canadian Foreign Policy, *Canada's Foreign Policy*: the Bloc's dissenting report, 1–26, and the Reform's dissenting opinion, 27–32.

[89] There was some cross-party consensus on Canada's participation in the Kosovo War of 1999: Kim Richard Nossal and Stéphane Roussel, "Canada and the Kosovo War: The Happy Follower," in Pierre Martin and Mark R. Brawley, eds., *Alliance Politics, Kosovo, and NATO's War: Allied Force or Forced Allies?* (New York: Palgrave, 2000), 181–99.

[90] *Globe and Mail*, January 28, 1994.

establishment of the International Criminal Court. By contrast, the Reform party toyed with isolationist positions, expressing distrust with international institutions and even Canada's commitment to peacekeeping. The party, which became the Canadian Alliance in 2000, became progressively more pro-American, particularly after George W. Bush was elected to the White House.

In the aftermath of 9/11, this divergence became more pronounced on the key foreign policy issues—the invasion of Afghanistan, defence spending, the Anglo-American invasion of Iraq in 2003, the issue of the Ballistic Missile Defense program, and the expansion of the Afghanistan mission. Not surprisingly, the Bloc tended to reflect the dominant views of voters in Québec on these issues, where unlike other parts of Canada, there was strong opposition to the Anglo-American invasion of Iraq, Canadian participation in the BMD program, and the intervention in Afghanistan. The Reform/Canadian Alliance tended to adopt radically opposite positions: They supported increases in military expenditures, the security measures taken after the attacks of 9/11, and participation in BMD. In March 2003, they criticized the Liberal government for its refusal to join the Anglo-American coalition against Iraq[91] and strongly supported the mission in Afghanistan.

The regionalization of the Canadian party system in the mid-1990s had two important consequences. First, between 1993 and 2003, opposition to the Liberals was fragmented, which provided the Chrétien government with a somewhat freer hand in international policy as in other areas of policy. This fragmentation also perhaps contributed to strengthening the capacities of the executive to the detriment of the legislature and to reducing Parliament's credibility, as Rempel has suggested.[92]

Second, the reuniting of the right that resulted in the emergence of the Conservative Party of Canada, the collapse of the Liberal party's majority in the 2004 elections, and the election of two successive Conservative minority governments in the January 2006 and October 2008 general elections have all continued to divide the vote so that the formation of a majority government becomes more difficult. Therefore, while minority governments were for much of Canada's history an exceptional phenomenon, it is likely that the present party system, with its regional cleavages that tend to divide the vote between the four parties, will make minority governments a more common part of the Canadian political landscape.

What impacts will minority governments have on international policy? One might expect that a minority government would be much more careful. One might point to the fate of the minority Diefenbaker government, which was defeated in 1963 because of its confused policies over the acquisition of nuclear weapons. On the other hand, the minority governments of both Martin and Harper suggest that a minority government does not necessarily dampen international activity. Martin was able to produce a new, if controversial, vision for Canadian international policy.[93] For his part, Harper did not hesitate to support Israel during the Lebanon war in the summer of 2006, despite the criticism that this provoked, particularly in Québec, where the Conservatives hoped to improve their electoral position.

---

91 See, for example, Stephen Harper, "Liberal Damage Control: A Litany of Flip-Flops on Canada–US Relations," *Policy Options* 24:6 (June/July 2003), 5–7.

92 Rempel, *Chatterbox*.

93 Canada, *A Role of Pride and Influence in the World: Canada's International Policy Statement* (Ottawa: April 2005).

However, while it must be more prudent, the main consequence of a minority govern-ment is its short life expectancy, which seldom exceeds a year or two. For this reason, it is difficult to undertake long-term initiatives, as the fate of Martin's *International Policy Statement* suggests. With the election of the Conservatives, the IPS disappeared from the website of the Department of Foreign Affairs and International Trade and went into the archives, less than a year after its publication.

CONCLUSION

In the early 1990s, the Liberals attributed the marginal role of Parliament in international policy to the Mulroney government. But to blame Mulroney is to miss the point. We have argued in this chapter that MPs play a relatively minor part in the development of inter-national policy in Canada for reasons that cannot be attributed to any single government but that are largely *structural*: the relative lack of legislation, the lack of interest of MPs themselves in international questions, the lack of resources available to the opposition, and, most importantly, the oppressive role of party discipline.

There is no better illustration of this than what became of the attempts by the new Liberal government in 1993 to change some of these structures. The Liberals came to power committed to "democratizing" Canadian foreign policy, not only by reforming par-liamentary institutions in order to make up a putative "democratic deficit" but also by embracing other mechanisms, partly financed by the government, that would involve civil society in the shaping of international policy. Beginning in 1993, the Chrétien government sought new ways to consult the population, a role traditionally associated with the House of Commons. The government organized an annual national forum on foreign policy and gave a new institution, the Canadian Centre for Foreign Policy Development, a mandate to establish a bridge between the government and civil society on international policy.

However, sixteen years later, it is not clear that any of the initiatives launched by the Liberals in 1993 made foreign policy in Canada more democratic. The Canadian Centre for Foreign Policy Development was closed in 2003 after a scathing internal audit; the kind of "dialogue" with civil society organizations that was a central feature of the Chrétien approach to international policy was abandoned by both Martin and Harper. In this sense, Canada's parliamentary institutions remain, by default if nothing else, important actors in the making of international policy in Canada. They may be inconsequential, marginalized, and hopelessly partisan, but they remain essential to the maintenance of democratic life.

CHAPTER 11

The Provinces and International Policy

Canada's federal structure has an important impact on international policy. While much of this book has focused on the international policies of the federal government in Ottawa, the provincial governments also make their own international policy, and in the process affect federal policymaking. In this chapter we explore the role and impact of Canada's provinces as international actors in their own right, focusing on what prompts provincial governments into international activity and what limits that activity. We begin by examining the nature of sovereignty and its impact on international policy in federal states like Canada.

SOVEREIGNTY, INTERNATIONAL RELATIONS, AND PARADIPLOMACY

The distinguishing feature of international politics has always been the existence of independent political communities that seek to preserve their autonomy against other states. This ideal was institutionalized as sovereignty by the Peace of Westphalia of 1648 and the treaties that prohibited European monarchs from interfering in the affairs of other political communities, and in particular religious conflicts, which had been the origin of the Thirty Years War (1618–1648). Sovereignty refers to the ability of a state to make decisions autonomously from other states.[1]

Over the past three centuries, the legal attributes of sovereignty have been carefully laid out. In international law, a sovereign state has four important legal and political rights: *jus belli*, a right to use force in defence of its interests; *jus legationis*, the right to send and receive diplomatic missions; *jus tractatuum*, the right to negotiate treaties or agreements with other sovereign states; and the *droit d'ester en justice*, the right to have access to legal processes and institutions at the international level. These rights and attributes of a sovereign state are possessed by a government within a defined territorial area, which exercises supreme authority over the population within those boundaries. Importantly, these rights and attributes are deemed to be indivisible: Only one sovereign authority can exercise them for a given territory and population. Sovereignty in international law is by nature subjective. In order to be sovereign, one must be recognized as such by other countries who enjoy sovereign status in international politics.

Paradoxically, at the very time that the principle of sovereignty—with its assumption of one supreme authority exercising political power within a polity—was gaining legitimacy in global politics, forms of government based explicitly on the necessary *divisibility* of sovereignty were being created—confederations and federations. A confederation is a voluntary union of states that choose to pool their sovereign powers. In a confederal system, each of the states retain their sovereignty but create a central government subject to international law. This government is not autonomous, in the sense that it depends on the constituent parts for its existence. Because of the instability inherent in this arrangement, there are no examples of confederations in history. Confederations tend to drift either toward greater integration or toward greater independence of its members.

---

1 Alan James, *Sovereign Statehood: The Basis of International Society* (London: Allen and Unwin, 1986); for critical analyses, see Jens Bartelson, *A Genealogy of Sovereignty* (Cambridge: Cambridge University Press, 1995) and Stephen Krasner, *Sovereignty: Organized Hypocrisy* (Princeton: Princeton University Press, 1999).

In a federal system, the central government and the governments of the constituent parts of the federation, or "non-central governments"[2]—states, provinces, Länder, republics, cantons, or communities (*comunidades autónomas* in Spain, *communautés* in Belgium), and so on—all retain their sovereign rights in defined areas of competence. The main principle of federalism is thus the necessary divisibility of sovereignty. This notion does not sit well with the Westphalian international order and the principles of international law enshrined in that order. On the contrary: Federalism assumes that sovereign political authority can be exercised in the same territory, over the same people, by more than one independent political authority.

The most important element is the sharing of powers between two orders of government. Depending on the federal constitution, certain powers will be assigned as the exclusive competence of the central government, while other powers will be assigned to the non-central governments. Some areas of competence—concurrent powers—will be shared by both levels of government. This division of powers will determine, in large part, the nature and form of the participation of the non-central governments in international policy, and thus the relations between the two orders of government in this sphere. The division of powers is also on occasion the source of ambiguous relationships, rivalries, and quarrels between the governments in a federation. Likewise, one of the problems arises from the fact that federal states are considered under international law as unitary actors, while the federal government must grapple with the constitutional division of powers when it negotiates with other countries, if only to ensure that it is able to implement obligations that it may incur in treaties or agreements it signs.

The role of non-central governments in the making of international policy in federal states leads to the fundamental question in contemporary political science: Who governs?[3] How are decisions about international affairs taken and implemented when the jurisdiction of non-central governments are involved? What is the role of non-central governments in the negotiation, signature, and implementation of international treaties when those treaties affect their powers?

Today virtually all government activity falls within the purview of at least one intergovernmental organization, and frequently many more.[4] Education, public health, cultural diversity, the environment, business subsidies, the treatment accorded to investors, the removal of non-tariff barriers, the liberalization of agricultural trade, the issue of

---

2 See Brian Hocking, *Localizing Foreign Policy: Non-central Governments and Multilayered Diplomacy* (New York: St. Martin's Press, 1993). We employ Hocking's central/non-central terminology because the other terms often used by students of federalism (subnational or substate governments, lower orders of government, constituent units or communities) are inappropriately hierarchical (e.g., the prefix *sub-* implies a subordination that does not appropriately reflect the shared sovereignty in a federation), too ambiguous (e.g., the central government is just as much a "constituent unit" in a federation as the non-central governments), or simply inappropriate in a Canadian context (e.g., subnational). The common term in French, *États fédérés*, with a capital *É*, involves an important distinction in French (*État* vs. *état*) that is lost in translation as "federated states."

3 Robert A. Dahl, *Who Governs? Democracy and Power in an American City*, 2nd ed. with Douglas W. Rae (New Haven: Yale University Press, 2005).

4 Margaret Karns and Karen Mingst, *International Organizations: The Politics and Processes of Global Governance* (Boulder: Lynne Rienner, 2004); Marie-Claude Smouts, "Que reste-t-il de la politique étrangère?" *Pouvoirs* 88 (1999), 11–29.

government procurement—all these policy areas are on the agendas of international organizations and summit meetings.

The enlargement of the international policy agenda has had important implications for decision-making at the national level. Today, as we saw in Chapter 9, some of the activities of most government departments are internationalized. At the federal level, this has had an impact on decision-making: The foreign ministry no longer has (if indeed it ever had) the ability to centralize decision-making, representation, and control functions concerning international policy.

As the international policy agenda has expanded, non-central governments have been increasingly aware that their political power and sovereignty—or, in other words, their ability to formulate and implement policy—are subject to negotiation in multilateral fora. This phenomenon is magnified in Europe by the process of European integration and in North America by the North American Free Trade Agreement (NAFTA). Thus, since the 1960s, there has been a noticeable increase in the number of non-central governments that have sought to participate actively in international questions. In the United States, for example, only four states maintained offices in other countries in 1970; by 2001, 42 states maintained 233 offices in 30 countries.[5] In Germany, the Länder have set up some 130 representative offices since 1970, of which 21 are located in the United States.[6] In Spain, the autonomous community of Catalonia operates some 50 representative offices abroad, and the Flemish government opened its hundredth office in September 2004.[7] This phenomenon is also evident in Japan, India, Russia, Brazil, and many other countries.[8]

Many international relations (IR) scholars maintain, at least implicitly, that global politics is primarily about sovereign states. The state-centric bias in much of the theorizing about IR—realist, liberal, and constructivist—tends to minimize the importance of semi-sovereign governments, such as Canadian provinces, because they do not have the qualifications to be considered "real international actors." In this perspective, only the decisions and policies of central governments are important enough to study; the international policy decisions of non-central governments are treated like other domestic actors such as nongovernmental organizations or social movements.[9]

---

5 Earl H. Fry, *The Expanding Role of State and Local Governments in U.S. Foreign Affairs* (New York: Council on Foreign Relations Press, 1998); Earl H. Fry, "Sub-state Strategies in an Era of Globalization and the Information Technology Revolution," in Guy Lachapelle and Stéphane Paquin, eds., *Mastering Globalization: New Sub-states' Governance and Strategies* (London: Routledge, 2005), 116–123.

6 Robert Kaiser, "Sub-state Governments in International Arenas: Paradiplomacy and Multi-level Governance in Europe and North America," in Lachapelle and Paquin, eds., *Mastering Globalization*, 90–103.

7 Stéphane Paquin, *Paradiplomatie identitaire en Catalogne* (Québec: Les Presses de l'Université Laval, 2003); Stéphane Paquin, "Les actions extérieures des entités subétatiques: quelle signification pour la politique comparée et la théorie des relations internationales?," *Revue internationale de politique comparée* 12:2 (2005), 129–142.

8 Purnedra Jain, *Japan's Subnational Governments in International Affairs* (New York: Routledge, 2005); Noé Cornago, "Paradiplomacy and International Customary Law: Subnational Governments and the Making of New Global Norms," in Klaus-Gerd Giesen and Kees van der Pijl, eds., *Global Norms in the Twenty-First Century* (Newcastle: Cambridge Scholars Press, 2006), 67–83.

9 The work of Anne-Marie Slaughter, *A New World Order* (Princeton: Princeton University Press, 2004), which focuses on intergovernmental networks, represents an important exception.

But in fact the international relations of non-central governments represent an important element of contemporary international policy. One could cite numerous examples: the state of Maryland imposing sanctions against South Africa in 1985; the Australian state of Victoria grappling with pressure to cancel contracts with French firms in protest against nuclear testing in the South Pacific in 1995; the participation of National Guard units of American states participating in international military exchange programs; the participation of the German Land of Baden-Württenberg in peacekeeping missions in Bangladesh, Russia, Bosnia-Herzegovina, Burundi, and Tanzania; Jordi Pujol i Soley, the president of the Generalitat of Catalonia, managing to secure face-to-face talks with every leader of the Group of Seven except Canada over the course of the 1990s; or the Mexican state of San Luis Potosí seeking to facilitate the transfer of cross-border funds from immigrants in the United States.[10]

Such international activity of non-central governments is called *paradiplomacy*—in the sense that it occurs alongside the diplomacy of central governments.[11] It has been a growing global phenomenon, and one that involves not only the governments in federations but also the governments of "world" or "global" cities such as London, Tokyo, New York, and Shanghai.[12] In this view, the international activities of the Canadian provinces must be put into a broader global perspective, but with the provinces playing the role of precursors in this area. And we must recognize that the paradiplomacy of Canada's provinces is intensive, extensive, and permanent. The provinces enjoy considerable autonomy in the elaboration of their international policies. They also devote considerable resources to paradiplomacy—sometimes more than some sovereign states devote to their diplomacy. And they have more and more influence not only on global politics but also on the definition of Canada's international policy.

As international actors, Canadian provinces have certain advantages over the federal government. These benefits come from their ambiguous status, which is, in the words of James Rosenau, both "sovereignty-bound" and "sovereignty-free."[13] Their sovereignty-bound

---

10 On these cases, see Hans J. Michelmann, "Federalism and International Relations in Canada and the Federal Republic of Germany," *International Journal* 41:2 (Summer 1986): 566–67; Peter Howard, "The Growing Role of States in U.S. Foreign Policy: The Case of the State Partnership Program," *International Security Perspectives* 5:2 (May 2004), 179–96; Paquin, *Paradiplomatie*, 86; Julián Durazo-Herrmann, "L'activité internationale des regions: Une perspective mexicaine," 31:3 (September 2000), 475–48.

11 The term was popularized by Panayotis Soldatos: Hans J. Michelmann and Soldatos, *Federalism and International Relations: The Role of Subnational Units* (Oxford: Oxford University Press, 1990). See also Brian Hocking, "Regionalism: An International Relations Perspective," in Michael Keating and John Loughlin, eds., *The Political Economy of Regionalism* (London: Frank Cass, 1995); Francisco Aldecoa and Michael Keating, eds., *Paradiplomacy in Action: The Foreign Relations of Subnational Governments* (London: Frank Cass, 1999); and Stéphane Paquin, *Paradiplomatie et relations internationales: Théorie des stratégies internationales des régions face à la mondialisation* (Brussels: Les presses interuniversitaires européennes–Peter Lang, 2004).

12 For example, John Friedman, "The World City Hypothesis," *Development and Change* 17:1 (January 1986), 69–83; Paul Knox and Peter Taylor, eds., *World Cities in a World-System* (New York: Cambridge University Press, 1995); Neil Brenner, "Global Cities, Glocal States: Global City Formation and State Territorial Restructuring in Contemporary Europe," *Review of International Political Economy* 5:1 (Spring 1998), 1–37.

13 James N. Rosenau, *Turbulence in World Politics: A Theory of Change and Continuity* (Princeton: Princeton University Press, 1990), 36.

status within Canada allows the provinces to have access to federal decision-makers, including those who make international policy for Canada. Thus, unlike NGOs and other civil society actors, provincial governments enjoy a privileged access to the diplomatic networks, international organizations, and negotiating forums available to the federal government in Ottawa. It now common for provincial officials to speak in the name of Canada in international forums or to participate in the drafting of international agreements when the subject matter falls within their constitutional jurisdiction.[14]

On the other hand, the provinces also enjoy a "sovereignty-free" status in global politics. Since they are not recognized as sovereigns in their own right, they are able to act more freely than the federal government. In that sense, provinces enjoy some of the benefits of civil society actors. It is easier for provinces to adopt idealistic positions, and they have more latitude to take firm positions on sensitive subjects; for example, condemning violations of human rights. By contrast, the federal government must always adopt a more nuanced and a more diplomatic approach on such questions since it cannot ignore the constraints of coalition politics or the effects its policies on Canada's political or commercial interests.[15] Likewise, the provinces can go and defend their interests before foreign courts, as Ontario did on the acid rain issue or as British Columbia did during the "salmon war," when both governments pleaded their case directly to an American judge. Such an option is not available to the federal government.

The range of tools available to the provinces in their international activities is almost as wide as those tools available to the central government in its diplomacy—with the obvious exception of the use of force.[16] Many provinces have offices or "mini-embassies" abroad that develop bilateral or multilateral relations with both sovereign governments and other non-central governments, including the creation of institutions of regional and transregional cooperation. Provincial officials are routinely included in Canadian delegations, and two provinces, Québec and New Brunswick, send their own separate delegations to La Francophonie, operating under the name "Canada Québec" and "Canada Nouveau-Brunswick," and maintain relations with other international institutions such as UNESCO, the World Health Organization, and the World Trade Organization. The provinces send missions abroad and participate in trade fairs and in private international forums such as the World Economic Forum in Davos. They also finance public relations campaigns to promote exports and attract foreign investment. They host official visits from leaders of other governments. Some provinces have a minister responsible for external relations.

However, the provinces also face a number of constraints. Because they are not recognized as actors under international law, most of the time they have to negotiate with the federal government the terms of some of their international activities, such as official missions to foreign countries or international organizations. But it is at the level of budgetary resources that the difference between the provinces and the federal government is most evident. Even though the international relations budget of some provinces is considerable,

---

14 Stéphane Paquin, "Quelle place pour les provinces canadiennes dans les organisations et les négociations internationales du Canada à la lumière des pratiques au sein d'autres fédérations?" *Canadian Public Administration* 48:4 (Winter 2005), 447–505.

15 Hocking, "Regionalism," 90.

16 For an exploration of this idea, see Eric Philippart, "Le Comité des Régions confronté à la 'paradiplomatie' des régions de l'Union européenne," in Jacques Bourrinet, ed., *Le Comité des Régions de l'Union européenne* (Paris: Editions économica, 1997), 6.

these budgets are dwarfed by the resources devoted to the Department of Foreign Affairs and International Trade. The annual budget of the Canadian embassy in Washington is equivalent to the entire annual budget of the Ministère des Relations internationales (MRI) in Québec, the province that is by far the most active in international policy.

It is sometimes argued that the emergence of the provinces as international actors is important because it suggests the disintegration and marginalization of the federal government. However, it is important to go beyond this image and examine in more detail the constraints and opportunities inherent in the international activities of the provinces. As a first step, we will look at the role of provinces in international policy; second, we will explore the international interests of the provinces.

FEDERALISM AND INTERNATIONAL RELATIONS

There are two schools of thought about federalism and international affairs: those who advocate centralization and those who suggest that multilevel governance provides a more appropriate approach. An example of the centralization school is Kenneth Wheare, one of the leading theorists of federalism, who asserted that a monopoly of foreign affairs is a "minimum power" of all federal governments.[17] In his landmark study, Wheare highlighted the negative consequences both for the national interest and for the functioning of the international system that would flow from an unbundling of central control over foreign affairs. In the same vein, Robert Davis maintained that questions concerning international relations are at the heart of federal regimes.[18] According to Bertrand Badie and Marie-Claude Smouts, central control over the foreign affairs power is a requirement of international law since a centralized political system is a necessary condition for states to be able to play the role they are assigned in international law and practice. In essence, without the existence of a central government that has a plenary authority on its territory in relation to foreign affairs and the ability to participate in international relations and to enforce international obligations in the domestic order, inter-state relations can only be seriously compromised.[19] If the two levels of government enjoy "co-decision" over international policy, its risks a version of what Fritz W. Scharpf called the "joint-decision trap"—in which a state cannot take decisive action in international policy because decisions have to reflect the lowest common denominator.[20] In Canada, a number of scholars have underlined the constitutional difficulties that the federal government encounters in negotiating and implementing international agreements when they involve provincial areas of jurisdiction.[21]

---

17 Kenneth C. Wheare, *Federal Government* (Oxford: Oxford University Press, 1967).

18 Robert Davis, "The Federal Principle Reconsidered," in Aaron Wildavsky, ed., *American Federalism in Perspective* (Boston: Little Brown, 1967).

19 Bertrand Badie and Marie-Claude Smouts, *Le retournement du monde: Sociologie de la scène internationale*, 3rd ed. (Paris: PFNSP et Dalloz, 1999).

20 Fritz W. Scharpf, "The Joint-Decision Trap: Lessons from the German Federalism and European Integration," *Public Administration* 66:3 (Autumn 1988), 239–78.

21 David M. Brown and Earl H. Fry, eds., *States and Provinces in the International Economy* (Berkeley: Institute of Governmental Studies Press, 1993); Grace Skogstad, "International Trade Policy and Canadian Federalism: A Constructive Tension," in Herman Bakvis and Grace Skogstad, eds., *Canadian Federalism: Performance, Effectiveness and Legitimacy* (Toronto: Oxford University Press, 2001).

Those who embrace the concept of multilevel governance take a different view.[22] In this view, regional integration, the growth of multilateralism, and globalization have all rendered the centralization approach obsolete. According to Brian Hocking, diplomacy and international policy cannot and should not be considered a monopoly of the central government. Non-central governments always have an important role, even if it is only for the purposes of implementing international agreements concluded by the central government. In addition, giving a monopoly over international policy to the central government in a federation risks upsetting what should be an equitable distribution of powers between the different orders of government, tipping it in favour of the central government.

Instead, Hocking suggests that international policy should be thought of as a complex system where different actors at the heart of a federal state structure tangle with each other.[23] Multilevel governance thus implies that there are "obligations of cooperation" that exist between central and non-central governments in federations. The only way to put coherent international policies in place is for both orders of government to set up intergovernmental mechanisms to consult on policy and secure agreement.

Because the requirements of cooperation are more and more important, we have seen in the negotiation of international treaties a noticeable increase in "executive federalism"— the process by which intergovernmental negotiation is dominated by the federal prime minister and provincial premiers.[24] While the temptation to govern from the centre remains dominant,[25] most students of federalism in Canada conclude that the culture of intergovernmentalism is largely informal and that intergovernmental arrangements mostly work by "soft" consensus.[26]

The Canadian Constitution and International Policy

While most federal constitutions explicitly assign exclusive power over foreign affairs to the central government, the British North America Act passed by the British parliament in 1867 was silent on the question. The provisions of the BNA Act (since 1982 called the Constitution Act, 1867) enumerating the division of powers—Sections 91 and 92—did not explicitly assign competence in foreign affairs to either the federal or provincial levels. Nor, importantly, did the BNA Act deny the provinces the possibility of an international role as other federal constitutions tend to do. Indeed, the only mention of international

---

22 Ian Bache and Matthew Flinders, eds., *Multi-level Governance* (Oxford: Oxford University Press, 2004). See also Liesbet Hooghe and Gary Marks, *Multi-level Governance and European Integration* (Lanham, MD: Rowman and Littlefield, 2001); Liesbet Hooghe and Gary Marks, "Unraveling the Central State, But How? Types of Multi-Level Governance," *American Political Science Review* 97:2 (May 2003), 233–43; Charlie Jeffery, "Sub-national Mobilization and European Integration: Does it Make Any Difference?" *Journal of Common Market Studies* 38:1 (March 2000), 1–23.

23 Hocking, *Localizing Foreign Policy.*

24 Ronald L. Watts, *Executive Federalism: A Comparative Analysis* (Kingston: Institute of Intergovernmental Relations, Queen's University, 1989), 3.

25 Donald J. Savoie, "Power at the Apex: Executive Dominance," in James Bickerton and Alain-G. Gagnon, eds., *Canadian Politics,* 4th ed. (New York: Broadview Press, 2004), 145–63.

26 See Richard Simeon and Amy Nugent, "Parliamentary Canada and Intergovernmental Canada: Exploring the Tensions," in Herman Bakvis and Grace Skogstad, eds., *Canadian Federalism: Performance, Effectiveness and Legitimacy,* 2nd ed. (Toronto: Oxford University Press, 2008).

affairs in the BNA Act was the now "spent" Section 132, designed to extend to the new dominion the power to implement Imperial treaties:

> The Parliament and Government of Canada shall have all Powers necessary or proper for performing the Obligations of Canada or any Province thereof, as Part of the British Empire, towards Foreign Countries, arising under Treaties between the Empire and such Foreign Countries.

The silence was entirely understandable since such an explicit allocation of powers was, in the circumstances, unnecessary. Perhaps somewhat shortsightedly, those who framed Canada's original constitution did not conceive that the new dominion might eventually enjoy the same autonomy in foreign policy as it was receiving in domestic affairs. Certainly as a member of the Empire, Canada could have no independent international personality. Instead, other states would continue to recognize only one sovereign entity, the British Empire. Correspondingly, the rights and responsibilities of sovereign statehood would be vested in, and exercised by, the Imperial government in London. The constitution was thus framed accordingly. As Roff Johannson noted, the BNA Act "was not designed to provide a constitution for an autonomous nation-state. Rather, what was involved was the sharing of authority between various levels of local government."[27]

And little effort has been made since that time to break the constitutional silence by amending the British North America Act to specify more clearly the powers and limitations of competence in international affairs. In the constitutional discussions that led to the Victoria Charter of 1971, a number of articles on international relations were proposed, but were dropped.[28] Since then, there have been two occasions when Canadian political elites negotiated changes to the Constitution, and thus could have modernized the Constitution by including a clearer reference to international policy: the patriation process of the early 1980s and the constitutional accords worked out at Meech Lake in 1987 and Charlottetown in 1992. However, in each case there were other, more pressing, issues to be negotiated. As a result, the Constitution Act, 1982, continues to leave the question of the competence of the provinces in the area of foreign affairs as constitutionally unclear as the BNA Act had in 1867. And in the absence of any constitutional prohibition against international activity, Canada's provincial governments have sought to project and protect their interests beyond their—and Canada's—borders.

International Treaties

However, with the Statute of Westminster of 1931 and the acquisition of sovereignty in all areas of policy, the question was raised rapidly in the context of Canadian federalism: Does the federal government have the power to force the provinces to implement treaties even when those treaties deal with subjects that fall exclusively within provincial jurisdiction? It was Ontario, in the *Labour Conventions* case, that challenged the ability of the federal government to legislate in provincial fields of jurisdiction in order to implement international agreements.[29] After the 1930 election, the Conservative government of R.B. Bennett ratified

---

27 P.R. (Roff) Johannson, "Provincial International Activities," *International Journal* 33:2 (Spring 1978), 359.

28 See Louis Sabourin, "Les dispositions internationales écartées de la Charte de Victoria de 1971: context et actualisation," unpublished paper, Montréal, May 2006.

29 André Patry, *Le Québec dans le monde* (Montréal: Leméac, 1980), 155.

three International Labour Organization (ILO) conventions on conditions of work. By implementing these conventions, the federal government intruded on the provincial right to legislate in the area of labour. The Judicial Committee of the Privy Council in London—at that time Canada's final court of appeal—gave its judgment in 1937. The judges observed that Canada is founded on federal principles, and that by virtue of the principle of parliamentary sovereignty, the provinces are not obliged to undertake legislative measures in order to implement a treaty concluded by the executive branch of the federal government.

Since then, international treaty-making in Canada has followed two distinct phases: first, the conclusion of the treaty—that is, its negotiation, signature, and ratification; and then its implementation. The first phase is the exclusive prerogative of the federal government (even though the government of Québec was to contest this with the Gérin-Lajoie doctrine of 1965, discussed in the next chapter). The second step, the adoption of the legislative measures necessary in order to apply a treaty as a matter of domestic law, belongs to both orders of government. It is therefore necessary to incorporate treaties as a matter of domestic law by legislative action at the appropriate level. In Canada, a treaty does not apply apart from applicable law. Judges in Canada adjudicate the law and not treaties.

Thus, the 1958 United Nations Convention on the Recognition and Enforcement of Foreign Arbitral Awards was concluded by the federal government (step 1) but was implemented (step 2) by both levels of government. By contrast, the Hague Convention on Civil Aspects of the Abduction of Children was concluded by the federal government (step 1) but implemented exclusively by the provinces (step 2).

This constitutional situation poses a sizeable problem for Canada: Provincial collaboration is inevitable when the provincial fields of power are affected by a treaty or international convention. This problem is even more obvious when it is a question of Canada's involvement in the work of international organizations that affect provincial areas of competence, such as UNESCO, the World Health Organization, or the ILO. The federal government has historically adopted three strategies: It has refused to participate or engage; it has invoked the federal clause; or it has created formal consultative mechanisms with the provinces.

The first possible solution is non-engagement. In other words, the federal government simply refuses to participate in the work of an international organization, as it did in the case of the Hague Conference on Private International Law. It was not among the founders in 1955 and did not become a member until 1968, and consistently refused invitations to join in this organization's work. Alternatively, the federal government simply abstained from participating in a final vote when a treaty that affects provincial spheres of competence is under consideration. Since 1938, a semi-official but detailed procedure has been put in place to define Canada's participation in the ILO, since labour is a matter of provincial jurisdiction. When a draft convention was at issue, the Canadian delegation had to vote in favour of taking the matter into consideration but was required to abstain from the final vote if the convention applied to a matter of provincial jurisdiction unless the "provinces had provided proof of sufficient support in order for reasonable hope that it would be effectively adopted in Canada."[30] As a result, by the end of the 1960s Canada had ratified only 18 of the 111 conventions adopted by the ILO and only 6 of 18 international human rights conventions.[31] The federal government has also tried to find ways to limit the convention

---

[30] Permanent Delegate of Canada to the League of Nations, memorandum, November 30, 1938, cited by Renaud Dehousse, *Fédéralisme et relations internationales* (Brussels: Bruylant, 1991), 191.

[31] Dehousse, *Fédéralisme*, 181, n27.

to matters falling under federal jurisdiction. For example, the Canadian delegation at the San Francisco Convention of 1945 objected to the inclusion of full employment as one of the aims of the United Nations because labour is a matter of provincial jurisdiction.[32]

Because these constraints affected Canada's ability to play the kind of constructive role at the United Nations it sought, a variant of the procedure was devised that left more room to manoeuvre. When any subject discussed in committee touched on provincial jurisdiction, Canadian diplomats were instructed to mention the constitutional difficulties at home and then abstain in the committee vote. But, when the issue was brought before the General Assembly, the delegation could take a position in the final vote, honour having been satisfied with the mention of the constitutional difficulty. This is what happened in 1948 when the draft convention on human rights was considered by the UN. In committee, Canada abstained on the grounds that the convention dealt with rights that were within provincial jurisdiction; but in the General Assembly, Lester Pearson, who headed the delegation, claimed that Canada "approves and supports the general principles contained in the Declaration and would not wish to do anything which might appear to discourage the effort" and voted for the convention.[33]

The second strategy when an international negotiation affects a field of provincial jurisdiction is for the federal government to try to secure the addition of a federal clause in the final text. Sometimes referred to as the "Canada Clause," this provision links the implementation of the treaty to Canada's constitutional requirements and confirms that the federal government undertakes to observe the treaty only within the limits of its constitutional competencies.[34] The proliferation of such federal clauses, particularly in commercial agreements, eventually prompted the federal government to secure adoption of international agreements by the provinces.

This transformation of federal clauses, together with the enunciation of the Gérin-Lajoie Doctrine in Québec in 1965, whereby Québec affirmed the right to represent itself when its fields of competence were involved, forced the federal government to adopt the third strategy—of consulting the provinces when international treaties affect their powers.[35] A number of consultative mechanisms between the federal government and the provinces were established.[36] The first federal–provincial understanding, in 1974, dealt with the Hague Conference on Private International Law. Under this agreement, the federal minister of justice created a consultative group composed of civil servants from provincial ministries of justice to provide recommendations on Canada's negotiating position that were then discussed with provincial ministers. Moreover,

---

32 James Eayrs, "Canadian Federalism and the United Nations," *Canadian Journal of Political Science* 16:2 (May 1950), 175.

33 Government of Canada, *Canada and the United Nations, 1948* (Ottawa, 1948), 248–249.

34 André Patry, *La compétence internationale des provinces canadiennes* (Montréal: André R. Dorais éditeur, 2003), 6.

35 Stéphane Paquin, ed., *Les relations internationales du Québec depuis la doctrine Gérin-Lajoie (1965–2005)* (Sainte-Foy, QC: Presses de l'Université Laval, 2006).

36 John Zeigel, "Treaty Making and Implementation Powers in Canada: The Continuing Dilemma," in Bin Cheng and E.D. Brown, eds., *Contemporary Problems of International Law: Essays in Honour of Georg Schwarzenberger on His Eightieth Birthday* (Agincourt: Carswell, 1988); Daniel Turp, *Pour une intensification des relations du Québec avec les institutions internationales* (Québec: Ministère des Relations internationales, November 2002).

provincial representatives were included on the Canadian delegation to sessions of the Hague Conference. Afterward, the Uniform Law Conference of Canada prepared model laws that the provinces could adopt if they wished.[37] A similar mechanism was instituted on human rights issues. In 1975, a Federal/Provincial/Territorial Continuing Committee of Officials on Human Rights was created to serve as a consultation mechanism between the different orders of government with respect to the domestic implementation of human rights instruments.[38]

In the field of education, in 1977 the Department of External Affairs concluded an understanding with the Canadian Council of Ministers of Education (CCME) that bestowed that in all international matters involving questions related to education, the CCME would recommend the composition of the Canadian delegation and designate the head of mission who would negotiate on behalf of the provinces. This understanding, agreed to by all provinces including Québec, has since regulated Canada's international relations in the field of education.

In the area of international trade, the federal government also instituted consultative mechanisms with the provinces, even though responsibility for trade is clearly federal. Beginning with the Tokyo Round of trade negotiations, from 1973 to 1979, the federal government started to consult the provinces when negotiations began to touch upon matters clearly within provincial jurisdiction. Since the subsequent rounds have also involved provincial jurisdiction, the trade consultation mechanisms remained in place.[39]

Because of the impact of trade agreements on provincial economies, the provincial governments were impelled into the Canada–United States free-trade debate in the 1980s and the North American free-trade debate in the early 1990s. Although the implementation of such an agreement would affect provincial responsibilities, the federal government refused provincial requests to be invited to sit at the table.[40] Instead, the provinces moved to make their positions known, not only personally via First Ministers' Conferences, but also at the official level via representatives to the Continuing Committee on Trade Negotiations established by Canada's chief negotiator, Simon Reisman.[41] The richer provinces hired high-profile consultants to represent their free-trade views in Ottawa: Bob Latimer, a former federal official with both the Department of Industry, Trade and Commerce and the Department of External Affairs worked for Ontario; Québec hired Jake Warren, who had been Canada's negotiator in the Tokyo Round of the GATT negotiations. The smaller provinces sent officials drawn from their own bureaucracies.

---

37 For details of the ULCC and its harmonization functions, see Jacob S. Ziegel, "Harmonization of Private Laws in Federal Systems of Government: Canada, the USA and Australia," in Ross Cranston, ed., *Making Commercial Law: Essays in Honour of Roy Goode* (Oxford: Clarendon Press, 1997), 131–66.

38 See the Heritage Canada site at http://www.pch.gc.ca/pgm/pdp-hrp/docs/core-eng.cfm.

39 H. Scott Fairley, "Jurisdictional Limits on National Purpose: Ottawa, the Provinces and Free Trade with the United States," in Marc Gold and David Leyton-Brown, eds., *Trade-Offs on Free Trade: the Canada–US Free Trade Agreement* (Toronto: Carswell, 1988), 107ff. Ivan Bernier, "La Constitution canadienne et la réglementation des relations économiques internationales au sortir du 'Tokyo Round,'" *Cahiers de Droit* 20(1979), 673ff.

40 Michael Hart, Bill Dymond, and Colin Robertson, *Decision at Midnight: Inside the Canada–US Free-Trade Negotiations* (Vancouver: UBC Press, 1994), 139.

41 For a good overview of the provincial positions, see G. Bruce Doern and Brian W. Tomlin, *Faith and Fear: The Free Trade Story* (Toronto: Stoddart, 1991), 126–51.

Throughout the negotiating process, the premiers were active in pressing their concerns. David Peterson, alarmed at rumours that the Auto Pact of 1965 was going to be put on the negotiating table, flew to Washington in January 1987 to press American officials to keep it excluded. The implications of the agreement negotiated by the federal government were assessed by each province. By the summer of 1988, all of the provincial governments except those of Ontario and Prince Edward Island had endorsed the agreement. A similar process was followed in the NAFTA negotiations, with the provinces once again seeking to make their views known and the federal government trying to coordinate provincial concerns via such mechanisms as the federal–provincial Committee for North American Free Trade Negotiations (CNAFTN).[42]

With the embrace of the North American Free Trade Agreement, the federal government maintained the structure of this consultative process. Recognizing the difficulties of negotiating trade treaties that did not touch on provincial jurisdiction, the government systematized the consultative process with the provinces, putting in place methods for developing negotiating positions. The Federal/Provincial/Territorial Committee on Trade (C-Trade) meets four times a year to review the general trade agenda and exchange views on the positions and strategies that the federal negotiators should take in global and bilateral negotiations. Recognizing the difficulties of negotiating trade treaties that did not touch on provincial jurisdiction, the federal government systematized the consultative process with the provinces, instituting methods for developing negotiating positions. These intergovernmental negotiations were pursued in a number of forums that included federal, provincial, and territorial officials. Since then, the consultative basis has been widened to include the Federation of Canadian Municipalities, nongovernmental organizations, and citizen input. However, as Christopher J. Kukucha has noted, Québec has pressed for a more formal European Union–like process that would see provincial representatives as direct participants in the negotiating process.[43]

In May 2009, the government of Stephen Harper and the European Union announced the launching of free-trade negotiations. This "new generation" free-trade agreement was going to focus on labour mobility, a provincial responsibility. Because of that, the EU wanted to ensure that the federal government in Ottawa had provincial representatives on the negotiating team (prompting Jean Charest, the Québec premier, to quip that the EU had a better understanding of Canadian federalism than Ottawa).[44] Charest named Pierre Marc Johnson, a former Parti Québécois premier who had represented Québec in the softwood lumber negotiations with the United States, as Québec's negotiator.

It is not only trade issues that interest the provinces. Québec and Alberta, for diametrically opposed reasons, are interested in the United Nations Framework Convention on Climate Change (UNFCCC) and the Kyoto protocol of 1997. This convention, were it to

---

42 Donald E. Abelson and Michael Lusztig, "The Consistency of Inconsistency: Tracing Ontario's Opposition to the North American Free Trade Agreement," *Canadian Journal of Political Science* 29:4 (December 1996), 681–98; Stephen de Boer, "Canadian Provinces, US States and North American Integration: Bench Warmers or Key Players?" *Choices* 8:4 (November 2002), 4.

43 For details, see Christopher J. Kukucha, *The Provinces and Canadian Foreign Trade Policy* (Vancouver: UBC Press, 2008); Christopher J. Kukucha, "An Independent Foreign Policy for Canadian Provinces? International Trade and Sub-federal Autonomy," in Brian Bow and Patrick Lennox, *An Independent Foreign Policy for Canada* (Toronto: University of Toronto Press, 2008), 168.

44 Antoine Robitaille, "Sommet Canada-EU-Québec compte sur l'appui de Bruxelles," *Le Devoir*, May 7, 2009.

be implemented, would have profound—and irreversible—effects on Canada's provinces and municipalities, particularly their policies on energy, transport, and urban planning. Canada's policy on climate change embraced at the Kyoto conference in 1997 emerged from negotiations between the federal and provincial governments, but at the last minute the prime minister intervened to set its Kyoto targets.[45]

Some provinces have increasingly become involved in the field of public health at an international level, recognizing that it would fall to local and provincial officials to deal with pandemics.[46] Following the SARS pandemic of 2003, Ontario and Québec asked the federal government to include provincial representatives on the Canadian delegation to the World Health Organization in order to monitor developments in this field. The response of the federal government has been to deny the provinces' request; indeed, in October 2005 the government of Paul Martin refused to agree to a Québec request to send representatives to an international conference on avian influenza in Montréal.

NAFTA and Province–State Relations

Globalization, regionalism, and interdependence has prompted an intensification of relations among the 10 Canadian provinces, the 50 states in the United States of America, and the 32 states in the United Mexican States. These non-central governments have concluded numerous bilateral and multilateral agreements and have established a number of transnational associations to respond to new common challenges. The phenomenal growth of trade with the United States since the signing of the free-trade agreements that went into force in 1989 and 1994, concentrated in some 20 north–south trade corridors, has prompted the provinces to consult and coordinate their actions with their neighbours.

At present there are about 400 agreements between American states and Canadian provinces. More than 100 of these have been concluded on issues of the environment and natural resources. Provincial officials conduct hundreds of missions to the United States and Mexico each year. Importantly, most of these linkages and agreements do not concern the federal governments in either Washington or Ottawa.[47] However, since so much provincial business focuses on the government in Washington, provincial governments have pressed to be allowed to establish a lobby there. In response, the federal government established a Washington Advocacy Secretariat in 2004 designed to coordinate federal and provincial lobbying activities in Washington and invited provincial governments to send a representative to the Washington embassy. Not all provinces took up the offer: While Alberta sent a representative in March 2005, Québec refused the invitation, since it has consistently wanted to establish its own office in Washington, separate from the Canadian embassy.

---

45 Steven Bernstein, "International Institutions and the Framing of Domestic Policies: The Kyoto Protocol and Canada's Response to Climate Change," *Policy Sciences* 35 (2002), 203–36; Heather A. Smith, "Canada and Kyoto: Independence or Indifference?" in Brian Bow and Patrick Lennox, eds., *An Independent Foreign Policy for Canada? Challenges and Choices for the Future* (Toronto: University of Toronto Press, 2008), 207–21.

46 Kumanan Wilson, "Pandemic Prescription," *Diplomat & International Canada* (May/June 2006), 14–16.

47 David W. Conklin, "NAFTA: Regional Impacts," in Michael Keating and John Loughlin, eds., *The Political Economy of Regionalism* (London: Frank Cass, 1997), 195–214.

The intensification of transnational relations between non-central governments in North America has led to the creation of a number of specialized organizations between Canadian provinces and American states.[48] These organizations cover a number of areas as varied as health, transboundary waters, energy, transborder security, firefighting, management of the electricity grid, and the administration of roads, highways, and bridges. As a result, an extensive network of linkages between Canadian provinces and American states has emerged. Numerous transnational organizations, such as the Conference of State and Provincial Health Administrators of North America, serve to provide a forum for state–provincial contacts. Canadian provinces are members of such American bodies as the Northeastern Interstate Forest Fire Protection Commission or the Midwestern and Western Associations of State Departments of Agriculture.[49] There are even regular "junior summits" that premiers can attend. In the east, there is the Conference of New England Governors and Eastern Canadian Premiers (NEG-ECP), who meet to discuss matters of common concern. The first summit was held in the summer of 1973 and was institutionalized thereafter in the wake of the first oil shock of October 1973, as governments sought to cooperate to take advantage of the complementarity of the electricity needs of New England and the ability of Canadian provinces to sell hydroelectricity. Although there are considerable differences in how the American governors and the Canadian premiers tend to transact business, there has nonetheless emerged a willingness to forge common policy perspectives, particularly for presentation to the two central governments.[50] In the west, British Columbia and Alberta joined the Western Legislative Conference, an organization of 13 western states, in 1989, adding an additional linkage to an already close institutional relationship between the governor of the state of Washington and British Columbia. In the centre, Ontario, for its part, has explored the possibility of joining the Council of Great Lakes Governors.

Some Canadian provinces are members of international groupings of non-central governments. Québec is one of the cofounders, with the German land of Bavaria, of the Partner Regions—which include Upper Austria, Shandong province, Western Cape, São Paulo, Florida, and Georgia. Québec also sits as an observer to the Conference of the regions with legislative powers and the Assembly of European regions. Ontario, for its part, has been an associate member of the "four motors of Europe" since 1990.

ORGANIZING FOR INTERNATIONAL POLICY

The growth of the external activities of the provinces has been matched by an expansion of bureaucratic establishments—"foreign offices" of a sort—that are charged with the management of the province's international relations. However, the importance of this bureaucracy will vary considerably from one province to the next. The main means of promoting

---

48 For details, see Canada, Policy Research Initiative, *The Emergence of Cross-Border Regions Between Canada and the United States: Final Report* (Ottawa: November 2008).

49 Gerard F. Rutan, "Legislative Interaction of a Canadian Province and an American State: Thoughts upon Sub-national Cross-Border Relations," *American Review of Canadian Studies* 11 (Autumn 1981), 67–69.

50 Martin Lubin, "The Routinization of Cross-Border Interactions: An Overview of the NEG/ECP Structures and Activities," in Brown and Fry, eds., *States and Provinces*, 145–166; Richard Vengroff and Jason Rich, "Foreign Policy by Other Means: Paradiplomacy and the Canadian Provinces," in Patrick James, Nelson Michaud, and Marc J. O'Reilly, eds., *Handbook of Canadian Foreign Policy* (Lanham, MD: Lexington Books, 2006), 117–120; *Cross-Border Regions*, 7.

these interests has been by establishing provincial offices abroad and developing bureaucratic capacity at home.

Representation Abroad

Section 92.4 of the Constitution Act, 1867, gives provinces authority over the "Establishment and Tenure of Provincial Offices." This permits provinces to establish provincial offices abroad if they wish. The first provincial office abroad was opened even before Confederation. In 1816, the province of Lower Canada opened an office in London, and in 1871 the Québec government sent agents to Britain and the United States to encourage emigration to Canada.

In 1882, Québec sent Hector Fabre, a Nationalist senator, to Paris as its agent-general; the province shared him with the federal government, which appointed Fabre as Canada's commissioner to Paris in 1883. On his death in 1910, he was replaced with an Alberta senator, Philippe Roy, but the Québec connection was severed. As Robert Borden noted in 1912, "It is undesirable that the representative of the Dominion government should represent one of the provinces as distinct."[51] Commercial offices were opened in Britain—by Ontario in 1908 and by Québec in 1911. In addition, Québec opened an agency in Brussels in 1915.[52]

But this early activity was relatively short-lived. Québec closed its agency in Paris in 1912 because the French business community was uninterested. The missions in Brussels and London were closed in the early 1930s in an effort to trim provincial expenditures. When the Union Nationale under Maurice Duplessis came to power in 1936, all of Québec's agencies abroad were abolished by law.[53]

If the Great Depression dampened the extension abroad of provincial interests, the Second World War greatly reduced the ability of the provinces to exercise their legislative powers in a number of important policy spheres. The War Measures Act was invoked by the federal government at the outset of the war, centralizing government, increasing federal regulation of most spheres of activity, greatly enhancing federal jurisdiction, and stripping the provinces—at least temporarily—of many of their prerogatives. As a result, Mackenzie King and "[m]ost of his ministers came to view the provinces, not as rivals or antagonists, as they had been in the thirties, but as irrelevancies to be stroked or prodded according to whether they had a Liberal government or not."[54]

---

51 Quoted in Louise Beaudoin, "Origines et développement du rôle international du gouvernement du Québec," in Paul Painchaud, ed., *Le Canada et le Québec sur la scène internationale* (Québec: Centre québécois de relations internationales, 1977), 447; see also John Hilliker, *Canada's Department of External Affairs*, vol. 1: *The Early Years, 1909–1946* (Montréal and Kingston: McGill-Queen's University Press, 1990), 17.

52 Canada, Department of External Affairs, *Documents on Canadian External Relations*, vol. 1: *1909–1918* (Ottawa: Department of External Affair, 1967), 17; Hilliker, *Canada's Department of External Affairs*, 19; Jean Hamelin, "Québec et le monde extérieur," *Annuaire statistique du Québec, 1968–69* (Québec: 1969), 19–26.

53 Beaudoin, "Origines et développement," 461. When the Liberals under Adélard Godbout came to power in the 1939 provincial elections, this law was repealed and legislation authorizing the government to appoint agents-general was introduced. Québec offices were opened in New York and in Ottawa. Duplessis and the Union Nationale were returned to power in 1944; the two offices were left in place, although the budget of the New York office was cut so much that the agent general could do virtually nothing.

54 Robert Bothwell, Ian Drummond, and John English, *Canada Since 1945: Power, Politics and Provincialism* (Toronto: University of Toronto Press, 1981), 74.

The end of the war brought the relaxation of federal centralization and a plethora of new spending programs, many involving the provincial governments. But in the decade and a half following the war, the growth of the modern welfare state increased the burden on the provinces to provide social and other services. This created a concomitant imperative for provincial governments to promote the growth of their economies to provide the funds necessary for the provision of expanded provincial services—an imperative that had an implicit electoral connection. Thus the expansion of provincial trade, and maintenance and expansion of a provincial infrastructure, and the raising of capital in foreign markets assumed increased importance in the post-1945 period. This economic imperative was one reason for the rapid growth of provincial activities abroad: By the early 1980s, seven provinces were operating over 35 agencies on three continents.[55]

On the other hand, provinces are often overwhelmed by the resources necessary to play the highly expensive game of operating in the international system. Maintaining provincial offices in other capitals—the most visible and most attractive form of international activity—is invariably a costly enterprise: space has to be rented in an appropriate part of town—usually in the overpriced central business district; housing for provincial representatives, schooling for their children, annual home leaves, and relocation expenses must be provided; joining the diplomatic cocktail circuit means having to provide for appropriate entertainment. Even if one runs a frugal operation, the costs involved invariably stand out. Moreover, the "returns" are not always visible to jaundiced-eyed provincial officials in the treasury back home who wonder to themselves what the province is getting out of what is invariably seen as an extravagance. And there is the added problem that it usually takes time for a representative to demonstrate "deliverables," particularly in those jurisdictions in which one has to spend not only energy but time developing relationships.

Because of this, offices abroad are a highly visible and attractive target for budget-cutting exercises. As a consequence, provincial offices abroad tend to open and close in tandem with the rhythms of the broader economic climate. Permanent foreign representation is expanded when the provincial economy is expanding—and contracted when budgets are tightened. It might be thought that it would be precisely during periods of recession that provinces would expand rather than contract foreign representation, in order to encourage international economic activity—and such logic appears to have driven the spate of provincial office openings in the early 1980s.

But hinging provincial representation abroad to the mood swings of the capitalist economy has produced a seemingly endless (and wasteful) procession of openings and closings. Ontario offers an interesting case study of this dynamic at work. In the thirty years between the late 1960s and 2009, it went through the cycle of opening and closing its missions abroad four times. In the boom years of the late 1960s and early 1970s, Queen's Park opened Ontario offices around the world, only to close many of them in the middle of the 1970s as a cost-cutting measure. In the early 1980s, the number of offices grew again, then contracted by the middle of the decade, and then grew once again under the Liberal government of David Peterson in the late 1980s. Then, once again, all Ontario offices abroad were closed by the New Democratic Party government of Bob Rae in the early 1990s, again as a means of trimming the provincial budget.

---

55 A.E. Blanchette, ed., *Canadian Foreign Policy, 1966–1976: Selected Speeches and Documents* (Ottawa: Carleton University Press, 1980), 302.

In December 2000, the Progressive Conservative government of Mike Harris embraced a new "global strategy," part of which involved reestablishing a modest provincial presence abroad. However, to avoid the huge waste involved in opening and closing offices, the government at Queen's Park embraced the policy of "co-location"—renting space in Canadian embassies, high commissions, or consulates. This saves money, allows the province to maintain a presence abroad, and avoids having to spend large amounts on startup costs. By early 2002, there were Ontario International Marketing Centres located in Canadian missions in Shanghai, New York, and Munich. When the provincial Liberals under Dalton McGuinty came to power in 2003, the network was expanded. As of 2009, Ontario maintains centres in Beijing, London, Los Angeles, Mexico City, Munich, New Delhi, New York, Paris, Shanghai, and Tokyo—all co-located in Canadian embassies or consulates.

Provincial offices abroad have numerous purposes: to promote trade and investment between the province and the foreign jurisdiction; to promote provincial products and services in the foreign market; and to identify local trade and investment opportunities for provincial businesses (and of course the obverse: to identify provincial trade and investment opportunities for local businesses). Other functions include the promotion of tourism; monitoring legislation and policy being considered by the foreign government that might have an impact on provincial interests; acting as the first line for lobbying foreign governments when necessary; encouraging "twinning" relations between the province and the local jurisdiction; and arranging local visits for provincial politicians.[56]

Bureaucratization at Home

The growth of provincial representation abroad has been mirrored by bureaucratic growth at home. This has proceeded at varying rates, however. At one end of the spectrum are those provinces that have eschewed anything more than the most rudimentary administrative and bureaucratic support systems for their international activities.

Smaller provinces, such as Prince Edward Island or Newfoundland and Labrador, have not created large bureaucracies to manage their international activities. Two or three officials attached to the cabinet or the premier's office oversee provincial activities abroad. This reflects in part the smaller budgetary bases of these provinces and their inability to fund such agencies. But lack of institutionalization may also be attributable to a simple lack of desire on the part of the premier and cabinet ministers to invest bureaucratic resources in international affairs. Nova Scotia, New Brunswick, Manitoba, and British Columbia have institutionalized somewhat more, but their governments are nonetheless content to conduct their international relations in an ad hoc and centralized fashion.

At the other end of the spectrum is Québec, which has sought to institutionalize the support system for its international relations in a way that comes close to being a fully developed foreign ministry. Today's Ministère des Relations internationales du Québec (MRI) began life in 1965 as an interdepartmental committee, the Commission interministérielle des relations extérieures du Québec. Under the leadership of Claude Morin, at the time the

---

56 Offices also assist in the negotiation of international agreements, network with consulates of other countries and develop educational exchanges: James D. McNiven and Dianna Cann, "Canadian Provincial Trade Offices in the United States," in Brown and Fry, eds., *States and Provinces*, 178–81; on "twinning" with China, see George MacLean and Kim Richard Nossal, "Triangular Dynamics: Australian States, Canadian Provinces, and Relations with China," in Brian Hocking, ed., *Foreign Relations and Federal States* (London: Leicester University Press, 1993), 170–89.

deputy minister of federal–provincial relations, the Commission grew from a coordinating body into a full-fledged bureaucracy charged with the development of external policy and the administration of a wide range of Québec government programs abroad. In 1967, the Commission was absorbed into the Ministère des Affaires fédérales–provinciales, which was restyled the Ministère des Affaires intergouvernementales du Québec (MAIQ) to reflect that its mission was not simply managing relations with the federal government but included relations across the world.[57]

Morin was a nationalist. After the government of Robert Bourassa was sworn in, he resigned from the civil service in the fall of 1971, and eventually joined the Parti Québécois and became the minister of intergovernmental affairs in René Lévesque's cabinet. His nationalism prodded him to develop a bureaucracy capable of identifying Québec's interests abroad and projecting the Québec government's presence internationally. By the early 1980s, the ministry was the most well-developed provincial agency charged with international relations. In size and structure it was a micro version of External Affairs in Ottawa, and in December 1984 the twin responsibilities of MAIQ were split. Responsibility for federal–provincial relations was given to the Secrétariat aux Affaires intergouvernementales, while the international activities of the province were assumed by the Ministère des Relations internationales. In December 1988, a new Ministère des Affaires internationales (MAI) was created. Mirroring the integration of the federal Department of Foreign Affairs and International Trade examined in Chapter 9, the MAI absorbed the international trade promotion function of the Ministère du Commerce extérieur et du Développement technologique and in June 1994 the immigration ministry was absorbed, creating the MAIICC: the Ministère des Affaires internationales, de l'Immigration et des Communautés culturelles. When the PQ returned to power, the bureaucracy was again reorganized. In January 1996, the trade responsibilities were moved back to the industry, commerce, science, and technology portfolio, and the old name—Ministère des Relations internationales—was restored.[58]

In the middle are provinces like Ontario, which has a modest bureaucratic capacity for international activity.[59] The international affairs bureaucracy enjoyed a slow growth in the 1960s, but an expansion in the 1970s as a separate unit for international relations evolved, first within the Ministry of Treasury, Economics and Intergovernmental Affairs. When this ministry was broken up in 1978, the international relations division moved to the new Ministry of Intergovernmental Affairs (MIA). As in Québec, the same tensions produced as the trade and political sides were pushed by an increasingly globalized economy also afflicted the Ontario bureaucracy. By the late 1980s, conflict over control of the activities of the Office of International Relations (OIR) developed between the MIA, with its emphasis on both trade and diplomacy, and the Ministry of Industry, Trade and Technology (MITT), which sought to use the OIR in a more single-minded way to expand Ontario's trade. Intergovernmental Affairs lost this turf war. In 1991, OIR was transferred to MITT. In the subsequent decade, this ministry underwent a number of name changes, most

---

57 Claude Morin, *L'art de l'impossible: La diplomatie québécoise depuis 1960* (Montréal: Boréal, 1987), 43, 75–78.

58 Nelson Michaud and Isabelle Ramet, "Québec et politique étrangère: contradiction ou réalité?," *International Journal* 59:2 (Spring 2004), 303ff.

59 David K.M. Dyment, "Substate Paradiplomacy: The Case of the Ontario Government," in Hocking, ed., *Foreign Relations and Federal States.*

recently the Ministry of Economic Development and Trade. Since then, some of the international relations functions migrated back to the intergovernmental affairs portfolio. In 2004, the Office of International Relations and Protocol (OIRP) was formally moved back to the Ministry of Intergovernmental Affairs.[60] After the 2007 provincial election, Dalton McGuinty, the premier, took over the intergovernmental affairs portfolio, moving it and the OIRP as a division into the Cabinet Office. However, Economic Development and Trade retains responsibility for international trade.

Figure 11.1 provides an overview of the different patterns of bureaucratization at the provincial level. Whatever the institutional arrangement, bureaucratic capability remains a key factor in explaining why the provincial governments have maintained their high level

FIGURE 11.1	Provincial Management of International Policy
Province	**Responsibility for International Policy**
Newfoundland and Labrador	Minister of Intergovernmental Affairs, supported by a secretariat; an assistant deputy minister is designated as a resource person on international issues
Prince Edward Island	Premier is minister of Intergovernmental Affairs; coordinator for intergovernmental affairs in the Executive Council Office is responsible for international issues
Nova Scotia	Premier is minister of Intergovernmental Affairs; deputy minister is responsible for international policy
New Brunswick	Premier is minister of Intergovernmental Affairs; Department of Intergovernmental Affairs covers international issues
Québec	Minister of International Relations, supported by the Ministère des Relations internationales
Ontario	Premier is also minister of Intergovernmental Affairs; Office of International Relations and Protocol is located in the Cabinet Office
Manitoba	Premier is responsible for federal-provincial relations, supported by a deputy minister of federal-provincial relations
Saskatchewan	Minister of Intergovernmental Relations, supported by a Ministry of Intergovernmental Relations, which is responsible for international policy
Alberta	Minister of International and Intergovernmental Relations, supported by the Ministry of International and Intergovernmental Relations
British Columbia	Minister of State for Intergovernmental Affairs, supported by a Secretariat, which includes a section responsible for international policy

Source: Louis Ranger, Jeff Heynen, and John Higginbotham, *Advancing Canadian Interests in the United States: A Practical Guide for Canadian Public Officials* (Ottawa: Canada School of Public Service, 2004), 38-39.

60 Vengroff and Rich, "Foreign Policy by Other Means," 117–18.

of international activity. The greater the number of civil servants who have a specialized expertise and who are hired to devote their attentions to defining provincial interests externally, the more likely that provincial ministers will be encouraged to seek an expanded external role for their province, acting on the advice received from their specialized agencies. Thus, while provincial international activities do not spring from the creation of a bureaucratic establishment whose raison d'être is to define provincial interests abroad, these agencies of the provincial state, once in existence, tend to strengthen and perpetuate a provincial international presence.

INTERNATIONAL INTERESTS OF THE PROVINCES

What propels provincial governments into international activity? While the provinces participate in the formulation of international policy at the federal level, they also have interests in international politics that parallel the international interests of the federal government. In the early years after Confederation, the external interests of the provinces—like those of the dominion government at the time—were quite limited: the promotion of immigration and the expansion of trade.[61] But in the years since, these concerns have multiplied. By the beginning of the twenty-first century, provincial governments had a range of international interests. We focus on four sets of interests: economic, environmental, security, and political.

Economic Interests

We noted above the impact that globalization has had on the growth of provincial international activity, particularly toward the United States. In fact, the vast majority of the international activities of Canada's provinces revolve around the advancement and protection of economic interests. The main reason why provincial governments maintain offices abroad, send trade missions to other countries, and conduct international diplomacy is to encourage economic growth through trade, investment, and tourism. Provinces seek to expand external markets for their products, particularly their agricultural and natural resources; to develop the secondary manufacturing sectors of their economies; and to find new sources of capital.

Canadian provinces also seek to defend their economic interests against the protectionist manoeuvres of their commercial competitors. In the trade dispute with the United States over softwood lumber, for example, the governments of Alberta, British Columbia, Ontario, and Québec fiercely sought to defend the interests of their provinces against the efforts of U.S. producers of softwood lumber to impose tariffs on imports of this product from Canada.

However, while the United States has been the most important target of provincial paradiplomacy, provinces have also had a more global focus. Premiers have gone to Europe, the newly industrializing countries of the Middle East and Latin America, and, particularly in the 1980s and 1990s, the Asia-Pacific region. For example, between 1993 and 2002, Prime Minister Jean Chrétien organized seven "Team Canada" trade missions to Europe, Latin America, and the Asia-Pacific—these always involved the provincial governments and generated considerable support from provincial premiers eager to expand

---

61 Howard A. Leeson and Wilfried Vanderelst, *External Affairs and Canadian Federalism: The History of a Dilemma* (Toronto: Holt, Rinehart and Winston, 1973), 45, 48–49.

their links. Likewise, the efforts of Jean Charest, premier of Québec, to secure approval for a Canadian free-trade agreement with the European Union is an example of this broader global push.

Environmental Interests

Although environmental concerns are usually related to the economic interests of a province and its citizens, these issues deserve separate mention. A province may be compelled to act to protect its environmental interests or practices. In the 1960s, Ontario played a central role in the management of environmental problems in the Great Lakes, establishing cooperative arrangements with neighbouring American states. In the 1980s, Ontario also actively cooperated with Ottawa in lobbying the United States Congress over the issue of acid rain, coordinating such efforts as speeches and information with Ottawa. Ontario was also active in pushing for environmental standards in the NAFTA negotiations in the early 1990s. And Clyde Wells, premier of Newfoundland and Labrador, supported Ottawa's efforts to stop European overfishing in international waters off the Grand Banks in the spring of 1995.[62]

These were cases when the environment of a province was threatened from outside its borders. But there are also occasions when it is the environmental practices of provincial governments that are seen to constitute threats to others and galvanize efforts abroad to change provincial government policy. This has occurred in the case of logging practices by British Columbia, Ontario, and Québec; in the case of Newfoundland and sealing; and in the case of Hydro-Québec's Great Whale hydroelectric development in northern Québec. Environmental groups, both foreign groups like Rainforest Action Network and transnational groups with branches in Canada like Greenpeace, have sought to change provincial policy—usually through consumer boycotts and negative advertising campaigns. In the 1980s, for example, Greenpeace was active in the campaign in Europe to boycott Canadian seal fur; in the early 1990s, Greenpeace led a campaign in Germany to boycott British Columbia wood products. In the Great Whale case, First Nations leaders like Matthew Coon Come, grand chief of the Crees, and Ethel Blondin, a Dene who was a Liberal MP from the western Arctic, travelled to the United States to argue that the project was environmentally unsound. Their intervention had an impact: On March 16, 1992, the New York State Assembly voted overwhelmingly to withhold approval for contracts to purchase $17 billion worth of electricity from Hydro-Québec until New York had conducted its own environmental assessment of the Québec project.[63]

When campaigns such as these are mounted, provincial governments will protect their constituents by defending their policies and practices. For example, in the case of the Greenpeace-led European boycott, the provincial government embarked on a high-profile lobbying campaign, directed not so much at European consumers, but at major corporate

---

62 On these cases, see David M. Dyment, "The Ontario Government as an International Actor," *Regional & Federal Studies* 11:1 (Spring 2001), 55–79; Donald E. Abelson, "Environmental Lobbying and Political Posturing: The Role of Environmental Groups in Ontario's Debate over NAFTA," *Canadian Public Administration* 38:3 (Fall 1995), 352–81; Donald Barry, "The Canadian–European Union Turbot War," *International Journal* 53:2 (Spring 1998), 252–84.

63 *Le Soleil*, March 31, 1992, B1. *Globe and Mail*, March 17, 1992, A4; on the international activities of First Nations, see Pierre-Gerlier Forest and Thierry Rodon, "Les activités internationales des autochtones du Canada," *Études internationales* 26:1 (March 1995), 35–58.

buyers of B.C. products. The premier and his forestry minister visited Europe on a number of occasions to defend B.C.'s record. Likewise, the Rainforest Action Network protested the clear-cutting policies of the B.C. government by running an ad campaign in the United States that used the province's own tourist slogan—"Visit Beautiful British Columbia"—but then added the admonition to "Picnic in the clearcut forests. Hike the eroded hillsides. See the dried-up salmon streams." The government in Victoria responded by mounting a counter-campaign. It enlisted forestry firms to run advertisements in American newspapers, and B.C. officials were sent to lobby foreign corporate buyers and policymakers.[64] In the case of the Great Whale, both the federal and Québec governments worked in tandem. From New York City, Alan Sullivan, the Canadian consul-general, and Leo Pare, Québec's delegate-general, lobbied legislators and the state governor in Albany.[65]

Security Interests

Issues of international security and territorial defence are generally activities that one associates with the federal government. And for good reason: In Canada, national defence and border control are exclusively federal. But the provinces do have an interest in security, in the sense that Section 92 of the Constitution gives them a central role in public safety. Until recently, however, the activities of both orders of government aimed at protecting the state against external threats were separated into tightly defined silos.

Several factors propelled the provinces into an interest in defence and security. As Québec's ministry of international relations put it in 2006: "In the 21st century, threats to international stability come increasingly from nonmilitary factors such as terrorism, transnational organized crime, the spread of infectious diseases and the deterioration of the environmental degradation. These emerging periods directly affect Québec's areas of responsibility, whether it is acting alone or jointly with the federal government."[66] To these issues one might add cyber-terrorism and identity theft.

But it was the emergence of Islamist terrorism in the 1990s, and the attacks of 9/11 in particular, that put international security issues more squarely on provincial agenda. The "global war on terror" after 2001 involved local and provincial governments—police, fire, and health services—as much, if not more, than federal agencies (the armed forces, the security forces, border protection). Moreover, given the importance of trade with the United States, all provincial governments had just as much interest as the federal government in doing what was necessary to keep the United States border open to the flow of goods to the American market after 9/11. Thus, for example, Québec reinforced its cross-border exchange of information with the neighbouring states of Vermont and New Hampshire and signed an anti-terrorism agreement with New York. Likewise, Ontario, Québec, and New Brunswick participate with 10 American states in the Northeast Regional Homeland Security Directors Consortium.

The provinces also took different measures to make the Canadian–American border more secure. On December 12, 2001, Canada and the United States signed the "Smart

---

64 *Globe and Mail*, March 21, 1994, B3; *Toronto Star*, May 28, 1995, F5.

65 *Le Soleil*, March 18, 1992, A5; *Globe and Mail*, March 17, 1992, A4.

66 Québec, Ministère des Relations internationales, *Québec's International Policy: Working in Concert* (Québec: Gouvernement du Québec, 2006), 67; available http://www.mri.gouv.qc.ca/en/pdf/Politique.pdf.

Border" agreement, as we saw in Chapter 5; but this agreement required the cooperation of the provincial governments in the implementation of such programs as NEXUS, which is intended to speed the movement of Canadians and Americans who frequently cross the border for work; FAST/EXPRES (Free and Secure Trade), designed to tighten security of just-in-time cross-border supply chains but subject goods to fewer delays; and C-TPAT (Customs–Trade Partnership Against Terrorism), which inspects and clears shipments before they arrive at the border.

Certain provincial international activities can be linked to international security interests. For example, it is not uncommon for provincial police or provincial election officials participate in peace-building and post-conflict reconstruction programs organized by the United Nations or institutions like the Organization for Security and Cooperation in Europe (OSCE). Likewise, the Ministère des Relations internationales du Québec has a development assistance program that funds projects for international cooperation to strengthen civil society in countries devastated by war or natural disasters. MRI has supported projects in Haiti, Guatemala, Nicaragua, and the Great Lakes region in Africa.

Political Interests

Provincial governments may be propelled into international activity by what Elliot J. Feldman and Lily Gardner Feldman call "political necessity"[67]—in other words, policy positions embraced for purely "political" reasons. Such "politics of necessity" can take different forms. First, provincial premiers may embrace foreign policy positions because an issue emerges on the provincial political agenda in a way that leaves them with no option but to involve themselves. Some issues—such as an earthquake in Italy, a coup d'état in Haiti, or an outbreak of war between Israel and its neighbours—affect provincial constituents, whether concretely or symbolically, and thus emerge on the provincial political agenda. Politicians in Canada's provinces are no less sensitive to agenda issues than elected officials anywhere else; they recognize the political costs of not pronouncing (or not acting) on such issues. They are impelled to have a position, even if they have little desire to do so. For elected officials recognize that resorting to the technically correct response—that such matters may fall more properly within the jurisdiction of the federal government—will tend to be criticized as pedantic at best, or buck-passing at worst.

Political necessity may emerge from an idiosyncratic mix of factors that are unlikely to be replicated. Certainly the "Team Canada" mission to China in the fall of 1994 falls into this category. While most provincial premiers were happy to join Jean Chrétien in this trade mission, the Parti Québécois premier of Québec, Jacques Parizeau, refused to join the mission because the political costs of a souverainiste premier being seen to be part of a pan-Canadian and overtly federalist "Team Canada" mission were simply too great. For Parizeau, political necessity demanded that he *not* go. However, once Parizeau refused, political necessity demanded that all other premiers accompany the prime minister—for to refuse would have been to be seen to be joining the souverainiste camp and "breaking" the unity of "Team Canada." Thus, even if some premiers had no interest at all in developing trade between their province and China, political necessity impelled them into this mission.

---

67 Elliot J. Feldman and Lily Gardner Feldman, "The Impact of Federalism on the Organization of Canadian Foreign Policy," *Publius: The Journal of Federalism* 14:4 (Fall 1984), 35.

Provincial governments were also drawn into the debates that preceded the war in Iraq in 2003. Ottawa's refusal to join the United States in the "coalition of the willing" being assembled by President George W. Bush was openly criticized by the Progressive Conservative premier of Alberta, Ralph Klein. The premier sent a letter to Bush through the U.S. ambassador in Ottawa not only expressing support for Bush's policies but also praising the president's "leadership" in the aftermath of the events of September 11. A few days later, the Progressive Conservative premier of Ontario, Ernie Eves, emulated his Alberta colleague.[68] The two statements, revealing the degree of division in Canada on the issue, deeply embarrassed the federal government. John Herd Thompson suggests that a concern for cross-border trade prompted these expressions of support,[69] but to the extent that Klein and Eves were echoing other voices in Alberta and Ontario calling for Canadian participation in the Iraq war, the two statements demonstrate that provincial leaders will express the views of their constituents on critical political issues.

CONCLUSION

From the perspective of the central government in Ottawa, Canada's federal structure places considerable constraints on the development of a "national" international policy in a number of key areas. The existence of provincial governments with parochial interests to project and maintain, and a constitution that does not explicitly deny the provinces the possibility of an international role, has precluded unilateralism in any but the high issues of war and peace. (And even then, electoral demands will on occasion propel provincial governments into pronouncing on those issues.) On those international policy issues that involve provincial jurisdiction, the imperatives of federalism demand that those who make international policy in Canada attempt to reflect the diversity of regional interests and concerns and try to leaven the impact of a centralist astigmatism. The nature of Canadian federalism also demands that in the process, the provincial governments at least be consulted, if not brought directly into the process of policymaking.

For their part, however, the provinces argue that *their* particular interests, important to the growth and health of the provincial economy and the province's citizens (and of course to the electoral fortunes of their political elites), can best be protected by the provincial government. Often the "provincial interest" must be defended against competing conceptions of the "national interest," and there is an occasional disagreement on basic elements of policy. Nor can provincial governments always be sure that the federal government is willing (or able) to represent their concerns and interests abroad satisfactorily.

Both levels of government may seek to dampen the political impact of conflicting interests by institutionalizing consultative and coordinating procedures, anticipating problems, and trying to accommodate each other's legitimate interests. But the potential for conflict always remains, rooted as it is in shared sovereignty and constitutional imprecision. In short, only a radical restructuring of the Canadian federal system would eliminate the constraints imposed on those who make international at the federal level by the existence of provincial governments with not so parochial interests.

---

68 Sheldon Alberts, "Klein Thanks Bush for Going to War Against 'Tyranny,' " *National Post*, March 22, 2003, A8; Antoine Robitaille, "Le ROC fissuré par la guerre," *Le Devoir*, March 22, 2003, B4.

69 John Herd Thompson, "Playing by the New Washington Rules: The U.S.–Canada Relationship, 1994–2003," *American Review of Canadian Studies* 33:1 (Spring 2003), 5–26, 21.

CHAPTER 12

Québec's *Paradiplomatie Identitaire*

In the previous chapter, we examined what propelled the provinces in Canada into the international sphere. But the view that Canada's provincial governments have essentially homogenous interests that they wish to advance in their international policy tends to overlook those unique interests the Québec government wishes to project internationally. In the international arena, as in so many other respects, Québec is unique. On the one hand, the Québec government does share with other provincial governments the desire to protect and project its interests. Like other provincial governments, it is jealous of its constitutional prerogatives. So too is it concerned about the raising of foreign capital for investment, the sale of its hydroelectricity, the export of its manufactured goods in offshore markets, and its economic relations with the United States. And it is propelled into relations with neighbouring jurisdictions by virtue of its geographical location. On the other hand, the Québec government is impelled into international activity by a factor not evident in other provinces: a desire to pursue a "paradiplomatie identitaire"—in other words, paradiplomacy directed at projecting and strengthening Québec's identity as a nation within Canada. In this chapter, we will examine the special nature of Québec's international policy.

QUÉBEC AS AN INTERNATIONAL ACTOR

Québec is one of the most active non-sovereign actors in international relations. In 2007–2008, the Québec government's ministère des Relations internationales (MRI) had a budget of nearly $116 million and some 562 civil servants, approximately 245 of whom were stationed abroad.[1] To this number one should add bureaucrats attached to other government departments who work on international affairs, including economic issues (such as the promotion of exports, strategies to attract foreign investment, and policies on trade liberalization), cross-border security (which has taken on increased importance since the attacks of September 11, 2001), not to mention immigration, environmental issues, education, and culture. Indeed, the MRI estimates that approximately $350 million of the Québec budget is devoted to international relations.

In 2009, Québec maintained 26 provincial representative offices—or "mini-embassies"—abroad, including a délégation-générale in Paris whose status is similar to that of an embassy.[2] This number includes six international representatives attached to Investissement Québec, the provincial agency responsible for encouraging foreign investment. Moreover, the government routinely conducts some 150–200 cultural, political, or commercial missions every year. And because Québec chooses to exercise the concurrent power over immigration granted to the provinces by the British North America Act, 1867, it maintains an active, even if limited, role in this area of policy. In 2003, Québec had 45 officials charged with recruiting immigrants to the province.

Since 1965, Québec has concluded over 550 international agreements, or ententes, with nearly 80 countries—either the governments of sovereign states or non-central governments of other federations. Most of these agreements were signed with France or Belgium; the most important ones focused on

---

1 Ministère des Relations internationales du Québec, *Rapport annuel de gestion, 2007–2008* (Québec: Gouvernement du Québec, 2008).

2 The Québec government includes délégations-générales, délégations, antennes (satellite offices), and foreign business agents who are under contract to Québec. The list of business agents is expansive, including, for example, the Italian Chamber of Commerce in Canada. MRI, *Rapport annuel de gestion, 2005–2006* (Québec: Gouvernement du Québec, 2006), 79.

issues of education, but there were also agreements on social security, energy, telecommunications, and the environment.

Québec is also involved in the negotiation of federal treaties when international agreements affect provincial competence. Since 2002 and the adoption by the Assemblée nationale of Loi 52, all important treaties concluded by the federal government that affect the legal competence of the province must be approved by the Québec legislature. Québec is the only province, and also the first legislature in the British parliamentary system, to be so closely involved in the conclusion of international agreements of the central government. (Indeed, the requirement that treaties must be approved by the legislature does not even exist at the federal level.)

As we noted in Chapter 7, the government of Québec is equally active as a "participating government" in the Organisation internationale de la Francophonie (OIF). Operating as "Canada Québec," the government in Québec City was intimately involved with the francophone summit since its origins and has hosted two summits itself. Québec has also participated in certain private international forums, such as the World Economic Forum in Davos, to which it has sent representatives since 1989. Under Parti Québécois governments, Québec has been represented in the World Social Forum, the annual meeting of the antiglobalization social movement. Québec representatives are also often included in Canadian delegations to other international organizations such as the World Trade Organization or the International Labour Organization. And in 2007 Québec appointed its first official representative to Canada's permanent delegation to the United Nations Economic, Social and Cultural Organization (UNESCO). In short, the government of Québec is more active in international affairs than other Canadian provinces, German *Länder,* or American states. The only non-central governments that rival Québec in international affairs are Flanders and Catalonia.[3]

The government of Québec is like that of the other provinces in that it seeks to defend its various interests, constitutional, economic, and environmental. But it is unique in that its international activities are also driven by a desire to maintain Québec's separate identity within the Canadian federation. It has been motivated by a factor not present in other provincial governments. While all provinces are motivated to various degrees in their international activities by the need to strengthen the role of the provincial government, only Québec is driven by the quest for identity and by what is called the "national project."[4] This quest is not limited to domestic politics, but also has an international dimension. In Québec, those who seek to project a separate identity for Québécois want to pursue a "paradiplomatie identitaire"; in other words, paradiplomacy that has as its key objective the reinforcement of the Québec nation within a Canadian context. This is a goal that is not only sought by souverainistes. As Jean Charest, the Liberal premier of Québec, said in July 2006, "sur la défense de notre identité, nous, fédéralistes, sommes aussi agressifs que les souverainistes peuvent l'être."[5]

---

3 On the foreign relations of these governments, see Stéphane Paquin, *Paradiplomatie identitaire en Catalogne* (Québec: Les Presses de l'Université Laval, 2003); Stéphane Paquin, "Paradiplomatie identitaire et la diplomatie en Belgique: Le cas de la Flandre," *Canadian Journal of Political Science* 33:3 (July 2003), 643–556.

4 Anne-Marie Jacomy-Millette, "Les activités internationales des provinces canadiennes," in Paul Painchaud, ed., *De Mackenzie King à Pierre Trudeau: quarante ans de diplomatie canadienne* (Québec: Les Presses de l'Université Laval, 1989), 89.

5 "In the defence of our identity, we federalists are just as aggressive as souverainistes can be." *L'Express*, July 27, 2006, quoted in Louis Sabourin, "Les dispositions internationales éscartées de la Charte de Victoria de 1971: context et actualisation," unpublished paper, Montréal, May 2006.

It is important to recognize that *paradiplomacy* is very different from *protodiplomacy*. Paradiplomacy, as we noted in the previous chapter, refers to the international activities of a non-central government that are conducted *alongside* the diplomacy of the central government. By contrast, in the context of international relations, protodiplomacy, as the prefix suggests, is a primitive or rudimentary diplomacy, usually pursued by a government-in-exile or a non-central government that is seeking to use its international activities to gain recognition by other states and thereby transform protodiplomacy into diplomacy pure and simple by the achievement of independence and sovereign statehood. In the case of Québec, we have seen sporadic episodes of protodiplomacy—in the late 1970s and the mid-1990s, for example. However, overall the international activities of the provincial government have been aimed at securing not independence for Québec as a sovereign state, but a paradiplomacy that strengthens Québec identity.

THE ORIGINS OF QUÉBEC'S *PARADIPLOMATIE IDENTITAIRE*

As we saw in the preceding chapter, Québec's international relations did not begin with the Quiet Revolution. While the international activities of the province were, before 1960, quite modest,[6] to understand the emergence of Québec's paradiplomacy it is necessary to put it in a broader historical context. The Quiet Revolution was a period of intense political, economic, and social transformation that had an enduring impact on contemporary Québec. The key concepts of the period were economic liberation, "rattrapage" (literally, catching-up, as in Québec "catching up" to English-speaking Canadians in Québec as well as to other industrialized societies in Europe and the Americas), and "maîtres chez nous" (masters of our own fate). The Quiet Revolution marked the emergence of greater intervention by the Québec state, a desire by French Canadians for greater control over their economy, the coming of age of the baby boom generation, the decline of the Roman Catholic Church, the rise of feminism, the "national question," and dreams of Québec independence.

In the first years of the Quiet Revolution, four important initiatives structured Québec's emerging relations with the world: the opening of the Maison du Québec in Paris in October 1961; the signing of the first agreement on education with France in February 1965; the articulation of the Gérin-Lajoie doctrine in April of that year; and finally Québec's participation in international conferences on education of francophone countries. These initiatives provided Québec with the kind of international personality that was unheard of for a non-central government during this period. And it was largely because of the support of the French government, and notably the president, Charles de Gaulle, that this was possible.[7]

To justify this new international activity, the Québec government did not just put the emphasis on economic arguments, it also articulated a resolutely nationalist tone. For

---

6 Louise Beaudoin, "Origines et développement du rôle international du gouvernement du Québec sur la scène internationale," in Paul Painchaud, ed., *Le Canada et le Québec sur la scène internationale* (Sainte-Foy, QC: Presse de l'Université du Québec-CQRI), 441–470.

7 On the relationship with France, see: Dale C. Thomson, *Vive le Québec libre* (Toronto: Denau, 1988); Frédéric Bastien, *Relations particulières: La France face au Québec après de Gaulle* (Montréal: Boréal, 1999); Frédéric Bastien, *Le poids de la coopération: Le rapport France-Québec* (Montréal: Québec Amérique, 2006).

example, in his speech formally opening the Maison du Québec in Paris in 1962, the premier, Jean Lesage, stressed that Québec was not just a Canadian province. On the contrary, he spoke of "l'État du Québec" (not the "la province du Québec") as the lever against the threat of assimilation in a North American context. For Lesage, Québec House "will be the continuation abroad of the work that we have undertaken in Québec itself."[8]

It is important to recognize that despite Lesage's language, his purpose was not to try and secretly secure Québec independence. The Québec Liberal party in the 1960s was resolutely federalist. According to Claude Morin, who was a deputy minister in the Québec government before joining the Parti Québécois, the international activities of Québec were not the result of politicians and civil servants who were quietly plotting independence. The desire to be active in international politics was a response to domestic determinants. As Morin put it, Québec's international policy was related to "problems or needs that were deeply felt during that period."[9]

An important factor, Morin suggests, was a widespread desire among both politicians and bureaucrats to open Québec to the world. Indeed, the neonationalism that emerged in Québec in the 1960s sought to break with the traditional nationalism associated with the politics of the Union Nationale under Maurice Duplessis and the fifteen years after the Second World War known in Québec as "la Grande Noirceur" (the Great Darkness). During the Quiet Revolution, there was a swing of the pendulum in the other direction as Québécois embraced this opening.

There was a certain naturalness to the fact that as Québec opened to the world, the government in Québec City—and Québécois more widely—should turn to France. The opportunities for francophones in the federal civil service in Ottawa were limited, and many Québécois went to study at French universities. In 1960, the provincial state in Québec was under construction and the relationship with France was seen as an important tool of nation-building.[10] Moreover, the French state had the resources to assist Québec in developing its own provincial capacities.

QUÉBEC'S PARADIPLOMACY, 1965–2010

If the Quiet Revolution propelled Québécois and their provincial government into the international sphere, the paradiplomacy of the government in Québec City took very different forms as it evolved in the years after the opening of the Maison du Québec in Paris. Four phases can be identified.

Projecting Outwards, 1965–1976

It was an outgrowth of the interconnections between education, the development of the state, and the importance of France that Québec began to expand its international competence and the range of its international activities in areas and in ways consistent with the

---

8 Quoted in Luc Bernier, *De Paris à Washington: La politique internationale du Québec* (Sainte-Foy, QC: Presses de l'Université du Québec, 1996), 30.

9 Claude Morin, *L'art de l'impossible: La diplomatie québécoise depuis 1960* (Montréal: Boréal, 1987), 35.

10 Ivo Duchacek, Daniel Latouche, and Garth Stevenson, eds., *Perforated Sovereignties and International Relations: Trans-sovereign Contacts of Subnational Governments* (New York: Greenwood, 1988).

role of champion of the Québec nation. In particular, the government in Québec City began sending delegates to international conferences on education and joined multilateral francophone organizations, the most important of which was l'Agence de coopération culturelle et technique (ACCT), discussed in Chapter 7.

The governments of both Lesage and Daniel Johnson also began to claim for Québec a special status in foreign affairs. The growing interest of the Lesage government in asserting a separate personality for Québec internationally was most concretely manifested in the agreement on educational exchanges. There was little doubt of the Québec government's interest in drawing on the expertise of the French educational system. Reversing the traditional lack of emphasis on scientific and managerial training in Québec's postsecondary educational system and developing an indigenous francophone cadre of Québécois professionals and managers were seen as critical to the ideals of the Quiet Revolution. In 1964, therefore, negotiations between the French and Québec governments culminated in the signing in February 1965 of an "Entente," or agreement, on educational exchanges between Québec and France.

But what began as an external expression of functional provincial interests was quickly transformed into an issue of symbolic national interest. Paul Gérin-Lajoie, Québec's minister of education and vice-premier, heralded the Entente as evidence of the province's competence in international affairs. Lesage and Gérin-Lajoie began to assert Québec's right to conclude agreements with other sovereign governments on issues under provincial jurisdiction and to participate as an actor in international conferences on issues such as education and culture.[11]

The key speech was given by Gérin-Lajoie to members of the consular corps in Montréal on April 12, 1965. In this speech, the minister asserted the idea that members of federations such as Québec should have the right to exercise the rights of a sovereign state, but only in those areas where the province had jurisdiction. Moreover, Gérin-Lajoie rejected efforts by the federal government to exercise control over the international activities of the provinces.[12] Such assertions, which came to be known as the "doctrine Gérin-Lajoie du prolongement externe des compétences internes du Québec"—the external continuation of domestic powers—challenged the position of the federal government, which had agreed to the Entente in the expectation that it would be a functional agreement with no political ramifications.

The Lesage government was not alone in pressuring for an expanded international role for Québec. In 1966, the Union Nationale under Daniel Johnson ran for office under the slogan "Québec d'abord," and once in power also claimed that the province should be given the international capacity to exercise the powers of a sovereign state in the two key areas under provincial jurisdiction: education and culture.

The response of the federal government to these initiatives demonstrated a progressive hardening of its position. While Ottawa had cooperated in the opening of the Maison du Québec in Paris in 1962, it did respond with increasing concern to the articulation of the Gérin-Lajoie doctrine. While Ottawa was willing to "discuss" agreements on matters within

---

11 Charlotte S.M. Girard, *Canada in World Affairs*, vol. 13: *1963–1965* (Toronto: Canadian Institute of International Affairs, 1980), chap. 4.

12 See Stéphane Paquin, ed., with the collaboration of Louise Beaudoin, Robert Comeau, and Guy Lachapelle, *Les relations internationales du Québec depuis la doctrine Gérin-Lajoie (1965–2005): Le prolongement externe des compétences internes* (Sainte-Foy, QC: Presses Université Laval, 2006).

provincial jurisdiction with other states, the federal government continued to insist on its constitutional right to sign treaties. It enshrined these claims in two white papers that were published in 1968, setting out its expectation that the federal government alone is empowered to sign treaties, and that the federal government is the only order of government empowered to attend international conferences and speak in Canada's name.[13]

The Québec City–Ottawa–Paris Triangle

The quarrels between Québec and Ottawa in the late 1960s were complicated by the interest that the French government under President Charles de Gaulle took in Québec's more independent role in international affairs. French support for Québec was driven by de Gaulle's idiosyncratic search for an independent role for France in the Western alliance. In the years after his election as French president in 1958, De Gaulle had grown increasingly annoyed at the domination of the alliance by the United States and Britain, and had eventually withdrawn from the North Atlantic Treaty Organization (NATO) in 1966. Moreover, de Gaulle was infuriated not only by the refusal of the Canadian government to sell uranium to France in 1950s and 1960s, but also by Canada's routine denunciations of French nuclear testing in the Sahara. He saw Ottawa's nuclear policy simply as part of a wider Anglo-Saxon effort suppress France.[14] Thus the overt encouragement of Québec separation was very much part of de Gaulle's *politique de grandeur*, designed to break the Anglo-American domination of the North Atlantic alliance and give an France an independent francophone ally in North America.

For this reason, the government in Paris engaged in a sustained campaign of interference in Canadian politics in the late 1960s, including the dispatch of French intelligence agents—Trudeau called one of them, Philippe Rossillon, "un agent plus ou moins secret"[15]—who were charged with the encouragement of francophone nationalist sentiment in Québec, New Brunswick, and Manitoba.[16] The most famous incident was de Gaulle's visit to Canada in July 1967. In a speech given from the balcony of old City Hall that was attended by thousands of Montréalers, de Gaulle claimed that "Ce soir ici, et tout le long de ma route [from Québec City to Montréal], je me suis trouvé dans une atmosphère du même genre que celle de la Libération [of France from the Nazis]."[17] It was at the end of this speech that he intoned, to the increasing cheers of the crowd, "Vive Montréal, vive le Québec, vive le Québec libre, vive le Canada français, vive la France." The federal government was furious; Lester B. Pearson, the prime minister, was particularly angered at de Gaulle's implicit comparison between anglophone Canada and the Nazis. While there was considerable concern in Ottawa that an overreaction by the federal government might

---

13 Canada, Secretary of State for External Affairs, *Federalism and International Relations* (Ottawa, 1968); Canada, Secretary of State for External Affairs, *Federalism and International Conferences on Education* (Ottawa, 1968); J.L. Granatstein and Robert Bothwell, *Pirouette: Pierre Trudeau and Canadian Foreign Policy* (Toronto: University of Toronto Press, 1990).

14 J.F. Bosher, *The Gaullist Attack on Canada, 1967–1997* (Montréal and Kingston: McGill-Queen's University Press, 2000), 203.

15 "L'Affaire Rossillon," *Le Nouvel Observateur*, September 23, 1968, 21.

16 Thomson, *Vive le Québec Libre*; Bastien, *Relations particulières*; Bosher, *The Gaullist Attack on Canada*.

17 "Tonight, and all along my route, I found myself in the same kind of atmosphere as the one during Liberation."

provoke nationalist sentiment in Québec, the Canadian government effectively declared de Gaulle persona non grata. He cut short his trip and returned to France.[18]

Much more serious were efforts by the French foreign ministry to secure for the Québec government an international presence at international conferences and as a member of a francophone organization separate from the federal government in Ottawa. In the late 1960s, a series of international conferences were held in West Africa, beginning with an international conference of education ministers in February 1968 in Libreville, Gabon. Apparently on the advice of officials the French foreign ministry, Gabon issued an invitation directly to the Québec government, without either inviting or informing the federal government in Ottawa. Indeed, when federal officials tried to secure an invitation to the conference in Libreville and the subsequent session in Paris, they were rebuffed.

Ottawa treated this incident with the utmost severity. Ivan Head, who was later to become Trudeau's principal adviser on foreign affairs, noted at the time that the Gabonese invitation to Québec was "one of the most serious threats to the integrity of Canada that this country has ever faced. . . . It contains the seeds of the destruction of Canada as a member of the international community."[19] Allan Gotlieb, who was at the time Trudeau's adviser on federal–provincial relations, revealed many years later the degree to which the issue was seen in existential terms. What France was doing in the 1960s, he wrote in 2004, posed "a growing threat to Canada's survival as a state," noting that this was "one of the most remarkable periods in Canadian diplomatic history. What other country experienced a prolonged attempt by a friendly ally to dismember it?"[20] For his part, the prime minister, Pierre Elliott Trudeau, was deeply angered at what he characterized in his foreign policy memoirs as "the mischief-makers in the Gaullist government."[21] He ordered that diplomatic relations with Gabon be severed immediately and issued some not-so-subtle reminders to other francophone African states that Québec was unlikely to be able to match federal development assistance programs.

The coercion worked. Further conferences of francophone countries were held in Kinshasa, Congo, in January 1969 and Niamey, Niger, in February. At both conferences, there was just one delegation, the result of an emerging cooperation between Ottawa and the new Québec government of Jean-Jacques Bertrand, who had become premier on Daniel Johnson's death in September 1968. However, once again France tried to interfere: although the president of Niger, Hamani Diori, wanted to invite Ottawa alone, Paris threatened to boycott the meeting if a separate invitation were not issued to Québec. Diori bowed to the pressure and issued separate invitations to Québec and Ottawa.[22] In February 1970,

---

18 For detailed accounts, see Girard, *Canada in World Affairs*, 153–67; Granatstein and Bothwell, *Pirouette*, 112–14; de Gaulle's speech in Montréal reproduced in A.E. Blanchette, ed., *Canadian Foreign Policy, 1966–1976: Selected Speeches and Documents* (Ottawa: Carleton University Press, 1980), 304.

19 *Montreal Star*, March 18, 1968.

20 Allan Gotlieb, "Romanticism and Realism in Canada's Foreign Policy," *Benefactors Lecture, 2004*, Toronto, November 3, 2004, 14.

21 Ivan L. Head and Pierre Elliott Trudeau, *The Canadian Way: Shaping Canada's Foreign Policy, 1968–1984* (Toronto: McClelland & Stewart, 1995), 286.

22 John P. Schlegel, "Containing Quebec Abroad: The Gabon Incident, 1968," in Don Munton and John Kirton, eds., *Canadian Foreign Policy: Selected Cases* (Scarborough, ON: Prentice-Hall Canada, 1992), 156–73; Granatstein and Bothwell, *Pirouette*, 141–44.

at the inaugural meeting of l'Agence de coopération culturelle et technique at Niamey, the francophone states voted for Canadian membership alone, with provincial representation subsumed within the Canadian delegation.

Relations with the United States

According to Louis Balthazar and Alfred O. Hero, one cannot really speak of relations between Québec and the United States for the simple reason that the government in Washington never treats Québec as an autonomous political actor. In the American government's view, no one speaks for Canada except the federal government in Ottawa.[23] As John Ciaccia, Québec's international relations minister in the Bourassa government from 1989 to 1994, liked to put it, if Québec wants to go to Washington, it has to go there with the Canadian government.[24]

While it is true that Québec opened a delegation in New York during the Second World War, it was not until the Quiet Revolution that the government of Jean Lesage began to think systematically about developing a policy toward the United States. In 1962, Lesage raised the status of the provincial representative in New York to a délégation-générale. The premier made five official visits to the United States and sought to establish links with Cajuns in Louisiana, strengthening links with the government in Lafayette. This new interest in the United States was not surprising given Québec's interest in completing the nationalization of electricity with the assistance of American investment capital. But it was also motivated by a desire to make Québec better known in the United States.

In April 1965, André Patry, a professor of international relations who had been appointed by Lesage as his senior adviser on international affairs in 1963 and had written the original draft of Gérin-Lajoie's 1965 speech,[25] was sent to Washington to meet two officials in the State Department to ask if the délégation-générale in New York might be given the same tax status as consulates of sovereign states. Although the U.S. consulate general in Montréal had suggested this route, the Québec government did not bother to inform the federal government in Ottawa of Patry's initiative. As it turned out, it did not matter: The State Department rejected the request on the grounds that it only dealt with sovereign states. And unlike France, which had a deep interest in fostering relations with Québec and thus had given the provincial government special status in Paris, the United States had little interest in Québec.

Lesage's numerous trips to the United States as premier set the pattern for increased connections with that country. Daniel Johnson, who became premier when the Union Nationale won the 1966 election, made two trips before his premature death in 1968, once to talk to the Council on Foreign Relations, the other time to address the Economic Club of New York. His successor, Jean-Jacques Bertrand, oversaw the rapid expansion of Québec's presence in the United States. Between October and December 1969, five new Québec offices were opened in Dallas, Chicago, Boston, Lafayette, and Los Angeles.

---

23 Louis Balthazar and Alfred O. Hero, *Le Québec dans l'espace américain* (Montréal: Québec-Amérique, 1999), 65.

24 For a perspective see John Ciaccia, "Le rôle essentiel du Québec sur la scène internationale," in Paquin, ed., *Les relations internationales du Québec*, 267–74.

25 On Patry, see Robin Stewart Gendron, *Towards a Francophone Community: Canada's Relations with France and French Africa, 1945–1968* (Montréal and Kingston: McGill-Queen's University Press, 2006); Robert Aird, *André Patry et la présence du Québec dans le monde* (Montréal: VLB éditeur, 2005).

The Liberal Interlude

When the Liberals under Robert Bourassa won the April 1970 elections, the cooperation between Ottawa and Québec City that had begun to emerge under Bertrand was intensified. The government in Québec City increased its international activities. Québec's presence abroad continued to expand dramatically, with new offices opened across the Europe and the United States. Bourassa travelled frequently to Europe and the Middle East, meeting government leaders. Québec representatives attended UN conferences on the prevention of crime, the law of the sea, and meetings of the Food and Agriculture Organization, the World Health Organization, and the Organisation for Economic Cooperation and Development. During this period, the Bourassa government continued to negotiate with the federal government on the possibility of Québec sending a delegation to the general meetings of the International Labour Organization. A new phase in Québec–United States relations also opened: Bourassa's plan to develop large-scale hydroelectricity generation in Québec's north required the raising of considerable capital, much of which came from New York. Bourassa visited the United States seven times as premier, mostly to raise capital.

The PQ and Protodiplomacy, 1976–1983

This period of relative calm came to an end on November 15, 1976, when the Parti Québécois under René Lévesque, which had won six seats in the 1973 elections, won a huge majority. Prior to the election, Québec's relationship with the United States was not prominent on the agenda; most PQ members of the Assemblée nationale had little affinity for the United States (with the notable exception of the premier, René Lévesque, who had served as a liaison officer and war correspondent with the United States Army in Europe during the Second World War). However, the relationship with the United States quickly assumed considerable importance as there was a certain nervousness in the States about the prospect of Québec independence. Moreover, not only did the government in Québec City have to worry about reassuring investors, it was equally important to reassure the administration in Washington about the PQ's positions on international relations. So in January 1977 Lévesque and Jacques Parizeau, his minister of finance, went to New York to reassure the Americans.

The trip was a political disaster for the PQ government. The evening before Lévesque's speech to the Economic Club of New York, Lévesque and Parizeau met with a number of members of the business community, including executives from Prudential Insurance and Metropolitan Life, which were primary underwriters of Hydro-Québec and Québec treasury bonds. Rather than reassure them about the security of their colossal investments in Québec, Lévesque focused on independence; according to Jean-François Lisée, many of the executives left the meeting convinced that an independent Québec would default on its debts.[26] Lévesque's speech the next day sowed even more doubt. Part of his speech to the assembled bankers, financiers, and business executives focused on foreign investment in Québec. Not only did Lévesque openly speak of nationalizing an asbestos company, he offered few clear assurances to his audience that an independent Québec would not engage in a wider policy of nationalization. He then tried, in Lisée's words, "to set the listeners' patriotic hearts beating to Québec's rhythm," quoting a passage from the American Declaration of Independence and assuring his audience that Québécois were only doing what Americans had done two centuries before. However, the speech fell flat: Whatever increased cardiac rhythms such an

---

26 Lisée, *Eye of the Eagle,* 218.

analogy might have caused in his audience came not from patriotism, but from concern over their investments in Québec. The reaction was not long in coming. Shareholders of Johns Manville, an American asbestos company with operations in the province, dumped 500,000 shares in one day, reducing the total share value 14 percent. Hydro-Québec bonds weakened significantly and did not rebound until September.[27]

In his New York speech, Lévesque had claimed that Québec sovereignty was "inevitable." The federal government decided to respond with a visit the United States in February 1977. Trudeau's foreign policy adviser, Ivan Head, called on his contacts in the Senate; Charles Mathias, a Republican senator from Maryland from 1969 to 1987; and Adlai Stevenson III, a Democrat who represented Illinois from 1970 to 1981, to secure an invitation to Trudeau to address a joint session of the United States Congress, at that time a rare privilege granted to few foreign leaders.[28] It was also an historic occasion, since it was the first time that a Canadian prime minister had addressed Congress.[29] The message Trudeau delivered was designed to reassure Americans: "I say to you with all the certainty that I can command that Canada's unity will not be fractured." But while the speech was greeted positively in the United States and in English Canada, some of the prime minister's rhetoric was overblown: "Most Canadians understand that the rupture of their country would be an aberrant departure from the norms they themselves have set, a crime against the history of mankind."[30] Likewise, the day afterward, he declared at the National Press Club that the secession of Québec would have more serious implications for the United States than the Cuban missile crisis.[31]

Trudeau's fulsome flourishes in Washington were being driven by a deep angst in Ottawa. Many federal officials worried that even the slightest sign of sympathy for the souverainiste cause by the administration in Washington would assure the disintegration of the country. As Allan Gotlieb, at the time the undersecretary of state for external affairs, put it, "It would have been so easy. . . . No need for the president to say anything publicly. It would have been enough for some diplomat to drop a few words of encouragement. . . . The capacity of the Americans to cause trouble was immense, immense."[32]

---

27 For an account of the New York speech and its aftermath, see Lisée, *Eye of the Eagle,* 122–28, 139, 145.

28 John English, "Two Heads Are Better Than One: Ivan Head, Pierre Trudeau, and Canadian Foreign Policy," in Greg Donaghy and Kim Richard Nossal, eds., *Architects and Innovators: Building the Department of Foreign Affairs and International Trade, 1909–2009* (Montréal and Kingston: McGill-Queen's University Press, 2009).

29 The first Canadian to address a joint meeting of Congress was the Governor General, Vincent Massey, on May 4, 1954.

30 United States, *Congressional Record*, 95th Congress, 1st sess., vol. 123, pt. 4, February 22, 1977, 4904. The official French version released by Prime Minister's Office in Ottawa translated "crime against the history of mankind" as "un crime contre l'humanité," which has a completely different meaning. The French-language press used the French version instead of looking at the English original, leaving the impression that Trudeau was calling Québec sovereignty a crime against humanity. See, for example, see "L'Unité du Canada ne sera pas rompue, affirme M. Trudeau à Washington/Un Crime contre l'humanité?" *Le Monde*, February 24, 1977, 1. René Lévesque was convinced that that is what had been said: In a press conference, he claimed that Trudeau was "raving" when he said that separation was a crime against humanity: "PM 'Desperate,' Levesque Says," *Globe and Mail*, February 24, 1977, 1.

31 "Separation Bad for U.S., PM Warns," *Globe and Mail*, February 24, 1977, 1.

32 Lisée, *Eye of the Eagle,* 199.

However, the fears in Ottawa proved overdrawn, as it became clear that the president, Jimmy Carter, was ready to assist the federal government on the issue of Canadian national unity. In an interview on the CTV television network in February 1977 given just before Trudeau's address to Congress, Carter claimed that "stability" in Canada was of "crucial importance" to the United States. He also said that if he were making the decision, confederation would be his preference. However, the decision would be for Canadians to make.[33]

This formulation—the United States prefers a united Canada, but this is a decision that should be made by Canadians themselves—became such a standard response that it was quickly dubbed "the mantra." Certainly all American administrations after Carter resorted to it. According to Balthazar, the American mantra had three elements: First, the United States would not intervene in Canada's internal affairs, and therefore it would not take any position in the Canadian constitutional debate. Second, the United States was in favour of anything that would reinforce Canadian unity, and expressed a preference for a united Canada rather than Québec secession. Finally, it was up to Canadians to decide the future of their country; the United States would therefore respect the popular will of Canada's citizens.[34]

It was in this context that Lévesque and Claude Morin, the minister of intergovernmental affairs, decided to launch what they called "Operation America." Both pragmatic politicians, Lévesque and Morin recognized that Québécois would not vote for sovereignty if the United States overtly opposed it. The objective of Operation America was not to secure the support of Americans, but to reassure them of the viability of an independent Québec, to demonstrate to them that an independent Québec would be deeply attached to the rule of law, and, above all, would honour obligations, particularly financial obligations.[35]

Operation America involved an organized blitz of presentations to the media, politicians, investors, and university audiences. PQ ministers travelled frequently to the United States to give speeches. The premier himself visited New York, Chicago, and the New England states. A Québec office was opened in Atlanta. Québec wanted to open a mission in Washington, but when the federal government in Ottawa refused, Québec had to content itself with opening a tourist office outside the Beltway (but which, according to Lévesque, was still able to provide Americans with political information). Overall the message to Americans was simple: Québécois were potential allies and were open for business.[36]

Part of the process of trying to maximize the attractiveness and the acceptability of the souverainiste option involved rewriting the Parti Québécois platform in order to expunge elements that might be regarded as contentious, particularly in the United States. This was particularly important in the case of international policy, since the PQ's formal platform attracted considerable attention in a Cold War context. When the party came to power in 1976, its platform called for an independent Québec to be a pacifist state that did not

---

33 Lisée, *Eye of the Eagle,* 152.

34 Louis Balthazar, "Les relations avec les États-Unis sous Lévesque, 1976–1985," in Paquin, ed., *Les relations internationales du Québec,* 158. On the "mantra," see David T. Jones, "An Independent Québec: Looking into the Abyss," *Washington Quarterly* 20:3 (Spring 1997), 21–36.

35 Bernier, *De Paris à Washington,* 98.

36 On Operation America, see Lisée, *Eye of the Eagle*, 312–32; Louis Balthazar, "Les relations Québec-États-Unis," in Balthazar, Louis Bélanger and Gordon Mace, eds., *Trente ans de politique extérieure du Québec (1960–1990)* (Québec: Septentrion-CQRI, 1993), 90–91; Bernier, *De Paris à Washington*, 107.

maintain any armed forces; it proposed that Québec would not be a member of NATO and would not participate in the North American Air Defence command (NORAD). It envisaged a turn toward the Third World. In short, the PQ's platform gave the impression that an independent Québec wanted to become a nonaligned country in global politics.

As long as the PQ was a minor party, such policies raised few concerns in Washington; after 1976, however, there was particular concern in some quarters in the United States government about the possibility that an independent Québec would jeopardize continental air defence. If it withdrew from NATO and NORAD, a large gap would appear in both air defence over Ungava and maritime defence in the Gulf of St. Lawrence. As one defence analyst put it—none too subtly—in 1977, "an independent Québec implies a fundamental change in one of the post–World War II military constants of the West, a strong and unified North America. The strategic reality demands that any attempt to make that change be thwarted—if not by Canada, then by the United States."[37]

So, between 1977 and 1979, the PQ modified its program. In preparation for the 1980 referendum, the Lévesque government released a white paper on sovereignty-association, which included a full foreign policy program for an independent Québec.[38] Gone were the simplicities of earlier PQ foreign policy platforms. Instead, the imprint of the professional bureaucrats in the Ministère des Affaires intergouvernementales was clearly evident. Québec pledged to continue commitments to NATO and NORAD, and even ironically contemplated membership in the Commonwealth. This conservative blueprint for the international policy of an independent Québec seemed to reflect a recognition that the same constraints and imperatives that mould Canada's international policy would also act on Québec, but all indications are that very little thought was given to strategic issues by the PQ leadership.[39] Rather, the change was driven by purely pragmatic considerations: to reassure foreigners, particularly Americans, and to dispel the image that a sovereign Québec would be a "Cuba of the North."[40]

With the election of the PQ in November 1976, there was a revival of interest in Québec affairs in Paris, but this time the French government was more restrained, limiting its support for Québec to providing some of that symbolic legitimacy necessary for the conduct of foreign relations, such as receiving the premier with the pomp usually reserved for heads of state.[41] Thus, for example, when Lévesque paid his first visit to France as premier in November 1977, Paris ignored a number of niceties of diplomatic propriety and gave him the kind of welcome normally reserved for leaders of sovereign

---

37 Nicholas Stethem, "Canada's Crisis (2): The Dangers," *Foreign Policy* 29 (Winter 1977–78), 59.

38 Québec, Conseil exécutif, *La nouvelle entente Québec-Canada: Proposition du gouvernement du Québec pour une entente d'égal à egal: la souveraineté-association* (Québec: Editeur officiel, 1979), 62, 104–105. On the evolution of PQ policy, see Stéphane Roussel and Chantal Robichaud, "L'élargissement virtuel: un Québec souverain face à l'OTAN (1968–1995)," *Les cahiers d'histoire* 20:2 (Winter 2001), 147–93.

39 Stéphane Roussel and Charles-Alexandre Théorêt, "A 'Distinct Strategy'? The Use of Canadian Strategic Culture by the Sovereignist Movement in Quebec, 1968–1996," *International Journal* 59:3 (Summer 2004), 557–577.

40 Anne Legaré, *Le Québec otage de ses alliés: les relations du Québec avec la France et les États-Unis* (Montréal: VLB éditeur, 2003), 22–23.

41 At times the hunt for indiscretions by the French government took on the elements of *opéra bouffe*: In February 1979, the *Globe and Mail* felt compelled to report that the Paris telephone directory listed

states. At a state luncheon given by President Valéry Giscard d'Estaing, Lévesque was made a grand officer of the Legion of Honour.

The results of the referendum of May 20, 1980—59.6 percent opposed and 40.4 percent in favour—put an end to the PQ's protodiplomacy. With the prospect of an independent francophone state on the North American continent somewhat dimmer, the French government appeared to lose interest in promoting the Québec cause. By 1983, Prime Minister Pierre Mauroy was publicly rebuffing Lévesque's attempts to bolster flagging French support for Québec's demand that the province be allowed to attend a summit of La Francophonie as a full participating government. At a dinner honouring Lévesque in June 1983, Mauroy stated that "France forbids itself from interfering in the affairs of others. This guiding principle [applies] to Québec as [to] anyone else."[42]

Conservatives and Liberals, 1984–1993

Instead, the paradiplomacy of the earlier period returned. Cooperation between the federal and provincial governments increased, first when the Progressive Conservatives under Brian Mulroney came to power in Ottawa in the September 1984 elections, and then when Robert Bourassa and the provincial Liberals, with their more pragmatic approach to relations with the federal government, returned to power in the December 1985 provincial elections.

As in the early 1970s, the transformation in the relationship was considerable. Mulroney, seeking to entrench support for the Progressive Conservatives in Québec, embraced a different attitude toward the international activities of Québec. Thus, for example, when Laurent Fabius, the French prime minister, visited Ottawa and Québec in November 1984, Mulroney declared that he saw nothing wrong with Québec and France enjoying direct and privileged relations with each other. Likewise, as discussed in Chapter 7, Mulroney took the initiative to put in place a francophone summit that included Québec's participation. The Mulroney government and the PQ government of René Lévesque negotiated an agreement, which was eventually signed in October 1985, just days after Pierre-Marc Johnson took over from Lévesque as premier.[43]

During this period, Québec's paradiplomacy intensified, with high-level visits to and from the province. Québec continued to maintain its presence abroad, with Ottawa and Québec cooperating by co-locating some of Québec's overseas missions in Canadian embassies.

Protodiplomacy Redux, 1994–1995

The Parti Québécois was returned to power in 1994, promising to hold a referendum on sovereignty as soon as possible. As in 1976, there was a souring of relations with the federal Liberal government under Jean Chrétien that had come to power in November 1993. The new premier, Jacques Parizeau, was warmly received by the government in Paris but

---

Québec's délégation-générale under "embassies." For its part, the French foreign ministry felt obliged to issue the helpful statement that the Québec mission could not possibly be an embassy since it was a délégation-générale. *Globe and Mail*, February 27, 1979.

42 "Don't Expect Help, French Tell Quebec," *Globe and Mail*, June 28, 1983, 1.

43 Luc Bernier, "Mulroney's International 'Beau Risque': The Golden Age of Québec's Foreign Policy," in Nelson Michaud and Kim Richard Nossal, eds., *Diplomatic Departures: The Conservative Era in Canadian Foreign Policy, 1984–1993* (Vancouver: UBC Press, 2001), 128–41.

coldly received by the American government. The souverainistes could, however, count on a new ally on the federal Canadian scene, the Bloc Québécois. Created in 1990 following the rejection of the Meech Lake Accord that had sought to bring Québec into the 1982 Constitution, the Bloc had become the official opposition in the wake of the October 1993 elections that had virtually wiped the Progressive Conservatives from the electoral map. The leader of the BQ was Lucien Bouchard, who had been appointed Canadian ambassador in Paris by Brian Mulroney in 1985 and then, in 1988, a minister in the Mulroney government before his resignation after the collapse of the Meech Lake accord.

The souverainiste strategy aimed at creating as much of a fait accompli as possible in the event of even a slim Yes victory. Thus, as in the 1980 referendum campaign, the PQ sought to project a reassuring image of the international policy of an independent Québec: to Québec voters, to the rest of Canada, and to the international community. The Partnership proposal, signed by Parizeau, Bouchard, and Mario Dumont of the Action Démocratique in June 1995, outlined a variety of areas in international affairs in which Canada and an independent Québec would undertake joint activities, including joint peacekeeping operations and even the possibility of "speaking with one voice" in certain international organizations.[44] Likewise, the text of the legislation that was submitted to the voters, Bill 1, An Act Respecting the Future of Québec (sometimes called the Sovereignty Bill), sent to Québec households in September 1995, explicitly committed an independent Québec to maintaining Canadian traditions of peacekeeping and multilateral involvement. Article 17 of the legislation stated:

> The Government shall take the necessary steps to ensure the continuing participation of Québec in the defence alliances of which Canada is a member. Such participation must, however, be compatible with Québec's desire to give priority to the maintenance of world peace under the leadership of the United Nations Organization.[45]

The souverainiste strategy of creating momentum in the wake of a Yes vote depended heavily on France. In July 1994, when Parizeau was provincial opposition leader, he had met with Alain Juppé, the French foreign minister. During this meeting, Parizeau had asked Juppé if France would be there for Québec in the event of a referendum victory. Juppé responded that if a majority of Québécois voted yes, "la France ne laisserait pas tomber le Québec et se manifesterait rapidement dans la reconnaissance d'un Québec souverain."[46] On a number of occasions, this position was reiterated by French politicians. For example, in January 1995, Jacques Chirac, the mayor of Paris who was running for the French presidency, claimed during Parizeau's official visit to Paris that France would never interfere in Canada's internal affairs. But in the event that the Québécois decided to become sovereign, he assured it that France "devrait être sans aucun doute au premier rang de ceux qui diraient au Québec que nous marchons avec lui."[47] And once he had been elected president in the elections of April and May, Chirac reminded Québec voters of the promise made by Juppé,

---

44 The official text of the Partnership agreement referred to in the October 30, 1995 referendum question is available at http://www.cric.ca/fr_html/guide/referendum/referendum1995_ententetripartite.html.

45 Text of Bill 1 is archived at http://www.sfu.ca/~aheard/bill1.html#text.

46 "France would not let Québec down and would move quickly to recognize a sovereign Québec."

47 "France would without any doubt be at the head of the line among those who will say to Quebec, 'We walk alongside you.'" *Le Devoir*, January 27, 1995, A1; also "French Leaders Give Lift to Parizeau: Presidential Candidates Favour Recognizing Independent Québec," *Globe and Mail*, January 27, 1995, A1.

who had by this time become the prime minister. On October 23, 1995, Chirac appeared on CNN's *Larry King Live* and indicated clearly that in the event of a referendum victory, France would recognize the result.

We have subsequently learned the full game plan for the referendum agreed to by the PQ and the French government. Once the results were known on the night of the referendum, the plan called for the délégation-générale du Québec in Paris to call Philippe Séguin, the president of the French Assemblée nationale and Chirac's special adviser on the Québec dossier. The next morning Parizeau would call Chirac, and the Elysée palace would immediately publish the following agreed-on communiqué:

> La France prend acte de la volonté démocratiquement exprimée par le peuple du Québec, le 30 octobre 1995, de devenir souverain après avoir formellement offert au Canada un nouveau partenariat économique et politique. Lorsque l'Assemblée nationale du Québec en viendra à proclamer la souveraineté du Québec selon la démarche prévue par la question référendaire et maintenant entérinée majoritairement par le peuple québécois, la France en tirera amicalement les conséquences. Soucieuse que ce processus se déroule dans les meilleures conditions, la France tient à réaffirmer son amitié pour au Canada et à son gouvernement. Ils peuvent être assurés de notre volonté de maintenir et d'approfondir les excellentes relations qui nous lient.[48]

It was believed that, once the government in Paris had made this announcement recognizing Québec's sovereignty, other members of La Francophonie would also recognize Québec, creating a bandwagon effect that would encourage other states to follow suit. The French government was also expected to undertake a campaign to gather support among the members of the European Union to recognize the results of the referendum.

As in 1980, the PQ government did not believe it would be possible to obtain the support of the United States for the souverainiste cause. Nonetheless, Parizeau wanted to reassure Washington about the policies of an independent Québec in hopes the Americans would remain neutral during the referendum campaign. It is true that throughout the campaign, the American ambassador to Canada, James Blanchard, was always careful to use a variation of the American "mantra" on the Québec question: "The United States enjoys excellent relations with a strong and united Canada." But it is "for Canadians to decide their own political future."[49] However, in fact he and the administration of Bill Clinton were deeply hostile to the souverainiste project and tried hard to use their influence to scuttle it.

When Clinton visited Ottawa in February 1995, he openly paid tribute to a united Canada. In a speech to the House of Commons, he noted that "In a world darkened by ethnic conflicts that literally tear nations apart, Canada has stood for all of us as a model of

---

48 "France takes note of the democratically expressed wish of the people of Québec on 30 October 1995 to become sovereign after formally offering Canada a new economic and political partnership. When the Assemblée nationale du Québec proclaims Québec's sovereignty according to the approach indicated in the referendum question and now approved by the majority of the Québécois people, France will in a friendly way accept the consequences. Concerned that this process occurs under the best conditions, France wishes to reaffirm its friendship for Canada and its government. They can be assured of our desire to maintain and deepen the excellent relations that bind us." Pierre Duchesne, "Diplomatie préférendaire," in Stéphane Paquin, ed., with the collaboration of Louise Beaudoin, *Histoire des relations internationales du Québec* (Montréal: VLB éditeurs, 2006), 202–203.

49 For example, *Globe and Mail*, September 29, 1995; see also James Blanchard, *Behind the Embassy Door: Canada, Clinton, and Quebec* (Toronto: McClelland & Stewart, 1998), 238, 248.

how people of different cultures can live and work together in peace, prosperity and understanding."[50] But much more important was the issue of whether an independent Québec would automatically become a member of the North American Free Trade agreement (NAFTA) as a "successor" state. Not surprisingly, souverainistes believe that were Québec to become independent, accession to NAFTA would be automatic. There is, however, another possibility: that an independent Québec would have to be admitted *de novo*, which would require the unanimous consent of all the parties to NAFTA, notably the approval of what remained of Canada. In that case, it was entirely possible that a rump Canada, aggrieved at the breakup of the country, would refuse to accept an independent Québec as a member. Moreover, it was entirely possible that the United States would also oppose admitting an independent Québec to NAFTA in solidarity with Canada. If that happened, an independent Québec would be left outside the free-trade regime—with the huge costs that that would impose on the newly independent economy.[51]

Thus the position taken on the NAFTA question by the United States was critical, since it was in a position to undermine the efforts of the souverainiste movement to paint accession to NAFTA by an independent Québec as unproblematic. For this reason, American officials decided, in preparation for President Bill Clinton's visit to Ottawa in February 1995, to amend the mantra. When Americans were asked what the position of the United States was on NAFTA accession, the response was "There are numerous and complicated legal issues. The United States has not given anybody any assurances on accession."[52]

In the event, the Clinton administration chose not to stick precisely to the script. Two weeks before the referendum, Warren Christopher, Clinton's secretary of state, said that no one should assume that agreements such as NAFTA would remain unchanged if Québec became independent. This prompted Bernard Landry, by this time Québec's minister of international affairs, to write Christopher a letter on October 19, threatening negative consequences if the United States did not stay out of the referendum campaign. "If the Yes side wins, as is now probable," Landry wrote,

> Québec voters . . . will remember that the sovereignty of Québec was achieved despite or even against the American will. If victory eludes the Yes side by a slim margin, as is plausible, those who did vote Yes—a clear majority of francophone Quebeckers—will be tempted to assign responsibility to the United States for part of their profound disappointment. I don't know how many decades it will take to dispel that feeling.[53]

The appearance of Jacques Chirac on *Larry King* on October 23 prompted the Clinton administration to depart, albeit slightly, from the mantra. The White House let Canadian reporters in Washington know that Clinton might have something interesting to say about Canada if he were asked at a press conference scheduled for October 25. At the conference, a Canadian reporter was included in the carefully scripted roster of those recognized to ask

---

50 Clinton's address on February 23, 1995 is in Canada, Parliament, House of Commons, *Debates*, 35th Parl., 1st sess., February 24, 1995, appendix, 10036–43. Also Blanchard, *Behind the Embassy Door*, 209–11.

51 See Louis Bélanger, "United States and the Formative Years of an Independent Québec's Foreign Policy," *American Review of Canadian Studies* 27:1 (Spring 1997), 11–25.

52 "Ambassador Sticks to Script on U.S. Approach to Quebec," *Globe and Mail*, September 29, 1995, A4.

53 Quoted in "Clinton Cites Canada as World Model," *Globe and Mail*, October 26, 1995, A7.

questions. When the reporter dutifully asked a question about the economic consequences of a possible breakup of Canada, Clinton took the opportunity to note that "a strong and united Canada has been a wonderful partner for the United States, and an incredibly important and constructive citizen throughout the entire world." Canada, he said, "has been a great model for the rest of the world and I hope that can continue."[54]

The cooperation of the administration in Washington added considerably to the forces inside and outside Québec arrayed against the souverainiste option. These included initiatives organized both within Québec and in other provinces to rally support for the No side and the votes by First Nations prior to the referendum that rejected independence and raised the possibility that if Québec seceded from Canada, the Crees and the Inuit would secede from Québec. On the other hand, the Québec government's protodiplomacy in the referendum campaign successfully secured the support of a key backer, France, whose recognition gambit in the event of a Yes vote, even a very narrow one, would likely have created an important bandwagon effect in the days after the referendum.

Paradiplomacy after 1995

The narrow failure of the referendum on October 30, 1995—50.58 percent voting no, 49.42 percent voting yes—brought an end to the souverainiste efforts of the PQ government. Parizeau resigned soon after the referendum; his successor, Lucien Bouchard, announced that another referendum would not be held until there were "conditions gagnantes" (winning conditions). While both Bouchard and Bernard Landry, who succeeded Bouchard after he retired from politics in 2001, remained committed souverainistes, in international policy a return to "normalcy" saw the PQ government under both premiers pursue paradiplomacy rather than protodiplomacy. In the immediate aftermath of the referendum, Bouchard sought to consolidate the province's finances and reduce the deficit; one of the consequences of the budget cuts that he introduced was the mass closing of 13 Québec missions in April 1996. Before long, however, the province was opening new offices abroad once again. Both Bouchard and Landry maintained an active schedule of overseas trips. The regularized biennial summit with the French prime minister was continued. The government was able to take advantage of the opening provided by the Mulroney Conservatives to continue activist participation in international summitry, attending not only the increasingly institutionalized summit of La Francophonie, but also attending a range of other international meetings, such as the summit on sustainable development in Johannesburg in 2002 and the annual meetings of the World Social Forum in Porto Alegre in 2002 and 2003. Québec even adopted a version of the Chrétien "Team Canada" model. "Mission Québec" teams went to Mexico in May 1999, to California in October of that year, to Argentina in April 2000, to Wisconsin in September, to Europe in January and February 2001, and to Chile and Peru in May 2002.

The victory of the Liberals under Jean Charest in the 2003 provincial elections and the victory of the Conservative Party of Canada under Stephen Harper in 2006 opened a new era in collaboration between Ottawa and Québec, marked in particular by an agreement in May 2006 between the two governments on Québec's participation in the United Nations Educational, Scientific and Cultural Organization (UNESCO).

The UNESCO agreement came from an initiative of the Québec minister of international relations, Monique Gagnon-Tremblay, who in September 2005 published a policy

---

54 Blanchard, *Behind the Embassy Door*, 248.

paper, *Le Québec dans les forums internationaux*, which laid out Québec's position on the province's participation in Canadian delegations to international organizations such as UNESCO and the World Trade Organization.[55] Québec's policy was not only the logical extension of the Gérin-Lajoie doctrine of 1965, but in effect it went further, because it pressed for a presence for Québec in international organizations that were clearly political, such as the WTO. For Stephen Harper and the Conservative Party of Canada, *Le Québec dans les forums internationaux* provided an opportunity to try to present the Conservatives as a party sympathetic to Québec's interests. On December 19, 2005, in the middle of the election campaign, Stephen Harper promised that if the Conservatives were elected, the federal government would arrange for Québec to be given a formal role in UNESCO. Once in power, Harper was as good as his word: An agreement between the two governments was negotiated, and on May 5, Harper went to the Assemblée nationale in Québec City for a symbolic signing with Jean Charest. His speech reveals the degree to which the Harper government, not unlike the Mulroney government in the 1980s, reflected an understanding of the importance of Québec's *paradiplomatie identitaire*:

> Today we welcome Québec into the UNESCO family. . . . Québec can now participate fully in all of UNESCO's activities, together with and through Canada's Permanent Delegation. . . . We are at the dawn of a new era, an era that will see us build a strong, united, free and inde-pendent Canada in which a confident, autonomous, proud and unified Quebec can develop its full potential.[56]

In February 2007, Michel Audet was appointed Québec's first official representative to the Canadian permanent delegation at UNESCO, fulfilling the vision articulated by Paul Gérin-Lajoie four decades earlier.

PARADIPLOMACY, PROTODIPLOMACY, AND INTERNATIONAL POLICY

In the literature on paradiplomacy, there are two divergent hypotheses about the impact of the international activities of non-central governments on international policy. The first is that the emergence of paradiplomacy significantly improves the international policy of nation-states. Paradiplomacy ensures better coordination of international activities between central and non-central governments, and this encourages national unity, discourages conflicts, and thus improves the efficacy of policy.[57] Jacques Palard, for example, argued that paradiplomacy is "a positive sum game," since the loss of centralizing power was overall less important than the gains that came from participation in decision-making at the international level.[58]

---

55 This document is reproduced in Stéphane Paquin, ed., *Les relations internationales du Québec*, appendix III.

56 "Prime Minister Harper and Premier Charest Sign Historic Agreement Establishing a Formal Role for Québec in UNESCO," May 5, 2006, available http://pm.gc.ca/eng/media.asp?id=1151.

57 Eric Philippart, "Le Comité des Régions confronté à la 'paradiplomatie' des régions de l'Union européenne," in Jacques Bourrinet, ed., *Le Comité des Régions de l'Union européenne* (Paris: Éco-nomica, 1997), 23; also Panayotis Soldatos and Hans J. Michelmann, *Federalism and International Relations: The Role of Subnational Units* (Oxford: Oxford University Press, 1990), 45.

58 Jacques Palard, "Les régions européennes sur la scène internationale: condition d'accès et systèmes d'échanges," *Études internationales* 30:4 (December 2003), 668.

For others, the emergence of paradiplomacy has done little more than create tensions and struggles for power. Moreover, paradiplomacy conducted by non-central governments where there is a minority, as in Flanders, Québec, or Catalonia, becomes even more conflictual. Nationalist movements seek to establish international relationships that are not controlled by the central government.[59] However, the internal conflicts are often exported, accentuating tensions and creating serious consequences for the unity of the country. At the domestic level, a struggle for power develops between the central government, which tries to preserve its monopoly over external representation on the one hand, and substate nationalist movements, which try to liberate themselves, at least partially, from the control of the central authorities.[60]

We cannot use the case of Québec in Canada to decide definitively between these two hypotheses. Québec's paradiplomacy sometimes complements, sometimes supports, and sometimes poses a threat to international policy in Canada. On the contrary: as we have seen, the response of the federal government when faced with Québec's paradiplomacy has varied, alternating between accommodation and intransigence, depending on who was in power in Ottawa and Québec City. Lester B. Pearson was not opposed to Québec's early initiatives, but the federal government's attitude changed after the France–Québec agreement on education and the formulation of the Gérin-Lajoie doctrine of 1965. For his part, Pierre Elliott Trudeau believed that international policy should serve the national interests, defined in particular as national unity. The conflict between the two governments reached a critical point after the election of the Parti Québécois in 1976. But the arrival of the Progressive Conservatives under Brian Mulroney marked a calming period in the relationship, both under the PQ and under Bourassa's provincial Liberals. The return of the federal Liberals to power under Jean Chrétien in November 1993 and the election of the PQ in 1994 reawakened the conflict. However, when the provincial Liberals under Jean Charest were elected in 2003 and the Conservative Party of Canada under Stephen Harper came to power in February 2006, there was a new era in collaboration.

Québec–Ottawa relations were generally only marked by conflict when they touched on politically sensitive subjects or when the government in Québec City engaged in protodiplomacy. In these cases, there was a struggle between the federal government and what it considered its international prerogatives and the Québec government, which was looking to create an international identity free of federal control. Given the preponderant place of relations with France and La Francophonie in the Québec's paradiplomacy, relations between Québec and Ottawa over international affairs tended to mirror relations between the federal and provincial governments in the area of domestic politics. It was indeed the "continuation abroad of internal conflicts."[61]

But even if relations between Québec and Ottawa tended toward conflict on some aspects of international relations, there was always a range of areas in which relations remained cooperative, such as immigration, trade, and foreign investment. According to a source close to Lucien Bouchard, Québec's relations with the federal government on trade

---

59 Renaud Dehousse, *Fédéralisme et relations internationales* (Bruxelles: Bruylant, 1991).

60 Brian Hocking, "Les intérêts internationaux des gouvernements régionaux: désuétude de l'interne et de l'externe?," *Études internationales* 25:3 (September 1994), 405–20.

61 Stéphane Paquin, "Le prolongement externe des conflits internes? Les relations internationales du Québec et l'unité nationale," *Bulletin d'histoire politique* 10:1 (2001), 85–98.

missions were marked by what one commentator termed an "exemplary synergy."[62] For his part, Graham Fraser has noted that in most foreign capitals, relations between the Québec délégation and the Canadian embassy were marked by "friendship and cooperation."[63] And, one might add, even in Paris there were friendly relations.

It is true that paradiplomacy can potentially lead to conflict. However, it in the contemporary global order, the international activities of non-central governments are inevitable. Not only are they widely seen as indispensable, whether for attracting foreign investment, for assisting in economic development, or for protecting a non-central government's constitutional jurisdiction. As a consequence, it makes little sense, from a national perspective, for a federal state to treat paradiplomacy by non-central governments as a threat to the integrity of the country's international policy. Rather, given the inevitability of these activities, it makes more sense to find new ways of collaborating and a better division of roles in international affairs. And the best way to limit conflict and promote unity is to clarify the responsibilities of each order of government in international affairs in a way that provides non-central governments with a role important enough for them to profit from globalization.

CONCLUSION

In a 1981 speech, Jacques-Yvan Morin, René Lévesque's deputy premier, noted that "L'activité internationale est en quelque sorte l'oxygène de notre société. . . . [C]'est une réalité quotidienne à tous les niveaux de notre société. . . . Le Gouvernement du Québec n'a d'autre choix que de refléter ces intérêts."[64] In this chapter we have seen that Québécois are impelled into international activity for reasons that are distinct and unique. And, for its part, the government of Québec has sought to project abroad some sense of the province's cultural and linguistic attributes that distinguish Québécois from other Canadians. In short, Québec's external impulses are, very simply, nationalistic, and its international interests as a result tend to be overlaid by the national question.

The paradiplomacy that results is a permanent feature of international policy in Canada. While the *atmospherics* of the province's international affairs have been and will be affected by who is in power in Québec City and Ottawa, the *patterns* of Québec's and Canada's international policy are unlikely to change. All governments in Québec City, regardless of which party is in power, can be counted on to maintain a highly developed bureaucratic agency, one that will remain almost indistinguishable from any foreign ministry; to maintain a range of offices abroad, at least when times are good; and to engage in a range of international activities, including summit meetings, international trips, and hosting foreign visitors. And, most importantly, all Québec governments can be counted on to project Québec's identity internationally. In that sense, Jacques-Yvan Morin was correct: International activities have become so deeply entrenched in Québec that they are indeed like oxygen—and just as essential.

---

62 Vincent Marissal, "Équipe Canada en Chine: Une synergie exemplaire entre Québec et Ottawa," *La Presse*, February 12, 2001.

63 Graham Fraser, "Préface," in Bernier, *De Paris à Washington*, xii.

64 "International activity is in a way the oxygen of our society. . . . It is a daily reality for all levels of our society. . . . The Quebec government has no other choice but to reflect these interests." Jacques-Yvan Morin, "Allocutions d'ouverture," *Choix* 14 (1982), 11–12.

APPENDIX

Chronology

What follows is a selection of defining events that shaped Canada's territorial evolution, politics, and foreign relations, and information on the dramatis personae—including key political figures in Canada, the United States, China, and Soviet Union/Russia. This is an expanded and updated version of the chronology first published in *The Politics of Canadian Foreign Policy* (1997). All entries are indexed.

BEFORE CONFEDERATION

19 June 1812	President James Madison proclaims the declaration of war against Britain passed by Congress (June 18), beginning the War of 1812, the last U.S. attempt to seize Canada by force
24 December 1814	Treaty of Ghent, ending the war, signed
29 April 1817	Rush-Bagot Agreement on warship deployment in the Great Lakes signed
20 October 1818	Anglo-American Convention of 1818 signed in London, *inter alia* fixing the border along the 49th parallel from Lake of the Woods to the Rocky Mountains
9 August 1842	Webster-Ashburton Treaty, settling border disputes on Maine–New Brunswick border and in Lake of the Woods, signed in Washington
1 February 1846	Repeal of the Corn Laws in Britain
15 June 1846	Oregon Treaty establishing boundary between Rocky Mountains and Pacific Ocean signed in Washington
6 June 1854	Reciprocity Treaty, removing tariffs on a wide range of goods, signed between Britain on behalf of the British North American colonies and the United States
12 April 1861	American civil war begins following secession of southern states and creation of Confederate States of America (February 4)
17 March 1866	Reciprocity Treaty of 1854 abrogated by United States in retaliation for British support of the Confederacy
10–16 April 1866	Fenian Brotherhood raids on Campobello Island, New Brunswick
1–7 June 1866	Fenian raids on Niagara (1st) and Ridgeway (2nd) in Canada West (now Ontario), Pigeon Hill (7th) in Canada East (now Québec)

THE IMPERIAL ERA

1 July 1867	Confederation: the British North America Act, 1867, unites the provinces of Canada, Nova Scotia, and New Brunswick as the Dominion of Canada
20 September 1867	First federal election: Sir John A. Macdonald's Conservatives win majority

18 October 1867	Alaska transferred to the United States from Russia for the purchase price of $7.2 million
25 May 1870	Battle of Eccles Hill, Québec: last major Fenian raid
23 June 1870	Rupert's Land and the NorthWestern Territory Order signed, transferring these lands from the Hudson's Bay Company to Canada as of July 15, 1870
15 July 1870	Manitoba enters Confederation
8 May 1871	Treaty of Washington signed with the United States laying out fishing and trade rights on Great Lakes
20 July 1871	British Columbia enters Confederation
21 October 1872	Arbitration settles final boundary in the Straits of Juan de Fuca
1 July 1873	Prince Edward Island enters Confederation
7 November 1873	Pacific Scandal: Macdonald resigns after vote of non-confidence; Mackenzie appointed prime minister
17 September 1878	Federal election: Conservatives under Macdonald defeat Liberals under Mackenzie
10 June 1880	Sir Alexander Galt presents credentials as Canada's first high commissioner to London
9 October 1880	Arctic islands ceded to Canada by Britain
20 June 1882	Federal election: Conservatives under Macdonald win second majority
12 July 1882	Hector Fabre appointed Canadian commissioner in Paris
15 September 1884	Nile Voyageurs depart for Sudan
18 March 1885	Northwest Rebellion under the leadership of Louis Riel begins
16 November 1885	Riel executed
22 February 1887	Federal election: Conservatives under Macdonald win third majority
5 March 1891	Federal election: Conservatives under Macdonald win fourth majority; trade with the United States key election issue
16 June 1891	Sir John Abbott prime minister after Macdonald's death
1 August 1894	Sino–Japanese war breaks out, weakening the Qing dynasty in China and establishing Japan as a regional power
23 June 1896	Federal election: Liberals under Laurier win majority
22 June 1897	Victoria's diamond jubilee marked the apogee of imperial sentiment in Canada
13 June 1898	Legislation creating Yukon Territory given royal assent
4 October 1899	Canadian troops depart for service in the Boer War
7 November 1900	Federal election: Liberals under Laurier win second majority
21 January 1901	Queen Victoria dies; Edward VII becomes king
14 September 1901	Theodore Roosevelt, Republican, takes office as U.S. president
31 May 1902	Treaty of Vereeniging signed, ending Boer War
25 March 1903	Alaska Boundary Dispute judgment rendered
3 November 1904	Federal election: Liberals under Laurier win third majority
1 September 1905	Alberta and Saskatchewan enter Confederation

26 October 1908	Federal election: Liberals under Laurier win fourth majority
11 January 1909	Boundary Waters Treaty signed with United States, creating International Joint Commission (IJC)
19 May 1909	Department of External Affairs created; Charles Murphy first secretary of state for external affairs
10 January 1910	Naval Service Bill introduced
4 May 1910	Royal Canadian Navy created
6 May 1910	Edward VII dies; George V becomes king
21 September 1911	Federal election: Conservatives under Borden win majority; reciprocity (free trade) with the United States and naval policy key issues
10 November 1911	Thomas Chase-Casgrain appointed chair of Canadian section of the IJC under the 1909 Boundary Waters Treaty
1 April 1912	Legislation making the prime minister the secretary of state for external affairs goes into effect
4 March 1913	Woodrow Wilson, Democrat, takes office as U.S. president

FIRST WORLD WAR (1914–1918)

4 August 1914	Great War begins: Britain declares war on Germany; all parts of the Empire are at war
3 October 1914	First Canadian troops leave for Europe
2 March 1917	First meeting of the Imperial War Cabinet, London
6 April 1917	United States declares war on Germany, enters First World War
9 April 1917	Beginning of the Battle of Vimy Ridge: for the first time, Canadian troops fight as a distinct national corps
18 May 1917	Conscription bill introduced in Parliament
29 August 1917	Conscription becomes law
7 November 1917	Bolshevik leader Vladimir Lenin leads revolt against Russian government
17 December 1917	Federal election: Unionists under Borden win majority; conscription is a major election issue
1 April 1918	Anti-conscription riot in Québec City; four killed
1 October 1918	Canadian forces arrive in northern Russia to assist in civil war against Bolsheviks
26 October 1918	Canadian troops arrive in Vladivostok for service in the Siberian intervention
11 November 1918	Armistice brings First World War to an end

INTERWAR PERIOD (1919–1939)

28 June 1919	Borden signs Versailles Peace Treaty on behalf of Canada
10 January 1920	League of Nations established; Canada a founding member

4 March 1921	Warren G. Harding, Republican, takes office as U.S. president
6 December 1921	Federal election: Liberals under King win a minority
15 September 1922	Chanak Crisis
2 March 1923	Halibut Treaty signed with the United States: first international treaty signed by Canada
1 July 1923	Chinese Immigration Act, barring Chinese from entering Canada
2 August 1923	Calvin Coolidge, Republican, takes office as U.S. president
24 February 1925	Lake of the Woods Treaty signed with United States
1 April 1925	O.D. Skelton appointed as undersecretary of state for external affairs
29 October 1925	Federal election: Conservatives under Meighen win 116 seats; Liberals under King win 99 seats; King governs with a minority
14 September 1926	Federal election: follows "King–Byng affair"; Liberals under King and Liberal-Progressives win majority
October 1926	Imperial Conference (October 27–November 19) agrees to grant Canada and other dominions full autonomy in domestic and international affairs
18 February 1927	Canada's first diplomatic mission—a legation in Washington—opens when Vincent Massey presents his credentials as envoy extraordinary and minister plenipotentiary
29 September 1928	Diplomatic status of Philippe Roy, Canada's commissioner general in Paris, raised to envoy extraordinary and minister plenipotentiary
4 March 1929	Herbert Hoover, Republican, takes office as U.S. president
18 September 1929	Diplomatic mission in Japan created; Sir Herbert Marler presents his credentials as minister
29 October 1929	New York Stock Exchange crash; beginning of the Great Depression
17 June 1930	U.S. adopts Smoot-Hawley tariff on imported goods
28 July 1930	Federal election: Conservatives under Bennett win majority
1 October 1930	Imperial Conference, London (ends November 14)
11 November 1930	Norway recognizes Canadian sovereignty over Sverdrup Islands
18 September 1931	Mukden Incident in China gives Japan pretext for invading Manchuria and establishing Manchukuo, a puppet state
11 December 1931	Statute of Westminster, 1931, gives Canada and other dominions full sovereignty
20 July 1932	Imperial Economic Conference in Ottawa creates preferential trade within the Empire
1 August 1932	Co-operative Commonwealth Federation (CCF) founded; J.S. Woodsworth selected as party leader
30 January 1933	Adolf Hitler, leader of the National Socialists (Nazis), appointed chancellor of Germany
3 March 1933	Franklin D. Roosevelt, Democrat, takes office as U.S. president
3 October 1935	Italy invades Ethiopia (Abyssinia)
14 October 1935	Federal election: Liberals under King win majority
20 January 1936	George V dies; Edward VIII becomes king

7 March 1936	German troops remilitarize the Rhineland, in violation of the Locarno treaties of 1925
17 July 1936	Spanish civil war begins
11 December 1936	Edward VIII abdicates; George VI becomes king
29 June 1937	Mackenzie King, visiting Germany, meets Hitler
7 July 1937	Marco Polo Bridge Incident leading to a full-scale invasion of China by imperial Japan
13 December 1937	Nanjing falls to Japanese forces, who rape between 20,000 and 80,000 women and murder an estimated 250,000 civilians in the "rape of Nanjing"
12 March 1938	*Anschluss:* Austrians welcome Hitler into Vienna and Austria's incorporation in a "Greater Germany"
18 August 1938	Roosevelt visits Queen's University, issues "Kingston Dispensation"
29 September 1938	Munich agreement: Britain and France agree to annexation of German-speaking Sudetenland in Czechoslovakia

SECOND WORLD WAR (1939–1945)

1 September 1939	Nazi Germany attacks Poland; Second World War begins
10 September 1939	Canada declares war on Germany, seven days after British declaration of war
April–May 1940	"Phoney war" ends: Germany invades Denmark and Norway (April 9) and France, Belgium, and the Netherlands (May 10)
10 June 1940	Canada declares war on Italy
June–September 1940	Battle of Britain
18 August 1940	Ogdensburg Agreement on defence signed with the United States
20 April 1941	Hyde Park Declaration on coordinated defence production
22 June 1941	Operation Barbarossa: German, Finnish, Hungarian, Italian, Romanian, and Slovak troops invade the Soviet Union
2 October 1941	Canadian war cabinet agrees to send troops to reinforce Hong Kong
7 December 1941	Japan attacks Pearl Harbor, Singapore, and Hong Kong; United States declares war on Japan and Germany; Canada declares war on Japan
25 December 1941	Allied troops in Hong Kong surrender after being overrun by Japanese forces; 2000 Canadians killed or captured
1 January 1942	In Washington, 26 states sign the Declaration by United Nations pledging cooperation in the defeat of Germany and Japan
27 April 1942	Referendum on conscription reveals strong support in English Canada and equally strong rejection in Québec
19 August 1942	Dieppe Raid: 3367 Canadian casualties in first European battle of the war
11 December 1942	John Bracken, Progressive premier of Manitoba, selected Conservative leader, on condition that the party changes its name to Progressive Conservative party

10 July 1943	Beginning of Italian campaign: British, Canadian and American troops land in Sicily
1–16 May 1944	First Commonwealth Prime Ministers' Meeting, London
6 June 1944	D-Day: Allied forces land at Normandy
1–22 July 1944	UN Monetary and Financial Conference at Bretton Woods, New Hampshire (Bretton Woods agreements)
21 August 1944	Closing of the "Falaise Pocket" marks end of the Battle of Normandy
21 August 1944	Conference at Dumbarton Oaks (Washington, DC) on the future world organization opens (ends October 7)
23 November 1944	Mackenzie King decides to implement conscription
12 April 1945	Roosevelt dies; Harry S. Truman becomes U.S. president
8 May 1945	"VE" (Victory in Europe) Day: Germany surrenders unconditionally: war in Europe ends; Germany divided; Berlin also divided into sectors among victorious powers
11 June 1945	Federal election: Liberals under Mackenzie King win majority government; Progressive Conservative John Bracken is leader of the official opposition
25 June 1945	UN Charter signed in San Francisco
August 1945	United States drops atomic bomb on Hiroshima (6th) and Nagasaki (9th)
15 August 1945	"VJ" (Victory in Japan) Day: Japan surrenders; war in the Pacific ends; Korea divided at the 38th parallel as Soviet Union takes surrender from Japanese forces in the north, the United States in the south

THE COLD WAR ERA (1945–1991)

5 September 1945	Igor Gouzenko, a clerk at the Soviet embassy in Ottawa, defects with evidence of a Soviet spy ring in Ottawa
1 February 1946	Trygve Lie (Norway) installed as first UN Secretary General
5 September 1946	Louis St. Laurent appointed as secretary of state for external affairs
19 December 1946	Civil war in Vietnam between French and Vietminh
13 January 1947	St. Laurent delivers Gray Lecture, outlining principles of Canadian foreign policy
15 May 1947	U.S. Congress votes funds to combat Communist insurgency in Greece and Turkey (Truman Doctrine)
5 June 1947	U.S. Secretary of State George Marshall outlines aid program for Europe (Marshall Plan)
9 July 1947	Brooke Claxton presents *Canada's Defence*, first white paper on defence
15 August 1947	Independence of India and Pakistan
30 October 1947	General Agreement on Tariffs and Trade (GATT) signed at Geneva
1 January 1948	Canada begins second two-year term on UN Security Council
20 February 1948	Communist takeover of Czechoslovakia begins

14 May 1948	Independence of Israel; first Arab–Israeli war
16 June 1948	Blockade of Berlin by Soviet Union begins (ends May 12, 1949)
2 October 1948	George Drew selected Progressive Conservative leader and leader of the official opposition
15 November 1948	King resigns; St. Laurent becomes prime minister; Lester B. Pearson appointed external affairs minister
31 March 1949	Newfoundland enters Confederation
4 April 1949	North Atlantic Treaty signed, Washington, DC
23 May 1949	Federal Republic of Germany (West Germany) established; German Democratic Republic (East Germany) created October 7, 1949
27 June 1949	Federal election: Liberals under St. Laurent returned with majority
1 October 1949	People's Republic of China proclaimed; Mao Zedong chairman of new government; Zhou En-lai premier; Kuomintang (Nationalist) government under Chiang Kai-shek moves to Taiwan
13 January 1950	Colombo Plan agreement
25 June 1950	Korean War begins; Canada sends destroyers and ground combat forces to serve with U.S.-led UN force
18 April 1951	European Coal and Steel Community (ECSC) treaty signed
1 August 1951	Exchange of notes between Canada and United States authorizing the Pinetree radar line project
6 February 1952	George VI dies; Elizabeth II becomes queen
18 February 1952	Greece and Turkey join NATO
4 November 1952	Republican candidate Dwight D. Eisenhower elected U.S. president
10 April 1953	Dag Hammarskjöld (Sweden) installed as second UN Secretary General
27 July 1953	Armistice agreement signed at Panmunjom ends Korean War
10 August 1953	Federal election: Liberals under St. Laurent returned with majority
30 June 1954	Canada approves the installation of the Distant Early Warning (DEW) radar line
21 July 1954	Vietnam divided into North and South at 17th parallel
6 May 1955	West Germany joins NATO; Warsaw Treaty Organization formed in response (May 14)
26 July 1956	Egypt nationalizes Suez Canal
29 October 1956	British, French, and Israeli forces attack Egypt; Lester Pearson proposes a UN peacekeeping force
1 November 1956	Soviet Union invades Hungary, removes coalition government of Imre Nagy
14 December 1956	John G. Diefenbaker named Progressive Conservative leader and leader of the official opposition
25 March 1957	Treaty of Rome establishes the European Economic Community (EEC)
10 June 1957	Federal election: minority Progressive Conservative government under Diefenbaker; Sidney Smith appointed external affairs minister
26 August 1957	Soviet Union launches first intercontinental ballistic missile (ICBM)
4 October 1957	Soviet Union launches Sputnik, first artificial earth satellite

14 October 1957	Pearson awarded Nobel Peace Prize
1 January 1958	Canada begins second two-year term on UN Security Council
16 January 1958	Pearson succeeds St. Laurent as Liberal leader and leader of the official opposition
27 March 1958	Khrushchev also assumes post of chairman of Council of Ministers
31 March 1958	Federal election: Conservatives under Diefenbaker returned with majority
12 May 1958	NORAD agreement signed
1 January 1959	Fidel Castro Ruz overthrows Fulgencio Batista in Cuba
20 February 1959	Diefenbaker announces the cancellation of the Avro Arrow, a Canadian-developed jet fighter
26 June 1959	St. Lawrence Seaway opens
17 March 1959	Sidney Smith dies in office; Howard Green subsequently appointed external affairs minister (4 June)
7 September 1959	Maurice Duplessis, Union Nationale premier of Québec, dies in office
13 February 1960	France explodes its first atomic weapon in the Sahara desert
1 May 1960	U-2 incident: U.S. spy plane shot down over Soviet Union
22 June 1960	Québec Liberals under Jean Lesage win provincial election, setting the stage for the Quiet Revolution
8 November 1960	Democratic candidate John F. Kennedy elected U.S. president
17 January 1961	Columbia River Treaty on the use and control of the Columbia River basin signed
2 February 1961	First Sino–Canadian grain sale announced
8–17 March 1961	Commonwealth Prime Ministers' Meeting, London; South Africa leaves the Commonwealth over the issue of apartheid (15th)
12 August 1961	East Germany closes border to the West; begins building the Berlin Wall
12 August 1961	CCF becomes New Democratic Party (NDP); Tommy Douglas, CCF premier of Saskatchewan, chosen party leader
18 September 1961	Hammarskjöld dies in suspicious plane crash; U Thant (Burma) installed as third UN Secretary General (3 November 1961)
18 June 1962	Federal election: Conservatives under Diefenbaker returned with minority
16–28 October 1962	Cuban missile crisis
8 April 1963	Federal election: minority Liberal government under Pearson; Paul Martin, Sr. appointed external affairs minister; Diefenbaker leader of the official opposition
22 November 1963	Kennedy assassinated; Lyndon B. Johnson becomes president
26 March 1964	Defence minister Paul Hellyer tables white paper on defence
4 May 1964	Kennedy Round of multilateral GATT negotiations begins (completed June 1967)
7 August 1964	Following naval incident in the Gulf of Tonkin, U.S. Congress passes Gulf of Tonkin resolution, giving Johnson the power to deploy U.S. forces for the defence of allies

15 October 1964	Khrushchev deposed, succeeded by Leonid Brezhnev as first secretary, Aleksei Kosygin as chairman of the Council of Ministers
16 October 1964	China explodes its first atomic weapon
3 November 1964	Johnson wins U.S. presidential elections
16 January 1965	Canada–U.S. Automotive Agreement (Auto Pact) signed by Pearson and Johnson
24 February 1965	Operation Rolling Thunder—sustained U.S. bombing of North Vietnam—begins
27 February 1965	Québec–France Entente in education
8 March 1965	First U.S. combat troops in Vietnam deployed to defend Danang
2 April 1965	Pearson's Temple University speech
12 April 1965	Paul Gérin-Lajoie, Québec minister of education, gives a speech articulating doctrine of Québec's competence in international affairs
8 November 1965	Federal election: Liberals under Pearson returned with minority
11 November 1965	White minority regime of Ian Smith in Rhodesia issues unilateral declaration of independence
11–12 January 1966	Special Commonwealth Prime Ministers' Meeting on Rhodesia, Lagos
16 May 1966	Mao and the Politburo issue a denunciation of a play, marking the beginning of the Great Proletarian Cultural Revolution
1 July 1966	France withdraws from integrated military command of NATO (but remains a signatory to the North Atlantic Treaty)
1 January 1967	Canada begins third two-year term on the UN Security Council
18 April 1967	Expo 67 opens in Montréal May 1967 Biafra secedes from Nigeria; civil war begins
5–10 June 1967	Arab–Israeli war (Six-Day War)
30 June 1967	Final act of Kennedy Round of trade negotiations signed, Geneva
24 July 1967	French president Charles de Gaulle's "Vive le Québec libre" speech, Montréal
9 September 1967	Robert Stanfield, premier of Nova Scotia, succeeds Diefenbaker as Conservative leader and leader of the official opposition (elected to Parliament November 6, 1967)
30 March 1968	NORAD renewed
20 April 1968	Pierre Elliott Trudeau replaces Pearson as Liberal leader and prime minister
25 June 1968	Federal election: majority Liberal government under Trudeau; Mitchell Sharp appointed external affairs minister
20 August 1968	Soviet and Warsaw Pact forces invade Czechoslovakia 5 November 1968 Republican candidate Richard M. Nixon elected U.S. president
25 August 1969	First *Manhattan* voyage through the Northwest Passage
20 March 1970	Agence de coopération culturelle et technique (ACCT) created
1 April 1970	Second *Manhattan* voyage; Parliament passes Arctic Waters Pollution Prevention Act (April 8)
25 June 1970	Trudeau government's foreign policy statement, *Foreign Policy for Canadians*, published

5 October 1970	1970 Kidnapping of British diplomat James Cross by FLQ begins "October Crisis" in Québec; War Measures Act invoked October 16
13 October 1970	Canada and China establish diplomatic relations
14–22 January 1971	Commonwealth Heads of Government Meeting held in Singapore, first CHOGM held outside Britain
24 April 1971	David Lewis elected NDP leader August 1971 Donald S. MacDonald, minister of national defence, tables a defence white paper, *Defence in the 70s*
15 August 1971	"Nixon Shocks": U.S. government imposes economic measures to stem balance of payments deficit; devalues the dollar and abandons fixed exchange rates
12 November 1971	Gray Report recommending foreign investment screening agency leaked
16 December 1971	East Pakistan declares independence as Bangladesh following civil war and war between India and Pakistan
22 January 1972	European Economic Community expanded to include Britain, Denmark, Ireland, and Norway (Norwegians reject membership in a national referendum, September 1972)
21 February 1972	Nixon visits China
15 April 1972	Great Lakes Water Quality Agreement between Canada and the United States signed in Ottawa
5 September 1972	Black September terrorists seize Israeli dormitory at Munich Olympics; 11 athletes killed
3 October 1972	Strategic Arms Limitation Treaty (SALT I) signed by United States and Soviet Union
30 October 1972	Federal election: Liberals under Trudeau returned with minority
7 November 1972	Nixon reelected U.S. president
18 December 1972	After peace talks break down, United States begins 11-day bombing campaign against Hanoi and Haiphong
22 December 1972	Kurt Waldheim (Austria) installed as fourth UN Secretary General
27 January 1973	Vietnam ceasefire agreement signed in Paris; last U.S. troops leave Vietnam (March 29); last U.S. prisoners of war released (April 1)
10 May 1973	Second NORAD renewal
2–10 August 1973	Canada hosts Commonwealth Heads of Government Meeting, Ottawa
11 September 1973	Coup d'état in Chile; President Salvador Allende Gossens commits suicide
12 September 1973	GATT meeting in Tokyo launches Tokyo Round of multilateral GATT negotiations (completed April 1979)
6–24 October 1973	Fourth Arab–Israeli war (Yom Kippur war)
19 October 1973	Oil embargo imposed by OPEC against the United States, later extended to Japan and Europe
23 November 1973	House of Commons passes foreign investment review bill
18 May 1974	India explodes nuclear device
8 July 1974	Federal election: Liberals under Trudeau returned with majority; Allan MacEachen appointed external affairs minister

9 August 1974	Nixon resigns as president following Watergate scandal; Gerald Ford becomes president
12 May 1975	Third NORAD renewal
26 June 1975	Indira Gandhi, prime minister of India, declares a state of emergency
7 July 1975	Ed Broadbent elected NDP leader
15–17 November 1975	Group of 6 economic summit, Rambouillet, France; Canada not invited
7 December 1975	Indonesia invades East Timor
22 February 1976	Joe Clark succeeds Stanfield as Progressive Conservative leader and leader of the official opposition
27–28 June 1976	Group of 7 (G7) economic summit, Puerto Rico; Canada invited by United States to attend
16 July 1976	Taiwan pulls out of the Montréal Olympics after quarrel with Canada
9 September 1976	Mao Zedong dies
14 September 1976	Don Jamieson appointed external affairs minister
2 November 1976	Democratic candidate Jimmy Carter elected U.S. president
15 November 1976	Québec elections: Parti Québécois under René Lévesque forms government
1 January 1977	Canada begins fourth two-year term on UN Security Council
7–8 May 1977	Third economic summit, London; G7 institutionalized
8–15 June 1977	Commonwealth Heads of Government Meeting, London; Gleneagles Declaration on apartheid in sport agreed to by Commonwealth leaders in London
15 December 1978	China and the United States announce the establishment of full diplomatic relations as of January 1, 1979
22 December 1978	Deng Xiaoping paramount leader of China
25 December 1978	Vietnam invades Cambodia; thousands of "boat people" begin to flee Vietnam
16 January 1979	Iranian revolution: Shah Mohammad Reza Pahlavi abdicates and leaves Iran
17 February 1979	China invades Vietnam
12 April 1979	Tokyo Round of trade negotiations concluded
22 May 1979	Federal election: minority Progressive Conservative government under Joe Clark; Flora MacDonald appointed external affairs minister; Trudeau is leader of the official opposition
1 June 1979	United States and Soviet Union sign SALT II (treaty is never ratified by the U.S.)
4 November 1979	U.S. embassy personnel in Tehran seized as "hostages" by Iran; Canada's ambassador to Iran, Kenneth Taylor, secretly helps six members of the U.S. embassy to escape disguised as Canadians; remaining Americans released January 1981
24 December 1979	Soviet Union invades Afghanistan; Soviet troops execute President Hafizullah Amin (27th)
18 February 1980	Federal election: majority Liberal government under Pierre Trudeau; Mark MacGuigan appointed external affairs minister; Clark is leader of the official opposition

22 April 1980	Canada joins boycott of 1980 Moscow Olympics
12 May 1980	Fourth NORAD renewal
22 May 1980	Québec referendum on sovereignty-association defeated
10 September 1980	Zhao Ziyang becomes premier of China
22 September 1980	Iraq invades Iran, beginning eight year war
4 November 1980	Republican candidate Ronald Reagan elected U.S. president
11 March 1981	Fifth NORAD renewal
20–21 June 1981	Canada hosts G7 summit at Montebello, Québec
13 October 1981	Anwar Sadat, president of Egypt, assassinated
21–23 October 1981	International Meeting on Cooperation and Development, Cancún, Mexico, chaired by Trudeau and Mexican president José Lopéz Portillo
15 December 1981	Javier Pérez de Cuéllar (Peru) installed as fifth UN Secretary General
12 January 1982	Department of External Affairs reorganized to incorporate Trade and Commerce
2 April 1982	Argentina invades the Falkland Islands
17 April 1982	Elizabeth II signs Constitution Act in Ottawa
10 September 1982	Allan MacEachen appointed external affairs minister
11 November 1982	Leonid Brezhnev dies, succeeded by Yuri Andropov
11 June 1983	Brian Mulroney elected Progressive Conservative leader and leader of the official opposition
1 September 1983	Korean Air Lines Flight 007 shot down by Soviet fighters
25 October 1983	United States invades Grenada
27 October 1993	Trudeau launches his "peace initiative"
9 February 1984	Andropov dies, succeeded by Konstantin Chernenko
6 March 1984	First cruise missile test over northern Canada
30 June 1984	John Turner replaces Trudeau as Liberal leader and prime minister; Jean Chrétien appointed external affairs minister
4 September 1984	Federal election: majority Progressive Conservative government under Mulroney; Clark appointed external affairs minister; Turner is leader of the official opposition
12 October 1984	Decision of a chamber of the International Court of Justice regarding the Canada–U.S. maritime boundary in the Gulf of Maine area
6 November 1984	Reagan reelected U.S. president
19 December 1984	U.S. withdraws from UNESCO as of December 31
10 March 1985	Chernenko dies, succeeded by Mikhail S. Gorbachev
17–18 March 1985	First "Shamrock Summit," Québec City; former Ontario premier William Davis and former U.S. secretary of transportation appointed to examine the acid rain issue
14 May 1985	Government green paper on foreign policy, *Competitiveness and Security*, published
23 June 1985	Double bombing of aircraft originating in Vancouver; bombing linked to Sikhs in British Columbia

1–11 July 1985	Transit through the Northwest Passage of the U.S. Coast Guard icebreaker *Polar Sea*
10 July 1985	French intelligence agents bomb the Greenpeace ship *Rainbow Warrior* in Auckland harbour, killing one person
5 September 1985	Report of the Royal Commission on the Economic Union and Development Prospects for Canada (Macdonald Commission) released
7 September 1985	Mulroney's "polite no" to the U.S. request for Canadian participation in the Strategic Defense Initiative
1 October 1985	Canada formally requests free trade negotiations with the United States
8 November 1985	Simon Reisman appointed Canada's chief negotiator for free trade
22 February 1986	First Francophone summit, Paris
19 March 1986	Second annual Canada–U.S. summit, Washington; NORAD renewed for the sixth time, for five years
14 April 1986	United States bombs cities in Libya
26 June 1986	Report of the Special Joint Committee of the Senate and House of Commons on Canada's International Relations, *Independence and Internationalism*, tabled in Parliament
25 September 1986	Uruguay Round of multilateral GATT negotiations launched (completed December 1993)
4 December 1986	Government statement on foreign policy tabled
5 April 1987	Third annual Canada–United States summit, Ottawa
3 June 1987	Meech Lake accord on constitutional amendment signed by first ministers
5 June 1987	Defence white paper, *Challenge and Commitment: A Defence Policy for Canada*, released
2–4 September 1987	Second Francophone summit, Québec City
3 October 1987	Canadian and American officials reach agreement on a free trade agreement
13 October 1987	Canada hosts Commonwealth Heads of Government Meeting, Vancouver (October 13–17)
19 October 1987	"Black Monday": global stock markets crash
8 December 1987	Intermediate-Range Nuclear Forces (INF) Treaty signed by Reagan and Gorbachev
2 January 1988	Mulroney and Reagan sign the Canada–U.S. Free Trade Agreement
11 January 1988	Canada–U.S. Arctic Cooperation Agreement signed
8 April 1988	Agreement reached for withdrawal of Soviet troops from Afghanistan
14 April 1988	France withdraws its ambassador after Canada seizes a French trawler off Newfoundland and charges all on board with illegal fishing
27–28 April 1988	Fourth Canada–U.S. summit, Washington
24 May 1988	Bill C-130, implementing the FTA, introduced into the House of Commons
19–21 June 1988	Canada hosts G7 summit, Toronto
20 August 1988	Ceasefire ends Iran–Iraq war

28 September 1988	Reagan signs the legislation implementing the FTA after it passed the House of Representatives (August 9) and the Senate (September 19)
29 September 1988	Nobel Peace Prize awarded to UN peacekeeping forces
8 November 1988	Republican candidate George H.W. Bush elected U.S. president
21 November 1988	Federal election: Conservatives under Mulroney returned with majority
5–9 December 1988	Montréal mid-term review of the Uruguay Round of multilateral trade negotiations
13 December 1988	Yassir Arafat, chairman of the PLO, renounces terrorism outside Israel
30 December 1988	Legislation implementing the FTA given Royal Assent after passing the Senate (December 30) and the House of Commons (December 24)
1 January 1989	Canada–U.S. Free Trade Agreement comes into effect
1 January 1989	Canada begins fifth two-year term on UN Security Council
4 June 1989	Beijing massacre
28 June 1989	Department of External Affairs renamed "External Affairs and International Trade Canada" (EAITC)
5 November 1989	First meeting of Asia-Pacific Economic Cooperation forum, Canberra
9 November 1989	Berlin Wall is breached
13 November 1989	Canada becomes 33rd member of the Organization of American States
2 December 1989	Audrey McLaughlin elected NDP leader
11 December 1989	*Concordia* incident: Canadian destroyer fires warning shots at American fishing vessel
20 December 1989	United States invades Panama
February 1990	African National Congress legalized by South Africa (2nd); Nelson Mandela released from jail (10th)
22 June 1990	Meech Lake constitutional accord defeated
23 June 1990	Jean Chrétien succeeds Turner as leader of the Liberal party and leader of the official opposition
11 July 1990	Oka/Kahnawake crisis begins
2 August 1990	Iraq invades Kuwait
29–30 September 1990	World Summit for Children, New York
3 October 1990	Germany is reunited
19–21 November 1990	Second CSCE summit, Paris, marks the formal end of the Cold War

POST–COLD WAR ERA (1991–2001)

13 March 1991	U.S.–Canada Air Quality Agreement signed in Ottawa
19 April 1991	Seventh NORAD renewal
21 April 1991	Barbara McDougall appointed external affairs minister
25 June 1991	Croatia declares independence; civil war breaks out in Yugoslavia

1 July 1991	Warsaw Pact dissolved
10 July 1991	Boris Yeltsin inaugurated as Russian president
31 July 1991	United States and Soviet Union sign Strategic Arms Limitations Treaty
30 September 1991	Coup d'état in Haiti overthrows President Jean-Bertrand Aristide
12 November 1991	Dili massacre, East Timor December 1991 Maastricht treaty, committing European Community to closer integration, signed
25 December 1991	Soviet Union declared dissolved by Mikhail Gorbachev
1 January 1992	Boutros Boutros-Ghali (Egypt) installed as sixth UN Secretary General
21 February 1992	Security Council approves the deployment of a peacekeeping force for Yugoslavia (UNPROFOR)
24 April 1992	UN Resolution 751 creates the first mission in Somalia (UNOSOM)
3–14 June 1992	UN Conference on Environment and Development (Earth Summit), Rio de Janeiro
10 June 1992	International court of arbitration decides on maritime boundary between Canada and the French territorial collectivity of St. Pierre and Miquelon
26 October 1992	Referendum on Charlottetown constitutional accord defeated
3 November 1992	Democratic candidate Bill Clinton elected U.S. president
8 December 1992	U.S. Marines land in Somalia, beginning Operation Restore Hope; Canadian troops arrive December 14–15
11 December 1992	Mulroney government announces that Canada will withdraw from the peacekeeping mission in Cyprus by June 1993
17 December 1992	NAFTA signed by Mexico, Canada, and the United States
26 February 1993	Islamists detonate a truck bomb in the North Tower of the World Trade Center, New York
March 1993	Somalia affair: members of the Canadian Forces kill Somali civilians caught stealing from Canadian base in Belet Huen: Ahmed Arush shot dead (4th), Shidane Arone beaten to death while in custody (16th)
27 March 1993	Jiang Zemin becomes president of China
14–25 June 1993	World Conference on Human Rights, Vienna
26 June 1993	Kim Campbell replaces Mulroney as Progressive Conservative leader and prime minister; Perrin Beatty appointed external affairs minister
21–25 October 1993	Commonwealth Heads of Government Meeting, Nicosia, Cyprus; first time a Canadian prime minister has not attended a CHOGM
25 October 1993	Federal election: majority Liberal government under Jean Chrétien; André Ouellet appointed minister of foreign affairs; Lucien Bouchard (Bloc Québécois) is leader of the official opposition
1 November 1993	Maastricht Treaty ratified, comes into force; European Community becomes European Union
5 November 1993	EAITC renamed Department of Foreign Affairs and International Trade (DFAIT)
14 December 1993	Jean Charest elected Progressive Conservative leader
15 December 1993	Uruguay Round of trade negotiations concludes

10 January 1994	NATO endorses "Partnership for Peace" program
6 April 1994	Plane carrying presidents of Rwanda and Burundi shot down; ethnic violence and genocide erupt in Rwanda, leaving 800,000 dead in 100 days
26–28 May 1994	First multiracial elections in South Africa; Nelson Mandela elected president
1 June 1994	South Africa returns to the Commonwealth
5 September 1994	5–13 UN International Conference on Population and Development, Cairo
19 September 1994	After U.S. invasion embarks for Haiti, military agrees to restore Aristide to power
15 November 1994	Special Joint (House of Commons and Senate) Committee Reviewing Canadian Foreign Policy tables its report *Canada's Foreign Policy: Principles and Priorities for the Future*
1 December 1994	David Collenette, minister of national defence, releases *1994 Defence White Paper*
1 January 1995	World Trade Organization comes into being
7 February 1995	Government statement on foreign affairs, *Canada in the World*, released
23–24 February 1995	Bill Clinton pays first bilateral visit to Canada 9 March 1995 "Turbot war": Canada arrests the Spanish fishing vessel *Estai* in international waters for overfishing
15–17 June 1995	Canada hosts G7 summit, Halifax
26 June 1995	Commemoration of the 50th anniversary of the signing of the UN Charter, San Francisco
10 July 1995	French navy boards and seizes Greenpeace ship *Rainbow Warrior II*
4–15 September 1995	Fourth UN World Conference on Women, Beijing
14 October 1995	Alexa McDonough elected NDP leader
30 October 1995	Referendum on Québec sovereignty narrowly defeated; Jacques Parizeau resigns as premier the next day
21 November 1995	Dayton General Framework Agreement for Peace in Bosnia and Herzegovina initialled; signed at Peace Implementation Conference, Paris, December 8–9
25 January 1996	Lloyd Axworthy appointed minister of foreign affairs; Pierre Pettigrew appointed minister of state for international cooperation and relations with La Francophonie
17 February 1996	Michel Gauthier elected as leader of Bloc Québécois after Lucien Bouchard resigns to move to provincial politics as leader of the Parti Québécois and premier of Québec
24 February 1996	Cuba shoots down two U.S.-registered Cessnas, killing four Cuban-Americans
1 January 1997	Kofi Annan (Ghana) installed as seventh UN Secretary General
15 March 1997	Gilles Duceppe elected Bloc Québécois leader
14 May 1997	International currency speculators assault Thai baht, marking the start of the Asian financial crisis

2 June 1997	Federal election: Liberals under Chrétien win a second majority; Preston Manning (Reform Party) is leader of the official opposition
20 June 1997	Russia joins G7 summit in Denver as a full member, forming the G8
1 July 1997	Hong Kong returned to Chinese sovereignty as the Hong Kong Special Administrative Region
8 July 1997	Czech Republic, Hungary and Poland invited to join NATO (formal accession occurs March 16, 1999)
21–25 November 1997	Canada hosts APEC summit, Vancouver
3 December 1997	Convention on the Prohibition of the Use, Stockpiling, Production and Transfer of Anti-Personnel Mines and on their Destruction (Ottawa Treaty) signed by 125 countries
11 December 1997	Kyoto Protocol to the UN Framework Convention on Climate Change adopted in Kyoto, Japan
28 May 1998	Pakistan explodes five nuclear devices underground
17 July 1998	Rome Statute of the International Criminal Court signed
7 August 1998	Al-Qaeda bombs U.S. embassies in Kenya and Tanzania
14 November 1998	Joe Clark elected as Progressive Conservative leader after Charest leaves federal politics to lead the Liberal party of Québec
2 December 1998	La Francophonie creates Organisation internationale de La Francophonie (OIF)
1 January 1999	Canada begins sixth two-year term on UN Security Council
1 January 1999	Euro becomes the official currency of the European Union
16 March 1999	Czech Republic, Hungary, and Poland become members of NATO
24 March 1999	NATO commences bombing of Serbia over Kosovo; Canadian CF-18s bomb Serb targets
1 April 1999	Nunavut created as a separate territory
3 September 1999	New Brunswick hosts eighth Francophonie summit, Moncton
20 September 1999	Security Council–sanctioned INTERFET forces intervene in East Timor to expel Indonesian militias; Canada's contribution (Operation Toucan) arrives by October 15
14 December 1999	Ahmed Ressam arrested entering the United States with materials for a bomb he was planning to detonate at Los Angeles International Airport on New Year's Eve
15 December 1999	First meeting of the G-20 finance ministers and central bank governors, Berlin, chaired by Paul Martin, Jr.
31 December 1999	Vladimir Putin becomes president of the Russian Federation
27 March 2000	Reform Party disbanded, becomes the Canadian Alliance
8 July 2000	Stockwell Day elected leader of the Canadian Alliance
17 October 2000	John Manley appointed minister of foreign affairs
7 November 2000	Republican nominee George W. Bush wins U.S. presidential election (not confirmed until the U.S. Supreme Court ruled on Florida recounts on December 12, 2000)
27 November 2000	Federal election: Liberals under Chrétien win a third majority; Stockwell Day (Canadian Alliance) is leader of the official opposition
20–22 April 2001	Summit of the Americas, Québec City

POST-9/11 ERA

11 September 2001	Al-Qaeda hijacks four airliners and flies three into World Trade Center towers and Pentagon; fourth airliner destined for U.S. Capitol or White House crashes into a Pennsylvania field
13 September 2001	NATO invokes Article 5, the collective security provision of the North Atlantic Treaty, 1949
20 September 2001	In an address to Congress, Bush demands that Afghanistan deliver Osama bin Laden and Al-Qaeda leaders to U.S. authorities
7 October 2001	NATO attack on Afghanistan begins
9 November 2001	Doha Development Round of trade negotiations launched at WTO Fourth Ministerial Conference, Doha, Qatar
10 November 2001	China admitted to the WTO
12 December 2001	"Smart Border" declaration
12 December 2001	Battle of Tora Bora forces last Taliban units in Afghanistan into Pakistan
20 December 2001	UN Security Council creates International Security Assistance Force (ISAF) for Kabul
16 January 2002	Bill Graham appointed minister of foreign affairs February 2002 Canadian troops deploy to Kandahar
20 March 2002	Stephen Harper elected leader of the Canadian Alliance
18 April 2002	American fighters accidentally bomb Canadian soldiers outside Kandahar, killing four
26–28 June 2002	Canada hosts G8 at Kananaskis; Russia inserted into the G8 rotation as of 2006
1 July 2002	International Criminal Court at The Hague enters into force
12 October 2002	Jemaah Islamiyah terrorist attacks in Bali, Indonesia kill 202 and injure 209
17 December 2002	Canada ratifies Kyoto Protocol
25 January 2003	Jack Layton elected NDP leader
12 March 2003	World Health Organization announces global health alert over SARS (severe acute respiratory syndrome) pandemic
17 March 2003	Chrétien announces that Canada will not join the U.S.-led "coalition of the willing" in using force against Iraq
19 March 2003	"Operation Iraqi Freedom" begins with U.S. bombing of Iraqi targets
23 March 2003	Hu Jintao becomes president of China
23 April 2003	Because of SARS pandemic, WHO recommends travellers postpone nonessential travel to Toronto (advice lifted April 29)
5 April 2003	Coalition forces enter Baghdad
31 May 2003	Peter MacKay elected Progressive Conservative leader
5 August 2003	Jemaah Islamiyah suicide bomber attacks Marriott Hotel, Djakarta
11 August 2003	NATO takes over command and coordination of ISAF in Afghanistan
7 December 2003	Canadian Alliance and Progressive Conservative Party merge as the Conservative Party of Canada
12 December 2003	Chrétien resigns as prime minister; Paul Martin, Jr. is sworn in

9 February 2004	Canadian Lt.-Gen. Rick Hillier assumes overall command of ISAF forces in Afghanistan
11 March 2004	Islamist attacks on Madrid trains (3/11), killing 191 people and injuring 1800
20 March 2004	Stephen Harper elected leader of Conservative Party of Canada
2 April 2004	Bulgaria, Estonia, Latvia, Lithuania, Romania, Slovakia, and Slovenia admitted to NATO
28 June 2004	Federal election: Liberals under Martin returned with a minority; Harper (Conservative Party of Canada) is leader of official opposition
20 July 2004	Pierre Pettigrew appointed foreign minister
5 August 2004	Canada–U.S. agreement giving NORAD a role in U.S. ballistic missile defense system
9 September 2004	Jemaah Islamiyah suicide bomber attacks Australian embassy, Djakarta
2 November 2004	Bush reelected U.S. president
26 December 2004	Indian Ocean tsunami
8 January 2005	Disaster Assistance Response Team (DART) arrives in Sri Lanka
22 February 2005	Martin government announces it will not participate in Ballistic Missile Defense plan with the United States
25 March 2005	Bush, Martin, and Vicente Fox of Mexico summit meeting; Security and Prosperity Partnership signed
19 April 2005	Martin government's *International Policy Statement* tabled in Parliament
7 July 2005	Four Islamist suicide bombers attack London transport system ("7/7" attack)
21 July 2005	Islamist suicide bombers launch 7/7 copycat attacks in London; all four bombs fail to detonate
16 August 2005	Canada assumes command of provincial reconstruction team in Kandahar City
2 September 2005	Canada deploys warships and a Canadian Coast Guard vessel to assist in the aftermath of Hurricane Katrina
1 October 2005	Three Jemaah Islamiyah suicide bombers attack Western tourists in Bali, Indonesia
29 November 2005	Martin government defeated in House of Commons on a non-confidence motion
15 January 2006	Suicide bomber kills Canadian diplomat Glyn Berry in Kandahar
23 January 2006	Federal election: Conservative Party of Canada under Stephen Harper wins minority
31 January 2006	London Conference on Afghanistan
1 February 2006	Martin resigns as parliamentary leader; Bill Graham is interim leader and leader of the official opposition
6 February 2006	Harper government sworn in; Peter MacKay is minister of foreign affairs, Gordon O'Connor is minister of national defence
5 May 2006	Québec given permanent representation at UNESCO within the Canadian delegation
8 May 2006	House of Commons votes to make NORAD agreement permanent

17 May 2006	House of Commons approves two-year extension of mission in Afghanistan
2 June 2006	Police arrest 17 Muslim men in Toronto, alleging a plot to detonate truck bombs against targets in Ottawa and Toronto and to decapitate Harper; 18th member of "Toronto 18" arrested August 3
12 July 2006	War between Israel and Hezbollah in southern Lebanon; Canadian government evacuates some of the 30,000 Canadian citizens in Lebanon
15 July 2006	Russia hosts G8 meeting for the first time, St. Petersburg
12 September 2006	Canada–U.S. agreement on softwood lumber
2 December 2006	Stéphane Dion elected Liberal leader and leader of the official opposition
1 January 2007	Ban Ki-moon (South Korea) installed as eighth UN Secretary General
14 August 2007	Maxime Bernier appointed foreign minister; Mackay appointed minister of national defence
12 October 2007	Harper appoints Independent Panel on Canada's Future Role in Afghanistan under John Manley
13 March 2008	House of Commons passes motion to extend Afghanistan mission to 2011
7 May 2008	Dmitry Medvedev inaugurated as president of the Russian Federation
7–16 August 2008	South Ossetian war between Russian Federation and Georgia
September 2008	Global financial crisis
14 October 2008	Federal election: Conservatives under Harper wins minority; Dion is leader of the official opposition
17 October 2008	Québec hosts twelfth Francophonie summit, Québec City
30 October 2008	Lawrence Cannon appointed foreign minister
4 November 2008	Democratic nominee Barack Obama wins U.S. presidential election
15 November 2008	G-20 Leaders' summit, Washington, DC, hosted by George W. Bush
26 November 2008	Islamists attacks in Mumbai, killing 173 and wounding 308
10 December 2008	Dion resigns; Michael Ignatieff becomes interim Liberal leader and leader of the official opposition
19 February 2009	Obama visits Canada, his first foreign visit
1 April 2009	Albania and Croatia join NATO
2 April 2009	Second G-20 Leaders' summit, London
17 July 2009	Jemaah Islamiyah suicide bombers attack Marriott and Ritz-Carlton hotels, Djakarta
3 September 2009	Saad Khalid, one of the "Toronto 18" terror cell, sentenced to 14 years in jail
24 September 2009	Third G-20 Leaders' summit, Pittsburgh; leaders decide to make G-20 summit meeting, co-hosted by Canada and South Korea in Huntsville in June 2010, the world's major economic forum, replacing the G8

Index*

3D approach, 5, 156, 247
9/11 (11 September 2001)
    attacks, 30, 42, 147, 342
    and Canada, 31, 201–202, 224,
        247, 261, 265
    Chrétien, 201, 201n
    impact of, 15, 31–32, 91–92, 97,
        100–101, 119, 147–51, 170, 278
    Kingston Dispensation, 31
    NATO, 47
    provinces, 301

A
Abbott, Sir John, 326
acid rain, 80–81, 165, 197n, 300
Act Respecting the Future
    of Québec, 317
Action Démocratique, 317
adjournment debates, 263
Afghanistan
    Afghanistan Compact, 69
    battle group deployment to
        Kandahar, 173, 343
    cabinet committee on, 225
    Canadian mission in, 5, 42, 66, 100,
        101, 108, 173, 257, 278
    extension until 2009, 344
    extension until 2011, 265, 344
    Independent Panel on Canada's
        Future Role in Afghanistan, 344
    International Security Assistance
        Force, 47, 173, 342
    London conference, 343
    parliamentary debates, 265, 269
    Québec opinion, 87
    Tarnak Farms deaths, 201n
    Soviet invasion, 73
    US–led invasion, 42, 47, 342
Africa, aid to, 183, 261
African Union, 38, 191
Agence de coopération culturelle et
    technique, 189, 190, 218, 308, 311
Agence intergouvernementale
    de la Francophonie, 190
Agence universitaire
    de la Francophonie, 191
agriculture
    agricultural producers, 40n, 41n
    Cairns Group, 42
    agricultural interests, 94–96
    grain exports, Argentina, 95
    grain sales, China, 95
    grain sanctions, 95
    producer associations, 95–96
    Quad meetings, 40
    supply management, 41n, 96
aid sanctions, 73
aid to the civil power, 71–72
Air India flight 182, 90, 336

Air Quality agreement, 338
Al Jazeera, 100
Alaska Boundary dispute, 23n,
    78–79, 326
Al-Bashir, Omar, 77
Albo, Greg, 61
Allende, Salvador, 334
alliances, 44–48
Al-Mashat, Mohammed, 243, 251
Al-Qaddafi, Muammar, 37
Al-Qaeda
    attacks, 97n, 147, 341, 342
    anti-western orientation of, 77
    Los Angeles airport plot, 91
    Maher Arar, 202n
    Osama bin Laden, 100
    sanctions against, 74
Alverstone, Lord [Richard Webster, 1st
    Viscount Alverstone], 79–80
American Recovery and
    Reinvestment Act, 92
American Revolution, 276
Amin, Hafizullah, 335
Amin Dada, Idi, 86
"anarchical society," 4, 20
Anastakis, Dimitry, 199
Andropov, Yuri, 336
Anglo–American Convention, 325
Anglo–Japanese alliance, 186
Anglo–Russian Treaty, 79
Anglo–Saxon racism, 122
Annan, Kofi, 340
Anschluss, 329
anti-Americanism, 93, 115, 118n,
    171, 202, 276
anti-submarine warfare, 70
Antony, Nancy Hughes, 111
apartheid: *see* South Africa
Arab League, 191
Arab Palestine Association, 88
Arafat, Yassir, 338
Arar, Maher, 202n
Arctic
    "Arctic card," 71
    Arctic Co-operation Agreement, 337
    Arctic policy, 71n, 193, 195, 237
    Arctic Waters Pollution Prevention
        Act, 256, 333
    Canada as an Arctic nation, 21n,
        21–22, 146
    Canadian Forces in, 70–71
    Canadian Rangers, 71
    Inuit Circumpolar Conference, 22
    Harper and, 173, 173n
    Mulroney and, 195–96
    sovereignty, 70, 173n, 195, 237
    See also: Manhattan, Polar Sea
Argentina, sanctions against, 73
Aristide, Jean-Bertrand, 73, 339

Armenia, genocide in, 104
Armenian Revolutionary Army, 90
Arone, Shidane, 68
Aroostook war, 23n
Article 2: *see* North Atlantic Treaty
    Organization
Article 5: *see* North Atlantic Treaty
    Organization
Article X: *see* League of Nations
Asian financial crisis, 340
Asia-Pacific Economic Cooperation
    (APEC) forum, 38, 105, 107,
    112, 146, 168, 177, 338
Asselin, Martial, 218, 220
Association des universities de langue
    française, 188
Association internationale des maires
    francophones, 191
Association québécoise des organismes
    de coopération internationale, 103
Association of Southeast Asian Nations
    (ASEAN), 107
Atatürk, Kemal, 129
Atlantic Alliance: *see* North Atlantic
    Treaty Organization
"Atlanticism," 45
Attlee, Clement, 161
Audet, Michel, 321
Auto Pact: *see* Canada–United States
    Auto Products Trade Agreement
autonomism, 127, 130, 153
avian influenza, 292
Avro Arrow, 332
Axworthy, Lloyd
    foreign minister, 209, 213, 340
    "francophone lieutenant" for, 220
    human security, 144, 153, 207, 214
    Internet, use of, 109
    International Commission on
        Intervention and State
        Sovereignty, 144
    landmines, 111, 143, 211
    on "national interest," 143
    Nobel Prize nomination, 111n
    soft power, 76–77

B
backbench revolts, 266
Badie, Bertrand, 285
balance of payments, 195
Baldwin, David, on power, 64
Balfour committee: *see* inter-imperial
    relations committee
Balfour, Arthur, 1st Earl of Balfour, 127
Bali bombings, 342, 343
Ballistic Missile Defense program
    2004 decision on, 31
    2005 decision on, 31, 36, 343
    American pressure, 77–78, 171n

*Entries for footnotes are indicated by "*n*."